Special Educational Needs and Disability in Education – A Legal Guide

To Helen

Special Educational Needs and Disability in Education – A Legal Guide

Simon Whitbourn

MA (Cantab), Dip.LG

Butterworths
LexisNexis™

Members of the LexisNexis Group worldwide

United Kingdom	LexisNexis Butterworths Tolley, a Division of Reed Elsevier (UK) Ltd, Halsbury House, 35 Chancery Lane, LONDON, WC2A 1EL, and 4 Hill Street, EDINBURGH EH2 3JZ
Argentina	LexisNexis Argentina, BUENOS AIRES
Australia	LexisNexis Butterworths, CHATSWOOD, New South Wales
Austria	LexisNexis Verlag ARD Orac GmbH & Co KG, VIENNA
Canada	LexisNexis Butterworths, MARKHAM, Ontario
Chile	LexisNexis Chile Ltda, SANTIAGO DE CHILE
Czech Republic	Nakladatelství Orac sro, PRAGUE
France	Editions du Juris-Classeur SA, PARIS
Hong Kong	LexisNexis Butterworths, HONG KONG
Hungary	HVG-Orac, BUDAPEST
India	LexisNexis Butterworths, NEW DELHI
Ireland	Butterworths (Ireland) Ltd, DUBLIN
Italy	Giuffrè Editore, MILAN
Malaysia	Malayan Law Journal Sdn Bhd, KUALA LUMPUR
New Zealand	Butterworths of New Zealand, WELLINGTON
Poland	Wydawnictwo Prawnicze LexisNexis, WARSAW
Singapore	LexisNexis Butterworths, SINGAPORE
South Africa	Butterworths SA, DURBAN
Switzerland	Stämpfli Verlag AG, BERNE
USA	LexisNexis, DAYTON, Ohio

© Reed Elsevier (UK) Ltd 2002

A CIP Catalogue record for this book is available from the British Library.

ISBN 0 406 94635 3

Typeset by M Rules, London
Printed and bound in Great Britain by
Thomson Litho Ltd, East Kilbride, Scotland

Visit Butterworths LexisNexis *direct* at www.butterworths.com

Foreword

In the twenty-five years that I have been practising law, education law has developed from virtually nothing into a major part of the daily work of all public lawyers and, since the decision in *E (a minor) v Dorset County Council* [1995] 2 AC 633, of those who practise in the field of negligence as well.

This has been the result of the convergence of a number of factors. Firstly, following the changes in High Court procedure in the early 1980s which resulted in the replacement of the old prerogative writs of certiorari, mandamus and prohibition with the procedure for applying for judicial review under Order 53 of the Rules of the Supreme Court, there was a massive expansion in the work of the Crown Office (now the Administrative Court). Secondly, the extension of Legal Aid in this area, caused by the simple fact that as the applicant was a minor she was almost invariably entitled to legal aid. Thirdly, the change in society whereby the citizen was no longer willing blindly to accept the decision of a public body but was prepared to challenge the decision-taker. This shift in the social welfare field, reflecting as it does the more individually orientated and rights-based society that has evolved in the latter part of the twentieth century, has in turn impacted upon the courts.

At the beginning of the twenty-first century these processes continue. The coming into force of the Human Rights Act 1998 on 2 October 2000 has further reinforced the rights-based approach, particularly with respect to the vulnerable. This has gone hand-in-hand with the procedural changes brought about by Woolf Reforms in civil procedure and the Community Legal Service Funding Code which prioritises human rights and public law claims.

The source of most public law challenges has been the Education Acts. It is surely a comment on what was happening in society that following the passing of the Education Act 1944 there were few changes in the basic structure of state education for over thirty years. Even the major educational change, the emergence of comprehensive education in the 1960s and 1970s, was not reflected in any major statutory change. Then, in the 1980s, starting with the revolution in special educational needs arising from the Education Act 1981 through to the Education Reform Act 1988, which introduced, amongst other things, local management of schools and grant maintained schools, and continuing with the changes in further and higher education in the 1990s, there was not an area of education which was not examined and changed. Given that the process was not always fully understood by the local education authorities (LEAs) or the professionals in the field, it is not surprising that a huge amount of hotly-contested litigation ensued.

Following the election of a new government in 1997, the focus on education and the introduction of new legislation developed apace. Today there are new questions to be asked about the proper role for local democracy and LEAs. It is also becoming apparent that 'choice' is no panacea when it comes to social welfare rights as one person's 'choice' may be another person's detriment, and thus questions of 'quality for all' rather than 'choice for the few' become relevant. We are, after all, concerned with very fine matters of judgment in a highly sensitive area. These are things over which reasonable minds can disagree, and change, as Lord Browne-Wilkinson said in the case of *X* (*supra*):

> 'Is it right to superimpose on the statutory machinery for the investigation and treatment of the plaintiff's special educational needs a duty of care to exercise the statutory discretion carefully? I find this a difficult question on which my views have changed from time to time.'

The balance is between, on the one hand, someone's (often a child's) need for compensation in what are usually desperate circumstances, and on the other hand the broader need to have a system that works for the majority without the caution that flows from the fear of litigation. As my colleague Conor Gearty has said recently, one of the difficulties in drawing this balance is the fact that one concern is real and the other, intangible:

> 'Who can dare to place such intangible public concerns on the weighing scales against a tragically unfortunate litigant with the rhetoric of human rights firmly behind him or her?' (*Unravelling Osman* [2001] 64 MLR 159, 186)

No area of education has undergone such a profound change of emphasis and an explosion of the use of legal challenges as the area of special educational needs. The timely publication of Simon Whitbourn's excellent book coincides with the coming into force of the Special Educational Needs and Disability Act 2001. The Act both builds on the progress that has been made in the last twenty years and reflects a welcome emphasis on inclusion of those with disabilities and an acknowledgement of their right to be treated with respect. As the Disability Rights Task Force acknowledged in their report in 1999:

> 'the inclusion of disabled people throughout their school and college life is one of the most powerful levers in banishing stereotypes and negative attitudes towards disabled people amongst the next generation' (*From Exclusion to Inclusion: A Report of the Disability Rights Task Force on Civil Rights for Disabled People* (DfEE, London, 1999), chap 4, para 3).

The importance of this task is reflected in the figures for children with special educational needs. In 2001 approximately 21.6% of all pupils in primary and secondary schools (or 1,670,600 pupils in total) were identified as having such needs (*Statistics of Education Schools in England* (HMSO, 2001), Table 34). Of this group, some 3% (258,000 pupils) had statements of special educational needs requiring additional support over and above that normally provided in mainstream schools. This represents a substantial need, and an equally substantial bill for the taxpayer.

The aim of the 2001 Act is to ensure that the needs of these special children are identified quickly and fully to enable them to reach their full potential. Building on the experience of the past twenty years, the aim is to provide a framework of rights which is transparent and easy to navigate for all involved in the process – the child, the parents, the schools and the LEAs. If this aim is to be achieved then it is important that the practitioners in this area, whether acting on behalf of the parents or the LEAs, have access to the comprehensive and detailed narrative that Simon Whitbourn's book provides. In this way the original decisions will be got right in the first place, avoiding the need for expensive appeals and directing resources to the individual children and schools where they are most needed.

Cherie Booth QC
Matrix Chambers
Griffin Building
Gray's Inn
London WC1R 5LN

Preface

The Special Educational Needs and Disability Act (SENDA) 2001 received Royal Assent on 11 May 2001. This book has been written in response and as a guide to the effect that the 2001 Act, along with the various subordinate legislation which accompanies it, will have on special educational needs and disability discrimination in education.

Most of the SENDA 2001, certainly as far as special educational needs is concerned, is not, however, new, and this whole area has been subject to development and scrutiny through the courts, especially over the last few years. Consequently, the opportunity has been taken to bring together both the old and the new to provide a comprehensive guide to the law of special educational needs in England and Wales.

Where the SENDA 2001 does innovate, though, is in the area of disability discrimination. Previously, and, as many disability groups have commented, erroneously, the provision of education was exempt from the Disability Discrimination Act (DDA) 1995. Teachers and lecturers in schools and colleges could claim disability discrimination if they were unfavourably treated as employees and other disabled people could complain if they were badly treated when accessing educational premises and facilities – but the children and students themselves were unable to complain at being subjected to disability discrimination.

The SENDA 2001 remedies this by applying the DDA 1995 to the whole area of education, including admissions, exclusions and the provision of education and educational services themselves. A large number of people – teachers and headteachers, school and college governors, local education authority officers and parents – will therefore be required to have, or wish to obtain, knowledge of an area of law that they have never had to worry about before. This book attempts to provide not only an analysis of these new provisions, but also to offer guidance on the interrelationship between those provisions and the other sections of the DDA 1995 and the pre-existing guidance and case law on disability discrimination.

As will be seen, the coming into force of, especially, the special educational needs provisions of the SENDA 2001 has not been smooth. Regulations implementing the detail of the Act have had to be amended and then consolidated, and intended commencement dates have been revoked. In order to try to keep step with revised commencement dates (principally 1 January 2002 for special educational needs and 1 September 2002 for disability discrimination), this book has been written as draft Codes of Practice have been issued, but not yet finalised, and has been finished before delayed sets of regulations have been approved. In particular, reference has had to be made to the two draft Codes of Practice relating to disability discrimination rather than, as would have been ideal, the approved versions. Similarly, at the time of writing, regulations dealing with the procedure of the newly-named Special Educational Needs and Disability Tribunal for disability discrimination claims had not been produced.

The SENDA 2001 itself makes changes to two pieces of significant and substantial legislation: the Education Act 1996 and the DDA 1995. Beneath it are, or will be, numerous sets of regulations, three Codes of Practice, various guidance circulars and that new creature of the Department for Education and Skills, the 'SEN Toolkit'. For what should be an area of practice with very simple rules and regulations to help those who use them on a daily basis understand what has to be done, there does appear to be an awfully large amount of material, often from different sources, although hopefully not giving different views. Some might query whether a book of this nature helps this situation – indeed, the criticism might even be it adds even more. I hope not. What I have tried to achieve in one single volume is as comprehensive a guide as possible, bringing together all the various sources and adding, for good measure, a fair element of case law, in order to provide readers with as much practical advice as possible on this fundamentally important area of education law.

In writing this book, I have been grateful for the assistance of individuals too numerous to mention. Special thanks should, however, go to Andrew Seber, County Education Officer of Hampshire County Council (and his predecessor, Peter Coles), and Hampshire's education officers who have provided me with the opportunity to advise on this area of law and especially to Felicity Dickinson who assisted me in getting to grips with some of the more practical aspects of the SENDA 2001. My thanks also go to Cherie Booth QC for kindly contributing the Foreword, and to Victoria Smith and Rachel Turner at Butterworths for their help, and patience, in seeing this work through to completion.

Despite all the difficulties with the new regulations and codes of practice, I have attempted to state the law as I understand it as of 1 February 2002.

Simon Whitbourn
February 2002

About the author

Simon Whitbourn has been working, speaking and writing in the area of education law for many years.

Simon received his MA from Cambridge University, where he was a Squire Scholar and Edward, Lord North Scholar in Law. Following that, he worked for Hampshire County Council from 1988, ultimately as Principal Solicitor, specialising in education law. As well as advising on a day-to-day basis over that period on special educational needs issues, he was also involved with a significant number of cases – judicial reviews, high court appeals and claims – concerning children with special educational needs.

Simon is currently principal of his own firm, Simon Whitbourn & Co, and is a school governor at his local primary school.

Simon has been a speaker at events organised by the Society of Education Officers, provided training at numerous courses for headteachers, teachers, education officers and educational psychologists and is an Associate Tutor with Hampshire's Governor Training Service. He has written the book *What is the LEA for? An Analysis of the Functions and Roles of the Local Education Authority*, and has contributed articles to the *Solicitors Journal*, *Local Government Chronicle*, *Education Public Law and the Individual* and the *Education Law Association Bulletin*.

Contents

Contents

Appendices

Abbreviations

CA	Court of Appeal
Code of Practice	Special Educational Needs Code of Practice (2001)
Code of Practice (Post 16)	Code of Practice (Post 16) – New duties (from 2002) in the provision of post-16 education and related services for disabled people and students
Code of Practice (Schools)	Code of Practice (Schools) – New duties (from 2002) not to discriminate against disabled pupils and prospective pupils in the provision of education and associated services in schools, and in respect of admissions and exclusions
Code of Practice for Securing Effective Relationships	Code of Practice on Local Education Authority – School Relations (2001)
Commission	Disability Rights Commission
CRE	Commission for Racial Equality
DDA 1995	Disability Discrimination Act 1995
DES	Department of Education and Science
DfE	Department for Education
DfEE	Department for Education and Employment
DfES	Department for Education and Skills
DRC	Disability Rights Commission
DRCA 1999	Disability Rights Commission Act 1999
EA 1981	Education Act 1981
EA 1993	Education Act 1993
EA 1996	Education Act 1996
EAT	Employment Appeals Tribunal
ELR	Education Law Reports
EOC	Equal Opportunities Commission
FE	Further education
FEFC	Further Education Funding Council
FHEA 1992	Further and Higher Education Act 1992
HE	Higher education
HEFC	Higher Education Funding Council
HL	House of Lords
HMI	Her Majesty's Inspectors
HRA 1998	Human Rights Act 1998
IEP	Individual Education Plan

Abbreviations

LEA	Local Education Authority
LGA 1974	Local Government Act 1974
NDC	National Disability Council
OFSTED	Office for Standards in Education
PRU	Pupil Referral Unit
QBD	Queen's Bench Division
SEN	Special educational needs
SENCO	Special educational needs co-ordinator
SENDA 2001	Special Educational Needs and Disability Act 2001
SENDT	Special Educational Needs and Disability Tribunal
SENT	Special Educational Needs Tribunal
SIA 1996	School Inspections Act 1996
SOC	School Organisation Committee
SSFA 1998	School Standards and Framework Act 1998
Tribunal	Special Educational Needs and Disability Tribunal
WHO	World Health Organisation

Table of statutes

References are to paragraph numbers. References in *italics* refer to page numbers of the appendices, and references in **bold** indicate where a section is set out in part or in full.

Table of statutory instruments

References are to paragraph numbers.

Table of cases

References are to paragraph number.

Chapter 1

Introduction

'Special education is a challenging and intellectually demanding field for those engaged in it . . . Those who work with children with special educational needs should regard themselves as having a crucial and developing role in a society which is now committed, not merely to tending and caring for its handicapped members, as a matter of charity, but to educating them, as a matter of right and to developing their potential to the full.'

Report of the Committee of Enquiry into the Education of Handicapped Children and Young People (1978)

Background   1.1

It is perhaps a sad comment on the development of special education since   **1.1.1**
1978 that these words of the Warnock Report[1] are still apt today, some twenty years after they were first made. It is true that the Warnock Report itself marked a significant change in the official attitude towards children with special needs and disabilities, and the period since then has seen a tremendous improvement in the system for assessing and providing educational support for these children. Nonetheless, after twenty years of continuous improvement it was still considered necessary in 1999 for a Disability Rights Task Force reviewing the civil rights of disabled children to comment that the statement in the Warnock Report 'is as relevant today as it was two decades ago. It is applicable to all stages of education and is a reminder to educators of their duties to all in society who seek equal access to education'[2].

1 Officially titled *Report of the Committee of Enquiry into the Education of Handicapped Children and Young People* (1978, Cmnd 7212); Chairman: Mary Warnock.
2 *From Exclusion to Inclusion: A Report of the Disability Rights Task Force on Civil Rights for Disabled People* (DfEE, London, 1999), Chap 4, para 51.

As the Disability Rights Task Force recognised, 'with all the challenges   **1.1.2**
facing disabled people, a high quality education that meets their needs is essential. It will increase their chances of living independent and fulfilling lives: something which the rest of society regards as a right'[1]. This statement echoed comments made by the Warnock Report:

'The purpose of education for all children is the same; the goals are the same. But the help that individual children need in progressing towards them will be different. Whereas for some the road they have to travel towards the goal is smooth and easy, for others it is fraught with obstacles. For some obstacles are so daunting that, even with the greatest possible help, they will not get very far. Nevertheless, for them too, progress will be possible, and their educational needs will be fulfilled, as they gradually overcome one obstacle after another on the way.'[2]

1 *From Exclusion to Inclusion: A Report of the Disability Rights Task Force on Civil Rights for Disabled People* (DfEE, London, 1999), Chap 4, para 1.
2 *Report of the Committee of Enquiry into the Education of Handicapped Children and Young People* (1978, Cmnd 7212), para 1.4.

1.1.3   This area of education is not simple. It can lead to diametrically opposed views: the arguments of those seeking the inclusion into mainstream education of children, despite their special educational needs or disabilities; and the counter-arguments of others who insist that such inclusion can prejudice the education of children without such needs. The education system must therefore seek to ensure a middle course, protecting the rights of disabled and special needs children to be educated, whilst ensuring that a policy of inclusion does not lead to the education of other pupils being compromised.

1.1.4   At times, it is a confrontational and litigious area. In the twenty years between the Education Act (EA) 1981 and the Special Educational Needs and Disability Act (SENDA) 2001, great steps forward have been taken by schools, colleges and Local Education Authorities (LEAs) to improve both the identification of, and provision of support to, children with special educational needs. Some of the improvements have been forced through legal action: cases specifying what needs warranted support[1], what support had to be provided and by whom[2] and how specific an LEA had to be when describing the provision so that parents could be sure that their children were receiving their due entitlement. More recent cases have shown how important early identification of a child's needs can be; if schools and LEAs are negligent in assessing children and then in meeting their needs, they will in principle be liable to pay compensation[3].

1 See, for example, *R v Hampshire Education Authority ex p J*, (1985) 84 LGR 547, QBD.
2 See, for example, *R v Lancashire County Council, ex p M* [1989] 2 FLR 279, CA; and *Bromley London Borough Council v Special Educational Needs Tribunal* [1999] ELR 260, [1999] Ed CR 907, CA.
3 See, for example, *X v Bedfordshire County Council; M (A Minor) v Newham London Borough Council; E (A Minor) v Dorset County Council; Christmas v Hampshire County Council; Keating v Bromley London Borough Council* [1995] 2 AC 633, [1995] ELR 404, HL; *Phelps v London Borough of Hillingdon; Anderton v Clwyd County Council; G v London Borough of Bromley;* and *Jarvis v Hampshire County Council* [2001] 2 AC 619, [2000] ELR 499, HL.

1.1.5   However, although the case law may have improved the lot of some children, and at the same time helped create a specialism of education law, most accept that the best way to secure provision for children in need is not through the courts. It is now accepted that tribunals will be a necessary part of the process, but with the introduction of and emphasis on dispute resolution and conciliation, it is hoped that even they will become the last, rather than the first, resort of dissatisfied parents.

The education of children with special educational needs or disabilities (it **1.1.6** does not always follow that a disabled child will have special educational needs, or vice versa) and their entitlements cannot – indeed, must not – be ignored. In 1978, it was estimated that approximately 20% of the total school population would, at some time during their school career, have some form of special educational need[1]. In January 2001, approximately 21.6% of all pupils in primary and secondary schools, or 1,670,600 pupils in total, were identified as having such needs[2]. Of this figure, 258,000 pupils, approximately 3% of the total number, had statements of special educational needs[3] requiring additional support to that provided in their normal schools. Of this latter group of children, 61% were educated in mainstream schools (nursery, primary or secondary); 35% in either maintained special schools or pupil referral units; and 4% in independent or non-maintained special schools[4]. In 2001, there were 1,113 maintained special schools and a further 62 non-maintained special schools meeting the needs of many of these children[5]. There are some 8.5 million disabled people in the UK[6].

1 *Report of the Committee of Enquiry into the Education of Handicapped Children and Young People* (May 1978, Cmnd 7212), para 3.17.
2 Statistics of Education Schools in England (HMSO, 2001), Table 34.
3 Statistics of Education Schools in England (HMSO, 2001), Table 32.
4 Statistics of Education Schools in England (HMSO, 2001), Table 33.
5 Statistics of Education Schools in England (HMSO, 2001), Table 2.
6 Hansard HL, vol 620, col 636(2R).

These are significant numbers of children, and whilst their levels of need **1.1.7** may vary, as the Task Force, and Warnock before it, pointed out, the early identification of the needs of all these children followed by prompt and appropriate support is essential to ensure that they can enjoy and benefit from education without discrimination.

The legislation from the EA 1981 onwards has tried to address this dis- **1.1.8** crimination. However, the good intentions have not always been successful and, particularly within the area of disability discrimination, the needs of children have at times been neglected. SENDA 2001 and the changes it brings to both the education legislation and the Disability Discrimination Act (DDA) 1995 are aimed at remedying some of these defects and ensuring that children with either special needs or disabilities are included within the education system and that, by their inclusion, some of the prejudice they suffer may be reduced:

> 'Education is vital to the creation of a fully inclusive society, a society in which all members see themselves as valued for the contribution they make. We owe all children – whatever their particular needs and circumstances – the opportunity to develop to their full potential, to contribute economically, and to play a full part as active citizens.'[1]

1 The then Secretary of State for Education and Employment, David Blunkett, quoted in *From Exclusion to Inclusion: A Report of the Disability Rights Task Force on Civil Rights for Disabled People* (DfEE, London, 1999).

In making recommendations with respect to the education of disabled chil- **1.1.9** dren and students, recommendations which have mainly been introduced through SENDA 2001, the Disability Rights Task Force in 1999 concluded:

'The 1978 Warnock Report laid the ground for a transformation in the education of children with special education needs. Although, we would not claim that the recommendations we have made will lead to a similar transformation two decades later, they offer a real opportunity for increasing the rights of disabled people to a quality education, free from unfair discrimination and segregation. However, Government legislation and new resources on their own will not be effective. As important is a real change in the attitude of all those engaged in all stages of education.'[1]

1 *From Exclusion to Inclusion: A Report of the Disability Rights Task Force on Civil Rights for Disabled People* (DfEE, London, 1999), Chap 4, para 51.

A BRIEF HISTORY OF SPECIAL EDUCATION IN ENGLAND AND WALES

1.2 Early history

1.2.1 Special education in England and Wales has a long, but not necessarily proud, history[1]. Schools for blind or deaf children date back to the eighteenth century, but for the majority of the period between then and 1944, the provision for children with what we would now term 'special needs' or 'disabilities' relied on either philanthropic individuals or the pure luck of living within an area with enlightened schools and local education authorities. Physically disabled children and children with mental disabilities frequently were categorised as 'defective', and for many the only 'provision' made by the state was in workhouses or infirmaries[2].

1 For a full summary of the history of special education, see *Report of the Committee of Enquiry into the Education of Handicapped Children and Young People* (1978, Cmnd 7212), Chap 2.
2 See *Report of the Committee of Enquiry into the Education of Handicapped Children and Young People* (1978, Cmnd 7212), para 2.6.

Nineteenth and early-twentieth century developments

1.2.2 The development of special educational provision since that time has relied on various commissions and committees, many bearing titles which we would now consider outrageous. In 1886 the Royal Commission on the Blind and Deaf was constituted[1], which ultimately led to the Elementary Education (Blind and Deaf Children) Act 1893. In 1896 a Committee on Defective and Epileptic Children was established, which proposed that school authorities should have the duty to make special provision for all 'defective' children in their area. Sadly, the enlightenment of the Committee was not matched by Parliament, and the ensuing Elementary Education (Defective and Epileptic Children) Act 1899 merely provided school boards with the power to provide for the education of mentally and physically 'defective' and epileptic children. The Elementary Education (Defective and Epileptic Children) Act 1914 did, however, for the first time impose a duty on school authorities to make provision for the 'mentally defective', and the Education Act 1918 imposed similar obligations in respect of the 'physically defective and epileptic'.

1 *Report of the Committee of Enquiry into the Education of Handicapped Children and Young People* (1978, Cmnd 7212), para 2.11.

In 1908, the Royal Commission on the Care and Control of the Feeble- **1.2.3**
Minded considered that provision for the mentally handicapped in special
schools was inappropriate; instead, they were to receive occupational provision. Nonetheless, the Mental Deficiency Act 1913 imposed a duty on
LEAs to identify and certify children between 7 and 16 who were 'defective'.
Once identified, these children were to be taught in special schools, except
those who were judged incapable of being taught in these settings and who
would be left to the care of mental deficiency committees. The education of
these children was again considered by the Mental Deficiency Committee in
1924 and, foreshadowing the vision of inclusion by seventy years, this
Committee proposed much closer involvement of these children in mainstream education. In a marked change from earlier commissions, the
Committee also proposed the abolition of certification and a move towards
the integration of all children, removing the separate regime which 'dealt
with' handicapped or 'defective' children. Unfortunately those proposals
were not implemented, although their spirit lives on in developments sixty or
so years later.

The Education Act of 1944

The 'great' Education Act of 1944 took further faltering steps towards inte- **1.2.4**
gration by removing the education of handicapped children as a separate
category of education and replacing it with a duty imposed on LEAs to meet
the educational needs of these children through their general duty to provide
sufficient primary and secondary places for all pupils. The duty of LEAs to
ascertain 'defective' and epileptic children was extended to children with all
types of disability – described, slightly more liberally, as children who suffered from any disability of mind or body. Less liberally, the implementing
regulations[1] set out 11 categories of pupils in 'need': blind, partially-sighted,
deaf, partially-deaf, delicate, diabetic, the (in modern eyes, wholly inappropriate term) 'educationally sub-normal', epileptic, maladjusted,
physically handicapped and those with speech defects.

These categories remained in use (with the exception of diabetic children
being merged into the 'delicate' category) until 1981. 'Educationally sub-
normal' children, a term which should make those who derived it cringe
from shame, included children of limited ability and those 'retarded by
other conditions' such as irregular attendance, ill-health, lack of continuity
in their education or unsatisfactory school conditions; in fact, a broad cross-
section of children experiencing difficulties for a variety of reasons, but
normal children nonetheless.

1 Handicapped Pupils and School Health Service Regulations 1945, SI 1945/1076.

The recommendations of the Warnock Report of 1978

In 1978, the Committee of Enquiry into the Education of Handicapped **1.2.5**
Children and Young People published its findings and recommendations
(the Warnock Report)[1]. It marked the high point of official consideration of
the needs of children with particular educational needs, either through learning difficulties or disability. The Warnock Report's recommendations led to
the EA 1981 and a system of provision for children with special needs, both
in terms of the definition of such children and assessing and meeting their
needs, which largely lives on through the subsequent legislation to this day.

The Report recognised the importance of research and training to develop methods of identifying and remedying special educational needs[2] and stressed the need for the involvement of parents and early identification and intervention to deal with any problems:

> 'If a close and, so far as possible, equal relationship between parents of children with special educational needs and professionals is established and if prompt and effective educational help for such children is provided as soon as their special needs become apparent, the whole of the children's subsequent education will benefit. The education service will also benefit, since early intervention will mean that many children will be less dependent upon support in later years and will be able to take their place in ordinary schools.'[3]

1   Cmnd 7212.
2   See *Report of the Committee of Enquiry into the Education of Handicapped Children and Young People* (1978, Cmnd 7212), Chaps 18 and 19.
3   *Report of the Committee of Enquiry into the Education of Handicapped Children and Young People* (1978, Cmnd 7212), para 19.10.

1.2.6   Altogether the Warnock Report made 225 recommendations, such as:

- introducing a system of recording as in need those children who, on the basis of a detailed profile of their needs prepared by a multi-disciplinary team, were judged by their LEAs to require special educational provision not generally available in ordinary schools[1];
- giving LEAs the power to require the multi-professional assessment of children of any age (after due notice to parents) and to impose on them a duty to comply with a parental request for such an assessment[2];
- that the progress of a child with special educational needs should be reviewed at least annually[3];
- that parents should have a right of appeal to the Secretary of State[4];
- that the facilities and expertise of special schools should be more widely available to provide intensive specialised help[5];
- that firm links should be developed between special and ordinary schools in the same area[6];
- that parents should be partners in the whole process[7]; and
- that every LEA should re-structure and, if necessary, supplement its existing advisory staff and resources to provide effective advice and support to teachers concerned with children with special educational needs[8,9].

1   *Report of the Committee of Enquiry into the Education of Handicapped Children and Young People* (1978, Cmnd 7212), para 3.31.
2   *Report of the Committee of Enquiry into the Education of Handicapped Children and Young People* (1978, Cmnd 7212), para 4.28.
3   *Report of the Committee of Enquiry into the Education of Handicapped Children and Young People* (1978, Cmnd 7212), para 4.53.
4   *Report of the Committee of Enquiry into the Education of Handicapped Children and Young People* (1978, Cmnd 7212), para 4.74.
5   *Report of the Committee of Enquiry into the Education of Handicapped Children and Young People* (1978, Cmnd 7212), para 8.9.
6   *Report of the Committee of Enquiry into the Education of Handicapped Children and Young People* (1978, Cmnd 7212), para 8.13.
7   *Report of the Committee of Enquiry into the Education of Handicapped Children and Young People* (1978, Cmnd 7212), Chap 9.
8   *Report of the Committee of Enquiry into the Education of Handicapped Children and Young People* (1978, Cmnd 7212), para 13.3.

9 All the recommendations can be found in the Summary of Recommendations at *Report of the Committee of Enquiry into the Education of Handicapped Children and Young People* (1978, Cmnd 7212), pp 338 to 366.

In the light of all the various recommendations, Warnock believed that the underlying assumption that should inform LEA planning was that one in six children at any time, and up to one in five children at some time during their school career, would require some form of special educational provision[1]. **1.2.7**

1 *Report of the Committee of Enquiry into the Education of Handicapped Children and Young People* (1978, Cmnd 7212), para 3.17.

The Education Act 1981 and the cementing of rights **1.3**

The EA 1981 came into force on 1 September 1983. It implemented many of the Warnock Report's recommendations. Use of the term 'educationally sub-normal' and the other categorisations disappeared and the Act replaced them with definitions of 'learning difficulties', 'special educational needs' and 'special educational provision', along the lines recommended by Warnock, which are still used today and which remain virtually unaltered in the current legislation[1]. **1.3.1**

LEAs were given the general responsibility for ensuring that children with special educational needs were identified[2], and, in securing the provision of primary and secondary school places, LEAs had to take into account the need for securing that special educational provision was made for children with special educational needs[3]. Arrangements for assessing the needs of children were set down[4], and the procedure for issuing a formal document setting out a child's special educational needs, special educational provision and appropriate placement (ie a statement of special educational needs) was first established[5]. The detail of the assessment process and the format of the statements was set out in regulations, which included the requirement for an LEA to obtain advice from a multi-disciplinary team of professionals[6].

For the first time, parents could appeal against the special educational provision specified in statements (or amended statements) to locally-arranged appeal committees. The committees' powers were, however limited to confirming the provision or remitting the case back to the LEA which arranged them for reconsideration in the light of the committee's observations[7]. A further appeal against the decision of the appeal committee to confirm the provision or against the LEA's decision following remission could be made to the Secretary of State[8]. Parents could not, however, appeal (for example) against a refusal by the LEA to assess their child or to issue a statement.

1 EA 1981, s 1, now Education Act (EA) 1996, s 312.
2 EA 1981, s 4, now EA 1996, s 321.
3 EA 1981, s 2.
4 EA 1981, ss 5 and 6.
5 EA 1981, s 7.
6 Education (Special Educational Needs) Regulations 1983, SI 1983/29.
7 EA 1981, s 8.
8 EA 1981, s 8(6).

The EA 1981 provided the first real statement in legislation of the entitlements of children with special educational needs and the rights of their parents. For the first time parents could appeal against decisions, albeit **1.3.2** that the local appeal panels were inconsistent in their abilities and decisions, and the Secretary of State could be notoriously slow. Further, as parents aspired to secure the rights granted by the 1981 Act, they resorted to the courts for the first time in order to cement and develop those rights. Ably assisted by campaigning organisations and lawyers, once the EA 1981 had bedded down, parents started to litigate in order to secure their children's rights and to see how far the Act would go in terms of the provision to which affected children were entitled. As with most things involving the law and the courts, there was initially some delay, but between 1987 and 1991 the higher courts first started to look at the EA 1981 and the condition of children with special educational needs. This litigation and judicial activity not only helped to develop and expand this specific area of law but also helped establish 'education law' as a recognised specialism.

1.3.3   Three cases in particular established that the courts were willing to uphold the rights of children with special educational needs. First, *R v Hereford and Worcestershire County Council, ex p Lashford*[1] examined the circumstances in which an LEA was required to determine the special educational provision to be made for a child with special educational needs. Then in 1989, in *R v Lancashire County Council, ex p M*[2] the Court of Appeal considered the nature of educational and non-educational provision in a statement of special educational needs. Even more of a landmark, however, was the Court of Appeal's 1991 decision in *R v Secretary of State for Education and Science, ex p E*[3].

1   [1987] 1 FLR 508, [1987] Fam Law 162, CA.
2   [1989] 2 FLR 279, CA.
3   [1993] 2 FCR 753.

1.3.4   In preparing statements of special educational needs under the EA 1981 and the 1983 Regulations[1], there had been a tendency for some statements to be written in (what might be described charitably as) general terms. The needs and provision required for a child could often be described in one sentence. Although the statement in *Ex p E* was not that bad, the Court of Appeal established that if a statement was to have any meaning it had to be sufficiently specific as to enable a parent, and hence the child's teacher, to understand the nature of the child's needs and the provision which had to be made in terms of type, time and anticipated outcomes. LEAs had to set out all the child's needs and all the provision required if the LEA was under an obligation to determine any of the child's needs.

1   Education (Special Educational Needs) Regulations 1983, SI 1983/29.

1.3.5   *Ex p E*, together with a number of other judicial reviews brought before and after the Court of Appeal's decision, showed that parents could secure redress through the courts, and the number of challenges against LEA decisions increased significantly. Partly as a result of the number of these cases and partly as concerns at the process and provision being made which prompted them increased, the EA 1981 was reviewed and changes to the system were included in the Education Act (EA) 1993, the relevant parts of which came into force in September 1994.

1.3.6   The EA 1981 had lasted for 12 years – an era in terms of some education legislation. Despite the advances it brought to the field of special educational needs, there were nonetheless a number of faults with the system it created. Parents were concerned that there was inconsistency in terms of the provision made across the country and in securing that the provision set out in statements was actually made; the appeals to local appeal committees were seen as ineffective and the grounds of appeal limited; and the increasing amount of litigation by way of judicial review also caused alarm.

The Education Act 1993 and 'failing to educate' cases   1.4

The EA 1993, whilst leaving in place the majority of the Warnock Report   **1.4.1** recommendations about definitions, assessment and provision, answered the criticisms of the EA 1981 by introducing a statutory Code of Practice to which all involved had to have regard, expanding the number and type of decisions against which parents could appeal and transferring the determination of appeals to an independent tribunal.

The provisions of the EA 1993 were later consolidated into the Education   **1.4.2** Act (EA) 1996, but the relevant sections remained unchanged; the 1996 Act remains the source of the law relating to children with special educational needs.

At about this time, a number of claims were received by LEAs from pupils or   **1.4.3** ex-pupils seeking compensation for alleged failures of schools and LEAs to identify and address their special educational needs. This was a new development. As has been seen, under the EA 1981 parents had reverted to the courts to seek orders that LEAs comply with their duties – but now parents were seeking compensation for the negligence of those working with their children.
 In the groundbreaking case of *X v Bedfordshire County Council; M (a minor) v Newham London Borough Council; E (a minor) v Dorset County Council; Christmas v Hampshire County Council; Keating v Bromley London Borough Council*[1], the House of Lords held that although compensation was unlikely to be awarded if a school or LEA failed to perform its statutory duties, teachers and LEA staff could owe duties to take reasonable care to identify and take remedial action to address children's special educational needs. The initial decision, as will be seen[2], caused some confusion, and it took a further case in 2000, *Phelps v London Borough of Hillingdon; Anderton v Clwyd County Council; G v London Borough of Bromley; Jarvis v Hampshire County Council*[3] to uphold the earlier House of Lords decision and establish beyond doubt that such duties could be owed by teachers, headteachers, education psychologists and LEA staff.

1 [1995] 2 AC 633, [1995] ELR 404, HL.
2 See 10.9.
3 [2001] 2 AC 619, [2000] ELR 499, HL.

The Disability Discrimination Act 1995   1.5

Developments were also taking place in the field of disability discrimination.   **1.5.1** Anti-discrimination legislation had been introduced in the US[1], Australia[2] and New Zealand[3]. Pressure within the UK for similar legislation developed, and although initially resistant[4] the then Conservative government relented and published a Green Paper in 1994 entitled *A Consultation on Government Measures to Tackle Discrimination Against Disabled People*[5], followed by a White Paper in early 1995, *Ending Discrimination Against Disabled People*[6]. The DDA 1995 was the result.

1 Americans with Disabilities Act 1990.
2 Disability Discrimination Act 1992.
3 In the New Zealand Human Rights Act 1993.
4 See the comments of John Major HC Deb, vol 217, col 485.
5 Department of Social Security, 1994.
6 Cm 2729.

1.5.2 The DDA 1995 made it unlawful to discriminate against disabled people on the grounds of their disability. It applied to the fields of employment; the provision of goods, facilities and services; and the disposal and management of premises. However, apart from requiring certain information to be published by governing bodies and further and higher education institutions[1], the DDA 1995 was expressly precluded from applying to the provision of education services by maintained and independent schools or any services funded or secured by LEAs and the various further and higher education funding councils[2]. Members of staff employed at such institutions could still bring claims under the employment aspects of the DDA 1995, and parents and other users of schools etc for non-educational purposes could complain under the provisions of the DDA 1995 relating to access to goods, facilities and services – but disabled pupils and students could not complain under the DDA 1995 that they had suffered discrimination.

1 DDA 1995, Pt IV.
2 DDA 1995, s 19(5) and (6).

1.5.3 The rationale for this exclusion was that the protection was best secured through other legislation, notably the EA 1993 and subsequently the EA 1996 Act, and the provisions relating to special education[1]. This explanation was always dubious: the EA 1996 should ensure that children's special educational needs are met, but that is not the same thing as protecting children from discrimination. Nor are the definitions, and hence the qualifications for protection, the same.

1 See *A Consultation on Government Measures to Tackle Discrimination Against Disabled People* (Department of Social Security, 1994), para 4.9.

1.6   Inclusion and the Disability Rights Task Force

1.6.1 In 1997, the newly-elected Labour government and a Secretary of State for Education who had a more personal interest in special education and disability than most, pushed for a review of the provisions relating to disability discrimination. At the same time, the same Secretary of State took forward an agenda in education marked by a desire for greater inclusion, both in social terms but also in terms of a greater integration of pupils with special educational needs in mainstream schools.

1.6.2 In October 1997 a Green Paper, *Excellence for All Children: Meeting Special Educational Needs,* was published[1], which provoked responses from 3,600 parents and organisations[2]. In response, the Department for Education and

Skills (DfES) published its Programme of Action[3], which set out the steps the government proposed to introduce between 1998 and 2001 to improve the educational achievements of children with special educational needs. These included:

- improving parent and LEA/school partnerships[4];
- increasing the rights of children to be involved in the special educational needs process[5];
- improving the statutory framework for addressing children's needs by, for example, introducing a simplified Code of Practice[6] and strengthening the power of the Special Educational Needs Tribunal[7];
- improving the working relationships between the various agencies involved[8];
- developing the knowledge and skills of all staff working with children with special educational needs[9]; and
- generally developing a more inclusive education system by promoting further inclusion and developing the role of special schools[10].

1 *Excellence for All Children: Meeting Special Educational Needs* (Cmnd 3785); in Wales, *The BEST for Special Education* (Cm 3792).
2 SEN Programme of Action (DfES, 1998); or Shaping the Future for Special Education, published in Wales.
3 SEN Programme of Action (DfES, 1998); or Shaping the Future for Special Education, published in Wales.
4 SEN Programme of Action (DfES, 1998), Chap 1.
5 SEN Programme of Action (DfES, 1998), Chap 1.
6 SEN Programme of Action (DfES, 1998), Chap 2; though it might be noted that while the first Code of Practice on the identification and assessment of special educational needs ran to 166 pages, the new Code of Practice published in 2001 comprises 207 and is also accompanied by statutory guidance: *Inclusive Schooling – Children with Special Educational Needs* (DfES Guidance, DfES/0774/2001) and the SEN Toolkit, containing practical advice on implementing the Code of Practice.
7 SEN Programme of Action (DfES, 1998), Chap 2, paras 24 to 26.
8 SEN Programme of Action (DfES, 1998), Chap 5.
9 SEN Programme of Action (DfES, 1998), Chap 4.
10 SEN Programme of Action (DfES, 1998), Chap 3.

1.6.3 Although many improvements were a matter of changing practice or providing additional support, the DfES identified the need for legislative action to bring about some of the recommended improvements.

At around the same time, the government established a Disability Rights Task Force to review all aspects of civil rights legislation for disabled people. The Task Force's report, *From Exclusion to Inclusion: A Report of the Disability Rights Task Force on Civil Rights for Disabled People*[1], was published in December 1999. The Task Force made 156 recommendations for action across all areas of disabled people's lives, but its recommendations in respect of education were perhaps the most significant and most critical[2].

1 DfEE, London, 1999.
2 *From Exclusion to Inclusion: A Report of the Disability Rights Task Force on Civil Rights for Disabled People* (DfEE, London, 1999), Chap 4.

1.6.4 Recognising that 'the inclusion of disabled people throughout their school and college life is one of the most powerful levers in banishing stereotypes and negative attitudes towards disabled people amongst the next generation'[1], the Task Force considered that the exemptions for education in the DDA 1995 could not be sustained. They made 18 specific recommendations to assist the inclusion of disabled children in and through education, the key ones of which were[2]:

(a) in schools:
  (i) a strengthened right for parents of children with statements of special educational needs to a place at a mainstream school, unless they favoured a special school and a mainstream school would not meet the needs of the child or the wishes of either the parent or the child;
  (ii) a new right for disabled pupils not to be discriminated against unfairly by schools and LEAs and to have reasonable adjustments made to policies, practices and procedures which placed them at a substantial disadvantage to others;
  (iii) a new duty on schools and LEAs to plan strategically and make progress in increasing accessibility for disabled pupils to school premises and the curriculum; and
(b) in further, higher and LEA-secured adult education:
  (i) a separate section on further, higher and LEA-secured adult education should be included in civil rights legislation to secure comprehensive and enforceable rights for disabled people; similar rights should apply in relation to the Youth Service;
  (ii) the legislation should have an associated statutory Code of Practice, explaining the new rights.

1 *From Exclusion to Inclusion: A Report of the Disability Rights Task Force on Civil Rights for Disabled People* (DfEE, London, 1999), Chap 4, para 3.
2 *From Exclusion to Inclusion: A Report of the Disability Rights Task Force on Civil Rights for Disabled People* (DfEE, London, 1999), Chap 4, para 6.

1.6.5   The government's response was to announce its intention to implement the recommendations in respect of civil rights in education. An interim response was published to the full report in March 2000, and a full response was published in the summer of 2001[1].

1 *Towards Inclusion: Civil Rights for Disabled People* (DfES, 2001).

1.6.6   By the time of this full response, the government had already introduced the Special Educational Needs and Disability Bill, which brought together both strands of reform – to special educational needs and to disability discrimination – in one piece of legislation. The Bill received Royal Assent on 11 May 2001.

1.7   The Special Educational Needs and Disability Act 2001

1.7.1   The SENDA 2001 substantially amends two pieces of primary legislation, the EA 1996[1] and the DDA 1995[2], and makes consequential changes to other legislation, including the School Standards and Framework Act 1998 and the Disability Rights Commission Act 1999.

1 EA 1996, Pt IV.
2 DDA 1995, Pt III and a new Pt IV.

Special educational needs provisions

In respect of special educational needs, in pursuing the inclusion agenda[1]   **1.7.2**
the SENDA 2001:

(a) strengthens the right of children with special educational needs to be educated in mainstream schools where parents want this and the interests of other children can be protected[2];

(b) requires LEAs to make arrangements to provide parents of children with special educational needs with advice and information and a means of resolving disputes with schools and LEAs;

(c) requires LEAs to comply, within prescribed periods, with orders of the Special Educational Needs Tribunal (which will become the Special Educational Needs and Disability Tribunal from 1 September 2002); and

(d) requires schools to inform parents where they are making special educational provision for their children and allow schools to request a statutory assessment of a pupil's special educational needs.

The special educational needs provisions of the SENDA 2001 apply only to England and Wales.

1 See SENDA 2001, Explanatory Notes.
2 And see particularly EA 1996, s 316 and DfES Guidance *Inclusive Schooling: Children with Special Educational Needs* (DfES/0774/2001).

Disability provisions

The disability provisions, which apply to England, Wales and Scotland[1],   **1.7.3**
remove the exemption from the DDA 1995 previously enjoyed by schools and further and higher education colleges. They establish duties[2] on the bodies responsible for conducting schools and LEAs[3]:

(a) not to treat disabled pupils less favourably, without justification, for a reason which relates to their disability;

(b) to make reasonable adjustments so that disabled pupils are not put at a substantial disadvantage compared to pupils who are not disabled; and

(c) to plan strategically and make progress in increasing accessibility to schools' premises and to the curriculum and in improving the ways in which written information provided to pupils who are not disabled is provided to disabled pupils.

Duties are placed on further and higher education institutions and LEAs in respect of adult education and youth services[4]:

(a) not to treat disabled students less favourably, without justification, for a reason which relates to their disability; and

(b) to make reasonable adjustments to ensure that people who are disabled are not put at a substantial disadvantage compared to people who are not disabled in accessing further, higher and LEA secured education.

1 Please note, however, that this book is concerned only with the law in England and Wales.
2 See SENDA 2001, Explanatory Notes, para 14.
3 For the definition of 'responsible bodies', see 13.3.
4 See SENDA 2001, Explanatory Notes, para 15.

1.7.4 The Disability Rights Commission is given powers to issue explanatory and guiding codes of practice in relation to disability and to make arrangements for the provision of conciliation services[1]. The Special Educational Needs Tribunal (or, as it will be from 1 September 2002, the Special Educational Needs and Disability Tribunal) will be given jurisdiction to hear most complaints relating to disability in school based education, the county court in respect of post-16 based education and independent admission and exclusion appeal panels will deal with any claim of disability discrimination arising in respect of admission and most exclusion decisions.

1.8 Commencement of the Special Educational Needs and Disability Act 2001

1.8.1 The commencement of the various provisions of the SENDA 2001 has been fraught with difficulties. The main amendments to the DDA 1995 were always intended to take effect from 1 September 2002, and are still planned to come into force on this date (with the consequence that the Special Educational Needs Tribunal will become the Special Educational Needs and Disability Tribunal on this date too). The amendments imposing obligations on responsible bodies for post-16 education to make reasonable adjustments relating to auxiliary aids and services and in respect of premises are, however, intended to come into force on 1 September 2003 and 1 September 2005 respectively. The amendments to the EA 1996 and the introduction of a new Code of Practice and Regulations has, however, had to be changed from the original timetable. The intention was that the substantive provisions would come into force on 1 September 2001. At the same time a new special educational needs Code of Practice would take effect. However, the draft Code of Practice tabled before Parliament in June 2001 received some criticism over particular aspects of its guidance, and this first draft was withdrawn. This meant that the Code would not be ready for a September 2001 start and, consequently, the Secretary of State decided to put back implementation of all the special educational needs provisions until 1 January 2002 (with the exception of the new regulations requiring the publication of certain information by schools and LEAs[1]).

1 See Special Educational Needs (Provision of Information by Local Education Authorities) (England) Regulations 2001, SI 2001/2218.

1.8.2 In Wales, the commencement of the special educational needs provisions of the SENDA 2001 has been more gradual. The enabling and regulation-making powers came into force on 21 January 2002, but the substantive parts of the Act take effect from 1 April 2002.

1 See SENDA 2001 (Commencement) (Wales) Order 2002, SI 2002/74 (W.8) (C.1).

1.9 Codes of practice, regulations and other materials

Codes of practice

1.9.1 The original Code of Practice on the identification and assessment of special educational needs, introduced by the EA 1993, was a fairly successful document, and although certain aspects of its guidance were questioned[1] and there had been criticism of the workload imposed on teachers, it was seen as a good basis to build on. Similarly, under the DDA 1995 a number of codes of practice had been issued which provided practical advice and had been well received by users and the tribunals which had to have regard to their provision.

1 For example, its interpretation of the responsibilities of LEAs for children post-16: see Code of Practice, para 6:36.

Consequently, the EA 1996 and the DDA 1995, as amended by the SENDA 2001, now put even greater emphasis on the use of codes of practice and the importance of regard being had to them. In special educational needs terms, a draft Code of Practice was issued for consultation in January 1999 and the first revised Code laid before Parliament on 21 June 2001. That, however, met opposition and was withdrawn and a second revised Code was issued and approved by Parliament in November 2001. **1.9.2**

In disability terms, the Disability Rights Commission issued two draft codes of practice for consultation in July 2001: a draft code relating to schools[1] and a draft code relating to post-16 education[2]. At the time of writing, the final versions of the codes had not been approved and so references to the disability discrimination codes, unfortunately, can only be to the draft versions. Other codes of practice and guidance previously issued under the DDA 1995 will also affect the work of schools and LEAs in this area. Of particular importance will be the *Guidance issued on matters to be taken into account in determining questions relating to the definition of disability*[3]. **1.9.3**

1 Draft Code of Practice (Schools) New duties (from 2002) not to discriminate against disabled pupils and prospective pupils in the provision of education and associated services in schools, and in respect of admissions and exclusion.
2 Draft Code of Practice (Post 16) New duties (from 2002) in the provision of post-16 education and related services for disabled people and students.
3 HMSO, 1996.

Regulations

Regulations will also provide much of the detail needed to implement fully the changes in the SENDA 2001. The process for assessing, identifying and providing for children with special educational needs was contained in the Education (Special Educational Needs) Regulations 1994[1]. Although much of the procedures these laid down continue to apply, they were in need of review and, with the changes in the SENDA 2001, needed to include maters such as the changed process for amending statements and complying with Tribunal orders. Consequently, the Education (Special Educational Needs) (England) Regulations 2001[2] were issued. These were, though, quickly followed by the Education (Special Educational Needs) (England) (Amendment) Regulations 2001[3] and the Education (Special Educational Needs) (England) (Amendment No 2) Regulations 2001[4]. These were all then replaced by the Education (Special Educational Needs) (England) (Consolidation) Regulations 2001[5]. In addition, the Special Educational Needs (Provision of Information by Local Education Authorities) (England) Regulations 2001 set out the information which must be published by both LEAs and schools to inform parents of children with special educational needs of the services available[6]. **1.9.4**

1 SI 1994/1047.
2 SI 2001/2216.

15

3 SI 2001/2468.
4 SI 2001/2612.
5 SI 2001/3455.
6 SI 2001/2218.

1.9.5 Regulations will also provide the detail to the disability discrimination provisions in the amended DDA 1995. Pre-existing Regulations will be relevant
to certain functions, most important perhaps being the Disability
Discrimination (Meaning of Disability) Regulations 1996[1], which assist in
the definition of 'disability'. Drafts were issued for consultation in respect of
the student services which will fall within the new education provisions[2],
rules relating to the alteration of leasehold premises[3], and certain justifications for discriminating against students[4], all of which should be finalised in
time for the coming into force of the disability discrimination elements in
September 2002.

1 SI 1996/1455.
2 Draft Disability Discrimination (Student Services) Regulations.
3 Draft Disability Discrimination (Educational Institutions) (Alterations of Leasehold
   Premises) Regulations.
4 Draft Disability Discrimination (Justifications) Regulations.

1.9.6 The Tribunal, in contrast, seems to have escaped lightly. A review of its procedures had already led to the Special Educational Needs Tribunal
Regulations 2001[1], which came into force on 1 September 2001 and which
have applied to appeals to the Tribunal brought after that date. New regulations will be required to set out the procedure for appeals to what will
become the Special Educational Needs and Disability Tribunal, but at the
time of writing these had not been drafted.

1 SI 2001/600.

Other materials

1.9.7 Beneath regulations, there will be guidance both on the special educational
needs and the discrimination aspects of the legislation. In November 2001
the DfES published guidance, *Inclusive Schooling: Children with Special
Educational Needs*[1], and more will come in relation to disability accessibility
strategies and plans and other aspects of the disability discrimination provisions. For special educational needs practitioners, the DfES has also
published an SEN Toolkit, a 12-section practical guide for those working
with children with special educational needs, giving guidance on such matters as statement writing, dispute resolution, parent partnership and the
review of statements.

1 DfES/0774/2001.

1.9.8 One of the aims set out in the DfEE's *Meeting Special Educational Needs: A
Programme of Action*, was 'introducing a simplified SEN Code of Practice'[1].
It might be a moot point whether the Code of Practice itself has been simplified: the new Code comprises 207 pages compared to 164 in the old
version. But with all the other materials required in order to gain an understanding of the responsibilities in schools, further and higher education
institutions and LEAs – at a rough count, two pieces of primary legislation,
three codes of practice, a toolkit, at least six sets of regulations and untold
guidance – the task is hardly simple. For parents who may not necessarily

have access to the printed versions of these materials (however accessible they may have to be in the future) or to the web versions, the task may be Herculean. It is hoped, however, that this book may be of some assistance to all of them.

1 *Meeting Special Educational Needs: A Programme of Action* (DfEE, 1998), p 14.

Chapter 2

Special educational needs: definitions and general principles

---

Introduction   2.1

One of the many ironies of the law and practice of special educational needs   2.1.1
is the large number of definitions and, at times, ambiguous general principles which direct and guide parents, schools and Local Education
Authorities (LEAs) in their work with children with special educational
needs. With respect to many parents, often parents of children with special
educational needs have special educational needs themselves and it is therefore particularly unfortunate that there has not been greater clarity in the
concepts and terminology used.

To understand the various duties and powers imposed on LEAs and schools,   2.1.2
it is necessary to have an appreciation of key definitions and principles,
firstly, in order to establish whether a child has special educational needs
and, secondly, to know what assistance and support may follow. This chapter will therefore attempt to explain some of these most important
definitions and principles.

Codes of Practice   2.2

Before turning to those definitions and principles, however, it is first of all   2.2.1
important to consider the Codes of Practice introduced, firstly, under the
Education Act (EA) 1993 and, now, the Education Act (EA) 1996, which
were intended, at least in part, to provide a clearer explanation of the work-
ings of the special educational needs legislation and also offer practical
guidance to LEAs, schools and parents.

The Secretary of State is under a duty to issue, and may from time to time   2.2.2
revise, a code of practice giving practical guidance in respect of the discharge
by LEAs and the governing bodies of maintained schools of their functions
towards children with special educational needs[1].

1 EA 1996, s 313(1).

In exercising their functions in respect of these children, LEAs and govern-   2.2.3
ing bodies, and any other person exercising any function for the purpose of

the discharge by LEAs and governing bodies of their functions, must have regard to the provisions of this statutory code of practice[1]. On any appeal to the Tribunal, it must also have regard to any provision of the Code of Practice which appears to the Tribunal to be relevant to any question arising on the appeal[2].

1 EA 1996, s 313(2).
2 EA 1996, s 313(3).

2.2.4   Codes of practice are statutory in nature and the process by which they are issued is prescribed in the EA 1996[1]. Where the Secretary of State proposes to issue or revise a code of practice, he is required to prepare a draft[2]. The Secretary of State must then consult such persons about the draft as he thinks fit and shall consider any representations made by the consultees[3]. If the Secretary of State determines to proceed with the draft (either in its original form or with such modifications as he thinks fit), he shall lay it before both Houses of Parliament[4]. If the draft is approved by resolution of each House, the Secretary of State shall issue the code of practice in the form of the draft and, the code of practice shall come into effect on such day as the Secretary of State may by order appoint[5].

1 EA 1996, s 314.
2 EA 1996, s 314(2).
3 EA 1996, s 314(2).
4 EA 1996, s 314(3).
5 EA 1996, s 314(4).

2.2.5   In the debate in the House of Lords on the EA 1993, the then Minister of State, Baroness Blatch, explained that the government saw the Code, together with the provisions of the EA 1993 and the regulations made under it, as setting the future framework for special education. The Code would 'deal with matters which are not susceptible to hard and fast rules, matters where an element of judgment is always required'[1]. The Code should also promote a consistent and coherent approach to special education across England and Wales. The Code would deal with the identification and assessment of both children under five and those of school age who have special educational needs – both the 18% who have such needs but do not require a statement, and the 2% whose needs are best met through a statement[2].

1 Hansard, 29.4.93, 485–492.
2 Hansard, 29.4.93, 485–492.

2.2.6   The Secretary of State issued the first Code, the Code of Practice on the Identification and Assessment of Special Educational Needs, in 1993. This came into effect on 1 September 1994. In March 1998 a supplement to the Code was issued to provide 'guidance on the application of the Code to providers outside the maintained sector of education who provide nursery education as part of an Early Years Development Plan'.

2.2.7   A review of the Code took place in 2000, and a revised Code of Practice was originally laid before Parliament in June 2001 with the intent that it would come into effect on 1 September 2001, at the same time as the special educational needs provisions in the Special Education Needs and Disability Needs and Disability Act (SENDA) 2001. In view of comments made on parts of the revised Code, especially the degree of specificity required when drafting statements, the government withdrew it and carried out further consultation. The final revised Code (referred to throughout this book as the 'Code of Practice') was subsequently issued in November 2001 and came into effect on 1 January 2002.

The Code of Practice takes account of the special educational needs provisions of SENDA 2001 and provides[1]: **2.2.8**

- a stronger right for children with special educational needs to be educated at mainstream schools;
- new duties on LEAs to arrange for parents of children with special educational needs to be provided with services offering advice and information and a means of resolving disputes;
- a new duty on schools and relevant nursery education providers to tell parents when they are making special educational provision for their child; and
- a new right for schools and relevant nursery education providers to request a statutory assessment of a child.

1 Code of Practice, Foreword, para 8.

SPECIAL EDUCATIONAL NEEDS: DEFINITIONS

Special education 2.3

Before turning to these new principles and the other general concepts, it is important to understand some of the terminology used in the field of special educational needs. **2.3.1**

A child has 'special educational needs' for the purposes of the EA 1996 if he has a learning difficulty which calls for special educational provision to be made for him[1]. In *B v Isle of Wight Council*[2], McCullough J held that the 'needs' in Pt II of a statement of special educational needs are for the 'provision' in Pt III. A child did not have special *educational* needs unless his difficulty called for special *educational* provision. Not every learning difficulty called for special *educational* provision. Although an exceptionally gifted child may appear to require educational provision which is additional to, or different from, the educational provision made generally for children of his age, he will not have special educational needs simply by reason of being intellectually abler than his peers. Only where a gifted child has learning difficulties, such as dyslexia, will such a child have special educational needs within the EA 1996[3]. **2.3.2**

1 EA 1996, s 312(1).
2 [1997] ELR 279.
3 See *R v Secretary of State for Education, ex p C* [1996] ELR 93.

A child has a 'learning difficulty' if either: (a) he has a significantly greater difficulty in learning than a majority of children of his age; (b) he has a disability[1] which either prevents or hinders him from making use of educational facilities of a kind generally provided for children of his age within the area of the LEA; or (c) he is under compulsory school age and is, or would be if special educational provision were not made for him, likely to fall within (a) or (b) when of that age[2]. A child is not to be taken as having **2.3.3** a learning difficulty solely because the language (or form of the language) in which he is, or will be, taught is different from a language (or form of language) which has at any time been spoken in his home[3].

> 1 'Disability' is not defined in the EA 1996: it must have the same meaning as in Disability Discrimination Act 1995 (DDA 1995), s 1 (see Chapter 10). But a different definition of disability is also contained in s 17(11) of the Children Act 1989 which states that a child is disabled if he is blind, deaf or dumb or suffers from a mental disorder of any kind or is substantially and permanently handicapped by illness, injury or congenital deformity or such other disability as may be prescribed. For SEN purposes, a child may therefore have a disability if he or she falls within either or both definitions – see Code of Practice para 1:3.
> 2 EA 1996, s.312(2).
> 3 EA 1996, s 312(3).

2.3.4 In one of the first cases to consider the definition of 'learning difficulties'[1], an LEA argued that dyslexia was not a learning difficulty on the (somewhat tendentious) basis that if educational provision was available generally for children, including those with dyslexia, the child could not require *special* educational provision. In dismissing that argument, the judge noted that the child was highly intelligent but suffered from some degree of dyslexia, which caused a significant weakness in his capacity for continuous reading, spelling and continuous essay-writing. The interaction of his high intelligence and his dyslexia caused him to be depressed and frustrated. The judge held that:

> '[i]t is very difficult to see how one could come to any other conclusion than that J had a learning difficulty . . . His dyslexia would appear to give him significantly greater difficulty in learning than the majority of children of his age. The fact that he has a very high intelligence and may therefore be able, to some extent, to compensate for that difficulty is neither here nor there. Again . . . his dyslexia is clearly a disability. Although it does not prevent him from making use of educational facilities, it is hard to see how one could come to any other conclusion than that it hindered him. Accordingly, it would seem to me that . . . the only reasonable conclusion one could reach would be that [he] does . . . have a learning difficulty.'

> 1 *R v Hampshire Education Authority, ex p J* (1985) 84 LGR 547.

2.3.5 'Special educational provision' means: (a) in relation to a child who has attained the age of two, educational provision which is additional to, or otherwise different from, the educational provision made generally for children of his age in schools maintained by the LEA (other than special schools); and (b) in relation to a child under that age, educational provision of any kind[1].

> 1 EA 1996, s 312(4).

2.3.6 The meaning of 'special educational provision' was also considered in *R v Hampshire Education Authority, ex p J*[1]. The LEA argued that if an educational provision was made available generally for children of the applicant's age by an LEA in their schools, then it was not a special educational provision. Thus, if there was provision generally available in the LEA's schools to cope with deaf children or dyslexic children, then such provision would not be special educational provision. The judge quite rightly rejected this argument as potentially driving a coach and horses through the new special educational needs legislation.

> 1 (1985) 84 LGR 547.

The definitions refer to a 'child' with special educational needs and requir-   **2.3.7**
ing special educational provision. In this context, a 'child' includes any
person who has not attained the age of 19 and is not a registered pupil at a
school[1], as well as including children of compulsory school age.

1 EA 1996, s 312(5).

'Children for whom responsibility lies'   **2.4**

An LEA is required to exercise its powers with a view to securing that, of the   **2.4.1**
children for whom it is responsible, it identifies those children who have special educational needs, and further it is necessary for the LEA to determine
the special educational provision which any learning difficulties call for[1].
  An LEA is responsible for a child if he is in their area and:

(a) he is a registered pupil at a maintained school;
(b) education is provided for him at a school which is not a maintained
    school but is so provided at the expense of the LEA;
(c) where (a) or (b) above do not apply, but he is a registered pupil at a
    school and has been brought to the LEA's attention as having or prob-
    ably having special educational needs; or
(d) he is not a registered pupil at a school but is not under the age of two
    or over compulsory school age and has been brought to their attention
    as having or probably having special educational needs[2].

1 EA 1996, s 321(1) and (2).
2 EA 1996, s 321(3).

A 'child' includes any person who has not attained the age of 19 and is a reg-   **2.4.2**
istered pupil at a school[1].
  A 'pupil' is defined as a person for whom education is being provided at
a school, other than (a) a person who has attained the age of 19 for whom
further education is being provided; or (b) a person for whom part-time
education suitable to the requirements of persons of any age over compulsory school age is being provided[2].
  A 'school' is an educational institution which is outside the further education sector and the higher education sector and is an institution for
providing (a) primary education, (b) secondary education, or (c) both primary and secondary education, whether or not the institution also provides
part-time education suitable to the requirements of junior pupils or further
education[3].
  'Secondary education' is defined as meaning (a) full-time education suitable
to the requirements of pupils of compulsory school age who are either senior
pupils, or junior pupils who have attained the age of ten years and six months
and whom it is expedient to educate together with senior pupils of compulsory
school age; and (b) full-time education suitable to the requirements of pupils
who are over compulsory school age but under the age of 19 which is provided
at a school at which education within para (a) is also provided[4].

1 EA 1996, s 312(5).
2 EA 1996, s 3(1).
3 EA 1996, s 4(1).
4 EA 1996, s 2(2) and (5).

2.4.3 The net effect of all these confusing definitions is that an LEA remains responsible for a child until he attains the age of 19 so long as he remains a pupil at a school. It follows, therefore, that once he attains the age of 19 or, before attaining that age, he leaves school, for example, to go into employment or to receive further education at a further education college, the LEA will cease to be responsible. In these cases, the statement will lapse simply by reason of the change of situation; there will be no need for the LEA formally to cease to maintain the statement. This was reflected in the original Code[1] which stated: 'a statement will remain in force until the LEA ceases to maintain it, or until the child is no longer the responsibility of the LEA, for example, if he or she moves into the further or higher education sector, or to social services provision, in which case the statement will lapse'. The inclusion of the words 'or to social services provision' caused some confusion, as it is a rather ambiguous phrase and 'social services provision' is not defined.

1 Code of Practice, para 6:36.

2.4.4 Under the current Code of Practice[1] it appears that a statement will lapse if a young person leaves school at age 16 plus to seek employment or training and there will be no need for the LEA to cease to maintain the statement in accordance with the statutory procedures[2]. Where a young person moves onto further or higher education the statement will lapse provided that the young person, the parents, the LEA and the further education institution are all in agreement about the child's transfer. There is therefore no need to formally cease the statement since the young person will cease to be a pupil for whom the LEA is responsible after leaving school, and so the statement will lapse[3]. If however there is agreement all round that the child should stay at school post 16, and the LEA or other LEAs, have appropriate school provision, the LEA should normally continue to maintain the statement[4]. Where, however, there is disagreement over the appropriate provision and the parents want their child to remain at school post 16, but the LEA considers that the young person's needs would be better met in a further education institution, the statement will not lapse. Instead, if the LEA are satisfied that the FE institution can meet his needs and has offered a place, the LEA should take steps to cease to maintain the statement[5]. The key difference between codes is therefore the introduction of advice to the effect that when a child moves into the further education (FE) sector, the statement will lapse only if everyone is agreed that that should happen.

1 Code of Practice, paras 8:121 to 8:123.
2 Code of Practice, para 8:122.
3 Code of Practice, para 8:121.
4 Code of Practice, para 8:122.
5 Code of Practice, para 8:123.

2.4.5 In *R v Dorset County Council and Further Education Funding Council, ex p Goddard*[1] an LEA misinterpreted the relevant provisions and had attempted to pass responsibility for a child to the Further Education Funding Council (FEFC). The child involved was aged 16 and had severe speech and language problems. The LEA had maintained a statement for him which specified he should attend an independent special school up to the age of 16. After he reached 16, his parents wanted him to attend another residential special school. The LEA initially thought that this placement would be funded by the FEFC, but the FEFC refused. The LEA did not amend or cease to maintain the statement and the child reached 16, at which point the LEA indicated that he should be able to attend the FE college and stated that as he was over compulsory school age they were no longer responsible for him. The FE college could not, in fact, meet his needs and the parents sought to argue that the statement still applied to the child and that the LEA were responsible. The LEA refused and were therefore challenged by judicial review. The judge held that the LEA recognised that the independent residential school suggested by the parents was the one institution appropriate to the child's needs and that it was only when it was suggested that the LEA should pay for the placement that it sought to suggest an FE college could meet his needs. Because his needs could, therefore, only be met in a school, the LEA continued to remain responsible. Only if they decided to cease to maintain the statement in accordance with the relevant statutory provisions could an LEA end its responsibility. On the facts, though, the LEA could not have ceased to maintain the statement as it was clearly still necessary for it to be maintained. The judge further held that the FEFC's (and now its successor, the Learning and Skills Council's) duty to 16 to 18 year olds was secondary to that of the LEA where the LEA was responsible and maintained, or should have maintained, a statement for a pupil requiring education in a school.

1 [1995] ELR 109, QBD.

SPECIAL EDUCATIONAL NEEDS: GENERAL PRINCIPLES

Inclusion – children with special educational needs should normally be educated in mainstream schools

2.5

One of the key changes brought about by the SENDA 2001, possibly reflecting the then Secretary of State's own personal circumstances and own experience of the special educational needs system, was the fundamental principle that children with special educational needs should have a stronger right to be educated in mainstream schools. To a certain extent, the aim of increasing the inclusion of special needs children in mainstream schools had been apparent since the Warnock Report, the Education Act 1981 and the Education Act 1993 (and hence into the EA 1996 consolidation). Nonetheless, the government identified a need for further work to be done on achieving inclusion, supported by clearer responsibilities in the primary legislation[1]. The provisions of the Special Educational Needs and Disability Bill relating to this were the most debated, with concerns being raised that, particularly with children with emotional and behavioural difficulties, a greater emphasis on placing these children in mainstream schools, certainly without adequate support, could harm the education of other children in the school.

2.5.1

1 See the Green Paper, *Excellence for all children: meeting special educational needs.*

The position is now that a child who has no statement of special educational needs (and who should be educated in a school[1]) must[2] be educated in a mainstream school[3].

2.5.2

Thus, children without statements should not be admitted to a special school unless one of the following apply[4]:

(a) the child is admitted to a special school for the purposes of an assessment of his educational needs and his admission to that school is with the agreement of the LEA, the headteacher (or in Wales, the governing body), the parent and any person whose advice is to be sought as part of the assessment[5];

(b) he remains admitted to a special school, in prescribed circumstances following an assessment of his educational needs at that school[6];

(c) he is admitted to a special school, following a change in his circumstances, with the agreement of the LEA, headteacher of the school (or in Wales, the governing body) and his parent[7];

(d) he is admitted to a community or foundation special school which is established in a hospital[8].

1 EA 1996, s 316(1).
2 EA 1996, s316(2); and see also *Inclusive Schooling: Children with Special Educational Needs* (DfES/0774/2001).
3 A 'mainstream school' being any school other than (a) a special school, or (b) an independent school which is not a (i) city technology college, (ii) city college for the technology of the arts, or (iii) a city academy: EA 1996, s 316(4).
4 EA 1996, s 316A(2).
5 EA 1996, s 316A(2)(a).
6 EA 1996, s 316A(2)(b).
7 EA 1996, s 316A(2)(c).
8 EA 1996, s 316A(2)(d).

2.5.3 In principle, if a child has a statement of special educational needs, he must be educated in a mainstream school unless that is incompatible with:

(a) the wishes of his parents, or
(b) the provision of efficient education for other children[1].

> 'It is reasonable to expect [an LEA] to be able to provide a mainstream education for nearly all children with special educational needs. However, it is not reasonable or practical to expect all schools to provide for every possible type of special educational need. When making decisions about individual schools the Government believes that it is right to consider: what parents want; an individual school's suitability to provide for the needs of the pupil; the impact their inclusion would have on resources and the efficient education of others.'[2]

1 EA 1996, s 316(3); and see *Inclusive Schooling: Children with Special Educational Needs* (DfES/0774/2001), paras 22 to 24.
2 *Inclusive Schooling: Children with Special Educational Needs* (DfES/0774/2001), para 29.

2.5.4 So far as the provision of efficient education is concerned, an LEA may, in relation to their mainstream schools taken as a whole, rely on this exception only if they show that there are no reasonable steps that they could take to prevent the incompatibility[1]. In relation to a particular mainstream school, the LEA, or governing body, may rely on the exception only if it shows that there are no reasonable steps that it or another LEA, or governing body, in relation to the school could take to prevent the incompatibility[2]. Detailed statutory guidance on what steps are reasonable is contained in *Inclusive Schooling: Children with Special Educational Needs*[3]. This exception, in addition, does not permit a governing body to fail to comply with the duty imposed on it[4] to admit a child to the school, if the school is named in the child's statement[5].

1 EA 1996, s 316A(5).

2 EA 1996, s 316A(6).
3 DfES/0774/2001, at paras 23, 45 and 46.
4 EA 1996, s 324(5)(b).
5 EA 1996, s 316A(7).

In performing their duties under these provisions, LEAs and governing   **2.5.5**
bodies must have regard to guidance issued by the Secretary of State, or in
Wales, by the National Assembly for Wales[1]. That guidance shall, in particular, relate to steps which may, or may not be regarded as reasonable for
the purposes of considering steps taken to prevent any incompatibility with
the provision of efficient education for other children[2].

1 EA 1996, s 316A(8); and see *Inclusive Schooling: Children with Special Educational Needs*
  (DfES/0774/2001) (separate guidance will be issued for Wales).
2 EA 1996, s 316A(9).

These provisions thus have a different emphasis than the original provi-   **2.5.6**
sions under the EA 1996 to reflect the need for greater inclusion. The old
provisions stated that that an LEA had to secure, subject to certain conditions, that a child was to be educated in a school which was not a special
school unless it was incompatible with the wishes of his parent. The conditions were that so educating a child was compatible with (a) his receiving the
special educational provision which his learning difficulty calls for, (b) the
provision of efficient education for the children with whom he will be educated, and (c) the efficient use of resources[1]. The key difference is,
apparently, the deletion of the condition enabling an LEA to declare provision in a mainstream school to be incompatible if it is contrary to the
efficient use of resources.

1 EA 1996, s 316 prior to amendment by the Special Educational Needs and Disability Act
  2001.

The *Consultation Document on the SEN and Disability Rights in Education Bill*   **2.5.7**
suggested that the government wanted to strengthen the right to a mainstream place (by replacing s 316) whilst simultaneously giving parents the
right to insist on a special school. The consultation was worded:

> 'The principles of the new provision would be that a child with SEN *shall*
> be educated within a mainstream setting unless:
>
> (a)   this is incompatible with the wishes of his or her parents; or
> (b)   a school or local authority[1] cannot take reasonable steps to adapt its
>   provision to secure a place for them in a mainstream setting without:
>   (i)   prejudicing the efficient education of the children with whom he
>   or she will be educated; or
>   (ii) incurring unreasonable public expenditure [emphasis added].'[2]

1 Presumably this means LEA in practice.
2 *Consultation Document on the SEN and Disability Rights in Education Bill.*

In practice, it is not clear what effect the changes will actually have. In fact,   **2.5.8**
whilst the paramount duty has been changed, the underlying duties which
determine whether LEAs must comply with a parent's preference for a
maintained placement[1] or consider their representations for non-maintained
provision remain unaltered[2]. Some assistance may, however, be gleaned
from *Inclusive Schooling: Children with Special Educational Needs*[3].

1 EA 1996, Sch 27, para 3.

2 See EA 1996, s 316(3).
3 DfES/0774/2001.

2.5.9 The provisions are not easy to understand. It will be difficult for LEAs to understand how this will work, let alone explain it to parents who may have been led to believe that their child has the right to a mainstream placement. What it means is that whether an LEA can have regard to the efficient use of resources in making a placement will depend upon how a particular placement has come to be proposed[1].

1 See *Inclusive Schooling: Children with Special Educational Needs* (DfES/0774/2001), paras 27 to 39 and Annex C.

2.5.10 Thus, if following an assessment of a child's special educational needs, an LEA proposes to make a statement of special educational needs, and a parent exercises his right to express a preference for a maintained school he wishes his child to attend[1], the LEA must comply with that preference unless the school is unsuitable to the child's age, ability or aptitude or to his special educational needs or that attendance of the child at the school would be incompatible with the provision of efficient education for the children[2] with whom he would be educated or the efficient use of resources[3]. Ie the LEA may take into account the efficient use of resources when considering complying with the parent's request. Where, however, a mainstream placement is against the wishes of the parent, the LEA may educate the child in a special school; the decision though is the LEA's[4], thus it need not educate the child in a special school if it does not believe the school to be suitable.

1 EA 1996, Sch 27, para 3(1); and see *Inclusive Schooling: Children with Special Educational Needs* (DfES/0774/2001), para 27.
2 For guidance on the meaning of efficient education for children with whom he would be educated, see *Inclusive Schooling: Children with Special Educational Needs* (DfES/0774/2001), paras 40 to 44, but especially para 42: it should mean only those children with whom the child will directly come into contact on a day-to-day basis.
3 EA 1996, Sch 27, para 3(3).
4 *Inclusive Schooling: Children with Special Educational Needs* (DfES/0774/2001), para 34.

2.5.11 Similarly, if following an assessment and a proposal to issue a statement, a parent makes representations that their child should attend an independent mainstream school (ie a city technology college or city academy), a non-maintained special school or an independent school, the LEA must consider those representations[1] but is permitted to disregard the parent's wish if the school is unsuitable to the child's age, ability or aptitude or to his special educational needs or that attendance of the child at the school would be incompatible with the provision of efficient education for the children with whom he would be educated or the efficient use of resources[2]. Ie the LEA may take into account the efficient use of resources when considering complying with the parent's request.

1 EA 1996, s 9 and Sch 27, para 4; and see *C v Buckinghamshire County Council and the Special Educational Needs Tribunal* [1999] ELR 179, CA; and see 2.6.
2 EA 1996, Sch 27, para 3(3); and see also *Inclusive Schooling: Children with Special Educational Needs* (DfES/0774/2001), para 37.

2.5.12 If, however, on proposing to make a statement, a parent does not express a preference or if a parent for whose child a statement is already maintained asks the LEA to substitute the name of a different maintained school to that specified in the current statement[1], it will not be permissible for an LEA to take account of the efficient use of resources when determining the appropriate placement for that child; the general presumption that the child should be educated in a mainstream school will apply unless, but only unless, the placement is incompatible with the wishes of his parent or the provision of efficient education for other children[2]. *Inclusive Schooling: Children with Special Educational Needs*[3], on the other hand[4], suggests that in the latter case, the normal procedures outlined in 2.5.11 and 2.5.12 will apply. That suggestion may not, however, accord with the provisions of s 316A(3) of the EA 1996 when read with paragraph 8 of Schedule 27 of the same Act, and should therefore be questioned.

1 Under EA 1996, Sch 27, para 8.
2 EA 1996, s 316(3); and see *Inclusive Schooling: Children with Special Educational Needs* (DfES/0774/2001), para 30.
3 DfES/0774/2001.
4 *Inclusive Schooling: Children with Special Educational Needs* (DfES/0774/2001), para 33.

Although there is therefore now, in effect, a presumption that children **2.5.13** should be educated in mainstream schools, it should be noted that this does not prevent a child from being educated in (a) an independent school which is not a mainstream school[1], or (b) an approved non-maintained special school, if the cost is met otherwise than by an LEA (ie if the parent pays or the child benefits from a scholarship or other charitable funding)[2]. As has been seen, if one of the exceptions[3] applies, a child can be educated in a special school. Nor does the presumption affect the power of LEAs[4] to name, and pay the fees of, a non-maintained special school which is named in a child's statement of special educational needs[5].

1 City technology colleges and city academies are independent schools which are also maintained schools – see *Inclusive Schooling: Children with Special Educational Needs* (DfES/0774/2001), para 31.
2 EA 1996, s 316A(1).
3 EA 1996, s 316A(2).
4 Under EA 1996, s 348.
5 EA 1996, s 316A(3)(a).

Parental wishes

2.6

One area which has caused the courts some problems when interpreting the **2.6.1** EA 1996 is the actual effect of parental wishes and preferences on the duties of LEAs to secure an appropriate placement for the child. As has been seen[1], the duty to educate in mainstream schools is subject to the qualification that the duty does not apply if a mainstream placement would be incompatible with the wishes of the child's parent[2]. In addition, another factor which complicates an LEA's task is the interrelationship between the special educational needs provisions of the EA 1996 and the general overriding duty placed on LEAs to have regard to parental wishes[3]. In exercising or performing their respective powers and duties under the Education Acts, LEAs shall have regard to the general principle that pupils are to be educated in accordance with the wishes of their parents, so far as that is compatible with the provision of efficient instruction and training and the avoidance of unreasonable public expenditure[4].

1 See 2.5.

2 EA 1996, s 316(3).
3 EA 1996, s 9.
4 EA 1996, s 9.

2.6.2 Initially, it was thought that the duty in s 9 of the EA 1996 did not apply in respect of children with special educational needs and the general duty was overridden by the specific special educational needs provisions of the EA 1996. However, this view was disabused by the Court of Appeal in *C v Buckinghamshire County Council and the Special Educational Needs Tribunal*[1].

1 [1999] ELR 179, CA.

2.6.3 In *C*[1], the Court of Appeal, whilst dismissing the actual appeal, pointed out that the general duty in s 9 applied equally to children with special educational needs as it did to children without such needs. The interrelationship of the general provision with the specific special educational needs provisions means that:

(a) if a parent expresses a preference for a maintained school, an LEA *must* comply in the absence either of the placement being incompatible with the parent's wishes (which, unless the child's parents are themselves in dispute with each other, will not patently apply) or it is incompatible with the provision of efficient education for other children[2]; and

(b) if a parent expresses a preference for an independent or non-maintained school, an LEA need only *consider* rather than *comply* with that preference, having regard to its general duty under s 9 and therefore its ability to disregard the parent's expressed preference if that was incompatible with the provision of efficient instruction and training and the avoidance of unreasonable public expenditure.

1 *C v Buckinghamshire County Council and the Special Educational Needs Tribunal* [1999] ELR 179, CA.
2 EA 1996, s 316(3).

2.6.4 The Court of Appeal also emphasised that s 9 of the EA 1996 did not provide parents with a veto over the LEA's proposed placement. If[1] the LEA's proposed school and the parent's preferred independent or non-maintained school were both adequate, but the LEA's proposed school was markedly more suitable than the other, neither the LEA or a Tribunal could 'ignore the difference and abdicate its judgement in favour of the parent's. To do so, since a section 9 choice may lawfully include an independent school, would be to extend the mandatory range of parental choice beyond that to which it is expressly limited by paragraph 3(1) Schedule 27 [EA 1996]'[2]. The Court of Appeal considered that on the facts of the case, the LEA's proposed school was more suitable than the parent's preference and upheld the Tribunal's decision naming the LEA's school.

1 See *C v Buckinghamshire County Council and the Special Educational Needs Tribunal* [1999] ELR 179, at p 188.
2 *C v Buckinghamshire County Council and the Special Educational Needs Tribunal* [1999] ELR 179, per Sedley LJ at p 188.

2.6.5 What, however, *C*[1] did not really address was the situation where the parent's preferred maintained school was either as suitable or more suitable than the LEA's proposed placement. In *C v Lancashire County Council*[2],

Popplewell J was faced with the situation where the child's parents had expressed a preference for a mainstream maintained secondary school, whilst the LEA wished to place the child at a special school. The LEA argued before the Tribunal that the cost of meeting the parent's preference would be £37,000 whilst provision at the special school would cost only £15,000. Evidence produced by the parents at the Tribunal however showed that the mainstream school could meet all his needs. The Tribunal concluded that given the disparity in costs, educating the child in a mainstream school could not be an efficient use of resources. On appeal to the High Court, Popplewell J held that the question of suitability of placement was a question of fact for the Tribunal. Having decided it, no question of balancing in favour, or considering whether there was a presumption in favour, of the parent's wishes arose. Where an LEA raised the issue of efficient use of resources[3], a balancing exercise had to be carried out: 'One has to look at the figures, decide whether there is additional cost, and then do a balancing exercise weighing the additional cost against the parents' preference.' Although the Tribunal's decision could have been better worded, the judge held that the Tribunal had accepted that the parents' preferred school could not have met his needs without additional expertise or specialised resources and that would have been double the expenditure. There was no educational gain in incurring the extra costs and therefore the parent's preference had been correctly outweighed by the inefficient use of resources involved.

1 *C v Buckinghamshire County Council and the Special Educational Needs Tribunal* [1999] ELR 179, CA.
2 [1997] ELR 377.
3 *C v Lancashire County Council* [1997] ELR 377 at p 388.

Subsequently, in *W-R v Solihull Metropolitan Borough Council and Wall (Chairman of the Special Educational Needs Tribunal)*[1], the Tribunal had decided in favour of the LEA's proposed maintained day special school placement and not the parent's expressed wish that he should attend an independent boarding school. Her appeal to the High Court was dismissed not least because the judge concluded that the parent herself was resolutely opposed to residential education. Nonetheless, the judge held that the Tribunal had accurately considered the preference she had expressed at the hearing, but, having come to a proper conclusion as to the merits of the proposals in relation to the two alternative schools, the mere fact that the parent preferred one to the other was of little significance. **2.6.6**

1 [1999] ELR 528, QBD.

The relationship between efficient use of resources and parental preference was considered further by the Court of Appeal in *Lane v Worcestershire County Council*[1], where the Court of Appeal held that a Tribunal could, having taken into account s 9 of the EA 1996, decide that a suitably adapted mainstream maintained school could meet the needs of a child with Turner's syndrome and cerebral palsy and that placement at the independent school preferred by the mother would on the facts be an unreasonable use of public resources. **2.6.7**

1 [2000] All ER (D) 333.

Clarification on what costs an LEA, and subsequently the Tribunal, may take into account have been provided by the courts. In *B v Harrow London* **2.6.8**

Borough Council[1] the LEA named a school which it maintained, but the parent expressed a preference for her child to attend another maintained school located in a neighbouring LEA. The placement in the neighbouring LEA's school would have cost the LEA £11,000–£12,000 a year. On that basis the LEA and the Tribunal concluded that complying with the parent's preference would not be an efficient use of resources. On appeal, the House of Lords agreed. Firstly, they concluded that the principles applying to the efficient use of resources argument in the case of admissions of children without statements of special educational needs[2] did not necessarily apply to the definition of inefficient use of resources in respect of children with statements. The relevant provisions referred to '*the* LEA's resources', not to LEA resources generally, which the parents were arguing, and therefore what fell to be considered were the responsible LEA's resources and their use; not the resources of any other LEA. Thus, the parent's preferred placement could properly be considered an inefficient use of the responsible LEA's resources. Lord Slynn[3] added that:

> 'I do not consider that s 9 [of the EA 1996] means that parental preference is to prevail unless it involves unreasonable public expenditure. In dealing with special schools, the [LEA] must also observe the specific provisions of Schedule 27, paragraph 3(3). This does not mean that the parent loses the right to express a preference. A preference may be expressed but it is subject to the qualifications set out in paragraph 3(3)[4], one of which is the efficient use of resources – in my opinion, the responsible LEA's resources. It may be as a result that a child seeking to go to a special school out of his own LEA's area may have more difficulty in doing so than a child seeking to go to another school. But that is what . . . parliament has clearly provided.'[5]

1 [2000] 1 WLR 223, [2000] ELR 109, HL.
2 See School Standards and Framework Act 1998, ss 88ff.
3 *B v Harrow London Borough Council* [2000] ELR 109 at p 116.
4 *Viz* wishes of the parent and compatibility with efficient education and the efficient use of resources.
5 *B v Harrow London Borough Council* [1 [2000] 1 WLR 223, [2000] ELR 109 at p 116.

2.6.9 Most recently, in *Oxfordshire County Council v GB*[1], the cost which an LEA could cite was clarified. In that case, the question for determination was whether, in making a comparison between two appropriate schools, one an independent specialist school, the other a mainstream LEA school with a specialist unit, the cost of the latter is to be taken as the global cost of LEA provision (either in total or for the school in question) divided by the relevant number of pupils, or simply the additional budgetary cost of placing the child there. In its broader form, it is whether the cost of placing a child in the state sector should be taken to be an individual fraction of the global cost of local state provision, or whether that provision is to be regarded as given and the relevant expenditure quantified as the additional amount which the placement will cost the LEA[2]. The Tribunal, in that case, when calculating the respective costs had included within the cost of the child attending the LEA's proposed placement an element for transport and teaching support which the LEA would have had to bear in respect of other children, whether or not the child had actually attended the unit. In effect, there was double counting, as those amounts could equally have been allocated to the costs of sending other children to that unit. The cost of the LEA provision, it was argued, and accepted by the Court of Appeal, was higher than it should have been and hence that meant that the differential between the cost of the parent's preference and the LEA's proposed provision was, perhaps unusually, greater than had been assessed by the Tribunal.

1   [2002] ELR 8, CA.
2   [2002] ELR 8, CA.

Sedley LJ concluded that[1]:

2.6.10

'the chief object of the last part of s 9 [ie compatibility with the efficient use of resources] is to prevent parental choice placing an undue or disproportionate burden on the education budget. When one considers that a single placement in the independent sector may well cost a ring-fenced education budget more than a teacher's salary, one can readily see why . . . The parental preference for an independent school, while perfectly reasonable, may have difficult cost implications for the LEA. In that event it is for the LEA, or on appeal the Tribunal, to decide whether those cost implications make the expenditure on the independent school unreasonable. This means striking a balance between (a) the educational advantages of the placement preferred by the parents and (b) the extra cost of it to the LEA as against what it will cost the LEA to place the child in a maintained school. In cases where the state system simply cannot provide for the child's needs, there will be no choice: the LEA must pay the cost. In cases where the choice is between two independent schools, it is accepted on all hands that the second criterion is simply the respective annual fees, whatever the comparative capital costs or other sources of income of the two establishments . . . In cases where the choice is between two maintained schools, by Schedule 27, paragraph 3, the [EA 1996] substitutes a test of suitability to the particular child, efficiency in education (for example because of possible disruption) and efficient use of resources. The latter will intelligibly include comparative on-costs, such as transport and personal support, but in most cases it is unlikely to be helped by apportioning the LEA's accounts or balance sheet . . . If so, there is no intelligible reason why a comparison of public expenditure as between an appropriate independent school and an appropriate school should be at large . . . That means, generally speaking, that the existing costs of providing [the maintained school] and of staffing it and its hearing-impaired unit do not come into account . . . It seems to us that what parliament has called for in the ordinary run of cases is a consideration of the burden which the respective placements will throw on the annual education budget when matched against their educational advantages and drawbacks for the child in question. Costs which either the private provider or the LEA would be incurring with or without the proposed placement are accordingly not in general relevant.'

1   *Oxfordshire County Council v GB* (22 August 2001, unreported), CA at para 15ff.

Advice and information for parents

2.7

A further new general responsibility imposed on LEAs is the obligation to provide advice and information to parents[1]. An LEA must arrange for the parent of any child in their area with special educational needs to be provided with advice and information about matters relating to those needs[2]. In making these arrangements, the LEA must have regard to any guidance given by the Secretary of State, or, in Wales, the National Assembly[3]. The

2.7.1

LEA must also[4] take such steps as they consider appropriate for making the services provided to parents known to:

(a) the parents of children in their area;
(b) the headteachers and proprietors of schools in their area; and
(c) such other persons as they consider appropriate.

1 EA 1996, s 332A.
2 EA 1996, s 332A(1).
3 EA 1996, s 332A(2).
4 EA 1996, s 332A(3).

2.7.2   As will be seen[1], LEAs are responsible for making arrangements with a view to avoiding or resolving disagreements between LEAs and parents of children in their area[2]. In addition, LEAs must also make arrangements with a view to avoiding or resolving, in each relevant school[3], disagreements between the parents of a relevant child[4] and the proprietor of the school about the special educational provision made for that child[5]. These arrangements must provide for the appointment of independent persons with the function of facilitating the avoidance or resolution of such disagreements[6]. In making such arrangements, LEAs must have regard to any guidance given by the Secretary of State, or, in Wales, the National Assembly[7]. An LEA must then take such steps as they consider appropriate for making these arrangements known to the parents of children in their area, the headteachers and proprietors of schools in their area and such other persons as they consider appropriate[8]. These arrangements cannot, however, affect the entitlement of a parent to appeal to the Tribunal[9].

1 See 10.2.
2 EA 1996, s 332B(1).
3 A school is a 'relevant school' in relation to a child if it is: (a) a maintained school or a maintained nursery school, (b) a pupil referral unit, (c) a city technology college, a city college for the technology of the arts or a city academy, (d) an independent school named in the statement of special educational needs maintained for the child, or (e) a non-maintained special school approved by the Secretary of State under EA 1996, s 342. See EA 1996, s 332B(8).
4 A child who has special educational needs and is a registered pupil at a relevant school: EA 1996, s 332B(7).
5 EA 1996, s 332B(2).
6 EA 1996, s 332B(3).
7 EA 1996, s 332B(4).
8 EA 1996, s 332B(5).
9 EA 1996, s 332B(6).

Chapter 3

Special schools and schools providing for children with special educational needs

Introduction 3.1

The majority of children with special educational needs will be taught in mainstream schools[1]. Indeed, as has been seen[2], subject to certain exceptions, a Local Education Authority (LEA) is under a duty[3] to educate children with special educational needs in mainstream schools. This applies whether or not a statement is maintained in respect of the child[4]. The exceptions to this principle which justify educating the child outside of a mainstream setting are: (a) if that is incompatible with the wishes of the parent or (b) the provision of efficient education for other children[5]. **3.1.1**

1 'Mainstream schools' being defined as any school other than a special school or an independent school which is not a city technology college, city college for the technology of the arts or a city academy: Education Act (EA) 1996, s 316(4).
2 See 2.5 and 2.6.
3 EA 1996, s 316.
4 EA 1996, s 316(2) and (3).
5 EA 1996, s 316(3); and see 2.5.

This being the case, most children with special educational needs will therefore be taught in maintained community, foundation or voluntary schools. **3.1.2**

For those children, however, whose needs cannot be met within such schools, it is necessary for there to be schools both inside and outside the maintained sector to make the necessary provision. These children will thus be taught at maintained special schools, non-maintained special schools and independent schools approved by the Secretary of State to take children with statements. **3.1.3**

A 'special school' is one specially organised to make special educational provision for pupils with special educational needs[1]. It may be maintained by an LEA as a community or foundation special school[2] or alternatively be approved by the Secretary of State under s 342 of the EA 1996 as a non-maintained special school and be subject to prescribed requirements[3]. **3.1.4**

An 'independent school'[4], which is not a special school as such, may be approved by the Secretary of State as suitable for the admission of children for whom statements of special educational needs are maintained by LEAs[5].

1 EA 1996, s 337(1).
2 EA 1996, s 337(2)(a).
3 EA 1996, s 337(2)(b).

4 For a definition of 'independent school' see 3.10.1.
5 EA 1996, s 347(1).

3.1.5   *Scope of the chapter*

This chapter will first consider the establishment, conduct and discontinuance of maintained special schools, and will then examine the establishment and conduct of non-maintained special schools and approved independent schools. With respect to the latter, however, it should be borne in mind that the Department for Education and Skills (DfES) has recently published a consultation paper[1] which proposes the introduction of a stricter regime of registration and inspection of independent schools[2].

1 *Registration and Monitoring of Independent Schools*, DfES, 5 September 2001.
2 See Education Bill, Pt 10, which will become the Education Act 2002 if it receives Royal Assent.

MAINTAINED SPECIAL SCHOOLS

3.2   **Establishment and approval of community and foundation special schools**

3.2.1   In order to fulfil their functions, LEAs have the power to establish community and foundation special schools[1]. Where an LEA intends to establish such a school, it must publish statutory proposals[2]. Such proposals shall (a) contain such information, and (b) be published in such manner as may be prescribed[3]. Before publishing any proposals the LEA is required to consult such persons as appears to it to be appropriate and in discharging this duty the LEA must have regard to any guidance given from time to time by the Secretary of State[4]. Where any proposals relate to a school or proposed school in England, the LEA must send (a) a copy of the proposals, and (b) such information in connection with those proposals as may be prescribed to the School Organisation Committee (SOC) for the area of the LEA which it is proposed should maintain the school[5]. Where any proposals relate to a proposed school in Wales, the LEA shall send (a) a copy of the proposals, and (b) such information in connection with those proposals as may be prescribed to the Secretary of State[6]. The LEA must also send a copy of any proposals to such other bodies or persons as may be prescribed[7]. The procedure for dealing which these proposals is set out in Schedule 6 of the School Standards and Framework Act (SSFA) 1998[8].

1 SSFA 1998, s 31.
2 SSFA 1998, s 31(1).
3 SSFA 1998, s 31(3).
4 SSFA 1998, s 31(4).
5 SSFA 1998, s 31(5).
6 SSFA 1998, s 31(6).
7 SSFA 1998, s 31(7).
8 SSFA 1998, s 31(8).

3.2.2   Once the proposals are published, any person may make an objection to them[1], which should be sent to the promoting LEA within two months of the date of publication[2]. The LEA must then send copies of all objections to the SOC (in Wales, the Secretary of State)[3] together with its comments. If no objections are received, or the objections which have been received are subsequently withdrawn, the LEA determines whether the proposals should be implemented within four months of the date of publication[4]. If, however, objections have been received and not withdrawn or no objections are outstanding, but the LEA has failed to make a determination within four months, it is necessary for the SOC to consider the proposals[5]. The SOC, or the Secretary of State in Wales, has the power to reject the proposals, approve them without modification or approve them with such modification as it thinks desirable after consulting with the prescribed persons and bodies and having had regard to guidance from the Secretary of State and the LEA's School Organisation Plan. The decision of the SOC needs to be unanimous; if it is not, the proposal is referred to the adjudicator.

1 SSFA 1998, Sch 6, para 2.
2 Education (School Organisation Proposals) (England) Regulations 1999, SI 1999/2213 (or, in Wales, Education (School Organisation Proposals) (Wales) Regulations 1999, SI 1999/1671), reg 7.
3 SSFA 1998, Sch 6, para 8.
4 SSFA 1998, Sch 6, para 4.
5 SSFA 1998, Sch 6, para 3.

Where the proposals are approved, or approved subject to modification, it is for the LEA to implement them[1].   **3.2.3**

1 SSFA 1998, Sch 6, para 15.

Proposals may also be published and dealt with in a similar fashion in respect of alterations to established community and foundation special schools, except that, in the case of foundation special schools, the proposals shall be published by the governing body of the school, not the LEA, and the governing body shall implement the proposals, if they are approved[1].   **3.2.4**

1 SSFA 1998, s 31(2)(a) and Sch 6, para 15.

The process described above provides the framework for the establishment of maintained special schools and does not differ substantially from the procedure for establishing mainstream community and foundation schools. In addition, however, maintained special schools must satisfy certain, specific procedural requirements as well as meeting certain criteria in respect of their premises and the special educational provision to be made[1].   **3.2.5**

1 See the Education (Maintained Special Schools) (England) Regulations 1999, SI 1999/2212, or in Wales, the Education (Maintained Special Schools) (Wales) Regulations 1999, SI 1999/1780.

Any proposals for the establishment of a school shall be published in at least one newspaper circulating in the area of the LEA which it is proposed should maintain the school[1]. The published proposals must contain the following information[2]:   **3.2.6**

(1) the name of the LEA publishing the proposals;
(2) the date on which the proposals are planned to be implemented or, where the proposals are planned to be implemented in stages, the date on which each stage is planned to be implemented;
(3) a statement explaining the rights of persons to object to the proposals including (a) the date by which objections should be sent to the relevant

LEA or school organisation committee; and (b) the address of the LEA or school organisation committee to which objections should be sent;

(4) the location of the site of the proposed school (including, where appropriate, the postal address);

(5) the category (ie community special or foundation special) into which the proposed school will fall; and

(6) information as to the numbers, age group, sex and special educational needs of the pupils (distinguishing boarding and day pupils) for whom provision is proposed.

1 Education (Maintained Special Schools) (England) Regulations 1999, SI 1999/2212, reg 5(2).
2 SI 1999/2212, Sch 2, Parts I and II.

3.2.7   Where the proposals for the establishment of the school need to be sent to the SOC, the LEA should send to the SOC the following[1]:

(1) the objectives of the proposals;

(2) a statement indicating how the proposals would contribute to enhancing the quality of education and how they support the policy for provision for children with special educational needs as set out in the LEA's education development plan;

(3) evidence of the consultation before the proposals were published including copies of the consultation documents and the views and responses from the persons consulted;

(4) a statement indicating the consequences for the education of pupils with special educational needs in the area if the proposals were rejected;

(5) a map showing the location of the school or proposed school;

(6) a list of all special schools and other schools maintained by a LEA at which there is provision that is recognised by the LEA as reserved for children with special educational needs in the area of the LEA who maintain or who it is proposed should maintain the school, together with information as to the number of pupils at each such schools;

(7) information as to the numbers of pupils with special educational needs of each type for whom the LEA maintain a statement of special educational needs in the current school year together with a forecast of such numbers for each of the subsequent five school years.

(8) a forecast of the projected number of pupils at the school by sex and, where appropriate, type of special educational need for which provision is made, for the four school years following the current school year;

(9) details of proposed arrangements for the provision of transport to the proposed school;

(10) details of the curriculum to be provided at the proposed school;

(11) details of the proposed staffing including details of the time at which it is expected to appoint the headteacher;

(12) the following information relating to the proposed accommodation (including temporary accommodation):
(a) the location of the accommodation;
(b) a site plan of the accommodation;
(c) whether the proposed school is to occupy a single or split site;
(d) how accessible the accommodation will be; and

   (e) details of the general and specialist accommodation (both teaching and non-teaching);

(13) details of the capital costs of establishment of the proposed school and how it is intended to fund implementation of the proposals together with a statement as to whether, as a result of the proposals, premises used for the purposes of another school will no longer be required and if so a statement as to whether those premises are to be sold, and if so the estimated sale proceeds;

(14) an estimate of the recurrent costs for the proposed school and any savings in expenditure as a result of implementation of the proposals;

(15) where the establishment of the new school involves development for the purpose of the Town and Country Planning Act 1990 a statement as to whether planning permission has been obtained and, if such permission has not been obtained, details of the reasons (if known) why it has not been obtained.

1 Education (Maintained Special Schools) (England) Regulations 1999, SI 1999/2212, reg 6.

Copies of the proposals must also be sent to each LEA whose area adjoins that of the LEA which is proposing to maintain the school and, where it is proposed to maintain the school in an area of another LEA, that LEA[1]. Under the 1999 Regulations, the LEA was also required to send a copy of the proposals to the Further Education Funding Council if it was likely to be affected[2]. Under the new arrangements, under the Learning and Skills Act 2000, it is likely that, in place of the now abolished FEFC, the proposals will have to be sent to the local Learning and Skills Council.   **3.2.8**

1 Education (Maintained Special Schools) (England) Regulations 1999, SI 1999/2212, reg 7(2)(d); SSFA 1998, s 31(7).
2 SI 1999/2212, reg 7(2)(a).

Any person may make objections to the proposals[1]. Any such objections must be sent to the LEA which published the proposals within two months after the date of publication[2] (except if the new school is being established on the site of a failing school which is being discontinued[3]).   **3.2.9**

1 SSFA 1998, Sch 6, para 2(1).
2 SSFA 1998, Sch 6, para 2(2); and Education (Maintained Special Schools)(England) Regulations 1999, SI 1999/2212, reg 8(2).
3 SI 1999/2212, reg 8(2)(b)(ii).

If the objections are not subsequently withdrawn, the LEA must refer the proposals to the local SOC[1]. The SOC, in deciding whether or not to give approval, shall have regard to any guidance issued by the Secretary of State and the school organisation plan for the SOC's area and shall not give any approval unless the SOC is satisfied that adequate financial resources will be available to allow the proposals to be implemented[2]. The SOC, after considering the proposals, may either reject the proposals, approve them without modification or approve them with such modifications as the SOC think desirable after consulting the LEA and any other bodies specified[3] by the Secretary of State[4].   **3.2.10**

1 SSFA 1998, Sch 6, para 3(1).
2 SSFA 1998, Sch 6, para 3(4).
3 No other bodies are currently prescribed in respect of proposals by LEAs to establish special schools.
4 SSFA 1998, Sch 6, para 3(2)(c).

3.2.11 Any approval from the SOC may be expressed to take effect only if an event specified in the approval occurs by the date specified[1]. These events[2] are:

(a) the grant of planning permission under Part III of the Town and Country Planning Act 1990;

(b) the acquisition of a site on which a new school, a proposed enlargement of the premises of a school or other alteration to the premises of the school is to be constructed;

(c) the acquisition of playing fields to be provided for the school;

(d) the securing of any necessary access to a site referred to in sub-paragraph (b) or playing fields referred to in sub-paragraph (c);

(e) the making of any scheme relating to any charity connected with the school or proposed school; and

(f) the entering into of a private finance transaction within the meaning of regulation 16 of the Local Authorities (Capital Finance) Regulations 1997[3].

1 SSFA 1998, Sch 6, para 3(3).
2 Education (Maintained Special Schools) (England) Regulations 1999, SI 1999/2212, reg 10.
3 SI 1997/319.

3.2.12 If at the end[1] of two months from the date on which the SOC receive copies of all objections from the LEA or, if later, two months from the date the SOC receive the statutory information[2], the SOC have not voted on whether to give approval or the LEA request the SOC to refer the proposal to the adjudicator, the SOC must refer the proposals to the adjudicator[3]. If the SOC do vote on the proposal, but fail to reach a decision because of a lack of unanimity amongst the SOC members, the proposal must also be referred to the adjudicator[4] within two weeks from the failure to reach a decision[5]. If proposals are referred to the adjudicator, he must consider them afresh and may reach a decision which was open to the SOC[6].

1 See Education (Maintained Special Schools) (England) Regulations 1999, SI 1999/2212, reg 11.
2 See 3.2.7.
3 SSFA 1998, Sch 6, para 3(5).
4 SSFA 1998, Sch 6, para 3(6); and see SI 1999/2212, reg 14.
5 Education (Maintained Special Schools) (England) Regulations 1999, SI 1999/2212, reg 15(2).
6 SSFA 1998, Sch 6, para 3(7).

3.2.13 Where the LEA have published the proposals, but no objections were made or all objections were withdrawn in writing within the objection period, then the LEA may, instead of the SOC, determine whether the proposals should be implemented[1]. Such a determination must be made within the period of four months beginning with the date of publication of the proposals and the LEA must notify the SOC of any such determination[2]. If the LEA fail to determine the proposals within this time, the proposal requires approval by the SOC[3].

1 SSFA 1998, Sch 6, para 4(1).
2 SSFA 1998, Sch 6, para 4(2).
3 SSFA 1998, Sch 6, para 4(5).

3.2.14 Where either a proposal has been approved by a SOC (whether or not with modifications or conditions) or the LEA has itself been able to determine the proposals, then the proposals must be implemented in the form in which they were approved or implemented[1] by the LEA[2].

1 SSFA 1998, Sch 6, para 5(1).
2 SSFA 1998, Sch 6, para 15.

Maintenance of maintained special schools: premises, funding and staffing   **3.3**

Once established, a community or foundation special school is maintained by the LEA which established it.   **3.3.1**

The concept of maintenance often invokes images of building repairs, but in terms of the SSFA 1998 maintenance connotes a wider responsibility on the part of the LEA to provide and maintain buildings, but also to fund and, in community special schools, employ staff. Detailed consideration of these factors is outside the scope of this work.   **3.3.2**

For the purposes of this book, however, it is sufficient to know that as part of their duty to maintain schools, LEAs are under an obligation to finance all maintained schools within their areas. LEAs are therefore required to maintain not only community special schools, but also foundation special schools, even though the LEA does not own the land nor employ the staff at the latter type of school.   **3.3.3**

To provide for the financing of all maintained schools under the framework introduced by the SSFA 1998, new arrangements, known as Fair Funding, were introduced with effect from 1 April 1999. These were intended to produce a clearer division of responsibility between LEAs and schools and to ensure further delegation of funds to governing bodies. A Department for Education and Employment (DfEE) Consultation Paper, entitled *Fair Funding: Improving Delegation to Schools*, was issued in May 1998 and the implementing regulations, the Financing of Maintained Schools Regulations 1999[1], soon followed. These Regulations are renewed on an annual basis and the latest provisions can be found in the Financing of Maintained Schools (England) Regulations 2001[2].   **3.3.4**

1 SI 1999/101.
2 SI 2001/475. The applicable regulations for Wales are the 1999 regulations as amended by the National Assembly for Wales.

The aims of the new financial framework included raising standards, developing the self-management of schools, increasing accountability and transparency, achieving equality in distribution and ensuring value for money. To promote the other main aim of providing clarity in the division of responsibility between LEAs and maintained schools, the Regulations identify those areas for which the LEA must still retain responsibility for expenditure and those areas where schools should be given freedom to spend.   **3.3.5**

LEA expenditure is divided into non-school expenditure, which includes education (except in primary and special schools) for children under five, adult and community education, student awards, the youth service and   **3.3.6** revenue funding of capital expenditure relating to these services; ongoing school-related commitments, which includes servicing and repayment of school-related capital debts, early redundancy and retirement costs arising from decisions taken before 1 April 1999 and expenditure on recruitment and retention schemes. All other LEA expenditure is known as the 'local schools budget'.

3.3.7 Each maintained school within an LEA's area should have an allocated budget share[1] calculated in accordance with ss 46 and 47 of the SSFA 1998 and annually issued Financing of Maintained Schools (England) Regulations[2]. The 'local schools budget' consists of the LEA's central expenditure, together with the amounts which will ultimately be delegated to the governing bodies of the maintained schools in the LEA's area. The LEA's central expenditure is limited to the four areas of LEA responsibility: strategic management, access, LEA support for school improvement and special educational expenditure[3].

1 SSFA 1998, s 45.
2 SI 2001/475.
3 Special educational expenditure encompasses LEA expenditure on: educational psychology services, statementing of pupils, support for pupils with special educational needs, education otherwise than at school and the preparation of Behaviour Support Plans and Pupil Referral Units.

3.3.8 The elements of central LEA expenditure under the above headings are deducted from the local schools budget to leave the sum which should be distributed to schools, known as the Individual Schools Budget[1]. Each school's budget share is then determined by the LEA dividing up the Individual Schools Budget amongst the maintained schools in its area[2], but subject to the rules laid down in the Financing of Maintained Schools Regulations[3]. In particular, the Regulations set out the factors the LEA must take into account when determining each school's budget share and the procedure for consultation on the allocation methods the LEA proposes to use.

1 SSFA 1998, s 46(2).
2 SSFA 1998, s 47.
3 SI 2000/475.

3.3.9 Every LEA must prepare a scheme dealing with such matters relating to the financing of schools maintained by the LEA as are required to be dealt with in the scheme or by Regulations made by the Secretary of State. These may include details of how surpluses and deficits may be carried forward into the next financial year, amounts which may be charged by the LEA against a school's budget share, the terms on which services and facilities are to be provided to schools by the LEA and the imposition of conditions, which must be complied with by schools, in relation to the management of their delegated budgets[1]. Before submitting a scheme to the Secretary of State, the LEA must consult the governing body and head teacher of every school maintained by the LEA[2].

1 The procedure for preparing and publishing the scheme is set out in SSFA 1998, Sch 14.
2 SSFA 1998, Sch 14, para 1(3)(b).

3.3.10 The approved scheme must be published by sending a copy to the governing body and head teacher of every school maintained by the LEA and making a copy available for reference at all reasonable times and without charge at each school maintained by the LEA and at the LEA's principal office.

Each LEA is then under a duty to provide every maintained school with a delegated budget in accordance with the published scheme[1]. The only exception is if the governing body's right to a delegated budget has been suspended[2]. By delegating a budget to a school, however, the LEA does not give or transfer the ownership of that money to the governing body. Any amount made available to the governing body by the LEA remains the property of the LEA until spent by the governing body or headteacher[3]. When the budget is spent, it is taken to have been spent by the governing body or headteacher as the LEA's agent. Thus any contract entered into by the governing body using money from its delegated budget is in law a contract between the LEA and the supplier and the governing body is not a contracting party, even in the case of a foundation special school[4].

3.3.11

1 SSFA 1998, s 49(1).
2 SSFA 1998, s 51.
3 SSFA 1998, s 49(5).
4 And see *R v Yorkshire Purchasing Organisation, ex p British Educational Suppliers Ltd* [1998] ELR 195 where the Court of Appeal held that a maintained school with a delegated budget, even though incorporated, was an agent of the LEA.

Where a maintained school has a delegated budget in respect of the whole or part of a financial year, the LEA has the duty to secure that there is available to be spent by the governing body a sum equal to the school's budget share for the year[1]. The governing body then has the power to spend the amounts made available for any purposes of the school or for such purposes as may be prescribed in regulations[2].

3.3.12

1 Or if it only has delegation for part of that year, a sum equal to that portion of the school's budget share for the year which has not been spent.
2 SSFA 1998, s 50(3).

To regulate the delegation of budget shares to schools, LEAs are required to produce financial statements before the beginning of each financial year ('the budget statement') and after the end of each financial year ('the outturn statement')[1]. The LEA must supply the governing body and headteacher of each maintained school with a copy of the relevant parts of every budget and outturn statement[2] and shall publish the statements by supplying a copy to the Secretary of State and making a copy available for reference by parents and other persons at all reasonable times and without charge at each education office of the LEA.

3.3.13

1 SSFA 1998, s 52.
2 SSFA 1998, s 52(4).

LEAs are responsible for monitoring the management of delegated budgets by governing bodies[1]. An LEA may suspend the governing body's right to a delegated budget where it appears to the LEA that the governing body of a school which has a delegated budget has (a) been guilty of a substantial or persistent failure to comply with any delegation requirement or restriction, or (b) are not managing in a satisfactory manner the expenditure or appropriation of the school's delegated budget share[2]. An LEA must have regard

3.3.14

to the Code of Practice for Securing Effective Relationships in exercising these powers[3]. One month's notice of suspension, specifying the grounds, should normally be given unless, by reason of any gross incompetence or mismanagement on the part of the governing body or other emergency, it appears to the LEA to be necessary to give the governing body a shorter period of notice or to give the governing body notice suspending their right to a budget with immediate effect[4].

1 SSFA 1998, s 51 and Sch 15.
2 SSFA 1998, Sch 15, para 1.
3 Thus an LEA must consider the following:
   (a) suspension of delegation should only happen in exceptional circumstances and is not a mechanism for improving school financial management or performance;
   (b) the LEA must be clear in its notice to explain to the governing body if it is acting under its powers of intervention to improve standards or to address financial mismanagement or non-compliance with scheme requirements;
   (c) suspension of delegation must be used with a constructive purpose;
   (d) the LEA should always explain the reasons which led to suspension, the evidence upon which it relies and how it believes suspension will help;
   (e) suspension is a transitional mechanism, not a permanent state; and
   (f) suspension of delegation should only be used as a means of creating an opportunity in which positive action can be taken, to resolve the immediate problem and ensure that it does not recur.
4 SSFA 1998, Sch 15, para 1(2).

3.3.15 Once the right of a governing body to a delegated budget has been suspended, the LEA may review the suspension at any time when it thinks it appropriate and must review every suspension before the beginning of the next financial year, unless the suspension took effect less than two months before the beginning of that financial year[1].

1 SSFA 1998, Sch 15, para 2(1)(a) and (b).

3.3.16 The governing body, but not the headteacher, may appeal against the imposition of the suspension or the decision not to revoke the suspension to the Secretary of State[1]. Such an appeal must be brought within two months of the LEA's decision. The Secretary of State may allow or reject the appeal and in determining the appeal must have regard to the gravity of the default on the part of the governing body and the likelihood of it continuing or recurring[2].

1 SSFA 1998, Sch 15, para 3(1).
2 SSFA 1998, Sch 15, para 3(4).

3.4 The staffing of community and foundation special schools

3.4.1 Again, detailed consideration of the law relating to the staffing of maintained special schools is outside the scope of this book.

3.4.2 In summary, every LEA is under a duty to ensure that at any school there shall be employed a staff of teachers suitable and sufficient in numbers for the purpose of securing the provision of education appropriate to the ages, abilities, aptitudes and needs of the pupils and having regard to any arrangements for the utilisation of the services of teachers employed otherwise than at the school in question[1].

1 Education (Teachers' Qualifications and Health Standards) (England) Regulations 1999, SI 1999/2166, reg 4.

An incorporated governing body of a community special school cannot   **3.4.3**
enter into contracts of employment[1] and so cannot in law be an 'employer'.
The legal employer in community special schools is therefore the LEA,
although the governing body, if the school has a delegated budget, is responsible for appointing, filling vacancies, disciplining, suspending and where
necessary, dismissing staff[2]. If the community special school does not have
a delegated budget, the number of teachers and non-teaching staff to be
employed at the school is determined by the LEA and the LEA may
appoint, suspend staff as it thinks fit[3].

1 EA 1996, s 88 and Sch 7, para 2(2)(b).
2 In accordance with the procedures set out in SSFA 1998, Sch 16.
3 SSFA 1998, s 54.

In contrast, in foundation special schools, the governing body has the power   **3.4.4**
to employ staff and so the governing body, not the LEA, is the legal
employer of staff so long as the school has a delegated budget[1]. The procedure for the appointment of staff etc is different to that for community
special schools[2]. If, however, the foundation special school's delegated
budget is withdrawn, the number of teachers and non-teaching staff to be
employed at the school is determined by the LEA and the governing body
may not appoint or dismiss any member of staff without the consent of the
LEA[3].

1 SSFA 1998, s 55.
2 See SSFA 1998, Sch 17.
3 SSFA 1998, s 55(2).

Staff employed in maintained special schools should meet certain staff qual-   **3.4.5**
ification requirements[1]. These requirements relate to the qualifications held,
registration, health and physical capacity and fitness of teachers or other persons employed or otherwise engaged to provide their services in work that
brings them regularly into contact with persons who have not attained the
age of 19[2].

1 SSFA 1998, Sch 16, para 21; and see, currently, the Education (Teachers' Qualifications
   and Health Standards) Regulations 1999, SI 1999/2166.
2 For more detailed guidance on the various requirements, see DfEE Circular 4/99, *Physical
   and Mental Fitness to Teach of Teachers and of Entrants to Initial Teacher Training.*

In addition to ensuring that teachers meet the educational qualifications set   **3.4.6**
out in these Regulations, the LEA is under a duty to carry out pre-employment checks to ensure that it does not employ anyone barred from teaching
by the Secretary of State[1] and should also check the criminal backgrounds
of staff whose posts involve substantial unsupervised access to children[2].

1 Known as 'List 99'.
2 For further information on the procedures for placing teachers on List 99 and the effect of
   such action, see DFE Circular 11/95, *Misconduct of Teachers and Workers with Children and
   Young Persons.* For guidance on pre-employment checks on criminal backgrounds, see
   DFE Circular 9/93, *Protection of Children: Disclosure of Criminal Background of those with
   Access to Children* (or, for Wales, Welsh Office Circular 54/93).

Where the LEA has any serious concerns about the performance of the   **3.4.7**
headteacher of a school, it must make a written report of its concerns to
the chairman of the governing body, at the same time sending a copy to the
headteacher. The chairman of the governing body must notify the LEA in

writing of the action which he proposes to take in the light of that report. In determining whether to make a report, the LEA must have regard to any guidance given from time to time by the Secretary of State[1].

The report must state the grounds for the LEA's concern and the evidence upon which it relies. The LEA should also advise the chairman of governors on action which it may be appropriate to take. The LEA must also allow the headteacher the opportunity to make representations to the chairman of the governing body and to the LEA about the report, if necessary being accompanied by a friend.

1 Triggers would include eg situations where:
    (a) the school has been found following inspection to require special measures or to have serious weaknesses and the LEA considers that the post-inspection plan is seriously deficient;
    (b) standards of performance in assessments or public examinations have worsened significantly for reasons attributable to the headteacher's performance;
    (c) there has been a pattern of repeated and serious complaints over a period of time from parents, staff, governors or pupils which have not been satisfactorily addressed; or
    (d) there is significant evidence of continuing and systematic weaknesses in the management of the school or in its financial controls which, if not tackled, risk serious disruption to the school's continuing operation.

3.5 Admission of pupils to maintained special schools

3.5.1 No child may be admitted to a maintained special school[1] unless:

(a) a statement of special educational needs is maintained for the child; or
(b) the child is admitted for the purposes of an assessment of his or her special educational needs[2] and the child's admission to the school is with the agreement of the LEA, the head teacher of the school, the child's parent and any person whose advice is to be sought[3]; or
(c) the child is admitted following a change in his or her circumstances, with the agreement of the LEA, the head teacher of the school and the child's parent.

1 Education (Maintained Special Schools) (England) Regulations 1999, SI 1999/2212, reg 19(1) or, in Wales, Education (Maintained Special Schools) (Wales) Regulations 1999, SI 1999/1780, reg 13(1); and see EA 1996, s 316A(2).
2 In accordance with EA 1996, s 323.
3 As part of the standard assessment process.

3.5.2 The admission of a child following such a change of circumstances as in (c) above must be reviewed at the end of every term[1].

1 Education (Maintained Special Schools) (England) Regulations 1999, SI 1999/2212, reg 19(3) or, in Wales, Education (Maintained Special Schools) (Wales) Regulations 1999, SI 1999/1780, reg 13(3).

3.5.3 A child may be admitted to a special school established in a hospital provided that he requires hospital treatment[1].

1 Education (Maintained Special Schools) (England) Regulations 1999, SI 1999/2212, reg 19(2) or, in Wales, Education (Maintained Special Schools) (Wales) Regulations 1999, SI 1999/1780, reg 13(2).

3.5.4 An issue which has arisen concerns the categorisation of the maintained special school and the 'match' with the needs of the child. To a certain extent the problem has been resolved by the implementation of the two separate sets of regulations relating to maintained and non-maintained special schools[1], but the issue may still arise in respect of certain placements.

1 Education (Maintained Special Schools) (England) Regulations 1999, SI 1999/2212 and Education (Non-Maintained Special Schools) (England) Regulations 1999, SI 1999/2257.

When making or amending a statement, an LEA is required to name the **3.5.5** type of school and, subject to certain conditions, to name the school which they consider would be appropriate for the child[1]. That appears to provide a wide discretion to the LEA to name the school which they believe will best meet the child's needs. In *Sunderland City Council v P and C*[2], however, the judge took a more restrictive view of the LEA's powers based on his interpretation of the regulations then applying to both maintained and non-maintained special schools[3]. In that case, the issue concerned whether or not a child could be placed at a maintained special school when that school had not been approved by the Secretary of State to take children of the child's age.

1 EA 1996, s 324(4).
2 [1996] ELR 283, QBD.
3 Education (Special Schools) Regulations 1994, SI 1994/652.

The 1994 Regulations stated that a governing body could not admit a child **3.5.6** to a school unless he fell within the category specified in the arrangements approved by the Secretary of State in respect of (i) the number, age and sex of day and of boarding pupils, and (ii) their respective educational needs[1]. Brooke J held that a child whose age was beyond the approved age range for the school could not lawfully be admitted by the school's governing body. Similarly, in *Re B*[2] Latham J held that an LEA could decline to name a special school if to do so would lead to the approved number of places for the school being exceeded.

1 Education (Special Schools) Regulations 1994, SI 1994/652, Schedule, Pt II, paras 1 and 7.
2 (4 August 1999, unreported), QBD.

In contrast, however, in *Ellison v Hampshire County Council*[1] Tucker J held **3.5.7** that where the issue was not about a child's age or sex[2], but related to the subjective assessment of the child's special educational needs, the *Sunderland* case could be distinguished.

> 'The question of what school is appropriate is not necessarily determined by the designation of a particular school although that is obviously a factor to be taken into account. If other or extra provision can be made for a child's educational needs as recognised in the statement, then a school may, despite certain initial apparent disadvantages, be an appropriate school.'

It would therefore follow that a child could not be placed in a school if he or she was not of the same sex or age as the designation or their admission would put the school above its designated number, but a child could be admitted if the school was 'appropriate', even if the child's special educational needs did not match, or match precisely, the type of need for which the school was approved. Tucker J's judgment was upheld by the Court of

Appeal[3] although the Court preferred to find that placement was a question of educational judgment properly left to the LEA and Tribunal.

1   (30 July 1999, unreported), QBD.
2   Ie the objective criteria under (i) in 3.5.6 above.
3   *Ellison v Hampshire County Council* [2000] ELR 651, CA; and see *S v Dudley MBC* [2000] ELR 330, QBD and 6.9.20.

3.5.8   The difficulties have probably been resolved by the changes brought about by the Education (Maintained Special Schools) (England) Regulations 1999[1]. The provisions which have caused problems, however, still apply in the case of admission to non-maintained special schools[2].

1   SI 1999/2212, reg 19(1) or, in Wales, Education (Maintained Special Schools) (Wales) Regulations 1999, SI 1999/1780, reg 13(3).
2   See SI 1999/2257, Schedule, Pt II, paras 1 and 7.

3.6   The conduct of maintained special schools

3.6.1   As with the maintenance and staffing of schools, the provisions governing the conduct of community and foundation special schools are virtually identical to those applying to mainstream maintained schools.

3.6.2   Each special school will have a governing body consisting of a number[1] of different categories of governor[2]. The actual composition of the governing body of each special school will be set out in its instrument of government. The one difference between the governing body of a mainstream maintained school and a maintained special school is that a representative governor may, or in the case of a community special school established in a hospital must, be appointed in place of one co-opted governor[3].

1   SSFA 1998, ss 36 and 37 and Schs 9 to 12.
2   Including those elected by parents, appointed by the LEA, co-opted by the governing body and those drawn from staff at the school.
3   SSFA 1998, Sch 9, para 10.

3.6.3   Where a community special school is established in a hospital, if the hospital is vested in the Secretary of State for Health, the representative governor will be appointed by the health authority. Where it is vested in an NHS trust, he or she will be appointed by that trust[1]. If the community special school is not situated in a hospital, the LEA may designate an appropriate voluntary organisation concerned with special educational needs catered for at the school. If the LEA does so designate such an organisation, that organisation shall appoint the representative governor. If more than one voluntary organisation is designated for that particular school, they should act jointly to appoint one representative governor.

1   SSFA 1998, Sch 9, para 10(5).

3.6.4   The conduct of the maintained special school is the responsibility of the governing body, save where the responsibilities must be discharged by the headteacher, teaching staff or the LEA. A useful laypersons' guide to the responsibilities of the governing body of a maintained special school can be found in *A Guide to the Law for School Governors – Community Special Schools*[1].

1   DfES Publications, ISBN 1 84185 332 1, available free from the DfES Publications Centre.

The detailed provisions relating to the conduct of a maintained special   **3.6.5**
school can be found in that guide and in Chapter III of the SSFA 1998 and
include, for example:

- the curriculum[1];
- behaviour and discipline[2];
- attendance[3];
- annual parents reports and meetings[4].

1 EA 1996, Part V; Education Act 1997, Pts IV and VII; and SSFA 1998, Pt II.
2 EA 1996, ss 494 and 548; and SSFA 1998, ss 41, 64 to 68 and Sch 18.
3 EA 1996, ss 437 to 448.
4 SSFA 1998, s 43.

Inspection   3.7

As with all maintained schools, maintained special schools are subject to   **3.7.1**
inspection by the Office for Standards in Education (OFSTED)[1].

1 Schools Inspection Act 1996.

Alterations and discontinuance   3.8

Similar procedures to those for the establishment of special schools apply to   **3.8.1**
their alteration and discontinuance, with one exception[1]. Thus, where an LEA
wishes to make a prescribed alteration[2] it must publish statutory proposals[3].

1 See 3.2.1.
2 A 'prescribed alteration' is one prescribed by Regulations, currently the Education
   (Maintained Special Schools) (England) Regulations 1999, SI 1999/2212 and the
   Education (Maintained Special Schools) (Wales) Regulations 1999, SI 1999/1780; and
   see 3.8.2.
3 SSFA 1998, s 31(1).

'Prescribed alterations'[1] are defined as follows[2]:   **3.8.2**

(a) Except where the school is established in a hospital, any increase in the
    number of pupils for whom the school is organised to make provision
    which, when taken together with all such previous increases in the
    number of pupils would increase the number of such pupils by 10% or
    the relevant number of pupils[3] (whichever is the lesser) as compared
    with (a) the number of such pupils on the appropriate date[4]; or (b) if,
    at any time after that date the number of such pupils was lower than on
    that date, the lowest number at any such time[5].
(b) Except where the school is established in a hospital, any decrease in the
    number of pupils for whom the school is organised to make provision[6].
(c) The alteration of the upper or lower age limits of the school (that is to
    say the highest and the lowest ages of pupils for whom education is nor-
    mally provided at the school)[7].
(d) An alteration to a school to provide that (i) a school which was an
    establishment which admitted pupils of one sex only becomes an estab-
    lishment which admits pupils of both sexes; or (ii) a school which was
    an establishment which admitted pupils of both sexes becomes an
    establishment which admits pupils of one sex only[8].

(e) The introduction or ending of a boarding provision and where the school makes provision for day pupils and boarding pupils, the alteration of boarding provision such that the number of pupils for whom boarding provision is made is increased or decreased by five pupils[9].

(f) A change in the type of special educational needs for which the school is organised to make provision[10].

(g) The transfer of a school to a new site except the transfer to a site which formerly consisted of playing fields[11] used by the school, provided that the main entrance of the school on its new site will be within 3.218688 kilometres (two miles) of the main entrance of the school on its old site[12].

1 Which are set out in Education (Maintained Special Schools) (England) Regulations 1999, SI 1999/2212, reg 3 and Sch 1.
2 SI 1999/2212, Sch 1.
3 The 'relevant number of pupils' is five where the school only makes boarding provision and 20 in any other case.
4 The 'appropriate date' means whichever is the latest of the following dates: (i) the date falling five years before the date on which the LEA or, as the case may be, the governing body, form the intention to increase the number of pupils for which the school is organised to make provision; (ii) the date when the school was established; (iii) where any proposals for the making of a prescribed alteration to the school consisting of an increase in the number of pupils for which the school is organised to make provision have been approved under EA 1993, s 184, EA 1996, s 340 or Sch 6, para 3 or Sch 7, para 8 or 9, the date (or latest date) on which any such proposals were implemented; and (iv) where the LEA has determined under Sch 6, para 4 to implement any proposals for the making of a prescribed alteration to the school consisting of an increase in the number of pupils for which the school is organised to make provision, the date (or latest date) on which any such proposals were implemented.
5 SI 1999/2212, Sch 1, para 1.
6 SI 1999/2212, Sch 1, para 2.
7 SI 1999/2212, Sch 1, para 3.
8 SI 1999/2212, Sch 1, para 4.
9 SI 1999/2212, Sch 1, para 5.
10 SI 1999/2212, Sch 1, para 6.
11 Within the meaning of SSFA 1998, s 77.
12 SI 1999/2212, Sch 1, para 7.

3.8.3 In the case of a foundation special school, if the governing body wish to make a prescribed alteration, it must publish the statutory proposals[1].

1 SSFA 1998, s 31(2).

3.8.4 In either case, the statutory proposals must contain such information and be published in such manner as may be prescribed[1]. Before publishing these proposals either the LEA or governing body must consult such persons as appear to them to be appropriate[2]. A copy of the proposals plus the prescribed information must be sent to the SOC for the area of the LEA which maintains the school[3] and to other prescribed bodies[4]. The procedure for dealing with the proposals is set out in Schedule 6 of the SSFA 1998 and is identical to that for the establishment of a maintained special school[5]. No alterations may be made unless the procedure set out above has been followed and approval obtained as required[6].

1 SSFA 1998, s 31(3).
2 SSFA 1998, s 31(4).
3 SSFA 1998, s 31(5).
4 SSFA 1998, s 31(7).
5 See 3.2.1ff.
6 SSFA 1998, s 33(1).

The process is also identical if either the LEA, in the case of a community   **3.8.5**
special school or a foundation special school, or the governing body, in the
case of a foundation special school, decide to discontinue the school[1]. The
proposals for discontinuance must be published in the prescribed form,
there must be the necessary consultation with relevant parties and a copy of
the proposals must be sent to the SOC for the area[2].

1 SSFA 1998, s 31(1) and (2).
2 SSFA 1998, s 31 and Sch 6.

One additional provision, however, which is unique to maintained special   **3.8.6**
schools, is the power given to the Secretary of State to give a direction
requiring an LEA to discontinue a community or foundation special school[1].
Under this provision, the Secretary of State may, if he considers it expedient
to do so in the interests of the health, safety or welfare of pupils at a community or foundation special school, give a direction to the LEA by whom
the school is maintained requiring the school to be discontinued on a date
specified in the direction[2]. Such a direction may require the LEA to notify
any persons or class of persons specified in the direction[3]. Before giving a
direction the Secretary of State[4] shall consult:

(a) the LEA;
(b) any other LEA who would in his opinion be affected by the discontin-
    uance of the school;
(c) in the case of a foundation special school which has a foundation, the
    person who appoints the foundation governors; and
(d) such other persons as the Secretary of State considers appropriate.

On giving a direction, the Secretary of State shall give notice in writing of
the direction to the governing body of the school and its head teacher[5].
Where an LEA is given a direction by the Secretary of State, it shall discontinue the school in question on the date specified in the direction[6].

1 SSFA 1998, s 32.
2 SSFA 1998, s 32(1).
3 SSFA 1998, s 32(2).
4 SSFA 1998, s 32(3).
5 SSFA 1998, s 32(4).
6 SSFA 1998, s 32(5).

NON-MAINTAINED SPECIAL SCHOOLS

Establishment and conduct of non-maintained special schools   **3.9**

A special school may also be established as a non-maintained special school   **3.9.1**
if approved by the Secretary of State, subject to it meeting prescribed
requirements[1]. Independent schools, which are not primarily intended to be
special schools may nonetheless be approved by the Secretary of State for
children with statements of special educational needs[2].

1 EA 1996, s 342.
2 EA 1996, s 347; and see 3.10.

3.9.2 A school which is specially organised to make special educational provision for pupils with special educational needs and which is not a community or foundation special school may be approved by the Secretary of State[1]. Such approval may be given before or after the school is established[2]. Any school, however, which was a special school immediately before 1 September 1994 is to be treated, subject to anything in the relevant regulations, as approved[3].

1 EA 1996, s 342(1).
2 EA 1996, s 342(1).
3 EA 1996, s 342(3).

3.9.3 The requirements necessary for approval are set out in the regulations made by the Secretary of State[1]. Such regulations may make provision as to the conditions which are to be complied with by a school in seeking approval, while approved and as to the withdrawal of approval[2]. The regulations must make provision for securing that, so far as practicable, every pupil attending a non-maintained special school receives religious education and attends religious worship or is withdrawn from receiving such education or from attendance at such worship in accordance with the wishes of his parent[3]. The current regulations applying to non-maintained special schools are the Education (Non-Maintained Special Schools) (England) Regulations 1999[4].

1 EA 1996, s 342(2).
2 EA 1996, s 324(4).
3 EA 1996, s 342(6).
4 SI 1999/2257.

3.9.4 In order to obtain initial approval, a non-maintained special school must meet certain conditions[1]. These conditions are:

(a) the school may not be conducted for profit and no member of the staff may have a financial interest in the school otherwise then by being employed at the school on a salary unrelated to the financial performance of the school[2];

(b) the arrangements as respects: (i) the pupils for whom provision is made categorised by reference to the number, age and sex of day and boarding pupils and their respective special educational needs; and (ii) the special educational provision made for those pupils must be such as have been approved[3] by the Secretary of State[4];

(c) the arrangements as respects the governing body (including, in particular, its composition and functions and the appointment and election of its members) shall be such as have been approved by the Secretary of State[5];

(d) the governing body shall make such arrangements for safeguarding and promoting the health, safety and welfare of the pupils as the school as are approved by the Secretary of State and shall secure so far as is practicable that such arrangements are carried out[6]; and

(e) the school premises must conform to the appropriate standards prescribed by the Secretary of State[7] and applicable to maintained schools. These Regulations are currently the Education (School Premises) Regulations 1999[8]. However, if the Secretary of State is satisfied that it would be unreasonable to require conformity with a premises requirement for a particular school, he may give a direction that the school premises shall, while the direction remains in force, be deemed to conform to the prescribed standards as respects matters with which the direction deals if such conditions, if any, as may be specified in the direction are observed by the school[9].

1 Education (Non-Maintained Special Schools) (England) Regulations 1999, SI 1999/2257, reg 3 and Schedule.
2 SI 1999/2257, Schedule, para 4.
3 An approval may be expressed to have effect for only a limited period and is subject to such conditions, if any, as are specified: SI 1999/2257, Schedule, para 1(2).
4 SI 1999/2257, Schedule, para 1.
5 SI 1999/2257, Schedule, para 2.
6 SI 1999/2257, Schedule, para 3.
7 Under EA 1996, s 542.
8 SI 1999/2.
9 SI 1999/2257, Schedule, para 5(2).

A list of non-maintained special schools is published by the Secretary of **3.9.5** State. The lists are renewed on a regular basis but the latest version is the Non-Maintained Special Schools List Approved under s 342 Education Act 1996[1]. These lists set out the schools approved by the Secretary of State by categorisation of need[2].

1 DfEE Guidance 336/2000, December 2000.
2 The categories of need used by the Secretary of State are currently: ADHD – Attention Deficit Hyperactivity Disorder; AUT – Autism; DEL – Delicate/Medical Problems; DYS – Specific Learning Difficulties (Dyslexia); EBD – Emotional and Behavioural Difficulties; EPI – Epilepsy; HI – Hearing Impaired; MLD – Moderate Learning Difficulties; MSI – Multi-sensory Impairment (Deaf/Blind); PD – Physical Disabilities; PMLD – Profound and Multiple Learning Difficulties; SLD – Severe Learning Difficulties; SP&L – Speech and Language Disorders; and VI – Visual Impairment (DfEE Guidance 336/2000, December 2000).

Once approved, non-maintained special schools must meet what are **3.9.6** referred to as 'further continuing requirements'[1]. Firstly, schools must meet the relevant requirements necessary to obtain approval in the first place[2] together with a number of further conditions. In summary these include provision as to[3]:

(a) admissions and special educational provision[4];
(b) pupil numbers[5];
(c) health of pupils[6];
(d) collective worship and religious education[7];
(e) sex education[8];
(f) milk, meals and refreshment[9];
(g) incident and punishment books[10];
(h) reports to LEAs[11];
(i) access to the school by LEAs and participation in annual reviews[12];
(j) non-teaching staff[13];
(k) the prohibition of discrimination against staff on religious grounds[14];
(l) accounts[15];
(m) reports and returns to the Secretary of State[16];
(n) the school prospectus[17];
(o) changes to the special educational provision or governing body[18].

1 Education (Non-Maintained Special Schools) (England) Regulations 1999, SI 1999/2257, reg 4 and Schedule, Pts I and II.
2 See 3.9.4.
3 SI 1999/2257, Schedule, paras 6 to 20.

4 SI 1999/2257, Schedule, para 7; see also 3.9.8 and 3.9.9.
5 SI 1999/2257, Schedule, para 8.
6 SI 1999/2257, Schedule, para 9.
7 SI 1999/2257, Schedule, para 10.
8 SI 1999/2257, Schedule, para 11.
9 SI 1999/2257, Schedule, para 12.
10 SI 1999/2257, Schedule, para 13.
11 SI 1999/2257, Schedule, para 14.
12 SI 1999/2257, Schedule, para 19.
13 SI 1999/2257, Schedule, para 15.
14 SI 1999/2257, Schedule, para 16.
15 SI 1999/2257, Schedule, para 17.
16 SI 1999/2257, Schedule, para 18.
17 SI 1999/2257, Schedule, paras 20 and 21.
18 SI 1999/2257, Schedule, para 6.

3.9.7 The continuing requirements are wide ranging, but perhaps the most important are those relating to admissions and pupil numbers, the health of pupils, milk meals and refreshments, incident and punishment books, reports and access to LEAs and participation in annual reviews.

3.9.8 As far as admissions are concerned, no pupil shall be admitted to the school unless he falls within the category of need specified in the approved arrangements which were submitted to the Secretary of State[1]. The special educational provision made in pursuance of those arrangements shall be suited to the pupils at the school (having regard to their different ages, abilities and aptitudes and, in particular, special educational needs) and shall be efficiently provided[2]. The number of pupils at the school shall at no time exceed the number specified in the same approved arrangements[3].

1 Under Education (Non-Maintained Special Schools) (England) Regulations 1999, SI 1999/2257, reg 1 and Schedule, para 1.
2 SI 1999/2257, Schedule, para 7.
3 SI 1999/2257, Schedule, para 8.

3.9.9 These provisions are now different from those applying to maintained special schools[1]. So long as a child has a statement (or is admitted on a trial basis) he can be admitted to a maintained special school irrespective of its categorisation. With non-maintained special schools, however, a child can only be admitted if his needs fall within the category specified in the approved arrangements, the special educational provision specified in those approved arrangements and the pupil numbers approved by the Secretary of State. The case law[2] on admission will therefore still assist in determining whether a particular child can be admitted to a non-maintained special school. Thus, a child cannot be admitted if their admission would cause the approved number of pupils to be exceeded, the school is single sex and they are the 'wrong' sex or their age exceeds the school's approved age range[3]. If the issue is whether their needs fall within the school's categorisation, the approved arrangements should not be applied so harshly and, rather than attempting to fit the child within a particular category of need and then see if that category falls within the school's approved arrangements, a wider, more flexible view should be taken to consider whether the special educational provision available in the school (either internally or with additional external support) can meet the child's needs[4].

'The question of what school is appropriate is not necessarily determined by the designation of a particular school although that is obviously a factor to be taken into account. If other or extra provision can be made for a child's educational needs as recognised in the statement, then a school may, despite certain initial apparent disadvantages, be an appropriate school.'[5]

1 See 3.5.
2 See *Sunderland City Council v P and C* [1996] ELR 283, QBD and *Ellison v Hampshire County Council* (30 July 1999, unreported), QBD, and [2000] ELR 651, CA.
3 Per *Sunderland City Council v P and C* [1996] ELR 283, QBD.
4 Per Tucker J in *Ellison v Hampshire County Council* (30 July 1999, unreported), QBD.
5 Per Tucker J in *Ellison v Hampshire County Council* (30 July 1999, unreported), QBD.

The health and safety of pupils placed in non-maintained special school is **3.9.10** obviously of paramount concern to the Secretary of State. Thus, the person or body responsible for the management of the school (the 'relevant person')[1] must make provision (a) for the care and supervision of the health of the pupils at the school by appropriately qualified persons with, in the case of a school providing for pupils with a particular type of disability, relevant experience of those disabilities, and (b) for the maintenance of medical and dental records[2]. In addition, provision shall be made for the medical and dental inspection at appropriate intervals of the pupils and their medical and dental treatment[3].

1 Education (Non-Maintained Special Schools) (England) Regulations 1999, SI 1999/2257, reg 2(1).
2 SI 1999/2257, Schedule, para 9(1).
3 SI 1999/2257, Schedule, para 9(2).

The relevant person must keep an incident book in which there shall be **3.9.11** recorded (a) any incident, involving a person who either is a pupil or is employed or is a volunteer working at the school, which results in personal injury (to that or some other person) or damage to property, and (b) any loss of, theft of, or damage to, property (otherwise than as a result of such incident) where the property is that of any such person or school property[1]. A punishment book must also be kept in which there shall be recorded disciplinary measures taken against pupils[2].

1 Education (Non-Maintained Special Schools) (England) Regulations 1999, SI 1999/2257, Schedule, para 13(1).
2 SI 1999/2257, Schedule, para 13(2).

As non-maintained special schools will primarily deal with children placed **3.9.12** there by LEAs, it is essential that placing LEAs receive reports and have access to the schools. Consequently, a report on each pupil at a school in respect of whom an LEA maintain a statement[1] shall be furnished to that LEA at least once a year[2]. To enable LEAs to inspect the provision being made and check on the welfare of a placed pupil, a person authorised by an LEA which arranges for pupils to attend the school shall be afforded access to the school at all reasonable times[3]. To ensure that annual reviews can take place, at the request of the LEA, the governing body, head teacher and staff shall participate in any annual review which relates to any registered pupil at the school, making no charge to the LEA for such participation[4].

1 Under EA 1996, s 324.
2 Education (Non-Maintained Special Schools) (England) Regulations 1999, SI 1999/2257, Schedule, para 14.

3   SI 1999/2257, Schedule, para 19(1).
4   SI 1999/2257, Schedule, para 19(2).

3.9.13   Arrangements shall be made to secure that every pupil who is provided with secondary education will receive sex education[1], or will be wholly or partly excused from such education (except in so far as it is comprised in the National Curriculum) if his parent so requests[2]. The governing body shall, in relation to pupils who are provided with secondary education at the school (a) make and keep up to date a separate written statement of their policy with regard to sex education, and (b) make copies of the statement available for inspection, at all reasonable times, by parents of pupils at the school and provide a copy of the statement free of charge to any such parent who asks for one[3].

1   'Sex education' includes education about Acquired Immune Deficiency Syndrome and Human Immunodeficiency Virus, and any other sexually transmitted disease: Education (Non-Maintained Special Schools) (England) Regulations 1999, SI 1999/2257, Schedule, para 11(3).
2   SI 1999/2257, Schedule, para 11(1).
3   SI 1999/2257, Schedule, para 11(2).

3.9.14   The governing body of a non-maintained special school must provide such facilities as they consider appropriate for the consumption of any meals or refreshments brought to school by day pupils, and shall provide a school lunch where requested to do so by, or on behalf of a registered day pupil[1]. But the governing body is not to be required to provide a school lunch if, in the circumstances, it would be unreasonable for them to do so, or where the pupil in question has not reached compulsory school age and is being provided with part-time education[2]. To bring the provision of meals etc into line with those provided in maintained schools, unless a pupil's parents are entitled to free school meals[3], the governing body must charge for anything provided by them to day pupils by way of milk, a meal or other refreshment and must charge every pupil the same price for the same quantity of every item[4]. However, these provisions do not prevent the governing body of a school, when determining the tuition and other fees from taking into account the net cost to them of providing for milk, meals and other refreshments and the facilities to enable pupils to enjoy them[5]. School lunches provided by the governing body must meet the nutritional standards prescribed by the Secretary of State[6].

1   Education (Non-Maintained Special Schools) (England) Regulations 1999, SI 1999/2257, Schedule, para 12(1).
2   SI 1999/2257, Schedule, para 12(1)(b).
3   SI 1999/2257, Schedule, para 12(3).
4   SI 1999/2257, Schedule, para 12(2).
5   SI 1999/2257, Schedule, para 12(5).
6   SI 1999/2257, Schedule, para 12(6); and see SSFA 1998, s 114.

3.9.15   If a governing body of a non-maintained special school proposes to make any changes to the approved arrangements in respect of the school, it must give written notice to the Secretary of State and the proposal may not take effect unless and until the changed arrangements have been approved by the Secretary of State[1]. If the approved arrangements in respect of the composition of the governing body do not provide for the governing body to include (a) at least one member appointed by one or more local education authorities, (b) at least one member elected by teachers at the school from among their number, and (c) at least one member elected by, or appointed to represent, parents of children at the school[2], then, at the request of the Secretary of State and by a date specified by him, changed arrangements shall be proposed (to take effect as soon as is reasonably practicable) which would result in the governing body including such members appointed or elected as are specified by the Secretary of State. Any steps necessary or expedient for the purpose of making such a change shall be taken[3].

1 Education (Non-Maintained Special Schools) (England) Regulations 1999, SI 1999/2257, Schedule, para 6(1).
2 The person who is elected or appointed shall be (a) a person who is the parent of a registered pupil at the school; (b) a person who is the parent of a child of compulsory school age with special educational needs; (c) a person who is the parent of a person of any age with special educational needs; or (d) a person who is the parent of a child of compulsory school age: SI 1999/2257, Schedule, para 6(3).
3 SI 1999/2257, Schedule, para 6(2).

Approval may be withdrawn by the Secretary of State if there has been any failure by a non-maintained special school to comply with any requirement applicable to the school[1]. The requirements applicable to the school are those contained in:

3.9.16

(a) the Education (Non-Maintained Special Schools) (England) Regulations 1999[2] and considered above;
(b) regulations from time to time in force relating to the employment of teachers and their qualifications[3]; and
(c) regulations relating to the standard of school premises[4].

1 Education (Non-Maintained Special Schools) (England) Regulations 1999, SI 1999/2257, reg 5(1).
2 SI 1999/2257.
3 Under Education Reform Act 1988, s 218 and, currently, the Education (Schools and Further and Higher Education) Regulations 1989, SI 1989/351 and the Education (Teachers) Regulations 1993, SI 1993/543.
4 Under EA 1996, s 542 and, currently, the Education (School Premises) Regulations 1999, SI 1999/2.

Normally, the Secretary of State may not withdraw approval without consulting the governing body of the school and, if the governing body so request, affording the school a period specified by the Secretary of State within which to comply with the relevant requirement. If the Secretary of State so directs, however, pending compliance with that requirement, the arrangements as respects the matters to which it relates shall be such as are temporarily approved by him[1].

3.9.17

1 Education (Non-Maintained Special Schools) (England) Regulations 1999, SI 1999/2257, reg 5(2).

The Secretary of State may, however, if he is of the opinion that it is necessary or expedient to do so in the interests of the health, safety or welfare of pupils at the school, withdraw his approval without consulting the governing body[1].

3.9.18

1 Education (Non-Maintained Special Schools) (England) Regulations 1999, SI 1999/2257, reg 5(2).

3.9.19 An approval may be withdrawn voluntarily if the relevant person requests in writing that the Secretary of State do so[1].

> 1 Education (Non-Maintained Special Schools) (England) Regulations 1999, SI 1999/2257, reg 5(3).

INDEPENDENT SCHOOLS

3.10 Establishment and approval of independent schools

3.10.1 As briefly mentioned at the beginning of this chapter, independent schools[1] are not in themselves 'special schools'. It is therefore not appropriate to consider in detail how they are established, registered and conducted[2]. Independent schools may, however, admit children with special educational needs, and it is the circumstances in which such children can be admitted that will be examined in this section.

> 1 Currently, an 'independent school' is a school at which full-time education is provided for five or more pupils of compulsory school age and which is neither a maintained school nor a non-maintained special school: EA 1996, s 463. However, if the Education Bill 2001 receives Royal Assent this definition will change to: 'any school at which full-time education is provided for five or more pupils of compulsory school age or at least one pupil of that age for whom a statement is maintained under section 324 of the Education Act 1996 or who is looked after by a local authority (within the meaning of section 22 of the Children Act 1989) and which is not a school maintained by an LEA or a special school not so maintained': Education Bill, clause 168 (as at 22 November 2001) (proposing to amend EA 1996, s 463).
> 2 Especially as the regime of registration of independent schools and their standards will be changed by the Education Act 2002.

3.10.2 The requirements for approval are set out in regulations[1] which may make provision as to:

(a) the requirements which are to be complied with by a school as a condition of its approval under this section;

(b) the requirements which are to be complied with by a school while an approval under this section is in force in respect of it; and

(c) the withdrawal of approval from a school at the request of the proprietor or on the ground that there has been a failure to comply with any prescribed requirement.

Any approval may be given subject to such conditions (in addition to those prescribed) as the Secretary of State sees fit to impose[2]. The requirements are currently set out in the Education (Special Educational Needs) (Approval of Independent Schools) Regulations 1994[3].

> 1 EA 1996, s 347(2).
> 2 EA 1996, s 347(3).
> 3 SI 1994/651.

3.10.3 The arrangements for independent schools are broadly similar to, but more extensive than, those for non-maintained special schools. Thus, in order to be approved to admit children with statements, an independent school must first meet the following criteria[1]:

(1) Every person who is a proprietor of the school shall be a fit and proper person so to act[2].

(2) The proprietor shall ensure that the school has a staff of teachers suitable and sufficient in number for the purpose of securing the provision of education appropriate to the ages, abilities, aptitudes and special educational needs of the children in the school; and the staff shall include a head teacher[3]. Teachers must be suitably qualified[4] and if teachers are required to teach sensory impaired children, they will not be suitable[5] unless they possess an appropriate qualification to teach visually impaired and/or hearing impaired children[6]. Teachers solely employed to give instruction in a craft, trade or domestic subject are exempt from the requirement to have an appropriate qualification[7].

(3) In the case of an independent school which is also a boarding school, there shall be employed staff suitable and sufficient in numbers for the purposes of securing the proper care and supervision of the boarders, and of attending to their welfare[8]. Such staff shall include an appropriately qualified and experienced person who is the head of care[9] and who is designated as such. The head of care shall not also be the head teacher of the school[10].

(4) The proprietor shall adopt and give effect to arrangements for the admission of children to the school in order to secure that a child shall not be admitted to the school where:

   (a) the school would not be capable of providing him with full-time education appropriate to his age, ability, aptitude and special educational needs in the form of a balanced and broadly based curriculum adapted for that purpose;

   (b) his admission would be incompatible with a condition imposed by the Secretary of State pursuant to s 347(3) of the EA 1996; or

   (c) his admission would result in the maximum number of children at the school, specified in a condition imposed by the Secretary of State being exceeded[11].

The proprietor shall use his best endeavours to secure that the number of new pupils admitted to the school in every school year is sufficient to ensure that the total number of children attending the school is either equal to, or not substantially less than, the maximum number specified in any condition[12].

(5) The proprietor shall make and maintain arrangements to secure that children shall not be excluded from the school otherwise than on reasonable grounds[13]. Before any decision is taken as to whether any child is to be excluded the proprietor or head teacher shall give, unless it would not be appropriate to do so in any case, written notice to his parents, the LEA or, as the case may be, the local authority who have arranged for the placing of the child at the school and the local authority in whose area the school is situated, stating the grounds for the proposed exclusion, and shall take into account any representation made by them[14].

(6) A proprietor must make provision for the care and supervision of the health of the children at the school by appropriately qualified persons with, in the case of a school providing for children with a particular type of disability, or particular types of disabilities, relevant experience with those disabilities[15]. In a boarding school, such steps as may

be necessary to be taken to safeguard and promote the welfare of the boarders at all times must be taken and medical and dental records relating to the children at the school must be maintained[16]. Arrangements for regular medical and dental checks should also be made.

(7) Arrangements shall be made to secure that, so far as practicable, every child with a statement at the school who has been placed there pursuant to arrangements made by a LEA will attend daily collective worship and receive religious education, or will be withdrawn from attendance at such worship or from receiving such education, in accordance with the wishes of his parents[17].

(8) An incident book must be kept in which there shall be recorded any incident involving a person who either is a child or is employed or a volunteer working at the school which results in personal injury (to that or some other person) or damage to property, and any loss of, theft of, or damage to, property (otherwise than as a result of such an incident) where the property is that of such a person or school property[18]. A punishment book must also be kept with details of disciplinary measures taken against children at the school[19].

(9) The school's premises must conform to prescribed standards[20] which are applicable to maintained special schools[21] unless the Secretary of State is satisfied that requiring conformity with those regulations would be unreasonable[22]. If this applies the Secretary of State should give a direction specifying which exemptions apply.

(10) Before certain radioactive substances and electrical equipment[23] are used at the school, the Secretary of State shall be notified in writing of the proposed use[24].

1 Education (Special Educational Needs) (Approval of Independent Schools) Regulations 1994, SI 1994/651, reg 3 and Sch 1.
2 SI 1994/651, Sch 1, para 1.
3 SI 1994/651, Sch 1, para 2(1).
4 SI 1994/651, Sch 1, para 2(2).
5 Subject to limited exceptions: SI 1994/651, Sch 1, para 2(4) to (6).
6 In accordance with the Education (Teachers' Qualifications and Health Standards) (England) Regulations 1999, SI 1999/2166.
7 SI 1994/651, Sch 1, para 2(7).
8 SI 1994/651, Sch 1, para 3(1).
9 'Head of care' means a person who is in daily charge of the care and welfare of boarders: SI 1994/651, reg 2(1).
10 SI 1994/651, Sch 1, para 3(2).
11 SI 1994/651, Sch 1, para 4(1).
12 SI 1994/651, Sch 1, para 4(2).
13 SI 1994/651, Sch 1, para 5(1).
14 SI 1994/651, Sch 1, para 5(2).
15 SI 1994/651, Sch 1, para 6(1).
16 SI 1994/651, Sch 1, para 6(1).
17 SI 1994/651, Sch 1, para 8.
18 SI 1994/651, Sch 1, para 9.
19 SI 1994/651, Sch 1, para 9(2).
20 Currently the Education (School Premises) Regulations 1999, SI 1999/2.
21 SI 1994/651, Sch 1, para 10(1).
22 SI 1994/651, Sch 1, para 10(22).
23 SI 1994/651, Sch 1, para 7(1).
24 SI 1994/651, Sch 1, para 7(2).

Once approved, a school must continue to meet the original criteria for **3.10.4** approval set out in 3.10.3 and the following further requirements[1]. Certain information must be set out in the school's prospectus[2], but more importantly requirements are imposed concerning the care and safety of pupils. Thus:

(1) Each child with a statement admitted to the school shall receive special educational provision suited to his age, ability, aptitude and special educational needs[3].

(2) Any change in the proprietor, principal, head teacher or head of care at the school, or the staff employed at the school such as to constitute a significant change in the character of the school, must be notified forthwith in writing to the Secretary of State[4].

(3) Any proposed substantial alteration to the premises of the school, any proposed rebuilding of the premises and any proposed transfer of the school to other premises shall be notified forthwith in writing to the Secretary of State[5]. Within five years of approval and at five yearly intervals thereafter, the proprietor of the school shall request the fire authority in whose area the school is situated to provide advice as to fire prevention, restriction of the spread of fires, and means of escape in case of fire. Any specific recommendations contained in such advice must be implemented forthwith[6].

(4) If any person is dismissed from employment as a member of the staff of the school on grounds of his misconduct (whether or not he is convicted of a criminal offence), or would have been so dismissed or considered for dismissal but for his resignation, the facts of the case shall be reported within one month of the dismissal or, if given, of any notice of dismissal or, as the case may be, resignation to the Secretary of State, the LEA in whose area the school is situated, any LEA or local authority who have arranged the placing of a child at the school and the local authority in whose area the school is situated[7].

(5) The school must comply with the provisions, so far as they apply to special schools, of the Education (Schools and Further Education) Regulations 1981 which relate to the duration of the school year and day[8], leave of absence for employment[9] and leave of absence for annual holiday[10].

(6) A written report on each child with a statement at the school shall be furnished to the relevant LEA at least once a year. This report must be capable of assisting the LEA in reviewing their assessment of the special educational needs of the child and of the special educational provision to be made for the purpose of meeting those needs, and to perform their duties under the Disabled Persons (Services, Consultation and Representation) Act 1986[11] The report should be compiled in consultation with the professional staff who, for the period in respect of which the report is compiled, were regularly concerned with the education or care of the child, and any other persons who have been regularly in contact with the child at the school and whom it would be appropriate to consult[12]. The report shall, where appropriate, refer to any involvement of the parents of the child in the preparation of the report, in any assessment of his special educational needs and in any review of such assessment[13]. If requested by the LEA, the proprietor, head teacher and professional staff of the school shall participate in any

annual review conducted by the LEA making no charge for such participation[14].

(7) If a child with a statement leaves the school and becomes a pupil at either another school or an institution which provides further education (whether within or outside the further education sector), the person responsible for the running of the new educational body or institution shall be furnished with such information concerning the education of that child at the school which he has left (including information as to his special educational needs) as they reasonably require of that school[15]. The Secretary of State shall be furnished with such reports, returns and information relating to the school as he may reasonably require of the school[16].

(8) Where the death of a child occurs at the school, or in the course of any activities organised by the school, the proprietor or head teacher shall report the death forthwith to the child's parents (in the case of a child with a statement), the relevant LEA (in the case of a child without a statement), any local authority who arranged for the placement of the child at the school and the local authority in whose area the school is situated and the Secretary of State[17]. The proprietor or head teacher shall not be required to report any such death to the parents or LEA where, in any particular case, it would be inappropriate for him to do so[18]. Where a child suffers any serious illness or serious injury at the school, the proprietor or head teacher shall forthwith notify the child's parents (unless, in any particular case, it would be inappropriate for him to do so) (in the case of a child with a statement), the relevant LEA (in the case of a child without a statement), any local authority who arranged for the placement of the child at the school and the local authority in whose area the school is situated[19].

(9) Where an LEA or local authority have arranged for a child to be placed at the school, access to the school shall be afforded at all reasonable times to any person authorised by that authority for the purpose of inspecting that child and the facilities and provision available to him[20]. In a boarding school, reasonable opportunities and encouragement to visit a child with a statement who is a boarder at the school shall be afforded to his parents and to any person authorised by a local authority or the relevant LEA[21].

1 Education (Special Educational Needs) (Approval of Independent Schools) Regulations 1994, SI 1994/651, reg 4 and Schs 1 and 2.
2 SI 1994/651, Sch 2, para 12.
3 SI 1994/651, Sch 2, para 2.
4 SI 1994/651, Sch 2, para 2.
5 SI 1994/651, Sch 2, para 4.
6 SI 1994/651, Sch 2, para 5(1).
7 SI 1994/651, Sch 2, para 6.
8 Education (Schools and Further Education) Regulations 1981, reg 10.
9 Education (Schools and Further Education) Regulations 1981, reg 11.
10 Education (Schools and Further Education) Regulations 1981, reg 12; SI 1994/651, Sch 2, para 7.
11 SI 1994/651, Sch 2, para 8(1) and (2).
12 SI 1994/651, Sch 2, para 8(3).
13 SI 1994/651, Sch 2, para 8(4).
14 SI 1994/651, Sch 2, para 8(5).
15 SI 1994/651, Sch 2, para 9(1).
16 SI 1994/651, Sch 2, para 9(2).
17 SI 1994/651, Sch 2, para 10(1).

18 SI 1994/651, Sch 2, para 10(2).
19 SI 1994/651, Sch 2, para 10(3).
20 SI 1994/651, Sch 2, para 11(1).
21 SI 1994/651, Sch 2, para 11(2).

Withdrawal of approval from independent schools

The Secretary of State may withdraw approval of a school on the ground   **3.10.5**
that there has been a failure on the school's part to comply with any of the
requirements of approval or continuing approval considered in 3.10.3 and
3.10.4[1]. Normally, approval should not be withdrawn without the Secretary
of State consulting the proprietor and, if the proprietor requests, affording
the school a period specified by the Secretary of State in which to comply
with the relevant requirement. Where the Secretary of State is of the opinion, however, that it is necessary or expedient to do so in the interests of the
health, safety or welfare of children at the school, it is not necessary to consult the proprietor[2].

1 Education (Special Educational Needs) (Approval of Independent Schools) Regulations
   1994, SI 1994/651, Sch 2, para 10(3).
2 SI 1994/651, reg 5(2).

The Secretary of State shall withdraw the approval if the proprietor of the   **3.10.6**
school requests in writing that that he does so[1].

1 Education (Special Educational Needs) (Approval of Independent Schools) Regulations
   1994, SI 1994/651, reg 5(3).

Chapter 4

General responsibilities for children with special educational needs

Introduction 4.1

This chapter will examine the general obligations placed on those involved 4.1.1 with children with special educational needs to ensure that their needs are identified and appropriate provision put in place. The more detailed obligations and powers will be considered in subsequent chapters.

As can been seen throughout this work, children with special educational 4.1.2 needs fall into two categories:

(a) first, those children who have special educational needs, but for whom it is *not* necessary for the Local Education Authority (LEA) to determine the special educational provision which any learning difficulty they have calls for (in effect, children without statements of special educational needs); and
(b) second, those children with special educational needs for whom it is necessary for the LEA to determine the special educational provision which any learning difficulty they have calls for.

It is to the second category of children that LEAs owe specific duties enforceable either through the Tribunal, the courts or the Secretary of State. That does not, however, mean that duties are not owed to children in the first category – those children are owed duties, but not by the LEA (except in the case of maintained nursery schools) rather by the governing bodies of maintained schools.

Invariably, when considering legal responsibilities, attention focuses on schools 4.1.3 and LEAs. It should not be forgotten, however, that other agencies, health and social services in particular, also owe duties towards such children and are often in the best position initially to identify and draw attention to their special educational needs. Their responsibilities must therefore be considered.

Ironically, however, the people who play the most important role in the child's education are often forgotten and their responsibilities overlooked – the parents. Parents must have the most fundamental role in supporting their children and it is unfortunate that in the litigation which has sought to establish responsibility, and most recently liability, against the statutory bodies, the important role and obligations of the child's parents have not been as fully examined as perhaps they should have.

Scope of the chapter

4.1.4 This chapter will examine the role of all agencies and persons who have some form of responsibility for children with special educational needs – parents, schools, LEAs and other agencies (such as health, social service and housing departments) – beginning with the child's parents.

4.2 Responsibilities of parents of a child with special educational needs

Securing suitable education

4.2.1 All parents[1] have an obligation to secure the education of their children if they are of compulsory school age[2]. Thus the parent of every such child must cause him to receive efficient full-time education suitable (a) to his age, ability and aptitude, and (b) to any special educational needs he may have either by regular attendance at school or otherwise[3].

1 Education Act (EA) 1996, s 7.
2 A person begins to be of compulsory school age (a) when he attains the age of five, if he attains that age on a prescribed day, and (b) otherwise at the beginning of the prescribed day next following his attaining that age.
   A person ceases to be of compulsory school age at the end of the day which is the school leaving date for any calendar year (a) if he attains the age of 16 after that day but before the beginning of the school year next following, (b) if he attains that age on that day, or (c) (unless (a) applies) if that day is the school leaving date next following his attaining that age: EA 1996, s 8.
3 EA 1996, s 7.

4.2.2 In *Harrison v Stevenson*[1], the Court held that education is suitable to a child's age, ability and aptitude if, and only if, the education (a) prepares the child for life in modern civilised society, and (b) enables the child to achieve his full potential.

1 (1981) unreported, Worcester Crown Court.

4.2.3 Where children are not in school and it becomes apparent to the LEA that a child of compulsory school age in its area is not receiving suitable education, either by regular attendance at school or otherwise, the LEA is under a duty to serve a notice in writing on the parent of the child requiring the parent to satisfy the LEA that, within the period specified in the notice, the child is receiving suitable education[1].

'Suitable education' for these purposes means efficient full-time education suitable to the child's age, ability and aptitude and to any special educational needs the child may have[2].

1 EA 1996, s 437(1).
2 EA 1996, s 437(8).

School attendance orders

4.2.4 If the parent fails to satisfy the LEA that the child is receiving suitable education and the LEA believes it is expedient that the child should attend school, the LEA shall serve on the parent an order (known as a 'school attendance order') requiring the parent to cause the child to become a registered pupil at a school named in the order[1].

1 EA 1996, s 437(2).

Before issuing a school attendance order, the LEA must first serve a written   **4.2.5**
notice on the parent informing him of their intention to serve the order,
specifying the school which the LEA intend to name and, if they think fit,
suitable alternatives and informing the parent of his ability to apply for
places at alternative schools in certain circumstances[1]. If the parent applies
for the child to be admitted to one of those alternative schools, that school
will generally be named in the order. If the parent does not put forward such
a school then the school which the LEA indicated they intended to name,
will be named in the order.

1 EA 1996, s 438(2).

Where the LEA intend to name a school, they must first consult the gov-   **4.2.6**
erning body[1] and if the school is the responsibility of another LEA, that
LEA[2]. A school cannot be named in an order if (a) the effect of admitting
the child would be to take the school above its fixed admissions number,
and (b) the LEA is not responsible for determining the admissions
arrangements at the school, ie is not the admissions authority, unless there
is no other maintained school within a reasonable distance of the child's
home[3].

1 EA 1996, s 439(5)(a).
2 EA 1996, s 439(5)(b).
3 EA 1996, s 439(1) to (3).

Once the school attendance order is made it continues in force for so long   **4.2.7**
as the child is of compulsory school age unless it is revoked by the LEA or
a court directs that it should cease[1]. The LEA must inform the governing
body and headteacher of the maintained school named in the order that the
order has been made and the governing body are then under a duty to
admit the child[2].

1 EA 1996, s 439(1) to (3).
2 EA 1996, s 437(5) and (6).

Once a school attendance order is in force, the parent of a child without a   **4.2.8**
statement of special educational needs may request that it be amended or
revoked.

If at any time the parent applies for the child to be admitted to a maintained   **4.2.9**
school other than the one named in the order, the child is offered a place
and the parent requests that the order be amended accordingly, the LEA
must comply with the request[1].

1 EA 1996, s 440(2).

If the parent applies to the LEA for education to be provided at a school   **4.2.10**
which is not maintained by an LEA, the child is offered a place under
arrangements made by the LEA under which it pays the fees and the parent
requests that the LEA amend the order, the LEA shall comply with the
request[1].

1 EA 1996, s 440(3).

4.2.11 If the parent applies for the child to be admitted to a non-maintained school, where the LEA is not responsible for the arrangements, the child is offered a place and the school is suitable to his age, ability, aptitude and to any special educational needs he may have and the parent requests that the order be amended, the LEA shall comply with that request[1].

1 EA 1996,s 440(4).

4.2.12 If the parent applies to the LEA requesting that the order be revoked on the ground that arrangements have been made for the child to receive suitable education otherwise than at school, the LEA are obliged to comply with the request unless they are of the opinion that no satisfactory arrangements have been made for the education of the child[1]. If the LEA refuse to revoke the order, the parent may refer the question to the Secretary of State[2] who may give such direction as he thinks fit. Perhaps most importantly, in the context of this book, a parent cannot apply for the order to be revoked if his child has a statement of special educational needs and the name of the school in the order is the school specified in the statement[3].

1 EA 1996, s 442(2).
2 EA 1996, s 442(3).
3 EA 1996, s 442(5).

4.2.13 If a parent on whom a school attendance order is served fails to comply with the requirements of the order, the parent is guilty of an offence, unless he proves to the court that he is causing the child to receive suitable education otherwise than at school[1].

1 EA 1996, s 443(1).

Parents' responsibility to ensure their child attends school

4.2.14 School attendance orders work only where a child is *not* a registered pupil at a school. Where a child of compulsory school age is a registered pupil, if he fails to attend regularly, his parent is guilty of an offence[1]. The offence is one of strict liability[2], although a parent prosecuted has a number of defences available.

First, a child should not be taken to have failed to attend regularly by reason of his absence from the school:

(a) with authorised leave;
(b) at any time when the child was prevented from attending by reason of sickness or any unavoidable cause; or
(c) on any day exclusively set apart for religious observance by the religious body to which the child's parent belongs[3].

Secondly, the child shall not be taken to have failed to attend regularly at the school if the parent proves:

(a) that the school at which the child is a registered pupil is not within walking distance of the child's home; and
(b) that no suitable arrangements have been made by the LEA for any of the following:
    (i)   the child's transport to and from the school,
    (ii) boarding accommodation for the child at or near the school, or

(iii) enabling the child to become a registered pupil at school nearer to his home[4].

Specific provision is made to protect children of traveller families[5].

1 EA 1996, ss 444(1) and 444(1A).
2 See *Bath and North East Somerset District Council v Warman* [1999] ELR 81, [1999] Ed CR 517 and *Jarman v Mid-Glamorgan Education Authority* [1985] LS Gaz R 1249.
3 EA 1996, s 444(3).
4 EA 1996, s 444(4); and see *Essex County Council v Rogers* [1987] AC 66, sub nom *Rogers v Essex County Council* [1986] 3 All ER 321, HL.
5 EA 1996, s 444(6).

With both types of prosecution[1], the LEA has the discretion to prosecute, and although prosecution is the only way of promoting good attendance in certain cases, in many cases it is not. For example, in the case of separated parents, although one parent is absent from the home and child and so has no ability to influence attendance, that parent will in principle be as guilty as the parent with whom the child resides. In other cases, the parents may do all they can to get the child to school, but the child may be stronger than the parents and there is no physical way in which the parents can secure that the child attends. In these circumstances fairness might persuade an LEA not to exercise its discretion to prosecute.   **4.2.15**

1 EA 1996, s 444(6).

In any event, before instituting any proceedings against a parent, the LEA must consider whether it would be appropriate (instead of, or as well as, instituting proceedings) to apply for an education supervision order with respect to the child[1]. One recent innovation is also available to magistrates, namely 'parenting orders', which can require parents to attend for counselling or guidance sessions for up to three months, and may include other requirements to help prevent further pupil absence such as ensuring the child is escorted to and from school for up to 12 months[2].   **4.2.16**

1 EA 1996, s 444(6).
2 Circular 11/99, *Social Inclusion: the LEA role in pupil support*, para 2.12.

The Secretary of State has issued guidance to LEAs as to how they should exercise their functions relating to the promotion and enforcement of attendance[1].   **4.2.17**

1 See Circular 11/99, *Social Inclusion: the LEA role in pupil support*, especially Chaps 1 and 2 'Managing Attendance' and 'Legal Action to Enforce Attendance'.

Parents' responsibility to ensure child's attendance at special educational needs examinations

Where an LEA decides, or is considering whether, to make an assessment of a child's special educational needs, the child will usually need to be examined by a number of professionals, including educational psychologists, doctors and therapists. Normally, parents have no objection and recognise that it is in the child's best interests. If, however, parents are uncooperative, they can be required to ensure that their child attends such examinations. Where, therefore, an LEA is considering whether to make an assessment, it may serve a notice on the parent of the child requiring the child's attendance for examination in accordance with the provisions of   **4.2.18** the notice[1]. The parent of the child may be present at the examination if he so desires[2].

The notice issued by the LEA must:

(a) state the purpose of the examination;
(b) state the time and place at which the examination will be held;
(c) name an officer of the LEA from whom further information may be obtained;
(d) inform the parent that he may submit such information to the LEA as he may wish; and
(e) inform the parent of his right to be present at the examination[3].

Attendance at the examination, if the notice has been properly issued, is compulsory. Any parent who fails without reasonable excuse to comply with any requirements of the notice commits an offence if the notice relates to a child who is not over compulsory school age at the time stated in the notice as the time for holding the examination[4]. A person guilty of this offence is liable on summary conviction to a fine not exceeding level 2 on the standard scale[5].

1 EA 1996, Sch 26, para 4(1).
2 EA 1996, Sch 26, para 4(2).
3 EA 1996, Sch 26, para 4(3).
4 EA 1996, Sch 26, para 5(1).
5 EA 1996, Sch 26, para 5(2).

4.3 Responsibilities of schools to children with special educational needs

4.3.1 *Overview of responsibilities*

The governing body of a community, foundation or voluntary school[1] shall:

(a) use their best endeavours, in exercising their functions in relation to the school, to secure that, if any registered pupil has special educational needs, the special educational provision which his learning difficulty calls for is made[2];
(b) secure that, where the responsible person[3] has been informed by the LEA that a registered pupil has special educational needs, those needs are made known to all who are likely to teach him[4]; and
(c) secure that the teachers in the school are aware of the importance of identifying, and providing for, those registered pupils who have special educational needs[5].

1 And the LEA, currently, in the case of a maintained nursery school.
2 EA 1996, s 317(1)(a).
3 'Responsible person' means, in the case of a community, foundation or voluntary school, the headteacher or the appropriate governor (ie the chairman of governors or the designated special educational needs governor) and, in the case of a nursery school, the headteacher: EA 1996, s 317(2).
4 EA 1996, s 317(1)(b).
5 EA 1996, s 317(1)(c).

4.3.2 To the extent that it appears necessary or desirable for the purpose of co-ordinating provision for children with special educational needs, the governing bodies of community, foundation and voluntary schools shall, in exercising functions relating to the provision for such children, consult the LEA and the governing bodies of other such schools[1].

1 EA 1996, s 317(3)(a).

Where a child who has special educational needs is being educated in a com- **4.3.3** munity, foundation or voluntary school (or a maintained nursery school), those concerned with making special educational provision for the child shall secure, so far as is reasonably practicable and is compatible with:

(a) the child receiving the special educational provision which his learning difficulty calls for;
(b) the provision of efficient education for the children with whom the child will be educated; and
(c) the efficient use of resources,

that the child engages in the activities of the school together with children who do not have special educational needs[1].

1 EA 1996, s 317(4).

When producing their annual report[1] to parents, the governing body must **4.3.4** ensure that that report includes such information as may be prescribed about the implementation of the governing body's policy for pupils with special educational needs[2]. The current Regulations are the Education (Governors' Annual Reports) (England) Regulations 1999[3], and the Education (Governors' Annual Reports) (Wales) Regulations 1999[4]. Thus every governing body's annual report must[5] contain a statement on the success in implementing the governing body's policy for pupils with special educational needs and a description of any significant changes to that policy during the reporting school year[6].

1 See School Standards and Framework Act (SSFA) 1998, s 42.
2 EA 1996, s 317(5).
3 SI 1999/2157.
4 SI 1999/1406.
5 SI 1999/2157, reg 3.
6 SI 1999/2157, Schedule, para 9.

With regard to specific children, the governing body of community, foun- **4.3.5** dation and voluntary schools must inform the parent of certain children that special educational provision is being made for them at the school because it is considered that the child has special educational needs[1]. This requirement will apply to a child if:

(a) the child attends a community, foundation or voluntary school or pupil referral unit[2] and no statement is maintained in respect of him;
(b) special educational provision is made for the child at the school because it is considered that he has special educational needs; and
(c) the child's parent has not previously been informed of special educational provision made for him at the school[3].

1 EA 1996, s 317A(3).
2 In the case of a pupil referral unit, the LEA must secure that the headteacher informs the child's parent that special educational provision is being made for the child at the school because it is considered that the child has special educational needs: EA 1996, s 317A(2).
3 EA 1996, s 317A(1).

4.3.6   In respect of children who do have a statement of special educational needs, if the name of a maintained school is specified in the statement, the governing body of the school must admit the child to the school[1].

1 EA 1996, s 324(5)(b).

4.3.7   Governing bodies of maintained schools are also required to provide access to any person authorised by an LEA, at any reasonable time, to the premises of their schools for the purposes of monitoring the special educational provision made in pursuance of a statement maintained for a child at the school[1]. The EA 1996 states that this obligation only arises where the child is educated at a school maintained by another LEA to the LEA which maintains the statement[2]. It must therefore be implicit that an authorised LEA officer may have access on the same terms to schools maintained by the officer's LEA for similar purposes.

1 EA 1996, s 327(2).
2 EA 1996, s 327(1)(b).

4.3.8   Finally, although perhaps most importantly in practice, each governing body must have regard to the Code of Practice[1] when carrying out its duties toward all pupils with special educational needs[2].

1 See 2.2.6 and 2.2.7.
2 EA 1996, s 313; and see particularly Chaps 1 to 6 of the Code of Practice.

Responsibility of schools to publish information

4.3.9   As far as publishing details of their policies and other information relating to children with special educational needs is concerned, certain requirements are imposed on governing bodies[1].

1 EA 1996, s 317; and SSFA 1998, ss 92(3) and (6) and 138(7) and (8).

4.3.10   Accordingly, the governing body of every maintained school must publish information about the following matters[1]:

(1) the objectives of the governing body in making provision for pupils with special educational needs, and a description of how the governing body's special educational needs policy will contribute towards meeting those objectives;

(2) the name of the person who is responsible for co-ordinating the day to day provision of education for pupils with special educational needs at the school (whether or not the person is known as the SEN co-ordinator);

(3) the arrangements which have been made for co-ordinating the provision of education for pupils with special educational needs at the school;

(4) the admission arrangements for pupils with special educational needs who do not have a statement in so far as they differ from the arrangements for other pupils;

(5) the kinds of provision for special educational needs in which the school specialises and any special units;

(6) facilities for pupils with special educational needs at the school including facilities which increase or assist access to the school by pupils who are disabled;

(7) how resources are allocated to and amongst pupils with special educational needs;

(8) how pupils with special educational needs are identified and their needs determined and reviewed;

(9) arrangements for providing access by pupils with special educational needs to a balanced and broadly-based curriculum (including the National Curriculum);

(10) how pupils with special educational needs engage in the activities of the school together with pupils who do not have special educational needs;

(11) how the governing body evaluate the success of the education which is provided at the school to pupils with special educational needs;

(12) any arrangements made by the governing body relating to the treatment of complaints from parents of pupils with special educational needs concerning the provision made at the school;

(13) any arrangements made by the governing body relating to in-service training for staff in relation to special educational needs;

(14) the use made of teachers and facilities from outside the school including links with support services for special educational needs;

(15) the role played by the parents of pupils with special educational needs;

(16) any links with other schools, including special schools, and the provision made for the transition of pupils with special educational needs between schools or between the school and the next stage of life or education; and

(17) links with child health services, social services and educational welfare services and any voluntary organisations which work on behalf of children with special educational needs.

1 Education (Special Educational Needs) (Information) (England) Regulations 1999, SI 1999/2506, reg 3(1) and Sch 1; or, in Wales, Education (Special Educational Needs) (Information) (Wales) Regulations 1999, SI 1999/1442.

The governing body of a maintained special school, other than one established in a hospital, must publish information about the following[1]: **4.3.11**

(1) the objectives of the governing body in making provision for pupils with special educational needs, and a description of how the governing body's special educational needs policy will contribute towards meeting those objectives;

(2) the kinds of special educational needs for which provision is made at the school;

(3) facilities for pupils at the school including facilities which increase or assist access to the school by pupils who are disabled;

(4) how resources are allocated amongst pupils;

(5) how the needs of pupils are identified and reviewed;

(6) arrangements for providing access by pupils to a balanced and broadly based curriculum (including the National Curriculum);

(7) how the governing body evaluate the success of the education which is provided at the school to pupils;

(8) any arrangements made by the governing body relating to the treatment of complaints from parents of pupils concerning the provision made at the school;

(9)   any arrangements made by the governing body relating to in-service training for staff in relation to special educational needs;

(10)   the use made of teachers and facilities from outside the school including the links with support services for special educational needs;

(11)   the role played by parents of pupils;

(12)   any links with other schools, and any arrangements for managing the transition of pupils between schools or between the school and the next stage of life or education; and

(13)   links with child health services, social services and educational welfare services and any voluntary organisations which work on behalf of children with special educational needs.

1   Education (Special Educational Needs) (Information) (England) Regulations 1999, SI 1999/2506, reg 3(2) and Sch 2; or, in Wales, Education (Special Educational Needs) (Information) (Wales) Regulations 1999, SI 1999/1442.

4.3.12   In special schools in hospitals, only the following information need be published[1]:

(1)   the name of the person who is responsible for co-ordinating the day-to-day provision of education for pupils with special educational needs at the school (whether or not the person is known as the SEN co-ordinator);

(2)   how pupils with special educational needs are identified and their needs determined and reviewed;

(3)   how resources are allocated to and amongst pupils with special educational needs;

(4)   how the educational progress of pupils with special educational needs is monitored;

(5)   how the contents of a pupil's statement are ascertained and made known to staff;

(6)   the arrangements for ensuring continuity of the educational provision set out in a pupil's statement differentiating where necessary between long stay and short stay patients;

(7)   arrangements for providing access by pupils with special educational needs to a balanced and broadly based curriculum; and

(8)   the use made of teachers and facilities from outside the school including links with support services for special educational needs.

1   Education (Special Educational Needs) (Information) (England) Regulations 1999, SI 1999/2506, reg 3(3) and Sch 3; or, in Wales, Education (Special Educational Needs) (Information) (Wales) Regulations 1999, SI 1999/1442.

4.3.13   In all cases, the information should be published in a single document by making copies available free-of-charge (a) for distribution to parents of pupils or prospective pupils and to the LEA, district health authority for the area in which the school is situated at the school or through the post, and (b) for reference at the school[1].

1   Education (Special Educational Needs) (Information) (England) Regulations 1999, SI 1999/2506, reg 4; or, in Wales, Education (Special Educational Needs) (Information) (Wales) Regulations 1999, SI 1999/1442.

Responsibilities of LEAs to children with special educational needs

An LEA's responsibilities for special education fall into two categories: (a) **4.** general duties owed towards all children; and (b) specific duties owed towards individual children and/or their parents. It is the number and precision of the latter type of duties which has caused so much difficulty for LEAs in the courts and which has also enabled parents to obtain far greater redress through the Tribunal and, on appeal, to the High Court in recent years. The more specific obligations will be considered in later chapters[1]; what is considered here are the general, overarching responsibilities of LEAs.

1 See Chapters 5, 6 and 7.

Keeping arrangements under review

The first general responsibility on LEAs is the duty to keep under review **4.4.2** the arrangements it makes for special educational provision[1]. In carrying out this duty (as with all other duties and powers towards children with special educational needs) the LEA must have regard to the Code of Practice[2]. It must also, to the extent that it appears necessary or desirable for the purpose of co-ordinating provision for children with special educational needs, consult the governing bodies of maintained[3] schools in the LEA's area[4].

1 EA 1996, s 315.
2 EA 1996, s 313(2).
3 Ie community, foundation, voluntary, community special and foundation special schools.
4 EA 1996, s 315(2).

This obligation to keep arrangements under review is general and does not **4.4.3** apply to specific pupils whose progress and review of needs is covered by s 328(5) of the EA 1996. It does not, therefore, impose a duty on an LEA, for which damages can be recovered, to, in effect, 'keep an eye on' specific children placed by an LEA in residential schools[1].

1 See *P v Harrow London Borough Council* [1993] 2 FCR 341.

General responsibilities of LEAs

LEAs are required to exercise their powers with a view to securing that, of **4.4.4** the children for whom they are responsible, (a) they identify those children who have special educational needs, and (b) they determine the special educational provision which any learning difficulty any such children may have calls for[1].

An LEA is responsible for a child if the child is in its area and:

(a) the child is a registered pupil at a maintained school;
(b) education is provided for the child at a school which is not a maintained school but is so provided at the expense of the authority;
(c) items (a) or (b) above do not apply, but the child is a registered pupil at a school and has been brought to the LEA's attention as having or probably having special educational needs, or
(d) the child is not a registered pupil at a school but is not under the age of two or over compulsory school age and has been brought to

their attention as having or probably having special educational needs[2].

1 EA 1996, s 321(1) and (2).
2 EA 1996, s 321(3).

4.4.5 A 'child' includes any person who has not attained the age of 19 and is a registered pupil at a school[1].

A 'pupil' is defined as a person for whom education is being provided at a school, other than (a) a person who has attained the age of 19 for whom further education is being provided, or (b) a person for whom part-time education suitable to the requirements of persons of any age over compulsory school age is being provided[2].

A 'school' is an educational institution which is outside the further education sector and the higher education sector and is an institution for providing (a) primary education, (b) secondary education, or (c) both primary and secondary education, whether or not the institution also provides part-time education suitable to the requirements of junior pupils or further education[3].

'Secondary education' is then defined as meaning (a) full-time education suitable to the requirements of pupils of compulsory school age who are either senior pupils, or junior pupils who have attained the age of ten years and six months and whom it is expedient to educate together with senior pupils of compulsory school age; and (b) full-time education suitable to the requirements of pupils who are over compulsory school age but under the age of 19 which is provided at a school[5].

1 EA 1996, s 312(5).
2 EA 1996, s 3(1).
3 EA 1996, s 4(1).
4 EA 1996, s 2(2) and (5).

4.4.6 The net effect of all of these, at times confusing, definitions is that an LEA remains responsible for a child until the child attains the age of 19 so long as the child remains a pupil at a school. It follows, therefore, that once the child attains the age of 19 or, before attaining that age, the child leaves school, for example, to go into employment or to receive further education at a further education college, the LEA will cease to be responsible.

The extent of the LEA's responsibilities is considered in more detail in Chapters 5, 6 and 7.

4.4.7 The duties of governing bodies have been considered above[1], but it should not be forgotten that the LEA will have the same duties in respect of nursery schools which it maintains[2] at least until the provisions of the Education Act 2002, if enacted, create governing bodies for such schools[3]. The LEA must, therefore, in respect of those nursery schools:

(a) use its best endeavours, in exercising its functions in relation to the school, to secure that, if any registered pupil has special educational needs, the special educational provision which the pupil's learning difficulty calls for is made[4];

(b) secure that, where the responsible person[5] has been informed by the LEA that a registered pupil has special educational needs, those needs are made known to all who are likely to teach him[6]; and

(c) secure that the teachers in the school are aware of the importance of identifying, and providing for, those registered pupils who have special educational needs[7].

The LEA must also in relation to maintained nursery schools, to the extent that it appears necessary or desirable for the purpose of co-ordinating provision for children with special educational needs, consult the governing bodies of community, foundation and voluntary schools[8]. Where a child with special educational needs is being educated at a maintained nursery school, the LEA shall secure, so far as is reasonably practicable and is compatible with:

(a) the child receiving the special educational provision which his learning difficulty calls for;
(b) the provision of efficient education for the children with whom he will be educated; and
(c) the efficient use of resources,

that the child engages in the activities of the school together with children who do not have special educational needs[9].

1 See 4.3ff
2 EA 1996, s 317(1).
3 See Education Bill, Part 3, as at 30 January 2002.
4 EA 1996, s 317(1)(a).
5 'Responsible person' means, in the case of a nursery school, the headteacher: EA 1996, s 317(2).
6 EA 1996, s 317(1)(b).
7 EA 1996, s 317(1)(c).
8 EA 1996, s 317(3)(b).
9 EA 1996, s 317(4).

4.4.8 The LEA is also under the duty in pupil referral units for which it is responsible to secure that the headteacher informs children's parents where special educational provision is being made for them in the unit because it is considered that they have special educational needs[1].

1 EA 1996, s 317A(2).

4.4.9 The majority of children with special educational needs will be educated in schools, either maintained schools, maintained special schools, non-maintained special schools or independent special schools. There may, however, be occasions where the needs of a child are such that it is necessary to make special educational provision for him otherwise than in schools. Thus, where an LEA is satisfied that it would be inappropriate for (a) the special educational provision which a learning difficulty of a child in their area calls for, or (b) any part of any such provision, to be made in a school, the LEA may arrange for the provision (or, as the case may be, for that part of it) to be made otherwise than in school[1]. Before making such an arrangement, however, the LEA must consult the child's parent[2].

1 EA 1996, s 319(1).
2 EA 1996, s 319(2).

4.4.10 Similarly, there may be occasions where a child's needs cannot be met by an institution within England or Wales. For example only a school in Scotland may be suitable or possibly the institute may be overseas, for example, the

Peto Institute in Budapest or the Institute for the Maximisation of Human Potential in Philadelphia, US. An LEA may therefore make such arrangements as it thinks fit to enable a child for whom it maintains a statement to attend an institution outside England and Wales which specialises in providing for children with special educational needs[1]. The arrangements made by the LEA may, in particular, include contributing to or paying (a) fees charged by the institution, (b) expenses reasonably incurred in maintaining him while he is at the institution or travelling to or from it, (c) his travelling expenses, and (d) expenses reasonably incurred by any person accompanying him while he is travelling or staying at the institution[2].

1 EA 1996, s 320(1).
2 EA 1996, s 320(3).

Responsibility of LEAs to publish information

4.4.11 Finally, LEAs are required to publish certain information about their functions[1]. The specific information relating to their functions with regard to children with special educational needs which must be published is currently set out in the Special Educational Needs (Provision of Information by Local Education Authorities) (England) Regulations 2001[2]. Unlike the other special educational provisions flowing from the Special Educational Needs and Disability Act 2001, these Regulations did come into force on 1 September 2001, although the information required only had to be published on or before 1 April 2002[3].

1 EA 1996, s 29.
2 SI 2001/2218. The equivalent regulations for Wales had not been produced at the time of writing.
3 Special Educational Needs (Provision of Information by Local Education Authorities) (England) Regulations 2001, SI 2001/2218, reg 3(2).

4.4.12 Consequently, an LEA must publish the following information[1]:

(1) an explanation of that element of special educational provision for children with special educational needs (but without statements) which the LEA expect normally to be met from maintained schools' budget shares and that element of such provision that the LEA expect normally to be met by the LEA from funds which it holds centrally[2];

(2) the broad aims of the LEA's policy in respect of children with special educational needs together with information about the action the LEA is taking to:
   (a) promote high standards of education for children with special educational needs;
   (b) encourage such children to participate fully in their school and community and to take part in decisions about their education;
   (c) encourage schools in their area to share their practice in making special educational provision for children with special educational needs; and
   (d) work with other statutory and voluntary bodies to provide support for such children[3]; and

(3) the general arrangements made by the LEA, including any plans, objectives and timescales, for[4]:
   (a) identifying children in their area with special educational needs;
   (b) monitoring the admission of children with special educational needs

(whether or not those children have a statement) to maintained schools in their area;

(c) organising the assessment of children's educational needs in the LEA's area including any local protocols for so doing;

(d) organising the making and maintaining of statements in their area including any local protocols for so doing;

(e) providing support to schools in their area with regard to making special educational provision for children with special educational needs;

(f) auditing, planning, monitoring and reviewing provision for children with special educational needs in their area, both generally and in relation to individual children;

(g) securing training, advice and support for staff working in their area with children with special educational needs; and

(h) reviewing and updating the arrangements referred to in (a) to (g) above.

1 Special Educational Needs (Provision of Information by Local Education Authorities) (England) Regulations 2001, SI 2001/2218, reg 2(a).
2 SI 2001/2218, Schedule, para 1.
3 SI 2001/2218, Schedule, para 2.
4 SI 2001/2218, Schedule, para 3.

The LEA must publish all this information by[1]:   **4.4.13**

(a) providing a written copy of the information to any health authority or social services authority which in the LEA's opinion has an interest in that information;

(b) making the information available on a website which the LEA maintains on the internet; and

(c) providing a written copy of the information to any person on request.

The published information must be kept under review[2]. Where there is a significant change in any of that information, the LEA must revise the information accordingly and publish the revised information in the same way as on initial publication[3].

1 Special Educational Needs (Provision of Information by Local Education Authorities) (England) Regulations 2001, SI 2001/2218, reg 3(1).
2 SI 2001/2218, reg 2(b).
3 SI 2001/2218, reg 2(c).

Power of LEAs to supply goods or services to governing bodies

Before leaving this area of LEAs' general responsibilities, it is necessary, for   **4.4.14**
the sake of completeness, to mention one general *power* which enables LEAs
to supply certain goods and services to governing bodies to assist them in
exercising their functions. An LEA may, for the purpose only of assisting:

(a) the governing bodies of community, foundation or voluntary schools in their or any other area in the performance of their duty to use its best endeavours to secure that special educational provision which a child's learning difficulty calls for, is made; or

(b) the governing bodies of community or foundation special schools in its area or any other area in the performance of the governing bodies' duties,

supply goods or services to those bodies[1]. The terms on which goods or services are supplied by LEAs may, in such circumstances as may be prescribed[2], include such terms as to payment as may be prescribed[3]. An LEA may supply goods and services to any authority or other person (other than a governing body mentioned above) for the purpose only of assisting them in making for any child, who is receiving nursery education or in respect of whom education grants are made, any special educational provision which any learning difficulty of the child calls for[4]. These specific powers are without prejudice to the generality of any power[5] of LEAs to supply goods or services[6].

1   EA 1996, s 318(1).
2   See Education (Payment for Special Educational Needs Supplies) Regulations 1999, SI 1999/710.
3   EA 1996, s 318(2).
4   EA 1996, s 318(3) and (3A).
5   For example, under the Local Authorities (Goods and Services) Act 1970.
6   EA 1996, s 318(4).

4.5   Responsibilities of other agencies to children with special educational needs

General

4.5.1   While discussing the issue of responsibility, whether general or specific, it is important to consider the role of other agencies which may be involved in providing support to children with special educational needs. In many ways these agencies – principally NHS bodies and social services – are likely to encounter a child with special educational needs or potential special educational needs at a far earlier stage than LEAs.

4.5.2   Consequently, if, in the course of exercising any of their functions in relation to a child who is under compulsory school age, a health authority, primary care trust or NHS trust form the opinion that the child has (or probably has) special educational needs, the authority or trust must inform the child's parents of their opinion and of their duty to, after giving the parent an opportunity to discuss that opinion with an officer of the authority or trust, bring it to the attention of the appropriate LEA[1].

1   EA 1996, s 332(1) and (2).

4.5.3   If the authority or trust are of the opinion that a particular voluntary organisation is likely to be able to give the parent advice or assistance in connection with any special educational needs that the child may have, they shall inform the parent accordingly[1].

1   EA 1996, s 332(3).

4.5.4   Health bodies and local authority social service or housing departments also have limited duties to help LEAs in carrying out their functions. Where it appears to an LEA that any health authority, primary care trust or local authority[1] could, by taking any specified action, help in the exercise of any of its functions, the LEA may request the help of that authority or trust, specifying the action in question[2]. An authority or trust whose help is requested shall comply with the request unless:

(a)   it considers that the help requested is not necessary for the purpose of the exercise by the LEA of those functions[3]; or

(b) in the case of a health authority or primary care trust, if that authority or trust consider that, having regard to the resources available to them for the purpose of the exercise of their functions under the National Health Service Act 1977, it is not reasonable for them to comply with the request[4]; or

(c) in the case of a local authority, if that authority considers that the request is not compatible with its own statutory or other duties and obligations or unduly prejudices the discharge of any of its functions[5].

Although the duty placed on the social services department is, in effect, a secondary duty to that of the LEA, if help is requested by the LEA the social services department must justify any decision to refuse to help by pointing to one of the grounds contained in EA 1996, s 322(3)(b). The duty also applies internally, ie to a social services department within the local authority which is also the LEA. Although it was initially thought that the duty to assist could only apply to a request from an LEA to another LEA or the social services department of another local authority, it is now established[6] that the section can apply to a request from an authority's LEA to the same authority's social services department.

1 'Local authority' for these purposes means a county council, a county borough council, a district council (other than one for an area for which there is a county council), a London borough council or the Common Council of the City of London: EA 1996, s 322(5).
2 EA 1996, s 322(1).
3 EA 1996, s 322(2)(a).
4 EA 1996, s 322(2)(b) and (3)(a).
5 EA 1996, s 322(2)(b) and (3)(b).
6 See *G v Wakefield City Metropolitan District Council* (1998) 96 LGR 69, QBD.

Regulations may provide that where an authority or a trust are under a duty   **4.5.5**
to comply with an LEA's request for assistance in the making of an assessment or a statement it must, subject to prescribed exceptions, comply with the request within a prescribed period[1]. Thus, where an LEA seeks medical advice from a health authority[2] or advice from a social services authority[3], the health or social services authority should comply with the request within six weeks of the date on which they receive it[4]. Neither authorities, however, need comply with that time limit if it is impractical to do so because:

(a) exceptional personal circumstances affect the child or the child's parent during the six-week period;

(b) the child or parent is absent from the area of the LEA for a continuous period of not less than four weeks during the six-week period; or

(c) the child fails to keep an appointment for an examination or a test by the health or social services authority during the six-week period[5].

If a social services authority has not produced or maintained any information or records relevant to the assessment of the child, it need not comply with the request[6]. In the case of a health authority which has not produced or maintained any information or records relevant to the assessment of the child, it need not comply with the time limit[7] but by implication should nonetheless obtain information upon which it can advise the LEA[8].

1 EA 1996, s 322(4).
2 Under Education (Special Educational Needs) (England) (Consolidation) Regulations 2001, SI 2001/3455, reg 7(1)(c).
3 Under SI 2001/3455, reg 7(1)(e).

4   SI 2001/3455, reg 12(8).
5   SI 2001/3455, reg 12(9).
6   SI 2001/3455, reg 12(11).
7   SI 2001/3455, reg 12(10).
8   SI 2001/3455, reg 12(10).

Co-operation, competition and conflict between agencies

4.5.6   Although there has been a welcome move in recent years towards greater co-operation between agencies and, indeed, government initiatives are moving towards pooled funding for certain aspects of special education provision (for example therapy services[1]), there is still the potential for conflict between agencies, each having limited resources and competing priorities.

> 1   See *Meeting Special Educational Needs – A programme of action* (DfEE 1998), Chap 5 'Working in Partnership to Meet Special Needs'.

4.5.7   This competition has led to a number of disputes over the respective roles and responsibilities, although, even if it was not clear before, it is now well-established that in virtually all cases the ultimate or primary responsibilities rest with LEAs.

4.5.8   The potential conflict between LEAs and health bodies was analysed in the linked cases of *R v London Borough of Harrow, ex p M*[1] and *R v Brent and Harrow Health Authority, ex p London Borough of Harrow*[2]. The girl involved in this case had cerebral palsy. The LEA had issued a statement of special educational needs which, in Part 3[3] stated that she needed occupational therapy and physiotherapy and specified the time and amounts. However, she did not receive it. The LEA blamed the health authority for failing to provide it. When it was judicially reviewed by the girl's mother, the LEA in turn attempted to judicially review the health authority. The girl's mother succeeded against the LEA, but the LEA failed against the health authority. The judge held that whilst the health authority could ration its resources and, in so doing, not provide therapy services specified in a statement, once that provision was specified in Part 3 of a statement, the LEA was under a duty, ie had the primary responsibility, to provide it. Thus, if the health authority failed for whatever reason, the LEA could not rely on that failure to justify its own breach of duty; instead, the LEA had to make the provision in some other way to ensure that the provision it had specified in the statement was made.

> 1   [1997] 3 FCR 761, [1997] ELR 62, QBD.
> 2   [1997] 3 FCR 765, [1997] ELR 187, QBD.
> 3   As to the various parts of a statement and the issue of educational or non-educational provision, see Chapter 6.

4.5.9   Therefore whilst partnership working between the respective agencies[1] is crucial, the ultimate duty to make the educational provision specified in a statement will always lie with the LEA. That provision will be covered in more detail in Chapter 6.

> 1   With the various initiatives and statutory attempts to assist joined-up working between health, social services and education (for example under the Health Act 1999 and the NHS Bodies and Local Authorities Partnership Arrangements Regulations 2000, SI 2000/617), it is hoped that there should soon be an improvement with, for example, pooled budgets, enabling more co-operation and co-ordination with services such as speech and occupational therapy.

Chapter 5

Identification and assessment of children with special educational needs

Introduction   5.1

Putting to one side the legal niceties of the statutory powers and duties   5.1.1
under the Education Acts, the key concern for any parent of a child with
special educational needs, and the teachers who have to teach him or her, is
ensuring that the child's needs are properly identified at the earliest possible
opportunity. If those needs are missed, all the legal action in the world,
including claims for compensation (which are looked at later[1]), cannot make
up for that failure and the remedial education which is likely to have been
missed.

1 See Chapter 10.

The Education Act (EA) 1996 makes detailed provision for the identification   5.1.2
and assessment of children with special educational needs by Local
Education Authorities (LEAs), but the most important work on the identification of needs is, and often can only be, the action taken by a child's school.

Scope of the chapter

This chapter will therefore consider both the obligations imposed on schools 5.1.3
and LEAs and the good practice set out in the Code of Practice[1] to spot,
diagnose and provide for children with special educational needs.

1 As to which, see 2.2.6 and 2.2.7.

IDENTIFICATION OF CHILDREN WITH SPECIAL EDUCATIONAL NEEDS

School-based identification   5.2

The governing body of each community, foundation or voluntary school   5.2.1
(and the LEA in the case of a maintained nursery school) are under a duty
to:

(a) use their best endeavours, in exercising their functions in relation to the
    school, to secure that, if any registered pupil has special educational
    needs, the special educational provision which his learning difficulty
    calls for is made[1]; and

(b) secure that the teachers in the school are aware of the importance of identifying, and providing for, those registered pupils who have special educational needs[2].

1 EA 1996, s 317(1)(a).
2 EA 1996, s 317(1)(c).

5.2.2   To the extent that it appears necessary or desirable for the purpose of co-ordinating provision for children with special educational needs, the governing bodies of maintained schools shall, in exercising functions relating to the provision for such children, consult the LEA and the governing body of other maintained schools[1].

1 EA 1996, s 317(3)(a).

5.2.3   This is, however, all that the EA 1996 prescribes in respect of schools. More important for setting out the school-based responsibility for assessment is the Code of Practice[1]. And, as we have seen, governing bodies of maintained schools exercising their functions towards children with, or potentially having, special educational needs, must have regard to the Code of Practice[2].

1 See 2.2.6 and 2.2.7.
2 EA 1996, s 313(2).

5.2.4   The Code of Practice deals with the question of assessment by providing advice for each of the three educational phases: (i) identification and assessment in the early education settings[1], (ii) the primary phase[2], and (iii) the secondary phase[3]. The guidance has been divided in this way for ease-of-access by school staff in the three phases, but, with minor variation, most of the advice is broadly similar irrespective of the age of the pupils concerned. The general principles of identification and assessment should, after all, be consistent whatever the school setting.

1 Code of Practice, Chap 4.
2 Code of Practice, Chap 5.
3 Code of Practice, Chap 6.

Early education

5.2.5   The importance of early identification, assessment and provision cannot be overemphasised[1]. To help identify children who may have special educational needs, schools can measure pupils' progress by referring to[2]:

- evidence from teacher observation and assessment;
- their performance monitored by the teacher as part of ongoing observation and assessment;
- the outcomes from baseline assessment results;
- their progress against the objectives specified in the National Literacy and Numeracy Strategy Frameworks;
- their performance against the level descriptions within the National Curriculum at the end of a key stage; and
- standardised screening or assessment tools.

Schools should also be open and responsive to views expressed by parents and should take into account any information provided by the child's parents[3].

1 Code of Practice, paras 5:11 and 6:10.

2 Code of Practice, paras 5:13 and 6:12.
3 Code of Practice, paras 5:14 and 6:13.

In the early years setting, where early identification is vitally important, **5.2.6**
early education settings[1] should monitor individual children's progress and,
where a child appears not to be making progress, may need to present different opportunities or use alternative approaches[2]. The key test for action
is evidence that the child's current rate of progress is inadequate[3].

1 'Early education settings' is defined as providers in receipt of government funding to
  deliver early education including maintained mainstream and special schools, maintained
  nursery schools, independent schools, non-maintained special schools, local authority day
  care providers such as day nurseries and family centres, other registered day care
  providers, such as pre-schools, playgroups and private day nurseries, local authority
  portage schemes and accredited childminders working as part of an approved National
  Childminding Association network (Code of Practice, Glossary).
2 Code of Practice, para 4:9.
3 Code of Practice, para 4:13.

In an early education setting, if a child is identified as having special educa- **5.2.7**
tional needs, interventions additional to or different from those provided as
part of the setting's usual curriculum should be devised (known as 'Early
Years Action')[1]. The suggested triggers for intervention through Early Years
Action are evidence of a child[2]:

(a) making little or no progress even where teaching approaches are par-
    ticularly targeted to improve the child's identified area of weakness;
(b) continuing to work at level significantly below those expected for chil-
    dren of a similar age in certain areas;
(c) presenting persistent emotional and/or behavioural difficulties, which
    are not ameliorated by the behaviour management techniques usually
    employed in the setting;
(d) having sensory or physical problems and continuing to make little or
    no progress despite the provision of personal aids and equipment;
(e) having communication and/or interaction difficulties and requiring
    specific individual interventions in order to access learning.

1 Code of Practice, para 4:20.
2 Code of Practice, para 4:21.

In all phases of education the role of the school's special educational needs **5.2.8**
co-ordinator (SENCO) is central to the identification and assessment of
pupils' needs. Every early education setting and school must identify a
member of staff to take responsibility for co-ordinating special educational
needs provision within their school. In a small school, the headteacher or
deputy may take on this role; in larger schools there may be an special educational needs co-ordinating team[1].

1 In the case of accredited childminders who are part of an approved network, the SENCO
  role may be shared between individual childminders and the co-ordinator of the network:
  Code of Practice, para 4:15.

In the early education setting, the SENCO should be responsible for or lead **5.2.9**
on[1]:

(a) ensuring liaison with parents and other professionals in respect of chil-
    dren with special educational needs;

(b) advising and supporting other practitioners in the setting;

(c) ensuring that appropriate Individual Education Plans (IEPs) are in place;

(d) ensuring that relevant background information about individual children with special educational needs is collected, recorded and updated;

(e) further assessing the child's particular strengths and weaknesses;

(f) planning future support for the child in discussion with colleagues;

(g) monitoring and reviewing the subsequent action taken;

(h) ensuring that appropriate records are kept including a record of children at Early Years Action and Early Years Action Plus and those with statements.

1 Code of Practice, paras 4:15 and 4:16.

Primary and secondary education

5.2.10 In primary and secondary schools, the SENCO's role includes[1]:

(a) in collaboration with the headteacher and governing body, playing a key role in helping to determine the strategic development of special educational needs policy and provision in the school to raise the achievement of pupils with special educational needs;

(b) day-to-day responsibility for the operation of the special educational needs policy and co-ordination of the provision made for individual pupils with special educational needs, working closely with staff, parents and carers, (in secondary schools) with the Connexions Personal Adviser and other agencies;

(c) providing related professional guidance to colleagues with the aim of securing high quality teaching for pupils with special educational needs;

(d) with the support of the headteacher and colleagues, seeking to develop effective ways of overcoming barriers to learning and sustaining effective teaching through the analysis and assessment of pupils' needs, by monitoring the quality of teaching and standards of pupils' achievements and by setting targets for improvement;

(e) collaborating with heads of departments, the literacy and numeracy co-ordinators to ensure that learning for all pupils is given equal priority and that available resources are used to maximum effect.

1 Code of Practice, paras 5:30 to 5:36 and 6:32 to 6:40.

5.2.11 Schools should record the steps taken to meet the needs of individual children. The SENCO should have responsibility for keeping proper records[1]. The pupil record or profile for children with special educational needs should include information about the pupil's progress and behaviour from the school itself, from the pupil's previous school(s), from the parents and from health and social services and other outside agencies, including Connexions. It should also include the pupil's own perception of any difficulties and how they might be addressed. It may also be necessary to record details about the pupil's needs in relation to the general strategies to be used to enable access to the curriculum and the school day[2]. The records should contain information on the different perceptions of those concerned with the child, any immediate educational concerns and an overall picture of the child's strengths and weaknesses[3].

1 Code of Practice, paras 4:18, 5:24 and 6:26.
2 Code of Practice, paras 4:18, 5:25 and 6:27.
3 Code of Practice, paras 4:19, 5:26 and 6:28.

Provision for special educational needs in schools   **5.3**

The majority of children with special educational needs will be educated in   **5.3.1**
their own early education settings or schools and LEA intervention will not
be necessary. Apart from the statutory responsibilities of governing bodies to
make provision for these children[1], they are, by and large, dealt with without recourse to the statutory processes considered below[2].

1 See Chapter 4.
2 See 5.4, 5.5 and 5.6 and Chapter 6.

As we have seen[1], one of the duties imposed on a governing body of a   **5.3.2**
school, or the LEA in the case of a maintained nursery school, is to use their
best endeavours to secure that, if any registered pupil has special educational
needs, the special educational provision which the pupil's learning difficulty calls for is made[2].

1 See 5.2.1.
2 EA 1996, s 317(1)(a).

The Code of Practice offers guidance on the type and nature of provision that   **5.3.3**
early education settings[1], primary schools[2] and secondary schools[3] should make.

1 Code of Practice, paras 4:5 to 4:14.
2 Code of Practice, paras 5:7 to 5:10, 5:17 to 5:23 and 5:43 to 5:61.
3 Code of Practice, paras 6:6 to 6:9, 6:17 to 6:25 and 6:41 to 6:69.

In early education settings, practitioners should work closely with all parents   **5.3.4**
to build on the child's previous experiences, knowledge, understanding and
skills and provide opportunities to develop in six areas of learning[1]:

(1) personal, social and emotional development;
(2) communication, language and literacy;
(3) mathematical development;
(4) knowledge and understanding of the world;
(5) physical development; and
(6) creative development.

Children who make slower progress do not necessarily have special educational needs, but such children will need carefully differentiated learning
opportunities to help them progress and monitoring of that progress[2]. The
Code advises early education settings to adopt a graduated response to provide specific help to individual children. This approach recognises that there
is a continuum of special educational needs and allows an increasingly specialist expertise to be brought to the child[3].

1 Code of Practice, para 4:6.
2 Code of Practice, para 4:8.
3 Code of Practice, para 4:10.

Early Years Action and School Years Action and Action Plus

5.3.5   Where a child is identified as having special educational needs in an early education setting, the setting should 'devise interventions that are additional to or different from those provided as part of the setting's usual curriculum offer and strategies'[1], which are known as 'Early Years Action'. The SENCO and the child's teacher, in consultation with the parent, should decide on the action needed to help the child to progress. This does not necessarily involve the deployment of staff to give one-to-one tuition, but will comprise effective individualised arrangements for learning and teaching[2]. The arrangements and strategies used should be recorded in an 'Individual Education Plan', including information about short-term targets, strategies, the provision put in place, review and outcome of the action to be taken[3].

1   Code of Practice, para 4:20.
2   Code of Practice, para 4:26.
3   Code of Practice, para 4:27.

5.3.6   If the setting needs to involve external support services, the child moves onto what is known as 'Early Years Action Plus'[1]. The triggers for initiating this support will include[2]:

(a)   the child continuing to make little or no progress in specific areas over a long period;
(b)   continuing working at an early years curriculum substantially below that expected of children of a similar age;
(c)   having emotional or behavioural difficulties which substantially and regularly interfere with the child's own learning or that of the group, despite having an individualised behaviour management programme;
(d)   having sensory or physical needs and requires additional equipment or regular visits for direct intervention or advice from specialist practitioners; and
(e)   having ongoing communication or interaction difficulties that impede the development of social relationships and cause substantial barriers to learning.

1   Code of Practice, para 4:29.
2   Code of Practice, para 4:31.

5.3.7   In the primary and secondary school phases, the Code of Practice lays down similar tiers of intervention and provision with similar triggers (see 5.2.5 and 5.2.6) known as 'School Action'[1] and 'School Action Plus'[2]. As with early education settings, schools should adopt a graduated response that encompasses an array of strategies[3] and IEPs should be created which will record the strategies used to enable the child to progress and which set out provision which is additional to or different from the differentiated curriculum plan[4]. Each IEP should therefore include information about[5]:

(a)   the short-term targets set for or by the child;
(b)   the teaching strategies to be used;
(c)   the provision to be put in place;
(d)   when the plan is to be reviewed;

(e) success and/or exit criteria; and
(f) outcomes.

1 Code of Practice, paras 5:43 to 5:53 for primary schools and 6:50 to 6:61 for secondary.
2 Code of Practice, paras 5:54 to 5:61 for primary and 6:62 to 6:69 for secondary.
3 Code of Practice, paras 5:20 and 6:22.
4 Code of Practice, paras 5:51 and 6:57.
5 Code of Practice, paras 5:50 and 6:58.

School Action Plus will be triggered when, despite receiving an individu- **5.3.8**
alised programme and/or concentrated support, the pupil[1]:

(a) continues to make little or no progress in specific areas over a long
     period;
(b) continues working at National Curriculum levels substantially below
     that expected of children of a similar age;
(c) continues to have difficulty in developing literacy and mathematics
     skills;
(d) has emotional or behavioural difficulties which substantially and regu-
     larly interfere with the child's own learning or that of the class group,
     despite having an individualised behaviour management programme;
(e) has sensory or physical needs and requires additional equipment or
     regular visits for direct intervention or advice from specialist practi-
     tioners; and
(f) has ongoing communication or interaction difficulties that impede the
     development of social relationships and cause substantial barriers to
     learning.

1 Code of Practice, paras 5:56 and 6:64.

Where, despite implementation of Early Years Action Plus or School Action **5.3.9**
Plus the child is still not progressing adequately or at all, the setting or
school should consider inviting the LEA to assess the child's needs or formally requesting that it should do so.

ASSESSMENT OF CHILDREN WITH SPECIAL EDUCATIONAL NEEDS

Assessments at the initiative of the LEA   **5.4**

Although the importance of school-based identification and assessment **5.4.1**
cannot be over-emphasised, the fundamental duty for identifying and assessing children with special educational needs rests on LEAs. Indeed, amidst
the recent re-defining of the role of LEAs, 'ensuring that individual children's needs are quickly and accurately identified and matched by
appropriate provision'[1] is seen as a core function. Whilst it is recognised that
this can, in many cases, be secured by delegating the necessary funding to
schools, the Department for Education and Skills (DfES) accept that for
some children, with specific learning difficulties, emotional needs and more
complex needs, the support from high quality education psychology services
and support teaching services and developing close inter-agency partnerships with health and social services should be the responsibility of LEAs[2].

1 *The Role of the Local Education Authority in School Education* (DfEE 2000), para 13.
2 *The Role of the Local Education Authority in School Education* (DfEE 2000), para 13.

5.4.2 The obligation to assess a child derives principally from the LEA's general duty towards children for whom they are responsible. As was considered in Chapter 4, an LEA shall exercise its powers with a view to securing that, of the children for whom it is responsible, (a) it identifies children[1] who have special educational needs, and (b) it is necessary for the LEA to determine the special educational provision which any learning difficulty they may have calls for[2].

1 EA 1996, s 321(1).
2 EA 1996, s 321(2).

5.4.3 An LEA is responsible for a child if the child is in its area and:

(a) the child is a registered pupil at a maintained school;
(b) education is provided for the child at a school which is not a maintained school, but is so provided at the expense of the LEA;
(c) the child does not come within (a) and (b) above but is a registered pupil at a school and has been brought to the LEA's attention as having (or probably having) special educational needs; or
(d) the child is not a registered pupil at a school but is not under the age of two or over compulsory school age and has been brought to their attention as having (or probably having) special educational needs[1].

1 EA 1996, s 321(3).

5.4.4 Where an LEA is of the opinion that a child for whom it is responsible has, or probably has, special educational needs and it is necessary for the LEA to determine the special educational provision which his learning difficulty may call for, the LEA is under a duty to carry out an assessment of the child's special educational needs[1]. The procedure for carrying out such an assessment is considered below[2].

1 EA 1996, s 323(1) and (2).
2 See 5.5 and 5.6.

5.4.5 Although the prime duty is therefore towards children between the age of two and up to compulsory school age, the LEA also has responsibility towards children under two. Where the LEA is of the opinion that a child in its area who is under the age of two has, or probably has, special educational needs and it is necessary for the LEA to determine the special educational provision which any learning difficulty he may have calls for, the LEA may, with the consent of the parent, make an assessment of the child's educational needs, and shall make such an assessment if requested to do so by the child's parent[1]. Such an assessment does not, however, have to follow the statutory assessment process outlined below[2]. Instead, it can be made in such manner as the LEA consider appropriate[3]. After making this type of assessment, the LEA may make a statement of the child's special educational needs and may maintain that statement in such manner as it considers appropriate[4].

1 EA 1996, s 331(1) and (2).
2 See 5.5 and 5.6 and Chapter 6.
3 EA 1996, s 331(3).
4 EA 1996, s 331(4).

Assessments requested by parents and schools   **5.5**

Although the main responsibility for initiating assessments lies with LEAs,   **5.5.1**
parents may also request that the LEA carry out an assessment of their
child's special educational needs[1]. The LEA is under a duty to comply with
such a request where:

(a) the LEA is responsible for the child but for whom no statement is
    maintained;
(b) no assessment has been made within the period of six months ending
    with the date on which the request is made; and
(c) it is necessary for the LEA to make an assessment because the child
    has, or probably has, special educational needs and it is necessary for
    the LEA to determine the special educational provision which any
    learning difficulty he may have calls for[2].

If the LEA determines not to comply with the request, but (a) and (b)
above apply, it must give notice of that decision to the parent and inform the
parent that he may appeal to the Tribunal against the determination[3]. On an
appeal the Tribunal may dismiss the appeal or order the LEA to arrange for
an assessment to be made[4].

1 EA 1996, s 329.
2 EA 1996, s 329(1).
3 EA 1996, s 329(2).
4 EA 1996, s 329(3).

Under the EA 1996, the right to appeal against an LEA's refusal to assess   **5.5.2**
only arose if the parent had requested the assessment. If the child's school
had requested the assessment instead, however, no appeal to the Tribunal
was available. This omission has been corrected by the Special Educational
Needs and Disability Act 2001, and now there is express provision enabling
a school[1] to make a request and for the parent to have a right of appeal if
that request is turned down.

1 Including certain early education settings.

If[1]:   **5.5.3**

(a) a child is a registered pupil at a 'relevant' school (which means a main-
    tained school, a maintained nursery school, a pupil referral unit, an
    independent school or a non-maintained special school approved by
    the Secretary of State[2]);
(b) the 'responsible body' (ie in relation to maintained nursery schools and
    pupil referral units, the headteacher and, in relation to all other schools
    the proprietor or headteacher[3]) ask the LEA to arrange for an assess-
    ment to be made in respect of that child;
(c) no such assessment has been made within the period of six months
    ending with the date on which the request is made; and
(d) it is necessary for the LEA to make an assessment,

the LEA must comply with the request[4].

1 EA 1996, s 329A(1).
2 EA 1996, s 329A(12).
3 EA 1996, s 329A(13).
4 EA 1996, s 329A(2).

5.5.4 Before deciding whether to comply with such a request, the LEA must serve on the child's parent a notice informing the parent[1]:

(a) that they are considering whether to make an assessment of the child's educational needs;
(b) of the procedure to be followed in making the assessment;
(c) of the name of the officer from whom further information may be obtained; and
(d) of the parent's right to make representations and submit written evidence to the LEA before the end of the period specified in the notice, which must not be less than 29 days beginning with date on which the notice is served[2].

The LEA cannot decide whether to comply with the request until the specified period has expired[3]. The LEA must take into account any representations made, and any evidence submitted, in response to the notice[4].

1 EA 1996, s 329A(3).
2 EA 1996, s 329A(4).
3 EA 1996, s 329A(5).
4 EA 1996, s 329A(6).

5.5.5 If the LEA decides to make an assessment, it must give written notice to the child's parent and to the school or Pupil Referral Unit (PRU) which made the request of that decision and the reasons for it[1]. If, however, the LEA decide not to assess the educational needs of the child, they must give written notice of their decision and of their reasons for making it to the parent and the school or PRU which made the request[2]. The parent may appeal against the decision to the Tribunal[3] and the parent must be informed of this right in the notice[4]. On an appeal, the Tribunal may dismiss the appeal or order the LEA to arrange for an assessment to be made[5].

1 EA 1996, s 329A(7).
2 EA 1996, s 329A(8)(a).
3 EA 1996, s 329A(8)(b).
4 EA 1996, s 329A(9)(a).
5 EA 1996, s 329A(10).

5.5.6 Where a request for a statutory assessment is made by a school to an LEA, the pupil should have demonstrated significant cause for concern[1]. The LEA will seek evidence from the school that any strategy or programme implemented for the pupil has been continued for a reasonable period of time without success and that alternatives have been tried or the reasons why this has not occurred. The LEA will need information about the pupil's progress over time and clear documentation about the pupil's special educational needs and any action taken to deal with those needs, including any resources or special arrangements put in place[2]. The school should therefore be able to provide written evidence of or information about[3]:

(a) the school's action through School Action or School Action Plus;
(b) individual education plans for the pupil;
(c) records of regular reviews and their outcomes;
(d) the pupil's health, including the child's medical history if relevant;
(e) National Curriculum levels;

(f)   attainments in literacy and mathematics;
(g)   educational and other assessments, for example from an advisory sup-
       port teacher or an educational psychologist;
(h)   views of the parents and the pupil;
(i)   involvement of other professionals; and
(j)   any involvement by social services or education welfare.

1   Code of Practice, paras 5:62 and 6:71.
2   Code of Practice, paras 5:62 and 6:71.
3   Code of Practice, paras 5:64 and 6:72.

It should be noted, however, that whilst parents can appeal against a refusal   **5.5.7**
to carry out an assessment, they cannot appeal against the LEA's decision to
carry out an assessment.

Making an assessment of special educational needs   **5.6**

The procedure and requirements in respect of the making of an assessment are   **5.6.1**
set out in s 323 of and Schedule 26 to the EA 1996, and in the Education
(Special Educational Needs) (England) (Consolidation) Regulations 2001[1].

1   SI 2001/3455.

Where the LEA is of the opinion that a child for whom it is responsible has,   **5.6.2**
or probably has, special educational needs and it is necessary for the LEA to
determine the special educational provision, the LEA must serve notice on
the child's parent informing the parent that it is considering whether to
make an assessment of the child's educational needs, of the procedure to be
followed, of the name of an officer who can provide information and of the
parent's right to make representations and submit written representations to
the LEA within a specified period[1]. This period must not be less than 29
days beginning with the date on which the notice is served.

1   EA 1996, s 323(1).

Where the specified period has expired and the LEA remains of the opinion   **5.6.3**
that, having taken into account any representations made and evidence submitted, the child has, or probably has, special educational needs and it is
necessary for the authority to determine the special educational provision
which his learning difficulty may call for, the LEA is under a duty to make
an assessment of the child's educational needs[1]. The LEA must accordingly
give notice to the child's parent, in writing, of that decision and the reasons
for it[2].

1   EA 1996, s 323(3).
2   EA 1996, s 323(4).

The critical question for the LEA when deciding whether to make a statu-   **5.6.4**
tory assessment is whether there is convincing evidence that, despite the
school (with the help of external specialists) taking relevant and purposeful
action to meet the child's learning difficulties, those difficulties remain or
have not been remedied sufficiently and may require the LEA to determine
the child's special educational needs[1]. The LEA will have to take account of
a wide range of evidence, including the school's assessment of the child's

needs, the input of other professionals such as educational psychologists and specialist support teachers, the action the school has taken to meet those needs, the factors associated with the child's levels of academic attainment and rate of progress, along with other evidence that will vary according to the child's age and the nature of the learning difficulty[2].

1 Code of Practice, para 7:34.
2 Code of Practice, para 7:34.

5.6.5 When deciding whether a statutory assessment is necessary, the Code of Practice requires LEAs to have particular regard[1] to:

(a) evidence that the school has responded appropriately to the requirements of the National Curriculum, especially the section entitled 'Inclusion: Providing effective learning opportunities for all children';
(b) evidence provided by the child's school, parents and other professionals where they have been involved with the child, as to the nature, extent and cause of the child's learning difficulties;
(c) evidence of action already taken by the child's school to meet and overcome those difficulties;
(d) evidence of the rate and style of the child's progress;
(e) evidence that where some progress has been made, it has only been as the result of much additional effort and instruction at a sustained level not usually commensurate with provision through Action Plus.

1 Code of Practice, para 7:35.

5.6.6 The Code of Practice[1] sets out guidance on the evidence LEA's should seek from schools, early education settings and parents, including evidence of attainment[2], evidence of the special educational provision being made for the child[3] and other factors[4]. The Code stresses[5] that decisions must be made by LEAs in the light of all the circumstances of each individual case and, always, in the closest consultation with parents and schools and recommends[6] that, in the interest of establishing agreed local interpretation, LEAs may operate moderating groups to support the LEA in making consistent decisions, comprising headteachers, SENCOs, governors, educational psychologists and colleagues from health and social services.

1 Code of Practice, paras 7:36 to 7:67.
2 Code of Practice, paras 7:38 to 7:41.
3 Code of Practice, paras 7:46 to 7:49.
4 Code of Practice, paras 7:42 to 7:45.
5 Code of Practice, para 7:36.
6 Code of Practice, para 7:37.

5.6.7 Where the balance of evidence presented to and assessed by the LEA suggests that the child's learning difficulties have not responded to relevant and purposeful measures taken by the school or setting and external specialists, and thus may call for special educational provision which cannot reasonably be provided within the resources normally available to mainstream maintained schools and settings in the area, the LEA should consider very carefully the case for a statutory assessment of the child's special educational needs[1].

1 Code of Practice, para 7:50.

Although the Code of Practice does not set out hard and fast categories of **5.6.8**
special educational needs, it recognises that each child is unique and that
there is a wide spectrum of special educational needs which are frequently
interrelated. Dispensing with the categorisation of need contained in the old
Code of Practice, the new Code of Practice asserts that children's educational needs and requirements will fall into at least one of four areas (with
guidance on each type of need then set out at the paragraphs shown):

(1) communication and interaction (paragraphs 7:55 to 7:57);
(2) cognition and learning (paragraphs 7:58 to 7:59);
(3) behaviour, emotional and social development (paragraphs 7:60 and
    7:61); and
(4) sensory and/or physical[1] (paragraphs 7:62 and 7:63).

The Code of Practice recognises that pupils may have needs which span two
or more areas[2], but advises that the accumulation of low-level difficulties
may not in itself equate with a school being unable to meet a child's needs
through school-based provision[3]. In considering, therefore, whether to carry
out an assessment, LEAs should bear in mind the needs and particular
requirements of each child and whether these requirements can be met
from resources already available to mainstream schools and settings in the
context of school-based intervention, monitoring and review arrangements[4].

1 Code of Practice, para 7:52.
2 Code of Practice, para 7:53.
3 Code of Practice, para 7:53.
4 Code of Practice, para 7:54.

If, after deciding to initiate an assessment, the LEA decides to discontinue **5.6.9**
the assessment or not to assess the child, it shall give notice in writing to the
child's parent[1].

1 EA 1996, s 323(6).

The manner and timing of assessments, together with the requirements as to **5.6.10**
the advice to be sought by LEAs, are contained in the Education (Special
Educational Needs) (England) (Consolidation) Regulations[1] and are considered below.

1 SI 2001/3455: EA 1996, Sch 26, paras 2 and 3.

Where an LEA is considering whether to make an assessment, it may serve **5.6.11**
a notice on the parent of a child requiring the child's attendance for examination in accordance with the provisions of the notice[1]. The notice shall[2]:

(a) state the purpose of the examination;
(b) state the time and place at which the examination will be held;
(c) name an officer of the LEA from whom further information may be
    obtained;
(d) inform the parent that he may submit such information to the LEA as
    he may wish; and
(e) inform the parent of his right to be present at the examination[3].

This examination does not necessarily have to be a medical examination,
but can include an examination by the LEA's educational psychologist.
Any parent who fails, without reasonable excuse, to comply with any

requirements of such a notice commits an offence if the notice relates to a child who is not over compulsory school age at the time stated for the examination[4]. A person guilty of this offence is liable on summary conviction to a fine not exceeding level 2 on the standard scale[5].

1 EA 1996, Sch 26, para 4(1).
2 EA 1996, Sch 26, para 4(3).
3 EA 1996, Sch 26, para 4(2).
4 EA 1996, Sch 26, para 5(1).
5 EA 1996, Sch 26, para 5(2).

5.6.12 In order to carry out an assessment, the LEA must seek[1]:

(a) advice from the child's parent;
(b) educational advice from the headteacher of the school which the child is currently attending[2];
(c) medical advice from the health authority, who shall obtain advice from a fully registered medical practitioner[3];
(d) psychological advice[4];
(e) advice from the social services authority; and
(f) any other advice which the LEA considers appropriate for the purposes of arriving at a satisfactory assessment.

1 Education (Special Educational Needs) (England) (Consolidation) Regulations 2001, SI 2001/3455, reg 7(1).
2 See 5.6.8 and 5.6.9; and see SI 2001/3455, reg 8(1).
3 See SI 2001/3455, reg 9.
4 See 5.6.10; and see SI 2001/3455, reg 10.

5.6.13 The educational advice required should ordinarily be obtained from the headteacher of the school which the child is currently attending[1]. If the headteacher has not himself taught the child within the preceding 18 months, the advice must be given only after the headteacher has consulted a teacher who has taught the child within that period[2]. The advice provided by the headteacher should include advice relating to the steps which have been taken by the school to identify and assess the special educational needs of the child and to make provision for the purpose of meeting those needs[3].

1 Education (Special Educational Needs) (England) (Consolidation) Regulations 2001, SI 2001/3455, reg 8(1).
2 SI 2001/3455, reg 8(4).
3 SI 2001/3455, reg 8(5).

5.6.14 If advice cannot be obtained from a headteacher, usually because the child is not attending a school, educational advice should be obtained from a person who the LEA is satisfied has experience of teaching children with special educational needs or knowledge of the differing provision which may be called for in different cases to meet those needs[1]. If this is not possible, the educational advice should be obtained from a person responsible for educational provision for the child[2]. In both cases, the advice cannot be sought from any person who is not a qualified teacher[3]. If, however, the child is receiving education from an early educational provider and that provider is not a qualified teacher, the advice shall be sought from the person responsible for his educational provision even if that person is not a qualified teacher[4]. In the case of an early education provider, the advice sought shall include details relating to the steps which have been taken by the provider to identify and assess the special educational needs of the child and to make provision for meeting those needs[5].

1 Education (Special Educational Needs) (England) (Consolidation) Regulations 2001, SI 2001/3455, reg 8(1)(b).
2 SI 2001/3455, reg 8(1)(c).
3 SI 2001/3455.
4 SI 2001/3455, reg 8(3).
5 SI 2001/3455, reg 8(6).

The psychological advice required must be sought from a person regularly **5.6.15** employed by the LEA as an educational psychologist or engaged by the LEA as an educational psychologist in the case in question[1]. If this person has reason to believe that another psychologist has relevant knowledge of, or information relating to, the child, the advice should be given after consultation with that other psychologist[2]. This applies whether the other psychologist is employed or retained by the LEA or by the parents or has had contact with the child through other agencies.

1 Education (Special Educational Needs) (England) (Consolidation) Regulations 2001, SI 2001/3455, reg 10(1).
2 SI 2001/3455, reg 10(2).

If, following receipt of the medical advice[1] or otherwise, it appears to the **5.6.16** LEA that the child is hearing impaired or visually impaired or both, and the education advice has been sought from a person who is not qualified to teach hearing or visually impaired children, the LEA should ensure[2] that the educational advice is only given after there has been consultation with a teacher who is qualified to teach such children[3].

1 Obtained under Education (Special Educational Needs) (England) (Consolidation) Regulations 2001, SI 2001/3455, reg 9.
2 SI 2001/3455, reg 8(7).
3 A teacher is qualified to teach such children if the teacher is qualified to be employed at a school as a teacher of a class of pupils who are hearing or visually impaired or both otherwise than to give instruction in a craft, trade or domestic subject: SI 2001/3455, reg 8(8).

The advice required (whether educational, medical, psychological or other) **5.6.17** shall be given in writing and shall relate to features of the child's case which appear to be relevant to the child's educational needs (including the child's likely future needs)[1]. It shall say how those features could affect the child's educational needs[2] and shall relate to the provision which is appropriate for the child in the light of those features, whether by way of special educational provision or non-educational provision, but should not relate to the specification of the school or other institution which the child should attend[3]. Where any person is requested to provide advice, that person may consult such other persons as it appears to him expedient to consult. If the LEA specifies that other persons have relevant knowledge of, or information relating to, the child, it must consult such persons[4]. When seeking advice, the LEA must provide the person from whom the advice is sought with copies of any representations made by the parent and any evidence submitted at the request of the parent[5].

The LEA is not required to seek educational, medical or psychological advice or advice from the social services if the LEA has obtained that advice within the preceding 12 months and the LEA, the person who provided the advice and the child's parent are satisfied that the existing advice is sufficient for the purpose of arriving at a satisfactory assessment[6]. It should be noted, therefore, that it is not just for the LEA to decide whether it can use the existing advice; the parent must be happy for it do so. If the parent or advisor is not happy, the LEA must obtain fresh advice.

1 Education (Special Educational Needs) (England) (Consolidation) Regulations 2001, SI 2001/3455, reg 7(2)(a).
2 SI 2001/3455, reg 7(2)(b).
3 SI 2001/3455, reg 7(2)(c).
4 SI 2001/3455, reg 7(3).
5 SI 2001/3455, reg 7(4).
6 SI 2001/3455, reg 7(2)(a).

5.6.18 The LEA should also seek to ascertain the views of the child as part of the assessment[1]. The child's views about his needs and aspirations should, wherever possible, be recorded as part of the assessment process. The Code of Practice suggests that LEAs may wish to include a pupil report form where pupils who are able to do so could submit their views. Where children need help, the Code encourages LEAs to make special arrangements for obtaining the child's views, including asking parents (although the parent's view may not always necessarily coincide with the child's), educational psychologists or teachers[2].

1 Code of Practice, para 7:85.
2 Code of Practice, para 7:85.

5.6.19 When making an assessment, the LEA must take into consideration[1]:

(a) any representations made by the child's parent;
(b) any evidence submitted by, or at the request of, the child's parent[2]; and
(c) the educational, medical, psychological and other advice obtained by the LEA.

1 Education (Special Educational Needs) (England) (Consolidation) Regulations 2001, SI 2001/3455, reg 11.
2 See EA 1996, s 323(1)(d) or s 329A(3)(d).

Time limits for considering whether to make an assessment

5.6.20 Where the LEA serve notice on a parent informing the parent that it is considering whether to make an assessment, the LEA shall within six weeks[1] of the date of service give notice to the parent of (a) its decision to make an assessment and of its reasons for making that decision, or (b) its decision not to assess the educational needs of the child and of its reasons for making that decision. In either case, the LEA must also notify the parent of the availability of advice and information on matters related to the child's special educational needs from the parent partnership service[2].

1 For the purpose of all time limits, where something is required to be done within a period after an action is taken, the day on which that action was taken does not count in the calculation of that period. Where it has to be done within a period and the last day of that period is not a working day, the period is extended to include the following working day: Education (Special Educational Needs) (England) (Consolidation) Regulations 2001, SI 2001/3455, reg 2(4).
2 SI 2001/3455, reg 12(1).

5.6.21 Where a parent asks the LEA to arrange for an assessment to be made[1] and the LEA agrees to make an assessment, the LEA shall, within six weeks of the date of the receipt of the request, give notice to the child's parent (a) of its decision to make an assessment and of its reasons, and (b) the availability to the parent of advice and information on matters related to the child's special educational needs from the parent partnership service[2]. If, however, the LEA decide not to carry out an assessment, within six weeks of the date of receipt of the request the LEA must give the parent notice:

(a) of its decision not to comply with the request;
(b) its reasons;
(c) the availability to the parent of advice and information on matters related to their child's special educational needs from the parent partnership service;
(d) the availability to the parent of arrangements for the prevention and resolution of disagreements between parents and LEA made by the LEA;
(e) the parent's right to appeal to the Tribunal against the determination not to make an assessment;
(f) the time limit within which an appeal to the Tribunal must be made; and
(g) the fact that the arrangements for the prevention and resolution of disagreements cannot affect the parent's right to appeal to the Tribunal[3].

The LEA should also set out the provision that it considers would meet the child's needs appropriately[4].

1 Under either EA 1996, s 328(2) or s 329(1).
2 Education (Special Educational Needs) (England) (Consolidation) Regulations 2001, SI 2001/3455, reg 12(2)(a).
3 SI 2001/3455, reg 12(2)(b).
4 Code of Practice, para 7:69.

Where the LEA has received a request for an assessment from the child's **5.6.22** school or early education setting, it must, within six weeks of the date of receipt of that request, give notice to the headteacher[1] of its decision to make an assessment or for not making an assessment and the reasons for this decision[2]. Where, following a request from a school, the LEA have notified the parent that it is considering making an assessment, and it has been decided to carry out an assessment, within six weeks of the date of service of that notice, the LEA must give notice to the parent of its decision to make an assessment, its reasons and the availability of advice and information on matters related to the child's special educational needs from the parent partnership service[3]. If the decision is that the LEA will not carry out an assessment, within the same period, the LEA must give notice to the parent of:

(a) its decision not to comply with the request;
(b) its reasons;
(c) the availability to the parent of advice and information on matters related to their child's special educational needs from the parent partnership service;
(d) the availability to the parent of arrangements for the prevention and resolution of disagreements between parents and LEA made by the LEA;
(e) the parent's right to appeal to the Tribunal against the determination not to make an assessment;

(f) the time limit within which an appeal to the Tribunal must be made; and
(g) the fact that the arrangements for the prevention and resolution of disagreements cannot affect the parent's right to appeal to the Tribunal[4].

The LEA should also set out the provision that they consider would meet the child's needs appropriately[5].

1 Or person or body of persons responsible, in the case of a provider of nursery education.
2 Education (Special Educational Needs) (England) (Consolidation) Regulations 2001, SI 2001/3455, reg 12(3).
3 SI 2001/3455, reg 12(4)(a).
4 SI 2001/3455, reg 12(4)(b).
5 Code of Practice, para 7:69.

5.6.23 The LEA will be exempt from the six-week time limits if it is impractical to comply because:

(a) the LEA has requested advice from a headteacher during a period beginning one week before any date on which the school was closed for a continuous period of not less than four weeks from that date and ending one week before the date on which it re-opens;
(b) the LEA has requested advice from the head of special educational needs or person responsible for a child's education at an early education provider during a period beginning one week before any date on which the provider was closed for a continuous period of not less than four weeks from that date and ending one week before the date on which it re-opens;
(c) exceptional personal circumstances affect the child or his parent during the six-week period; or
(d) the child or his parent are absent from the area of the LEA for a continuous period of not less than four weeks during the six-week period[1].

1 Education (Special Educational Needs) (England) (Consolidation) Regulations 2001, SI 2001/3455, reg 12(5).

Time limits for making an assessment

5.6.24 Where an LEA decides to carry out an assessment of the child's special educational needs and has given notice of that decision to the parent, the LEA must complete the assessment within ten weeks of the date on which it gave notice of its decision to the parent[1].

1 Education (Special Educational Needs) (England) (Consolidation) Regulations 2001, SI 2001/3455, reg 12(6).

5.6.25 An LEA will not be required to comply with the ten-week time limit in the following circumstances[1]:

(a) in exceptional cases, after receiving educational, medical, psychological or other advice, it is necessary for the LEA to seek further advice;
(b) the child's parent has indicated to the LEA that the parent wishes to provide advice after the expiry of six weeks from the date on which the request for such advice was received and the LEA has agreed to consider such advice before completing an assessment;
(c) the LEA has requested advice from a headteacher during a period beginning one week before any date on which the school was closed for

a continuous period of not less than four weeks from that date and ending one week before the date on which it re-opens;

(d) the LEA has requested advice from the head of special educational needs or person responsible for a child's education at an early education provider during a period beginning one week before any date on which the provider was closed for a continuous period of not less than four weeks from that date and ending one week before the date on which it re-opens;

(e) the LEA has requested advice from a health authority or a social services authority and the authority has not complied with that request within six weeks from the date on which it was made[2];

(f) exceptional personal circumstances affect the child or his parent during the ten-week period;

(g) the child or his parent are absent from the LEA's area for a continuous period of not less than four weeks during the ten-week period; or

(h) the child fails to keep an appointment for an examination or test during the ten-week period.

1 Education (Special Educational Needs) (England) (Consolidation) Regulations 2001, SI 2001/3455, reg 12(7).

2 Where an LEA requests advice from a health authority or social services authority, the authority is under a duty to comply with that request within six weeks of the date on which they receive it: Education (Special Educational Needs) (England) (Consolidation) Regulations 2001, SI 2001/3455, reg 12(8).

The health authority or social services authority need not, however, comply with this time limit if it is impractical to do so because (a) exceptional personal circumstances affect the child or his parent during the six-week period; (b) the child or his parent are absent from the LEA's area for a continuous period of not less than four weeks during the six-week period; or (c) the child fails to keep an appointment for an examination or test during the six-week period: SI 2001/3455, reg 12(9).

A health or social services authority also need not comply with the time limit if it has not, before the date on which it was served with a copy of a notice, produced or maintained any information or records relevant to the assessment of the child: SI 2001/3455, reg 12(10) and (11).

Chapter 6

Statements of special educational needs: content and procedure

Introduction   **6.1**

Following the completion of an assessment, a Local Education Authority   **6.1.1**
(LEA) must decide whether to make and issue a statement of special educational needs. This chapter will consider the basis upon which an LEA can
make this decision; what an LEA should do if it decides not to issue a statement; the process once a decision has been made to issue a statement; and
what a statement of special educational needs should contain.

The conclusion of the assessment process   **6.2**

Once an assessment has been completed and the LEA has considered all   **6.2.1**
representations made to it by the child's parents, it has to decide whether or
not the child's special educational needs are such as to warrant the LEA
making and issuing a statement. The question for the LEA is, having considered all the information, 'Is it necessary for the LEA to determine the
special educational provision which any learning difficulty the child may
have calls for?'[1].

1 See Education Act (EA) 1996, s 324(1).

What this rather unwieldy test means has been considered in a number   **6.2.2**
of cases, the most important of which was the decision of the Court of
Appeal in *R v Secretary of State for Education and Science, ex p E*[1]. The
pupil concerned in this case had literacy and numeracy difficulties. The
LEA had issued a statement recognising those needs which stated that
there was a consequent need for a mainstream curriculum with additional support from a teacher from the special educational needs support
service. The parents contended that the child should be educated at a
specialist non-maintained school at the LEA's expense. At first instance,
Nolan J drew an analogy between Part 2 of the statement, which could
be compared to a medical diagnosis, and Part 3, which was akin to a prescription for the needs so diagnosed. In the Court of Appeal[2], Balcombe
LJ agreed and set out when and in what circumstances it would be necessary for an LEA to determine the special educational provision for a
child:

'A child has special educational needs if he has a learning difficulty which requires special educational provision. Of course a child may have more than one learning difficulty. If the special educational provision which the child requires for all his needs can be determined, and provided, by his ordinary school then no statement is necessary. But once the LEA have decided that they are required to determine that some special educational provision should be made for him, they have to maintain a statement . . . in respect of that child, not in respect of any particular learning difficulty that he may have. Then the statement must specify in Part [2] the [LEA]'s assessment of the special educational needs of the child . . . and in Part [3] the special educational provision to be made for the purpose of meeting those needs . . . In my judgment the judge's analogy with a medical diagnosis and prescription is entirely apt. It then becomes the duty of the [LEA] to arrange that the special educational provision specified in the statement is made for the child . . . Whilst the [LEA] can undoubtedly take the view that some part of the child's special educational needs can be adequately provided by his ordinary school, once the [LEA] are bound to make and maintain a statement, that statement must in Part [3] specify all the special educational provision to be made for the purpose of meeting those needs, whether provided by the [LEA] or by the school . . . However, the duty of the [LEA] is then to arrange that the special educational provision specified in the statement is made for the child. It may be that in some cases, or in relation to some particular needs, it will not be possible for the [LEA] to fulfil that duty without themselves providing the requisite special educational provision. But where the [LEA] take the view that the school is able to provide some part of the special educational provision which the child requires, then they will fulfil their duty by arranging that the school does so provide that part of the special educational provision . . . .'

1   [1993] 2 FCR 753.
2   [1993] 2 FCR 753.

6.2.3   The LEA therefore should decide to make a statement when it considers that the special educational provision necessary to meet the child's needs cannot reasonably be provided within the resources normally available to mainstream schools and early education settings in the area[1]. As has been seen[2] maintained schools, other than special schools, should have within their delegated budget funding to cover the additional needs of pupils with special educational needs. This funding should permit schools to provide support under Schools Action and Schools Action Plus (or Early Years Action and Early Years Action Plus in early education settings)[3]. Where a child's needs cannot be met wholly from within these resources, an LEA will need to consider whether it is necessary for it to determine the special educational provision and thus draw up a statement.

1   Code of Practice (as to which, see 2.2.6 and 2.2.7), para 8:2.
2   See Chapter 3.
3   See 5.3.5ff.

6.2.4   The Code of Practice provides guidance to LEAs on the criteria for deciding to draw up a statement[1]. The LEA should consider the following[2]:

(a)   The child's learning difficulties: Does the information on the child's learning difficulties broadly accord with the original evidence provided by the school? If not, are there aspects of the learning difficulties which the school may have overlooked and which, with the benefit of advice, equipment or other provisions, the school could effectively address through School Action or School Action Plus?

(b) The child's special educational provision: Do the proposals for the child's special educational provision arising from any of the assessment advice indicate that the special educational provision being made by the school, including teaching strategies or other approaches is appropriate to the child's learning difficulties? If not, are there approaches which, with the benefit of advice, equipment or other provision, the school could effectively adopt within its own resources through School Action or School Action Plus?

(c) If the assessment confirms that the assessment and provision made by the school or early education setting is appropriate, but the child is nonetheless not progressing, or not progressing sufficiently well, the LEA should consider what further provision may be needed and whether that provision can be made within the school's or setting's resources or whether a statement is necessary[3].

Examples of possible approaches are given in paragraph 8:13 of the Code of Practice.

1 Code of Practice, paras 8:8 to 8:14.
2 Code of Practice, para 8:11.
3 Code of Practice, para 8:12.

The ultimate decision as to whether to make a statement should be: **6.2.5**

> 'determined by the child's identifiable special educational needs in the context of arrangements for funding schools in the area. LEAs should, of course, arrange for the provision specified in a child's statement to be made in a cost-effective manner, but that provision must be consistent with the child's assessed needs. The efficient use of resources must be taken into account when an LEA is considering the placement of a child with a statement, once the parents have had an opportunity to express a preference.'[1]

1 Code of Practice, para 8:14.

WHERE THE LEA DECIDES NOT TO MAKE A STATEMENT

General **6.3**

If the LEA decides not to make a statement, because it believes that it is not **6.3.1** necessary for the LEA to determine the special educational provision, the LEA must give the parent notice in writing of its decision[1] and of the right of the parent to appeal to the Tribunal, the time limits for appeal and the availability of parent partnership and disagreement resolution services[2]. This notice should be sent to the parent within two weeks of the date on which the assessment was completed[3]. On an appeal, the Tribunal may dismiss the appeal, order the LEA to make and maintain a statement or remit the case to the LEA for it to reconsider whether, having regard to any observations made by the Tribunal, it is necessary for the LEA to determine the special educational provision which any learning difficulty the child has may call for[4].

1 Education Act (EA) 1996, s 325(1).
2 EA 1996, s 325(2) and (2A).
3 Education (Special Educational Needs) (England) (Consolidation) Regulations 2001, SI 2001/3455, reg 17(1).
4 EA 1996, s 325(3).

6.4 Notes in lieu

6.4.1 Although not a statutory requirement, the Code of Practice[1] recommends that an LEA should issue what is termed a 'note in lieu' to parents where it decides not to make a statement. In this note, the LEA should set out the reasons for its conclusion not to make a statement, together with the evidence collected through the assessment. It is also helpful for the information collected, with the parent's agreement, to be sent to the child's school and to any other professionals who have provided advice. In many cases the note in lieu will take the form of a statement[2], although it will have none of the consequences[3].

1 Code of Practice, paras 8:15 to 8:20.
2 See 6.6.
3 See Code of Practice, para 8:19.

MAKING A STATEMENT: THE PROPOSED STATEMENT

6.5 Overview of the proposed statement

6.5.1 If, however, the LEA decides that it is necessary for it to determine the special educational provision which the child's learning difficulties call for, it should draw up a proposed statement. The LEA must serve a copy of the proposed statement and a written notice on the child's parent within two weeks of the date on which the assessment was completed[1]. The notice accompanying the proposed statement must contain the information specified in Part A of Schedule 1 to the Education (Special Educational Needs) (England) (Consolidation) Regulations 2001[2].

1 EA 1996, Sch 27, para 2; and Education (Special Educational Needs) (England) (Consolidation) Regulations 2001, SI 2001/3455, reg 17(1).
2 SI 2001/3455, reg 14.

6.5.2 The proposed statement should be in a form substantially corresponding to that set out in Schedule 2 to the Education (Special Educational Needs) (England) (Consolidation) Regulations 2001[1]. The statement should[2]:

(a) contain the information specified in Schedule 2;
(b) be dated and authenticated by the signature of a duly authorised officer of the LEA;
(c) set out whether it is the first statement made by the LEA for the child or a subsequent statement;
(d) indicate on the front page if it is:
    (i) amended pursuant to an annual review and the date of any such annual review;

(ii) amended pursuant to a review other than an annual review and the date of any such review;

(iii) amended pursuant to an order of the Tribunal and the date of any such order; or

(iv) amended pursuant to a direction of the Secretary of State and the date of any such direction.

1 SI 2001/3455. EA 1996, s 324(2); and SI 2001/3455, reg 16(a).
2 SI 2001/3455, reg 16.

In particular, the statement shall: **6.5.3**

(a) give details of the LEA's assessment of the child's special educational needs[1], and

(b) specify the special educational provision to be made for the purpose of meeting those needs[2], including:

(i) the type of school or other institution which the LEA considers would be appropriate for the child[3];

(ii) if the LEA is not required to specify under Schedule 27 (ie in order to comply with the parent's preferred school) the name of any school in the statement, specify the name of any school or institution (whether in the UK or elsewhere) which it considers would be appropriate for the child and should be specified in the statement[4]; and

(iii) specify any provision for the child for which they make arrangements otherwise than at school[5] and which it considers should be specified in the statement[6].

1 EA 1996, s 324(3)(a).
2 EA 1996, s 324(3)(b).
3 EA 1996, s 324(4)(a).
4 EA 1996, s 324(4)(b).
5 See EA 1996, s 319.
6 EA 1996, s 324(4)(c).

Thus, the statement shall (a) give details of the LEA's assessment of the child's **6.5.4** special educational needs[1], and (b) specify the special educational provision to be made for the purpose of meeting those needs[2]. Whilst the final statement will specify a type of school or name a specific school or other institution in Part 4, the proposed statement cannot include this information[3]. It may not contain any details relating to where the proposed special educational provision should be made[4]. In all other respects, however, the proposed statement should contain the LEA's assessment of the child's special educational needs, the special educational provision the LEA believes it is necessary to specify and non-educational needs and provision that the LEA considers appropriate[5].

1 EA 1996, s 324(3)(a).
2 EA 1996, s 324(3)(b).
3 EA 1996, Sch 27, para 2(4).
4 Code of Practice, para 8:54.
5 EA 1996, Sch 27, para 2(1).

The content of the statement **6.6**

A statement of special educational needs should be in a form substantially **6.6.1** corresponding to that set out in Schedule 2 to the Education (Special

Educational Needs) (England) (Consolidation) Regulations 2001[1] and containing the information specified therein[2].

1 SI 2001/3455.
2 SI 2001/3455, reg 16(a) and (b).

6.6.2 Schedule 2 provides that a statement should comprise[1] the following parts:

(1) *Part 1: Introduction* – This will include a notice informing the parent that the statement is made on a certain date by the LEA in respect of his child in accordance with s 324 of the EA 1996 and the Education (Special Educational Needs) (England) (Consolidation) Regulations 2001[2]; the child's name and address and date of birth; the child's home language and religion; the names and address(es) of the child's parent(s); and a list of the evidence and advice taken into consideration by the LEA.

(2) *Part 2: Special educational needs* – In this part the LEA will set out (in accordance with Code of Practice, paragraph 8.29 and *R v Secretary of State for Education, ex p E*[3]), each and every one of the child's special educational needs, in terms of the child's learning difficulties that call for special educational provision, as assessed by the LEA.

(3) *Part 3: Special educational provision* – In this Part the LEA will set out the special educational provision which the LEA considers necessary to meet the child's special educational needs and (a) the objectives that the special educational provision should aim to meet; (b) the special educational provision which the LEA considers appropriate to meet the needs set out in Part 2 and these objectives; and (c) the arrangements to be made for monitoring progress in meeting those objectives, particularly for setting short-term targets for the child's progress and for reviewing the child's progress on a regular basis.

(4) *Part 4: Placement* – Here the LEA should specify: (a) the type of school which the LEA considers appropriate for the child and if the LEA is required to specify the name of a school for which the parent has expressed a preference, the name of that school, or, where the LEA is otherwise required to specify the name of a school or institution, the name of the school and/or institution which it considers would be appropriate for the child and should be specified; or (b) any provision for the child's education otherwise than at school which the LEA make under s 319 of the EA 1996, and consider it appropriate to specify.

(5) *Part 5: Non-educational needs* – The LEA should specify the non-educational needs of the child for which the LEA considers provision is appropriate if the child is to properly benefit from the special educational provision specified in Part 3.

(6) *Part 6: Non-educational provision* – The LEA should specify any non-educational provision which the LEA proposes to make available or which it is satisfied will be made available by a health authority, a social services authority or some other body, including the arrangements for its provision. The LEA should also specify the objectives of the provision and the arrangements for monitoring progress in meeting those objectives.

(7) *Appendices A to G* – Setting out the advice, evidence and representations received.

1 See Education (Special Educational Needs) (England) (Consolidation) Regulations 2001, SI 2001/3455, Sch 2; and Code of Practice, para 8:29.

2 SI 2001/3455.
3 [1993] 2 FCR 753.

The Code of Practice[1] and the SEN Toolkit[2] provide particular guidance on   **6.6.3**
what should actually appear in the respective parts of the statement. Certain
areas have, however, been particularly contentious in the past: (a) the specificity and detail of the special educational provision; (b) the distinction
between special educational provision and non-educational provision; and
(c) the question of placement and parental preference. The rest of this section will therefore examine these issues in detail.

1 See 2.2ff.
2 See 2.2.9.

Specificity and detail   **6.7**

The detail of the special educational provision specified in Part 3 has fre-   **6.7.1**
quently led to dispute between parents and LEAs. In the early days of
statementing, some statements could amount to only one or two sentences
of bland generalisations, which were of no use to either the child or the
school. It is hoped that such a practice should by now have died out, as it is
clear from the legislation, the SEN Code and case law that statements must
be detailed enough to enable all concerned in a child's education to understand what special educational provision is required. However, the debate
over the content of the new Code of Practice and its advice on this area,
which led to the first revised Code presented to Parliament being withdrawn, suggests that this area is still as contentious as ever[1].

1 DfES Press Release, 12 July 2001, 'New Draft Code on Special Educational Needs'.

The point was first considered in *R v Secretary of State for Education ex p E*[1]. **6.7.2**
This decision has already been considered above[2] in respect of the question
of necessity for the LEA to determine provision, but it also considered, in
broad terms, the question of detail. The Court of Appeal held that if the
LEA decide that it, as opposed to the school, is required to make arrangements itself for the special educational provision that a child requires, the
LEA is under an obligation to make a statement. That statement must set
out *all* the child's special educational needs and *all* the special educational
provision that he requires whether provided by the child's ordinary school or
the LEA (emphasis added).

1 [1993] 2 FCR 753.
2 See 6.2.2.

This decision led to what could be described as a radical change in practice   **6.7.3**
by LEAs and most statements post-*E* followed the guidance provided by the
Court of Appeal. There was, however, always argument over the degree of
specificity required in a statement especially with regard to the special educational provision. LEAs argued that the provision needed to be recorded in
terms which allowed both the LEA and schools a degree of flexibility in
teaching the child; parents on the other hand, believed that their children
would not receive the education to which they were entitled unless the provision was detailed with precision. Surprisingly, the issue was not litigated

until 1997 when the case of *L v Clarke and Somerset County Council*[1] came before Laws J.

1 [1998] ELR 129, QBD.

6.7.4 In *L*[1], it was held that a statement had to be sufficiently specific and clear so as to leave no room for doubt as to what has been decided is necessary in the individual case. Although in some cases flexibility should be retained, in most others greater detail, including the specification of the number of hours per week, will be required of the LEA. *L* did, however, concern a pupil with special educational needs placed in a mainstream school. It may be possible that, where a pupil is placed in a special school, the degree of specificity may be less to ensure greater flexibility within an environment specifically designed to meet the needs of such children.

1 [1998] ELR 129, QBD.

6.7.5 Subsequent to *L*[1], the point has been considered in a number of cases. In *C v Special Educational Needs Tribunal and London Borough of Greenwich*[2], the child's needs were identified in Part 2 of his statement as including immature fine motor control for his age which was affected by his dyspraxia. It was agreed that the child needed occupational therapy, but this was recorded as 'occupational therapy . . . delivered by an occupational therapist or someone with at least those skills'. This did not specify that the therapy was required to assist with handwriting. The Court held that the wording was not sufficiently specific.

Similarly, in *S v Swansea City Council and Confrey*[3], the Court held that the Tribunal had erred in not being more specific in its order. In that case, the child had ADHD, Asperger's Syndrome and dyspraxia and, again, had a need for occupational therapy but the proposed placement did not have identified the specific time given to it by an occupational therapist. Sullivan J applied the test propounded by Laws J in *L*, but explained that the question had to be answered not in the abstract, but against the background of the matters in dispute between the parties. He said:

> 'If the parties' contentions lack particularity, the Tribunal might be forgiven for describing what it decides is required in Part 3 in less specific terms, for example, that provision shall be made weekly. On the other hand, where parents have advanced a detailed case based upon experts' reports, setting out their view of the required level of provision expressed in numbers of hours of support or therapy, a statement which merely requires unspecified provision to be made weekly may not be an adequate response. If there is dispute as to whether therapy or support is required for, say, two hours or ten hours per week, simply directing that it be provided "weekly" leaves room for doubt as to what has been decided.'

On the facts, it was held that the statement was not sufficiently specific. Although relating to a statement amended by the Tribunal which would have heard considerable expert evidence on the amount of support required, the same principles will, it is submitted, apply to LEAs when first making a statement. If the parents' representations include reports suggesting the number of hours support required, the LEA should respond by stating what provision is required in similarly specific terms.

1 [1998] ELR 129, QBD.
2 [1999] ELR 5, QBD.
3 [2000] ELR 315, QBD.

To address concerns over specificity and detail the revised Code of Practice   **6.7.6**
provides some guidance. Originally, having repeated the requirements in the
relevant statutory instrument[1], the Code of Practice was going to advise[2]:

> '8.36 A statement should specify clearly the provision necessary to meet
> the needs of the child. It should detail appropriate provision to meet each
> identified need and quantify provision as necessary. It will be helpful to the
> child's parents and teachers if the provision in [Part 3] is set out in the
> same order as the description of needs in Part 2.
>
> 8.37 LEAs must make decisions about which actions and provision are
> appropriate for which pupils on an individual basis. This can only be
> done by a careful assessment of the pupils' difficulties and consideration of
> the educational setting in which they may be educated. *There is a need for
> flexibility to ensure that the provision meets the needs of the individual child, and
> that it is responsive to their changing needs. In detailing appropriate provision for
> the child, there may often be a need to express it in terms of hours, equipment or
> personnel.* It will always be necessary for LEAs to monitor, with the school
> or other setting, the child's progress towards identified outcomes, however
> provision is described. LEAs must not, in any circumstances, have blanket
> policies not to quantify provision.'

1 Education (Special Educational Needs) (England) (Consolidation) Regulations 2001, SI
   2001/3455, Sch 2, Pt 3.
2 Draft Code of Practice, paras 8:36 and 8:37.

In the final, approved, version of the Code of Practice[1] the words in italics   **6.7.7**
above were replaced with '*Provision should normally be quantified (eg in terms
of hours of provision, staffing arrangements) although there will be cases where some
flexibility should be retained in order to meet the changing special educational needs
of the child concerned*'. The remainder of the guidance is the same.

1 Code of Practice, paras 8:36 and 8:37.

The effect of the changes would appear to be to reverse a presumption. The   **6.7.8**
presumption must now be that provision in terms of quantity such as hours
of provision and staffing arrangements *should* be specified. There is still
room for argument about the extent of the quantification, especially in an
holistic special school setting, but there can be no doubt that a degree,
probably high degree, of quantification will be required in the future, certainly if a child with a statement is being placed in a mainstream setting.

Educational and non-educational provision   6.8

As has been seen, a statement must[1] be in a form substantially correspon-   **6.8.1**
ding to that set out in Schedule 2 to the Education (Special Educational
Needs) (England) (Consolidation) Regulations 2001[2] and contain the information therein specified. Hence, as has been seen[3], the statement should set
out in Part 2 the child's special educational needs, in Part 3 the special educational provision, in Part 4, the placement, in Part 5, the non-educational
needs and in Part 6, the non-educational provision.

1 Education (Special Educational Needs) (England) (Consolidation) Regulations 2001, SI
   2001/3455, reg 16; and see 6.5.2.
2 SI 2001/3455.
3 See 6.5.2.

6.8.2 Under Part 3, the LEA is required to specify the special educational provision which the LEA considers appropriate to meet the needs specified in Part 2[1] and to meet the objectives which are specified by the LEA in Part 3. In particular, the LEA should specify[2]:

(a) any appropriate facilities and equipment, staffing arrangements and curriculum;

(b) any appropriate modifications to the application of the National Curriculum;

(c) any appropriate exclusions from the application of the National Curriculum, in detail, and the provision which it is proposed to substitute for any such exclusions in order to maintain a balanced and broadly-based curriculum; and

(d) where residential accommodation is appropriate, that fact.

The LEA should also set out in Part 3 the objectives which the special educational provision should aim to meet and the arrangements for monitoring the provision, but for present purposes the important wording is that concerning what may be considered as special educational provision.

1 Ie special educational needs.
2 Education (Special Educational Needs) (England) (Consolidation) Regulations 2001, SI 2001/3455, Sch 2.

6.8.3 Under Part 6, non-educational provision, the LEA should specify any non-educational provision which the LEA proposes to make available or which it is satisfied will be made available by a health authority, a social services authority or some other body, including the arrangements for its provision. The LEA should also specify the objectives of the provision, and the arrangements for monitoring progress in meeting those objectives[1]. The Code of Practice[2] puts a gloss of this definition by providing that Part 6 should contain 'details of relevant non-educational provision required to meet the non-educational needs of the child as *agreed* between the health services and/or social services and the LEA, including the *agreed* arrangements for its provision'(emphasis added).

1 Education (Special Educational Needs) (England) (Consolidation) Regulations 2001, SI 2001/3455, Sch 2, Pt 6.
2 See para 8:29.

6.8.4 The distinction between the two types of provision is important because, whilst the LEA is under a statutory duty (ie 'shall') to arrange for the special educational provision specified in the statement to be made for the child[1], it only has the discretion or power (ie 'may') to arrange that any non-educational provision specified in the statement is made for him in such manner as the LEA considers appropriate[2].

1 EA 1996, s 324(5)(a)(i).
2 EA 1996, s 324(5)(a)(ii).

6.8.5 This distinction between 'special educational provision' and 'non-educational provision' has provoked much debate and resulted in a number of cases in the courts, commencing with the 1989 decision of *R v Lancashire County Council, ex p M*[1] and culminating in the Court of Appeal's 1999 decision in *Bromley London Borough Council v C and Special Educational Needs Tribunal*[2]. The *Bromley* case is now the leading authority on this point and will be considered below, but before that it is worth setting out the series of cases which have examined the special educational provision/non-educational provision dichotomy.

1 [1989] 2 FLR 279, CA.
2 [1999] ELR 260, CA.

R v Lancashire County Council, ex p M[1] involved a child who required inten- **6.8.6**
sive speech therapy as a result of a congenital speech deformity. After considering the history of speech therapy provision, the Court of Appeal held that the identity of the provider of the therapy was immaterial. The crucial test was whether the nature of the provision itself could be characterised as educational or non-educational. Finding that the speech therapy in that case was educational in nature and therefore should have appeared under Part 3 of the statement, Balcombe LJ set out a method of comparison which was adopted in a number of subsequent decisions:

> 'To teach an adult who has lost his larynx because of cancer might well be considered as treatment rather than education. But to teach a child who has never been able to communicate by language, whether because of some chromosomal disorder . . . or because of some social cause (eg because his parents are themselves unable to speak, and thus he cannot learn by example as normally happens) seems to us just as much educational provision as to teach a child to communicate by writing.'

1 [1989] 2 FLR 279, CA.

Although the judgment left open the possibility that some forms of speech **6.8.7**
therapy could be non-educational, the reality of Balcombe LJ's analysis was that most forms of speech therapy, whether implemented by speech therapists or teachers (or special needs assistants), would be likely to be educational and should appear in Part 3 of a statement.

This decision caused problems for many LEAs. Under the National Health **6.8.8**
Service Reorganisation Act 1973, 'educational' speech therapists had transferred to the NHS together with the funding, so the *Lancashire* decision left LEAs with the duty to provide the therapy but without, in many cases, the resources to do a proper job. A further flaw in the decision was that the Court only considered the role of speech therapists in providing speech therapy. In concluding that speech therapy could only be provided by a speech therapist, the court omitted to consider the role of teachers and learning support assistants (particularly in special schools) in delivering speech therapy or improving communication skills in the classroom as an integral part of the teaching task.

As a consequence, some LEAs started to employ their own therapists. **6.8.9**
Others tried to frame Parts 3 and 6 of statements so as to ensure some input from speech therapists in Part 6, but with the majority of programmes being implemented by school staff under Part 3. In many cases this ensured that a child could receive therapy throughout the school day (something that occasional visits from NHS speech therapists could not achieve), but it was still unsatisfactory for parents, especially when the re-prioritisation of NHS resources meant that no speech therapists were available.

6.8.10 Such a situation arose in Harrow in 1996, where the Local Health Authority, for reasons of financial stringency, was only able to provide one-half of the therapy (which in this case included speech therapy, occupational therapy and physiotherapy) specified in a child's statement. When the parents became aware of the reduction in provision, they launched a judicial review against the LEA, and the LEA in turn initiated judicial review proceedings against the Local Health Authority. The two cases came before Turner J in *R v London Borough of Harrow, ex p M*[1] and *R v Brent and Harrow Health Authority, ex p London Borough of Harrow*[2]. Acknowledging that the dispute arose from the 'chronic underfunding of public bodies who have a statutory duty to fulfil, but only a limited budget out of which to meet, their statutory obligations', the judge held that the duty on an LEA under s 324 of the EA 1996 was personal. If the LEA requested help from a health authority or a social services department and that help was provided, the LEA would have made the required arrangements. If, however, that help was not, for whatever reason, available, the LEA was under a continuing obligation to ensure that the provision was made available. The duty on the LEA was not an 'ultimate' one, but it was a duty for which the LEA was, and continued to be, primarily responsible.

1 [1997] ELR 62, QBD.
2 [1997] ELR 187.

6.8.11 Although a number of cases subsequent to the *Lancashire* decision have pointed out that the Court of Appeal only said that speech therapy is capable of being special educational provision, not that it has to be[1], the reality for LEAs is that most cases of speech therapy will, in law, be special educational provision and should appear in Part 3 of statements.

1 See *Re L* [1994] ELR 16, QBD and *C v Special Educational Needs Tribunal* [1997] ELR 390, QBD.

6.8.12 The question, however, of whether occupational therapy, physiotherapy, nursing care and social welfare provision are special educational provision or non-educational provision is still not resolved and the case law, certainly pre-*Bromley*, was to a certain extent inconsistent.

6.8.13 In some cases, judges had been reluctant to interfere in educational, or perhaps more correctly, non-educational decisions unless the LEA had acted *Wednesbury* unreasonably, ie in a way no reasonable LEA would have acted. See, for example, *C v Special Educational Needs Tribunal*[1].

1 [1997] ELR 390 at p 400, QBD.

6.8.14 In other cases, however, judges have been prepared to state categorically that certain types of provision cannot, as a matter of law, be considered educational. In *B v Isle of Wight Council*[1], McCullough J concluded that the occupational therapy and physiotherapy envisaged in that case was not capable of amounting to educational provision.

1 [1997] ELR 279, QBD.

6.8.15 In *R v London Borough of Lambeth, ex p MBM*[1], Owen J held that the provision of a lift to enable a child to access the upper floors of her school was non-educational provision:

'If the provision of a lift is necessary, it is necessary to assist M's mobility and not as special educational provision. The installation of a lift would be no more special educational provision than is the provision of M's wheel chair.'

1   [1995] ELR 374, QBD.

In *Bradford Metropolitan Council v A*[1], the issue was whether nursing care for   **6.8.16**
a child, who was severely visually impaired, epileptic and had cerebral palsy, was educational or medical. Brooke J held that although certain types of provision fell in a borderline area where it was a mater of discretion for the LEA into which part of the statement they placed the provision, nursing care was not such a provision. In his view, such care 'fell fairly and squarely into the category of non-educational needs, which are the needs of the child for which the [LEA] consider that provision is appropriate if a child is to properly benefit from the special educational provision'.

1   [1997] ELR 417, QBD.

In *C v Special Educational Needs Tribunal*[1], Dyson J considered occupational   **6.8.17**
therapy and physiotherapy in respect of a child with limited movement, epilepsy and poor visual awareness and who could not stand or take steps without assistance. In the event, the judge did not find it necessary to decide whether occupational therapy or physiotherapy was lawfully placed in Part 5 of the statement. Instead, he adopted the position that there was room for a difference of opinion 'as to which side of the line the therapy specified for [the child] in Part 5 fell . . . In borderline cases where the Special Educational Needs Tribunal does not interfere with the LEA's classification, I think that the Court should be very slow to find that the Tribunal has erred in law. It is only in the clearest cases that the Court should find an error of law arising from a failure by a Tribunal to interfere with an LEA's classification of provision.' Nonetheless, he went on to express the opinion that occupational therapy and physiotherapy were not special educational provision[2].

1   [1997] ELR 390, QBD.
2   [1997] ELR 390 at p 400, QBD.

Residential care and the provision of a 24-hour curriculum have also   **6.8.18**
become areas of contention. In *G v Wakefield City Metropolitan District Council*[1], G suffered from profound and multiple learning difficulties, but her biggest problem was her home environment, which was not suitable for her needs and her mother was disabled and therefore incapable of carrying or lifting her. Laws J concluded that the provision of, in effect, residential and/or respite care was not special educational provision:

'Economic problems faced by the child's parents, where for example different and perhaps more spacious living accommodation would in an ideal world be suitable for the family because of the child's physical difficulties are not ordinarily within the remit of the SEN Tribunal. Nor are difficulties associated with a parent's disabilities, where the effect is that the child is, in physical terms, more difficult to look after.'

1   (1998) 96 LGR 69, QBD.

In view of this, it is very difficult to draw any conclusions from the case law   **6.8.19**
or, indeed, to find any true principles to assist in determining whether a particular type of provision is educational or non-educational. With one or two

exceptions identified above, there is clearly no hard and fast rule, no distinct line between educational and non-educational. All that can perhaps be said is, as per Laws J in *G*[1], that there must be a direct relation between the therapy or provision and the child's learning difficulties in order for it to be regarded as educational.

1   (1998) 96 LGR 69, QBD.

6.8.20   It was hoped that the decision of the Court of Appeal in *Bromley London Borough Council v C and Special Educational Needs Tribunal*[1] would settle the point, but unfortunately, though probably for the very valid reason that the judiciary felt unwilling to interfere in areas of educational judgement, this did not happen. Thus the law may still be open to differing interpretations on a case-by-case basis. According to Sedley LJ:

> 'special educational provision is, in principle, what ever is called for by a child's learning difficulty. A learning difficulty is anything inherent in the child, which makes learning significantly harder for him than for most others or which hinders him from making use of ordinary school facilities . . . the LEA is required to distinguish between special educational provision and non-educational provision . . . Two possibilities arise here; either the two categories share a common frontier so that one stops where the other begins; or there is between the unequivocally educational and the unequivocally non-educational shared territory of provision which can intelligibly be allocated to either . . . to interpose a hard edge or common frontier does not get rid of definitional problems; it simply makes them more acute. And this is one of the reasons why, in my judgement, the second approach is the one to be attributed to Parliament. The potentially large intermediate area of provision which is capable of ranking as educational or non-educational is not made the subject of any statutory prescription precisely because it is for the local authority, and if necessary the SENT, to exercise a case by case judgement which no prescriptive legislation could ever hope to anticipate . . . It is true that the LEA's functions (which include both powers and duties: see Section 579(1) [of the EA 1996]) will include the elective making of arrangements for non-educational provision as well as the mandatory making of arrangements for educational provision pursuant to Section 324(5)(a) [of the EA 1996]; but it is the fact that Health, Social Services and other authorities can be enlisted to help in the making of special educational provision which gives some indication of a possible breadth of the duty. [Consequently] the Tribunal's conclusion that physiotherapy, occupational therapy and speech therapy were all measures which related directly to [the child's] learning difficulties and therefore amounted to a special educational provision was a conclusion properly open to it provided that it is not read as meaning that these therapies were exclusively educational.'

1   [1999] ELR 260.

6.8.21   Having considered all this case law, perhaps the best advice for an LEA is to fall back on McCullough J's comments in *B v Isle of Wight Council*[1]:

> 'All that anyone can do when judging whether a "provision" is "educational" or "non-educational" is to recognise that there is an obvious spectrum from a clearly educational (in the ordinary sense of the word) at one end to the clearly medical at the other, take all the relevant facts into account, apply common sense and do one's best.'

1   [1997] ELR 279, QBD.

In such circumstances, however, it is inevitable that disputes between LEAs   **6.8.22**
and parents will continue, particularly as the more complex types of provision are developed and more holistic approaches to a child's needs are
encouraged. So long as the various agencies involved have different statutory
obligations and responsibilities, with limited resources and differing, often
conflicting, priorities, the educational/non-educational dichotomy is likely to
continue to exercise tribunals and courts.

Placement   **6.9**

An equally contentious area is the placement specified in Part 4 of the state-   **6.9.1**
ment. LEAs have the power to specify a maintained or maintained special
school in Part 4 or, where appropriate, an independent school or non-
maintained special school. Where it is inappropriate for the special
educational provision to be made in a school, the LEA also has power to
arrange for the provision, or part of it, to be made otherwise than in a
school[1]. In extreme cases, an LEA may arrange for the provision to be made
outside England and Wales in an institution which specialises in providing
for children with special educational needs[2].

1   EA 1996, s 319.
2   EA 1996, s 320.

The process by which a school or other institution may be named in the   **6.9.2**
statement is complicated by the fact that a school may not be specified in
a proposed statement, only in the 'final' statement. The basis for this is
that it enables a parent, who has been served with a proposed statement,
to exercise a degree of preference over the school which his child will
attend.

Every LEA must make arrangements for enabling a parent on whom a copy   **6.9.3**
of a proposed statement has been served to express a preference as to the
maintained school at which the parent wishes education to be provided for
his child and give reasons for this preference[1]. The parent is only able to
express a preference for a *maintained* school; he cannot therefore express a
preference for a non-maintained special school or an independent school. In
respect of these latter schools, the parent may only make representations. A
parent must express or make his preference within the period of 15 days
beginning (a) with the date on which the required written notice was served
on the parent, or (b) if a meeting has (or meetings have) been arranged with
the parents[2] with the date fixed for that meeting (or the last of those meetings)[3].

1   EA 1996, Sch 27, para 3(1).
2   See 6.11.1.
3   EA 1996, Sch 27, para 3(2).

Where the LEA makes a statement in a case where the parent has so   **6.9.4**
expressed a preference as to the school at which he wishes education to be
provided for his child, the LEA shall specify the name of that maintained
school in the statement unless (a) the school is unsuitable to the child's
age, ability or aptitude or to his special educational needs, or (b) the attendance of the child at the school would be incompatible with the provision

of efficient education for the children with whom he would be educated or the efficient use of resources[1].

1 EA 1996, Sch 27, para 3(3) which is expressly stated not to be affected by the duty in EA 1996, s 316 by s 316A(3)(b).

6.9.5 If a parent who has been sent the correct notice and has been given the opportunity to express a preference does not do so, the LEA cannot take account, in theory, of the efficient use of resources in deciding which school to name. They must comply with the general principle in EA 1996, s 316 and only consider whether the proposed placement is incompatible with parental wishes or the provision of efficient education for other children[1]. In reality, in going ahead and selecting a school in the absence of any preference from the parent, the LEA will most probably choose a financially cost-effective place, and will probably be required to do so to meet its general fiduciary obligations to council tax payers.

The difficulties may, however, arise if, after issuing a final statement, a parent appeals and then expresses the wish that his child should attend another school, as occasionally happens. Could the LEA at appeal stage argue that the parent's preferred school should not be named because it would be an inefficient use of resources? Arguably it should be able to do so. If the parent is expressing a preference for a maintained school, if he had done so at the time when he had the chance to do so as part of the statutory process, the LEA would have been able to have regard to efficient resources, so it would not seem unreasonable to allow the same arguments to apply if the preference is expressed later. If the school named is not a maintained school, however, for the reasons set out below[2] it is submitted that the LEA would be permitted to raise arguments on whether such a placement would be unreasonable public expenditure.

1 EA 1996, s 316(3); and see *Inclusive Schooling: Children with Special Educational Needs* (DfES/0774/2001), paras 30 and 32.
2 See 6.9.7.

6.9.6 Where a parent has made representations for his child to attend a non-maintained special school or an independent school (including independent mainstream schools, ie city technology colleges and city academies[1]), the LEA is not under an obligation to accede to those representations, but must take them into account when deciding on the appropriate placement. In considering the appropriate placement, though, the general duty in EA 1996, s 316 will apply and not the more qualified duty in paragraph 3(3) of Schedule 27. Although s 316 will raise the presumption that the LEA should not accede to the request as the child should, under s 316, be educated in a mainstream school, if a mainstream placement is incompatible with a parent's wishes (which is going to be likely if they are making representations for a non-mainstream non-maintained school), does this mean that an LEA cannot use the efficient use of resources argument to support a decision not to accede to the parent's request[2]?

1 See *Inclusive Schooling: Children with Special Educational Needs* (DfES/0774/2001), para 31.
2 Per EA 1996, s 316.

6.9.7 The author, although suspecting that this may well not be resolved until decided by the Tribunal and courts, believes that it does not[1]. In making representations for a non-maintained special or independent school, the parent is not utilising any express right specific to the special educational needs part of the EA 1996, which he would be if he was expressing a preference for a maintained school. Those representations must therefore, in effect, be made under the general provision requiring all pupils, whether having special educational needs or not, to be educated in accordance with their parent's wishes[1]. This provision requires LEAs, when exercising or performing their powers and duties, to have regard to the general principle that pupils are to be educated in accordance with the wishes of their parents. This duty is, however, qualified in that it only applies so far as it is 'compatible with the provision of efficient instruction and training and *the avoidance of unreasonable public expenditure*' (emphasis added). Consequently, it is submitted that the issue of the efficient use of resources or, at least, unreasonable public expenditure (if these two phrases mean different things) can be a factor to be taken into account when considering parental representations for a non-maintained special school or independent school. Support for this view can now also be found in the guidance issued by the Department for Education and Skills (DfES), *Inclusive Schooling: Children with Special Educational Needs*[2], which makes clear[3] that the LEA must have regard to the general duty imposed by s 9 of the EA 1996 when considering parental representations for an independent or non-maintained school.

1 EA 1996, s 9.
2 DfES/0774/2001.
3 *Inclusive Schooling: Children with Special Educational Needs* (DfES/0774/2001), paras 37 and 38 and Annex C.

Perhaps somewhat surprisingly, if, once a statement is made, a parent asks **6.9.8** for the school named in that statement to be changed for a maintained school requested by the parent[1], the LEA may no longer be able to use the efficient use of resources argument in rejecting the parent's request. This qualification does still appear in the relevant provision[2] but unlike the case of the similar provision in respect of parental preferences made in response to a proposed statement, s 316A[3] of EA 1996 does not stipulate that this provision is unaffected by the new general duty in s 316. Whether this was a drafting oversight remains unclear, but it does mean that there is a degree of ambiguity as to whether or not efficient use of resources can be an argument against complying with a parent's request to substitute a different maintained school for the school in the existing statement[4].

1 EA 1996, Sch 27, para 8; and see 7.5 where this issue is considered in more detail.
2 EA 1996, Sch 27, para 8(2)(b).
3 EA 1996, s 316A(3).
4 This point is considered further in 2.5 and 7.5.

Frequently, disputes arise where parents wish their children to attend spe- **6.9.9** cialist independent or non-maintained schools, whereas the LEA believes that either a mainstream maintained or maintained special school are appropriate for the child. The argument is important, not only in terms of finding the right school for the child, but also in respect of ascertaining responsibility for funding the placement. If a non-maintained or independent school is named either initially by the LEA, or on appeal by the Tribunal, the LEA becomes responsible for meeting the fees[1].

1 Under EA 1996, s 324(5).

6.9.10   Cases on this point include *R v Hackney London Borough Council, ex p C*[1], *R v Kent County Council, ex p W*[2], *C v Special Educational Needs Tribunal*[3], *Surrey County Council v P and P*[4] and *White v Ealing London Borough Council, Richardson v Solihull Metropolitan Borough Council, Solihull Metropolitan Borough Council v Finn*[5], although not all with consistent results.

1   (1995) Times, 7 November, CA.
2   [1995] ELR 362, QBD.
3   [1997] ELR 390, QBD.
4   [1997] ELR 516, QBD.
5   [1998] ELR 203, QBD; affd [1998] ELR 319, CA.

6.9.11   The *Surrey* case[1] is important as a reminder that LEAs are not obliged to make the best possible education available, but only to meet the needs of the child. *C v Special Educational Needs Tribunal*[2] re-iterated the point that an LEA was entitled to conclude that educating a child at the parent's preferred school was an inefficient use of resources when that school, while suitable, was much more expensive than the LEA's preferred option. In calculating the cost, the costs of provision specified in Part 5 of the statement should be excluded since, in that case, they were to be borne by the health authority. The reasoning in this decision was followed by the House of Lords in *B v Harrow London Borough Council and Special Educational Needs Tribunal*[3]. Overturning the decision of the Court of Appeal, the House of Lords held that, in determining whether placement of a child in a school maintained by an adjoining LEA was incompatible with the efficient use of resources, only the resources of the placing LEA should be considered[4] and not the resources of the LEA responsible for the maintenance of the school which the child would attend. That appears to decide the issue so far as the resources of other public bodies are concerned. One issue which remains, though, is whether the resources of other departments within the LEA's own authority, particularly social services, should be taken into account in deciding what is incompatible with the efficient use of resources. The reasoning in *C* should, however, apply in that social service provision is usually non-educational provision, albeit provided by the same authority, and its cost should be excluded from consideration.

1   [1997] ELR 516, QBD.
2   [1997] ELR 390, QBD.
3   [2000] ELR 109, HL.
4   For details of what costs an LEA can include see *R v Oxfordshire County Council, ex p GB* [2002] ELR 8, CA, considered at 2.6.9.

6.9.12   In *R v Hackney London Borough Council ex p C*[1], the Court of Appeal held that naming a school in Part 4 of a statement did not automatically render the LEA liable for all the fees at the school. The parents wanted their child to attend a non-maintained school, which the LEA considered suitable, but only with additional support which the LEA was willing to provide. The Court held that the naming of the school in these circumstances did not impose a duty of the LEA to fund all the fees. Whether this is correct is debatable in the light of *R v Kent County Council ex p W*[2], where Turner J appeared to take the opposite view. In this case it was held that the LEA had failed to make suitable arrangements to make the necessary special educational provision for the child; the LEA could not in the circumstances argue that this was a case of the parents making arrangements. The LEA therefore had an obligation to fund the entire cost of the placement.

1   (1995) Times, 7 November, CA.
2   [1995] ELR 362, QBD.

The result of these cases is that an LEA, contemplating naming the parent's   **6.9.13**
preferred school in such circumstances, needs to be very careful how it
words Part 4 of the statement. This doubt is supported by the decision of
Dyson J in the *White* case[1]. There it was held that although there was no
absolute duty to name a school in a statement, if a school was named, the
LEA was under a duty to arrange and pay for the placement. The normal
solution therefore was to first name the maintained school that the LEA
believes to be appropriate and then to record that the parents have chosen to
place their child at the non-maintained school for which they are making
suitable arrangements, other than for the support which the LEA is willing
to fund. This could, however, mean that a place would be kept open in the
maintained school, thus denying another child a place there.

1   [1998] ELR 203 QBD; affd [1998] ELR 319, CA.

The Special Educational Needs and Disability Act (SENDA) 2001[1] has   **6.9.14**
now introduced some clarification to avoid some of the confusion over the
naming of schools in Part 4 of a statement where the parent has made alternative provision for the child than that proposed by the LEA. Consequently,
an LEA is not required to specify the name of a school or institution if the
child's parent has made suitable arrangements[2] for the special educational
provision specified in the statement to be made for the child[3]. This therefore
avoids, in those circumstances, the LEA naming a school in the statement
and having to keep a place open for the child at that school, even where the
LEA knows that the child will not be attending so allowing the place to be
taken up by another child[4].

1   SENDA 2001, s 9, inserting EA 1996, s 324(4A).
2   Typically by paying for a place at an independent school: see SENDA 2001, Explanatory
    Notes, para 64.
3   EA 1996, s 324(4A).
4   See SENDA 2001, Explanatory Notes, para 64.

Another issue relating to placement concerns the ability of an LEA or the   **6.9.15**
SEN Tribunal to place a child in a school beyond its 'designation'. To a certain extent the problem has been resolved by the implementation of the two
separate sets of regulations relating to maintained and non-maintained special schools[1], but the issue may still arise in respect of certain placements.

1   Education (Maintained Special Schools) (England) Regulations 1999, SI 1999/2212 and the
    Education (Non-Maintained Special Schools) (England) Regulations 1999 SI 1999/2257.

Under s 324(4) of the EA 1996, the LEA is required to name the type of   **6.9.16**
school and, subject to certain conditions, to name the school which it considers would be appropriate for the child. That appears to provide a wide
discretion to the LEA to name the school which it believes will best meet the
child's needs. In *Sunderland City Council v P and C*[1], however, the judge took
a more restrictive view of the LEA's powers based on his interpretation of the
regulations then applying to both maintained and non-maintained special
schools[2]. In that case, the issue concerned whether or not a child could be
placed at a maintained special school when that school had not been approved
by the Secretary of State to take children of the child's age.

1 [1996] ELR 283, QBD.
2 Education (Special Schools) Regulations 1994, SI 1994/652.

6.9.17 The Regulations stated that a governing body could not admit a child to a school unless he fell within the category specified in the arrangements approved by the Secretary of State in respect of (a) the number, age and sex of day and of boarding pupils, and (b) their respective educational needs[1]. Brooke J held that a child whose age was beyond the approved age range for the school could not lawfully be admitted by the school's governing body.

1 Education (Special Schools) Regulations 1994, SI 1994/652, Sch, Pt II, paras 1 and 7.

6.9.18 Similarly, in *Re B*[1], Latham J held that an LEA could decline to name a special school if to do so would lead to the approved number of places for the school being exceeded.

1 (4 August 1999, unreported), QBD.

6.9.19 In contrast, in *Ellison v Hampshire County Council*[1], Tucker J held that where the issue was not a child's age or sex (ie the objective criteria under (a) above), but was the subjective assessment of the child's special educational needs, the *Sunderland* case[2] could be distinguished:

> 'The question of what school is appropriate is not necessarily determined by the designation of a particular school although that is obviously a factor to be taken into account. If other or extra provision can be made for a child's educational needs as recognised in the statement, then a school may, despite certain initial apparent disadvantages, be an appropriate school.'

1 (30 July 1999, unreported), QBD.
2 [1996] ELR 283, QBD.

6.9.20 The position was therefore that a child could not be placed in a school if the child was not of the same sex or age as the designation or his admission would put the school above its designated number, but a child could be admitted if the school was 'appropriate', even if the child's special educational needs did not match the type of need for which the school was approved. Tucker J's judgment was upheld by the Court of Appeal in *Ellison v Hampshire County Council*[1], although the Court preferred to find that placement was a question of educational judgment properly left to the LEA and Special Educational Needs Tribunal.

Similarly, in *S v Dudley Metropolitan Borough*[2], a mother expressed a preference for a school which was oversubscribed. The LEA declined to name it and, on appeal, the Tribunal felt unable to order that the child attend that school if the effect of its order would be to cause the school to exceed its approved number. The Court held that the Tribunal had erred: simply because the school would exceed its approved numbers did not mean that the child's admission would be incompatible with the efficient education of other children at the school or an efficient use of resources. Distinguishing the *Sunderland* case[3], the Court said, in effect, that the LEA and Tribunal should have considered whether the child's needs justified admitting him beyond the approved number.

1 [2000] ELR 651, CA.
2 [2000] ELR 330, QBD.
3 [1996] ELR 283, QBD.

These provisions still apply in the case of admission to non-maintained spe-   **6.9.21**
cial schools, as paragraphs 1 and 7 of Part II of the Schedule to the 1994
Regulations[1] now appear in the same form in the Education (Non-
Maintained Special School) (England) Regulations 1999[2].

1   Education (Special Schools) Regulations 1994, SI 1994/652.
2   See Education (Non-Maintained Special School) (England) Regulations 1999, SI
    1999/2257, Schedule, paras 1 and 7.

In the case of admission to maintained special schools however, the regula-   **6.9.22**
tions have changed significantly and the only restrictions on a child's
admission to such a school are found in regulation 19 of the Education
(Maintained Special Schools) (England) Regulations 1999[1]. These provide
that no child is to be admitted into a maintained special school unless:

(a) a statement of special educational needs is maintained for him;
(b) the child is admitted for the purposes of an assessment of his special
    educational needs and his admission is with the agreement of the LEA,
    the headteacher of the school, the child's parent and any person whose
    advice is sought as part of that assessment; or
(c) the child is admitted following a change in his circumstances, with the
    agreement of the LEA, the headteacher of the school and the child's
    parent[2].

1   SI 1999/2212.
2   SI 1999/2212, reg 19(1).

Thus, the only real condition attached to a child's admission to a maintained   **6.9.23**
special school is that he has a statement naming that school. Although an
LEA must clearly have regard to the child's age and sex, the numbers at the
school and the special educational provision which the school provides (otherwise the LEA's decision could be challenged on normal administrative law
principles of unreasonableness), the important factor in future will be the
appropriateness of the placement. If, with additional support, a child with
particular needs can be accommodated at a school designated for a different
type of need it will not be unlawful for that school to admit him.

Other special educational provision   **6.10**

Similar problems over wording have arisen with respect to school trans-   **6.10.1**
port. In *R v Havering London Borough Council ex p K*[1], the LEA agreed to
name the parents' preferred school, on condition that the parents meet the
transport costs. This was not, however, recorded in the statement. Later, the
parents could not afford to pay the transport costs and the LEA attempted
to alter the placement and require the child to attend the LEA's originally
preferred school. This was held to be unlawful by the court, as the non-
maintained school was the named school in Part 4 and, in the absence of the
LEA lawfully amending the statement, the LEA continued to be responsible
for the placement, together now with the transport costs. The lesson of this
case is that if an LEA is prepared to name a school on the basis that the parents will meet the transport costs that agreement needs to be recorded in the
statement.

1   [1998] ELR 402, QBD.

6.11   The response to a proposed statement

6.11.1   A parent who has been served with a copy of a proposed statement may (a) make representations (or further representations) to the LEA about the content of the statement; or (b) require the LEA to arrange a meeting between the parent and an officer at which the statement can be discussed[1]. If, after having attended such a meeting, the parent disagrees with any part of the assessment, the parent may require the LEA to arrange such meeting or meetings as the LEA consider will enable the parent to discuss the relevant advice with the appropriate person or person, usually the person who prepared the report for the assessment[2]. Representations under (a) above must be made within a period of 15 days beginning with the date on which the written notice was served on the parent or the date of the meeting or last of the meetings arranged with an LEA officer[3]. A requirement for a meeting to be arranged must be made within a period of 15 days beginning with the date on which the written notice was served on the parent[4]. A requirement to discuss advice given as part of the assessment must be made within 15 days beginning with the date fixed for the first meeting arranged between the LEA and parent[5].

1   EA 1996, Sch 27, para 4(1).
2   EA 1996, Sch 27, para 4(2).
3   EA 1996, Sch 27, para 4(4).
4   EA 1996, Sch 27, para 4(5).
5   EA 1996, Sch 27, para 4(6).

6.11.2   Every LEA must make arrangements for enabling a parent on whom a copy of a proposed statement has been served to express a preference as to the maintained school at which the parent wishes education to be provided for his child and give reasons for this preference[1]. The parent is only able to express a preference for a *maintained* school; he cannot therefore express a preference for a non-maintained special school or an independent school. In respect of these latter schools, the parent may only make representations. A parent must express or make his preference within the period of 15 days beginning (a) with the date on which the required written notice was served on the parent, or (b) if a meeting has (or meetings have) been arranged with the parents with the date fixed for that meeting (or the last of those meetings)[2]. The implications of expressing a preference and the obligations of the LEA in response have been considered above when the question of placement was considered[3].

1   EA 1996, Sch 27, para 3(1).
2   EA 1996, Sch 27, para 3(2).
3   See 6.9.

6.11.3   Where representations are made to the LEA in response to the proposed statement, the LEA shall not make the statement until it has considered the representations and the period or the last of the periods allowed for making requirements for meetings or representations has expired[1]. The statement may be in the form originally proposed (except as to matters required to be excluded from the copy of the proposed statement, such as the name of the school) or in a form modified in light of the representations[2]. It is not even necessary for an LEA which has issued a proposed statement, to make a statement. After receiving further representations on the proposed statement, the LEA may decide that, although the child may have special educational needs, it is not necessary for the LEA to determine the special educational provision which any learning difficulty he may have calls for ie the child's ordinary school should be able to meet his needs without any intervention from the LEA[3]. If, however, the LEA decides not to issue a final statement, it must give notice of this fact to the parents and inform them of their right to appeal to the Tribunal[4].

1 EA 1996, Sch 27, para 5(1).
2 EA 1996, Sch 27, para 5(2).
3 See *R v Isle of Wight County Council, ex p S* (1992) Times, 2 November, CA.
4 EA 1996, s 325.

If an LEA is considering specifying the name of a maintained school in a statement, it must (a) serve a copy of the proposed statement on, and (b) consult the governing body of any school which the LEA is considering specifying and, if such a school is maintained by another LEA, that LEA[1]. **6.11.4**

1 EA 1996, Sch 27, para 3A.

MAKING A STATEMENT: THE 'FINAL' STATEMENT

Overview of the 'final' statement 6.12

Having issued a proposed statement and considered any representations received in response, particularly with regard to the parent's preferred placement, if the LEA still believes that it is necessary for it to determine the special educational provision which any learning difficulties the child has calls for, they will make a statement, often known as the 'final' statement. **6.12.1**

As with the proposed statement, the final statement must be in the prescribed form and must: **6.12.2**

(a) give details of the LEA's assessment of the child's special educational needs[1]; and
(b) specify the special educational provision to be made for the purpose of meeting those needs[2], including:
  (i) the type of school or other institution which the LEA consider would be appropriate for the child[3];
  (ii) if the LEA is not required to specify under Schedule 27 (ie in order to comply with the parent's preferred school) the name of any school in the statement, specify the name of any school or institution (whether in the UK or elsewhere) which it considers would be appropriate for the child and should be specified in the statement[4]; and
  (iii) specify any provision for the child for which it makes arrangements otherwise than at school[5] and which it considers should be specified in the statement[6].

1 EA 1996, s 324(3)(a).
2 EA 1996, s 324(3)(b).
3 EA 1996, s 324(4)(a).
4 EA 1996, s 324(4)(b).
5 See EA 1996, s 319.
6 EA 1996, s 324(4)(c).

6.12.3 Where an LEA makes a statement, it must be served on the parent[1]. At the same time, the LEA must give the parent written notice of such matters as may be prescribed[2] and of his right to appeal against:

(a) the description in the statement of the LEA's assessment of the child's special educational needs;

(b) the special educational provision specified in the statement (including the name of a school specified in the statement), or if no school is named in the statement, that fact[3].

1 EA 1996, Sch 27, para 6(1).
2 EA 1996, Sch 27, para 6(3).
3 EA 1996, Sch 27, para 6(2).

6.12.4 The 'final' statement and notice must be served on the parent within eight weeks of the date on which the proposed statement was served[1]. The LEA need not comply with this time limit if it is impractical to do so because[2]:

(a) exceptional personal circumstances affect the child or his parent during the eight-week period;

(b) the child or his parent are absent from the area of the LEA for a continuous period of not less than four weeks during the eight-week period;

(c) the child's parent indicates that he wishes to make representations to the LEA about the content of the statement after the expiry of the 15-day period for representations;

(d) a meeting between the child's parent and an officer of the LEA has been held and the child's parent has either required that another such meeting be arranged or has required a meeting with the appropriate person to be arranged[3];

(e) the LEA has sent a written request to the Secretary of State seeking his consent to the child being educated at an independent school which is not approved by him and such consent has not been received by the LEA within two weeks of the date on which the request was sent.

1 Education (Special Educational Needs) (England) (Consolidation) Regulations 2001, SI 2001/3455, reg 17(3).
2 SI 2001/3455, reg 17(4).
3 See EA 1996, Sch 27, para 4.

6.12.5 When the statement is sent to the parent, the parent may appeal to the Tribunal against any of the following:

(a) the description in the statement of the LEA's assessment of the child's special educational needs;

(b) the special educational provision specified in the statement (including the name of the school so specified);

(c) if no school is specified in the statement, that fact[1].

1 EA 1996, s 326(1) and (1A).

6.12.6 On such an appeal, the Tribunal may:

(a) dismiss the appeal;

(b) order the LEA to amend the statement, so far as it describes the LEA's assessment of the child's special educational needs or specifies the special educational provision and make such other consequential amendments to the statement as the Tribunal think fit; or

(c) order the LEA to cease to maintain the statement[1].

Before determining an appeal, the Tribunal may, with the agreement of the parties, correct any deficiency in the statement[2]. The Tribunal, however, shall not order the LEA to specify the name of any school in the statement (either in substitution for an existing name or in a case where no school is named) unless:

(a) the parent has expressed a preference for the school in accordance with the statutory arrangements allowing him to do so[3]; or

(b) in the proceedings the parent, the LEA or both have proposed the school[4].

1 EA 1996, s 326(3).
2 EA 1996, s 326(5).
3 See EA 1996, Sch 27, para 3; and see 6.9
4 EA 1996, s 326(4).

Maintaining a statement   6.13

Where an LEA maintains a statement then, unless the child's parent has   **6.13.1**
made suitable arrangements, the LEA (a) shall arrange that the special educational provision specified in the statement is made for the child, and (b)
may arrange that any non-educational provision specified in the statement is
made for him in such manner as the LEA considers appropriate[1].

1 EA 1996, s 324(5)(a).

If the statement specifies the name of a maintained school, the governing   **6.13.2**
body of the school shall admit the child to the school[1]. The governing body
has no discretion in the matter; it has the right to be consulted before the
school is named in the statement but if, having responded to the consultation, the LEA nonetheless decides to name the school in Part 4 of the
statement, the governing body must admit the child. This duty applies even
if the governing body is required to take measures to reduce infant class
sizes[2]. It also applies even if the LEA responsible for the child is different
from the LEA responsible for the school[3]. It does not, however, mean that
once the child is admitted, the child cannot be excluded if his behaviour is
such that exclusion is justified[4].

1 EA 1996, s 324(5)(b).
2 EA 1996, s 324(5A); and see School Standards and Framework Act 1998, s 1(6).
3 See *R v Chair of Governors and Headteacher of A and S School, ex p T* [2000] ELR 274,
   QBD.
4 EA 1996, s 324(6).

The keeping and disclosure of statements is governed by the Education   **6.13.3**
(Special Educational Needs) (England) (Consolidation) Regulations 2001[1].
These Regulations also make provision, where an LEA becomes responsible
for a child for whom a statement is maintained by another LEA, for the
transfer of the statement to it and for the duty to maintain the transferred
statement to become its duty in place of the transferor LEA[2].

1 SI 2001/3455; and EA 1996, Sch 27, para 7(1).
2 EA 1996, Sch 27, para 7(2).

6.13.4 Thus, where a child with a statement moves from the area of one LEA (the old LEA) to another (the new LEA), the old LEA shall transfer the statement to the new LEA[1]. From the date of the transfer, the statement shall be treated as if it had been made by the new LEA on the date on which it was made by the old LEA and, where the new LEA make an assessment and the old LEA have supplied the new LEA with advice obtained in pursuance of a previous assessment, the effect will be as if the new LEA had obtained the advice on the date the old LEA obtained it[2].

1 Education (Special Educational Needs) (England) (Consolidation) Regulations 2001, SI 2001/3455, reg 23(1) and (2); and see Code of Practice, paras 8:113 to 8:115.
2 SI 2001/3455, reg 23(3).

6.13.5 Within six weeks of the date of transfer, the new LEA must serve a notice on the child's parent informing him[1]:

(a) that the statement has been transferred;
(b) whether they propose to make an assessment, and
(c) when they propose to review the statement.

The statement must be reviewed by the new LEA within whichever of two periods expires later. The two periods are either (a) the period of 12 months beginning with the date of making the statement, or, as the case may be, the previous review, or (b) the period of three months beginning with the date of transfer[2].

1 Education (Special Educational Needs) (England) (Consolidation) Regulations 2001, SI 2001/3455, reg 23(4).
2 SI 2001/3455, reg 23(5).

6.13.6 A problem in the past has been, what happens if a statement transfers but the child had no possibility of continuing to attend the school named in Part 4 of his statement? Where, by reason of the transfer of the statement, the new LEA is, in principle, under a duty to arrange the child's attendance at a school specified, but which, in light of the child's move, it is no longer practicable for him to attend, the new LEA may arrange the child's attendance at another school appropriate for the child until such time as it is possible to amend the statement[1].

1 Education (Special Educational Needs) (England) (Consolidation) Regulations 2001, SI 2001/3455, reg 23(6).

6.13.7 As to disclosure of a statement, the general principle is that a statement[1] may not be disclosed without the child's consent[2]. A child may consent to the disclosure of a statement if his age and understanding are sufficient to allow him to understand the nature of that consent[3]. This provision differs from the similar provision under the Education (Special Educational Needs) Regulations 1994[4] which only gave the parent the power to consent to disclosure, not the child. If the child does not have such age or understanding, his parent may consent on his behalf[5].

1 A statement includes any representations, evidence, advice or information which is set out in the appendices: Education (Special Educational Needs) (England) (Consolidation) Regulations 2001, SI 2001/3455, reg 24(5); and see also Code of Practice, paras 8:111 and 8:112.
2 SI 2001/3455, reg 24(1).
3 SI 2001/3455, reg 24(2).

4 SI 1994/1047, reg 19.
5 SI 2001/3455, reg 24(3).

There is, however, provision to permit disclosure of a statement without the   **6.13.8**
child's, or parent's, consent in the following circumstances[1]:

(a) to persons to whom, in the opinion of the LEA, it is necessary to dis-
    close the statement in the interests of the child;
(b) for the purposes of any appeal to the Tribunal;
(c) for the purposes of educational research which, in the opinion of the
    LEA, may advance the education of children with special educational
    needs, if, but only if, the person engaged in that research undertakes
    not to publish anything contained in, or derived from, a statement oth-
    erwise than in a form which does not identify any individual concerned
    including, in particular, the child concerned and his parents;
(d) on the order of any court or for the purpose of any criminal proceed-
    ings;
(e) for the purposes of an investigation into maladministration by the
    Ombudsman[2];
(f) to the Secretary of State where he requires such disclosure for the pur-
    poses of deciding to give directions or make an order in response to a
    complaint made to him[3];
(g) for the purposes of an assessment of the needs of the child with respect
    to the provision of any statutory services for him being carried out by
    officers of a social services authority[4];
(h) for the purposes of a local authority, principally the children services
    part of the social services authority in the performance of their duties[5];
(i) to Her Majesty's Chief Inspector of Schools, one of Her Majesty's
    Inspectors of Schools, or to a registered inspector or a member of an
    inspection team who requests the right to inspect or take copies of a
    statement[6];
(j) to the Connexions Service for the purposes of writing or amending a
    transition plan; or
(k) to a Young Offenders Institution for the purposes of the performance
    of its duties[7].

1 Education (Special Educational Needs) (England) (Consolidation) Regulations 2001, SI
   2001/3455, reg 24(1).
2 Under Local Government Act 1974, Pt III.
3 Under EA 1996, ss 496, 497 and 497A.
4 By virtue of Disabled Persons (Services, Consultation and Representation) Act 1986,
   s 5(5).
5 Under Children Act 1989, ss 22(3)(a), 85(4)(a), 86(3)(a) and 87(3).
6 In accordance with School Inspections Act 1996, s 2(8) or 3(3), or Sch 3, para 7.
7 Under Young Offender Institution Rules 2000, SI 2001/3371, r 38.

An LEA must make arrangements for keeping statements so as to ensure, so   **6.13.9**
far as is reasonably practicable, that unauthorised persons do not have
access to them[1].

1 Education (Special Educational Needs) (England) (Consolidation) Regulations 2001, SI
   2001/3455, reg 24(4).

Chapter 7

Statements of special educational needs: re-assessment, review, amendment and cessation

Introduction	**7.1**

Statements of special educational needs may be reconsidered after a further **7.1.1** assessment (otherwise known as a 're-assessment') or following a review of the statement, which is required to occur on a regular, annual basis through-out the duration of the statement. It is also possible for a Local Education Authority (LEA) to decide to amend a statement (or for a parent to request to change the named school) or to cease to maintain a statement provided it is no longer necessary for it to maintain the statement. Where a child ceases to be the responsibility of an LEA, the child's statement will lapse. All these changes to a statement are considered in this chapter.

Re-assessment of statements	**7.2**

An LEA may choose to carry out a further assessment in respect of a state- **7.2.1** ment maintained by it whenever it considers it appropriate to do so.

Alternatively, the parent of a child for whom a statement is maintained may **7.2.2** ask an LEA to arrange for an assessment to be made[1]. If no such assessment has been made within the period of six months ending with the date on which the request is made and it is necessary for the LEA to make a further assessment, the LEA must comply with the request[2]. If, in a case where an assessment has not been made for six months, the LEA determines not to comply with the request, it must give notice of that fact to the parent and inform the parent that he may appeal to the Tribunal[3]. On appeal, the Tribunal may dismiss the appeal or order the LEA to arrange for an assess-ment to be made[4]. If, however, an assessment has been made within the previous six months, if the LEA decides not to comply with the request, there is no right of appeal.

1 Education Act (EA) 1996, s 328(2)(a).
2 EA 1996, s 328(2).
3 EA 1996, s 328(3).
4 EA 1996, s 328(4).

The Special Educational Needs and Disability Act (SENDA) 2001 has **7.2.3** introduced a further mechanism to enable the special educational needs of a child with a statement to be re-considered. It is therefore now possible for the responsible body[1] of a relevant school[2] at which a child with a statement is registered to ask the LEA to arrange for further assessment of his special educational needs[3]. If no such assessment has been made within the period of six months ending with the date on which the request is made, and it is necessary for the LEA to make a further assessment, the LEA must comply with the request[4]. As with an initial request for an assessment from a relevant school[5], the LEA, before deciding whether to comply with the request, must serve a notice on the child's parent[6] informing him that it is considering whether to make a further assessment, of the procedure, of the name of an officer and of the right to make representations and submit written evidence. If the LEA decides not to make a further assessment, it must give written notice of its decision and the reason for making it to the parent and the responsible body which requested the assessment and inform the parent that he may appeal against the decision to the Tribunal[7]. On an appeal, the Tribunal may dismiss the appeal or order the LEA to arrange for the further assessment to be made[8].

1 'Responsible body' means the headteacher, in relation to a maintained nursery school or pupil referral unit, the proprietor or headteacher, in relation to any other relevant school and, in relation to a provider of relevant nursery education, the person or body of persons responsible for the management of the provision of that nursery education: EA 1996, s 329A(13).
2 'Relevant school' means a maintained school, a maintained nursery school, a pupil referral unit, an independent school or a non-maintained special school: EA 1996, s 329A(12).
3 EA 1996, s 329A(1).
4 EA 1996, s 329A(2).
5 See Chapter 5.
6 EA 1996, s 329A(3).
7 EA 1996, s 329A(8).
8 EA 1996, s 329A.

7.2.4 In all cases, where the LEA determines that it is necessary to make a further assessment, it will then carry out the assessment in accordance with the procedure and timetable for an initial assessment considered in Chapter 5.

7.3 Review of statements

7.3.1 Once a statement of special educational needs is issued and maintained by an LEA, it is under an obligation to keep that statement under review[1].

1 EA 1996, s 328.

7.3.2 Thus a statement must be reviewed by an LEA (a) on the making of an assessment (ie a further assessment) in respect of the child under EA 1996, s 323[1], and (b) in any event, within the period of 12 months beginning with the making of the statement or, as the case may be, with the previous review[2]. Regulations may make provision[3] (a) as to the manner in which reviews of such statements are to be conducted, and (b) as to the participants in the review and in connection with such other matters relating to such reviews as the Secretary of State considers appropriate.

1 See 7.2ff.
2 EA 1996, s 328(5).
3 EA 1996, s 328(6).

The detailed requirements for the conduct of reviews are now contained in   **7.3.3**
the Education (Special Educational Needs) (England) (Consolidation)
Regulations 2001[1].

1   SI 2001/3455.

Notice of review   **7.3.4**

Not less than two weeks before the first day of every school term, an LEA
shall serve a notice on the headteacher of every school[1] listing those pupils
with statements registered at that school (a) for whom the LEA is responsible, and (b) whose annual reviews fall to be carried out before the
commencement of the second term after the notice is given[2].

1   For these purposes, a 'school' is a maintained school or maintained special school, a
maintained nursery school, a pupil referral unit, a school approved by the Secretary of
State under EA 1996, s 342 or s 347, and a city technology college, a city college for
technology and the arts or a city academy at which a pupil for whom the LEA is
responsible is a registered pupil: Education (Special Educational Needs) (England)
(Consolidation) Regulations 2001, SI 2001/3455, reg 18(2).
2   SI 2001/3455, reg 18(1).

Not less than two weeks before the first day of a school year an LEA shall   **7.3.5**
serve on the Connexions Service for its area (or where no Connexions
Service has been established at that date, the Careers Service for its
area), a notice listing all the children with statements for whom the LEA
is responsible and who will be in their tenth year of compulsory education in that school year, and indicating the school attended by each of
those children or the educational provision made in respect of each of
them[1].

1   Education (Special Educational Needs) (England) (Consolidation) Regulations 2001, SI
2001/3455, reg 18(5).

Not less than two weeks before the first day of every school term, an LEA   **7.3.6**
shall serve a notice on the health authority and on the social services
authority (a) listing those children with statements living in the area of the
health or social services authority for whom the LEA is responsible and
whose annual reviews fall to be carried out before the commencement of
the second term after the notice is given; and (b) indicating the school
attended by those children or the educational provision made in respect of
them[1].

1   Education (Special Educational Needs) (England) (Consolidation) Regulations 2001, SI
2001/3455, reg 18(6).

Phase transfers

If a statement is maintained for a child who is within 12 months of a trans-   **7.3.7**
fer between phases of schooling, an LEA must ensure that the child's
statement is amended so that before 15 February in the calendar year of the
child's transfer, the statement names the school or other institution which
the child will be attending following that transfer[1]. A transfer between phases
of schooling means[2] a transfer from (a) primary school to middle school, (b)
primary school to secondary school, (c) middle school to secondary school,
or (d) secondary school to an institution which is maintained by an LEA and
is principally concerned with the provision of full-time education suitable to

the requirements of pupils who are over compulsory school age but under the age of 19[3].

1 Education (Special Educational Needs) (England) (Consolidation) Regulations 2001, SI 2001/3455, reg 19(1) and (3).
2 SI 2001/3455, reg 19(2).
3 EA 1996, s 2(2A), although reg 19(2) mistakenly refers to 's 2A' which does not exist.

Annual reviews of statements of children attending school (except for children in their tenth year of compulsory education)

7.3.8 Annual reviews will need to be carried out for all children with statements. Notice initiating a review will be given either in the notice served two weeks before the start of the term[1] or by the LEA giving written notice requiring a headteacher of the child's school to submit a report to the LEA by a specified date, not less than two months from the date the notice is given[2]. In order to prepare his report, the headteacher is required to seek written advice in respect of[3]:

(a) the child's progress towards meeting the objectives specified in the statement;
(b) the child's progress towards attaining any targets established in furtherance of the objectives specified in the statement;
(c) where the school is a community, foundation, voluntary school or a community or foundation special school (other than a special school established in a hospital) the application of the provisions of the National Curriculum to the child, and the progress made in relation to those provisions by the child since the statement was made or the last annual review;
(d) the application of any provision substituted for the provisions of the National Curriculum in order to maintain a balanced and broadly based curriculum and the progress made in relation to those provisions by the child since the statement was made or the last review;
(e) the progress made by the child since the statement was made or the last annual review in his behaviour and attitude to learning;
(f) where appropriate, and in any case where a transition plan exists, any matters which are the appropriate subject of such a plan;
(g) whether the statement continues to be appropriate;
(h) any amendments to the statement which would be appropriate; and
(i) whether the LEA should cease to maintain the statement.

1 See 7.3.4 and Education (Special Educational Needs) (England) (Consolidation) Regulations 2001, SI 2001/3455, reg 18(1).
2 SI 2001/3455, reg 20(2).
3 SI 2001/3455, reg 20(5).

7.3.9 This advice should be sought from[1]:

(a) the child's parent (in respect of all the matters listed above);
(b) any person whose advice the LEA considers appropriate for the purpose of arriving at a satisfactory report and whom the LEA specifies in the notice served on the headteacher (in relation to such of the matters listed above as the headteacher considers are within that person's knowledge or expertise); and
(c) any person whose advice the headteacher considers appropriate for the

purpose of arriving at a satisfactory report (in relation to such matters listed as the headteacher considers are within that person's knowledge or expertise).

1   Education (Special Educational Needs) (England) (Consolidation) Regulations 2001, SI 2001/3455, reg 20(4).

In respect of each child specified in the notice served by the LEA on the headteacher, the headteacher shall, before the annual review report is to be submitted invite the following to attend a meeting in respect of each child specified[1]:   **7.3.10**

(a) the representative of the LEA specified in the notice;
(b) the child's parent;
(c) a member or members of staff of the school who teach the child or who are otherwise responsible for the provision of education for the child whose attendance the headteacher considers appropriate;
(d) any other person whose attendance the headteacher considers appropriate; and
(e) any person whose attendance the LEA considers appropriate and who is specified in the LEA's notice.

Not later than two weeks before this meeting, the headteacher shall send to all persons invited, and who have not informed the headteacher that they will not be attending, copies of the written advice he has received and, by written notice accompanying the copies, shall request the recipients to submit to him before or at the meeting, written comments on that advice and any other advice which they think appropriate[2].

1   Education (Special Educational Needs) (England) (Consolidation) Regulations 2001, SI 2001/3455, reg 20(6).
2   SI 2001/3455, reg 20(7).

At the meeting, those present shall consider the aspects of the child's education listed in 7.3.8 above and any significant changes in the child's circumstances since the date on which the statement was made or last reviewed[1]. The meeting must recommend[2]:   **7.3.11**

(a) any steps which it concludes ought to be taken, including whether the LEA should amend or cease to maintain the statement (although it should be noted that this can only be a recommendation; the LEA need not comply with it);
(b) any targets to be established in furtherance of the objectives specified in the statement which it concludes the child ought to meet during the period until the next review; and
(c) where a transition plan exists, the matters which it considers ought to be included in such a plan.

If the meeting cannot agree these recommendations, the persons who attend the meeting shall make differing recommendations as appears necessary to each of them[3].

1   Education (Special Educational Needs) (England) (Consolidation) Regulations 2001, SI 2001/3455, reg 20(8).
2   SI 2001/3455, reg 20(9).
3   SI 2001/3455, reg 20(10).

7.3.12 After the meeting has been held, the headteacher shall complete the report of the annual review and in this shall include his assessment of the matters listed in 7.3.8 of any significant changes in the child's circumstances, and his recommendations on the matters referred to in 7.3.11. If there is any difference between his assessment and recommendations and those of the meeting, he shall refer to them[1]. When the headteacher sends his report to the LEA, he must also at the same time send copies to[2]:

(a) the child's parent;
(b) any other person who submitted written advice;
(c) any other person to whom the LEA considers it appropriate that a copy be sent and to whom the LEA directs the headteacher to send a copy; and
(d) any other person to whom the headteacher considers it appropriate to send a copy.

1 Education (Special Educational Needs) (England) (Consolidation) Regulations 2001, SI 2001/3455, reg 20(11).
2 SI 2001/3455, reg 20(12).

7.3.13 In the light of the annual review report and any other information or advice which it considers relevant, the LEA shall review the statement[1], record in writing its decision on the recommendations made by the review meeting and, where a transition plan exists, make written recommendations for amendments to the plan as they consider appropriate[2]. Within one week of completing its review, the LEA shall send copies of its decisions and recommendations to[3]:

(a) the child's parent;
(b) the headteacher; and
(c) any other person to whom the LEA considers it appropriate that a copy should be sent.

The headteacher then becomes responsible for making any necessary amendments to any transition plan[4].

1 Under EA 1996, s 328(5).
2 Education (Special Educational Needs) (England) (Consolidation) Regulations 2001, SI 2001/3455, reg 20(13).
3 SI 2001/3455, reg 20(14).
4 SI 2001/3455, reg 20(16).

Annual reviews of statements where child in his tenth year of compulsory education attends school

7.3.14 Where the child with a statement is in his tenth year of compulsory education, the process of the review is broadly similar to that for other years[1] except that the headteacher must also seek written advice from, in addition to those persons set out in 7.3.10 above, a representative of the Connexions Service, or if no Connexions Service has been established at the date the advice is requested, a representative of the Careers Service. The representative's advice should relate to any matters which are the appropriate subject of a transition plan and such other matters as the headteacher considers are within the representative's knowledge and expertise[2].

1 See Education (Special Educational Needs) (England) (Consolidation) Regulations 2001, SI 2001/3455, reg 21(1) to (3).
2 SI 2001/3455, reg 21(4)(c).

The headteacher should also ensure that, in addition to the persons invited **7.3.15**
to the annual review meeting[1], he invites a representative of the social services authority and a representative of the Connexions Service or, if no Connexions Service has been established at the date of the request to attend, a representative of the Careers Service[2].

1 Education (Special Educational Needs) (England) (Consolidation) Regulations 2001, SI 2001/3455, reg 21(6) and set out in 7.3.10.
2 SI 2001/3455, reg 21(6)(c) and (d).

In all other respects, the process, outcomes and consequences of the review **7.3.16**
meeting are the same in the child's tenth year of compulsory schooling as in all other years[1]. Thus the meeting shall recommend:

(a) any steps which it concludes ought to be taken, including whether the LEA should amend or cease to maintain the statement;
(b) any targets to be established in furtherance of the objectives specified in the statement which it concludes the child ought to meet during the period until the next review; and
(c) the matters which it concludes ought to be included in the transition plan[2].

The headteacher will submit his own report, assessment and recommendations[3] and is responsible for ensuring that the transition plan is drawn up[4].

1 See Education (Special Educational Needs) (England) (Consolidation) Regulations 2001, SI 2001/3455, reg 21(7) to (16).
2 SI 2001/3455, reg 21(9).
3 SI 2001/3455, reg 21(11).
4 SI 2001/3455, reg 21(15).

Annual review of statement where child does not attend school

Where a child with a statement does not attend school, the LEA is respon- **7.3.17**
sible for preparing a report[1]. The report shall address all the matters upon which the LEA is required to obtain written advice in the case of children who attend schools[2] and, in the case of a child who is in his tenth year of compulsory education, any matters which are the appropriate subject of a transition plan. To achieve this, the LEA should seek advice from the child's parent and on such of the specified matters from any other person whose advice they consider appropriate in the case in question for the purpose of arriving at a satisfactory report[3]. Before the review is required to be completed, the LEA shall invite the following to attend a meeting:

(a) the child's parent;
(b) where the review is the first review commenced after the child has begun his tenth year of compulsory education, a representative of the social services authority and a representative of the Connexions Service, or if no Connexions Service has been established, a representative of the Careers Service; and
(c) any person or persons whose attendance the LEA considers appropriate[4].

1 Education (Special Educational Needs) (England) (Consolidation) Regulations 2001, SI 2001/3455, reg 22(1) and (2).
2 SI 2001/3455, reg 22(2) and 7.3.8
3 SI 2001/3455, reg 22(2).
4 SI 2001/3455, reg 22(3).

7.3.18 Not later than two weeks before the meeting is due to be held, the LEA shall send to all persons invited to attend the meeting a copy of the report which they propose to make. By written notice accompanying the copy of the report, the LEA shall request the recipients to submit to the LEA written comments on the report and any other advice which they think appropriate[1].

1 SI 2001/2216, reg 22(4).

7.3.19 A representative of the LEA must attend the review meeting[1] and the meeting must consider all the matters listed at 7.3.11 above[2]. If the child is in the tenth year of his compulsory education, the meeting must consider any matters which are the appropriate subject of a transition plan[3]. The meeting shall make recommendations on:

(a) any steps which it concludes ought to be taken, including whether the LEA should amend or cease to maintain the statement;
(b) any targets to be established in furtherance of the objectives specified in the statement which it concludes the child ought to meet during the period until the next review; and
(c) the matters which it concludes ought to be included in the transition plan[4].

1 Education (Special Educational Needs) (England) (Consolidation) Regulations 2001, SI 2001/3455, reg 22(5).
2 SI 2001/3455, reg 22(6).
3 SI 2001/3455, reg 22(6).
4 SI 2001/3455, reg 22(6).

7.3.20 After the meeting, the LEA must complete its report. The report shall contain the LEA's assessment of the matters required to be considered by the meeting and their recommendations as to the matters required to be recommended. If there are any differences between the LEA's assessment and recommendations and those of the meeting, the report shall refer to those differences[1]. Within one week of the meeting, the LEA shall send copies of the completed report to the child's parent and any person to whom the LEA considers it appropriate to send a copy[2]. In the light of its report and any other advice or information which it considers relevant, the LEA shall review the statement[3]. It shall make written recommendations on any steps which it concludes ought to be taken, including whether the LEA should amend or cease to maintain the statement, any targets to be established in furtherance of the objectives specified in the statement which it concludes the child ought to meet during the period until the next review and the matters which it concludes ought to be included in the transition plan (or in the tenth year of the child's compulsory education, and a transition plan exists, amend the transition plan as appropriate)[4]. Within one week of completing the review, the LEA shall send copies of the recommendations and the transition plan to the child's parent and any other persons to whom the LEA considers it appropriate to send copies[5].

1 Education (Special Educational Needs) (England) (Consolidation) Regulations 2001, SI 2001/3455, reg 22(7).
2 SI 2001/3455, reg 22(8).
3 Under EA 1996, s 328.
4 SI 2001/3455, reg 22(9).
5 SI 2001/3455, reg 22(10).

Amendments to statements   **7.4**

A child's special educational needs will change over the course of his edu-   **7.4.1**
cation and it is therefore important for his statement to be a living document
able to change to reflect those changing needs. Consequently, provision is
made in the legislation to allow and require an LEA to amend his statement.
The principles applying to the content of an amended statement are the
same as for an initial statement[1] and will therefore not be reconsidered here.
Instead, this section will concentrate on the previously complicated and
ambiguous provisions setting out the procedure by which a statement can be
amended.

1 See Chapter 6.

Before SENDA 2001, it is fair to say that here was some confusion within   **7.4.2**
LEAs as to when a statement should be amended and how those amendments would be effected. Practice differed between LEAs: some would
amend following an annual review, others only after a further assessment.
Some would amend even if minor alterations were required; others would
only amend if significant changes were necessary. Some would issue a 'new'
statement as an amended statement; others would add the amendments to
the old statement, not always making it clear what needs and what provision
were still current. In order to bring some clarity (although some of these
issues remain unresolved), SENDA 2001 has strengthened the provision in
the EA 1996 relating to amendments and provided parents with greater entitlement to information and involvement in the amendment process[1].

1 See SENDA 2001, Sch 1.

It may be obvious, but a prerequisite for any amendment must be that the   **7.4.3**
LEA maintains an existing statement in respect of a child. If a child had a
statement and his needs improved so that the LEA ceased to maintain the
statement, if his needs then deteriorate the LEA must issue a new statement,
not amend the statement he had before it was ceased. Nor can a note in lieu
be amended to become a statement.

If a statement is maintained for a child who is within 12 months of a trans-   **7.4.4**
fer between phases of schooling, an LEA must ensure that the child's
statement is amended so that before 15 February in the calendar year of the
child's transfer, the statement names the school or other institution which
the child will be attending following that transfer[1]. A transfer between phases
of schooling means[2] a transfer from (a) primary school to middle school, (b)
primary school to secondary school, (c) middle school to secondary school,
or (d) secondary school to an institution which is maintained by an LEA and
is principally concerned with the provision of full-time education suitable to
the requirements of pupils who are over compulsory school age but under
the age of 19[3].

1 Education (Special Educational Needs) (England) (Consolidation) Regulations 2001, SI
   2001/3455, reg 19(1) and (3).
2 SI 2001/3455, reg 19(2).
3 EA 1996, s 2(2A), although reg 19(2) mistakenly refers to 's 2A' which does not exist.

7.4.5 An LEA cannot amend a statement except[1]:

(a) in compliance with an order of the Tribunal;
(b) as directed by the Secretary of State[2]; or
(c) in accordance with the procedure set out in Schedule 27 of the EA 1996.

1 EA 1996, Sch 27, para 2A(1).
2 Under EA 1996, s 442(4) (in respect of a school attendance order).

Amendment following re-assessment review

7.4.6 If, following a re-assessment review, an LEA proposes to amend the child's statement, it shall serve on the child's parent a copy of the proposed amended statement[1]. The proposed amended statement may not specify any prescribed matter or the type of school or other institution which the LEA considers would be appropriate for the child[2]. With the proposed amended statement, the LEA must also serve on the parent a written notice explaining, so far as they are applicable, the following[3]:

(a) the arrangements for enabling the parent to express a preference for the maintained school he wishes his child to attend;
(b) the parent's right to make representations about the content of the proposed statement, to require the LEA to arrange a meeting with an officer; and to arrange meetings with one of more of the people who have provided advice to the re-assessment process to enable the parent to discuss their advice; and
(c) the parent's right to appeal to the Tribunal against the description of the child's special educational needs, the special educational provision to be made in the amended statement or, if no school is named in the amended statement, that fact.

1 EA 1996, Sch 27, para 2A(2).
2 EA 1996, Sch 27, para 2A; and see EA 1996, s 324(4).
3 EA 1996, Sch 27, para 2B(2).

7.4.7 Similarly, if the LEA is considering amending a statement, if a school is not specified in the original statement, so that a maintained school will be specified or, if a school was named in the original, by specifying a different maintained school, the LEA shall serve a copy of the proposed amended statement on the governing body of any and each school the LEA is considering specifying[1]. If the proposed school is maintained by another LEA, the LEA should also serve a copy of the proposed amended statement on the other LEA[2].

1 EA 1996, Sch 27, para 3A.
2 EA 1996, Sch 27, para 3A(3)(b).

7.4.8 The LEA must also inform the parent of his rights to make representations about the content of the statement as it will have effect if amended in the way proposed[1] and to require the LEA to arrange a meeting between the parent and an officer of the LEA to discuss the effect of the amendment[2]. If a parent attends this meeting but disagrees with any part of the re-assessment, he may require the LEA to arrange such meeting or meetings as it considers will enable him to discuss the advice given in connection with the re-assessment with the appropriate person or persons[3]. Any representations should be made within 15 days of service of the proposed amended statement on the parent or the meeting or, if more than one has been arranged, the last meeting[4]. A requirement from the parent to hold a first meeting with an LEA officer must be made within 15 days of receipt of the notice explaining the effect of the proposed amended statement and the parent's rights[5] and for further meetings, 15 days from the date of the first meeting[6].

1 EA 1996, Sch 27, para 4(1)(a).
2 EA 1996, Sch 27, para 4(1)(b).
3 EA 1996, Sch 27, para 4(2).
4 EA 1996, Sch 27, para 4(4).
5 EA 1996, Sch 27, para 4(5).
6 EA 1996, Sch 27, para 4(6).

Where representations have been made, the LEA may not amend the state- **7.4.9**
ment until it has considered the representations and the period or the last of the periods for the parent to request a meeting has expired[1]. The amended statement may be made in the same form as originally proposed or in a form modified in light of representations made[2]. A copy of the amended statement shall be served on the child's parent[3]. At the same time, the LEA must give the parent written notice of his right to appeal to the Tribunal against (a) the description in the amended statement of the LEA's assessment of the child's special educational needs, (b) the special educational provision specified, or (c) if no school is specified, that fact[4]. It should be noted that the parent's right of appeal is not just limited to the part or parts of the statement which have been amended. The parent can appeal against any part of the description of special educational needs or special educational provision specified, even if that has not been amended.

1 EA 1996, Sch 27, para 5(1).
2 EA 1996, Sch 27, para 5(2A); and see *R v Isle of Wight County Council, ex p S* (30 September 1992, unreported), CA (an LEA may decide, even after issuing a proposed statement that, in light of representations, that it need not actually go on and make a final statement).
3 EA 1996, Sch 27, para 6(1).
4 EA 1996, Sch 27, para 6(2).

Amendment following periodic review

Where the LEA decides to amend a statement following a periodic review **7.4.10**
(otherwise known as an annual review) or at any time other than following a re-assessment, the process is slightly different. In these cases, if the LEA proposes to amend a statement after such a review, the LEA must serve on the child's parent a copy of the existing statement and a document called an 'amendment notice'[1]. An amendment notice is a notice in writing giving details of the amendments to the statement proposed by the LEA[2]. With the amendment notice, the LEA must also[3] serve a written notice explaining (to the extent that they are applicable):

(a) the arrangements for enabling a parent to express a preference as to the maintained school at which he wishes education to be provided for his child and to give reasons for his preference[4];
(b) the right of the parent to make representations (or further representations) to the LEA about the content of the statement as it will have effect if amended in the way the LEA proposes; to require the LEA to arrange a meeting between the parent and an officer of the LEA to discuss the proposed amended statement[5];

(c) the right to appeal against the description of the child's special educational needs, the special educational provision specified or, if no school is specified in the statement once amended, that fact[6].

1 EA 1996, Sch 27, para 2A(4).
2 EA 1996, Sch 27, para 2A(6).
3 EA 1996, Sch 27, para 2B.
4 Under EA 1996, Sch 27, para 3.
5 Under EA 1996, Sch 27, para 4.
6 Under EA 1996, s 326.

7.4.11 As with an initial statement, the parent on whom an amendment notice has been served should be able to express a preference as to the maintained school at which he wishes education to be provided for his child and to give reasons for his preference[1]. This preference must be expressed or made within the period of 15 days beginning on the day the amendment notice was served on the parent or, if a meeting or meetings have been arranged to discuss it, the date fixed for the meeting or the last of the meetings[2]. Where the parent expresses a preference for a maintained school, the LEA shall specify the name of that school in the amended statement unless (a) the school is unsuitable to the child's age, ability or aptitude or to his special educational needs, or (b) the attendance of the child at the school would be incompatible with the provision of efficient education for children with whom he would be educated or the efficient use of resources[3].

1 EA 1996, Sch 27, para 3(1).
2 EA 1996, Sch 27, para 3(2).
3 EA 1996, Sch 27, para 3(3).

7.4.12 If a school is not specified in the original statement, but the LEA intends to specify a school in the amended statement or, if a school was named in the original, specify a different maintained school, the LEA shall serve a copy of the existing statement and the amendment notice on the governing body of any and each school the LEA is considering specifying[1]. If the proposed school is maintained by another LEA, the LEA should also serve copies on the other LEA[2].

1 EA 1996, Sch 27, para 3A.
2 EA 1996, Sch 27, para 3A(3)(b).

7.4.13 The LEA must also inform the parent of his rights to make representations about the content of the statement as it will have effect if amended in the way proposed[1] and to require the LEA to arrange a meeting between the parent and an officer of the LEA to discuss the effect of the amendment[2]. In the case of an amendment proposed through an amendment notice, the parent does not have the ability to require the LEA to arrange a meeting or meetings with those persons who contributed advice, because there will not have been an assessment as such to which such persons contributed. Any representations should be made within 15 days of service of the amendment notice on the parent or the meeting or the meeting[3]. A requirement from the parent to hold a meeting with an LEA officer must be made within 15 days of receipt of the notice explaining the effect of the amendment notice and the parent's rights[4].

1 EA 1996, Sch 27, para 4(1)(a).
2 EA 1996, Sch 27, para 4(1)(b).

3 EA 1996, Sch 27, para 4(4).
4 EA 1996, Sch 27, para 4(5).

Where representations have been made, the LEA may not amend the   **7.4.14**
statement until it has considered the representations and the period or the
last of the periods for the parent to request a meeting has expired[1]. The
amended statement may be made in the same form as originally proposed
in the amendment notice or in a form modified in light of representations
made[2]. A copy of the amended statement shall be served on the child's
parent[3]. At the same time, the LEA must give the parent written notice of
his right to appeal to the Tribunal against (a) the description in the
amended statement of the LEA's assessment of the child's special educational needs, (b) the special educational provision specified, or (c) if no
school is specified, that fact[4]. It should be noted that the parent's right of
appeal is not just limited to the part or parts of the statement which have
been amended. The parent can appeal against any part of the description of
special educational needs or special educational provision specified, even if
that has not been amended.

1 EA 1996, Sch 27, para 5(1).
2 EA 1996, Sch 27, para 5(2B); and see *R v Isle of Wight County Council, ex p S* (30
   September 1992, unreported), CA (an LEA may decide, even after issuing a proposed
   statement that, in light of representations, that it need not actually go on and make a final
   statement).
3 EA 1996, Sch 27, para 6(1).
4 EA 1996, Sch 27, para 6(2).

Parent's request to change named school   **7.5**

If a statement specifies the name of a school or institution, the child's parent   **7.5.1**
may ask the LEA to substitute for that name the name of a maintained
school specified by the parent[1]. If a parent does ask the LEA to change the
name of the school, and the request is not made less than 12 months after
an earlier request, the service of a statement or amended statement or, if
there has been an appeal to the Tribunal, the date when the appeal was concluded, the LEA must comply with the request unless:

(a) the school is unsuitable to the child's age, ability or aptitude or to his
     special educational needs; or
(b) the attendance of the child at the school would be incompatible with
     the provision of efficient education for the children with whom he
     would be educated or the efficient use of resources[2].

However, as has been seen[3] there may be some ambiguity over the LEA
being able to justify refusing to comply on the grounds of the efficient use of
resources. The DfES do not believe that there is a problem[4] and that the
LEA can take resources into account. That does not, however, appear to fit
with a reading of the relevant provisions in the EA 1996[5]. Whilst the provisions enabling parents to express a preference when a statement is first
made or amended are said[6] to be unaffected by the changes to the duty to
educate in a mainstream setting and thus the efficient use of resources condition may be applied, the same opt out is not applied to the provision
enabling parents to ask for the name of the school to be substituted[7]. It is
therefore possible that if an LEA were to refuse on the grounds of efficient

use of resources, that decision could be challenged and the Department for Education and Skill's advice will be of little comfort.

1 EA 1996, Sch 27, para 8(1).
2 EA 1996, Sch 27, para 8(2).
3 See 2.5 and 6.9.
4 *Inclusive Schooling: Children with Special Educational Needs* (DfES/0774/2001), para 33.
5 EA 1996, s 316A(3) and Sch 27, para 8.
6 EA 1996, s 316A(3).
7 Ie EA 1996, Sch 27, para 8.

7.5.2   If the LEA determines not to comply with the request, it shall give notice of that fact and of the parent's right of appeal to the Tribunal against the determination[1]. This does, it should be remembered, apply only if the parent names a maintained school. If the parent asks that any other school be named, there is no right of appeal. On the appeal, the Tribunal may dismiss the appeal or order the LEA to substitute for the name of the school or other institution specified in the statement the name of the school specified by the parent[2]. On this appeal, it should be noted that the Tribunal is limited to ordering the LEA to name the school specified by the parent. It cannot order the LEA to name any other school. Where it is ordered to specify the parent's preferred school, the LEA must do so within two weeks of the Tribunal's order[3].

1 EA 1996, Sch 27, para 8(3).
2 EA 1996, Sch 27, para 8(4).
3 Education (Special Educational Needs) (England) (Consolidation) Regulations 2001, SI 2001/3455, reg 25(2)(g).

7.6   Ceasing to maintain a statement

7.6.1   Once a child has been issued with a statement of special educational needs it does not necessarily follow that he will continue to require that statement for the rest of his education. Indeed, if the provision required by the statement has been put in place, in many cases the child's special educational needs may be addressed and in some cases improved to such an extent that the child may no longer have those needs. In such cases it will be unnecessary for the LEA to continue to maintain the statement as the provision will either not be required or, if special educational provision is needed, it may be provided in the child's school from the school's own resources. The LEA will therefore be able to cease to maintain the statement.

Has a statement ceased to be maintained or has it lapsed?

7.6.2   Some confusion has arisen over the circumstances in which a statement 'ceases to be maintained', in accordance with the statutory meaning, and those circumstances where a statement is said to 'lapse'. This confusion has not been helped by ambiguity in terminology, particularly in some references to the process in the old Code of Practice[1].

1 As to which, see 2.2.6.

7.6.3   Under the EA 1996, 'ceasing to maintain a statement' refers to a positive act by an LEA in accordance with the statutory process to terminate a statement[1], usually following an annual review or a further assessment. It does not refer to the situation where the child ceases to be the responsibility of the LEA[2] or the LEA is ordered to cease to maintain the statement by the Tribunal[3].

1 In EA 1996, Sch 27, paras 9 and 11.
2 EA 1996, Sch 27, para 9(2)(a).
3 EA 1996, Sch 27, para 9(2)(c).

The distinction, in practice, can be important and, with the reference to statements lapsing in the old Code of Practice[1], the confusion has led to a number of challenges, especially in respect of children reaching the end of their compulsory education.   **7.6.4**

1 Old Code of Practice, para 6:36.

An LEA is responsible for a child if the child is in its area and: **7.6.5**

(a) the child is a registered pupil at a maintained school;
(b) education is provided for the child at a school which is not a maintained school but is so provided at the expense of the authority;
(c) items (a) or (b) above do not apply, but the child is a registered pupil at a school and has been brought to the LEA's attention as having or probably having special educational needs; or
(d) the child is not a registered pupil at a school but is not under the age of two or over compulsory school age and has been brought to their attention as having or probably having special educational needs[1].

The LEA is therefore no longer responsible for a child when the above do not apply.

1 EA 1996, s 321(3).

A 'child' includes any person who has not attained the age of 19 and is a registered pupil at a school[1]. A 'pupil' is defined as a person for whom education is being provided at a school, other than (a) a person who has attained the age of 19 for whom further education is being provided, or (b) a person for whom part-time education suitable to the requirements of persons of any age over compulsory school age is being provided[2].   **7.6.6**

A 'school' is an educational institution which is outside the further education sector and the higher education sector and is an institution for providing (a) primary education, (b) secondary education, or (c) both primary and secondary education, whether or not the institution also provides part-time education suitable to the requirements of junior pupils or further education[3].

'Secondary education' is then defined as meaning (a) full-time education suitable to the requirements of pupils of compulsory school age who are either senior pupils, or junior pupils who have attained the age of ten years and six months and whom it is expedient to educate together with senior pupils of compulsory school age; and (b) full-time education suitable to the requirements of pupils who are over compulsory school age but under the age of 19 which is provided at a school at which education within para (a) is also provided[4].

1 EA 1996, s 312(5).
2 EA 1996, s 3(1).
3 EA 1996, s 4(1).
4 EA 1996, s 2(2) and (5).

7.6.7 The net effect of all these confusing definitions is that an LEA remains responsible for a child until the child attains the age of 19 so long as the child remains a pupil at a school. It follows, therefore, that once the child attains the age of 19 or, before attaining that age, he leaves school, for example, to go into employment or to receive further education at a further education college, the LEA will no longer be responsible. In these cases, the statement will lapse simply by reason of the change of situation; there will be no need for the LEA formally to cease to maintain the statement. This was reflected in the old Code of Practice[1] which stated: 'a statement will remain in force until the LEA ceases to maintain it, or until the child is no longer the responsibility of the LEA, for example, if he or she moves into the further or higher education sector, or to social services provision, in which case the statement will lapse'. The inclusion of the words 'or to social services provision' caused some confusion as it is a rather ambiguous phrase and social services provision is not defined.

1 Old Code of Practice, para 6:36.

7.6.8 In *R v Dorset County Council and Further Education Funding Council, ex p Goddard*[1] an LEA misinterpreted the relevant provisions and had attempted to pass responsibility for a child to the Further Education Funding Council (FEFC). The child involved was aged 16 and had severe speech and language problems. The LEA had maintained a statement for him which specified he should attend an independent special school up to the age of 16. After he reached 16, his parents wanted him to attend another residential special school. The LEA initially thought that this placement would be funded by the FEFC, but the FEFC refused. The LEA did not amend or cease to maintain the statement and the child reached 16, at which point the LEA indicated that he should be able to attend a further education college and stated that as he was over compulsory school age they were no longer responsible for him. The FE college could not, in fact, meet his needs and the parents sought to argue that the statement still applied to the child and that the LEA were responsible. The LEA refused and were therefore challenged by judicial review.

The judge held that the LEA recognised that the independent residential school suggested by the parents was the one institution appropriate to the child's needs and that it was only when it was suggested that the LEA should pay for the placement, that it sought to suggest an FE college could meet his needs. Because his needs could, therefore, only be met in a school, the LEA continued to remain responsible. Only if they decided to cease to maintain the statement in accordance with the relevant statutory provisions could an LEA end its responsibility. On the facts, though, the LEA could not have ceased to maintain the statement as it was clearly still necessary for it to be maintained. The judge further held that the FEFC's (and now its successor the Learning and Skills Council's) duty to 16 to 18 year olds was secondary to that of the LEA where the LEA was responsible and maintained, or should have maintained, a statement for a pupil requiring education in a school.

1 [1995] ELR 109, QBD.

7.6.9 In contrast, in *R v Oxfordshire County Council, ex p B*[1], the Court of Appeal held that an LEA had been correct to say that a statement had lapsed. The

Court thought that some of the statements in *Goddard* had gone too far and that the suggestion in that case that there remained a duty upon all LEAs to continue to maintain a statement until it was amended or ceased to be maintained on a proper proposal by the authority, was far too wide. In this case, the child had left school to go onto a further education college which could meet his special educational needs. Once the child had left school, whether to go into employment or to go on to further education in a college, he would no longer be registered at a school maintained by an LEA and the LEA would therefore no longer be responsible for the child. The Court held that 'the LEA's responsibility for the registered child ends upon the child ceasing to be registered and the maintenance of the statement would cease [again, this shows confusing terminology – the Court here meant lapse] with the cessation of that responsibility and registration'.

1 [1997] ELR 90, CA.

The new Code of Practice[1] has attempted to clarify this, although it still **7.6.10** does not provide a particularly clear explanation of when statements will lapse and when they will have to be ceased.

> 'A statement will generally remain in force until and unless the LEA ceases to maintain it. A statement will lapse automatically when a young person moves into further or higher education. Therefore, if a young person, the parents, the LEA and the further education institution are all in agreement about the young person's transfer, there is no need to formally cease the statement since the young person will cease to be a pupil for whom the LEA is responsible after leaving school and so the statement will lapse.'[2]

Similarly:

> 'a young person may leave school at age 16 plus to seek employment or training, again there is no need to formally cease to maintain the statement since the young person would cease to be a pupil for whom the LEA is responsible once they leave school. By contrast, where there is agreement all round that the pupil should stay at school post-16 and the LEA or other LEAs have appropriate school provision, the LEA should normally continue to maintain the statement.'[3]

And:

> 'Where the parents want their child to remain at school post-16, but the LEA considers that the young person's special educational needs would be better met in a further education institution, the LEA cannot know whether the child still requires a statement until it has contacted the FE institution . . . and confirmed that it is both able to meet the young person's needs and has offered a place. The LEA should satisfy itself on both counts before taking formal steps to cease to maintain the young person's statement. At that time the LEA must also notify the parents of the right of appeal to the Tribunal . . . It is not sufficient for LEAs to have a general expectation that an FE institution should be able to meet a young person's needs.'[4]

1 As to which, see 2.2.6 and 2.2.7.
2 Code of Practice, para 8:121.
3 Code of Practice, para 8:122.
4 Code of Practice, para 8:123.

7.6.11 In summary, what this means is:

(a) if the child leaves school for employment or training, the statement will lapse;

(b) if the child moves into further education and the parents, LEA and FE institute all agree it can meet his needs, the statement will lapse;

(c) if the parents and LEA agree the child should attend a school for his post-16 education, the statement will continue unless and until the LEA formally cease to maintain it;

(d) if the LEA believes the child's needs can be met at an FE institution, but the parent disagrees and believes they can only be met in school, the statement will continue unless and until the LEA formally cease to maintain it.

7.6.12 If, for some exceptional reason, a child with special educational needs attends a higher education institution, the LEA has no responsibility to meet the child's needs[1].

1 *R v Portsmouth City Council, ex p Faludy* [1998] ELR 619; affd [1999] ELR 115, CA.

Procedure to cease a statement

7.6.13 Where an LEA is required to cease a statement, Schedule 27, paragraph 11 of the EA 1996 lays down the procedure. First, an LEA may cease to maintain a statement only if it is no longer necessary for the LEA to maintain it[1]. Where an LEA determines to cease to maintain a statement, it must give notice of that fact to the child's parent and also inform him of his right to appeal to the Tribunal against that determination[2]. On an appeal, the Tribunal may dismiss the appeal or order the LEA to continue to maintain the statement in its existing form or with amendments. The amendments can be to the description in the statement of the LEA's assessment of the child's special educational needs or the special educational provision specified and such other consequential amendments as the Tribunal may determine[3]. The LEA must then cease the statement within the prescribed period, unless the parent appeals to the Tribunal. If the parent does appeal, the LEA may not cease to maintain the statement until the appeal has been determined by the Tribunal or withdrawn[4].

1 EA 1996, Sch 27, para 11(1).
2 EA 1996, Sch 27, para 11(2).
3 EA 1996, Sch 27, para 11(3).
4 EA 1996, Sch 27, para 11(4) and (5).

Chapter 8

Appeals to the Special Educational Needs and Disability Tribunal[1]

1 The Special Educational Needs Tribunal will be renamed the Special Educational Needs and Disability Tribunal from 1 September 2002.

ESTABLISHMENT, CONSTITUTION AND JURISDICTION OF THE TRIBUNAL

Background to appeal procedures   8.1

Prior to 1993, if parents wished to contest a statement of special educational needs issued by a Local Education Authority (LEA), their options were limited. LEAs were required to make arrangements for enabling the parent of a child for whom they maintained a statement to appeal against the special educational provision specified in the statement following the first or any subsequent assessment of the child's special educational needs or the amendment of the special educational provision specified[1]. Any appeal had to be made to an appeal committee appointed by the LEA[2]. The appeal committee could uphold the LEA's decision or remit the case back to the LEA for re-consideration. In any case where the appeal committee confirmed the decision of the LEA or where the LEA, having had the matter remitted to it, informed the parent of its decision following such reconsideration, the parent could appeal in writing to the Secretary of State[3]. On appeal, the Secretary of State could, after consulting the LEA, confirm the special educational provision specified; amend the statement so far as it specified the special educational provision and make such other consequential amendments as he considered appropriate; or direct the LEA to cease to maintain the statement[4].

8.1.1

1 Education Act (EA) 1981, s 8(1).
2 EA 1981, s 8(2).
3 EA 1981, s 8(6).
4 EA 1981, s 8(7).

This system of appeal was, however, unpopular with parents and their representatives. The so-called independence of the local appeal committees was often cast into doubt[1], because many parents felt that they were, in effect, appealing to the same organisation that had issued the statement. Councillors who sat on the committees were usually members of the LEA's education committee and so were perceived as having an interest in not allowing appeals where the consequences might have had an impact on the LEA's budget. Even if the committees could achieve the necessary degree of independence, they were fairly toothless. They could remit cases to the

8.1.2

LEA, but they themselves were unable to impose requirements on LEAs or indeed, partly because they were unlikely to have SEN 'experts' sitting on the panels, were they able to amend statements or direct what provision was to be made.

1 See, for example, *R v Gloucestershire County Council, ex p P* [1994] ELR 334, QBD and *R v Mid-Glamorgan County Council, ex p B* [1995] ELR 168, QBD.

8.1.3 Appeals to the Secretary of State were, or were certainly perceived to be, even more ineffectual. True, the Secretary of State could impose a decision on an LEA, but the biggest problem for any person bringing an appeal was the time it took for the Secretary of State to reach a decision: it was not uncommon for appeals to take 18 months to be determined. There were also concerns about the procedures adopted by the Secretary of State[1].

1 See, for example, *R v Secretary of State for Education, ex p S* [1995] ELR 71, CA.

Establishment of the Tribunal

8.1.4 As a consequence, in 1992 the government, in its consultation document *Special Educational Needs: Access to the System*[1], proposed the creation of a tribunal to determine all appeals under the EA 1981. This proposal was repeated in the government's 1992 White Paper, *Choice and Diversity*[2] and was implemented in the Education Act (EA) 1993.

1 DFE, 1992.
2 Cmnd 2021.

8.1.5 The Special Educational Needs Tribunal thus came into being and first started hearing appeals from 1 September 1994. The provisions establishing the Tribunal and governing its jurisdiction were subsequently consolidated in the Education Act (EA) 1996[1]. The process of appeal and the detailed rules regarding the Tribunal's procedure were first set out in the Special Educational Needs Tribunal Regulations 1994[2], followed by the Special Educational Needs Tribunal Regulations 1995[3].

1 See EA 1996, Pt IV.
2 SI 1994/1910.
3 SI 1995/3113.

8.1.6 The constitution, jurisdiction and powers of the Tribunal (which will be renamed the Special Educational Needs and Disability Tribunal from 1 September 2002) in respect of children with special educational needs, are now contained in ss 325 to 336A of the EA 1996, as amended by the Special Educational Needs and Disability Act (SENDA) 2001. The current regulations governing the procedure of the Tribunal, made by the Secretary of State under ss 333(5), 334(2), 336(1) and (2) and 569(4) of the EA 1996 and in accordance with s 8 of the Tribunals and Inquiries Act 1992, are now contained in the Special Educational Needs Tribunal Regulations 2001[1].

1 SI 2001/600.

8.1.7 To assist parties to appeals, and also to give guidance to individual tribunals, the President of the Tribunal has issued a number of Practice Statements and Guidance[1]. The President has also arranged for digests of tribunal decisions to be published regularly[2]. Although these are not binding on subsequent tribunals and therefore have no effect as precedents, they are useful to gain an overview of the decisions made by tribunals, especially on procedural issues such as jurisdiction and applications to strike out.

1 See the Special Educational Needs Tribunal President's Guidance – Applications to Review Decisions [1996] ELR 278; and the following Special Educational Needs Tribunal President's Statements: Attendance of Solicitors with Counsel [1996] ELR 280; Prompt Delivery of Replies by LEAs [1996] ELR 281; Attendance at Hearings [1997] ELR 141; Documenting Partial Agreements [1997] ELR 275; Recorded Evidence [1997] ELR 276; Lodging Notice of Appeal [1998] ELR 234; Conditional Non-Opposition to Appeals [1999] ELR 249; Translations of Decisions [2000] ELR 469; and Postal Delays [2000] ELR 637

2 See the following Special Educational Needs Tribunal Digests of Decisions: (Number 1) [1996] ELR 117; (Number 2) [1996] ELR 265; (Number 3) [1996] ELR 270; (Number 4) [1996] ELR 340; (Number 5) [1996] ELR 435; (Number 6) [1997] ELR 135; (Number 7) [1997] ELR 267; (Number 8) [1997] ELR 525; (Number 9) [1998] ELR 227; (Number 10) [1998] ELR 447; (Number 11) [1999] ELR 75; (Number 12) [1999] ELR 335; (Number 13) [1999] ELR 535; (Number 14) [2000] ELR 103; (Number 15) [2000] ELR 339; (Number 16) [2000] ELR 631; and (Number 17) [2001] ELR 119.

Constitution and membership of the Tribunal   8.2

The Special Educational Needs and Disability Tribunal ('the Tribunal') is   **8.2.1**
established and continues in existence under s 333 of the EA 1996. Under
the EA 1996, it was named the Special Educational Needs Tribunal, but by
virtue of s 28H of the Disability Discrimination Act (DDA) 1995, from the
coming into force of s 17 of the SENDA 2001, it will be renamed the
Special Educational Needs and Disability Tribunal.

The Tribunal comprises a President[1], a chairmen's panel[2] and a lay panel[3].   **8.2.2**

1 EA 1996, s 333(2)(a).
2 EA 1996, s 333(2)(b).
3 EA 1996, s 333(2)(c).

The President and members of the chairmen's panel are appointed by the   **8.2.3**
Lord Chancellor[1]. No person may be appointed President or as a member
of the chairmen's panel unless the person has a seven-year general qualification within the meaning of s 71 of the Courts and Legal Services Act
1990[2].

1 EA 1996, s 333(3).
2 EA 1996, s 334(1).

Members of the lay panel are appointed by the Secretary of State[1] and must   **8.2.4**
satisfy prescribed requirements[2]. These requirements were originally that no
person could be appointed as a member of the lay panel unless the Secretary
of State was satisfied that they had knowledge and experience in respect of
(a) children with special educational needs, or (b) local government[3]. Under
the 2001 Regulations[4], however, that requirement has changed. No person
can now be appointed as a member of the lay panel unless the Secretary of
State, and the National Assembly for Wales in respect of Wales, is satisfied
that he has knowledge and experience of children with special educational
needs and that he is not eligible for appointment to the chairmen's panel[5].
As a consequence, no person will in future be able to be appointed to the lay

panel simply because of their knowledge of local government or indeed knowledge of education in local government generally. Only if they have specific knowledge and experience of children with special educational needs will they be eligible.

1 EA 1996, s 333(4).
2 EA 1996, s 334(2).
3 Special Educational Needs Tribunal Regulations 1995, SI 1995/3113, reg 3.
4 Special Educational Needs Tribunal Regulations 2001, SI 2001/600.
5 SI 2001/600, reg 3.

8.2.5 If, in the opinion of the Lord Chancellor, the President is unfit to continue in office or is incapable of performing his duties, the Lord Chancellor may revoke his appointment[1]. Each member of the chairmen's panel or lay panel shall hold and vacate office under the terms of the instrument under which he is appointed[2]. The President or a member of the chairmen's or lay panel may resign office by notice in writing to the Lord Chancellor or the Secretary of State, as appropriate, and is eligible for re-appointment if he ceases to hold office[3].

1 EA 1996, s 334(4).
2 EA 1996, s 334(4).
3 EA 1996, s 334(5).

8.2.6 The Secretary of State may pay to the President and any other person in respect of his service as a member of the Tribunal, such remuneration and allowances as the Secretary of State may, with the consent of the Treasury, determine[1].

1 EA 1996, s 335(1).

8.2.7 The Secretary of State may, with the consent of the Treasury, provide such staff and accommodation as the Tribunal may require[1] and may defray the expenses of the Tribunal to such amount as he may, with the consent of the Treasury, determine[2].

1 EA 1996, s 333(6).
2 EA 1996, s 335(2).

8.2.8 The responsibility for exercising the Tribunal's jurisdiction may be, and is, provided for in the 2001 Regulations[1]. The President may therefore from time to time determine the number of tribunals to exercise the jurisdiction of the Tribunal[2] and these tribunals shall sit at such times and in such places as may from time to time be determined by the President[3].

1 EA 1996, s 333(5)(a); Special Educational Needs Tribunal Regulations 2001, SI
   2001/600, regs 4 and 5.
2 SI 2001/600, reg 4(1).
3 SI 2001/600, reg 4(2).

8.2.9 Each Tribunal should consist of a chairman and two other members[1]. For each hearing, the chairman shall be the President or a person selected by him from the chairmen's panel and the two other members shall be selected from the lay panel by the President[2].

1 Special Educational Needs Tribunal Regulations 2001, SI 2001/600, reg 5(1).
2 SI 2001/600, reg 5(2).

Jurisdiction of the Tribunal: decisions against which an appeal may lie   **8.3**

The types of appeal possible under the EA 1981 were criticised as being   **8.3.1**
unduly limited and consequently the EA 1993 widened the appeal rights
available to parents. There were, however, still some omissions, for example
there was no right of appeal against the refusal of the LEA to carry out an
assessment or re-assessment if the request for the assessment or re-assessment
came from the child's school, not his parents. This appeared illogical –
often a school would be in the best position to request assistance, but if the
school made the request, not the parent, the parent would be deprived of
any right of appeal. There was also no power to appeal against a decision of
the LEA to carry out an assessment.

The SENDA 2001 does not address the lack of a parental right of appeal   **8.3.2**
against a decision to carry out an assessment, but it does introduce a right
of appeal for parents where a request for an assessment or further assessment
is made by the child's school[1].

1   EA 1996, s 329A.

Consequently, parents may now appeal to the Tribunal against decisions of   **8.3.3**
LEAs in respect of their child's special educational needs in the following
circumstances:

(1) Where the LEA has carried out an assessment of a child's special educational needs and proposes not to make a statement of special educational needs[1]. The Tribunal may dismiss the appeal, order the LEA to make and maintain such a statement, or remit the case to the LEA for them to reconsider whether, having regard to any observations made by the Tribunal, it is necessary for the LEA to determine the special educational provision which any learning difficulty the child may have calls for[2].

(2) Where the LEA has carried out an assessment of a child's special educational needs and has decided to issue and maintain a statement of special educational needs for the first time, the parents may appeal to the Tribunal against:
 (a) the description in the statement of the LEA's assessment of the child's special educational needs;
 (b) the special educational provision specified in the statement (including the name of a school so specified); or
 (c) if no school is named in the statement, that fact[3].
 The Tribunal may dismiss the appeal, order the LEA to amend the statement so far as it describes the assessment of the child's special educational needs or specifies the special educational provision and make such other amendments to the statement as the Tribunal think fit, or order the LEA to cease to maintain the statement[4]. It is not unlawful for the Tribunal to order that the LEA should make provision for a child, but leave the detail of that provision to be based on a report to be carried out[5].

(3) Where a statement is already maintained for a child and the LEA has decided to amend the statement, an appeal may be brought against:
 (a) the description in the statement of the LEA's assessment of the child's special educational needs;

(b) the special educational provision specified in the statement (including the name of a school so specified); or

(c) if no school is named in the statement, that fact[6].

The Tribunal may dismiss the appeal, order the LEA to amend the statement so far as it describes the assessment of the child's special educational needs or specifies the special educational provision and make such other amendments to the statement as the Tribunal think fit, or order the LEA to cease to maintain the statement[7].

(4) Where a statement is already maintained for a child, the LEA has conducted a further assessment of the child, but the LEA decides not to amend the statement, an appeal may be brought against:

   (a) the description in the statement of the LEA's assessment of the child's special educational needs;

   (b) the special educational provision specified in the statement (including the name of a school so specified); or

   (c) if no school is named in the statement, that fact[8].

The Tribunal may dismiss the appeal, order the LEA to amend the statement so far as it describes the assessment of the child's special educational needs or specifies the special educational provision and make such other amendments to the statement as the Tribunal think fit, or order the LEA to cease to maintain the statement[9].

(5) Where a statement is already maintained for a child, the parent asks the LEA to arrange for a further assessment to be made, but the LEA decides not to comply with the request for a further assessment[10]. This right of appeal, however, only arises if no assessment has been made within the period of six months ending with the date on which the request is made and it is necessary for the LEA to make a further assessment[11]. The Tribunal may dismiss the appeal or order the LEA to arrange for an assessment to be made in respect of the child under s 323 of the EA 1996[12].

(6) Where, in respect of a child who does not have a statement of special educational needs, the parent asks the LEA to arrange an assessment, but the LEA declines to comply with that request[13]. This right of appeal only applies if such an assessment has not been made within the period of six months ending with the date on which the request is made and it is necessary for the LEA to make an assessment[14]. The Tribunal may dismiss the appeal or order the LEA to arrange for an assessment to be made in respect of the child under s 323 of the EA 1996[15].

(7) Where a headteacher or proprietor of a school asks the LEA to carry out an assessment of a child registered at the school, but the LEA decides not to comply with the request, the child's parent may appeal[16]. This only applies if no assessment has been made within the period of six months ending with the date on which the request is made[17]. The Tribunal may dismiss the appeal or order the LEA to arrange for an assessment to be made in respect of the child under s 323[18].

(8) Where the parent of a child who has a statement which specifies the name of a school or institution is maintained has asked the LEA to substitute for that name the name of a maintained school specified by the parent, but the LEA has declined to comply with that request[19]. This right of appeal only applies if the request is not made less than 12 months after:

(a) an earlier similar request;

(b) the service of a copy of a statement;

(c) if the statement has been amended, the date when notice of the amendment was given; or

(d) if the parent has appealed to the Tribunal, the date when the appeal was concluded[20].

The Tribunal may dismiss the appeal or order the LEA to substitute for the name of the school or other institution specified in the statement the name of the school specified by the parent[21].

(9) Where the LEA determines to cease to maintain a statement[22]. The Tribunal may dismiss the appeal or order the LEA to continue to maintain the statement in its existing from or with such amendments of:

(a) the description in the statement of the LEA's assessment of the child's special educational needs; or

(b) the special educational provision specified in the statement, and such other consequential amendments, as the Tribunal may determine[23].

1   EA 1996, s 325(1).
2   EA 1996, s 325(3).
3   EA 1996, s 326(1)(a) and (1A).
4   EA 1996, s 326(3).
5   See *M v Hampshire County Coucnil and Special Educational Needs Tribunal* [2002] EWHC 32 (Admin), QBD.
6   EA 1996, s 326(1)(b) and (1A).
7   EA 1996, s 326(3).
8   EA 1996, s 326(1)(c) and (1A).
9   EA 1996, s 326(3).
10   EA 1996, s 328(2)(a) and (3).
11   EA 1996, s 328(2)(b) and (c).
12   EA 1996, s 328(4).
13   EA 1996, s 329(2).
14   EA 1996, s 329(1)(b) and (c).
15   EA 1996, s 329(3).
16   EA 1996, s 329A(8).
17   EA 1996, s 329A(1)(c).
18   EA 1996, s 329(3).
19   EA 1996, Sch 27, para 8(3).
20   EA 1996, Sch 27, para 8(1)(b).
21   EA 1996. Sch 27, para 8(4).
22   EA 1996, Sch 27, para 11.
23   EA 1996, Sch 27, para 11(3).

As can be seen, there is still no right of appeal against a decision of an LEA   **8.3.4** to carry out an assessment or a further assessment. Nor is there a right of appeal against the description of the non-educational needs or the non-educational provision specified in a statement, which is partly why the distinction between educational and non-educational needs and provision has assumed such importance[1]. There is also no right of appeal against the refusal of a health authority, primary care trust or local authority (Social Services) to help in the exercise of the LEA's functions under s 322 of the EA 1996.

1   See 6.8.

THE TRIBUNAL'S PROCEDURE

8.4 Statutory foundations

8.4.1 The proceedings of the Tribunal and the detailed rules for the initiation of an appeal are contained in the Special Educational Needs Tribunal Regulations 2001[1].

1 EA 1996, s 336(1).

8.4.2 Section 336(2) of the EA 1996 permits the Regulations, in particular, to include provision:

(a) as to the period within which, and the manner in which, appeals are to be instituted;

(b) where the jurisdiction of the Tribunal is being exercised by more than one tribunal (i) for determining by which tribunal any appeal is to be heard, and (ii) for the transfer of proceedings from one tribunal to another;

(c) for enabling any functions which relate to matters preliminary or incidental to an appeal to be performed by the President, or by the chairman;

(d) for the holding of hearings in private in prescribed circumstances;

(e) for hearings to be conducted in the absence of any member other than the chairman;

(f) as to the persons who may appear on behalf of the parties;

(g) for granting any person such discovery or inspection of documents or right to further particulars as might be granted by a county court;

(h) requiring persons to attend to give evidence and produce documents;

(i) for authorising the administration of oaths to witnesses;

(j) for the determination of appeals without a hearing in prescribed circumstances;

(k) as to the withdrawal of appeals;

(l) for the award of costs or expenses;

(m) for taxing or otherwise settling any such costs or expenses (and, in particular, for enabling such costs to be taxed in the county court);

(n) for the registration and proof of decisions and orders; and

(o) for enabling the Tribunal to review its decisions, or revoke or vary its orders, in such circumstances as may be determined in accordance with the regulations.

The detailed provisions contained in the Special Educational Needs Tribunal Regulations 2001 are considered below.

8.5 The status of statements pending appeal to the Tribunal

8.5.1 The effect of an appeal on the child's statement was not originally expressly set out in the legislation. This led to some confusion, especially where the LEA's decision was to cease to maintain a statement; an appeal could take up to seven months to determine, during which time a child might lose the benefit of the support in the statement, even though his parents might subsequently win on appeal and require the LEA to reinstate the statement. To address this problem amendments have been introduced by the SENDA 2001[1].

1 See EA 1996, Sch 27, para 11(5).

The position pending the determination of appeals to the Tribunal in respect of each right of appeal is now as follows: **8.5.2**

(1) Where the parent appeals against a decision not to make a statement after an assessment[1], no statement will have been created, although a notice in lieu should have been issued. This situation will continue unless and until the Tribunal orders the LEA to issue and maintain a statement or such a course of action is agreed between the LEA and the parents.

(2) Where the LEA has issued a statement of special educational needs for the first time and the parent appeals against the content of the statement[2], the issued statement remains in force unless and until amended by the Tribunal or by agreement between the parties to the appeal.

(3) Where the parent appeals against amendments to the content of a statement[3], the amendments take effect as soon as the amendments are issued and continue to have effect unless and until amended by the Tribunal or by agreement between the parties.

(4) Where the parent appeals against the LEA's refusal to amend the statement following a further assessment[4], the original statement remains in force unless and until the Tribunal orders the LEA to amend the statement or the parties agree to do so.

(5) Where the parent appeals against the LEA's refusal to carry out a further assessment[5], the original statement remains in force. Even if the parent succeeds on appeal, it does not mean that the statement will be amended. Under this right of appeal the Tribunal can only order the LEA to carry out the requested further assessment.

(6) Where the parent appeals against the LEA's refusal to carry out an assessment[6], the child will not have a statement. Even if the parent succeeds on appeal, the Tribunal cannot order the LEA to issue and maintain a statement. Under this right of appeal, the Tribunal can only order the LEA to carry out an assessment. This right of appeal also only applies if such an assessment has not been made within the period of six months ending with the date on which the request is made and it is necessary for the LEA to make an assessment[7].

(7) Where the parent appeals against an LEA's refusal to carry out an assessment at the request of the child's school[8], again, no statement will be in existence. The Tribunal can only order the LEA to carry out an assessment, not to issue and maintain a statement.

(8) Where the parent appeals against the LEA's refusal to change the name of the school specified in the child's current statement[9], the name of the school originally specified remains the appropriate school unless and until the Tribunal orders the LEA to substitute the name of the parent's preferred school or the parties agree to the change. The parent will therefore be required to ensure that the child continues to attend the school named in the statement (unless they can make suitable alternative provision), otherwise the parent may be in breach of his duty to ensure that the child receives efficient full-time education suitable to his age, ability and aptitude and to any special educational

needs he may have either by regular attendance at school or otherwise[10].

(9) Where the parent appeals against the LEA's decision to cease to maintain a statement[11], the statement will continue in effect unless and until the Tribunal determines that the decision should be upheld or the LEA agrees to continue to maintain the statement[12]. In practice LEAs should ensure that they do not cease to maintain any statement until the period for the parent making an appeal to the Tribunal has passed.

1 EA 1996, s 325(1).
2 EA 1996, s 326(1)(a) and (1A).
3 EA 1996, s 326(1)(b) and (1A).
4 EA 1996, s 326(1)(c) and (1A).
5 EA 1996, s 328(2)(a) and (3).
6 EA 1996, s 329(2).
7 EA 1996, s 329(1)(b) and (c).
8 EA 1996, s 329A(8).
9 EA 1996, Sch 27, para 8(3).
10 EA 1996, s 7.
11 EA 1996, Sch 27, para 11.
12 EA 1996, Sch 27, para 11(5).

8.6 Who may appeal to the Tribunal?

8.6.1 In all cases, the EA 1996 provides for appeals to be brought by 'the parent of a child'[1].

1 EA 1996, ss 325(2), 326(1), 328(3), 329(2), 329A(8) and Sch 27, paras 8(3) and 11(2).

8.6.2 For these purposes, a 'parent' is defined, in relation to a child or young person, as including 'any person (a) who is not a parent of his but who has parental responsibility for him, or (b) who has care of him'[1].

1 EA 1996, s 576(1).

8.6.3 This has always been something of an ambiguous definition. What it does mean is that a 'parent' will include the child's natural parents, whether married or not, any individual with parental responsibility for the child and any other person who is neither a natural parent nor a person with parental responsibility, but who does have care of the child.

8.6.4 A local authority can be a parent if it has a care order in respect of the child (a care order will give it parental responsibility)[1], and foster-parents will also be parents as they will have care of the child. In *Fairpo v Humberside County Council*[2] Laws J held that a foster-parent with whom a child had been placed by the local authority, could bring an appeal to the Tribunal. Although he felt that such a person did not immediately and easily fall within the definition of a 'parent' in EA 1996, s 576(1), the definition did include someone involved in the full-time care of the child on a settled basis. His Lordship's interpretation would, however, appear to preclude a short-term foster parent being able to exercise similar rights.

1 The social services department of the same authority may therefore, through a social worker, appeal to the Tribunal against a decision of the LEA, part of the same council – see, for example, Digest of Decisions (Number 4) 96/25 [1996] ELR 341.
2 [1997] 1 All ER 183, QBD.

THE TRIBUNAL APPEAL PROCESS

Introduction   8.7

The following paragraphs will outline the process in respect of appeals made   **8.7.1**
to the Tribunal on or after 1 September 2001. Appeals lodged before that
day will continue to be dealt with in accordance with the Special
Educational Needs Tribunal Regulations 1995[1]. Where reference is made
below to 'Regulations', unless the contrary is indicated, references will be to
the Special Educational Needs Tribunal Regulations 2001[2].

1 SI 1995/3113.
2 SI 2001/600.

Initiating an appeal to the Tribunal   8.8

Lodging a notice of appeal

An appeal to the Tribunal must be made by notice[1]. The notice must state: **8.8.1**

(a) the name and address of the parent making the appeal and if more than
    one address is given, the address to which the Tribunal should send
    notices or replies concerning the appeal;
(b) the name and date of birth of the child;
(c) that the notice is a notice of appeal;
(d) the name of the LEA which made the disputed decision and the date
    on which the parent was notified of it;
(e) if the parent seeks an order that the child's statement be amended, to
    which part or parts of the statement the appeal relates;
(f) if the parent seeks an order that a school (other than one already
    named in the child's statement) be named in it, either the name and
    address of that school or a sufficient description of the type and nature
    of the school which the parent considers would constitute an appro-
    priate placement for the child. (This last requirement was introduced
    in the 2001 Regulations and ensures that parents notify the Tribunal of
    the school they want named at the start of an appeal, so allowing the
    school's confirmation to be given well in advance of any hearing, so
    avoiding any potential delay[2].)

1 Special Educational Needs Tribunal Regulations 2001, SI 2001/600, reg 7(1).
2 SI 2001/600, reg 7(1)(a).

The notice of appeal must be accompanied by[1]:   **8.8.2**

(a) a copy of the disputed decision (usually the LEA's decision letter);
(b) where the appeal is made against the content of the statement or
    amended statement, a copy of the child's statement;
(c) where the notice of appeal states the name of a school which the par-
    ent seeks to have named in the statement, written confirmation that the
    parent has informed the school that he proposes that it be named in the
    statement (usually a copy of a letter sent by the parent to the school
    saying exactly this).

1 Special Educational Needs Tribunal Regulations 2001, SI 2001/600, reg 7(1)(b).

8.8.3 The notice must also include or be accompanied by a statement of the parent's reasons for appealing[1]. If the parent does not include, or sends with the notice reasons for appealing which the President does not consider sufficient to enable the LEA to respond to the appeal, the President shall direct the parent to send particulars of the reasons to the Secretary of the Tribunal ('the Secretary') within ten working days of his direction[2]. Particulars of reasons sent in response to such a direction shall be treated as part of the notice of appeal[3]. The parent must sign the notice of appeal[4]. A pro forma notice of appeal can be found in the booklet issued by the Tribunal offering guidance on making an appeal. If the notice of appeal does not fully comply with the requirements of the Regulations, it is likely that the Tribunal will follow the practice previously set out in the Special Educational Needs Tribunal President's Statement – Lodging Notice of an Appeal[5]. This advised that if a notice of appeal is substantially complete, but wanting in certain particulars or not accompanied by all the papers which should have been sent with it[6], rather than reject the appeal, the Secretary will nonetheless register it and the President will direct that the omissions have to be corrected or the papers supplied within a limited time.

1 Special Educational Needs Tribunal Regulations 2001, SI 2001/600, reg 7(1)(c).
2 SI 2001/600, reg 8(1).
3 SI 2001/600, reg 8(3).
4 SI 2001/600, reg 7(3).
5 [1998] ELR 234.
6 Where a statement of special educational needs has to accompany the notice of appeal, the copy should include all the appendices to the statement.

8.8.4 The notice of appeal must be delivered by the parent, or his representative, to the Secretary so that it is received no later than the first working day after the expiry of two months from the date on which the LEA gave the parent notice that he had a right of appeal[1]. In *S and C v Special Educational Needs Tribunal*[2], Latham J held that mistakes by legal advisers could not, on their own, be a good reason for extending time for entering an appeal. This principle was considered in respect of a 'lay' adviser in *R v Special Educational Needs Tribunal, ex p J*[3]. In that case, the notice of appeal was lodged two days outside the time limit specified by the Regulations. The reason for the delay was a failure by the parent's adviser to send in the appeal. As soon as the parent discovered the adviser's failure, she lodged the appeal, but the President refused to grant an extension of time as there were not, in his view, exceptional reasons. The court refused to overturn that decision and held that even though the adviser was dilatory and possibly inept, mistakes by legal advisers could not properly be described as exceptional. In the court's view, exceptional circumstances justifying an extension of time would involve sudden illness or accident preventing the delivery of the notice of appeal[4].

1 Special Educational Needs Tribunal Regulations 2001, SI 2001/600, reg 7(3).
2 [1997] ELR 242, QBD.
3 [1997] ELR 237, QBD.
4 [1997] ELR 237, QBD at p 240.

The Tribunal's receipt of the notice of appeal

Upon receipt of the notice of appeal, the Secretary shall[1]: **8.8.5**

(a) enter particulars of it in the records;
(b) send to the parent:
   (i) an acknowledgement of its receipt and a note of the case number entered in the records;
   (ii) a note of the address to which notices and communications to the Tribunal or to the Secretary should be sent;
   (iii) notification that advice about the appeals procedure may be obtained from the office of the Tribunal; and
   (iv) a notice stating the time for submitting a statement of the parent's case and written evidence[2];
(c) send to the LEA:
   (i) a copy of the notice of appeal and any accompanying papers;
   (ii) a note of the address to which notices and communications to the Tribunal or to the Secretary should be sent; and
   (iii) a notice stating the time for submitting a statement of the LEA's case and written evidence[3] and the consequences of failing to do so;
(d) if the notice of appeal names a maintained school, other then one maintained by the LEA, give the headteacher of that school notice of the appeal, stating the name and date of birth of the child and the name of the LEA.

1 Special Educational Needs Tribunal Regulations 2001, SI 2001/600, reg 17(1).
2 See 8.10.
3 See 8.10.

Where the Secretary is of the opinion that, on the basis of the notice of **8.8.6** appeal, the parent is asking the Tribunal to do something which it cannot do, he may give notice to the parent:

(a) stating the reasons for his opinion; and
(b) informing the parent that the notice of appeal will not be entered in the records unless, within a specified time (which shall not be less than five working days), the parent notifies the Secretary of State of the Tribunal that he wishes to proceed with it[1].

In such cases, the notice of appeal shall only be treated as having been received for the purposes of the steps which the Secretary needs to take, when the parent notifies the Secretary that he wishes to proceed with the appeal[2]. This does not, however, affect the time limit for submitting the appeal. Even if the Secretary is of the opinion that the notice of appeal is asking the Tribunal to do something it cannot do, if it was received at the Tribunal within the two-month time limit, it will be a valid appeal for those purposes, even if the parent's response that he wishes to proceed with the appeal is received after the two-month deadline.

1 Special Educational Needs Tribunal Regulations 2001, SI 2001/600, reg 17(2).
2 SI 2001/600, reg 17(4).

Where the Secretary is of the opinion that there is an obvious error in the **8.8.7** notice of appeal, he may correct that error and if he does so shall notify the parent accordingly. Such notification shall state that, unless within five working days the parent notifies the Secretary that he objects to the correction, the notice of appeal so corrected shall be treated as the notice of appeal[1].

1 Special Educational Needs Tribunal Regulations 2001, SI 2001/600, reg 17(3).

8.9 Service of notices

8.9.1 Notices under the Regulations must be in writing and where a party is required to notify a matter to the Secretary, he must do so in writing[1]. Notices and documents required to be sent or delivered to the Secretary or to the Tribunal may be sent by post, by facsimile transmission (fax) or by electronic mail to or delivered at the office of the Tribunal or such other office as the Secretary may notify to the parties[2].

1 Special Educational Needs Tribunal Regulations 2001, SI 2001/600, reg 50(1).
2 SI 2001/600, reg 50(2).

8.9.2 Notices or documents which the President or Secretary of the Tribunal are authorised or required to send, may either be sent by first class post or by fax to or delivered at:

(a) in the case of a party:
   (i) his address for service specified in the notice of appeal or in a written reply or in a notification of a change of address[1], or
   (ii) if no address for service has been so specified, his last known address; and
(b) in the case of any other person, his place of residence or business or if such person is a corporation, the corporation's registered or principal office[2].

The only exception to this is where the Secretary or President is required to serve a witness summons, in which case the summons must be served using the recorded delivery service instead of first class post[3].

1 A party may at any time, by notice to the Secretary, change his address: Special Educational Needs Tribunal Regulations 2001, SI 2001/600, reg 50(4).
2 SI 2001/600, reg 50(3).
3 SI 2001/600, reg 50(5).

8.9.3 A notice or document sent by the Secretary by post, and otherwise in accordance with the Regulations, and not returned, shall be taken to have been delivered to the addressee on the second day for normal postal deliveries after it was posted[1]. A notice or document sent by fax or electronic mail shall be taken to have been delivered when it is received in legible form[2].

1 Special Educational Needs Tribunal Regulations 2001, SI 2001/600, reg 50(6).
2 SI 2001/600, reg 50(7).

8.9.4 Where, for any sufficient reason, service of any document or notice cannot be effected in the manner prescribed under the Regulations, the President may dispense with service or make an order for substituted service in such manner as he may deem fit and such service shall have effect as service in the manner prescribed under the Regulations[1].

1 Special Educational Needs Tribunal Regulations 2001, SI 2001/600, reg 50(8).

The case statement period

Under the 1995 Regulations[1], once an appeal was received it would be sent **8.10.1**
to the LEA and the LEA would then have the period of 20 working days in
which to submit its response. Once the LEA's response had been received,
the parent was then entitled to reply to the response, in effect commenting
on the LEA's case. Under the 2001 Regulations[2] that sequential approach
has been replaced by a contemporaneous 'case statement period'.

1 Special Educational Needs Tribunal Regulations 1995, SI 1995/3113.
2 Special Educational Needs Tribunal Regulations 2001, SI 2001/600.

Once the Secretary has received an appeal and notified both the LEA and **8.10.2**
the parent of the time for submitting the parent's and LEA's case and written evidence[1], the parent and the LEA shall be allowed the same period of
30 working days from the date on which notification is taken to have been
delivered[2] to send a statement of their respective cases and written evidence
to the Secretary[3].

1 Special Educational Needs Tribunal Regulations 2001, SI 2001/600, reg 17(1)(b)(iv) and
  (c)(iii).
2 See 8.9.
3 SI 2001/600, reg 18(1).

Where, however, the President has issued a direction because he considers **8.10.3**
that the notice of appeal does not include and is not accompanied by reasons for appealing which are sufficient to enable the LEA to respond to the
appeal[1], the 30 working day period shall not start, and the Secretary shall
not send notification or any documents, until particulars of reasons are
received in response to the President's direction[2].

1 See Special Educational Needs Tribunal Regulations 2001, SI 2001/600, reg 8(1); and see
  8.8.3.
2 SI 2001/600, reg 18(2).

During the case statement period, the parent may deliver to the Secretary a **8.10.4**
written statement of his case, which may include the views of the child and
all written evidence which he wishes to submit to the Tribunal[1].

1 Special Educational Needs Tribunal Regulations 2001, SI 2001/600, reg 9(1).

In exceptional circumstances[1], the parent may amend the notice of appeal, **8.10.5**
deliver a supplementary statement of reasons for appealing or statement of
case or amend a supplementary statement of reasons for appealing or statement of case if permission is given by (a) the President at any time before the
hearing, or (b) the Tribunal at the hearing[2]. If the President gives permission
before the hearing, he is obliged to consider extending the case statement
period[3]. The parent shall deliver to the Secretary a copy of every amendment and supplementary statement for which permission was given[4].

1 'Exceptional circumstances' are not defined in the Regulations. They may include illness
  or accident (per *R v Special Educational Needs Tribunal, ex p J* [3 [1997] ELR 237, QBD)
  or significant change in the circumstances of a child since the original papers were filed.
2 Special Educational Needs Tribunal Regulations 2001, SI 2001/600, reg 9(2).
3 SI 2001/600, reg 9(4).
4 SI 2001/600, reg 9(3).

8.10.6 During the case statement period, the LEA must deliver to the Secretary a written statement of its case and all written evidence which it wishes to submit to the Tribunal[1].

1 Special Educational Needs Tribunal Regulations 2001, SI 2001/600, reg 13(1).

8.10.7 The statement of the LEA's case shall be signed by an officer of the LEA who is authorised to sign such documents and shall state whether or not the LEA intends to oppose the appeal[1]. If it does intend to oppose the appeal, it should state:

(a) the grounds on which it relies;
(b) the name and profession of the representative of the LEA and the address for service of the LEA for the purposes of the appeal;
(c) a summary of the facts relating to the disputed decision;
(d) the reasons for the disputed decision, if they are not included in the decision; and
(e) the views of the child concerning the issues raised by the appeal, or the reasons why the LEA has not ascertained those views[2].

1 Special Educational Needs Tribunal Regulations 2001, SI 2001/600, reg 13(2).
2 SI 2001/600, reg 13(2)(a) to (e).

8.10.8 In exceptional circumstances[1], the LEA may amend its statement of case, deliver a supplementary statement of case or amend a supplementary statement of case if permission is given by the President at any time before the hearing or the Tribunal at the hearing[2]. If the President gives such permission, he is obliged to consider extending the case statement period[3]. The LEA shall deliver to the Secretary a copy of every amendment and supplementary statement for which permission was given[4].

1 See 8.10.5, note 1.
2 Special Educational Needs Tribunal Regulations 2001, SI 2001/600, reg 13(3).
3 SI 2001/600, reg 13(5).
4 SI 2001/600, reg 13(4).

8.11 Representatives

8.11.1 The parent may, in the notice of appeal or by giving written notice to the Secretary at any later time:

(a) appoint a representative;
(b) appoint another representative to replace the representative previously appointed, whose appointment is cancelled by the later appointment;
(c) state that no person is acting as the parent's representative, which cancels any previous appointment[1].

To appoint a representative, the parent must give the name, address and profession of the representative[2].

1 Special Educational Needs Tribunal Regulations 2001, SI 2001/600, reg 12(1).
2 SI 2001/600, reg 12(2).

8.11.2 If a person appointed by the parent notifies the Secretary in writing that he is not prepared, or is no longer prepared to act in that capacity, the Secretary shall notify the parent and the appointment of that representative shall be cancelled[1].

1 Special Educational Needs Tribunal Regulations 2001, SI 2001/600, reg 12(3).

Where the parent has appointed a representative, and that appointment has **8.11.3** not been cancelled, the Secretary shall send all documents and notices concerning the appeal to the representative instead of to the parent (unless the parent notifies the Secretary that he does not wish this to apply)[1]. Reference in the Regulations to sending documents and notice to the parent shall be construed as sending documents to or giving notice to the representative[2]. The only exceptions are that the Tribunal's decision letter (or any corrected document containing reasons[3]) must be sent to the parent as well as to the representative[4].

1 Special Educational Needs Tribunal Regulations 2001, SI 2001/600, reg 12(5)(a).
2 SI 2001/600, reg 12(4).
3 SI 2001/600, reg 49(5).
4 SI 2001/600, regs 12(6) and 36(6).

The LEA is required to give details of its representative in the statement of **8.11.4** its case[1]. The LEA may at any time change its representative for the purposes of the appeal by notifying the Secretary of the name and profession of its new representative[2].

1 Special Educational Needs Tribunal Regulations 2001, SI 2001/600, reg 13(2)(b).
2 SI 2001/600, reg 14(1).

The use of solicitors and barristers by the parties initially caused some **8.11.5** problems, especially when the Tribunal was attempting to retain informality to its proceedings. The problem led the President to issue a statement[1]. In this, the President gave notice that he would not automatically give permission for a solicitor to attend with counsel. He would, however, entertain an application for permission in advance of the hearing. Such an application has to show why, in the interests of justice, permission should be allowed. It will not normally be sufficient to say it would be convenient to have a notetaker or that counsel is unknown to the client.

1 Special Educational Needs Tribunal President's Statement – Attendance of Solicitors with Counsel [1996] ELR 280.

Withdrawal of appeal

8.12

The parent may withdraw his appeal (a) at any time before the hearing of the **8.12.1** appeal by sending to the Secretary a notice signed by the parent[1], or (b) at the hearing of the appeal itself[2]. The parent should, however, be aware of the rules concerning costs[3] if the Tribunal takes the view that the parent acted frivolously or vexatiously or that the parent's conduct in making and/or pursuing the appeal was wholly unreasonable.

1 Special Educational Needs Tribunal Regulations 2001, SI 2001/600, reg 10(a).
2 SI 2001/600, reg 10(b).
3 See 8.21.

8.13 LEA's failure to deliver a statement of case and absence of opposition

8.13.1 If the Secretary does not receive a statement of case from the LEA within the case statement period or if the LEA states in writing that it does not resist the appeal, or withdraws its opposition to the appeal, the Tribunal shall:

(a) determine the appeal on the basis of the notice of appeal without a hearing; or

(b) without notifying the LEA, hold a hearing at which the LEA is not represented[1].

Where the parent's appeal relates to the content of the child's statement, the notification from the LEA that it does not resist the appeal or that it withdraws its opposition shall not take effect until the LEA sends the Tribunal a written statement of the amendments (if any) to the child's statement which it has agreed to make[2].

1 Special Educational Needs Tribunal Regulations 2001, SI 2001/600, reg 15(1).
2 SI 2001/600, reg 15(2).

8.13.2 This provision does, however, appear to conflict with the new provision in the EA 1996 dealing with unopposed appeals[1]. This provides that where an LEA notifies the Tribunal that the LEA has decided that it will not, or will no longer, oppose the appeal, the appeal is to be treated as having been determined in favour of the appellant[2] and the Tribunal is not required to make any order[3]. Where it does not oppose an appeal, an LEA will be under a duty to take certain steps, depending upon the nature of the appeal, within a prescribed period[4]. If the appeal is against a refusal to make a statement, the LEA must make a statement; if the appeal is against a refusal to assess or carry out a further assessment, the LEA must carry out such an assessment; and if the LEA has refused to substitute the name of the parent's preferred school, the LEA must comply with the request.

Given this conflict, it is suggested that the Regulations will need to be changed. Until they are, clearly, the provisions in the EA 1996 should prevail, with the effect that where an LEA gives notice that it will not resist an appeal, there will be no need for the appeal to proceed any further.

1 EA 1996, s 326A.
2 EA 1996, s 326A(2).
3 EA 1996, s 326A(3).
4 EA 1996, s 326A(4); and Education (Special Educational Needs) (England) (Consolidation) Regulations 2001, SI 2001/3455, regs 25 and 26.

8.14 Striking out an appeal

8.14.1 The Secretary shall, at any stage of the proceedings, if the LEA applies[1] or the President so directs, serve a notice on the parent stating that it appears that the appeal should be struck out for want of prosecution (ie that the parent appears not to be pursuing the appeal[2]) or on one or both of the following grounds:

(a) that the appeal is not, or is no longer, within the jurisdiction of the Tribunal; and/or

(b) that the notice of appeal is, or the appeal is or has become, scandalous, frivolous or vexatious[3].

1 An application for striking out should be made in the form set out in the Special Educational Needs Tribunal President's Statement – Applications to Strike Out Appeals [1998] ELR 641.
2 See *Decision 97/30* [1997] ELR 526 in which parents prior to a hearing indicated they wanted to withdraw. The hearing was cancelled, but the parents never formally withdrew. No further steps were taken for some months, so the Tribunal struck out the appeal. See also *Decision 96/72* [1996] ELR 441.
3 Special Educational Needs Tribunal Regulations 2001, SI 2001/600, reg 44(1) and (2).

The notice sent by the Secretary must invite the parent to make represen- **8.14.2**
tations on the proposal[1]. The notice must inform the parent that he may, within a specified period (not being less than five working days), either make written representations or request an opportunity to make oral repre-sentations[2]. Representations are duly made if written representations are made within the specified period and, in the case of oral representations, the parent requests an opportunity to make them within the specified period[3]. The Tribunal may, after considering any representations made by the parent, order that the appeal should be struck out for want of prosecution or on one or both of the grounds set out above[4]. Such an order may be made without holding a hearing, unless the parent requests the opportunity to make oral representations. If the Tribunal holds a hearing, it may be held at the beginning of the hearing of the substantive appeal[5].

1 Special Educational Needs Tribunal Regulations 2001, SI 2001/600, reg 44(3).
2 SI 2001/600, reg 44(8)(a).
3 SI 2001/600, reg 44(8)(b).
4 SI 2001/600, reg 44(4).
5 SI 2001/600, reg 44(5).

The President may, if he thinks fit, at any stage of the appeal proceedings, **8.14.3**
order that a statement of a party's case should be struck out or amended on the grounds that it is scandalous, frivolous or vexatious[1]. However, before making such an order, the President must give to the party against whom he proposes to make the order a notice inviting representations and he shall consider any representations duly made[2]. The notice must inform the party against whom the order is proposed that he may, within a specified period (not being less than five working days), either make written representations or request an opportunity to make oral representations[3]. Representations are duly made if written representations are made within the specified period and, in the case or oral representations, the party requests an opportunity to make them within the specified period[4].

1 Special Educational Needs Tribunal Regulations 2001, SI 2001/600, reg 44(6).
2 SI 2001/600, reg 44(7).
3 SI 2001/600, reg 44(8)(a).
4 SI 2001/600, reg 44(8)(b).

The power to strike out has been considered in two cases: *White v Aldridge* **8.14.4**
QC and London Borough of Ealing[1] and *G v London Borough of Barnet and Aldridge QC*[2].

White was a complicated case involving appeals in respect of twin boys and appeals on points of law to the High Court. Whilst the appeal against the decision of the first tribunal was being pursued, the LEA amended the statements in accordance with the decision of the first tribunal. The mother appealed again, but her appeal was struck out as the only 'new' evidence was contained in one fax. The Court of Appeal held that the second tribunal had been correct to strike out the appeal. The tribunal had the power to prevent the re-litigation of issues already decided and, although the power to strike out should be used with care and discretion and with an element of flexibility, that power could be used in such circumstances.

In *G*, the parents had made one unsuccessful appeal, but the LEA then issued a fresh statement. The parent appealed, but, on the application of the LEA, the President struck it out. Collins J held, following *White*, that there should be flexibility in the way that a tribunal approached strike outs. In this case, there was fresh speech therapy advice and advice about the child's Jewishness. The test which should have been adopted was, was there any evidence that the provisions required to meet the child's special educational needs had changed? Holding that there was, the court quashed the striking out of the appeal.

1 [1999] ELR 150, CA.
2 [1999] ELR 161, QBD.

8.14.5 A number of applications for striking out have been considered by the Tribunal and reported in the Digests of Decisions. In *Decision 96/26*[1], the parents had been unable to obtain the Secretary of State's approval for the school they wished their child to attend. The President applied to strike out the appeal as the tribunal did not therefore have jurisdiction to name the school. In *Decision 96/27*[2] an LEA tried to obtain a striking out on the rather odd grounds that the child had a record of non-attendance. The Tribunal, rightly, held that this did not render the appeal frivolous or vexatious. In *Decision 97/29*[3], a parent lodged a second appeal which the tribunal considered was being used as an inappropriate way to reopen questions settled at an earlier appeal. The second appeal was therefore struck out as frivolous or vexatious. In *Decision 24/98*[4] parents had appealed against the contents of their child's statement two years before and appealed on substantially the same grounds. The LEA applied for the appeal to be struck out, but the parents had moved house in the meantime and the child attended a different school. The Tribunal rejected the application and held that the appropriateness of the provision was a central issue and that provision in two schools was seldom identical. A potentially important decision on the use of striking out appears in *Decision 59/00*[5]. The child's statement named a school favoured by his parents, but added that his needs could be met at a nearer school, therefore his parents would be responsible for transport costs. The LEA applied for the appeal to be struck out because the parents were appealing against having to pay transport costs (ie non-educational provision). The appeal was not struck out because it nonetheless raised a ground within jurisdiction, namely whether a nearer school could make appropriate education provision.

1 [1996] ELR 342.
2 [1996] ELR 342.
3 [1997] ELR 526.
4 [1998] ELR 448.
5 [2001] ELR 120.

Preparing for an appeal hearing

8.15

If the parent amends their notice of appeal during the case statement period, the Secretary should send a copy of the amendment forthwith to the LEA[1]. At the end of the case statement period, the Secretary shall send a copy of each party's statement of case and written evidence to the other party[2]. Similarly, the Secretary shall forthwith send copies of any amendments, supplementary statements, written representations, written evidence (other than written evidence which is submitted at the hearing) or other documents received from a party after the end of the case statement period to the other party[3].

8.15.1

1 Special Educational Needs Tribunal Regulations 2001, SI 2001/600, reg 19(1)(a).
2 SI 2001/600, reg 19(1)(b).
3 SI 2001/600, reg 19(1)(c).

If a notice of appeal, a statement of case, amendment, supplementary statement, written representation, written evidence or other document is delivered after the time prescribed or set by order for its delivery, the Secretary shall not send a copy of it to the other party, unless the President extends the time limit[1].

8.15.2

1 Special Educational Needs Tribunal Regulations 2001, SI 2001/600, reg 19(2).

If a notice of appeal is amended so that a parent seeks an order that a maintained school, other than the one already named in the child's statement, or a different maintained school to the one previously stated, be named in the statement, the Secretary shall give the headteacher of that school notice of the appeal, providing him or her with the name and date of birth of the child and the name of the LEA, unless the school is maintained by that LEA[1].

8.15.3

1 Special Educational Needs Tribunal Regulations 2001, SI 2001/600, reg 19(3).

The Secretary shall[1], at any time after he has received notice of appeal:

8.15.4

(a) ask each party:
    (i)   whether or not the party intends to attend the hearing;
    (ii) whether the party wishes to be represented at the hearing and, if so, the name of the representative;
    (iii) whether the party wishes the hearing to be in public;
    (iv) whether the party intends to call witnesses and, if so, the names of them;
    (v) whether the party or a witness will require the assistance of an interpreter;
(b) enquire of the parent whether he wishes any persons (other than his representative or a witness) to attend the hearing, if the hearing is in private, and, if so, the name of such persons; and
(c) inform each party of the fact that the Tribunal may exclude from the hearing a representative or a witness whom a party omitted to name, without reasonable cause[2].

1 Special Educational Needs Tribunal Regulations 2001, SI 2001/600, reg 20.
2 SI 2001/600, 30(4)(c).

In response to this enquiry, the parent shall give the Secretary the information requested[1]. If the parent does not intend to attend or be represented at

8.15.5

the hearing he may, not less than five working days before the hearing, send to the Secretary additional written representations[2]. Similarly, the LEA shall give the Secretary the information requested[3] and if it does not intend to be represented at the hearing, it may, not less than five working days before the hearing, send to the Secretary additional representations[4].

1 Special Educational Needs Tribunal Regulations 2001, SI 2001/600, reg 11(1).
2 SI 2001/600, reg 11(2).
3 SI 2001/600, reg 16(2).
4 SI 2001/600, reg 16(3).

8.15.6 Where more than one appeal relates to the same child or requires a decision on substantially the same issue, the President may order that the appeals be heard together[1]. Such an order can only be made if it appears to be just and convenient to do so. Before an order is made, the parties to each appeal must be given the opportunity to be heard[2].

1 Special Educational Needs Tribunal Regulations 2001, SI 2001/600, reg 27(1).
2 SI 2001/600, reg 27(3).

8.16 Directions

8.16.1 Although the ability to request, and the power to give, directions has been relatively rarely used in the past, the President may, on the application of a party, or on his own initiative, at any time before the hearing give such directions as will enable the parties to prepare for the hearing or to assist the tribunal to determine the issues[1]. The directions are not, however, without limit[2]. The President may give directions:

(a) requiring any party to provide in or with that party's statement of case, such particulars or supplementary statements as may reasonably be required for the determination of the appeal[3];
(b) requiring a party to deliver to the tribunal any document or other material which the tribunal may require and which is in the power of that party to deliver[4]. It is, however, provided that the President shall impose a condition on the supply of a copy of any document or other material delivered in compliance with such a direction that the party receiving it shall use it only for the purposes of the appeal[5]. The President may require a written undertaking to observe such a condition before supplying a copy[6];
(c) granting to a party such disclosure or inspection of documents (including the taking of copies) as might be granted under the Civil Procedure Rules 1998[7]. Any person who without reasonable cause fails to comply with requirements regarding disclosure or inspection of documents shall be liable on summary conviction to a fine not exceeding level 3 on the standard scale[8].

1 Special Educational Needs Tribunal Regulations 2001, SI 2001/600, reg 21(1).
2 SI 2001/600, regs 21(1), 23 and 24.
3 SI 2001/600, reg 23.
4 SI 2001/600, reg 24(1)(a).
5 SI 2001/600, reg 24(1)(b).
6 SI 2001/600, reg 24(1)(c).
7 SI 2001/600, reg 24(2).
8 EA 1996, s 336.

If a party wishes to request directions, the application must be made in writ- **8.16.2**
ing to the Secretary. Unless it is accompanied by the written consent of the
other party, the Secretary shall serve a copy of the application on the other
party. If the other party objects to the directions sought, the President shall
consider the objection and, if he considers it necessary for the determination
of the application, shall give the parties an opportunity of appearing before
him[1]. If, in the opinion of the President, there would not be a reasonable
time before the hearing of the substantive appeal to comply with a direction
for which a party applies, the President shall refuse the application. The
practical consequence of this being that a party should consider and, if necessary apply for, directions at the earliest possible opportunity during the
proceedings.

1 Special Educational Needs Tribunal Regulations 2001, SI 2001/600, reg 21(2).

Any direction issued must: **8.16.3**

(a) include a statement of the possible consequences for the appeal of a
     party's failure to comply within the time allowed by the President[1]. The
     possible consequences[2] are that the tribunal may:
     (i) where the parent is the party in default, dismiss the appeal without
          a hearing;
     (ii) where the LEA is the party in default, determine the appeal without
          a hearing; or
     (iii) hold a hearing (without notifying the party in default) at which
          the party in default is not present or represented or, where the
          parties have already been notified of the hearing, direct that nei-
          ther the party in default nor his representative nor any person
          who is to give evidence on his behalf will be entitled to attend the
          hearing[3];
(b) if the direction relates to the disclosure and/ or inspection of docu-
     ments, contain a reference to the fact that, under s 336 of the EA 1996,
     any person who without reasonable cause fails to comply with the
     requirements regarding disclosure or inspection of documents shall be
     liable on summary conviction to a fine not exceeding level 3 on the
     standard scale[4]; and
(c) unless the person to whom the direction is addressed had an opportu-
     nity to object to the direction, or he gave his written consent to the
     application for it, contain a statement to the effect that he may apply to
     the President to vary or set aside the direction[5].

1 Special Educational Needs Tribunal Regulations 2001, SI 2001/600, reg 21(4)(a).
2 For examples of appeals where the parties have not complied with directions, see eg
   Decisions 96/73 [1996] ELR 435, *97/20* [1997] ELR 267 and *97/31* [1997] ELR 525.
3 SI 2001/600, reg 25.
4 SI 2001/600, reg 21(4)(b).
5 SI 2001/600, reg 21(4)(c).

If a person receiving a direction did not have the opportunity to object and **8.16.4**
did not consent to the application, that party may apply to the President, by
notice to the Secretary, to vary it or to set it aside. The President cannot,
however vary or set it aside without first notifying the other party and considering any representations that party may make[1].

1 Special Educational Needs Tribunal Regulations 2001, SI 2001/600, reg 22.

8.17 Witness summons

8.17.1 The President may require any person in England and Wales to attend as a witness at a hearing of an appeal. He does this by summons, which must specify the time and place of the hearing. At the hearing, which the person is summonsed to attend, the witness can be required to answer any questions or produce any documents or other material in his custody or under his control which relate to any matter in question in the appeal[1].

1 Special Educational Needs Tribunal Regulations 2001, SI 2001/600, reg 26(1).

8.17.2 There are, however, certain restrictions on the President's power to issue a summons. No person can be compelled to give any evidence or produce any document or other material that he could not be compelled to give or produce at a trial of an action in a court of law[1]. In exercising the power, the President is obliged to take into account the need to protect any matter that relates to intimate personal or financial circumstances or consists of information communicated or obtained in confidence[2]. No person can be required to attend unless they have been given at least five working days' notice of the hearing or the person informs the President that he is prepared to accept lesser notice[3]. The necessary expenses of the witness attending the hearing must also be tendered with the summons[4].

1 Special Educational Needs Tribunal Regulations 2001, SI 2001/600, reg 26(1)(a).
2 SI 2001/600, reg 26(1)(b).
3 SI 2001/600, reg 26(1)(c).
4 SI 2001/600, reg 26(1)(d).

8.17.3 The summons must contain reference to the fact that if the witness fails without reasonable excuse to comply with it, he shall be liable on summary conviction to a fine not exceeding level 3 on the standard scale[1]. The summons must also inform the witness that they can apply to vary it or set it aside[2].

1 Special Educational Needs Tribunal Regulations 2001, SI 2001/600 and s336 EA 1996, reg 26(3)(a).
2 SI 2001/600, reg 26(4).

8.17.4 In order to obtain a witness summons, a party must apply in writing to the Secretary at least eight working days before the hearing, or later, if the person to be summonsed consents in writing[1].

1 Special Educational Needs Tribunal Regulations 2001, SI 2001/600, reg 26(2).

8.17.5 The recipient of the summons may apply to the President, by notice in writing to the Secretary, to vary it or set it aside. The President may not, however, do so without first notifying the party who applied for the summons and considering any representations he may make[1].

1 Special Educational Needs Tribunal Regulations 2001, SI 2001/600, reg 26(4).

8.18 Notice of appeal hearing

8.18.1 Unless the appeal is to be determined without a hearing[1], the Secretary shall, after consultation with the parties, fix the time and place of the hearing and send to each party a notice giving those details[2]. This notice must be sent not less than five working days before the date fixed for the hearing of a preliminary matter or not less than ten working days before the date fixed for the substantive hearing[3]. A shorter notice period can, however, be agreed by the parties[4]. The date and place of hearing can be altered by the tribunal, provided that the Secretary must give the parties not less than five working days notice, unless the parties agree a shorter time. Unless the parties agree, the new date cannot be before the original date[5].

1   See 8.19.4.
2   Special Educational Needs Tribunal Regulations 2001, SI 2001/600, reg 28(1).
3   SI 2001/600, reg 28(2)(a) and (b).
4   SI 2001/600, reg 28(1)(c).
5   SI 2001/600, reg 28(4).

With the notice of hearing, the Secretary must include in or with the notice: **8.18.2**

(a)   information and guidance as to attendance at the hearing of the parties and witnesses, the bringing of documents and the right of representation or assistance; and

(b)   an explanation of the possible consequences of non-attendance and the rights to make representations in writing by (i) the parent if he does not attend and is not represented; and (ii) the LEA if it is not represented and if it has submitted a statement of case, unless it confirms it does not resist the appeal or has withdrawn its opposition[1].

1   Special Educational Needs Tribunal Regulations 2001, SI 2001/600, reg 28(3).

The appeal hearing and the determination of appeals   8.19

At the hearing, the parent may conduct his case himself (with assistance   **8.19.1** from one person if he wishes) or may appear and be represented by one person whether or not legally qualified. If, however, the parent requests, and the President gives permission before the hearing or the tribunal gives permission at the hearing, the parent may obtain assistance or be represented by more than one person[1].

1   Special Educational Needs Tribunal Regulations 2001, SI 2001/600, reg 12(6).

The LEA may be represented by one person whether or not legally qualified.   **8.19.2** If, however, the President gives permission before the hearing or the tribunal gives permission at the hearing, the LEA may be represented by more than one person[1]. The right of representation has caused some dispute between practitioners and the President and guidance was issued by the President in respect of the attendance at the hearing of solicitors and counsel[2] and in respect of attendance generally[3].

1   Special Educational Needs Tribunal Regulations 2001, SI 2001/600, reg 16(1).
2   Special Educational Needs Tribunal President's Statement – Attendance of Solicitors with Counsel [1996] ELR 280.
3   Special Educational Needs Tribunal President's Statement – Attendance at Hearings [1997] ELR 141.

A hearing will normally take place. The tribunal may, however, determine   **8.19.3** an appeal or any particular issue without a hearing if the parties so agree in writing or the LEA has failed to deliver its statement of case or a party has failed to comply with a direction[1]. Before disposing of an appeal in the absence of a party, the tribunal must, however, consider any representations made by that party[2].

1 Special Educational Needs Tribunal Regulations 2001, SI 2001/600, reg 29(1).
2 SI 2001/600, regs 29(2) and 31(2).

8.19.4 The hearing should be in private unless both parties have agreed or the President before, or the tribunal at, the hearing orders that it be heard in public[1]. The people who may be present at the hearing are as follows:

(a) the parties and their permitted representatives and witnesses;
(b) the child;
(c) any person the parent has requested to attend the hearing, unless the President has refused permission for that person to attend (if the parent has named more than two persons, only two will be entitled to attend, unless the President has given permission before the hearing, or the tribunal gives permission at the hearing[2]);
(d) a parent of the child who is not a party to the appeal ('parent' here has the wide definition[3]);
(e) the clerk to the tribunal and the Secretary;
(f) the President and a member of the chairmen's or lay panel (as observers);
(g) a member of the Council on Tribunals;
(h) a person undergoing training as a member of the chairmen's or lay panel or as a clerk to the tribunal;
(i) a person acting on behalf of the President in the training or supervision of clerks to tribunals; and
(j) an interpreter[4].

1 Special Educational Needs Tribunal Regulations 2001, SI 2001/600, reg 30(1).
2 SI 2001/600, reg 30(9).
3 See 8.6.
4 SI 2001/600, reg 30(2).

8.19.5 The tribunal may also permit, with the consent of the parties or their representatives, any other person to attend the hearing[1], although this power is rarely used. With the exception of the parties, the child and his parent, the clerk and an interpreter, none of the persons appearing in this list may take any part in the hearing or, where able to remain, in the tribunal's deliberations[2].

1 Special Educational Needs Tribunal Regulations 2001, SI 2001/600, reg 30(3).
2 SI 2001/600, reg 30(6).

8.19.6 As a reassurance to parties, it is unlikely that all on this list will ever attend one appeal. Normally, the tribunal strives to keep the hearing as informal and unintimidating as possible; indeed, the tribunal must, as far as appears to be appropriate, seek to avoid formality in its proceedings[1]. What this regulation does allow is the attendance of a certain number of specified individuals to what would otherwise be a closed, private hearing either in the interests of the appeal itself or in the wider interests of training members and clerks of tribunals. It does not, however, ordinarily permit solicitors acting for the parties to accompany the barristers they have instructed[2] nor does it allow LEAs or advocacy groups to send staff as observers and gain experience of a tribunal.

1 Special Educational Needs Tribunal Regulations 2001, SI 2001/600, reg 32(2).
2 Special Educational Needs Tribunal President's Statement – Attendance of Solicitors with Counsel [1996] ELR 280.

The tribunal may permit the child to give evidence and to address the tribunal[1]. This provision reflects the greater emphasis in the 2001 Regulations on the rights of the child[2]. Caution must, however, be exercised when a child gives evidence. In one case[3], the child witness was a boy of eight with specific learning difficulties. A witness for the parents insisted that the boy give evidence and asked him questions about being bullied at school. The child became tearful and distressed. The tribunal had to ask that the questioning be ended and that the child leave the hearing. The tribunal may also permit a parent, who is not a party to the appeal, to address the tribunal on the subject matter of the appeal[4]. Recorded evidence may be permitted and it is considered to be essentially the same as written evidence[5]. Parties may therefore submit recorded evidence at the same time as they are entitled to submit written evidence. Five copies of the tape must be supplied as the Tribunal does not have the facilities to copy such material nor will it guarantee to have facilities available at hearings to allow recorded evidence to be played[6]. **8.19.7**

1 Special Educational Needs Tribunal Regulations 2001, SI 2001/600, reg 30(7).
2 See also the requirement on the LEA to state in its case what it believes the views of the child are or the reasons why it has not ascertained those views: Special Educational Needs Tribunal Regulations 2001, SI 2001/600, reg 13(2).
3 *Digest of Decisions (Number 16) 37/00* [2000] ELR 631.
4 SI 2001/600, reg 30(8).
5 See Special Educational Needs Tribunal President's Statement – Recorded Evidence [1997] ELR 276.
6 Special Educational Needs Tribunal President's Statement – Recorded Evidence [1997] ELR 276.

The tribunal may exclude from the hearing: **8.19.8**

(a) a person whose conduct has disrupted or is likely to disrupt the hearing;
(b) a person, including the child, whose presence is likely to make it difficult for any person to adduce the evidence or make the representations necessary for the proper conduct of the appeal; and
(c) a representative or witness whom a party omitted to name, without reasonable cause, in response to the standard enquiry from the Secretary[1].

1 Special Educational Needs Tribunal Regulations 2001, SI 2001/600, reg 30(4).

In order to reach its decision, the tribunal must order all persons to leave the hearing room, other than the members of the tribunal and the clerk, the member of the Council on Tribunals, members and 'trainee' members and clerks of the Tribunal[1]. When considering questions of procedure, the tribunal may ask all persons, with the same exceptions, to leave the room[2]. **8.19.9**

1 Special Educational Needs Tribunal Regulations 2001, SI 2001/600, reg 30(5)
2 SI 2001/600, reg 30(5).

8.19.10   If a party fails to attend or be represented at the hearing and he has been properly notified, the tribunal may:

(a) unless it is satisfied that there is sufficient reason for his absence, hear and determine the appeal in the party's absence; or

(b) adjourn the hearing[1].

Even if a party does not appear, the tribunal are still required to consider any representations in writing submitted by that party during the course of the appeal[2].

1 Special Educational Needs Tribunal Regulations 2001, SI 2001/600, reg 31(1).
2 SI 2001/600, reg 31(2).

8.19.11   The procedure at the hearing is a matter for the tribunal and strict rules of procedure are not set down in the Regulations. The tribunal should conduct the hearing in such manner as it considers most suitable to the clarification of issues and generally to the just handling of the proceedings. The tribunal shall determine the order in which the parties are to be heard and the issues determined[1].

1 Special Educational Needs Tribunal Regulations 2001, SI 2001/600, reg 32(3).

8.19.12   This flexibility enables the tribunal to deal with different appeals in different ways, although this may appear to lead to some inconsistencies in procedure between tribunals. In some hearings the tribunal has expected one party to present its case and witnesses, followed by the other party, whereas other tribunals identify key issues beforehand and expect each party and witnesses to concentrate on those. This can result in the parties having to prepare two or more different presentations. The principle of flexibility is not wrong, indeed it has tremendous benefits for appellants and their children, but a way of avoiding the parties 'not knowing' what procedure is to be adopted could be for tribunals to let the parties know in advance, rather than waiting to the start of the hearing. Whatever is adopted, however, the chairman must explain at the beginning of the hearing the order of proceedings which the tribunal proposes to adopt[1].

1 Special Educational Needs Tribunal Regulations 2001, SI 2001/600, reg 32(1).

8.19.13   The tribunal may, if it is satisfied that it is just and reasonable to do so, permit:

(a) the parent to rely on grounds not stated in his notice of appeal or statement of his case and to adduce evidence not presented to the LEA before or at the time it took the disputed decision; and

(b) the LEA to rely on grounds not specified in its statement of case[1].

Again, experience suggests that the Tribunal, by and large (again, there is reported to be some inconsistency) are fairly strict in allowing such amendments to the parties' cases.

1 Special Educational Needs Tribunal Regulations 2001, SI 2001/600, reg 32(4).

8.19.14   Given the time it takes for a hearing to be arranged and the educational changes that may occur in relatively short periods, in many cases, parties have sought to introduce evidence close to and/or at the hearing. Under the

1995 Regulations[1], such evidence could only be accepted by the tribunal in exceptional circumstances. This led to argument and again apparent inconsistencies between tribunals over what were exceptional cases.

1   Special Educational Needs Tribunal Regulations 1995, SI 1995/3113.

To address this issue, the 2001 Regulations make express provision for the acceptance of late evidence. Now, at the beginning of the hearing, unless the tribunal, after considering any representations from the other party, is of the opinion that it would be contrary to the interests of justice, a party may submit further written evidence so long as: **8.19.15**

(a) the evidence was not, and could not reasonably have been, available to that party before the end of the case statement period; and
(b) a copy of the evidence was sent or delivered to the Secretary and to the other party to arrive at least five working days before the hearing; and
(c) the extent and form of the evidence is such that, in the opinion of the tribunal, it is not likely to impede the efficient conduct of the hearing[1].

1   Special Educational Needs Tribunal Regulations 2001, SI 2001/600, reg 33(1) and (2).

If, however, a party cannot meet these requirements, the tribunal may give permission for that evidence to be adduced at the hearing if the tribunal is of the opinion that: **8.19.16**

(a) the case is wholly exceptional; and
(b) unless the evidence is admitted, there is a serious risk of prejudice to the interests of the child[1].

1   Special Educational Needs Tribunal Regulations 2001, SI 2001/600, reg 33(3).

In the course of the hearing, the parties shall be entitled to give evidence, to call witnesses, to question any witness and to address the tribunal both on the evidence, including the written evidence submitted before the hearing, and generally on the subject matter of the appeal[1].   **8.19.17**

1   Special Educational Needs Tribunal Regulations 2001, SI 2001/600, reg 34(1).

The Regulations provide, however, that neither party shall be entitled to call more than two witnesses to give evidence orally unless the President has given permission before the hearing or the tribunal gives permission at the hearing[1].   **8.19.18**

1   Special Educational Needs Tribunal Regulations 2001, SI 2001/600, reg 34(1).

If there is a difficulty and permission cannot be obtained, a party should ensure that the witness who is not permitted to attend provides a written statement. Evidence before the tribunal can be given by written statement as well as orally, although the tribunal may at any stage require the personal attendance of a maker of a written statement[1]. However, a party needs to be aware at an early stage of which witnesses they intend to call as a written statement can only be given in evidence if it was submitted with the notice of appeal, the statement of case or it meets the conditions for late evidence[2].   **8.19.19**

1   Special Educational Needs Tribunal Regulations 2001, SI 2001/600, reg 34(2).
2   See 8.19.15.

8.19.20   Rules of hearsay and other court rules of evidence do not strictly apply. The tribunal may receive evidence of any fact which appears to the tribunal to be relevant[1]. The tribunal may require, though does not usually, any witness to give evidence on oath or affirmation or may require any written statement to be given by statement of truth[2].

1 Special Educational Needs Tribunal Regulations 2001, SI 2001/600, reg 34(3).
2 SI 2001/600, reg 34(4).

Adjournments

8.19.21   The tribunal may from time to time adjourn the hearing[1]. Tribunals are not however keen to allow adjournments and usually will only do so in exceptional circumstances. However, on occasion this position has been too severe and in a couple of cases the courts have held that tribunals have been too strict in declining to grant adjournments.

1 Special Educational Needs Tribunal Regulations 2001, SI 2001/600, reg 35(1).

8.19.22   In *LEA v Royal Borough of Kensington and Chelsea*[1], there was some confusion on the part of the parent who thought that a hearing would be to consider preliminary issues and not the substantive hearing. She had intended to call a witness from Norway to the substantive hearing. As the parent only found out about the true nature of the hearing seven days beforehand, it was impossible to secure the witness' attendance. She therefore applied for an adjournment which was refused. On appeal, the court considered that the evidence of the witness was of great importance as it related to a central issue in the appeal. In the interests of fairness, an adjournment should have been allowed so that the expert could have attended.

1 [1997] ELR 155, QBD.

8.19.23   In *R v Headteacher and Governing Body of Crug Glas School, ex p W*[1], the circumstances were even more unusual. The parent had engaged an educational psychologist to appear for her and to argue that Crug Glas was not an appropriate school for her child. Unknown to the parent, though, the educational psychologist had been a former headteacher of the predecessor school to Crug Glas and had given an undertaking not to have any contact with the school. The school therefore refused the educational psychologist permission to visit to assess it as an appropriate placement for the child. This meant that the educational psychologist could not provide a report in time for the scheduled hearing of the appeal. The parent therefore applied for an adjournment. This was refused on the basis that the tribunal would not become involved in the preparation of a party's case. The court declined to overturn that decision. The parent therefore had the choice of going ahead with her original educational psychologist or to ask for an adjournment for the purpose of obtaining another report from an educational psychologist who would be allowed to visit the school.

1 [1999] ELR 484, QBD.

8.19.24   More recently, in *S v London Borough of Hounslow and Vassie*[1], the court quashed a tribunal's refusal to grant an adjournment. The parent had arranged respite care for her child on the day of the hearing. Unfortunately, one week before the hearing she was told that the arrangements had fallen through. She then asked her neighbour to look after the child, but on the morning of the hearing, the neighbour pulled out. She then spoke to a social worker who offered to contact the tribunal. She did and told the parent that the appeal was adjourned. In the meantime, the parent's representative attended at the tribunal, which knew nothing of the adjournment. In the absence of the parent, who wanted to give evidence, the representative applied for an adjournment but this request was turned down. Tomlinson J held that it was highly desirable for the child's primary carer to attend the hearing, especially where the carer was the child's mother. The tribunal had also not been informed of the social worker's telephone call to the Tribunal offices. In these circumstances, the court considered that it was, or should have been, virtually inevitable that an adjournment should have been granted. There had therefore been procedural unfairness and the decision of the tribunal was quashed.

1 [2001] ELR 88, QBD.

When a hearing is adjourned, the tribunal may give directions to be com- **8.19.25**
plied with before or at the resumed hearing[1]. Such directions may require a
party to provide such particulars, evidence or statements as may reasonably
be required for the determination of the appeal[2]. If a party fails to comply
with a direction, the tribunal shall take account of that fact when determining the appeal or deciding whether to make an order for costs[3]. The
chairman may also announce provisional conclusions reached by the tribunal (although these are not a decision nor do they form part of the decision
of the tribunal)[4].

1 Special Educational Needs Tribunal Regulations 2001, SI 2001/600, reg 35(2(a).
2 SI 2001/600, reg 35(3).
3 SI 2001/600, reg 35(4).
4 SI 2001/600, reg 35(2).

The decision of the tribunal   8.20

If an agreed decision can be reached by the parties, the tribunal, if it thinks **8.20.1**
fit, may make a decision in the terms agreed by the parties[1].

1 Special Educational Needs Tribunal Regulations 2001, SI 2001/600, reg 42(2).

A decision of the tribunal may be taken by a majority. Where the tribunal **8.20.2**
consists of two members only, the chairman shall have a second or casting
vote[1]. The decision will not refer to the decision being made by a majority
nor can it make reference to the opinion of a minority[2]. The decision may be
given orally at the end of the hearing or, as is usually the case, reserved.
Whether there has been a hearing or not, the decision shall be recorded in
a document which, save in a case of a decision by consent, shall also contain,
or have annexed to it, a statement of the reasons (in summary form) for the
tribunal's decision. Each such document shall be signed and dated by the
chairman[3].

1 Special Educational Needs Tribunal Regulations 2001, SI 2001/600, reg 36(1).
2 SI 2001/600, reg 36(3).
3 SI 2001/600, reg 36(2).

8.20.3   As with many other tribunals and quasi-judicial and administrative bodies, the detail and specificity of the reasons given by tribunals have led to a number of challenges[1]. The general position on what reasons should be given was set out by Lord Clyde in *Stefan v General Medical Council*[2]:

> 'The extent and substance of the reasons must depend on the circumstances. They need not be elaborate or lengthy. But they should be such as to tell the parties in broad terms why the decision was reached. In many cases . . . a very few sentences should suffice to give such explanation as is appropriate to the particular situation.'

1 See, for example, *Brophy v Special Educational Needs Tribunal* [1997] ELR 291, QBD; *S v City and Council of Swansea and Confrey* [2000] ELR 315; *R v London Borough of Brent and Vassie, ex p AF* [2000] ELR 550; and *H v Kent County Council and the Special Educational Needs Tribunal* [2000] ELR 660.
2 [1999] 1 WLR 1293.

8.20.4   In the context of decisions made by tribunals, the position was most recently summarised by Grigson J in *H v Kent County Council and the Special Educational Needs Tribunal*[1]:

> 'The aggrieved party[2] should be able to identify the basis of the decision with sufficient clarity to be able to determine whether or not the Tribunal had gone wrong in law. Further, that statements of reasons should deal in short form with the substantial issues raised in order that the parties can understand why the decision has been reached; in other words, what evidence is rejected and what evidence is accepted.'[3]

Where substantial expert evidence is rejected, the tribunal should give reasons otherwise its decision will be quashed[4].

1 [2000] ELR 660, QBD.
2 *H v Kent County Council and the Special Educational Needs Tribunal* [2000] ELR 660 at p 669.
3 This might, however, conflict with the comments of Owen J in *R v London Borough of Brent and Vassie, ex p AF* [2000] ELR 550 that, whilst a claim that the tribunal's reasoning was not adequate might constitute a free-standing ground upon which a decision might be quashed in judicial review, it is not in an appeal to the High Court. Given the comments in other cases, for example, those of Latham J in *S v Special Educational Needs Tribunal and the City of Westminster* [1996] ELR 102, it is suggested that the summary of Grigson J is to be preferred.
4 See *J v Devon County Council and Strowger* [2001] EWHC Admin 958.

8.20.5   As soon as may be, the Secretary shall send a copy of the decision to each party, accompanied by guidance about the circumstances in which there is a right to appeal against the decision and the procedure to be followed[1]. Every decision is to be treated as having been made on the date on which a copy of the decision is sent to the parent (whether or not the decision was announced orally after the hearing)[2].

1 Special Educational Needs Tribunal Regulations 2001, SI 2001/600, reg 36(5).
2 SI 2001/600, reg 36(7).

8.20.6   One problem which arose under the old rules was the tribunal's lack of jurisdiction to enforce its orders. Parents would have to resort either to complaining to the Secretary of State or to the Ombudsman or else seek judicial review of the LEA's action, or more usually, inaction. To address this omission, the legislation now makes express provision for ensuring compliance with its orders. If the tribunal makes an order, the LEA concerned must comply with the order before the end of the prescribed period beginning with the date on which it is made[1]. The 'prescribed period' is[2] set out in regulations issued by the Secretary of State, which, in Wales, will require the agreement of the National Assembly[3]. Arguably, this does not add much to the previous provision for securing compliance with Tribunal orders, although now that it is expressly stated to be a duty imposed on an LEA to comply, it may make it easier for parents to obtain the action or provision required by the tribunal.

1 EA 1996, s 336A(1).
2 EA 1996, s 336A(2).
3 See Education (Special Educational Needs) (England) (Consolidation) Regulations 2001, SI 2001/3455, reg 25 and in Wales, Special Educational Needs Tribunal (Time Limits) (Wales) Regulations 2001, SI 2001/3982.

The time limits are[1] in respect of orders: **8.20.7**

(a) to make an assessment – the LEA must notify the parent it will make an assessment within four weeks[2];
(b) to make and maintain a statement – the LEA must make the statement within five weeks;
(c) to remit the case back to the LEA – the LEA shall take the action referred within two weeks;
(d) to amend a statement – the LEA shall serve an amendment notice within five weeks;
(e) to continue to maintain a statement – the statement shall be maintained with immediate effect[3];
(f) to continue to maintain and amend a statement – the statement will be maintained with immediate effect[4] and an amendment notice must be served within five weeks;
(g) to substitute the name of a school for that currently specified in the statement – the LEA shall specify the school within two weeks; and
(h) to dismiss an appeal against a decision to cease to maintain a statement – the LEA shall cease to maintain it immediately or on a date proposed by the LEA, which ever is the later.

1 Education (Special Educational Needs) (England) (Consolidation) Regulations 2001, SI 2001/3455, reg 25(2) and in Wales, Special Educational Needs Tribunal (Time Limits) (Wales) Regulations 2001, SI 2001/3982, reg 3(2).
2 In each case the period begins on the day after the issue of the Order: Education (Special Educational Needs) (England) (Consolidation) Regulations 2001, SI 2001/3455; reg 25(3) and in Wales, Special Educational Needs Tribunal (Time Limits) (Wales) Regulations 2001, SI 2001/3982, reg 3(3).
3 Although as the statement should have continued pending the appeal in any event (see EA 1996, Sch 27, para 11(5) and 8.5.2), this provision seems superfluous.
4 See note 3 above.

Costs and expenses   **8.21**

Normally, the tribunal should not make an order in respect of costs and   **8.21.1** expenses. It may, however, make such an order against:

(a) a party (including a parent who has withdrawn his appeal or an LEA which has withdrawn its opposition to an appeal) if it is of the opinion that that party has acted frivolously or vexatiously or that his or its

conduct in making, pursuing or resisting the appeal was wholly unreasonable;

(b) a party who has failed to attend or be represented at a hearing of which
he was duly notified;

(c) the LEA, where it has not delivered a statement of its case; or

(d) the LEA, where the tribunal considers that the disputed decision was
wholly unreasonable[1].

1 Special Educational Needs Tribunal Regulations 2001, SI 2001/600, reg 40(1).

8.21.2   An order may be made:

(a) as respects any costs and expenses incurred, or any allowances paid, or

(b) as respects the whole, or any part, of any allowance (other than
allowances paid to members of the tribunal) paid by the Secretary of
State to any person for the purposes of, or in connection with, his
attendance at the tribunal[1].

1 Special Educational Needs Tribunal Regulations 2001, SI 2001/600, reg 40(2).

8.21.3   An order may require one party to pay the other party either a specified sum
in respect of the costs and expenses incurred in connection with the proceedings or the whole or part of such costs as may be assessed, if not
otherwise agreed[1]. If an assessment is ordered, it shall allow the county
court to make a detailed assessment of fast track trial costs either on the
standard or indemnity basis, as the tribunal may specify, in accordance with
the Civil Procedure Rules 1998[2].

1 Special Educational Needs Tribunal Regulations 2001, SI 2001/600, reg 40(4).
2 SI 2001/600, reg 40(5).

8.21.4   No order can be made without first giving the party against whom the order
is sought, an opportunity of making representations[1].

1 Special Educational Needs Tribunal Regulations 2001, SI 2001/600, reg 40(3).

8.21.5   In *C v London Borough of Lambeth and the Special Educational Needs
Tribunal*[1], parents appealed to the court after their application for costs
against the LEA was refused. The basis of the original appeal was that the
LEA had refused to carry out an assessment of a child's special educational
needs. The LEA had made this decision on the basis that the child was following the Lovaas programme and was making good progress. The parents
appealed and, after the parents submitted further evidence, the LEA
reversed its decision. The appeal hearing went ahead, but the appeal was
withdrawn in view of the LEA's concession. The tribunal refused to award
the parents their costs. The tribunal concluded that in order for a decision
made by an LEA to be 'wholly unreasonable' it had to be 'unjustifiable and
unsustainable upon any view of the facts'. The court held that the tribunal
was entitled to conclude that the LEA's decision was not 'wholly unreasonable' and its decision was not perverse or wrong in law.

1 [1999] ELR 350, QBD.

8.21.6   The question of costs has also been considered in a number of appeals
reported in the Digests of Decisions. At one appeal[1], the parties agreed a
number of amendments to a statement, but when they were put in writing

the LEA denied it had agreed. The tribunal had to reconvene, only for the parties to concur with the agreed amendments, with very minor variations. The tribunal decided that the LEA had been frivolous or vexatious in denying that agreement had been reached and ordered the LEA to pay the parents' costs of the reconvened hearing. In *Decision 41/98*[2], the LEA refused to carry out an assessment until it received further evidence and a notice of appeal was issued. The parents claimed their costs. This was rejected as the tribunal felt that re-considering a decision in the light of new evidence was not wholly unreasonable behaviour by the LEA. In contrast, in *Decision 42/98*[3], costs were awarded against an LEA in respect of a decision to refuse to assess which the LEA subsequently reversed, where the LEA presented no evidence explaining its original decision or why it had changed its mind[4].

1 See *Decision 96/74* [1996] ELR 442.
2 [1998] ELR 452.
3 [1998] ELR 452.
4 For other decisions on costs where the tribunal did not consider that the LEA had acted wholly unreasonably, see *Decision 44/98* and *Decision 45/98* [1998] ELR 453.

Chapter 9

Challenging decisions of the Special Educational Needs and Disability Tribunal[1]

---

1 The Special Educational Needs Tribunal will be renamed the Special Educational Needs and Disability Tribunal from 1 September 2002.

Introduction

9.1

Where a party is dissatisfied with a decision of the Tribunal there are two principal methods of 'challenge' open to it: (a) requesting a review, or (b) appealing to the High Court on a point of law. Two other High Court methods, case stated and judicial review, may also be available, although, as shall be seen, they will rarely be appropriate.

REQUESTING A REVIEW

Overview of the review process

9.2

Review under the Special Educational Needs Tribunal Regulations 2001[1] (hereinafter 'the Regulations') is available both in respect of final decisions of the Tribunal[2] and also in respect of interlocutory decisions made by the President[3].

9.2.1

1 SI 2001/600.
2 SI 2001/600, reg 38.
3 SI 2001/600, reg 39.

Application and grounds for review

In respect of decisions of the President made prior to the hearing of an appeal, a party may apply to the Secretary of the Tribunal for the President to review his decision. Such an application must be made in writing stating the grounds in full and not later than 10 working days after the date on which the party was notified of the decision[1]. There is no power to extend this time limit. The President has the discretion to review and to set aside or vary any decision of his, provided that the conditions set out below[2] are met. The President himself may also, on his own initiative, review his decision[3] and set it aside or vary it, again, provided that the same conditions are met. If he proposes to do this, the President shall serve notice of that proposal on the parties not later than ten working days after they were notified of the decision[4].

9.2.2

1 Special Educational Needs Tribunal Regulations 2001, SI 2001/600, reg 39(2).
2 See 9.2.3.
3 SI 2001/600, reg 39(1).
4 SI 2001/600, reg 39(3).

9.2.3 The conditions which allow the President to review and set aside or vary a decision are that he is satisfied that:

(a) the decision was wrongly made as a result of an error on the part of the Tribunal staff;
(b) there was an obvious error in the decision; or
(c) the interests of justice so require[1].

1 Special Educational Needs Tribunal Regulations 2001, SI 2001/600, reg 39(1)(a) to (c).

9.2.4 The parties shall have the opportunity to be heard on any application or proposal for review and the review shall be determined by the President[1]. If any decision is set aside or varied, the Secretary of the Tribunal shall alter the entry in the records and shall notify the parties accordingly[2].

1 Special Educational Needs Tribunal Regulations 2001, SI 2001/600, reg 39(4).
2 SI 2001/600, reg 39(5).

9.2.5 A parent can also ask the President to review his decision not to extend the parent's time for delivering notice of appeal, even though such a parent is not a 'party' as the President's decision will mean there is no valid appeal. In this case the LEA is not entitled to be heard or notified[1].

1 Special Educational Needs Tribunal Regulations 2001, SI 2001/600, reg 39(6).

9.2.6 A party can also request a review of a tribunal's substantive decision. A party may therefore apply to the Secretary of the Tribunal for the decision of the tribunal to be reviewed on the grounds that:

(a) the decision was wrongly made as a result of an error on the part of the Tribunal staff;
(b) a party, who was entitled to be heard at the hearing, but failed to appear or be represented, had good and sufficient reason for failing to appear;
(c) there was an obvious error in the decision of the Tribunal; or
(d) the interests of justice require[1].

1 Special Educational Needs Tribunal Regulations 200, SI 2001/600, reg 37(1).

9.2.7 An application for a review must be made not later than ten working days after the date on which the decision was sent to the parties and be in writing stating the grounds for review in full[1]. There is no power to extend this time limit and it will be strictly enforced.

1 Special Educational Needs Tribunal Regulations 2001, SI 2001/600, reg 37(2).

9.2.8 An application for review may be refused by the President or by the chairman of the Tribunal which decided the case, if, in his opinion, it has 'no reasonable grounds of success'[1]. The test under the 1995 Regulations was that the application 'had no realistic prospect of success'[2] which suggests that the threshold for seeking a review may have been slightly relaxed. If, the application is not refused in this way, the application shall be determined, after the parties have had the opportunity to be heard, by the tribunal which made the original decision, or, where that is not practicable, by another tribunal appointed by the President[3].

1 Special Educational Needs Tribunal Regulations 2001, SI 2001/600, reg 37(3).

2 Special Educational Needs Tribunal Regulations 1995, reg 31(3).
3 SI 2001/600, reg 37(4).

The tribunal which made the original decision may on its own initiative pro-   **9.2.9**
pose to review its decision on any of the grounds set out in 9.2.6. If it
proposes to do so, the Secretary of the Tribunal shall serve notice on the
parties (although the Regulations, erroneously it is suggested, refer only to
service on the parents) not later than ten working days after the date on
which the decision was sent to them and the parties shall have an opportunity to be heard[1].

1 Special Educational Needs Tribunal Regulations 2001, SI 2001/600, reg 37(5).

If, following a request by a party or on the tribunal's own motion, the tri-   **9.2.10**
bunal is satisfied as to any of the grounds listed in 9.2.6, it shall order that
the whole or a specified part of the decision be reviewed and it may give
directions to be complied with before or at the hearing of the review[1]. A
direction may require a party to provide such particulars, evidence or statements as may reasonably be required for the determination of the review[2]. If
a party fails to comply with such a direction, the tribunal shall take account
of that fact when determining the review or deciding whether to make an
order for costs[3].

1 Special Educational Needs Tribunal Regulations 2001, SI 2001/600, reg 37(6).
2 SI 2001/600, reg 37(7).
3 SI 2001/600, reg 37(8).

The tribunal which then reviews all or part of a decision may: **9.2.11**

(a) by certificate under the chairman's hand, set aside or vary that decision
     and substitute such other decision as it thinks fit; or
(b) order a rehearing before the same or a differently constituted tribunal[1].

If the original decision is set aside or varied, the Secretary of the Tribunal
shall alter the entry in the records to conform to the chairman's certificate
and shall notify the parents accordingly[2].

1 Special Educational Needs Tribunal Regulations 2001, SI 2001/600, reg 38(1).
2 SI 2001/600, reg 38(2).

The power of review is therefore similar to that available to Employment   **9.2.12**
Tribunals and this was recognised by the President of the Tribunal in guidance issued in 1996[1]. The President made clear that the purpose of a review
is to reconsider a decision which is technically flawed and is not a substitute
for a right of appeal. The power to review should be exercised cautiously and
is appropriate in three types of case:

(a) where there has been a fundamental procedural error or lack of due
     process;
(b) fraud, appearing very soon after the decision; and
(c) simple cases of minor error or omission, 'very much as one would use
     the slip rule'.

Errors of law should be dealt with by way of appeal[2], but a procedural
mishap could be corrected by review. The tribunal should consider whether
it has jurisdiction, even if not raised by a party; where it does not do so, a

review is appropriate. The failings of a party's representatives, professional or not, however, will generally not constitute a ground for review but new factual evidence, becoming available immediately after the hearing, may be.

1 President's Guidance – Applications to Review Decisions [1996] ELR 278.
2 See 9.3ff.

Cases involving reviews

9.2.13   Examples of cases where the tribunal has considered reviewing its decisions can be found in the Digest of Decisions. In *Decision 37/99*[1], at the appeal the tribunal had ordered that the school of the parents' choice should be named. The LEA applied for a review on the grounds that the tribunal had been misled by the parent's evidence about the school. The tribunal accepted that the evidence was wrong, possibly due to confusion rather than dishonesty, and that it had been materially misled. The application for the review was allowed, although at the review, having heard further evidence about the school, the tribunal declined to vary its original order. In *Decision 38/99*[2], the parents had failed to comply with a direction from the President that they should submit details of the type of school they wished to see specified in Part 4 of their child's statement. As a result of this failure their appeal was dismissed. The parents asked for a review. As it appeared that a response to the direction had, in fact, been sent to the Tribunal within the time allowed, the tribunal agreed to hold a review. However, at the review the tribunal considered that the response which had been sent, nonetheless, failed to comply with the direction and, so, the decision to dismiss the appeal was confirmed. Most recently, in *Decision 36/00*[3], the tribunal had declined to order that the name of the school in the child's statement be changed on the grounds that the school the parents wanted cost unreasonably more than the school proposed by the LEA. The parents sought a review on later evidence that the school was prepared to reduce its fees so that it would cost no more than the LEA provision. The tribunal felt that it would not admit evidence which had become available only after the original hearing and which would result in the original case being re-argued. The application for a review was therefore dismissed.

1   [1999] ELR 540.
2   [1999] ELR 540.
3   [2000] ELR 339.

Correcting irregularities

9.2.14   Although not a review in itself, the Regulations also contain provision for the Tribunal to correct irregularities[1]. Any irregularity resulting from a failure to comply with any provision of the Regulations or of any tribunal direction before the tribunal has reached its decision shall not render the proceedings void[2]. Where, however, such an irregularity does come to the attention of the tribunal, the tribunal may, and shall if it considers that any person may have been prejudiced by the irregularity, give such directions as it thinks fit just before reaching its decision to cure or to waive the irregularity[3]. Clerical mistakes in any document recording the decision of the tribunal or decision of the President or errors arising in such documents from accidental slips or omissions may at any time be corrected by the chairman or the President (as the case may be) by certificate under his hand[4]. The Secretary of the

Tribunal shall, as soon as may be, send a copy of any corrected document containing reasons for the tribunal's decision to each party[5].

1 Special Educational Needs Tribunal Regulations 2001, SI 2001/600, reg 49.
2 SI 2001/600, reg 49(1).
3 SI 2001/600, reg 49(2).
4 SI 2001/600, reg 49(3).
5 SI 2001/600, reg 49(4).

CHALLENGE IN THE HIGH COURT

Appeal, case stated or judicial review?   **9.3**

The more popular methods of challenge are under s 11 of the Tribunals and   **9.3.1**
Inquiries Act (TIA) 1992, which allows a party to an appeal to either (a)
appeal to the High Court on a point of law, or (b) ask that the Tribunal state
a case for determination by the High Court. A number of applications for
judicial review have also been attempted, but, for the reasons set out below,
this approach has been discouraged by the courts.

When the Tribunal was first established there was uncertainty over the route   **9.3.2**
which could be used to bring a case before the High Court: should the challenge be by way of appeal[1], case stated[2] or judicial review[3]?

1 Under the then Rules of the Supreme Court (RSC), Ord 55, now Civil Procedure Rules
  1998 (CPR), Pt 52.
2 Under then RSC Ord 56, now CPR Pt 52 and Sch 1 RSC Ord 94.
3 Under then RSC Ord 53, now CPR Pt 54.

Judicial review

The use of judicial review was dismissed by the Court of Appeal in *R v*   **9.3.3**
Special Educational Needs Tribunal, ex p South Glamorgan County Council[1].
The judge at first instance had granted leave to the County Council to
apply for a judicial review, but the Court of Appeal quashed this decision on
the basis of the general principle that judicial review should not be granted
where an alternative remedy is available. An alternative remedy was available
under the TIA 1992 Act or RSC Order 55 (now CPR Part 52) and this
route should have been followed by the LEA. A similar decision was reached
in *R v Special Educational Needs Tribunal, ex p F*[2] in which Popplewell J,
although indicating that judicial review might be available in exceptional circumstances, held that if a statutory right of appeal was available it should be
exercised. One example of 'exceptional circumstances' appeared in *R v*
President of the Special Educational Needs Tribunal, ex p Hampshire County
Council[3], where leave to bring judicial review was granted to challenge the
issue by the President of a purported practice direction. The challenge did
not relate to an individual appeal, where judicial review may have been
inappropriate, but related to the general issue of the powers of the President
under the Regulations to issue directions. The challenge asserted that the
President had no power to issue directions, but could only issue guidance or
advice. There was never, however, a full hearing as the direction was withdrawn and replaced by guidance. Another case where judicial review was
permitted was *R v Special Educational Needs Tribunal, ex p Fisher*[4]. In that
case, concerning parents who had already appealed once to the High Court,

the Tribunal initially ordered that the High Court papers should be included in the papers to be considered by a freshly constituted tribunal. Ognall J held that that decision must be quashed and the High Court papers, given the circumstances of the case, should not be shown to the new tribunal.

1 [1996] ELR 326.
2 [1996] ELR 213.
3 1995 (unreported).
4 [1999] ELR 417.

Case stated

9.3.4 The decision in *Brophy v Special Educational Needs Tribunal*[1] settled the circumstances in which an application for a case to be stated could be used. Carnwath J held that the procedure under RSC Order 56[2] was not suitable where a full and final decision of the Tribunal was under challenge. The case stated procedure should only be available to challenge a decision made during the course of proceedings (for example, a Directions Order issued by the President) in order to ask the court to determine how an appeal should be dealt with. Appeal to the High Court alone should be used to challenge a final decision of the Tribunal. This decision was subsequently endorsed in *Altan-Evans v Leicester LEA and White*[3].

1 [1997] ELR 291.
2 Now CPR Pt 52 and Sch 1 RSC Ord 94, r 9.
3 [1998] ELR 237.

Appeal

9.3.5 A further issue which has been considered by the courts is whether, before issuing an appeal on a point of law, the dissatisfied party should apply for a review of the tribunal's decision under reg 38 of the 2001 Regulations[1]. In *South Glamorgan County Council v L and M*[2], Carnwath J considered that the purpose of the review provision was to enable the tribunal, with the assistance of the parties, further opportunity to get its decision right, without the delay and expense of an appeal. He held[3] that the power to review does not in terms provide for the tribunal to clarify its summary reasons, but felt that it did not exclude a request for elaboration of the reasons if one of the parties wished. It seemed, or so the judge thought, far more sensible for elaboration of the reasons to be asked for and given at that stage when the matter was fresh in minds, than to await a determination of a court some months later.

Then, and going further in potentially opening up review in far more cases than the President perhaps envisaged in his Statement[4], the judge suggested that if the concern from the party went further than a defect of reasons, and was that 'the decision had been reached on a radically flawed basis of fact . . . then that would seem an obvious case for review . . . The interests of justice would require the tribunal to look into the matter, and if it found the point justified, to review its decision. Again, it is much better that it should be done then, than months later, possibly after yet another hearing before a different tribunal'.

1 Special Educational Needs Tribunal Regulations 2001, SI 2001/600.
2 [1996] ELR 400.
3 [1996] ELR 400 at 414.
4 President's Guidance – Applications to Review Decisions [1996] ELR 278.

In *Bradford Metropolitan Council v A*[1], the LEA appealed to the High Court on a point of law. The parent respondents argued that the LEA should have applied for review first. Brooke J accepted that there would be some cases where it would be highly desirable for matters to be corrected or clarified by way of review, but held that this case raised a substantive point of law as to whether nursing care was capable, as a matter of law, of amounting to educational provision. He therefore felt that the LEA was entitled to pursue an appeal without first having requested a review. In any event the LEA had the statutory right of appeal which could not be refused. He distinguished judicial reviews where the court had a discretion to entertain the application from statutory appeals where the appellant had the right to appeal and the court the consequent obligation to entertain that appeal.

9.3.6

1 [1997] ELR 417.

The practice of the tribunal appears to follow the President's guidance and take an extremely cautious approach to the use of review, in contrast to Carnwath J's view in *South Glamorgan*. In summary, though, it would appear that, where the appellant wishes to allege a substantive point of law, he is entitled to appeal to the High Court without first requesting a review. If, however, the concern is that the tribunal's reasons require clarification or that the decision was reached on a radically flawed basis of fact, the party may wish to request a review. It would, however, be prudent, given the time limits involved and the likely reaction of the tribunal, to issue an appeal to the High Court in any event, if it is thought that some error of law is involved, to avoid the appeal time limit being missed because of the request for the review.

9.3.7

Appeal to the High Court

9.4

Parties to an appeal

An appeal on a point of law against a tribunal's decision can be brought by a person who was a party to the proceedings before the tribunal and is dissatisfied in point of law with the decision of the tribunal[1]. Appellants will therefore either be parents or the LEA. Where the dissatisfied party is the parent, the appeal to the High Court can likewise only be brought by the 'parent' of the child. A child cannot appeal on his own behalf. In *S v Special Educational Needs Tribunal and the City of Westminster*[2], the Court of Appeal held that the same rules which required the parents to be the appellant to an appeal before the Tribunal should also require the parents to be the appellants to an appeal to the High Court against decisions of the Tribunal. This decision was followed in *S and C v Special Educational Needs Tribunal*[3]. This distinction can be important when seeking public funding for the appeal as the financial means of the parents, not the child, will be assessed.

9.4.1

1 CPR Sch 1 RSC Ord 94 r 8.
2 [1996] ELR 228, CA.
3 [1997] ELR 242, QBD.

The definition of a 'parent' is, however, given a wide definition by s 576 of the Education Act (EA) 1996, which provides that a 'parent' in relation to a child or young person, includes any person '(a) who is not a parent of his, but

9.4.2

who has parental responsibility for him, or (b) who has care of him'. This therefore enables a foster-parent to appeal on behalf of his foster-child[1].

1 See *F v Humberside County Council* [1997] 1 All ER 183, [1997] ELR 12, QBD.

9.4.3 Where an appeal to the High Court is brought by a parent, an LEA should clearly be named as a respondent to the appeal. There was, however, initially some confusion over the position of the Tribunal itself. The procedure in the CPR[1] specifies that the appellant's notice commencing proceedings must be served on the chairman of the tribunal against whose decision the appeal is brought.

1 CPR Sch 1 RSC Ord 94 r 8(2) and Pt 52 PD 17.5.

9.4.4 In *S and C v Special Educational Needs Tribunal*[1], Latham J, overriding previous decisions to the contrary, held that the chairman of the tribunal was a proper respondent to an appeal brought by a parent and should be named. It was incorrect simply to bring an appeal naming the Tribunal. The chairman has however no right to appear or be heard, although he or she would be entitled to ask the court for permission to do so. Equally, the chairman cannot be compelled to give evidence and, normally, will only consider doing so where allegations are made against the conduct of the Tribunal. This has meant in practice that the Treasury Solicitor does not usually appear on behalf of the chairman and will only become involved, for example, where a breach of natural justice or bias is alleged[2]. The LEA is therefore normally left to defend the appeal to the High Court, even where it is alleged that the chairman misunderstood the parent's case or the rationality of the tribunal's decision is questioned[3].

1 [1997] ELR 242, QBD.
2 See, for example, *Joyce v Dorset County Council* [1997] ELR 26, QBD in respect of a case concerning alleged bias.
3 See *W-R v Solihull Metropolitan Borough Council and Wall (Chairman of the Special Educational Needs Tribunal)* [1999] ELR 528, QBD.

9.4.5 If the appeal is brought by the LEA the same considerations apply and the chairman of the tribunal should be served with the LEA's notice commencing the appeal[1]. In addition, the parent is also 'a party to the proceedings before the tribunal' and should, therefore, also be served with the notice, thus making the parent a respondent to the appeal. The child may, however, in light of comments made by Carnwath J in *South Glamorgan County Council v LEA and M*[2], be permitted to be represented at the hearing of that appeal. He accepted[3] that the parents were the proper respondents, but went on to say:

> 'However, it is clearly a decision which intimately affects the [child]. No doubt for this reason the Court of Appeal . . . also directed that [the child] be represented at the hearing. I take it that the power to do so . . . was based on the fact that [the child] is the person to whom the primary duty is owed. The practical significance of this point is that [the child] is eligible for legal aid, where as his parents, as I understand it, are not . . . It would be most unfortunate if, the LEA having sought as a matter of principle to challenge the decision of the tribunal, [the child] were deprived of legal representation to defend his interest.'

1 CPR Sch 1 RSC Ord 94 r 8(2).
2 [1996] ELR 400, QBD.
3 [1996] ELR 400, QBD at p 415.

Commencement of proceedings and time limits

A detailed discussion of the procedures for bringing an appeal to the High **9.4.6**
Court or requesting that a case be stated is outside the scope of this work.
This section will therefore simply briefly consider the rules for commencing
such proceedings (which are contained in CPR Part 52, the Practice
Direction (PD) to Part 52 and RSC Order 94 in Schedule 1 to the CPR),
concentrating mainly on those areas which have particular significance for
appeals against decisions of the Special Educational Needs and Disability
Tribunal.

Appeals to the High Court are commenced by an appellant's notice, which **9.4.7**
must be entered at the Administrative Court within 28 days after the date of
the Tribunal's decision[1]. The 28-day period is calculated from the date on
which notice of the decision was given to the appellant by the Tribunal.
After filing the notice at the Administrative Court, the appellant must serve
the notice on each respondent as soon as practicable and in any event not
later than seven days after it is filed[2]. As discussed above, the notice must be
served by the appellant on, in addition to the other party to the appeal
before the Tribunal, the chairman of the tribunal[3].

1 CPR Pt 52 PD 17.3.
2 CPR 52.4.
3 CPR Pt 52 PD 17.5.

The time limits are enforced rigorously. Extensions of time cannot be agreed **9.4.8**
by the parties; they can only be ordered by the court[1]. To obtain an extension of time[2], a party must show an acceptable explanation for the delay, but
even then, the court can refuse to exercise its discretion to extend time if the
delay is substantial or if to do so would cause significant prejudice to the
respondent. Neglect on the part of legal or lay, specialist advisers was not
considered to provide an acceptable explanation[3].

1 CPR 52.6(1).
2 Under CPR 52.6.
3 See *Phillips v Derbyshire County Council* [1997] ELR 461, QBD and *S and C v Special
   Educational Needs Tribunal* [1997] ELR 242, QBD.

In contrast, in *Ligouri v Salford and Special Educational Needs Tribunal*[1], the **9.4.9**
appellant's solicitor's holiday and delays caused by the long vacation were
held to provide a reasonable explanation, although the judge indicated that
his decision should not encourage appellants to seek an extension of time on
the ground that their application was delayed because of a delay in obtaining legal aid/ public funding. His decision should also be considered as an
exception to the general principle in light of *Phillips*[2] and *S and C v Special
Educational Needs Tribunal*[3] in which the judges clearly indicated that mistakes by advisers or other commitments could not per se amount to an
acceptable explanation. Delays caused by the failure of legal representatives to press the Legal Aid Board (now the Legal Services Commission) for
a response are also unacceptable[4].

1 [1997] ELR 455, QBD.
2 [1997] ELR 461, QBD.
3 [1997] ELR 242, QBD.
4 See *Wood v City of Westminster and Special Educational Needs Tribunal* (unreported).

9.4.10   In *Sage v South Gloucestershire County Council and Confrey*[1], an extension of time was granted, but that can be justified on the wholly exceptional circumstances. The appellant had been advised by a member of the Tribunal to seek a review of its decision which was eventually turned down, but only after the 28-day time limit had expired. The Judge found that this constituted a good explanation and considered that no prejudice arose by allowing the extension of time.

1   [1998] ELR 525, QBD.

9.4.11   The appellant's notice should be accompanied by a bundle of relevant documents[1], including the Tribunal's decision[2]. Other relevant documents may include any witness statement or affidavits in support of any application made as part of the appeal[3] and any other documents which the appellant considers necessary to enable the court to reach its decision at the hearing. Documents which are extraneous to the issues to be considered should be excluded[4]. Where bundles comprise more than 150 pages, only those documents which the court may reasonably be expected to pre-read should be included[5]. A full set of documents should be brought to the hearing for reference. The appellant should include a skeleton argument with the appellant's notice or should lodge and serve this on the respondents within 14 days of filing the appellant's notice[6]. Skeleton arguments should contain a numbered list of points stated in no more than a few sentences which should both define and confine the areas of controversy. Each point should be followed by references to any documentation on which the appellant proposes to rely[7]. The appellant should also consider what other information the court will need. This may include a list of persons who feature in the case or glossaries of technical terms. A chronology of relevant events will be necessary in most appeals. In the case of points of law, authorities relied on should be cited with reference to the particular pages where the principle concerned is set out[8].

1   CPR Pt 52 PD 5.6.
2   CPR Pt 52 PD 5.6(4).
3   CPR Pt 52 PD 5.6.
4   CPR Pt 52 PD 5.6(7).
5   CPR Pt 52 PD 5.8.
6   CPR Pt 52 PD 5.9.
7   CPR Pt 52 PD 5.10.
8   CPR Pt 52 PD 5.11.

9.4.12   The respondent may file at the Administrative Court a respondent's notice within 14 days of the date on which the respondent is served with the appellant's notice[1]. The respondent's notice must be served on the appellant and any other respondent as soon as practicable and in any event not later than seven days after it is filed[2].

1   CPR 52.5(1).
2   CPR 52.5(6).

9.4.13   The respondent is not required to file a respondent's notice and may therefore be a non-participating party to the appeal. Should, however, a respondent wish to uphold the decision of the Tribunal for additional or different reasons than those given by the Tribunal, that respondent must file and serve a respondent's notice[1]. If the respondent wishes to lodge any documents in addition to those filed by the appellant, they must be included in a supplemental bundle accompanying the respondent's notice[2].

1 CPR 52.5(2).
2 CPR Pt 52 PD 7.12.

A respondent, if it proposes to present arguments to the court at the hearing, should produce a skeleton argument[1]. This can be included in the respondent's notice or else can be filed and lodged within 21 days after service of the respondent's notice[2].   **9.4.14**

1 CPR Pt 52 PD 7.6.
2 CPR Pt 52 PD 7.7.

Interim relief

Part 52 allows parties to make interlocutory applications to the court[1]. This encompasses applications for extensions of time and, in the context of the Tribunal, has included applications for production of the notes of the Chairman of the Tribunal and/or a transcript of the hearing. It also addresses stays, amendments of appellants' notices and striking out.   **9.4.15**

1 CPR 52.6, 52.7 and 52.8.

The court may strike out the whole or any part of an appellant's notice or impose or vary conditions upon which an appeal may be brought[1]. The court will, however, only exercise these powers where there is a compelling reason for doing so[2].   **9.4.16**

1 CPR 52.9(1)(a) and (c).
2 CPR 52.9(2).

Unless the court orders otherwise, an appeal does not operate to stay any order or decision of the Tribunal[1]. Parties have, however, attempted to persuade the courts to grant stays, although without much success. In *Camden London Borough Council v Hadin and White*[2], the LEA sought a stay of the Tribunal's decision on the grounds that, if its appeal was successful, overturning the Tribunal's decision at a later stage could have an adverse effect on the child and disrupt their education. The court, although not dismissing the possibility of a stay, nonetheless held that in the circumstances a stay should not be granted. Similarly, in *R v Worcestershire County Council, ex p S*[3], albeit an application for judicial review, Popplewell J held that the court should not usurp the function of the LEA and that it therefore had no power to order the LEA to carry out a statutory assessment pending the outcome of court proceedings.   **9.4.17**

1 CPR 52.7.
2 [1996] ELR 430, QBD.
3 [1999] ELR 46, QBD.

Evidence

The evidence to be put before the court usually takes the form of written evidence in witness statements or affidavits. The hearing, as is proper for an appeal on a point of law, involves technical legal argument only and will not normally involve witnesses giving oral evidence.   **9.4.18**

9.4.19 The court will not usually receive evidence which was not before the tribunal as the appeal should be limited to a review of the decision of the tribunal[1]. Nonetheless, the court does have the power to order oral evidence or evidence which was not before the tribunal to be produced[2].

1 CPR 52.11(1) and (2).
2 CPR 52.11(2).

9.4.20 In the context of appeals from the Tribunal, issues have arisen over the production of the notes made by the chairman of the tribunal. Although it is not usually necessary for these notes to be available to the court, in some cases the parties have applied to the chairman of the tribunal for a signed copy of any note made by him of the proceedings and to furnish that copy for the use of the court. In *Staffordshire County Council v J and J*[1], the appellants applied for production of the chairman's notes. Collins J held that the chairman's notes or the transcript of the hearing[2] did not have to be produced in every case and their production would only be necessary if there was an issue, which depended upon the court having those notes. There is only likely to be such an issue if the ground of appeal was that the conclusion reached by the tribunal or a finding of fact was either based on no evidence or was contrary to the evidence put before the tribunal.

1 [1996] ELR 418, QBD.
2 The Tribunal's practice is now not to record the hearing so a transcript of the evidence is therefore no longer available.

9.4.21 In *Joyce v Dorset County Council*[1] Latham J stated that it would only be in very rare cases that a transcript would be necessary and the court would be unlikely to be impressed by any arguments based upon the transcript which have not been raised by the appeal. This judgment and Collins J's obiter comments in *Staffordshire County Council v J and J*[2] were adopted in *Fisher v Hughes and Hounslow London Borough Council*[3], although on the facts of the case an order was granted for the chairman to produce his notes and the transcript of proceedings. The test according to Keene J was 'was it necessary for the chairman's notes and/or the transcript to be produced in order to dispose properly of an issue raised in the appeal?'[4]. He continued:

> 'The courts are not going to be minded to make orders [for production of the chairman's notes and transcript of the hearing] if the purpose of it is really to conduct a fishing expedition and to add to the grounds or to seek to discover grounds on which an appeal can be pursued. None the less, there must remain a residuary situation, where it is necessary for the proper assessment of a ground raised that the notes and, in some cases, the transcript will be required.'[5]

1 [1997] ELR 26, QBD.
2 [1996] ELR 418, QBD.
3 [1998] ELR 475, QBD.
4 [1998] ELR 475 at p 477E.
5 [1998] ELR 475 at p 477H.

Disposal of appeals by consent

9.4.22 In a number of cases, it is possible for the appellant and respondents to resolve the issues raised in an appeal without the need for a full hearing. In other cases, having seen the respondent's notice, the appellant may be advised to withdraw his appeal.

Where an appellant does not wish to pursue an appeal, he may request that   **9.4.23**
the court make an order that his appeal be dismissed. Such a request must
contain a statement that the appellant is not a child or patient[1]. If such a
request is granted it will usually be on the basis that the appellant pays the
costs of the application or appeal[2]. If the appellant wishes to have the application or appeal dismissed without costs, his request must be accompanied
by a consent signed by the respondent or his legal representative stating that
the respondent is not a child or patient and consents to the dismissal of the
application or appeal without costs[3]. It must be remembered that, even if the
chairman of the tribunal has not submitted a respondent's notice, he is
nonetheless still a respondent to the appeal and will need to give his consent,
through the Treasury Solicitor, to its dismissal.

1 This will, of course, be possible as the child is not a party to the appeal – only his or her
   parent can be a party as such.
2 CPR Pt 52 PD 12.2.
3 CPR Pt 52 PD 12.3.

Where a settlement has been reached disposing of the appeal, the parties   **9.4.24**
may make a joint request to the court stating that none of them is a child or
patient, and asking that the application or appeal be dismissed by consent.
If the request is granted the application or appeal will be dismissed[1].

1 CPR Pt 52 PD 12.4.

The court will not make an order allowing an appeal unless satisfied that the   **9.4.25**
decision of the tribunal was wrong. Where the court is requested by all parties to allow an appeal, the court may consider the request on the papers. The
request should state that none of the parties is a child or patient and set out
the relevant history of the proceedings and the matters relied on as justifying
the proposed order and be accompanied by a copy of the proposed order[1].

1 CPR Pt 52 PD 13.1.

Powers available to the court at the hearing of the appeal

The court has wide powers when dealing with an appeal and has all the   **9.4.26**
powers possessed by the tribunal[1]. It may[2]:

(a) affirm, set aside, or vary any decision made by the tribunal;
(b) refer the case or any issue back for determination by the tribunal;
(c) order a new hearing to take place before the same or a differently con-
     stituted tribunal; and
(d) make an order for costs.

It may exercise it powers in relation to the whole or any part of the tribunal's
decision[3].

1 CPR 52.10(1).
2 CPR 52.10(2).
3 CPR 52.10(4).

The court has the power to draw any inference of fact which it considers jus-   **9.4.27**
tified on the evidence[1] although the court will be reluctant to do so given that
the tribunal and not the court will have heard the totality of the evidence[2].

1 CPR 52.11(4).
2 See, for example, *Ellison v Hampshire County Council* [2000] ELR 651, CA.

9.4.28 The court may allow the appeal if it determines that the tribunal's decision was:

(a) wrong; or

(b) unjust because of a serious procedural or other irregularity in the proceedings in the tribunal[1].

1 CPR 52.11(3).

9.4.29 In *R v Northamptonshire County Council, ex p M*[1], the court held that a failure by the Tribunal to give reasons is not in itself a ground to vitiate the decision (cf judicial review proceedings where it may be) unless it discloses an error of law. However, in *J v Devon County Council and Strowger*[2], the court held that where a tribunal had failed to give reasons for its rejection of substantial expert evidence, its decision should be quashed.

1 [1998] Ed CR 262, QBD.
2 [2001] EWHC Admin 958, QBD.

9.5 Case stated by the Tribunal

9.5.1 Although, as considered above[1], the procedure for stating a case is only appropriate in limited circumstances and is rarely used, for completeness, reference should be made to the process.

1 See 9.3.4.

9.5.2 The Tribunal may, of its own initiative or at the request of any party to proceedings before it, state in the course of proceedings before it, in the form of a special case for the decision of the High Court, any question of law arising in the proceedings[1]. Any party to proceedings before the tribunal who is aggrieved by the tribunal's refusal to state such a case may apply to the High Court for an order directing the tribunal to do so[2].

1 CPR Sch 1 RSC Ord 94 r 9(1).
2 CPR Sch 1 RSC Ord 94 r 9(2).

9.5.3 If the tribunal agrees to state a case, the case stated must be signed by the chairman or President[1]. The tribunal must serve the stated case on (a) the party who requested that the case be stated[2]. If the case is stated at the initiative of the tribunal, the tribunal must serve the stated case on those parties that it considers appropriate and give notice to every other party to the proceedings that the stated case has been served on the party named and on the date specified in the notice[3].

1 CPR Pt 52 PD 18.8.
2 CPR Pt 52 PD 18.9.
3 CPR Pt 52 PD 18.10.

9.5.4 The party on whom the stated case was served must file the appellant's notice and the stated case at the court and serve copies of the notice and stated case on (a) the tribunal, and (b) every party to the proceedings to which the stated case relates, within 14 days after the stated case was served on him.[1]. Where the tribunal has stated a case on its own initiative, the tribunal must file an appellant's notice and the stated case at the court and serve copies of those documents on those parties that it considers appropriate and give notice to every other party to the proceedings within 14 days after stating the case.[2].

1 CPR Pt 52 PD 18.11.
2 CPR Pt 52 PD 18.12.

Where a stated case has been served by the tribunal and the party on whom **9.5.5** the stated case was served does not file an appellant's notice, any other party may file an appellant's notice with the stated case at the court and serve a copy of the notice and the case within 14 days from the last day on which the party on whom the stated case was served.[1]. The court may amend the stated case or order it to be returned to the tribunal for amendment and may draw inferences of fact from the facts stated in the case[2].

1 CPR Pt 52 PD 18.13 and 18.14.
2 CPR Pt 52 PD 18.15.

Where a request for the tribunal to state a case has been refused, a party **9.5.6** may[1] apply to the court for an order directing the tribunal to state a case for determination by the court or refer a question of law to the court by way of case stated[2]. The application notice must contain the grounds of the application, the question of law on which it is sought to have the case stated and any reasons given by the tribunal for its failure to state a case[3]. The application notice must be filed at the court and served on the Secretary of the Tribunal and every party to the proceedings within 14 days after the party received notice from the tribunal of its refusal to state a case[4].

1 CPR Pt 52 PD 18.18.
2 The application must comply with and be made in accordance with CPR Pt 23.
3 CPR Pt 52 PD 18.19.
4 CPR Pt 52 PD 18.20.

In other respects, proceedings by way of case stated are governed by CPR **9.5.7** Part 52 and the Practice Direction to that Part in the same way as appeals on a point of law. The question of time limits, apart from those set out above[1] does not arise in respect of applications for cases to be stated as, for reasons made clear in *Altan-Evans v Leicester LEA and White*[2], the application must be made during the course of pending proceedings before the Tribunal, which impose their own time restraints.

1 See 9.5.4 and 9.5.6.
2 [1998] ELR 237, QBD.

Effect of the Court's decision   **9.6**

If any decision of the Tribunal is set aside, varied or altered in any way by **9.6.1** order of the Court, the Secretary of the Tribunal shall alter the entry in the records to conform to that order and shall notify the parties accordingly[1].

1 Special Educational Needs Tribunal Regulations 2001, SI 2001/600, reg 48(1).

If an appeal is remitted to the Tribunal by order of the court to be re-heard, **9.6.2** the Secretary of the Tribunal shall notify both parties that during a period of 15 working days (or such shorter period as the parties may agree in writing) each may submit a supplementary statement of case and further written evidence[1].

1 Special Educational Needs Tribunal Regulations 2001, SI 2001/600, reg 48(2).

9.6.3 If an order to strike out an appeal is quashed or set aside by the court, the Secretary of the Tribunal shall notify the parties[1]:

(a) in the case where the case statement period has not expired before the order to strike out took effect, that both parties shall be allowed the same period of 30 working days to send a statement of their respective cases and written evidence to the Secretary of the Tribunal[2];

(b) in any other case, that each party has a period of 15 working days (or such shorter period as the parties may agree in writing) to submit a supplementary statement of his case and further written evidence.

The Secretary of the Tribunal shall forthwith send a copy of all statements and written evidence received from a party during the period to the other party[3].

1 Special Educational Needs Tribunal Regulations 2001, SI 2001/600, reg 48(3).
2 SI 2001/600, reg 18(1).
3 SI 2001/600, reg 48(4).

Chapter 10

Dispute resolution, accountability and liability

Introduction   **10.1**

The rights of parents to appeal to the Special Educational Needs Tribunal[1] **10.1.1**
have been considered in Chapter 8, and the means of challenging the
Tribunal's decisions in Chapter 9. In this chapter we will consider the other
options open to parents who wish to complain about their children's treatment, either through statutory complaints mechanisms or by seeking
compensation through the courts.

1 Which will be renamed the Special Educational Needs and Disability Tribunal from
   1 September 2002; hereinafter 'the Tribunal'.

The formality and litigious nature of this area of education has caused some **10.1.2**
concern over the years. When first established in 1994, the Tribunal was
seen as a means of ensuring redress without parents having to go through
the courts. Unfortunately, though (as evidenced by the number of High
Court appeals, if nothing else), the Tribunal has become subject to a greater
formality than was originally intended, never being the 'lawyer-free zone' the
then Secretary of State, John Patten, intended. Further, the Tribunal
process itself has become too confrontational, with an 'us-and-them' men-
tality unfortunately all too often meaning that, whatever the outcome, the
relationship between the Local Education Authority (LEA) and the parent
can be harmed as a consequence.
   To address this problem, the Special Educational Needs and Disability
Act (SENDA) 2001 introduced dispute or disagreement resolution measures which are intended to reduce the potential confrontation and animosity
and may reduce the number of cases going to the Tribunal.

Scope of the chapter

This chapter will consider, first, the new dispute resolution arrangements. **10.1.3**
Next it will examine the statutory means of complaint and redress available
to parents. And finally it will consider redress in the courts, including judicial review and the impact of the Human Rights Act 1998, as well as an
analysis of the most recent development in this field – the possibility of
children, or their parents on their behalf, recovering compensation through
the courts.

DISPUTE RESOLUTION

10.2 Overview of arrangements and objectives

Dispute resolution arrangements

10.2.1 As has been seen, the role of the Tribunal is significant in resolving disputes between LEAs and parents. The number of cases and the formality has, although many could have predicted it, caused some concern and there was particular disappointment that the appeal process may have polarised the relationship between LEAs and parents, once an appeal was lodged. Although the introduction of parent partnership officers in LEAs and the old Code of Practice's[1] guidance on working together[2] sought to encourage more information sharing and greater co-operation, this did not necessarily produce the better relationships and less confrontational approach ministers desired. Consequently, the SENDA 2001 has introduced a statutory requirement for LEAs to put in place dispute resolution arrangements.

1 As to which, see 2.2.6.
2 Old Code of Practice, paras 2:28 to 2:32.

10.2.2 Parent partnership arrangements must still be made available by LEAs for the parent of any child in their area with special educational needs to be provided with advice and information about matters relating to those needs[1]. Each LEA take such steps as they consider appropriate for making those services known[2].

1 Education Act (EA) 1996, s 332A.
2 EA 1996, s 332A(3).

10.2.3 Now, however, every LEA must also make arrangements with a view to avoiding or resolving disagreements between the LEA and parents of children in its area about the exercise by the LEA of its functions in respect of children with special educational needs[1]. This duty is not limited to parents and children involved in the statutory assessment process, but applies across the whole range of an LEA's special educational needs functions.

1 EA 1996, s 332B.

Appointment of independent persons

10.2.4 Whatever arrangements are put in place, the LEA must provide for the appointment of independent persons with the function of facilitating the avoidance or resolution of such disagreements[1]. These persons should have a range of knowledge, experience and qualifications, such as counselling skills, training and experience in dispute resolution and knowledge of the relevant legislation and framework, the Code of Practice[2] and other educational issues[3]. In making the arrangements, an LEA must have regard to any guidance given by the Secretary of State or, in Wales, by the National Assembly[4]. The LEA must, once arrangements have been made, take such steps as it considers appropriate for making the arrangements known to the parents of children in their area, the headteachers and proprietors of schools in its area and such other persons as it considers appropriate[5]. The arrangements must not, however, affect the entitlement of a parent to appeal to the Tribunal[6].

1 EA 1996, s 332B(3).

2 As to which, see 2.2.6 and 2.2.7.
3 Code of Practice, para 2:28.
4 EA 1996, s 332B(4).
5 EA 1996, s 333B(5).
6 EA 1996, s 332B(6).

In addition, LEAs must also make arrangements with a view to avoiding or **10.2.5**
resolving in each relevant school[1] disagreements between the parents of a
relevant child[2] and the proprietor of the school about the special educational
provision made for that child[3]. These arrangements must provide for the
appointment of independent persons with the function of facilitating the
avoidance or resolution of such disagreements[4]. In making such arrangements, LEAs must have regard to any guidance given by the Secretary of
State, or, in Wales, the National Assembly[5]. An LEA must then take such
steps as it considers appropriate for making these arrangements known to
the parents of children in their area, the headteachers and proprietors of
schools in their area and such other persons as they consider appropriate[6].
These arrangements cannot, however, affect the entitlement of a parent to
appeal to the Tribunal[7].

1 A school is a 'relevant school' in relation to a child if it is: (a) a maintained school or a
   maintained nursery school; (b) a pupil referral unit; (c) a city technology college, a city
   college for the technology of the arts or a city academy; (d) an independent school named
   in the statement of special educational needs maintained for the child; or (e) a non-
   maintained special school approved by the Secretary of State under EA 1996, s 342: see
   EA 1996, s 332B(8).
2 A 'relevant child' is a child who has special educational needs and is a registered pupil at a
   relevant school: EA 1996, s 332B(7).
3 EA 1996, s 332B(2).
4 EA 1996, s 332B(3).
5 EA 1996, s 332B(4).
6 EA 1996, s 332B(5).
7 EA 1996, s 332B(6).

Minimum standards and structure of arrangements

The arrangements should meet certain minimum standards. Consequently, **10.2.6**
LEAs[1]:

- should take responsibility for the overall standard of the service and
  ensure it is subject to Best Value principles;
- should have clear funding and budgeting plans for the service;
- should ensure that the service is neutral and must involve an independent element;
- should ensure that the service, whether outsourced or provided in-
  house, has a development plan which sets out clear targets and is regularly reviewed. Such plans should specify arrangements for evaluation
  and quality assurance;
- must make the arrangements for disagreement resolution and how they
  will work known to parents, schools and others they consider appropriate;
- must inform parents about the arrangements for disagreement resolution at the time a proposed statement or amended statement is issued,
  and that entering disagreement resolution does not affect their right of
  appeal to the Tribunal;
- should ensure that the independent persons appointed as facilitators

have the appropriate skills, knowledge and expertise in disagreement resolution; an understanding of special educational needs processes, procedures and legislation; have no role in the decisions taken about a particular case, nor any vested interest in the terms of the settlement; are unbiased; maintain confidentiality; carry out the process quickly and to the timetable decided by the parties;

- should establish protocols and mechanisms for referring parents to disagreement resolution;
- should ensure that those providing the service receive appropriate initial and ongoing training and development to enable them to carry out their role effectively;
- should establish a service level agreement for delivering the service which ensures sufficient levels of resources and training, and sets out the appropriate standards expected of, and the responsibilities delegated to, the provider;
- whether the service is provided in-house or bought-in, should have appropriate arrangements for overseeing, regularly monitoring and reviewing the service, taking account of local and national best practice;
- should actively seek feedback from the service to inform and influence decisions on special educational needs policies, procedures and practices; and
- should monitor and evaluate the performance of the service.

The arrangements should ensure that practical educational solutions, acceptable to all parties, are reached as quickly as possible ensuring the minimum disruption to the children's education[2].

1 Code of Practice, para 2:25.
2 Code of Practice, para 2:26.

10.2.7   The structure of the arrangements are a matter for each LEA, but the Code of Practice suggests:

(a) using a panel of trained facilitators, affiliated to a recognised body in the field of disagreement resolution;
(b) expanding existing disagreement resolution services that cover a wide range of areas across the work of the LEA to include special educational needs expertise; or
(c) using regional panels funded by a number of neighbouring LEAs, perhaps using the SEN Regional Partnerships[1].

1 Code of Practice, para 2:29.

Use and purpose of dispute resolution

10.2.8   Dispute or disagreement resolution[1] can be entered into at any time, but will be more commonly used when parents are dissatisfied with the proposed provision for their children. Legal representation should not be necessary as the arrangements should be informal, but all participants, including the child, need to feel confident that their views and concerns will receive equal respect. The purpose of disagreement resolution is not to apportion blame but to achieve a solution to a difference of views in the best interest of the child[2].

1 Interestingly, the Code of Practice talks of 'disagreement' resolution, which is rather more friendly and less confrontational than the 'dispute' resolution referred to in EA 1996.
2 Code of Practice, para 2:27.

STATUTORY MEANS OF COMPLAINT AND REDRESS

Secretary of State for Education and Skills   **10.3**

Since 1944, the Secretary of State has always retained reserve powers to deal   **10.3.1**
with abuses committed by LEAs.

Any dispute between an LEA and a governing body of a school as to the   **10.3.2**
exercise of any power conferred or the performance of any duty imposed by
or under the Education Acts may be referred to the Secretary of State (who
may intervene despite any enactment which makes the exercise of a power or
the performance of a duty contingent upon the opinion of the LEA or of the
governing body)[1]. The Secretary of State has a discretion to determine any
dispute referred to him in this manner[2].

1   EA 1996, s 495.
2   EA 1996, s 495(2).

This procedure applies both ways. Thus, if a governing body is dissatisfied   **10.3.3**
with the exercise of an LEA's powers, it can complain to the Secretary of
State, just as in the same way that an LEA can complain to the Secretary of
State about the exercise of a governing body's power. Section 495 of the EA
1996 cannot, however, be utilised unless the dispute is referred to the
Secretary of State; it does not allow the Secretary of State to intervene of his
own volition.

If the Secretary of State is satisfied (either on a complaint by any person or   **10.3.4**
otherwise, including of his own volition) that any LEA and/or the governing
body of any maintained or maintained special school has acted or is proposing to act unreasonably with respect to the exercise of any power conferred or
the performance of any duty imposed by or under the Education Acts, the
Secretary of State may give such directions as to the exercise of the power or
the performance of the duty as appear to him to be expedient (and may do so
despite any enactment which makes the exercise of a power or the performance of a duty contingent upon the opinion of the body)[1].

1   EA 1996, s 496(1).

Although in the past there have been concerns that the Secretary of State has   **10.3.5**
not acted as quickly as the situation may warrant, recourse should really be
had to EA 1996, s 496 before any court action is contemplated. Although the
case law is inconsistent, a number of cases have indicated that before considering judicial review in particular, an aggrieved individual should first
complain to the Secretary of State. Similarly, a complaint to the Secretary of
State is not necessarily precluded where an LEA is alleged to have acted *ultra
vires* (ie outside its powers) or contrary to natural justice[1]. Here, the courts
have recognised that the Secretary of State is equally capable of considering
the unreasonableness of an LEA's or school's actions as a court. The question of when the statutory procedure should be invoked and when an
aggrieved parent or pupil should seek judicial review will be discussed below[2].

1   See *Herring v Templeman* [1973] All ER 581.
2   See 10.9.12.

10.3.6 The question of whether the LEA has acted or is proposing to act 'unreasonably' is to be decided in accordance with the legal definition of 'unreasonableness'. Thus in order to intervene the Secretary of State must show that the LEA have acted in a way in which no reasonable LEA would act[1].

1 See *Secretary of State for Education and Science v Tameside Metropolitan Borough Council* [1977] AC 1014.

10.3.7 In addition, the Secretary of State has a general default power where, if he is satisfied (either on a complaint by any person interested or otherwise) that either an LEA or a governing body of a maintained school or special school have failed to discharge any duty imposed on them by or for the purposes of the education legislation, he may make an order:

(a) declaring the LEA or governing body to be in default in respect of that duty; and

(b) giving such directions for the purpose of enforcing the performance of the duty as appear to him to be expedient[1].

1 EA 1996, s 497(1).

10.3.8 Any direction given shall be enforceable, on an application to the court made on behalf of the Secretary of State, by a mandatory order, ie a court order requiring the LEA or the governing body to comply with the direction.

10.3.9 The EA 1996, s 497 power is slightly different from the s 496 power in that it applies only to the discharge of duties, whereas s 496 allows the Secretary of State to intervene if he believes the LEA or school are unreasonably exercising a power. Because of the importance of the discharge of duties, however, s 497 does provide the Secretary of State with a far more effective means of enforcing his decision, first by direction and second by court order if necessary.

10.3.10 A further general power which can be applied to an LEA's performance in respect of its wider functions, rather than individual cases, is the ability of the Secretary of State to issue directions where he is satisfied (either on a complaint by any person interested or otherwise) that an LEA is failing in any respect to perform any function to an adequate standard (or at all)[1]. If the Secretary of State decides to exercise his powers he can direct an officer of the LEA to secure that the function which is being performed to an inadequate standard, or not at all, is performed in such a way as to achieve objectives set out in the Secretary of State's direction. The Secretary of State may give an LEA officer such directions as he thinks expedient for the purpose of securing that the function:

(a) is performed on behalf of the LEA and at their expense by such a person as is specified in the direction; and

(b) is so performed in such a way as to achieve such objectives as are specified in the direction[2].

1 EA 1996, s 497A(2).
2 EA 1996, s 497A(3) and (4).

Inspection of LEAs   **10.4**

A normal prerequisite for the exercise by the Secretary of State of the power   **10.4.1**
to deal with inadequate performance is a poor inspection report in respect
of a particular LEA. Again, this aspect of accountability will not provide a
remedy for individual cases, but may be applicable if an LEA is found to be
failing in its general provision for children with special educational needs.

Her Majesty's Chief Inspector of Schools in England, or his equivalent in   **10.4.2**
Wales, may arrange for any LEA to be inspected or shall arrange for such an
inspection if requested to do so by the Secretary of State[1]. An inspection
carried out by the Chief Inspector consists of a review of the way in which
the LEA is performing any of its functions (of whatever nature) which relate
to the provision of education, either for persons of compulsory school age
(whether at school or otherwise) or for persons of any age above or below
that age who are registered as pupils at schools maintained by the LEA[2].

1 Education Act (EA) 1997, s 38(1).
2 EA 1997, s 38(2).

The LEA is required to provide the Chief Inspector with such information   **10.4.3**
as may be prescribed and within such a period and in such a form as regulations may lay down[1]. An inspector has a right of entry to the premises of
the LEA and a right to inspect and take copies of any LEA records and other
documents containing information relating to the LEA which the inspector
considers relevant[2]. An LEA is required to give the inspector and any person
assisting him all assistance in connection with the inspection which they are
reasonably able to give[3]. The Chief Inspector may, when carrying out an
inspection, request the assistance of the Audit Commission[4].

1 EA 1997, s 38(6).
2 EA 1997, s 40(1).
3 EA 1997, s 40(2).
4 EA 1997, s 41.

Following an inspection, the inspector makes a written report on the matters   **10.4.4**
reviewed and sends copies to the LEA and the Secretary of State[1]. Where an
LEA receives a copy of a report it is under an obligation to prepare a written statement of the action which it proposes to take in the light of the
report and the period within which it proposes to take it[2]. The LEA is also
required to publish the report and its statement in response in accordance
with the Education (Publication of Local Education Authority Inspection
Reports) Regulations 1998[3]. The Chief Inspector may also arrange for the
report to be published in such manner as he considers appropriate[4].

1 EA 1997, s 39(1).
2 EA 1997, s 39(2).
3 SI 1998/880.
4 EA 1997, s 39(4).

Inspection of schools and intervention in schools causing concern   **10.5**

Again, this is not a remedy to address an individual case, but if a school is   **10.5.1**
failing in the education or support it provides to children with special

educational needs, this may well be picked up during a school's OFSTED[1] inspection.

1 Office for Standards in Education, officially the Office of Her Majesty's Chief Inspector of Schools in England.

10.5.2   In addition to inspection and advisory services which may be provided by agreement between LEAs and maintained schools, four types of statutory inspection are provided by the School Inspections Act (SIA) 1996[1].

1 SIA 1996, ss 10 to 25.

10.5.3   The most important type of inspection is (a) the inspection of a school by registered inspectors[1], but other forms of inspection include (b) *ad hoc* inspections, (c) inspections of religious education and (d) inspections carried out by the LEA for the area in which the school is located.

1 SIA 1996, s 10.

10.5.4   The Chief Inspector is to ensure that all maintained schools, LEA nursery schools, city technology colleges and academies, special schools and independent schools approved for children with statements of special educational needs are inspected by registered inspectors[1] who are to report in relation to particular schools on:

(a) the quality of the education provided and standards achieved;
(b) whether the financial resources are managed efficiently; and
(c) the spiritual, moral, social and cultural development of pupils.

1 Registered inspectors must be fit and proper persons, capable of conducting inspections competently and effectively. For the provisions relating to their appointment and removal see SIA 1996, ss 7 to 9.

10.5.5   Parents must be informed in advance of the inspections and a meeting must be arranged where parents can meet the inspector[1]. The inspector has a right of entry to the premises of the school and any other school attended by its pupils; and he may inspect and copy records and documents required for the purposes of the inspection[2]. Obstruction of an inspector or member of his team is an offence[3]. The inspection team then carries out an inspection of the school. The inspection must be completed within two weeks and the subsequent report within six weeks of the completion of the inspection[4].

1 SIA 1996, Sch 3, para 6.
2 SIA 1996, Sch 3, para 7.
3 SIA 1996, Sch 3, para 8.
4 Education (School Inspection) Regulations 1997, SI 1997/1966, reg 7.

10.5.6   Following an inspection, the registered inspector must prepare a written report and summary[1]. Where in his opinion the school is failing or likely to fail to give pupils an acceptable standard of education and therefore special measures are required[2], he must submit a draft of the report to the Chief Inspector[3], who may ask him for further information[4], and is to tell him whether he shares that opinion[5] and specific provisions apply if the registered inspector and Chief Inspector disagree[6].

1 SIA 1996, s 13(1).
2 SIA 1996, s 14(1).
3 SIA 1996, s 13(2).

4 SIA 1996, s 14(3).
5 SIA 1996, s 14(4).
6 See SIA 1996, s 14(5) and (6).

In the case of maintained schools, copies of reports and summaries are to be   **10.5.7**
sent by the person making the report to[1]:

(a) the governing body or the LEA where the governing body do not have
     a delegated budget (the appropriate authority);
(b) the Secretary of State, where the opinion is expressed that special
     measures are required and (if not expressed by an HMI) is shared by
     the Chief Inspector and the report is made by an HMI in which he
     expresses the opinion that special measures are required;
(c) the Chief Inspector (unless the report was by an HMI);
(d) the headteacher;
(e) whichever of the LEA and the governing body are not sent a copy
     under item (a) above;
(f) the person appointing foundation governors (if any) and (if different)
     the appropriate diocesan authority.

The governing body or LEA are to make public the report and summary,
and parents are to receive copies of the latter.

1 SIA 1996, s 16.

If the report recommends special measures, that appropriate authority must   **10.5.8**
prepare an action plan in response and state the period within which they
propose to take action[1]. Copies must be sent to the Chief Inspector[2] and a
summary should be available to parents if they require one[3]. Where the
LEA are not the appropriate authority, they should receive a copy from the
governing body[4] and then prepare a statement of the action they propose to
take (within a period they specify) in the light of the report, or an explanation of why they do not propose to take any action[5]. This should be sent to
the Secretary of State, the Chief Inspector and, in the case of a voluntary
aided school, the person appointing foundation governors and (if different)
the appropriate diocesan authority[6]. Further inspections will follow to monitor progress in implementing the action plan.

1 SIA 1996, s 17(1).
2 SIA 1996, s 17(3).
3 SIA 1996, s 17(6).
4 SIA 1996, s 17(3).
5 SIA 1996, s 18(2) and (3).
6 SIA 1996, s 18(3).

In the case of schools which are not maintained schools, copies of reports   **10.5.9**
and summaries are to be sent by the person making the report to[1]:

(a) the LEA (in the case of LEA nursery schools), or otherwise the pro-
     prietor or governing body;
(b) the Chief Inspector (unless the report was by an HMI);
(c) the Secretary of State where:
     (i)   the person making the report expresses the opinion that special
           measures are required which (if not expressed by an HMI) is shared
           by the Chief Inspector, or

(ii) the report is made by an HMI in which he expresses the opinion that special measures are required.

1 SIA 1996, s 20.

10.5.10 In the case of a non-maintained special school or an independent school, the proprietor or governing body must send a copy of the report or summary to any LEA which pays the fees of a registered pupil at the school. The report must be made public and parents should receive a copy of the summary. The same requirements as to actions plans and follow up inspections apply as with maintained schools[1].

1 SIA 1996, ss 20 to 22.

10.5.11 LEAs also have limited powers of intervention[1] by appointing additional governors or withdrawing a maintained school's delegated budget where a school is:

(a) subject to a warning notice;
(b) adjudged to have serious weaknesses; or
(c) requiring special measures.

1 School Standards and Framework Act 1998, ss 14 to 17.

10.6 The Commissioners for Local Administration or Ombudsmen

10.6.1 The Commissions for Local Administration were established by the Local Government Act (LGA) 1974 and their powers extended by the Local Government and Housing Act 1989. Their jurisdiction relates to complaints of injustice in consequence of maladministration in connection with action taken in the exercise of administrative functions by or on behalf of a local authority including LEAs[1].

1 LGA 1974, s 26(1).

10.6.2 The jurisdiction does not, however, extend to secular instruction in maintained schools, teaching and conduct of the curriculum, internal organisation and management or discipline in these schools[1]. Thus, decisions taken by schools in respect of children with special educational needs are normally outside the scope of the Ombudsman's powers.

1 LGA 1974, Sch 5, para 2.

10.6.3 As administrative functions have been held to include decision-making functions[1] but not the decision itself, the jurisdiction is, in effect, to examine the procedure rather than the merits of a decision and is to a certain extent akin to the court's supervisory functions in judicial review. Although neither 'maladministration' nor 'injustice' is defined, a working definition of 'maladministration' includes 'bias, neglect, inattention, delay, incompetence, ineptitude, adversity, turpitude, arbitrariness, and so on'[2]. Thus maladministration is concerned with faulty administration or inefficient or improper management of affairs. If the Ombudsman, having investigated, believes personally that the decision was wrongly taken, but is unable to point to any maladministration, he is prevented from questioning the decision[3].

'Injustice' has a wide meaning, but nonetheless should only apply in circumstances where an aggrieved complainant has no legal remedy. Thus injustice may include a 'sense of outrage' caused by unfair and incompetent administration even where no legal loss has occurred[4].

1 *R v Local Commission for Administration, ex p Croydon* [1989] 1 All ER 1033.
2 As per Lord Denning in *R v Local Comr for Administration ex p Bradford Metropolitan Borough Council* [1979] 1 QB 287.
3 See *R v Local Comr for Administration, ex p Bradford Metropolitan Borough Council* [1979] 1QB 287.
4 *R v Parliamentary Commission, ex p Balchin* [1997] COD 146.

Examples of circumstances where the Ombudsman has found maladminis-   **10.6.4**
tration in the special education context include:

- failure to keep parents informed during the course of the assessment of their child's special educational needs[1];
- failure to issue a statement of special educational needs, which led to a child being denied appropriate education for a school year[2];
- delay in dealing with a child's statement of special educational needs[3]; and
- failure to ensure speech therapy support was provided as specified in a statement[4].

1 See, for example, *Complaints 99/C/03072* and *00/C/05749 against Lancashire County Council*.
2 *Complaint No 95/B/2431 against Dorset County Council*.
3 See, for example, among numerous complaints, *Compliant No 00/A/1940 against Lewisham LBC*.
4 *Complaint No.95/A/2849 against Islington London Borough Council*.

The jurisdiction of the Ombudsman extends to any member or officer of the   **10.6.5**
local authority or anyone to whom the authority have delegated this function.

The Ombudsman cannot investigate a matter in respect of which the com-   **10.6.6**
plainant has, or had, a right of appeal or review to a Tribunal, a minister or a remedy by way of proceedings in court unless the Ombudsman is satisfied that in the particular circumstances of a case it is not reasonable to expect the person aggrieved to resort, or have resorted, to those procedures.

In *R v Comr for Local Administration, ex p H*[1], parents complained to the Ombudsman in an attempt to obtain compensation. The parents had previously issued judicial review proceedings against their LEA which had been compromised by an agreed settlement. The Ombudsman declined to investigate the complaint and the Court upheld this decision on the basis that the parents had already obtained a remedy by way of proceedings in a court of law and Parliament clearly intended that the Ombudsman should only investigate where such a route was not open. In *contrast*, in *R v Local Comr for Local Government for North and North East England, ex p Liverpool City Council*[2] the Court of Appeal declined to overturn a report of the Ombudsman on the basis that the complainants had alternative remedies available to them, in particular through judicial review. The Ombudsman had decided that it would be very difficult, if not impossible, for the complainants to obtain the necessary evidence in judicial review proceedings, whereas her powers allowed her to compel the disclosure of documents, interview staff and conduct a fact finding investigation. She had also taken the view that the complainants were a group in modest housing, unlikely to have the means to pursue the remedy. The Court of Appeal saw nothing wrong in this approach and felt that the Ombudsman had correctly exercised her discretion in concluding that it would have been unreasonable for the persons aggrieved to have had to resort to judicial review.

1   [1999] ELR 314.
2   [2001] 1 All ER 462.

10.6.7   Complaints must be in writing identifying the action alleged to constitute maladministration and must be made by or on behalf of a member of the public who claims to have sustained injustice in consequence of maladministration. The complaint may be made by an individual or a body corporate or incorporate, but not by a local authority or any other public authority or body which includes the governing body of a maintained school. The complaint must normally be made within 12 months of the time when the person aggrieved first had notice of the matters he believes constituted maladministration, although the Ombudsman may dispense with this time limit if it is reasonable to do so. Before investigating, however, the Ombudsman must be satisfied that the complaint has been brought to the notice of the local authority and that the local authority has been afforded a reasonable opportunity to investigate and reply to a complaint itself[1].

1   LGA 1974, s 26(5).

10.6.8   The Ombudsman has all the powers of the court in relation to the attendance and examination of witnesses and the production of documents (for example, to issue a witness summons or subpoena); he may require members and officers of the authority, and anyone else who he considers is able to furnish information or produce documents relevant to his investigation, to produce such information and documents. The Ombudsman cannot however be given information or documents which are legally privileged or protected by the privilege against self-incrimination[1].

1   LGA 1974, s 29 (7).

10.6.9   If the Ombudsman decides not to conduct an investigation, he must give a statement of his reasons for not doing so to the complainant. If, however, he decides to issue a report, the report will not normally identify any individual, but may name a member whose conduct constitutes maladministration and which constituted a breach of the National Code of Local Government Conduct. Within two weeks of receipt of the report, the authority must give public notice by way of newspaper advertisement or otherwise that the report is to be made available to the public for inspection without charge for a period of three weeks starting no later than one week after first notification. Anyone can take copies or extracts from the report during this period and the authority is obliged to provide copies on payment of the authority's reasonable charge. Obstruction of the right to inspect or copy the report is a criminal offence[1]. The authority must consider any report which concludes that injustice had been caused by maladministration[2] although the duty at this stage may be delegated to a committee, sub-committee, or even potentially an officer, within three months of receipt of the report, or such longer period as the Ombudsman allows. The authority must notify the Ombudsman what action it has taken or propose to take[3]. It is implicit that the authority is not bound to accept the Ombudsman's conclusions and could consider other reports, for example, from an officer.

1 LGA 1974, s 30(6).
2 LGA 1974, s 31(1).
3 LGA 1974, s 31(2).

If, however, the Ombudsman does not receive the necessary notification or **10.6.10** if he is not satisfied with the authority's actual or proposed course of action, or if within a further three months, he does not receive confirmation that the authority has taken action which satisfies him, the Ombudsman must make a further report setting out these facts and making his recommendations. The recommendations are within the discretion of the Ombudsman and should relate to the action which the authority should take both to remedy the injustice caused to the individual complainant and to prevent similar injustice in the future[1]. In addition, the Ombudsman may also require the authority by notice to arrange for publication of a statement to be agreed between himself and the authority containing details of any recommendations he has made in the further report which the authority has not taken, together with supporting material as to his reasons, and any statement from the authority as to why it proposes to take no action or other action to that recommended. Publication will be in two editions of a newspaper circulating in the authority's area and, if the authority does not arrange publication, the Ombudsman can step in and do so himself. If such a further report is issued, it must be considered by the full authority and cannot be delegated as can the first report.

1 LGA 1974, s 31(2B).

As far as the actual recommendations are concerned, the Ombudsman has **10.6.11** considerable freedom. This should clearly provide an adequate remedy for any injustice found and can include financial compensation. Often an award is made for time, distress and inconvenience caused to the complainant and for expenses properly incurred. An LEA has the power, whether or not recommended to do so (ie in an attempt to resolve the complaint amicably), to incur expenditure in making payments to a person who has suffered injustice in consequence of the maladministration[1].

1 LGA 1974, s 31(3).

Monitoring Officer   10.7

Another general means (not just applying to the education field) of chal- **10.7.1** lenging unlawful decisions, the Monitoring Officer is a statutory appointment which must be made by each local authority[1]. The Monitoring Officer is under a duty to prepare a report to the authority in respect of:

(a) any proposal, decision or omission of the authority or committee, sub-committee, or officer, or employee of the authority which appears to the Monitoring Officer to have given rise to, or be likely to, or would give rise to contravention by the authority or any committee or sub-committee of the authority, or by any person holding any office of employment under the authority, of any enactment or rule of law or of any Code of Practice made or approved by or under any enactment; or

(b) any injustice in consequence of maladministration in connection with administrative functions.

1 Local Government and Housing Act 1989, s 5.

REDRESS IN THE COURTS

10.8 Introduction

10.8.1 Although current press reports may suggest that there is a recent trend for aggrieved parents and pupils to take legal action in the courts against their schools or LEAs, this is not in a reality a new phenomenon and schools and LEAs have been used to being sued where physical injury has resulted due to their default for a number of years[1].

> 1 One of the earliest cases is *Smith v Martin and Kingston-upon-Hull Corpn* [1911] 2 KB 775, where a teacher ordered a pupil to attend an open fire which resulted in her being badly burnt.

10.8.2 Given the more recent claims brought alleging failure on the part of schools or LEAs to spot children with special educational needs, it might be assumed that most cases pursued by parents seek some form of compensation. In fact a considerable number, if not the majority, of legal actions brought against schools or LEAs have been by way of judicial review.

10.8.3 As a consequence, when considering the role of the civil courts in holding schools and LEAs to account, it is necessary to look, first, at the judicial review process and the effect of the Human Rights Act 1998 and, second, at the ability of pupils or parents to claim compensation.

10.9 Redress in the courts: (1) judicial review

10.9.1 Judicial review is the means by which the High Court exercises a supervisory jurisdiction over the activities of public bodies. Judicial review is not an appeal mechanism or an opportunity for the court to examine the merits of a decision; those are matters for statutory appeal. It is a means by which the court can consider the process adopted by a public body and ensure that it complied with all statutory requirements imposed in respect of a particular decision.

10.9.2 As the courts cannot intervene in the merits of a particular case it is important to recognise the circumstances when a court can interfere. Often reference is made to principles of '*Wednesbury* unreasonableness' or irrationality. What this means is that the courts can only intervene where an LEA has acted outside its powers or, in Latin terms, *ultra vires*. This does not however mean that an LEA acts unlawfully only when it fails to comply with a particular duty; the principles have been interpreted to ensure that when exercising discretionary powers the court has an equal supervisory jurisdiction.

The summary of the principle was first set out by Lord Greene in *Associated*   **10.9.3**
Provincial Picture Houses Ltd v Wednesbury Corpn[1] when he said:

> 'the exercise of . . . a discretion must be a real exercise of the discretion. If,
> in the statute confirming the discretion, there is to be found expressly or
> by implication matters which the authority exercising the discretion ought
> to have regard to, then in exercising the discretion it must have regard to
> those matters. Conversely, if the nature of the subject matter and the gen-
> eral interpretation of the Act make it clear that certain matters would not
> be germane to the matter in question, the authority must disregard those
> irrelevant collateral matters.'

Lord Greene felt that the word 'unreasonable' had often been used to cover
a wide range of unlawful administrative acts as a general description of
things that must not be done:

> 'For instance a person entrusted with a discretion must . . . direct himself
> properly in law. He must call his own attention to the matters which he is
> bound to consider. He must exclude from his consideration matters which
> are irrelevant to what he has to consider . . . Similarly, there may be some-
> thing so absurd that no sensible person could ever dream that it lay within
> the powers of the authority . . . Warrington LJ in *Short v Poole Corporation*[2]
> gave the example of the red-haired teacher, dismissed because she had red
> hair . . . It is so unreasonable that it might almost be described as being
> done in bad faith and, in fact, all these run into one another . . .'

1   [1948] 1 KB 223, [1947] 2 All ER 680.
2   [1926] Ch 66.

Lord Greene summarised the position as follows: **10.9.4**

> 'The court is entitled to investigate the action of the local authority with
> a view to seeing whether they have taken into account matters which they
> ought not to take into account, or, conversely, have refused to take into
> account or neglected to take into account matters which they ought to
> take into account. Once that question is answered in favour of the local
> authority, it may still be possible to say that, although the local authority
> have kept within the four corners of the matters which they ought to con-
> sider, they have nevertheless come to a conclusion so unreasonable that no
> reasonable authority could ever have come to it. In such a case, again, I
> think the court can interfere. The power of the court to interfere in each
> case is not as an appellate authority to override a decision of the local
> authority, but as a judicial authority which is concerned, and concerned
> only, to see whether the local authority have contravened the law by acting
> in excess of the powers which Parliament has confided in them.'

The principles were again considered in the *Council of Civil Service Unions v*   **10.9.5**
Minister for the Civil Service[1]. Lord Diplock identified three principles:

(1) 'Illegality' means that the decision-maker must understand correctly
    the law that regulates his decision-making power and must give effect
    to it.
(2) 'Irrationality' applies to a decision which is so outrageous in its defi-
    ance of logic or accepted moral standards that no sensible person who
    has applied his mind to the question to be decided could have arrived
    at it.
(3) Finally, 'procedural impropriety' covers a failure to observe procedu-
    ral rules that are expressly laid down in the statutory framework and

which regulate the decision under challenge and also a failure to observe the basic rules of natural justice or to act with procedural fairness.

1   [1985] AC 374, [1984] 3 All ER 935.

Effect of the Human Rights Act 1998

10.9.6   With the introduction of the Human Rights Act (HRA) 1998 in October 2000, however, it may be necessary to extend these general principles to include as another ground of challenge that an authority has acted in a way which is incompatible with one or more of the rights under the European Convention on Human Rights ('Convention rights').

10.9.7   The HRA 1998 will require all primary and subordinate legislation to be read and given effect in a way which is compatible with the Convention rights listed in the Schedule to the HRA 1998, so far as it is possible to do so[1]. More importantly for LEAs, the Act renders it unlawful for public authorities to act in a way which is incompatible with one or more of the Convention rights[2].

1   HRA 1998, s 3(1).
2   HRA 1998, s 6(1).

10.9.8   The principal Convention rights that will affect special education, are likely to be:

(a) *Article 6* – The right to a fair trial, which provides that everyone, in the determination of his civil rights and obligations, is entitled to a fair and public hearing within a reasonable time by an independent and impartial tribunal established by law. Judgment should be given in public, but the press may be excluded in certain specified circumstances.

(b) *Article 8* – The right to respect for private and family life, which includes the right to respect for a person's home and correspondence.

(c) *Article 9* – Freedom of thought, conscience and religion, which can only be limited in a way prescribed by law and necessary for reasons of public safety, public health or morals, public order or the rights or freedom of others.

(d) *Article 14* – Prohibition on discrimination. This is not a stand-alone Convention right but provides that the enjoyment of other Convention rights should be secured without discrimination on the grounds of sex, race, colour, language, religion, political or other opinion, national or social origin, association with a national minority, property, birth or other status.

(e) *First Protocol, Article 2* – No one shall be denied the right to education. In the exercise of any functions which it assumes in relation to education and to teaching, the state shall respect the right of parents to ensure such education and teaching in conformity with their own religious and philosophical convictions only in so far as it is compatible with the provision of efficient instruction and training and the avoidance of unreasonable public expenditure[1].

1   Ie the same qualification which applies to the obligation to educate children in accordance with their parents' wishes in EA 1996, s 9.

The effect of the HRA 1998 in the education field may, however, be muted   **10.9.9**
in light of one decision of the European Court of Human Rights[1] and the
initial judgments of the UK courts. In *Simpson v United Kingdom*[2], a dyslexic
child complained at an LEA's decision not to place him in a special school.
The child had appealed to an old-style local appeal panel, in the days before
the Special Educational Needs Tribunal, which had dismissed his appeal.
The Commission held that the right not to be denied education was not a
civil right within Article 6, and thus the requirement for a fair and impartial
hearing etc, was not a requirement under the Convention. Thus, although
UK legal principles of natural justice and due process must be observed by
the Tribunal, it would follow that as it is normally dealing with appeals
against placement, that will not invoke 'civil rights' and therefore it will not
be subject to the principles of Article 6[3].

1   *Simpson v United Kingdom* (1989) 64 DR 188, EComHR.
2   (1989) 64 DR 188, EComHR.
3   Similar decisions have been reached in cases involving admission and exclusion appeals –
    see *R (on the application of B) v Head Teacher of Alperton Community School* [2001] EWHC
    Admin 229, [2001] ELR 359.

Any action, or failure to act, on the part of an LEA or school[1] which   **10.9.10**
infringes a person's Convention rights can lead to challenge by way of judicial review or, if proceedings are being brought by the LEA against the
aggrieved individual, can be raised by way of collateral challenge to those
proceedings. In principle, the HRA 1998 will allow individuals aggrieved by
breach of their Convention rights to seek damages but damages recoverable
under the HRA 1998 are significantly limited. In comparison to damages
recoverable under private law actions, the amounts which may be awarded
will be significantly less and consequently any damages claim for breach of
Convention rights is likely to be made in types of proceedings other than
judicial review.

1   Maintained schools will be public bodies for the purposes of the HRA 1998.

The judicial review process

Only those with 'sufficient interest', often referred to as those persons having   **10.9.11**
'*locus standi*' in a matter, can make an application to the court. Within the
educational field it is usually quite clear whether a parent or a parent taking
action on behalf of his child has sufficient interest in a decision of an LEA
or school.

The court may, in certain circumstances, decline to allow a judicial review   **10.9.12**
to go ahead if alternative statutory remedies are available. This immediately
produces an issue in the educational field where the Secretary of State
retains default powers to deal with complaints about the performance of an
LEA[1]. Generally the courts will take the view that only in exceptional circumstances will a judicial review be allowed if a suitable, effective alternative
remedy is available. For example in *R v Newham London Borough Council, ex
p R*[2] it was held that the appeal mechanism to the Secretary of State was
more appropriate and effective than judicial review. Similar principles were
applied in *R v Special Educational Needs Tribunal, ex p F*[3], where it was held
that there must be exceptional circumstances for a judicial review of the
Tribunal to be allowed, if there was an alternative, statutory right of appeal.

Some judges, however, are stricter in the application of these principles than others and there have been cases, particularly where concern has been expressed at the delay inherent in a complaint to the Secretary of State, where judicial review has been allowed to go ahead in spite of the alternative statutory remedies. Other examples of the court ignoring alternative remedies have arisen where the court has decided that matters of law arise which the court and only the court can interpret or decide[4]. However, these latter decisions may now be questioned in light of *R (Cowl) v Plymouth City Council*[5] in which the Lord Chief Justice emphasised that parties to a judicial review should wherever possible use statutory mechanisms or alternative dispute resolution rather than resorting to the court.

1 See 10.3.
2 [1995] ELR 156.
3 [1996] ELR 213.
4 See, for example, *R v Barnet London Borough Council, ex p B* [1994] ELR 357.
5 [2001] EWCA Civ 1935, [2002] 1 WLR 803.

10.9.13   Judicial reviews should be brought promptly after the decision being challenged but in any event within three months from the date of the decision or failure. The period can be extended but exceptional grounds need to be shown. If the court believes that there has been undue delay it may refuse to allow permission for a judicial review to go ahead or may refuse relief if it considers that to do so would be likely to cause substantial hardship to or substantially prejudice the rights of any person or would be detrimental to good administration[1].

1 Supreme Court Act 1981, s 31(6).

10.9.14   Judicial review consists of a two-stage process. First, there is an application for permission. At this point it is necessary for the claimant to show that he has an arguable case and for the court to be convinced that he has sufficient interest and is not vexatious. The application for permission is usually heard *ex parte* and the public body whose action is under challenge is not notified of the application.

If permission is granted, the second stage, a full hearing, follows at which both the applicant and the challenged authority present their cases.

10.9.15   A number of discretionary remedies are available to the court, including the following:

- *Quashing order* – an order that the decision under challenge be quashed, often followed by an order that the matter should be remitted back for the body to reach a conclusion in accordance with the court's findings.
- *Mandatory order* – an order requiring the performance of a specified act or duty. This is normally only granted where the authority is under an absolute duty to do something or else the facts make it clear that the authority concerned has failed to perform its duty at all.
- *Prohibiting order* – an order which prevents the authority concerned acting or continuing to act unlawfully.
- *Declaration* – which is, as it says, simply a declaration by the court of the law and/or the rights of the parties concerned.
- *Injunction* – an order restraining a particular act or acts.

- *Damages* – an order very rarely made in judicial review proceedings. It can only be awarded if the court is satisfied that if a claim had been brought in a private law action the applicant would have been entitled to damages. In practice, because of the short time limits, it is rarely possible to provide evidence to support a claim for damages therefore applicants normally pursue compensation by way of private law remedies.

Judicial reviews brought against LEAs and schools have been numerous · **10.9.16** and many have concerned children with special educational needs. The following cases provide some examples, although other cases are referred to throughout this book:

- *R v Hampshire Education Authority, ex p J*[1] – This case involved a challenge to the LEA's decision that dyslexia did not constitute a 'learning difficulty'. The court held that the LEA's interpretation had been incorrect and that dyslexia was a special educational need.
- *R v Lancashire County Council, ex p M*[2] – An LEA was under a duty to provide speech therapy.
- *R v East Sussex County Council, ex p T*[3] – The arbitrary reduction of hours of home tuition as part of a cost cutting exercise was unlawful.

1   (1985) 84 LGR 547.
2   [1989] 2 FLR 279.
3   [1998] ELR 251.

Redress in the courts: (2) civil liability and claims for compensation   10.10

Judicial review is a mechanism for securing that a public body acts in accor- **10.10.1** dance with the relevant legislation or procedures and/or natural justice. As has been seen, it rarely provides pupils or parents with a means of obtaining compensation. If parents or pupils do wish to recover damages, it will be necessary for them to show that the LEA or school have broken duties which give rise to civil liability to pay compensation.

LEAs and schools enjoy no special status in law and may be held liable in **10.10.2** the courts for damages if they infringe the private law rights of individuals or other organisations by committing a tort against them. A 'tort' is a civil wrong, the redress for which is usually in the form of legal action for damages or an order of the court, such as an injunction. Although the most common types of action are for breach of statutory duty and/or negligence, this area of the law embraces such matters as trespass to persons, goods and land, nuisance, defamation and misfeasance in public office.

Although relevant to LEAs and schools, so far as special education is con- **10.10.3** cerned, trespass to goods and land, nuisance and defamation are unlikely to arise and need not be considered here. Instead, this section will examine those torts which have been applied to schools and LEAs in respect of their special educational needs functions.

Trespass to persons

'Trespass to persons' covers a range of torts including assault, battery and **10.10.4** false imprisonment. These are not usually committed directly by an LEA, but an LEA may find itself vicariously liable for the acts of its staff which constitute these torts.

10.10.5 'Battery' is the intentional and direct application of force to another person; 'assault' is an act which causes another person to apprehend the infliction of battery upon him by that other person.

10.10.6 These torts are of particular significance in the school setting where a number of claims have been made against teachers who have come into physical contact with their pupils for one reason or another. Corporal punishment, now outlawed, would clearly constitute battery, but what is often overlooked is that a mere touching can amount to the tort – a particular problem for staff in schools, especially where physical restraint may be required. To alleviate certain fears amongst school staff, s 550A of the EA 1996 was introduced by the EA 1997. This section provides reassurance by making clear that any teacher who works at the school and any other person who, with the authority of the headteacher, has lawful control or charge of pupils at the school, may use reasonable force to prevent a pupil committing an offence, causing personal injury to himself or others or damage to property, or engaging in behaviour prejudicial to the maintenance of good order and discipline at the school or among any of its pupils. This power applies both to actions on the school premises and off-site where the member of staff has lawful control or charge of the pupil. Guidance on the use of restraint by school staff can be found in *The Use of Force to Control or Restrain Pupils*[1].

1 DfEE Circular 10/98.

10.10.7 LEAs and schools are unlikely, if at all, to incur direct liability for assault or battery, but they may do so through the acts of their staff. There is always a fine line between civil assault and battery and a criminal act, and if a teacher was guilty of deliberate criminal misconduct, the act used to be outside the scope of the employee's employment and the LEA would not be vicariously liable. For example, in *Trotman v North Yorkshire County Council*[1], an LEA was held not to be vicariously liable for a sexual assault by a deputy head-teacher on a handicapped teenager in his charge whilst on an approved school trip abroad. However, this decision was overruled by the House of Lords in *Lister v Hesley Hall Ltd*[2], where the employer, the proprietors of independent schools, was held liable for the sexual and physical assaults carried out on pupils by a warden employed at one of their schools.

1 [1998] ELR 625.
2 [2001] UKHL 22, [2001] 2 All ER 769.

10.10.8 'False imprisonment' is another tort which would appear to be of little relevance to LEAs. However, claims have arisen in respect of the detention of pupils. In general terms, 'false imprisonment' is the infliction of bodily restraint which is not expressly or impliedly authorised by law. In 1980 an attempt was made to claim false imprisonment in respect of a class detention, but in an unreported decision, the judge in the Blackpool County Court dismissed the claim on the grounds that the school had lawful authority to impose the punishment.

The position, though, became confused where parents refused to allow their   **10.10.9**
children to take detentions. Could schools detain children against their parents' wishes? To avoid some of these problems, the EA 1997 tried to clarify
the position by inserting a new section into the EA 1996[1]. This provides that
where a pupil is required, on disciplinary grounds, to spend a period of time
in detention at school after the end of the school day, his detention shall not
be rendered unlawful by virtue of the absence of his parent's consent provided certain conditions are met[2]. These conditions are that the headteacher
must have made generally known within the school and to all parents that
detentions will be used; that the detention must be imposed by the headteacher or a teacher specifically authorised to do so; that the detention must
be reasonable in all the circumstances; and that the pupil's parent must
have been given at least 24 hours' notice in writing of the detention[3]. If these
conditions are met, the headteacher, and vicariously the LEA, should have
a defence to a claim for false imprisonment.

1 EA 1996, s 550B.
2 EA 1996, s 550B(1).
3 EA 1996, s 550B(2).

Misfeasance in public office

This tort is committed by an LEA and/or by individual officers where they   **10.10.10**
perform an *ultra vires* act (ie an act outside of the LEA's powers) mali-
ciously. The person acting needs to know that he or his authority had no
power to act in the way against which complaint is made and that he either
intended to injure or probably knew that so acting would injure the complainant. In recognition of the seriousness of the tort the Court of Appeal[1]
held that deliberate and dishonest abuse of power is necessary in every case
in which misfeasance is alleged.

1 *Three Rivers District Council v Bank of England* (No 3) [1996] 3 All ER 558.

Where the tort is alleged against a decision of a council or committee, as   **10.10.11**
opposed to the act of an individual, it is necessary to show that a majority of
the members voting in favour of the decision did so with the object of dam-
aging the claimant's interests[1].

1 *Jones v Swansea City Council* [1990] 3 All ER 737, [1990] 1 WLR 1453.

To the author's knowledge, a claim of misfeasance in public office has only   **10.10.12**
been pursued against an LEA officer in one case[1], where it was alleged that
an LEA officer had committed the tort when arranging for a child with special educational needs to be placed in a special school. The Court of Appeal
struck out the allegation as misconceived, on the grounds that, first, the
placement was made not by the officer against whom the allegations were
made, but by a multi-disciplinary panel; and second, because it was an
abuse of the process of the court to make allegations of dishonesty which
were inconsistent with all the known facts.

1 *Jarvis v Hampshire County Council* [2000] ELR 36, [2000] Ed CR 1.

Breach of statutory duty and/or negligence

The effect of this area of law on public authorities has troubled the courts   **10.10.13**
over the past few years and a relatively high number of cases have been

considered by the Court of Appeal and House of Lords. The liability of the police[1], ambulance services[2], fire services[3], highway authorities[4] and social services[5] have all been subject to judicial scrutiny, but unfortunately, not necessarily with consistent or unambiguous conclusions.

1   *Hill v Chief Constable of West Yorkshire* [1989] AC 53, [1988] 2 All ER 238.
2   *Kent v Griffiths* [2001] QB 36, [2000] 2 All ER 474.
3   *Capital and Counties plc v Hampshire County Council* [1997] 2 All ER 865, 95 LGR 831.
4   *Stovin v Wise (Norfolk County Council (third party))* [1996] AC 923, [1996] 3 All ER 801.
5   *X v Bedfordshire County Council* [1995] ELR 404.

10.10.14   Although the position with regard to schools and LEAs has now been clarified by the House of Lords in two cases, first, in *X v Bedfordshire County Council; M (a minor) v Newham London Borough Council; E (a minor) v Dorset County Council; Christmas v Hampshire County Council; Keating v Bromley London Borough Council* (referred to as *X*)[1] and, second, in *Phelps v London Borough of Hillingdon; Anderton v Clwyd County Council; G v London Borough of Bromley; Jarvis v Hampshire County Council* (referred to as *Phelps*)[2] the whole question of the liability of public authorities for breach of statutory duty and/or common law negligence can be difficult to fathom.

1   [1995] 2 AC 633; affd [1995] ELR 404, HL.
2   [2000] ELR 499, HL.

Breach of statutory duty

10.10.15   On the issue of breach of statutory duty, *X*[1] is the leading authority. As reference to this decision recurs throughout this section, it is worth examining the facts, such as there were, involved in this decision.

1   [1995] 2 AC 633; affd [1995] ELR 404, HL.

10.10.16   *X* was five cases in one, two involving claims against social service authorities and three against LEAs. The social services cases concerned allegations in *X v Bedfordshire* that social workers had failed to take action to protect children at risk of abuse and in *M v Newham London Borough Council* that children were taken into care when they should not have been. The three education cases, *Christmas v Hampshire County Council, E v Dorset County Council* and *Keating v Bromley London Borough Council*, involved claims respectively against a headteacher and advisory teacher for failing to spot and address a child's dyslexia, an educational psychologist on similar grounds and an LEA for placing a child in a special school and not mainstream education. In all five cases, the claims were based either on breaches of statutory duties by the various authorities and/or negligence on the part of the authorities and/or their staff.

10.10.17   So far as breach of statutory duties was concerned, Lord Browne-Wilkinson, in the leading judgment, made clear that the circumstances in which such claims could be successfully pursued would be rare, saying: 'The basic proposition is that in the ordinary case a breach of statutory duty does not, by itself, give rise to any private law cause of action.'[1] Thus if an LEA were to breach any of its various duties, although it might lead to challenge by way of judicial review, it would not normally lead to a claim for damages.

Lord Browne-Wilkinson continued: **10.10.18**

> 'However, a private law cause of action will arise if it can be shown, as a
> matter of construction of the statute, that the statutory duty was imposed for
> the protection of a limited class of the public and that Parliament intended
> to confer on members of that class a private right of action for breach of the
> duty . . . [I]t is significant that [we] were not referred to any case where it
> had been held that statutory provisions establishing a scheme of social wel-
> fare for the benefit of the public at large had been held to give rise to a
> private right of action for damages for breach of statutory duty. Although
> regulatory or welfare legislation affecting a particular area of activity does in
> fact provide protection to those individuals particularly affected by that
> activity, the legislation is not to be treated as having been passed for the ben-
> efit of those individuals but for the benefit of society in general . . . The cases
> where a private right of action for breach of statutory duty have been held
> to arise are all cases in which the statutory duty has been very limited and
> specific as opposed to general administrative functions imposed on public
> bodies and involving the exercise of administrative discretions.'

1 [1995] ELR 404 at p 415.

On this basis, in the education cases the House of Lords struck out a claim   **10.10.19**
that the LEA in the *Bromley* case had been in breach of the relevant education legislation. The Lords held that a claim that an LEA had failed to
provide sufficient school places[1] could not give rise to a private law claim for
damages. Lord Browne-Wilkinson also held that, although the legislation
relating to children with special educational needs protected individual children[2], Parliament did not intend to give those children a right of action for
damages if the duties in the legislation were not met.

1 Contrary to what is now EA 1996, s 14.
2 [1995] ELR 404 at p 454.

As a consequence of *X*, it is unlikely that many claims will succeed against   **10.10.20**
LEAs for breach of their statutory duties. This position was confirmed in
Holtom v Barnet London Borough Council[1] where it was held that an alleged
breach of the duties in respect of children with special educational needs in
the EA 1996 could not give rise to a private right of action for damages and
in *Phelps*[2].

1 [1999] ELR 255.
2 [2000] ELR 499, HL.

In *Phelps* the House of Lords considered that although the various duties   **10.10.21**
under the education legislation were intended to benefit a particular group,
mainly children with special educational needs, the legislation was essentially providing a general structure for all LEAs in respect of all children who
fell within the legislation's ambit:

> 'The general nature of the duties imposed on local authorities in the con-
> text of a national system of education and the remedies available by way of
> appeal and judicial review indicate that Parliament did not intend to create
> a statutory remedy by way of damages. Much of the [legislation] is con-
> cerned with conferring discretionary powers or administrative duties in an
> area of social welfare where normally damages have not been awarded
> when there has been a failure to perform a statutory duty.'[1]

1 *Phelps* [2000] ELR 499, HL per Lord Slynn at p 515.

10.10.22   The occasions when an LEA will be sued for a direct breach of its statutory duties are therefore likely to be rare. To stand a chance of succeeding a claimant must be able to show that Parliament has imposed the statutory duty for the benefit of a limited class of the public and intended that breach of that duty should lead to a claimant having a private right of action for damages. Given the circumstances considered in *X, Phelps* and *Holtom* it is suggested that few claims (if any) for breach of statutory duty will be successful against an LEA. Claims for negligence are, however, a different matter.

Common law negligence

10.10.23   'Negligence', in simple terms, is the breach of a duty to take care which results in damage. For the tort to arise the damage must result from a duty which the law will impose, there must have been a breach of that duty and damage or injury must result from that breach.

10.10.24   So far as establishing a duty of care is concerned, the law will not impose duties on all occasions. The circumstances where duties may arise were outlined by Lord Atkin in the landmark case of *Donoghue v Stevenson*[1], where he said: 'You must take reasonable care to avoid acts or omissions which you can reasonably foresee would be likely to injure your neighbour.'

1   [1932] AC 562.

10.10.25   Even if a *duty* of care can be established, a claimant then needs to show that there has been a *breach* of that duty. In most cases the test is whether there has been 'an omission to do something which a reasonable man, guided upon those considerations which ordinarily regulate the conduct of human affairs [in more modern language, in all the circumstances], would do, or doing something which a prudent and reasonable man would not do'[1].

1   *Blyth v Birmingham Waterworks Co* (1856) 11 Ex Ch 781.

10.10.26   This principle is modified where the actions of professionals (for example, doctors, psychologists, solicitors and headteachers) are called into question. In these cases the so-called *Bolam* test applies. Thus the standards to be applied in these circumstances are not those of the 'ordinary man', but the standards of reasonably competent fellow professionals at the time[1].

1   *Bolam v Friern Hospital Management Committee* [1957] 2 All ER 118, [1957] 1 WLR 582.

10.10.27   Assuming that a duty is owed and that there has been a breach of the duty, *damage* of a type recognised by law has to be thereby caused. This therefore requires a claimant to show that the act or omission which constitutes a breach of duty caused the injury for which the claimant is seeking compensation and was not so remote that it could not have been a contributory factor.

10.10.28   The claimant must also show that physical damage resulted and, except in a very few cases, that economic loss was not the only consequence of the act or omission. This latter point causes some difficulties, but is important in the context of the educational cases discussed below. An example was provided in *Murphy v Brentwood District Council*[1] where it was alleged that the local authority had negligently approved defective building plans causing a reduction in the value of the claimant's house. It was held that a duty of care could be owed in respect of personal injury or damage to property arising from a defect (ie physical damage), but no such duty was owed to those who acquired the house and suffered economic loss because of the effect of the defects on its value. Only if the local authority had accepted some additional responsibility, akin to that of an independent surveyor retained by a purchaser, would the local authority have been liable for any such economic loss. As it was, all it had done was carry out its statutory functions and no more and that could not give rise to any liability for the diminution in value.

1 [1991] 1 AC 398, [1990] 2 All ER 908, HL.

Those, then, are the general principles applying in 'simple' cases of negligence. Needless to say, negligence, so far as it affects local authorities generally and LEAs in particular, is not so simple. This is principally because a number of other factors come into play to recognise the discretionary nature of much decision making and public policy issues concerning the imposition of liability on public bodies. **10.10.29**

One initial factor which first needs to be considered is the distinction between (a) direct liability on the part of an LEA, or in rarer cases schools, and (b) the vicarious liability of LEAs and schools, as employers, for the acts or omissions of their employees. **10.10.30**

In X^1, the House of Lords drew a distinction between the direct liability of a local authority and the liability which can be incurred vicariously for the acts of their employees[2] in the context of claims for breach of statutory duties and/or negligence. Lord Browne-Wilkinson identified a number of areas where a local authority might owe direct duties of care to a claimant, either because the tort was committed through the action of the authority corporately (for example, as a result of a committee decision) or through the act of an officer which constituted a breach of a direct duty, an authority only being able to act through its servants in the majority of cases. These were, in his Lordship's view, to be distinguished from the separate, additional, usually professional duties, which an individual officer owed personally to a claimant and where the authority would not necessarily be directly liable, but where it would be vicariously liable. Indeed, in the education cases under consideration in X, the Lords held that vicarious liability, as opposed to direct liability, might arise in respect of the professional duties owed by educational psychologists and headteachers to pupils in their care. **10.10.31**

1 [1995] 2 AC 633, [1995] ELR 404, HL.
2 Vicarious liability will be imposed on an employer when an employee acts or omits to act in away which gives rise to liability, where that act or omission occurred in connection with his employment – see *Lister v Hesley Hall Ltd* [2001] UKHL 22, [2001] 2 All ER 769, HL.

The House of Lords in *Phelps*[1] also looked to the distinction and provided greater clarity, largely by recognising that in claims relating to education, it is better to concentrate on vicarious liability which will usually be at issue, rather than at direct liability, which will rarely be pleaded. Lord Slynn[2] recognised that since an LEA can only act through its employees and agents, and if they are negligent or breach other common law duties vicarious liability will arise, it may rarely be necessary to invoke a claim for direct **10.10.32** liability. He indicated that this was only likely to arise where, for example, an LEA appointed an educational psychologist or other professional who at the outset were neither qualified nor competent to carry out the duties.

1 [2000] ELR 499, HL.
2 [2000] ELR 499, HL at p 521.

10.10.33 Thus in summary, where employees of an LEA act in a way which breaches duties of care they owe to individuals, their employing LEA or school will be vicariously liable for those breaches of duty. LEAs, and to a lesser extent schools, will only be directly liable where they themselves are under a duty to take care, such as in the appointment of staff, or the decision under challenge is in the nature of a committee resolution.

10.10.34 The more substantive issue of when liability for common law negligence might arise in cases involving education were first comprehensively analysed by Lord Browne-Wilkinson in *X*. His Lordship[1] identified three categories of situation where a common law duty of care (ie the first requirement of negligence) might arise:

(1) where a statutory duty gives rise to a common law duty of care owed to a claimant by a local authority to do or refrain from doing a particular act;

(2) where, in the course of carrying out a statutory duty, a local authority has brought about such a relationship between itself and the claimant as to give rise to a duty of care at common law; or

(3) where, whether or not the authority is itself under a duty of care to the claimant, its officers or employees in the course of performing the statutory functions of the authority were under a common law duty of care for a breach of which the authority would be vicariously liable.

1 [1995] ELR 404, HL at p 418.

10.10.35 Whether duties will actually arise in these circumstances will depend on a number of other factors:

(a) Under categories (1) and (2) above, it is possible that common law duties of care may arise in the performance of statutory functions, but a distinction has to be made between, first, cases in which it is alleged that the LEA owes a duty of care in the manner in which it exercises a statutory discretion (for example, a decision whether or not to exercise the discretion to close a special school) and, second, cases in which a duty of care may arise from the manner in which the statutory duty has been implemented in practice (for, example, the running of a special school pursuant to statutory duties). In the first case no common law duty of care should arise, but in the second case it will.

(b) An LEA cannot be held liable for doing what Parliament authorised in legislation. To establish liability for negligence in the exercise of a discretion, it is necessary to show that the decision was outside the ambit of the discretion altogether; if it was not, an LEA cannot itself be directly in breach of any duty of care.

(c) A common law duty of care in relation to the taking of decisions involving policy matters cannot exist for Parliament will have conferred the discretion on the authority not the courts. Nothing which falls within the ambit of the statutory discretion can be actionable. If the matter complained of falls outside the statutory discretion, it may give rise to liability. If, however, factors relevant to the exercise of the discretion include matters of policy, the court cannot adjudicate on such policy matters and therefore cannot reach the conclusion that the decision was outside the ambit of the statutory discretion.

(d) If, however, the allegations concern negligence, not in the taking of a discretionary decision to do some act but in the practical manner in which that act has been performed, the question of whether or not a common law duty of care arises is determined by the general principles.

(e) In circumstances where no direct duty of care arises, LEAs may be vicariously liable for the acts or omissions of their officers and employees. However, where there is no allegation of a separate 'professional' duty of care being owed by an individual employee, the negligent acts of that employee are only capable of constituting a breach of a duty of care (if any) owed directly by the authority to the claimant.

Negligence cases involving LEAs and schools can best be split into two categories: (a) cases involving physical injury; and (b) cases where the allegation is of educational malpractice leading to an inadequate education or attainment (sometimes referred to as 'educational well-being', 'failure to educate' or 'educational malpractice' cases).   **10.10.36**

'PHYSICAL INJURY' CASES

The first category of negligence cases is relatively straightforward and such cases have been brought successfully against LEAs and schools for years. In these cases, the duty can best be expressed as a duty to take reasonable care for the health and safety of pupils (and, for that matter, other employees and visitors). In certain circumstances the duty may extend to require the taking of positive steps to protect a pupil from physical harm[1].   **10.10.37**

1 See *Hippolyte v Bexley London Borough* [1995] PIQR P 309.

The standard of care to which all staff must aspire in cases of physical harm (as opposed to educational malpractice cases where the standard is different) is that of a careful and/or reasonable parent[1]. The standard should though take account of the fact that a teacher will, unlike the reasonable parent, usually be responsible for a whole class or a large playground[2]. The courts have also been disinclined to 'wrap children in cotton wool' or require schools to be turned into secure fortresses[3].   **10.10.38**

1 *Williams v Eady* (1893) 10 TLR 41; *Rich v LCC* [1953] 2 All ER 376; and *Martin v Middlesborough Corpn* (1965) 63 LGR 385.
2 *Beaumont v Surrey County Council* (1968) 66 LGR 580 and *Lyes v Middlesex County Council* (1962) 61 LGR 443.
3 *Nwabudike v Southwark London Borough* [1997] ELR 35.

As it is part of a teacher's duty to take reasonable steps to protect pupils from injury[1] there is no reason why bullying claims will not succeed if, for example, supervision has been negligent. However, although schools are   **10.10.39** required to have anti-bullying policies, these claims should not fall into any special category, but will be considered in line with the general principles[2].

1 See *Beaumont v Surrey County Council* (1968) 66 LGR 580.
2 See *Bradford Smart v West Sussex County Council* [2001] ELR 138 and *E v Isle of Wight Council*, (23 February 2001, unreported), QBD.

10.10.40 Numerous examples of cases of schools or LEAs being sued for physical injury can be found in the law reports[1] and as they apply equally to children without special educational needs as they do to pupils with, no further reference will be made to them here. Of more importance when considering the law of special educational needs are the recent trend of cases in which compensation has been sought for the failure of schools and LEAs to detect a child's special educational needs and to address those needs adequately.

1 See, for example, *Barnes v Hampshire County Council* [1969] 3 All ER 746; *Moore v Hampshire County Council* (1981) 80 LGR 481, *Affutu-Nartoy v Clarke* (1984) Times, 9 February; and *Nwabudike v Southwark London Borough* [1997] ELR 35.

'EDUCATIONAL WELL-BEING', 'FAILURE TO EDUCATE' OR 'EDUCATIONAL MALPRACTICE' CASES

10.10.41 The second category of negligence cases, educational malpractice or educational well-being cases, are a much more recent phenomenon. Although the courts have provided some limits on the circumstances in which such claims can be brought, they are likely to increase significantly and provide pupils with a further means of seeking redress for failures in their special educational provision. Although these claims are discussed in the context of special educational needs, the principles apply across all areas of education, as was recognised by Lords Nicholls and Clyde in *Phelps*[1].

1 [2000] ELR 499, HL, at pp 531 and 534, respectively.

10.10.42 The catalyst for the development of these claims was the decision of the House of Lords in respect of the education cases in *X*. As has been seen, claims for physical injury had a long history, but, before *X*, no claim for a failure to educate or a failure to remedy an educational need had been brought in the courts.

10.10.43 In the *X* cases, it was alleged that LEAs, through their educational psychologists[1] or headteachers and advisory teachers[2] or education officers[3] owed duties to detect the special educational needs of pupils, provide appropriate remedial tuition or support and ameliorate those needs. No actual physical injury was alleged. Instead, it was claimed that the children had suffered an educational detriment so that their future career prospects were affected. In addition, in the *Dorset* claim, the recovery of the costs of educating the pupil in a private school was attempted.

1 *E v Dorset County Council* [1995] 2 AC 633, [1995] 3 All ER 353.
2 *Christmas v Hampshire County Council* [1995] 2 AC 633, [1995] 3 WLR 152.
3 *Keating v Bromley London Borough Council* [1995] 2 AC 633, [1995] 3 WLR 152.

10.10.44 It must be remembered, however, that the appeals before the House of Lords were against applications to the lower courts to 'strike out' claims. These were presented on the basis that, as a matter of law, none of the claims should succeed. As a consequence, no evidence had been given as to either the arrangements for educating pupils with special educational needs in the respective LEAs or on the specific details of what had happened to these particular pupils. The decision of the Lords therefore needs to be read in light of the fact that because there was no evidence, they had to make certain assumptions about the work of the education professionals involved. In particular, Lord Browne-Wilkinson probably did misunderstand the role of the educational psychology service, an error which he subsequently corrected in *Barrett v Enfield London Borough Council*[1].

1 [2001] 2 AC 550, [1999] 3 All ER 193.

Nonetheless, the Lords held that: **10.10.45**

(a) A headteacher, being responsible for a school, is under a duty of care to exercise the reasonable skills of a headteacher in relation to a pupil's educational needs. If it comes to the attention of a headteacher or teacher that a pupil is under-performing he owes a duty to take such steps as a reasonable teacher would consider appropriate to try to deal with such under-performance. If a headteacher gives advice to parents, he should exercise the skills and care of a reasonable headteacher in giving such advice. 'To hold that, in such circumstances, the headteacher could properly ignore the matter and make no attempt to deal with it would fly in the face, not only of society's expectations of what a school will provide, but also of the fine traditions of the teaching profession itself.'[1]

(b) An advisory teacher brought in to advise on the educational needs of a specific pupil, if he knows his advice will be communicated to the pupil's parents, owes a duty to the pupil to exercise the skill and care of a reasonable advisory teacher.

(c) Where educational psychologists carry out an assessment of an individual pupil as part of the statutory process, even though their advice is directed to the LEA, they could owe a duty of care to use reasonable professional skill and care in the assessment and determination of the pupil's educational needs.

(d) Actions for common law negligence should not however be brought where the imposition of a common law duty of care might cause a conflict with the LEA's statutory responsibilities.

(e) Damages might, in principle, be recoverable for educational detriment, but that was a matter for the trial judge when in possession of all the facts.

(f) LEAs would be vicariously liable for the breaches of duty committed by their teaching, advisory and educational psychology staff.

1 [1995] ELR 404, HL per Lord Browne-Wilkinson at p 451.

Although the Lords' decision seemed to quash any notion of damages being recovered from LEAs for breach of statutory duty[1] and emphasised that any claim would be difficult to pursue successfully, the decision was seen as a green-light for a number of claims against LEAs for the negligence of their staff. **10.10.46**

1 See 10.10.15 to 10.10.22.

This view was diminished, albeit briefly, by the decision of Kennedy J in **10.10.47** *Christmas v Hampshire County Council*[1], the first of the education cases considered in *X* to come to trial. Having heard the evidence, the judge concluded that neither the headteacher nor the advisory teacher had been negligent and therefore dismissed the claim.

1 [1998] ELR 1.

10.10.48 Next day, however, Garland J gave judgement at first instance in *Phelps v Hillingdon London Borough Council*[1] and found the LEA to be liable for what he considered were the negligent acts of the LEA's educational psychologist. The judge found that the educational psychologist owed a duty of care to a pupil and should have known that her findings in respect of the pupil would have been acted upon by the pupil's parents. There had been, in the judge's view, a failure to diagnose the claimant's dyslexia and a failure by the educational psychologist to review her opinion after she was aware that the claimant had failed to make progress. This amounted to negligence. Further, in failing to mitigate the adverse consequences of dyslexia, a congenital defect, the claimant had been injured for which she should be compensated with damages. The LEA was therefore held liable for the educational psychologist's negligence and was ordered to pay £46,000 damages.

1 [1998] ELR 38.

10.10.49 That decision was overturned by the Court of Appeal[1]. The Court of Appeal firstly rejected the notion that the claimant could have been injured by the educational psychologist's acts. Stuart-Smith LJ said that it was wrong to categorise dyslexia, or the failure to ameliorate or mitigate its effects, as an injury. Instead, in reality what the claimant was seeking to compensate was an economic loss and that, in law, the economic consequences of a failure to mitigate or ameliorate could only be recoverable if the educational psychologist had assumed responsibility to protect the claimant from the loss she had suffered. Although a private educational psychologist who had assumed responsibility to assess a child under a contract could be liable, an educational psychologist exercising or carrying out the LEA's statutory functions could not be sued to the same effect for negligence.

1 [1998] ELR 587, CA.

10.10.50 Secondly, and perhaps more importantly, the Court of Appeal held that the educational psychologist and, vicariously, the LEA owed no duty of care to the claimant. A number of reasons were given for this including the lack of assumption of responsibility beyond the statutory framework; the fact that, otherwise, the claimant could have circumvented the principle set out in *X* that an LEA owed no direct duty of care to a pupil for whom it was responsible under the Education Acts; the fact that the decision taken in respect of the child was made by a multi-disciplinary team of which the educational psychologist was just one member; the cost to LEAs of vexatious claims; the involvement of parents in the special educational needs process; the alternative remedies available; and the concern that if claims of this nature were allowed it would encourage 'defensive education'.

10.10.51 The court was also reluctant to impose duties of care because of the difficulty in showing that whatever the educational psychologist might have done or not done actually contributed to the loss which the claimant claimed to have suffered. In *Phelps*, the court felt that the claimant had to demonstrate that the teaching provided would have been different and more effective if the educational psychologist had identified the dyslexia and that significant improvement would have resulted. On the facts, the claimant was unable to show that if that had happened it would have made any meaningful difference. When other factors such as non-attendance and other physical, neurological, emotional, cultural and environmental factors were included in the equation, the court felt it would be nigh on impossible to establish a link between an educational psychologist's negligence and the claimed loss.

The Court of Appeal's view, especially on the nature of the 'loss' suffered, **10.10.52** was followed in *Anderton v Clwyd County Council*[1]. The same court as in *Phelps* found that even if dyslexia was regarded as an impairment of a person's mental condition, it could not be caused by an educational psychologist or LEA. Dyslexia is a congenital and constitutional condition and failure to diagnose it cannot exacerbate the condition. Consequently, the failure to mitigate or ameliorate the consequences of dyslexia could not amount to a personal injury.

1 [1999] ELR 1, CA.

In *Gower v Bromley London Borough Council*[1], the Court of Appeal distin- **10.10.53** guished the decision in *Phelps*. In this case, allegations of negligence were made against teachers at a maintained special school who were accused of being professionally incompetent and failing to provide a pupil with the computer teaching or aids necessary to enable him to communicate adequately in order to learn or socialise with his fellow pupils. On this occasion, the Court of Appeal declined to strike out the claim and set out the following propositions applicable to claims against teaching staff in schools:

(a) A headteacher and teachers have a duty to take such care of pupils in their charge as a careful parent would have in like circumstances, including a duty to take positive steps to protect their well-being.

(b) A headteacher and teachers have a duty to exercise the reasonable skills of their calling in teaching and otherwise responding to the educational needs of their pupils. Those responsible for teachers in breach of that duty may be vicariously liable for it.

(c) The justiciability of such a claim for vicarious responsibility is the same whether or not a headteacher and teachers are operating under a statutory scheme, such as that for children with special educational needs, and whether or not the school is in the public or private sector.

(d) The duty is to exercise the skill and care of a reasonable headteacher and/or teachers ie whether the teaching and other provision for a pupil's educational needs accords with that which might have been acceptable at the time by reasonable members of the teaching profession.

(e) It is plainly reasonably foreseeable by a headteacher and his staff that if they do not properly teach or otherwise provide for a pupil's educational needs he may suffer educationally and possibly psychologically.

(f) In normal circumstances of the headteacher and teacher/pupil relationship, there should be little difficulty in establishing proximity where, as in *Gower*, it is alleged that the teaching staff held themselves out as specialists in the teaching of pupils with special educational needs.

1 [1999] ELR 356, CA.

10.10.54 The principles set out by the Court of Appeal in *Phelps* were, however, preferred by the Court of Appeal in the next case to be considered[1], albeit that that case involved educational psychologists and education officers as opposed to teachers. This was another application to strike out a claim. In addition to alleging misfeasance in public office[2], compensation had been sought in respect of the LEA's alleged failure to provide the claimant with the education it should have done. He accordingly claimed the cost of remedial tuition and the loss of prospective future earnings. Relying on *Phelps*, the LEA applied for the claim to be struck out as disclosing no cause of action.

1 *Jarvis v Hampshire County Council* [2000] ELR 36, [2000] Ed CR 1.
2 Discussed at 10.10.10 to 10.10.12.

10.10.55 In summary, the claim was that, during the course of assessment and statementing under the Education Acts, an LEA educational psychologist had negligently offered advice to the LEA as to the appropriate placement for the claimant and that the LEA's officers had been negligent in arranging the claimant's placement at a school which it was alleged was inappropriate to meet his needs.

10.10.56 Perhaps surprisingly, in view of the cases which have cast doubt on the propriety of courts using their striking out powers[1], the Court of Appeal found that none of the allegations of negligence made against the educational psychologist and LEA officers were capable of giving rise to a duty of care. Nor could any of them be liable to the claimant so as to give rise to any vicarious liability on the part of the LEA.

1 See, for example, *Barrett v Enfield London Borough Council* [2001] 2 AC 550, [1999] 3 All ER 193, HL.

10.10.57 In reaching this conclusion, Morritt LJ tried to summarise the principles applying to educational malpractice claims as he saw them[1]:

(a) An LEA does not owe a direct common law duty of care in the exercise of its powers and discretions relating to children with special educational needs specifically conferred on them by the EA 1996.
(b) An LEA does not owe a direct duty of care in respect of the performance of any educational psychology service set up to advise it as to the performance of its educational functions unless, with the requisite statutory authority, it also provides psychology services to the public in a medical adviser/patient relationship.
(c) Where the exercise of professional skills by an individual agent or employee of the LEA within the scope of his authority or employment is such as to give rise to a duty of care at common law, the LEA will be vicariously liable if the existence of such a duty does not fetter or conflict with the proper exercise by the LEA of its statutory powers and discretions.
(d) The acts or omissions of such an agent or employee in advising the LEA how to exercise its statutory powers and discretions are not, without more, sufficient to constitute the assumption of responsibility in

those cases where such an assumption is necessary to give rise to the alleged duty of care.

(e) A claim for the recovery of compensation for a failure to diagnose or ameliorate the consequences of dyslexia (or other congenital constitutional conditions) is a claim for economic loss for which an assumption of responsibility is required if the relevant duty of care is to arise.

1 *Jarvis v Hampshire County Council* [2000] ELR 36, [2000] Ed CR 1.

That summary, however, left open some inconsistencies. First, it suggested that the failure to ameliorate certain non-congenital or constitutional conditions could amount to an injury. Second, the idea that LEA educational psychologists assume no responsibility to the children they assess was a way of avoiding significant litigation against educational psychologists, it hardly accorded with what educational psychologists assumed was their responsibility towards the child. Third, although the Court of Appeal had given the message that LEA educational psychologists would, in effect, be protected from negligence claims, the position of headteachers, teachers, advisory teachers and inspectors was unclear. *X* and *Gower* gave the clearest possible indication that they would be in breach of their legal duties if they failed to exercise the reasonable skills of their fellow professionals in relation to a pupil's educational needs. There was therefore still the potential for claims to be made against teaching staff, and vicariously, their LEAs for failing to detect a pupil's special educational needs and/or to provide adequate remedial assistance but not, surprisingly against educational psychologists (who after all were the nearest education professionals to medical professionals who had been subject to duties of care for many years) and education officers employed by LEAs. **10.10.58**

For these reasons and others, the House of Lords overturned the decisions of the Court of Appeal in *Phelps*, *Anderton* and *Jarvis* and upheld the decision in *Gower*[1]. Hearing all four appeals together, seven Law Lords unanimously held that various educational professionals could owe common law duties of care towards children for whom they were responsible and that their employers (LEAs or, in theory, schools) could be vicariously liable for those breaches of duty. **10.10.59**

1 [2000] ELR 499, HL.

The Lords could find no reason for finding some form of immunity as these were not cases where the LEA had had to weigh competing interests or which related to considerations which Parliament could not have intended to be justiciable. The question therefore was whether the damage alleged to have occurred was foreseeable, proximate and it was reasonable to recognise a duty of care. The Lords did not accept that a duty was prevented from arising simply because the advice was given only because an LEA, through its officers, had a statutory power to do so. Adopting the judgment of Lord Browne-Wilkinson in *X*, the Lords felt that only where the imposition of a common law duty would be inconsistent with the exercise of a statutory duty or power should the courts be wary of creating such a duty. **10.10.60**

In the Court of Appeal, it had been suggested that to establish liability there had to be some 'acceptance of responsibility' on the part of the educational **10.10.61** professional, the Court treating the damage as being in the nature of economic loss and therefore applied the principles required to found such a claim. The House of Lords, however, rejected that argument and considered that the damage in issue could amount to personal injury, psychological damage and a failure to diagnose a congenital condition and to take appropriate action as a result of which a child's level of achievement is reduced (which leads to a loss of employment and wages) were capable of being personal injuries to a person[1].

1 *Phelps* [2000] ELR 499, HL per Lord Slynn at p 529.

10.10.62 That being the case, the acceptance of responsibility was no longer a determinative factor. Instead, Lord Slynn, with whom the other Lords agreed, held[1] that it was elementary that persons exercising a particular skill or profession may owe a duty of care in the performance to people who it can be foreseen will be injured if due skill and care are not exercised. This would include doctors, accountants or engineers. So too would it include an educational psychologist or psychiatrist or a teacher including a teacher in a specialised area, such as a teacher concerned with children having special educational needs. Lord Slynn agreed[2] with Lord Browne-Wilkinson[3] that a headteacher or teacher owed duties of care to specific pupils. There was no reason why similar duties on specific facts should not arise for others engaged in the educational process, for example, an educational psychologist. The fact that the psychologist owed a duty to their employer to exercise skill and care should not oust any duty to the child.

1 [2000] ELR 499, HL at p 516.
2 [2000] ELR 499, HL at p 517.
3 *X v Bedfordshire County Council* [1995] ELR 404 at p 451.

10.10.63 In an attempt to offset criticism that the decision would 'open the flood gates', Lord Slynn[1] pointed out that this was only the start of the enquiry:

'It must still be shown that the educational psychologist is acting in relation to a particular child in a situation where the law recognises a duty of care. A casual remark, an isolated act may occur in a situation where there is no sufficient nexus between the two persons for a duty of care to exist. But where an educational psychologist is specifically called in to advise in relation to the assessment and future provision for a specific child, and it is clear that the parents, acting for the child, and the teachers will follow that advice, prima facie a duty of care arises.'

1 [2000] ELR 499, HL at p 517.

10.10.64 Applying these principles to the *Phelps* case, the Lords reinstated the decision of Garland J and the award of damages to the claimant. In the other cases, they decided that the claims should not be struck out and that full argument should occur.

10.10.65 As a consequence, in *Phelps* the Lords have clarified the law after *X* and made clear that teachers, headteachers and all other educational professionals involved with children having special educational needs may owe duties of care which, if broken, may enable a claim to be made for compensation. The logic of the decision and the need for equivalence between professionals cannot be doubted, but the potential effect, especially when applied to all pupils as it must be, could be a cause of concern. However, given the strict criteria which have to be met and which have been highlighted in both *X* and *Phelps*, the flood gates are unlikely to open too wide. Indeed, claims post-*Phelps* have not been extensive or numerous[1]. Perhaps the object lesson of all the legislation is that rather than adopt 'defensive education' as was suggested might occur during argument in the Lords, as long as proper procedures are followed and the guidance in the Code of Practice adhered to, there should, hopefully, be few failures that may give rise to litigation.

1 Only one case, *Liennard v Slough Borough Council* [2002] EWHC 398, QBD, has been reported and the teachers concerned were held not to have been negligent.

Chapter 11

Disability discrimination: definitions and general principles, claims and conciliation

---

INTRODUCTION TO DISABILITY DISCRIMINATION LAW

Statutory provisions   11.1

The Disability Discrimination Act 1995

The Disability Discrimination Act (DDA) 1995 was a response to an   **11.1.1**
increasing concern at the lack of protection from discrimination available to
disabled persons in the UK and was a belated attempt to catch up with the
protections available in other countries[1]. In the UK, efforts had been made
through private members' bills for some anti-discrimination measures to be
introduced[2], but these had been defeated. The groundswell of opinion
which demanded some form of protection did, however, persuade the government to publish a Green Paper in July 1994[3] setting out proposals to
prevent discrimination in employment and in access to goods and services.
A White Paper[4] and a Disability Discrimination Bill followed in January
1995.

1 See, for example, the Australian Disability Discrimination Act 1992 and the New Zealand
   Human Rights Act 1993, s 21.
2 Civil Rights (Disabled Persons) Bill 1991–92 and Civil Rights (Disabled Persons) Bill
   1993–94.
3 *A Consultation on Government Measures to Tackle Discrimination Against Disabled People*
   (Department of Social Security, 1994).
4 *Ending Discrimination Against Disabled People* (HMSO, London, 1995), Cmnd 2729.

The Bill received Royal Assent on 8 November 1995, and the resulting   **11.1.2**
DDA 1995 has remained the basis for anti-discrimination measures protecting disabled persons. It was not, however, without its critics, who
suggested that the 1995 Act did not go far enough. In education, in particular, there was criticism of the fact that the provision of education had been
specifically excluded from the protection the Act conferred[1]. Upon their
election in May 1997, the new Labour government proposed to reform the
DDA 1995 to provide greater protection for the disabled and set up the
Disability Rights Task Force to make appropriate recommendations. The
Task Force reported back in 1999[2].

1 See DDA 1995, s 19.
2 *From Exclusion to Inclusion: A Report of the Disability Rights Task Force on Civil Rights for
   Disabled People* (DfEE, London, 1999).

Report of the Disability Rights Task Force

11.1.3 The report covered all aspects of disability including employment, access to goods and services, travel and environment and housing[1]. So far as education was concerned, the Task Force recognised that the education of disabled persons caused much debate, but was vital as it would determine their future opportunities in life[2]. In looking at education, the Task Force ensured that the principle of inclusion underlined their considerations and recommendations[3].

> 1 *From Exclusion to Inclusion: A Report of the Disability Rights Task Force on Civil Rights for Disabled People* (DfEE, London, 1999), Chaps 5 to 8.
> 2 *From Exclusion to Inclusion: A Report of the Disability Rights Task Force on Civil Rights for Disabled People* (DfEE, London, 1999), Chap 4, para 1.
> 3 *From Exclusion to Inclusion: A Report of the Disability Rights Task Force on Civil Rights for Disabled People* (DfEE, London, 1999), Chap 4, para 2.

11.1.4 The Task Force set out 17 recommendations in total[1], but identified the key ones as[2]:

(1) In schools:
    (a) A strengthened right for parents of children with statements of special educational needs to a place at a mainstream school, unless they favour a special school and a mainstream school would not meet the needs of the child or the wishes of either the parent or the child.
    (b) A new right for disabled pupils not to be discriminated against unfairly by schools and Local Education Authorities (LEAs) and to have reasonable adjustments made to policies, practices and procedures which place them at a substantial disadvantage to others.
    (c) A new duty on schools and LEAs to plan strategically and make progress in increasing accessibility for disabled pupils to school premises and the curriculum.
(2) In further, higher and LEA-secured adult education:
    (a) A separate section on further, higher and LEA-secured adult education should be included in civil rights legislation to secure comprehensive and enforceable rights for disabled people; similar rights should apply in relation to the Youth Service.
    (b) The legislation should have an associated statutory Code of Practice, explaining the new rights.

> 1 *From Exclusion to Inclusion: A Report of the Disability Rights Task Force on Civil Rights for Disabled People* (DfEE, London, 1999), Chap 4, paras 9 to 48.
> 2 *From Exclusion to Inclusion: A Report of the Disability Rights Task Force on Civil Rights for Disabled People* (DfEE, London, 1999), Chap 4, para 6.

Government's proposals

11.1.5 The government responded with an interim report[1] to answer the Task Force's general recommendations, but produced a specific consultation document in response to the education recommendations[2]. In this, the government proposed legislation which would make it unlawful for education providers to discriminate against a disabled child by[3]:

(a) treating a disabled child less favourably on the grounds of their disability than a non-disabled child, without justification, in the arrangements made for the provision of education;

(b) failing to take reasonable steps to change any policies, practices or procedures which place a disabled child at a substantial disadvantage compared to a non-disabled child; and

(c) failing to take reasonable steps to provide education using a reasonable alternative method where a physical feature places a disabled child at a substantial disadvantage compared to a non-disabled child,

and also:

(d) extending the jurisdiction of the Special Educational Needs Tribunal.

1   *Interim Government Response to the Report of the Disability Rights Task Force* (DfEE, London, 2000).
2   *SEN and Discrimination Rights in Education Bill Consultation* (DfEE, London, 2000).
3   *SEN and Discrimination Rights in Education Bill Consultation* (DfEE, London, 2000), Annex A1.

In respect of further and higher education, the government proposed legislation which would make it unlawful for education providers, in relation to the provision of education and services provided primarily for students, to discriminate against a disabled person by[1]:   **11.1.6**

(a) failing to make a reasonable adjustment, where any arrangements, including physical features of premises, place him at a substantial disadvantage in comparison to persons who are not disabled; or

(b) unjustifiably treating him less favourably, for a reason which relates to his disability, than the provider treats others to whom that reason does not apply.

1   *SEN and Discrimination Rights in Education Bill Consultation* (DfEE, London, 2000), Annex A2, para 2.

Together with the legislative provisions, the government proposed that there would be associated Codes of Practice for schools and post-16 providers to be prepared by the Disability Rights Commission and approved by the Secretary of State[1]. These Codes would be distinct from the SEN Code of Practice[2] and would give practical guidance and advice on the new responsibilities.   **11.1.7**

1   *SEN and Discrimination Rights in Education Bill Consultation* (DfEE, London, 2000), Annex A, para 7.
2   As to which, see 2.2.6 and 2.2.7.

The Special Educational Needs and Disability Act 2001

Virtually everything proposed in the consultation document was subsequently incorporated into the Special Educational Needs and Disability Bill, which became the Special Educational Needs and Disability Act (SENDA) 2001 when it received Royal Assent on 11 May 2001.   **11.1.8**

The new provisions of the DDA 1995 are considered in detail below. In addition to the Act, the Secretary of State will make a number of regulations. At the time of writing, none had been made, although a number of drafts had been issued[1]. In addition, the Commission will issue two Codes of Practice, one for schools and the other for the post-16 sector. Drafts of the Codes of Practice had been circulated for consultation in July 2001:   **11.1.9**

(a) Code of Practice (Schools): New duties (from 2002) not to discriminate against disabled pupils and prospective pupils in the provision of education and associated services in schools and in respect of admissions and exclusions (hereinafter 'Code of Practice (Schools)'); and

(b) Code of Practice (Post 16): New duties (from 2002) in the provision of post-16 education and related services for disabled people and students (hereinafter 'Code of Practice (Post 16)').

Final versions of the two documents had not been produced, however, at the time of writing. Accordingly, references in this and following chapters to the 'Codes of Practices' are references to the draft versions. Paragraph numbers and the advice they contain may therefore change from those quoted below.

1 See, for example, the draft Disability Discrimination (Student Services) Regulations; Disability Discrimination (Educational Institutions) (Alteration of Leasehold Premises) Regulations; and the Disability Discrimination (Justification) Regulations, which are available on the DfES website: www.dfes.gov.uk

11.1.10   To clarify the position of sixth form provision, educational provision in school sixth forms will be covered by the Code of Practice (Schools). The Code of Practice (Post 16) will only apply to sixth form provision that is not made in a school[1].

1 See Code of Practice (Schools), para 2:3.

11.1.11   The majority of disability provisions introduced by the SENDA 2001 are, although no commencement has been made at the date of writing, intended to come into force on 1 September 2002[1]. Exceptions will be the duty in post-16 education to make adjustments which involve the provision of auxiliary aids and services, which will come into force on 1 September 2003, and the requirements for responsible bodies to make adjustments to physical features of premises, which will take effect from 1 September 2005. The Codes of Practice should, however, be finalised and approved in the spring of 2002, in order to enable the guidance to be applied and steps taken to ensure that the relevant obligations are met by the time the SENDA 2001 comes into force.

1 See, for example, Code of Practice (Schools), para 1:18; and the Foreword to the Code of Practice (Post 16).

11.2   Codes of Practice

11.2.1   The original DDA 1995 set out a process by which the Secretary of State could ask the National Disability Council to produce proposals for codes of practice or to review existing codes[1]. The content of these codes would be such as the Secretary of State had referred to the National Disability Council and therefore the extent of the codes could be, and was to a certain extent, limited.

1 DDA 1995, s 51(1).

11.2.2   The Disability Rights Commission Act 1999 changed all this. As part of its aim to give the Disability Rights Council, or after the Act, the Disability

Rights Commission ('the Commission'), autonomy and a status equivalent to that of the Equal Opportunities Commission and the Commission for Racial Equality, the government has removed[1] the Secretary of State's power to issue and revise codes of practice and, instead, will give the responsibility for the initiation, preparation and revision of codes of practice to the Commission.

1 With effect from 25 April 2000 – see Disability Rights Commission Act 1999 (Commencement No 2 and Transitional Provision) Order 2000, SI 2000/880.

Thus, the Commission has the power to prepare and issue codes of **11.2.3** practice giving practical guidance on how to avoid discrimination, or on any other matter relating to any provision of Parts II, III and IV of the DDA 1995, including the provisions on discrimination in education, to employers, service providers, responsible bodies for schools or further education and higher education institutes[1] and any other person to whom the provision of Parts II or III or Chapter 2 of Part IV of the DDA 1995 apply[2].

The Commission may also prepare and issue codes of practice giving practical guidance to any person on any other matters with a view to promoting the equalisation of opportunities for disabled persons and persons who have had a disability or encouraging good practice in the way such persons are treated in any field of activity regulated by any provision of Parts II, III or IV of the DDA 1995[3]. Such codes of practice may not, however, deal with or be issued in respect of, the duties imposed on LEAs and governing bodies to produce accessibility strategies and plans[4].

1 For consideration of responsible bodies, see 13.3 and 14.3.
2 DDA 1995, s 53A(1).
3 DDA 1995, s 53A(1A).
4 DDA 1995, s 53A(1B); and see DDA 1995, ss 28D and 28E, considered at 13.7.

Although the power of the Secretary of State to issue codes of practice will **11.2.4** be lost, the Secretary of State still retains the power to request that the Commission prepare a code of practice on matters specified in the request. The Commission must, in response to such a request, prepare a code of practice[1].

1 DDA 1995, s 53A(2).

In preparing a code of practice, the Commission must carry out such con- **11.2.5** sultation as it considers appropriate (which shall include the publication for public consultation of proposals relating to the code)[1].The Commission may not issue a code of practice unless a draft of it has been submitted to and approved by the Secretary of State and laid by him before both Houses of Parliament and the 40-day period has elapsed without either House resolving not to approve the draft[2]. If the Secretary of State does not approve the draft, he must provide the Commission with a written statement of his reasons[3].

1 DDA 1995, s 53A(3).
2 DDA 1995, s 53A(4).
3 DDA 1995, s 53A(5).

11.2.6 A code of practice issued by the Commission shall come into effect on such day as the Secretary of State may by order appoint and may be revised and re-issued by the Commission or can be revoked by the Secretary of State by order at the request of the Commission[1]. Where the Commission proposes to revise a code of practice it must carry out such consultations as it considers appropriate (including publishing the proposals relating to the code for public consultation). The other provisions governing the issue of a code apply to the publication and issue of a revised code[2].

1 DDA 1995, s 53A(6).
2 DDA 1995, s 53A(7).

11.2.7 Failure to observe any provision of a code of practice does not of itself make a person liable to any proceedings[1]. But, if any provision of a code which appears to a court or tribunal or other body (including admission and exclusion appeal panels) hearing any proceedings under Parts II, III or IV of the DDA 1995 to be relevant, it must take that provision into account[2].

1 DDA 1995, s 53A(8).
2 DDA 1995, s 53A(8A).

11.2.8 Codes of Practice have been issued under the provisions of the DDA 1995 by the Disability Rights Council, the Secretary of State or the Commission to provide guidance on matters to be taken into account in relation to the definition of disability[1], the elimination of discrimination in the field of employment[2], the right of access to goods, facilities, services and premises[3] and the duties of trade organisations to their disabled members and applicants[4]

1 *Guidance on matters to be taken into account in determining questions relating to the definition of disability* (1996).
2 Code of Practice for the elimination of discrimination in the field of employment against disabled persons or persons who have had a disability (1996), which is to be updated in 2002.
3 Code of Practice: Rights of access: goods, facilities, services and premises.
4 Code of Practice: Duties of trade organisations to their disabled members and applicants (1999).

DISABILITY DISCRIMINATION: DEFINITIONS AND GENERAL PRINCIPLES

11.3 Meaning of 'disability'

11.3.1 The notion of 'disability' and who may be a disabled person is obviously key to an understanding of the principles of disability discrimination in education. The DDA 1995 will only apply to a person who has a physical or mental impairment which has a substantial and long-term adverse effect on their ability to carry out normal day-to-day activities[1]. Because of its central importance, the meaning of disability is considered in detail in Chapter 12.

1 DDA 1995, s 1.

Meaning of 'discrimination'   **11.4**

The concept of 'discrimination' has been well-established in the fields of sex   **11.4.1**
and race since the mid-1970s. The disability discrimination provisions in the
DDA 1995 built on these foundations, although the nature of discrimination
against disabled persons is, especially outside the field of employment, slightly,
but importantly, different. Even in the employment field there are subtle variations between race and sex discrimination and disability discrimination.

In the education sphere, unlawful discrimination against a disabled child or   **11.4.2**
student can occur in two ways[1]:

(1) treating a disabled pupil/student or prospective pupil/student less
   favourably for a reason relating to his disability than someone to whom
   that reason does not apply is treated without justification; or
(2) failing to make reasonable adjustments to admission arrangements and
   in relation to education and associated services to ensure that disabled
   pupils/students or prospective pupils/students are not placed at a substantial disadvantage in comparison with their non-disabled peers
   without justification.

1 DDA 1995, ss 28B and 28R; and see Code of Practice (Schools), Chap 3; and Code of
  Practice (Post 16), Chaps 4 and 5.

'Less favourable treatment'

The first type of discrimination, 'less favourable treatment', is similar to the   **11.4.3**
concepts of direct discrimination in sex and race law. It requires a comparison to be made between the disabled person and a non-disabled person in
order to assess whether the treatment of the disabled person was less
favourable than that given to the non-disabled person. In sex and race discrimination, there is specific direction to compare like with like so that the
comparison has to be based upon a consideration of comparators in relevant
circumstances which are the same or not materially different[1]. Thus, for
example, if a lesbian claims sex discrimination, she has to show that she has
been treated less favourably than a male homosexual (taking all relevant circumstances into account) rather than a male heterosexual[2]. This specific
provision is missing from the definition of discrimination under the DDA
1995 so it is possible[3] that the courts will say that the comparison can be
broadly drawn or be drawn more broadly than in the case of race and sex
discrimination. The comparator may also be hypothetical; the legislation
uses the word 'would'.

1 See Sex Discrimination Act 1975, s 5(3) and Race Relations Act 1976, s 3(4).
2 See, for example, *Pearce v Governing Body of Mayfield School*, [2001] EWCA Civ 1347,
  [2002] ICR 198, [2001] IRLR 669.
3 And see *Clark v TDG Ltd (t/a Novacold)* [1999] IRLR 318, CA in the context of
  employment discrimination.

The comparison, whether actual or hypothetical, is between the disabled   **11.4.4**
pupil/student and a comparator to whom the reason relating to the disabled person's disability does not or would not apply. Although the
distinction is slight, it is important. The comparison is not a simple comparison between the disabled person and a non-disabled person; the reason
relating to the disability is the key.

11.4.5 There are, in fact, three tests to be met before this type of discrimination may apply[1]:

(1) the less favourable treatment is for a reason that is related to the child's disability;
(2) it is less favourable treatment then someone gets or would get if the reason does not apply to them; and
(3) it is less favourable treatment that cannot be justified.

1 And see Code of Practice (Schools), para 3:7.

11.4.6 The effect of this type of discrimination is considered in more detail when we look at the specific types of discrimination in Chapters 13 and 14.

'Failure to make reasonable adjustments'

11.4.7 The second type of discrimination, which is again considered in more detail when we examine the specific provision relating to discrimination in education[1], is 'failure to make reasonable adjustments'. This element does not appear in the equivalent legislation relating to sex and race discrimination.

1 See Chapters 13 and 14.

11.4.8 Although not expressed as such in the Codes of Practice, there are three tests under this heading as well:

(1) failing to make reasonable adjustments;
(2) as a consequence of which, the disabled person is placed at a substantial disadvantage in comparison with his or her non-disabled peers; and
(3) is a failure which cannot be justified.

11.4.9 Again, an element of comparison is involved. The duty only arises after a comparison has been made with the adverse effect on a non-disabled person. It is, again, suggested that the comparison may be wider than in the case of sex and race discrimination[1], but how wide will have to wait for the first case on this area of the DDA 1995.

1 And as in *Clark v TDG Ltd (t/a Novacold)* [1999] IRLR 318, CA.

11.5 Victimisation

11.5.1 A common concept in all aspects of discrimination law is the idea that an individual should be protected from victimisation if they assert or attempt to assert their rights under the respective legislation. The provisions in the DDA 1995[1] are slightly different from those in the Sex Discrimination Act 1975[2] and the Race Relations Act 1976[3], but the effect is similar and the case law under that legislation is informative and helpful.

1 DDA 1995, s 55.
2 Sex Discrimination Act 1975, s 4.
3 Race Relations Act 1976, s 2.

A person (A) discriminates against another person (B)[1] if: **11.5.2**

(a) A treats B less favourably than he treats or would treat other persons whose circumstances[2] are the same as B's; and
(b) A does so because B has either[3]:
  (i) brought proceedings against A or any other person under the DDA 1995;
  (ii) given evidence or information in connection with such proceedings brought by any person;
  (ii) otherwise done anything under the DDA 1995 in relation to A or any other person; or
  (iv) alleged that A or any other person has (whether or not the allegation so states) contravened the DDA 1995;
  or:
  (v) A believes or suspects that B has done or intends to do any of these things.

1 DDA 1995, s 55(1).
2 Where B, the victim, is a disabled person or a person who has had a disability, the disability should be disregarded in comparing B's circumstances with those of any other person: DDA 1995, s 55(3).
3 DDA 1995, s 55(2).

The victimisation provisions do not apply to a person who has made an alle-   **11.5.3**
gation if the allegation was false and not made in good faith[1].

1 DDA 1995, s 55(4).

Thus the victimisation provisions can apply to a disabled person who has   **11.5.4**
brought a claim under the DDA 1995, but also to a person who is not disabled but who gives evidence or information or makes an allegation.
Protection is also given, for the purposes of disability discrimination in
schools[1], but only for those purposes, to parents and siblings of B. Thus references to B in the paragraphs above, include references to a person who is
B's parent and a sibling of B[2].

1 Under DDA 1995, Pt 4, Chap 1.
2 DDA 1995, s 55(3A).

The sex discrimination cases have, to a certain degree, limited the extent of   **11.5.5**
the protection afforded by the victimisation provisions. In *British Airways
Engine Overhaul Ltd v Francis*[1], the claimant issued a statement to the press
criticising her union for not carrying out its policy of seeking equal pay for
women. She was reprimanded by her employer for making an authorised
press statement. She complained of victimisation, but failed as she was held
not to have been claiming that either her employer (A) or her union (another
person) was in breach of the Sex Discrimination Act 1975, merely that the
union wasn't pursuing its equal pay policy. Nor had she done anything
under the Act in relation to her employer or any other person.

1 [1981] IRLR 9, EAT.

Similarly, in *Cornelius v University College of Swansea*[1], Ms Cornelius had   **11.5.6**
complained she had been subject to unwanted attention from her manager.
She was transferred to another post, but became dissatisfied with that and
asked to be returned to her old job. When this was refused, she issued a

number of applications to the Tribunal under the Sex Discrimination Act 1975. While these were still pending, she asked to use the grievance procedure, but this was refused by her employer while her Tribunal proceedings were still live. She was eventually dismissed after refusing to carry out the duties of the post to which she had been transferred. She claimed under the victimisation provisions of the Sex Discrimination Act 1975.

Her application was dismissed by the Court of Appeal. The Court held that claims for victimisation were not claims of discrimination on the ground of sex (or race or disability) but discrimination on the grounds of the conduct specified and that, in order to succeed, it would have to appear that in refusing the transfer or access to the grievance procedure, (a) the employer treated her less favourably than it would in the same circumstances have treated other persons, and (b) it did so because she had brought proceedings against the employer under the relevant Act. The Court held that the College had deferred matters pending the Tribunal proceedings rather than taking that action as a result of those proceedings being issued against it and therefore the test had not been made out.

1 [1987] IRLR 141, CA.

11.5.7   A decision which is of more assistance to claimants is *Nagarajan v London Regional Transport*[1]. The claimant had brought numerous race discrimination claims against his employer. He applied for a job, but was unsuccessful and complained of race discrimination. There was no evidence that the employer had consciously discriminated against him because of his previous claims. However, the House of Lords held that conscious motivation was not necessary. If, consciously or subconsciously, the claimant's interviewers had been influenced by the fact that he had previously brought proceedings against the employer, he would succeed in his claim of victimisation. Aside from the difficulties of proving or disproving the subconscious thoughts of an employer, the decision does mean that an absence of an intention on the part of A to discriminate because of B's previous conduct, will not necessarily enable A to escape liability.

1 [1999] IRLR 572, HL.

11.5.8   In the context of disability discrimination in education, the following may be examples of acts which may be covered by the victimisation provisions:

- a non-disabled student/pupil acts as a witness in a complaint brought by a disabled student against a college lecturer/teacher; later, in retaliation, other staff lose the student's work and hand assignments back later than other students'/pupils'[1];
- a headteacher disciplines a non-disabled pupil because he acted as a witness to support a claim by a disabled pupil[2];
- an admissions authority refuses to admit a child to a school because the child's parent has previously complained to the Tribunal that her other child, who attends the school, has been discriminated against by the school;
- a school prevents a disabled pupil going on a school trip because his parent raised issues of disability discrimination during an admission appeal for admission to the school.

However, if (for example) a child with epilepsy makes a series of allegations that she and other disabled pupils are excluded from after-school activities and the allegations are found to be without foundation and based on a personal vendetta, it is unlikely that there has been victimisation[3].

1 Code of Practice (Post 16), para 8:2 and Code of Practice (Schools), para 8:15.
2 Code of Practice (Schools), para 8:15A.
3 Code of Practice (Schools), para 8:18 and Code of Practice (Post 16), para 8:4.

Aiding and abetting   **11.6**

A person who knowingly aids another person to do an act made unlawful by **11.6.1** the DDA 1995 is to be treated as himself doing the same kind of unlawful act[1]. An employee or agent for whose act the employer or principal is liable[2] shall be taken to have aided the employer or principal to do the act[3]. A person does not, however, knowingly aid another to do an unlawful act if (a) he acts in reliance on a statement made to him by that other person that, because of any provision of the DDA 1995, the act would not be unlawful, and (b) it is reasonable for him to rely on that statement[4]. A person who knowingly or recklessly makes such a statement which is false or misleading in a material respect is guilty of an offence[5] which on summary conviction shall make him liable to a fine not exceeding level 5 on the standard scale[6].

1 DDA 1995, s 57(1).
2 See 11.7.
3 DDA 1995, s 57(2).
4 DDA 1995, s 57(3).
5 DDA 1995, s 57(4).
6 DDA 1995, s 57(5).

These provisions, although applying to further education and higher edu- **11.6.2** cation institutes, do not apply to disability discrimination in schools[1].

1 Under DDA 1995, Pt 4, Chap 1; and see DDA 1995, s 57(6), inserted by SENDA 2001, s 38(1).

Two elements are required before there can be liability: (a) the act of aiding, **11.6.3** and (b) the mental element of 'knowingly' doing the act. It is closely connected with the principles of employer's liability, considered below[1], but does mean that an employee can be made liable as well as the employer[2].

1 See 11.7.
2 See *Armitage, Marsden and HM Prison Service v Johnson* [1997] IRLR 162, EAT.

In *Hallam v Avery*[1], a case brought under the equivalent provisions of the **11.6.4** Race Relations Act 1976, it was claimed that the police had aided a council to discriminate against gypsies. The police had provided the council with information about a proposed wedding, which led the council to impose extra conditions on the booking of a venue. The claim against the police officers for aiding and abetting failed in the Court of Appeal because it would have to be proved that the aider knew that the council was treating, or about to treat, the claimant less favourably on (in that case) racial grounds and that, with that knowledge or intention, the aid was provided. In the House of Lords, their Lordships dismissed the claim but on the basis that the police officers were not involved in, or party to, the decision which was unlawful, although Lord Bingham indicated that their decision should not be taken as authority for the view that where a person gives information to another on which that other relies in doing an unlawful discriminatory act, the first person can never be liable.

Thus, based on the Court of Appeal decision which, although not approved by the Lords, was not overturned, in cases where an employee is accused of aiding his employer, it will probably have to be proved that the employee either wanted the discrimination to be the result or knew that the employer would treat or was contemplating treating the victim in a discriminatory way.

1 [2000] ICR 583, CA; affd [2001] UKHL 15, [2001] 1 WLR 638, HL.

11.6.5 In *Anyanwu v South Bank Student Union*[1], the applicants, who were student union officials, were expelled from their university. As a result, the student union treated their employment contracts as at an end. The applicants claimed that the union and university had discriminated against them on racial grounds. They alleged that the university had made various allegations about them and encouraged other union officers to make allegations which, they claimed, had aided and abetted the racial discrimination. The same House of Lords as in *Hallam* held that the provision prohibiting aiding and abetting in the Race Relations Act 1976 was to be construed purposively. They therefore gave the word 'aids' its everyday and simple meaning rather than a technical or special one; it meant help or assistance given by one person to another which was more than trivial. It required the adjudicating body to identify an act of some kind which helped another person to commit an unlawful act. On the facts, the House of Lords held that there was an arguable case that the university had aided the union and therefore the case was remitted back to an employment tribunal.

1 [2001] UKHL 14, [2001] 2 All ER 353, [2001] 1 WLR 638.

11.6.6 Examples of aiding and abetting are given in the Code of Practice (Post-16). One example is where a college provides guidance to its part-time agency teaching staff that they should not agree extra time or other examination arrangements for disabled students because of the extra costs; then when a dyslexic student requests additional time for a class exam, an agency lecturer says this is not available, although she knows that this is likely to be against the law. It is likely that the governing body of the college is acting unlawfully and the agency which employs the lecturer may be liable for aiding the governing body's unlawful act[1]. Another example is where an LEA officer sends a memorandum to the LEA's part-time teachers saying that the DDA 1995 does not apply to part-time or evening class students. The officer knows this is not true. As a result a teacher refuses to provide electronic copies of overheads for a blind student. The LEA is likely to be acting unlawfully, although not criminally, because it had no knowledge of the officer's memo. The teacher is unlikely to be knowingly aiding an unlawful act because it may be reasonable to rely on the memorandum, but the officer is likely to have committed a criminal offence[2].

1 Code of Practice (Post 16), para 8:5A.
2 Code of Practice (Post 16), para 8:7A.

Liability of employers and principals   **11.7**

Anything done by a person in the course of his employment shall be   **11.7.1**
treated as also done by his employer, whether or not it was done with the
employer's knowledge or approval[1]. This does not, however, apply if the
act is the criminal offence of knowingly or recklessly making a statement
that an act would not be unlawful which is false or misleading in a material respect[2]. An employer does, however, have a defence in proceedings
brought in respect of an employee's act if the employer can prove that he
took such steps as were reasonably practicable to prevent the employee
from doing that act or doing, in the course of his employment, acts of that
description[3].

1   DDA 1995, s 58(1).
2   DDA 1995, s 58(4); and see DDA 1995, s 57(4) and 11.6.1.
3   DDA 1995, s 58(5).

Anything done by a person as agent for another person with the authority of   **11.7.2**
that other person shall be treated as also done by that other person, ie acts
of an agent are treated as the acts of the principal[1]. This applies whether the
authority given by the principal was express or implied or given before or
after the act in question was done[2]. As with an employer's liability, this does
not apply to a criminal act of the agent who makes a statement that an act
would not be unlawful which is false or misleading in a material respect[3].
The defence available to employers, to show that they had taken such steps
as were reasonably practicable to prevent the employee from doing the act or
doing, in the course of employment, acts of that description, is not available
to principals.

1   DDA 1995, s 58(2).
2   DDA 1995, s 58(3).
3   DDA 1995, s 58(4).

For a time, the extent of an employer's vicarious liability for discrimination   **11.7.3**
was wider than an employer's vicarious liability for common law torts.
Whether, in light of the House of Lords' decision in *Lister v Hesley Hall
Ltd*[1], that is still the case is debatable now that that judgment has extended
the concept of 'in the course of employment' to include criminal acts of
employees. So now, in practice, there may be little distinction. In the
sphere of discrimination, the words 'in the course of his employment'
have been given a purposive and wide meaning. In *Jones v Tower Boot Co
Ltd*[2], the Court of Appeal held that racist acts (and by extension sexist acts
and negative acts towards disabled persons) carried out by employees can
be committed in the course of the employee's employment, even if the
behaviour had nothing to do with the work the employee was employed to
do. Vicarious liability may also extend to out-of-hours activities: in *Chief
Constable of Lincolnshire v Stubbs*[3], a female police officer was subjected to
sexual harassment by a fellow officer in a pub after her shift had finished.
The Employment Appeal Tribunal (EAT) held that this could give rise to
vicarious liability; the words 'in the course of employment' were to be
widely construed. They should not, however, cover behaviour taking place
at a purely social gathering or during a meeting wholly unrelated to work
outside hours. Thus, in *Sidhu v Aerospace Composite Technology Ltd*[4], an
employer was not held liable for the racial discrimination of an employee

by a fellow employee out of work during a work organised social outing to a racecourse.

1 [2001] UKHL 22, [2001] 2 All ER 769.
2 [1997] 2 All ER 406, CA.
3 [1999] IRLR 81, EAT.
4 [2000] IRLR 602, CA.

11.7.4 Examples given in the Codes of Practice include:

- The case of a disabled pupil who, because other facilities are not available to meet her needs, has to use the staff toilet. If a member of staff objects and makes it impossible for the pupil to use the toilet, there is likely to be discrimination (less favourable treatment) and the teacher's employer will be liable for their unlawful acts[1].
- A school's director of music employs a number of specialist music teachers. Although the school has an equal opportunities and anti-discrimination policy, unknown to the school, one of the teachers is reluctant to teach two physically disabled pupils because they may reduce the chances of success of the school orchestra. The Code of Practice (Schools) suggests the school may have a defence to assuming vicarious liability for the unlawful acts of the music teacher because it took reasonable steps as required by DDA 1995, s 58(5)[2].
- A security guard employed at a college always takes a long time to open the barrier of a staff car park for a disabled student who has been allocated a place there. If this is less favourable treatment and unlawful, the guard's employer will be liable for his actions[3].
- As an example of a principal/agent, the Code of Practice (Schools) refers to the case of a parent running a martial arts club after school, which is authorised by the school. If the parent refuses to admit a visually impaired child, he may be acting unlawfully and the Code suggests the parent is an agent of the school and therefore the school is liable as principal[4], although there may be some question whether the parent is in fact an agent in this case or simply an independent contractor.
- Another example of principal liability is where the cleaning of a university is contracted out to an agency and an agency worker discriminates against a disabled student[5].

1 Code of Practice (Schools), para 8:19A.
2 Code of Practice (Schools), para 8:22A.
3 Code of Practice (Post 16), para 8:8A.
4 Code of Practice (Schools), para 8:23A.
5 Code of Practice (Post 16), para 8:10A.

11.8 Liability for acts of third parties

11.8.1 Schools and colleges cannot be vicariously liable for the acts of their pupils or students against fellow pupils/ students or indeed against members of staff; they are not employees. Nor are pupils agents of the school. Liability for the acts of third parties will therefore depend, not on principles of vicarious liability, but on whether the responsible body itself subjected the complainant to less favourable treatment through the acts of third parties over which the responsible body had 'control'.

The test of 'control' was first set out in *Burton and Rhule v De Vere Hotels*[1]. **11.8.2**
In that case, two black waitresses employed by the respondent hotel were
allegedly subjected to abuse by the comedian Bernard Manning, who had
been hired by the Round Table to perform at a function which was being
held in the hotel. The EAT found the hotel liable for the racial harassment
meted out to its employees. Smith J set out the principle which should
apply in such cases:

> 'We think [subjecting] connotes "control". A person "subjects" another to
> something if he causes or allows that thing to happen, in circumstances
> where he can control whether it happens or not. An employer subjects an
> employee to the detriment of racial [or sexual or disability] harassment if
> he causes or permits the racial [or sexual or disability] harassment to
> occur in circumstances in which he can control whether it happens or not.'

1 [1996] IRLR 596, EAT

In the school setting, the decision in *Burton* has been applied in three cases. **11.8.3**
First, in *Go Kidz Go v Bourdouane*[1], a member of staff of a playgroup was
subjected to sexual harassment by a parent of one of the children. Her
employer was held liable on the basis that they had sufficient control over the
parent's behaviour and that, by not dealing with it, they had subjected the
employee to sex discrimination.

Second, in *Bennet v Essex County Council*[2] the teacher claimant was
exposed at school to a number of incidents of racial abuse by pupils. The
school's response was somewhat muddled and uncertain and there was
some lack of action because a number of parents failed to support the
school's disciplinary sanctions by not allowing their children to attend detention. The EAT held that the Employment Tribunal had been correct to
direct themselves that, although the school and the LEA were not vicariously
liable for the acts of the children, the claimant could succeed in her claim for
race discrimination if she could show, adapting the principle in *Burton and
Rhule*, that the racial harassment by the pupils was something which was sufficiently under the control of the school that they could, by the application
of good education practice, have prevented the racial harassment or reduced
the extent of it. The EAT considered that the facts did amount to a case
where the school had sufficient control so that it had discriminated against
the teacher on the grounds of her race.

1 Unreported, EAT/1110/95.
2 (5 October 1999, unreported) EAT.

And third, in the most recent and important case of *Pearce v Governing* **11.8.4**
Body of Mayfield School[1], a number pupils at the school had subjected the
appellant, a lesbian teacher, to abuse both inside and outside school. Within
lessons in school, the teacher had been subjected to name calling from a
number of identified and unidentified pupils. Outside school, she had been
abused in the street and by her neighbours' children, some of whom
attended her school, some of whom did not. The teacher brought a claim for
sex discrimination against the governing body on the basis that they were
responsible for the acts of the pupils and/or for failing to address the homo-
phobic taunting. The claim failed on the substantive point that
discrimination on the grounds of sexual orientation did not fall within the
meaning of 'sex discrimination' under the Sex Discrimination Act 1975, but

the Employment Tribunal had held that if sex discrimination had been established on the facts, they would have held the school responsible for the acts of its pupils. Applying the test in *Burton and Rhule*, the Employment Tribunal concluded that the school had not taken appropriate steps and would therefore have been directly responsible for any sex discrimination.

On appeal[2], the EAT was persuaded that the Tribunal's application of the *Burton and Rhule* test had been too restrictive. The EAT said that the correct test was 'whether the event in question was something which was sufficiently under the control of the employer that he could . . . have prevented the harassment or reduced the extent of it'. Whilst accepting that it was not necessary for the claimant to show that steps which the school should have taken *would* have prevented the harassment, it was necessary to find that the steps identified by the Employment Tribunal *could* have prevented or reduced the discrimination.

The majority of the Court of Appeal agreed with the EAT. Judge LJ[3] commented on the nature of 'control' in the context of a school:

> 'For the purpose of testing whether the school authorities should be liable . . . the nature of the "control" which a school can exercise over its pupils is problematic . . . Disciplinary responsibility for the behaviour of children generally is shared by the teachers with the parents. Given the inevitable involvement of parents (with all their differing attitudes) as well as the statutory obligations on the school to provide education for large numbers of children from different homes, the enforcement of school discipline for the benefit of individual teachers as well as the necessary fulfilment of the school's obligations to all its pupils, predicate a much more subtle and complicated mechanism than that implied by the word "control".'

The Employment Tribunal had identified that the school should have dealt with the abuse through whole school assemblies or by removing children from classes. Judge LJ did not agree that these would have solved the problem. In assemblies:

> 'in this delicate area, one silly comment by a teenage boy or girl, out of sight of members of the staff, might convulse a large section of the assembled pupils, with tittering and barely controlled mirth, forcing the assembly to an undignified end. Again, some parents, particularly those of the younger children at the school, might have serious reservations about discussions relating to sexual orientation in open assembly . . . Some parents would prefer, and strongly prefer, to deal with them, with their own children, at home. As to practical support and changing classes, I cannot discern . . . how changing the appellant's class would have brought this nastiness by pupils to an end. It continued outside as well as within the school . . . The Appellant was, at all material times, a very experienced teacher. Schools are not and were not then awash with resources, or teachers, not already committed to their own teaching timetables. The Employment Tribunal did not acknowledge the potential dilemma that if the Appellant had been given "support" in the classroom itself, this step may very well have exacerbated the problem by highlighting it, giving those pupils behaving in this unseemly way the satisfaction of discovering that the Appellant was unable to handle it for herself.'

The majority decision recognises the difficulties faced by schools in dealing with the prejudices of its pupils, prejudices often nurtured at home. The test of 'control' expressed by the EAT and endorsed by the majority of the

Court of Appeal, with the need to show that a school should have taken steps which could have prevented or reduced the harassment, applies a realistic standard for schools.

1 [2001] EWCA, Civ 1347, [2002] ELR 16, CA, [2002] 1 CR 198.
2 [2000] ICR 920, EAT.
3 At para 60.

In principle, schools and colleges may be held responsible for the discriminatory acts of their pupils or students or, indeed, parents. Liability will, however, depend on the extent of control that school or college can reasonably be expected to exert over those who commit the discriminatory acts. Responsible bodies should therefore have in place strategies to deal with this type of behaviour. If they fail to take steps which could have prevented or reduced the extent to which the pupil, student or member of staff was subject to the detriment, they may be liable to pay compensation for disability discrimination. **11.8.5**

DISABILITY DISCRIMINATION: CLAIMS AND CONCILIATION

Bringing claims under the Disability Discrimination Act 1995   **11.9**

The majority of claims under the DDA 1995 to date have been brought in employment tribunals, principally because most claims have alleged disability discrimination in the workplace. Under the DDA 1995, however, certain claims could be brought in the county court in the case of disability discrimination in respect of goods, facilities, services and premises[1]. **11.9.1**

1 DDA 1995, s 25(1).

Claims for disability discrimination in employment and in respect of goods, services etc where they relate to education will continue to be brought in the Employment Tribunal and county court respectively. Claims specifically for disability discrimination in education (which will be dealt with in Chapters 13 and 14) will, however, be brought in a variety of forums. **11.9.2**

If it is claimed that the act of discrimination arises in respect of an admissions decision[1], the claim must be made under the appeal arrangements[2]. That means that in the case of an appeal decision made by an LEA as admission authority for community or voluntary controlled schools, the claim will have to be brought before the independent admission appeal panel established by the LEA. In the case, of an admission decision made by a foundation school, the claim will be made under the appeal arrangements to the independent appeal panel established by the governing body of the school. Similarly, if the claim relates to an admission decision made by the governing body of a voluntary aided school, the claim will have to made to the independent admission appeal panel established by the governing body[3]. In the case of an admission decision made in respect of the admission of a person to a city academy, the claim will have to be raised under the appeal arrangements made by the academy under the agreement it has entered into with the Secretary of State[4]. **11.9.3**

1 DDA 1995, s 28K; and see 13.10.6.

2   DDA 1995, s 28K(3).
3   DDA 1995, s 28K(2) and (5).
4   DDA 1995, s 28K(2) and (5).

11.9.4   If it is claimed that the act of discrimination arises in respect of a decision to permanently exclude a pupil[1], the claim similarly has to be made under the specific exclusion arrangements[2]. Thus a claim will have to be raised in the course of an appeal to an independent exclusions appeal panel established by the LEA in respect of exclusions from community, voluntary controlled, foundation and voluntary aided schools[3]. In the case of city academies, the claim will have to be raised under the arrangements established in pursuance of the agreement between the academy and the Secretary of State[4]. If the claim is in respect of a decision to exclude a child for a fixed term, which does not give a right of appeal to an independent exclusion appeal panel arranged by the LEA, any claim for discrimination will have to be brought in the Tribunal[5].

1   DDA 1995, s 28L; and see 13.10.11ff.
2   Under School Standards and Framework Act 1998, s 67(1) or Education Act 1996, s 482.
3   DDA 1995, s 28L(2) and (5).
4   DDA 1995, s 28L(2) and (5).
5   See 11.9.5.

11.9.5   In the case of all other claims in schools, or in respect of an LEA's residual duties[1] towards children or pupils, a claim for discrimination should be made to the Tribunal[2].

1   DDA 1995, s 28F; and see 13.10.
2   DDA 1995, s 28I.

11.9.6   Claims of discrimination in further and higher education (including further education provided by LEAs and schools)[1] should be brought in the county court[2] by way of civil proceedings in the same way as any other claim in tort[3].

1   DDA 1995, ss 28R to 28U; and see Chapter 14.
2   DDA 1995, s 28V(3); see 11.9.11.
3   DDA 1995, s 28V(1).

11.9.7   Because of the variety of forums in which claims can be brought, the procedures and time limits for making claims will vary from adjudicating body to adjudicating body. In the case of admission and exclusion appeals, the current process and time limits relating to appeals[1] will apply. Thus there are no statutory time limits for admission appeals. Exclusion appeals have to be heard within 15 school days of the date on which the parent is informed of the governing body's decision to uphold the permanent exclusion[2].

1   See School Standards and Framework Act 1998, s 94 and Sch 24 in respect of admission appeals and s 67 and Sch 18 in respect of exclusion appeals.
2   See School Standards and Framework Act 1998, Sch 18, para 1(1).

Claims made to the Tribunal

11.9.8   In the case of claims made to the Tribunal, it shall not consider a claim unless proceedings in respect of the claim are instituted before the end of the period of six months beginning when the act complained of was done[1].

This contrasts markedly with the time limits for an appeal to the Tribunal against an LEA's decision in respect of a child with special educational needs[2] which has to be made within two months of the day notice was given of the decision[3]. If the dispute is referred for conciliation[4] before the end of the six-month period, the period allowed for submitting the claim is extended by two months[5]. The Tribunal may also consider any claim which is made outside the time limit, either the original time limit or one extended because of conciliation, if, in all the circumstances, it considers that it is just and equitable to do so[6]. If an unlawful act of discrimination is attributable to a term in a contract, the act is treated as extending throughout the duration of the contract, so the claim must be brought within six months of the end of the contract term[7]. If the act extends over a period of time, it shall be treated as being done at the end of that period[8] and a deliberate omission[9] shall be treated as done when the person in question decided upon it[10].

1 DDA 1995, Sch 3, para 10(1).
2 See 8.8.4.
3 Special Educational Needs Tribunal Regulations 2001, SI 2001/600, reg 7(3).
4 See 11.10.
5 DDA 1995, Sch 3, para 10(2).
6 DDA 1995, Sch 3, para 10(3); for circumstances where it may be just and equitable for the Tribunal to extend time, see 8.8.4.
7 DDA 1995, Sch 3, para 10(5)(a).
8 DDA 1995, Sch 3, para 10(5)(b).
9 DDA 1995, Sch 3, para 10(6): 'In the absence of evidence establishing the contrary, a person shall be taken to decide upon an omission when he does an act inconsistent with doing the omitted act or, if he has done no such inconsistent act, when the period expires within which he might reasonably have been expected to do the omitted act if it was to be done.'
10 DDA 1995, Sch 3, para 10(5)(c).

The procedure to be adopted by the Tribunal for disability discrimination claims will be contained in regulations to be issued by the Secretary of State[1]. The regulations may, in particular, include provision[2]: **11.9.9**

(a) as to the manner in which a claim must be made;
(b) for enabling functions which relate to matters preliminary or incidental to a claim to be performed by the President or by the chairman;
(c) as to the persons who may appear on behalf of a party;
(d) for granting such disclosure or inspection or right to further particulars as might be granted by a county court;
(e) requiring persons to attend to give evidence and produce documents;
(f) for determining a claim without a hearing;
(g) for enabling the Tribunal to stay proceedings;
(h) for the award of costs or expense; and
(i) for reviewing decisions.

1 DDA 1995, s 28J; at the time of writing no such regulations had been issued.
2 For the full list of matters which may be contained in the Regulations, see DDA 1995, s 28J(2).

Proceedings will be held in private, except in prescribed circumstances[1]. **11.9.10** The Regulations may make provision for a claim under the DDA 1995 to be heard with an appeal against a decision of an LEA relating to a child with special educational needs[2] although care will need to be taken over the respective time limits. A person who, without reasonable excuse, fails to comply with a requirement in respect of the disclosure or inspection of documents or to attend to give evidence and produce documents, will be guilty of an offence and, on summary conviction, will be liable to a fine not exceeding level three on the standard scale[3].

1   DDA 1995, s 28J(3).
2   DDA 1995, s 28J(8).
3   DDA 1995, s 28J(9) and (10).

Further and higher education proceedings: county court

11.9.11   Proceedings for disability discrimination in further and higher education must be instituted in the county court before the end of the period of six months beginning when the act complained of was done[1]. As with the Tribunal[2], if the dispute is referred to conciliation before the end of the six-month period, the time limit is extended by two months[3]. A court may consider any claim which is out of time if, in all the circumstances of the case, it considers that it is just and equitable to do so[4]. The criteria for when time starts to run are identical to those relating to claims in the Tribunal[5].

1   DDA 1995, Sch 3, para 13(1).
2   See 11.9.8.
3   DDA 1995, Sch 3, para 13(2).
4   DDA 1995, Sch 3, para 13(3).
5   DDA 1995, Sch 3, para 13(4) and (5); and see 11.9.8.

11.9.12   Damages may be awarded by the county court, but the amount of any damages awarded as compensation for injury to feelings shall not exceed an amount to be prescribed[1]. In all other respects, the procedure for claims in the county court will be governed by the appropriate county court rules.

1   DDA 1995, Sch 3, para 14.

11.10   Conciliation

11.10.1   The original DDA 1995 had as a principle the idea that disputes should, if possible, be resolved without recourse to tribunals or courts. The Secretary of State was therefore given powers to make arrangements for the provision of advice and assistance with a view to promoting the settlement of disputes otherwise than by recourse to the courts[1].

1   DDA 1995, s 28(1).

11.10.2   With the introduction of the Disability Rights Commission under the Disability Rights Commission Act 1999, the Commission was given responsibility for making the arrangements for the settlement of disputes relating to the provision of goods, facilities or services[1]. There were no provisions for conciliation in respect of disputes relating to education, principally because so few education functions were originally covered by the DDA 1995.

1   DDA 1995, s 28(1) as amended by Disability Rights Commission Act 1999, s 10.

11.10.3   With the extension of the DDA 1995 to cover disability discrimination in education, the SENDA 2001 has also provided the Commission with power to make arrangements for the provision of conciliation services[1]. Thus the Commission may make arrangements with any other person for the provision of conciliation services[2] by, or by persons appointed by, that person in connection with disputes[3]. Neither the Commission itself nor any of its employees may provide the conciliation services[4]. In deciding what arrangements to make (if any), the Commission must have regard to the desirability of securing, so far as reasonably practicable, that conciliation services are available for all disputes which the parties may wish to refer to conciliation[5]. Even if arrangements are made, however, disputes may only be referred for conciliation if both parties agree and the conciliation does not have the power to impose a settlement[6].

1 DDA 1995, s 31B as inserted by SENDA 2001, s 37.
2 'Conciliation services' means advice and assistance provided to the parties to a dispute, by a conciliator, with a view to promoting its settlement otherwise than through a court, tribunal or other body: DDA 1995, s 31B(8).
3 DDA 1995, s 31B(1).
4 DDA 1995, s 31B(3).
5 DDA 1995, s 31B(2).
6 See Code of Practice (Schools), para 7:29 and Code of Practice (Post 16), para 9:3.

11.10.4 Except in the case of information disclosed with the consent of the parties to a dispute[1], the Commission must ensure that the conciliation arrangements include appropriate safeguards to prevent the disclosure to members or employees of the Commission of information obtained by any person in connection with the provision of the conciliation services[2]. This prohibition does not apply to information which does not identify a particular dispute or particular person and is reasonably required by the Commission for the purpose of monitoring the conciliation arrangements[3]. To assist the aim of avoiding the dispute going to court etc, anything communicated to a person providing the conciliation service is not admissible in evidence in any proceedings except with the consent of the party who communicated it[4].

1 DDA 1995, s 31B(5).
2 DDA 1995, s 31B(4).
3 DDA 1995, s 31B(6).
4 DDA 1995, s 31B(7).

11.10.5 The conciliation arrangements apply not just to those disputes which can be brought in the courts or the Tribunal, but also to disputes relating to disability claims in respect of admissions and exclusions which are considered by independent appeal panels. Whether the time limits applicable to these panels permits sensible conciliation will be something to be seen whenever the arrangements are put in place[1].

1 See also Code of Practice (Schools), para 7:30.

11.10.6 Although claims to the Tribunal will normally have to be brought within six months of the act complained of[1], where the dispute is referred for conciliation before the end of that six month period, the period allowed for submitting the claim to the Tribunal is extended by a further two months[2].

1 DDA 1995, Sch 3, para 10(1); and see 11.9.8.
2 DDA 1995, Sch 3, para 10(2).

Chapter 12

The meaning of 'disability'

<table>
<tr><td>**Introduction**</td><td>**12.1**</td></tr>
</table>

Fundamental to any understanding of the law of disability discrimination is **12.1.1**
the meaning of 'disability' for the purposes of the Disability Discrimination
Act (DDA) 1995. Only a person with a disability, a 'disabled person'
according to the Act's terminology, is entitled to the protection the Act
confers.

As with so much legislation, however, the definitions in the DDA 1995 are **12.1.2**
not especially comprehensive and, although providing a basic interpretation[1], the legislation leaves much to supplemental Regulations, statutory
guidance and case law.

1 DDA 1995, s 1(1).

A 'disabled person' is a person who has a 'disability'[1]. A person has a 'dis- **12.1.3**
ability' if he or she has a physical or mental impairment which has a
substantial and long-term adverse effect on his ability to carry out normal
day-to-day activities[2]. Although 'impairment' is not defined in the DDA
1995, the Act does provide assistance[3] in understanding what impairments
may fall within the ambit of the legislation, as do Regulations[4] and statutory
guidance[5].

1 DDA 1995, s 1(2).
2 DDA 1995, s 1(1).
3 DDA 1995, Sch 1.
4 Disability Discrimination (Meaning of Disability) Regulations 1996, SI 1996/1455.
5 *Guidance on matters to be taken into account in determining questions relating to the definition of
   disability* (1996, HMSO).

In *Goodwin v Patent Office*[1] the Employment Appeal Tribunal (EAT) set **12.1.4**
down the correct approach to be taken when seeking to establish whether a
person has a disability within the meaning of the DDA 1995. Although the
onus of proof will be on the person asserting that he is disabled, the EAT (in
an employment case, although the principles should apply in all other cases
as well), indicated that an adjudicating body[2] should adopt an inquisitorial
or interventionist[3] approach to the meaning of 'disability'. The adjudicating
body should also adopt a purposive approach to the construction and interpretation of the DDA 1995 itself, so that the language of the Act is

construed in a way which gives effect to the stated or presumed intention of Parliament, but with due regard to the ordinary and natural meaning of the words in question.

1 [1999] IRLR 4, EAT.
2 Ie a tribunal, court or any other person who, or body which, may decide a claim under DDA 1995, Pt IV: DDA 1995, s 3(3) and (3A) as amended by Special Educational Needs and Disability Act (SENDA) 2001, s 38(3) and (4).
3 Akin to the role of employment tribunals in equal pay claims.

12.1.5 The approach adopted by the EAT has been subsequently endorsed and followed in *Hutton v A E Proctor Ltd*[1], where the EAT repeated that it was important to look at the things that a claimant either could not do or could only do with difficulty, rather than upon the things that the claimant could do. An adjudicating body had to adopt an investigative role incorporating an inquisitional element and, because the legislation was 'social legislation' a purposive approach had to be adopted. Where a disabled person might, out of dignity, answer that they could cope, although their ability to lead what would generally be considered as a normal life had been compromised, there was an onus on the adjudicating body to go beyond that dignity in order to ensure that the claimant received the protection to which he was entitled under the DDA 1995. The *Goodwin* approach has also been followed in *Vicary v British Telecommunications plc*[2], *Kapadia v London Borough of Lambeth*[3] and *Law Hospital NHS Trust v Rush*[4].

1 (18 December 2000, unreported), EAT.
2 [1999] IRLR 680, EAT.
3 [2000] IRLR 699, CA.
4 (8 February 2000, unreported), EAT.

12.1.6 Adjudicating bodies are given explicit assistance by the Disability Discrimination (Meaning of Disability) Regulations 1996[1] and the *Guidance on matters to be taken into account in determining questions relating to the definition of disability*[2]. In addition, any further guidance issued by the Disability Rights Commission in respect of disability in education may provide assistance on this question[3].

1 SI 1996/1455.
2 HMSO, 1996.
3 See the draft Code of Practice (Schools) and Code of Practice (Post 16) (as to which, see 11.1.9).

12.1.7 Having established the correct approach, the EAT in *Goodwin*[1] laid down conditions which employment tribunals (and, it is submitted, now all other adjudicating bodies) must be satisfied exist in order for an applicant to establish that they are disabled within the meaning of the DDA 1995. These conditions, which all need to be answered in the affirmative, are:

(a) Does the applicant have an impairment?
(b) Does the impairment have an adverse effect on the ability of the person to carry out normal day-to-day activities?
(c) Is the adverse effect substantial?
(d) Is the adverse effect long term?

Each of these conditions will be considered in detail below.

1 [1999] IRLR 4, EAT.

The Guidance   12.2

In *Goodwin*[1], the EAT alluded to the type of guidance available to tribunals   **12.2.1**
and other adjudicating bodies. First, the Secretary of State may issue regulations which prescribe the circumstances in which certain conditions may
amount to disabilities or elements of disability[2]. As a consequence, the
Secretary of State issued the Disability Discrimination (Meaning of
Disability) Regulations 1996[3]. Perhaps more importantly with regard to the
practical application of the principles of the DDA 1995, the Secretary of
State could, and the Disability Rights Commission now may, also issue
guidance about the matters to be taken into account in determining (a)
whether an impairment has a substantial adverse effect on a person's ability
to carry out normal day-to-day activities, or (b) whether such an impairment
has a long-term effect[4]. This guidance may, among other things, give examples of:

(a) effects which it would be reasonable, in relation to particular activities,
    to regard for purposes of the DDA 1995 as substantial adverse effects;
(b) effects which it would not be reasonable, in relation to particular activ-
    ities, to regard for such purposes as substantial adverse effects;
(c) substantial adverse effects which it would be reasonable to regard, for
    such purposes, as long-term;
(d) substantial adverse effects which it would not be reasonable to regard,
    for such purposes, as long-term[5].

1 [1999] IRLR 4, EAT.
2 See DDA 1995, Sch 1, paras 1(2), 2(4) and (3), 4(2)(a) and 5(a).
3 SI 1996/1455.
4 DDA 1995, s 3(1).
5 DDA 1995, s 3(2).

Any adjudicating body[1] determining, for any purpose of the DDA 1995,   **12.2.2**
whether an impairment has a substantial and long-term adverse effect on a
person's ability to carry out normal day-to-day activities, shall take into
account any guidance which appears to it to be relevant[2]. In 1996 the
Secretary of State issued *Guidance on matters to be taken into account in determining questions relating to the definition of disability* (hereinafter 'the
Guidance')[3] which is the current guidance on the meaning of 'disability'.
Although, as will be seen[4], the Disability Rights Commission will issue
Codes of Practice to deal specifically with disability discrimination in education, this guidance will continue to apply to the fundamental issue of the
meaning of 'disability' in that context.

1 Which includes a tribunal, court or any other person who, or body which, may decide a
   claim under DDA 1995, Pt IV: DDA 1995, s 3(3) and (3A).
2 DDA 1995, s 3(3).
3 1996 HMSO.
4 See 11.2 and Chapters 13 and 14.

Past disabilities   12.3

The DDA 1995, insofar as it affects disability in education, applies to a   **12.3.1**
person who has had a disability in the past, as much as it applies to a person
who currently has that disability[1]. Schedule 2 of the DDA 1995 accordingly

modifies the provisions of the Act applying to current disabilities as if they apply to past disabilities[2]. When the DDA 1995 was enacted, it was recognised that persons who had had a disability in the past, although they might no longer be disabled, still required protection from discrimination[3]. This therefore provides practical protection to persons who may have recovered from particular disabilities, especially mental disabilities, where they might nonetheless encounter prejudice, as well as rendering unnecessary any detailed consideration or argument as to when the person may have or may not have been disabled.

1 DDA 1995, s 2(1).
2 DDA 1995, s 2(2).
3 See, for example, House of Lords Deb, vol 564, col 1655.

12.3.2   In order to protect persons with past disabilities, the DDA 1995 has retrospective effect. Thus, in any proceedings under the DDA 1995, the question of whether a person had a disability at a particular time ('the relevant time') shall be determined as if the provisions of, or made under, the DDA 1995 were in force when the act complained of was done[1]. The 'relevant time' may be a time before the passing of the Act, ie 8 November 1995[2].

1 DDA 1995, s 2(4).
2 DDA 1995, s 2(5).

THE ELEMENTS OF DISABILITY

12.4   Elements of disability: (1) impairment

12.4.1   Somewhat surprisingly, the first and perhaps key element in the definition of disability, 'impairment', is not defined in the DDA 1995. 'Mental impairment' is partially defined[1], but mention of 'physical impairment' is nowhere to be found. The 1996 Regulations[2] are also of little assistance as they only exclude certain conditions from the definition of 'impairment', so it is left to the Guidance and recent (though still limited) case law[3] to shed some light on the condition. Assistance can, however, be received from the World Health Organisation's (WHO) International Classification of Diseases[4] to discover what medical opinion might consider to be an impairment.

1 See DDA 1995, Sch 1, para 1.
2 Disability Discrimination (Meaning of Disability) Regulations 1996, SI 1996/1455.
3 See Guidance, Pt 1, para 14 and *Goodwin v Patent Office* [1999] IRLR 4, EAT.
4 World Health Organisation, *International Classification of Impairments, Disabilities and Handicaps: A Manual of Classifications Relating to the Consequences of Disease* (1980, Geneva: WHO).

12.4.2   The WHO Classification[1] defined 'impairment' as 'any loss or abnormality of psychological, physiological or anatomical structure or function'. The Classification then provides detailed listings and categorisation of functional impairments. The 1980 WHO Classification has been recognised as providing the most authoritative categorisation. The WHO, however, carried out a consultation in 1999–2000 and published a revised classification, *ICF – International Classification of Functioning, Disability and Health*, in November 2001[2]. This is now the source document for the medical understanding of impairments and a scientific model of disability.

1 World Health Organisation, *International Classification of Impairments, Disabilities and Handicaps: A Manual of Classifications Relating to the Consequences of Disease* (1980, Geneva: WHO).

2 *ICF WHO International Classification of Functioning, Disability and Health* (2001, Geneva: WHO) which can be found on the WHO website: www.who.int/classification/icf

That definition clearly only goes so far in assisting an understanding of the **12.4.3** meaning of 'impairment', and the Guidance provides little further help. It states that it is not necessary to consider how an impairment was caused[1], but goes no further in defining what may be included within a definition of 'impairment', preferring, like the 1996 Regulations, to assist by suggesting what may be excluded. The Guidance suggests[2] that in many cases there will be no dispute whether a person has an impairment, but whilst in many cases that may be so, there will be other cases where there may well be considerable argument over the existence of an impairment. In some cases therefore, unless the respondent is prepared to accept that the claimant has a disability, expert evidence may be required and the burden of proof will be on the claimant. If, however, the claimant produces uncontested medical evidence, the adjudicating body cannot ignore that[3] nor should it carry out its own test of the claimant's disability[4].

1 Guidance, Pt 1, para 11.
2 Guidance, Pt 1, para 10.
3 *Kapadia v London Borough of Lambeth* [2000] IRLR 14, EAT.
4 *London Underground Ltd v Bragg* (1999) EAT /847/98.

Perhaps, though, by considering what is *excluded*, it may be possible to provide **12.4.4** some idea, in the absence of case law on the point, of what may be included.

Mental impairment

'Mental impairment' includes an impairment resulting from or consisting of **12.4.5** a mental illness only if the illness is a clinically well-recognised illness[1]. Regulations may make provision, for the purposes of the DDA 1995 (a) for conditions of a prescribed description to be treated as amounting to impairments, and (b) for conditions of a prescribed description to be treated as not amounting to impairments[2]. Regulations may also make provision as to the meaning of 'conditions'[3].

1 DDA 1995, Sch 1, para 1(1).
2 DDA 1995, Sch 1, para 1(2).
3 DDA 1995, Sch 1, para 1(3).

Mental impairment includes a wide range of impairments relating to mental **12.4.6** functioning, including what are often known as 'learning disabilities' (formerly known as 'mental handicaps')[1]. A 'clinically well-recognised illness' is a mental illness which is recognised by a respected body of medical opinion. It is very likely that this would include those specifically mentioned in publications such as the WHO's Classification[2]. The DDA 1995 states that 'mental impairment' does not have the special meaning used in the Mental Health Act 1983, although this does not preclude a mental impairment within the meaning of that legislation from coming within the definition in the DDA 1995[3].

1 Guidance, Pt 1, para 13.
2 Guidance, Pt 1, para 14.
3 Guidance, Pt 1, para 15.

12.4.7   Thus 'mental impairment' includes an impairment resulting from or consisting of a mental illness, but only if the illness is a clinically well-recognised
illness. What illnesses are 'well-recognised' will be a question of fact for the
adjudicating body and, unless an illness is clearly well-recognised, may
require expert medical evidence. In *Goodwin v Patent Office*[1], the EAT suggested that where there is doubt reference should be made to the WHO
Classification. Mental illnesses falling within the definition will include clin-
ical depression, certain psychoses and, for example, schizophrenia. The use
of the word 'includes' does of course mean that a mental impairment may
fall within the DDA 1995 even if it does not amount to a mental illness. The
DDA 1995 should not, however, include moods or mild eccentricities or
mild or tendentious (ie not well-recognised) conditions[2].

1 [1999] IRLR 4, EAT.
2 HC Standing Committee E, cols 103-105.

12.4.8   A number of anti-social behaviours and addictions are excluded from the
definition of 'impairment'. Thus a tendency to set fires, to steal and to
physically or sexually abuse other persons are excluded[1]. The 1996
Regulations refer to abuse of 'other persons' which may leave open the possibility of a tendency to self-abuse or a tendency to self-mutilation to be able
to be classified as impairments, possibly important in the case of some children. Also excluded are exhibitionism and voyeurism[2].

1 Disability Discrimination (Meaning of Disability) Regulations 1996, SI 1996/1455, reg
4(1).
2 SI 1996/1455, reg 4(1).

12.4.9

Addictions, whether mental or physical, to alcohol, nicotine or any other
substance are to be treated as *not* amounting to an impairment[1]. The only
exception will be if the addiction was originally the result of the administration of medically prescribed drugs or other medical treatment[2].

1 Disability Discrimination (Meaning of Disability) Regulations 1996, SI 1996/1455, reg 3.
2 SI 1996/1455, reg 3(2).

Physical impairment
12.4.10
'Physical impairment' is even less well-defined in the DDA 1995. As has
been seen[1], addiction to alcohol and other substances cannot be an impairment unless caused by the administration of medically prescribed drugs or
other medical treatment[2]. The drugs must, however, be prescribed, so an
addiction to over-the-counter drugs would not be included. However,
because it is not necessary to consider how an impairment was caused[3],
impairments which are the consequence of addiction can still be considered
impairments. The Guidance provides the example of liver disease resulting
from alcohol dependency[4]. The only other statutory assistance is that seasonal allergic rhinitis (most commonly hayfever) is not to be treated as
amounting to an impairment[5] except where it aggravates the effect of
another condition[6], for example asthma.

1 See 12.4.9.
2 Disability Discrimination (Meaning of Disability) Regulations 1996, SI 1996/1455, reg 3.
3 Guidance, Pt 1, para 11.
4 Guidance, Pt 1, para 11.
5 SI 1996/1455, reg 4(2).
6 SI 1996/1455, reg 4(3).

Sensory impairments

The Guidance states that physical or mental impairment may include sensory impairments, such as those affecting sight or hearing[1]. Other types of sensory impairment, such as those affecting touch and smell, should also fall within the definition, although they may not meet the other conditions set out below.

1 Guidance, Pt 1, para 12.

12.4.11

Other impairments

Some conditions may involve both physical and mental impairment. In others, there may be considerable medical disagreement as to the nature of the impairment, some doctors considering it to be mental, others physical. For example, epilepsy exhibits both physical and mental effects, but must be an impairment.

12.4.12

Elements of disability: (2) inability to carry out normal day-to-day activities

12.5

An impairment is to be taken to affect the ability of a person to carry out normal day-to-day activities only if it affects one of the following:

12.5.1

(a) mobility;
(b) manual dexterity;
(c) physical co-ordination;
(d) continence;
(e) ability to lift, carry or otherwise move everyday objects;
(f) speech, hearing or eyesight;
(g) memory or ability to concentrate, learn or understand; or
(h) perception of the risk of physical danger[1].

Again, Regulations may prescribe impairments which may or may not have these effects[2].

1 DDA 1995, Sch 1, para 4.
2 DDA 1995, Sch 1, para 4.

The important point to stress is that this element is wholly subjective, ie the adjudicating body must consider the effect on the normal day-to-day activities of the individual complainant. The effect of the impairment generally is immaterial. In employment claims, the effect on the person's prescribed job is also immaterial[1]. In *Law Hospital NHS Trust v Rush*[2], the applicant was employed as a staff nurse in a hospital. The evidence was that, although she suffered a number of difficulties in her day-to-day activities because of back pain, she was able to do her job. The EAT held that the correct question was not what effect the impairment had on her work, but rather what effect did it have on her carrying out wider day-to-day activities. The fact that a person was able to carry out a particular job would not always mean that the person was able to carry out normal day-to-day activities.

12.5.2

1 *Law Hospital NHS Trust v Rush* (8 February 2000, unreported), EAT.
2 (8 February 2000, unreported), EAT.

12.5.3   The adjudicating body must also ensure that in considering the effect of the impairment, it should concentrate more on the things that a claimant cannot do as opposed to what the claimant can do. It must also decide for itself whether there is an effect on normal day-to-day activities and not simply rely on expert evidence[1]. In *Vicary v British Telecommunications plc*[2], the claimant suffered from a disability relating to the use of her right arm and hand. She suffered pain when doing repetitive light work, for example cutting vegetables, or more physical work, such as moving a chair. She also had difficulty doing what can only be considered 'day-to-day' activities such as ironing, grooming animals, polishing furniture, knitting and sewing. Surprisingly, but in reliance on expert medical evidence that these weren't considered by occupational health professionals at that time to be considered as day-to-day activities, the employment tribunal decided that the impairment did not have the necessary effect. In overturning that decision, the EAT considered that all these activities were of a type which most people do on a frequent or regular basis and so could not be dismissed as not being normal day-to-day activities. The EAT also said that it was not for a doctor called by a party to express an opinion as to what is a normal day-to-day activity; that it a matter for the adjudicating body to decide using their basic common sense after considering the evidence and having taken into account the Guidance.

This approach was followed in *Abadeh v British Telecommunications plc*[3] and *Pottage v Stonham Housing Association*[4]. In *Abadeh*[5], the EAT reiterated that the question of whether an impairment was substantial was to be decided by the adjudicating body, not by experts or others giving medical evidence. The purpose of the medical evidence was to address diagnosis, observation of a person's ability to carry out day-to-day activities, prognosis and the effect of medication; whether the impairment did in fact have a substantial adverse effect on the claimant's ability to carry out normal day-to-day activities was a matter for the adjudicating body alone.

1   *Vicary v British Telecommunications plc* [1999] IRLR 680.
2   [1999] IRLR 680.
3   [2001] IRLR 23, EAT.
4   (6 April 2000, unreported).
5   [2001] IRLR 23, EAT.

12.5.4   The Guidance emphasises that 'normal day-to-day activities' are not intended to include activities which are normal only for a particular person or group of people[1]. Therefore in deciding whether an activity is a 'normal day-to-day activity' account should be taken of how far it is normal for most people and carried out by most people on a daily or frequent and fairly regular basis. The term does not, for example, include work of any particular form, because no particular form of work is 'normal' for most people. In any individual case, the activities carried out might be highly specialised. The same is true of playing a particular game, taking part in a particular hobby, playing a musical instrument, playing sport, or performing a highly skilled task. Impairments which affect only such an activity and have no effect on 'normal day-to-day activities' are not covered[2].

1   Guidance, para C2.
2   Guidance, para C3.

12.5.5   In many cases the effect of the impairment will be obvious, but an impairment may also have an indirect effect on one or more of the matters listed in the DDA 1995[1]. This should be taken into account when the adjudicating body determines whether the definition is met. To assist, the adjudicating body should consider[2]:

(a) medical advice, for example, where a person has been professionally advised to change, limit or refrain from a normal day-to-day activity on account of an impairment or only do it in a certain way or under certain conditions;
(b) pain or fatigue, for example, where an impairment causes pain or fatigue in performing normal day-to-day activities, so the person may have the capacity to do something but suffer pain in doing so; or the impairment might make the activity more than usually fatiguing so that the person might not be able to repeat the task over a sustained period of time.

1 See 12.5.1.
2 Guidance, para C6.

Elements of disability: (3) is the adverse effect substantial?   12.6

A person's impairment must have a substantial adverse effect[1]. The   **12.6.1**
Guidance[2] makes clear that the effect must be substantial to reflect the general understanding of disability as going beyond the normal differences in ability which may exist. A 'substantial' effect is more than would be produced by the sort of physical or mental conditions experienced by many people which have only minor effects. A 'substantial' effect is one which is more than 'minor' or 'trivial'[3].

1 DDA 1995, s 1(1).
2 Guidance, Pt 2, para A1.
3 Guidance, Pt 2, para A1.

In determining whether the effect is substantial, an adjudicating body should   **12.6.2**
take into account:

(a) *Time:* The time taken to carry out an activity in comparison with the time that might be expected if the person did not have the impairment[1].
(b) *Method:* The way in which an activity is carried out in comparison with the way the person might be expected to carry out the activity if he or she did not have the impairment[2].
(c) *Cumulative effects of an impairment:* An impairment might not have a substantial adverse effect on a person in any one of the elements listed[3], but its effects in more than one of these respects taken together could result in a substantial adverse effect on the person's ability to carry out normal day-to-day activities. For example, although the great majority of people with cerebral palsy will experience a number of substantial effects, someone with mild cerebral palsy may experience minor effects in a number of the respects listed which together could create substantial adverse effects on a range of normal day-to-day activities: fatigue may hinder walking, visual perception may be poor, co-ordination and balance may cause some difficulties. Similarly, a person whose impairment causes breathing difficulties may experience minor effects in a number of

respects but which overall have a substantial adverse effect on their ability to carry out normal day-to-day activities. For some people, mental illness may have a clear effect in one of the respects. However, for others, depending on the extent of the condition, there may be effects in a number of different respects which, taken together, substantially adversely affect their ability to carry out normal day-to-day activities[4].

(d) *Effects of behaviour:* Account should be taken of how far a person can reasonably be expected to modify behaviour to prevent or reduce the effects of an impairment on normal day-to-day activities. If a person can behave in such a way that the impairment ceases to have a substantial adverse effect on his or her ability to carry out normal day-to-day activities the person would no longer meet the definition of disability[5]. In some cases people have such 'coping' strategies which cease to work in certain circumstances (for example, where someone who stutters or has dyslexia is placed under stress). If it is possible that a person's ability to manage the effects of an impairment will break down so that effects will sometimes still occur, this possibility must be taken into account when assessing the effects of the impairment[6].

(e) *Effects of environment:* For example, the temperature, humidity, the time of day or night, how tired the person is or how much stress he or she is under may have an impact on the effects. When assessing whether adverse effects are substantial, the extent to which such environmental factors are likely to have an impact should also therefore be considered[7].

1 Guidance, para A2.
2 Guidance, para A3.
3 See 12.5.1.
4 Guidance, paras A4 to A6.
5 Guidance, para A7.
6 Guidance, para A8.
7 Guidance, para A10.

Effects of treatment

12.6.3   An impairment which would be likely to have a substantial adverse effect on the ability of the person concerned to carry out normal day-to-day activities, but for the fact that measures are being taken to treat or correct it, is, nonetheless, to be treated as having that effect[1]. 'Measures' include, in particular, medical treatment and the use of prosthesis or other aids[2]. This provision does not, however, apply (a) in relation to the impairment of a person's sight, to the extent that the impairment is, in his case, correctable by spectacles or contact lenses or in such other ways as may be prescribed; or (b) in relation to such other impairments as may be prescribed in such circumstances as may be prescribed[3]. This applies even if the measures result in the effects being completely under control or not at all apparent[4]. For example, if a person with a hearing impairment wears a hearing aid, the question whether his or her impairment has a substantial adverse effect is to be decided by reference to what the hearing level would be without the hearing aid[5].

1 DDA 1995, Sch 1, para 6(1).
2 DDA 1995, Sch 1, para 6(2).
3 DDA 1995, Sch 1, para 6(3).
4 Guidance, para A12.
5 Guidance, para A13.

Progressive conditions

Where a person has (a) a progressive condition (such as cancer, multiple sclerosis or muscular dystrophy or infection by human immunodeficiency virus), and (b) as a result of that condition, has an impairment which has (or had) an effect on his ability to carry out normal day-to-day activities, but (c) that effect is not (or was not) a substantial effect, the person shall be taken to have an impairment which has a substantial adverse effect if the condition is likely to result in his having such an impairment[1]. Regulations may make provision for conditions of a prescribed description to be treated as being progressive or as not being progressive[2].

12.6.4

1 DDA 1995, Sch 1, para 8(1).
2 DDA 1995, Sch 1, para 8(2).

The Guidance adds that:

12.6.5

'The [DDA 1995] provides for a person with such a condition to be regarded as having an impairment which has a substantial adverse effect on his or her ability to carry out normal day-to-day activities before it actually does so. Where a person has a progressive condition, he or she will be treated as having an impairment which has a substantial adverse effect from the moment any impairment resulting from that condition first has some effect on ability to carry out normal day-to-day activities. The effect need not be continuous and need not be substantial. For this rule to operate medical diagnosis of the condition is not by itself enough.'[1]

1 Guidance, para A15.

Severe disfigurement

An impairment which consists of a severe disfigurement is to be treated as having a substantial adverse effect on the ability of the person concerned to carry out normal day-to-day activities[1]. Regulations may provide that in prescribed circumstances a severe disfigurement is not to be treated as having this effect and may make provision relating to deliberately acquired disfigurements[2].

12.6.6

1 DDA 1995, Sch 1, para 3(1).
2 DDA 1995, Sch 1, para 3(2) and (3).

Thus a severe disfigurement is not to be treated as having a substantial adverse effect on the ability of the person concerned to carry out normal day-to-day activities if it consists of (a) a tattoo (which has not been removed), or (b) a piercing of the body for decorative or other non-medical purposes, including any object attached through the piercing for such purposes[1].

12.6.7

1 Disability Discrimination (Meaning of Disability) Regulations 1996, SI 1996/1455, reg 5.

The Guidance suggests that examples of disfigurements would include scars, birthmarks, limb or postural deformation or diseases of the skin. Assessing severity will be mainly a matter of the degree of the disfigurement. However, it may be necessary to take account of where the feature in question is (eg on the back as opposed to the face)[1].

12.6.8

1 Guidance, para A17.

Babies and young children

12.6.9   Where a child under six years of age has an impairment which does not affect the ability of the child to carry out normal day-to-day activities, that impairment is, nonetheless, to be taken to have a substantial and long-term adverse effect on the ability of that child to carry out normal day-to-day activities where it would normally have a substantial and long-term adverse effect on the ability of a person aged six years or over to carry out normal day-to-day activities[1]. The 1996 Regulations[2] here recognise that in the case of many young children, an impairment may not have a significant effect on their abilities at that stage in their life. They therefore require an adjudicating body to consider the effect of that child's impairment on a person over six and if it would have the necessary effect on that person, then it is deemed to have a similar effect on the child under six.

1 Disability Discrimination (Meaning of Disability) Regulations 1996, SI 1996/1455, reg 6.
2 SI 1996/1455.

12.7   Elements of disability: (4) is the adverse effect long-term?

12.7.1   The effect of an impairment is 'long-term' if:

(a) it has lasted at least 12 months;
(b) the period for which it lasts is likely to be at least 12 months; or
(c) it is likely to last for the rest of the life of the person affected[1].

1 DDA 1995, Sch 1, para 2(1).

12.7.2   Where an impairment ceases to have a substantial adverse effect on a person's ability to carry out normal day-to-day activities, it is to be treated as continuing to have that effect if that effect is likely to recur[1], although the likelihood of an effect recurring shall be disregarded in prescribed circumstances[2]. Regulations may prescribe circumstances in which an effect which would not otherwise be a long-term effect is to be treated as having such an effect or an effect which would otherwise be a long-term effect is to be treated as not having such an effect[3]. Conditions which recur only sporadically or for short periods (eg epilepsy) can still qualify. Regulations specifically exclude seasonal allergic rhinitis (eg hayfever) from this category, except where it aggravates the effects of an existing condition[4]. An example given is a person with rheumatoid arthritis who may experience effects from the first occurrence for a few weeks and then have a period of remission. If the effects are likely to recur, they are to be treated as if they were continuing. If the effects are likely to recur beyond 12 months after the first occurrence, they are to be treated as long-term[5].

1 DDA 1995, Sch 1, para 2(2).
2 DDA 1995, Sch 1, para 2(3).
3 DDA 1995, Sch 1, para 2(4).
4 Guidance, para B3.
5 Guidance, para B4.

12.7.3   For the purpose of deciding whether a person has had a disability in the past, a long-term effect of an impairment is one which lasted at least 12 months[1]. It is not necessary for the effect to be the same throughout the relevant period. It may change, as where activities which are initially very difficult become possible to a much greater extent. The main adverse effect might even disappear, or it might disappear temporarily, while one or other effects on ability to carry out normal day-to-day activities continue or develop. Provided the impairment continues to have, or is likely to have, such an effect throughout the period, there is a long-term effect[2].

1 DDA 1995, Sch 2, para 5.
2 Guidance, para B5.

> 'Likelihood of recurrence should be considered taking all the circum- **12.7.4**
> stances of the case into account. This should include what the person
> could reasonably be expected to do to prevent the recurrence; for exam-
> ple, the person might reasonably be expected to take action which
> prevents the impairment from having such effects (eg avoiding substances
> to which he or she is allergic). This may be unreasonably difficult with
> some substances. In addition, it is possible that the way in which a person
> can control or cope with the effects of a condition may not always be suc-
> cessful because, for example, a routine is not followed or the person is in
> an unfamiliar environment. If there is an increased likelihood that the
> control will break down, it will be more likely that there will be a recur-
> rence. That possibility should be taken into account when assessing the
> likelihood of a recurrence.'[1]

1 Guidance, para B5.

POSSIBLE EXAMPLES OF DISABILITY

Sources of examples   **12.8**

Each case of claimed disability will depend on the facts and the circum- **12.8.1**
stances of the particular claimant. Although impairments may be, and may
increasingly become, recognised, it is only if that impairment has a substantial adverse long-term effect on the day-to-day activities of that person
will he or she be able to establish that they are disabled within the meaning
of the DDA 1995.

However, there does need to be some certainty to enable LEAs, schools, col- **12.8.2**
leges and universities to know when they are dealing with a disabled person
or a person who has been disabled. Assistance can therefore be gleaned from
the Guidance, case law and, when published, the Code of Practice (Schools)
and Code of Practice (Post 16)[1]. What follows therefore is an attempt to
show the types of disability recognised by the Guidance, the types of disability which have been accepted in the courts and employment tribunals
and the types of disability which the two Codes of Practice envisage having
an effect in the education field.

1 As to these Codes, see 11.1.9.

The Guidance

The Guidance helpfully sets out[1] indicators of what might be and what **12.8.3**
might not be reasonable to regard as impairments having substantial adverse

effects on day-to-day activities. It stresses, though, that they are indicators, not tests nor conclusive pointers[2]. Examples of effects which are obviously within the definition are not included in the Guidance's examples. Thus inability to dress oneself, inability to stand up, severe dyslexia or a severe speech impairment which the Guidance says would clearly be covered by the definition are not included. The purpose of the Guidance's lists is to provide help in cases where there may be doubt as to whether the effects on normal day-to-day activities are substantial[3].

1 Guidance, paras C10 to C21.
2 Guidance, para C10.
3 Guidance, para C12.

Mobility

12.8.4 'Mobility'[1] covers 'moving or changing position in a wide sense'[2]:

> 'Account should be taken of the extent to which, because of either a phys-ical or a mental condition, a person is inhibited in getting around unaided or using a normal means of transport, in leaving home with or without assistance, in walking a short distance, climbing stairs, travelling in a car or completing a journey on public transport, sitting, standing, bending, or reaching, or getting around in an unfamiliar place.'[3]

Examples of what might be regarded as a substantial adverse effect might be an:

- inability to travel a short journey as a passenger in a vehicle;
- inability to walk other than at a slow pace or with unsteady or jerky movements;
- difficulty in going up or down steps, stairs or gradients;
- inability to use one or more forms of public transport; or
- inability to go out of doors unaccompanied.

It would *not* be reasonable to regard as having a substantial adverse effect:

- difficulty walking unaided a distance of about 1.5 kilometres or a mile without discomfort or having to stop – the distance in question would obviously vary according to the age of the person concerned and the type of terrain; or
- inability to travel in a car for a journey lasting more than two hours without discomfort.

1 DDA 1995, Sch 1, para 4(1)(a).
2 Guidance, para C14.
3 Guidance, para C14.

Manual dexterity

12.8.5 'Manual dexterity'[1] covers the ability to use hands and fingers with preci-sion. Account should be taken of the extent to which a person can manipulate the fingers on each hand or co-ordinate the use of both hands together to do a task. This includes the ability to do things like pick up or manipulate small objects, operate a range of equipment manually, or com-municate through writing or typing on standard machinery. Loss of function in the dominant hand would be expected to have a greater effect than equiv-alent loss in the non-dominant hand[2].

Examples of manual dexterity impairments having a substantial adverse effect might include:

- loss of function in one or both hands such that the person cannot use the hand or hands;
- inability to handle a knife and fork at the same time; or
- ability to press the buttons on keyboards or keypads but only much more slowly than is normal for most people.

It would *not* be reasonable to regard as having a substantial adverse effect:

- inability to undertake activities requiring delicate hand movements, such as threading a small needle;
- inability to reach typing speeds standardised for secretarial work; or
- inability to pick up a single small item, such as a pin.

1 DDA 1995, Sch 1, para 4(1)(b).
2 Guidance, para C15.

Physical co-ordination

'Physical co-ordination'[1] covers balanced and effective interaction of body   **12.8.6**
movement, including hand and eye co-ordination. In the case of a child, it is necessary to take account of the level of achievement which would be normal for a person of the particular age. In any case, account should be taken of the ability to carry out 'composite' activities such as walking and using hands at the same time[2].
  Examples of substantial adverse effects might include:

- ability to pour liquid into another vessel only with unusual slowness or concentration; or
- inability to place food into one's own mouth with fork/spoon without unusual concentration or assistance.

It would *not* be reasonable to regard as having a substantial adverse effect:

- mere clumsiness; or
- inability to catch a tennis ball.

1 DDA 1995, Sch 1, para 4(1)(c).
2 Guidance, para C16.

Continence

'Continence'[1] refers to the ability to control urination and/or defecation.   **12.8.7**
Account should be taken of the frequency and extent of the loss of control and the age of the individual[2].
  Examples falling within the definition might include:

- even infrequent loss of control of the bowels;
- loss of control of the bladder while asleep at least once a month; or
- frequent minor faecal incontinence or frequent minor leakage from the bladder.

It would *not* be reasonable to regard as having a substantial adverse effect:

- infrequent loss of control of the bladder while asleep; or
- infrequent minor leakage from the bladder.

A frequent desire to urinate, which did not lead to incontinence, was not a disability[3].

1 DDA 1995, Sch 1, para 4(1)(d).
2 Guidance, para C17.
3 *Thornhill v London Central Bus Co Ltd* (2000), EAT/463/99.

Ability to lift, carry or otherwise move everyday objects

12.8.8 In considering whether a person is able to lift, carry or otherwise move everyday objects[1], account should be taken of a person's ability to repeat such functions or, for example, to bear weights over a reasonable period of time. Everyday objects might include such items as books, a kettle of water[2], bags of shopping, a briefcase, an overnight bag, a chair or other piece of light furniture[3].

Examples of a substantial adverse effect might be:

- inability to pick up objects of moderate weight with one hand; or
- inability to carry a moderately loaded tray steadily.

It would *not* be reasonable to regard as having a substantial adverse effect:

- inability to carry heavy luggage without assistance; or
- inability to move heavy objects without a mechanical aid.

1 DDA 1995, Sch 1, para 4(1)(e).
2 See also the comments of the EAT in *Vicary v British Telecommunications plc* [1999] IRLR 680.
3 Guidance, para C18.

Speech, hearing or eyesight

12.8.9 Impairments[1] affecting speech, hearing or eyesight would include the ability to speak, hear or see and includes face-to-face, telephone and written communication.

1 DDA 1995, Sch 1, para 4(1)(f).

12.8.10 With speech, account should be taken of how far a person is able to speak clearly at a normal pace and rhythm and to understand someone else speaking normally in the person's native language. It is necessary to consider any effects on speech patterns or which impede the acquisition or processing of one's native language, for example by someone who has had a stroke[1].

Examples might include:

- inability to give clear basic instructions orally to colleagues or providers of a service;
- inability to ask specific questions to clarify instructions; or
- taking significantly longer than average to say things.

It would *not* be reasonable to regard as having a substantial adverse effect:

- inability to articulate fluently due to a minor stutter, lisp or speech impediment;

- inability to speak in front of an audience;
- having a strong regional or foreign accent; or
- inability to converse in a language which is not the speaker's native language.

1 Guidance, para C19(i).

With hearing, if a person uses an aid, what needs to be considered is the effect that would be experienced if the person were not using the hearing aid or device. Account should be taken of effects where the level of background noise is within such a range and of such a type that most people would be able to hear adequately[1].   **12.8.11**

Examples would include:

- inability to hold a conversation with someone talking in a normal voice in a moderately noisy environment; or
- inability to hear and understand another person speaking clearly over the voice telephone.

It would *not* be reasonable to regard as having a substantial adverse effect:

- inability to hold a conversation in a very noisy place, such as a factory floor; or
- inability to sing in tune.

1 Guidance, para C19(ii).

With eyesight, because of the fact that impairment which can be corrected by wearing spectacles or contact lenses is to be disregarded, if a person's sight is corrected by spectacles or contact lenses, or could be corrected by them, what needs to be considered is the effect remaining while they are wearing such spectacles or lenses, in light of a level and type normally acceptable to most people for normal day-to-day activities[1].   **12.8.12**

A substantial adverse effect might therefore include:

- inability to see to pass the eyesight test for a standard driving test;
- inability to recognise by sight a known person across a moderately-sized room;
- total inability to distinguish colours;
- inability to read ordinary newsprint; or
- inability to walk safely without bumping into things.

It would *not* be reasonable to regard as having a substantial adverse effect:

- inability to read very small or indistinct print without the aid of a magnifying glass;
- inability to distinguish a known person across a substantial distance (eg a playing field); or
- inability to distinguish between red and green.

1 Guidance, para C19(iii).

Memory or ability to concentrate, learn or understand

12.8.13   With difficulties with memory or the ability to learn, concentrate or understand[1], account should be taken of the person's ability to remember, organise his or her thoughts, plan a course of action and carry it out, take in new knowledge, or understand spoken or written instructions. This includes considering whether the person learns to do things significantly more slowly than is normal. Account should be taken of whether the person has persistent and significant difficulty in reading text in standard English or straightforward numbers[2].

Examples having a substantial adverse effect would include:

- intermittent loss of consciousness and associated confused behaviour;
- persistent inability to remember the names of familiar people such as family or friends;
- inability to adapt after a reasonable period to minor change in work routine;
- inability to write a cheque without assistance; or
- considerable difficulty in following a short sequence such as a simple recipe or a brief list of domestic tasks.

It would *not* be reasonable to regard as having a substantial adverse effect:

- occasionally forgetting the name of a familiar person, such as a colleague;
- inability to concentrate on a task requiring application over several hours;
- inability to fill in a long, detailed, technical document without assistance;
- inability to read at faster than normal speed; or
- minor problems with writing or spelling.

1 DDA 1995, Sch 1, para 4(1)(g).
2 Guidance, para C20.

Perception of the risk of physical danger

12.8.14   Difficulties with the perception of physical danger[1] includes both the underestimation and overestimation of physical danger, including danger to well-being. Account should be taken, for example, of whether the person is inclined to neglect basic functions such as eating, drinking, sleeping, keeping warm or personal hygiene; reckless behaviour which puts the person or others at risk; or excessive avoidance behaviour without a good cause[2].

Examples of what it would be reasonable to regard as having a substantial adverse effect are:

- inability to operate safely properly-maintained equipment;
- persistent inability to cross a road safely;
- inability to nourish oneself (assuming nourishment is available); or
- inability to tell by touch that an object is very hot or cold.

It would *not* be reasonable to regard as having a substantial adverse effect:

- fear of significant heights;

- underestimating the risk associated with dangerous hobbies, such as mountain climbing; or
- underestimating risks, other than obvious ones, in unfamiliar workplaces.

1 DDA 1995, Sch 1, para 4(1)(g).
2 Guidance, para C20.

The Codes of Practice

When published, the Code of Practice (Schools) and the Code of Practice (Post 16)[1] may provide some assistance by indicating what impairments are, in the education context, considered by the Disability Rights Commission to be capable of amounting to a disability. Again, the fact that a particular disability is mentioned in a Code of Practice does not mean that it will always be a disability or that because a condition is omitted, it can not be. The examples in the Codes of Practice are therefore merely illustrations of what might be disabilities.   **12.8.15**

1 See 11.1.9.

Code of Practice (Schools)

In the Code of Practice (Schools), 'all the examples in the Code relate to pupils who have a disability as defined by the Act'[1] but 'are illustrative, not comprehensive, and they do not constitute an authoritative interpretation of the legislation'[2]. Thus, the following are mentioned in the examples provided by the Disability Rights Commission: epilepsy[3], muscle spasms and involuntary noises[4], Tourette's Syndrome[5], hearing impairment[6], visual impairment[7], Hirschprung's Disease[8], learning difficulties[9], learning and behaviour difficulties[10], moderate learning difficulties, poor muscle tone and speech and language difficulties[11], having only one arm[12], coeliac disease[13], diabetes[14], physical disability[15], severe asthma[16], cerebral palsy[17], leukaemia[18] and HIV[19].   **12.8.16**

1 Code of Practice (Schools), para 1:16.
2 Code of Practice (Schools), para 1:17.
3 Code of Practice (Schools), paras 3:9A, 3:12A, 3:18A, 8:18A and 9:21A.
4 Code of Practice (Schools), paras 3:9B, 3:12B and 3:18B.
5 Code of Practice (Schools), paras 3:9C, 3:12C, 3:18C and 3:19A.
6 Code of Practice (Schools), para 3:10A.
7 Code of Practice (Schools), paras 4:21B and 8:23A.
8 Code of Practice (Schools), para 3:23A.
9 Code of Practice (Schools), paras 3:23B and 3:29A.
10 Code of Practice (Schools), para 3:29A.
11 Code of Practice (Schools), para 4:20A.
12 Code of Practice (Schools), para 4:21C.
13 Code of Practice (Schools), para 5:8A.
14 Code of Practice (Schools), paras 5:10A and 9:21A.
15 Code of Practice (Schools), paras 8:19A, 9:6B and 9:7A.
16 Code of Practice (Schools), paras 4:21A and 5:11A.
17 Code of Practice (Schools), para 3:23C.
18 Code of Practice (Schools), para 5:14A.
19 Code of Practice (Schools), para 9:6A.

So far as the overlap between disability and special educational needs is concerned, the Code of Practice (Schools) offers the following guidance: **12.8.17**

> 'It is important to recognise that the definition of children with learning difficulties includes children with a disability where any special educational provision needs to be made. This does not mean that children with

277

a disability necessarily have learning difficulties in the everyday meaning of the word or that disabled children with learning difficulties have special educational needs. It means that all children with a disability have special educational needs if they have any difficulty in accessing education and if they need any special educational provision to be made for them, that is, anything that is additional to or different from what is normally available in schools in the area.'[1]

1   Code of Practice (Schools), para 1:53.

Code of Practice (Post 16)

12.8.18   Examples given in the Code of Practice (Post 16) include: learning difficulties[1], dyslexia[2], hearing impairment[3], facial disfigurement[4], Tourette's Syndrome[5], visual impairment[6], mobility difficulties[7], artificial limb[8], epilepsy[9], bi-polar disorder[10], long-term back problems[11], mental health problems[12], medical condition which causes fatigue[13], MS[14], Asperger Syndrome[15], Autistic spectrum disorder[16], emotional and behavioural difficulties[17], restricted growth[18], depression[19], requiring dialysis[20], cerebral palsy[21], heart condition[22], arthritis[23] and AIDS[24].

1   Code of Practice (Post 16), paras 3:6B, 4:9B, 4:26A, 5:8F, 6:3A (moderate LD), 6:11A (severe LD), 6:12A, 6:14A and 6:16A.
2   Code of Practice (Post 16), paras 4:4A, 4:11A, 4:21A, 4:27A (severely dyslexic), 4:27B, 5:8B, 6:3B, 6:11B and 8:5A.
3   Code of Practice (Post 16), paras 4:4B, 4:8B, 4:15A, 5:2A, 6:5A, 6:7B, 6:8A, 6:10A, 6:17A and 8:9A.
4   Code of Practice (Post 16), para 4:4C.
5   Code of Practice (Post 16), para 4:5B.
6   Code of Practice (Post 16), paras 4:8A, 4:13A, 4:28A, 5:2C, 5:8C, 5:11A, 5:12A, 6:6A, 6:19A and 8:10A.
7   Code of Practice (Post 16), paras 4:9A, 4:12A, 5:2D, 6:7A and 6:13A.
8   Code of Practice (Post 16), para 4:15B.
9   Code of Practice (Post 16), paras 4:10A and 5:8J.
10   Code of Practice (Post 16), para 4:14A.
11   Code of Practice (Post 16), para 4:16A.
12   Code of Practice (Post 16), paras 4:17A, 4:17B and 4:18A.
13   Code of Practice (Post 16), para 4:19A.
14   Code of Practice (Post 16), para 4:21B.
15   Code of Practice (Post 16), para 4:28B.
16   Code of Practice (Post 16), para 4:32A.
17   Code of Practice (Post 16), para 4:31A.
18   Code of Practice (Post 16), para 5:2B.
19   Code of Practice (Post 16), para 5:8D.
20   Code of Practice (Post 16), para 5:8E.
21   Code of Practice (Post 16), paras 5:8G and 6:9A.
22   Code of Practice (Post 16), para 5:10A.
23   Code of Practice (Post 16), para 6:4A.
24   Code of Practice (Post 16), para 6:20A.

Case law

12.8.19   The type of conditions which have been considered in the cases brought under the DDA 1995 may also be useful in suggesting what impairments are likely to be considered as disabilities in the future. Again, although of some help, total reliance cannot be put on the decisions as they either depended on their individual facts or it was accepted that the claimant had a particular disability. Nonetheless, as examples of what types of disabilities have prompted claims, they can only add to an understanding of what the law may regard as a disability.

Thus, in case law the following conditions have either been held to amount   **12.8.20**
to disabilities or have been accepted as such: 'thought broadcasting', misinterpretation of words and actions of colleagues in a paranoid fashion and auditory hallucinations[1], impaired use of arm and hand[2], permanent hearing loss[3], dyslexia[4], depressive illness[5], post-viral fatigue syndrome[6], diabetes and dependency on insulin[7], back pain[8], reactive depression[9], blindness[10], serious back injury[11], ME or Chronic Fatigue Syndrome[12] and cone dystrophy (a congenital disorder affecting the retina of both eyes)[13].

Cases where the Tribunal or court has *not* considered a claimant to be a disabled person include: post-viral/'Gulf War Syndrome'[14] and learning difficulty with poor standards of reading and writing[15].

1 *Goodwin v Patent Office* [1999] IRLR 4, EAT.
2 *Vicary v British Telecommunications plc* [1999] IRLR 680, EAT.
3 *Abadeh v British Telecommunications plc* [2001] IRLR 23.
4 *Hutton v A E Proctor Ltd* (18 December 2000, unreported), EAT.
5 *Pottage v Stonham Housing Association Ltd* (6 April 2000, unreported), EAT.
6 *Edwards v Mid-Suffolk District Council* [2001] IRLR 190.
7 *Jones v Post Office* [2001] EWCA Civ 558, [2001] IRLR 384.
8 *Law Hospital NHS Trust v Rush* (8 February 2000, unreported), EAT.
9 *Kapadia v London Borough of Lambeth* [2000] IRLR 699, CA.
10 *Rose v Raymond Bouchet* [1999] IRLR 463, Sh Ct.
11 *British Telecommunications plc v Wilding* (27 July 1999, unreported), EAT.
12 *H J Heinz Co Ltd v Kenrick* [2000] ICR 491, [2000] IRLR 144, EAT.
13 *McPhee v Fife Council* (7 February 2001, unreported), EAT
14 *Humphreys v Environment Agency* (19 November 1999, unreported), EAT.
15 *Cave v Goodwin and Goodwin* (14 March 2001, unreported), CA.

Future developments

With the extension of the DDA 1995 to education, it is likely that various   **12.8.21**
adjudicating bodies, whether the Tribunal, county courts or admission and exclusion panels will consider different conditions and the ambit of the definition of 'disability' will hopefully become clearer. In the education context, conditions such as ADHD, nut allergies and behavioural difficulties are likely to be the first to require consideration.

Chapter 13

Disability discrimination in primary and secondary education

Introduction   **13.1**

As has been seen[1], the Disability Discrimination Act (DDA) 1995 did very   **13.1.1**
little to protect disabled pupils. Although the employment of staff in schools
and the provision of certain goods, services and accommodation to parents
and others visiting schools was covered[2], the DDA 1995 did not impose any
duties on Local Education Authorities (LEAs) or schools towards pupils for
whom they were responsible.

1 See 11.1.
2 Within DDA 1995, Pts II and III; and see also *What the Disability Discrimination Act 1995
   means for Schools and LEAs* (DfEE Circular 3/97).

The underlying assumption behind this lack of protection was the idea that   **13.1.2**
the needs of disabled pupils would be addressed through the legislation
dealing with special education and the Code of Practice for the identification
and assessment of children with special educational needs[1].

1 As to which, see 2.2.6 and 2.2.7.

The DDA 1995 did, however, introduce limited recognition of the respon-   **13.1.3**
sibility of governing bodies and LEAs for disabled pupils. The governing
body of every maintained school must produce a report to parents each
year[1]. This annual report is required to include a report containing information on the arrangements for the admission of disabled pupils, steps
taken to prevent disabled pupils from being treated less favourably than
other pupils and the facilities provided to assist access to the school by disabled pupils[2]. The intention was that those schools which could not admit
disabled pupils or had difficulties in doing so would be identified and steps
could be taken to improving accessibility. These limited measures, when
combined with the special educational needs provisions, were intended to
encourage genuine and full integration of disabled pupils in mainstream
education as far as possible[3].

1 School Standards and Framework Act (SSFA) 1998, s 42.
2 Education Act (EA) 1996, s 317(6).
3 House of Lords Deb, vol 564, cols 1994–1995.

13.1.4 Unfortunately, these new obligations did not truly address the underlying problems of disability discrimination in schools, and there were criticisms that the provisions relating to children with special educational needs were not sufficiently wide to deal with the discrimination which could be encountered by some disabled pupils. Consequently, the Special Educational Needs and Disability Act (SENDA) 2001 amends the DDA 1995 to impose obligations on LEAs and governing bodies to avoid discrimination towards disabled pupils.

DEFINITIONS, RULES AND RESPONSIBILITIES

13.2 Unlawful discrimination

13.2.1 From the date of implementation of the disability provisions of the SENDA 2001[1], it will be unlawful for a body responsible for a school to discriminate against a disabled person:

(a) in the arrangements it makes for determining admission to the school as a pupil;

(b) in the terms on which it offers to admit a child to the school as a pupil; or

(c) by refusing or deliberately omitting to accept an application for his admission to the school as a pupil[2].

1 Anticipated to be 1 September 2002.
2 DDA 1995, s 28A(1).

13.2.2 It will also be unlawful for the body responsible for a school to discriminate against a disabled pupil in the education or associated services provided for, or offered to, pupils at the school by that body[1]. Although the Secretary of State may by regulations prescribe services which are, or services which are not, to be regarded as being education or an associated service[2], it is likely that they will include such services as school trips, extra-curricula lessons and activities, school transport and any other services normally associated with a child's time at school.

1 DDA 1995, s 28A(2).
2 DDA 1995, s 28A(3).

13.2.3 The Code of Practice (Schools)[1] suggests[2] that 'education and associated services' is a broad term covering all aspects of school life, including:

- preparation for entry to the school;
- the curriculum;
- teaching and learning;
- classroom organisation;
- timetabling;
- grouping of pupils;
- homework;
- access to school facilities;
- activities to supplement the curriculum, for example a drama group visiting the school;
- school sports;

- school policies;
- breaks and lunchtimes;
- the serving of school meals;
- interaction with peers;
- assessment and exam arrangements;
- school discipline and sanctions;
- school clubs and activities;
- school trips;
- the school's arrangements for working with other agencies; and
- preparation of pupils for the next phase of education.

1 As to which, see 11.1.9.
2 Code of Practice (Schools), para 2:13.

Further, it will be unlawful for the body responsible for a school to dis- **13.2.4** criminate against a disabled pupil by excluding him from the school, whether permanently or temporarily[1]. Given the fact that this duty will apply to independent and non-maintained special schools, this obligation may impose greater duties on these schools when considering excluding or expelling their pupils than has been the case in the past[2].

1 DDA 1995, s 28A(4).
2 See, for example, *R v Fernhill Manor School, ex p A* [1994] ELR 67, QBD.

Responsible bodies   13.3

The new provisions of the DDA 1995 impose duties on bodies responsible **13.3.1** for schools[1]. These bodies are defined by the Act but include schools in both the maintained and non-maintained sector[2].

1 DDA 1995, s 28A.
2 DDA 1995, s 28A(5) and Sch 4A.

Thus the relevant responsible body will be[1]:   **13.3.2**

(a) in relation to maintained schools, the LEA or the governing body according to which has the function in question;
(b) in relation to pupil referral units, the LEA;
(c) in relation to maintained nursery schools, the LEA;
(d) in relation to independent schools, the proprietor[2];
(e) in relation to a special school not maintained by an LEA, the proprietor[3].

1 DDA 1995, Sch 4A, para 1(1) and (2).
2 'Proprietor', in relation to a school, means the person or body of persons responsible for the management of the school: EA 1996, s 579(1); this will vary according to the type of school but would include the trustees, the governing body, private owner or the management group of the school: Code of Practice (Schools), para 2:6.
3 'Proprietor', in relation to a school, means the person or body of persons responsible for the management of the school: EA 1996, s 579(1).

The body responsible for a school is known for the purposes of the DDA **13.3.3** 1995 as 'the responsible body'[1]. It should be noted that whilst independent and non-maintained schools are included, in contrast to the special educational needs legislation, most early years or early education settings are not subject to the duty not to discriminate. The exceptions are maintained nursery schools which do fall within the DDA 1995. This does not mean that what goes on in early years settings may not fall within the DDA 1995 by other means; for example, where parents of early years children may be unable to voice their concerns LEAs should ensure that parents are provided with access to signers or interpreters[2]. If, in fact, in the provision of these services the LEA discriminated on grounds of disability, the LEA could be liable albeit that the setting in which the child is being educated would not be.

1 DDA 1995, s 28A(5).
2 SEN Code of Practice, para 4:25.

13.3.4   By including independent and non-maintained special schools, for perhaps one of the first times, therefore, the DDA 1995 will impose statutory duties on schools which are not otherwise subject to the same statutory regimes as maintained schools.

13.3.5   In addition, as will be seen[1], LEAs will be under a general duty not to discriminate against disabled persons in respect of their wider, non-school based educational functions[2]. Here, clearly, the LEA will be the body responsible for meeting the relevant duties under the DDA 1995.

1 See 13.8.
2 DDA 1995, ss 28F and 28G.

13.4   Meaning of 'discrimination'

13.4.1   Discrimination under the DDA 1995 may occur in two ways. First, a responsible body will discriminate against a disabled person if:

(a) for a reason which relates to his disability, it treats him less favourably than it treats or would treat others to whom that reason does not or would not apply; and
(b) it cannot show that the treatment in question is justified[1].

This discrimination, known as 'less favourable treatment' (discussed at 13.5), will apply to all education functions covered by the DDA 1995.

1 DDA 1995, s 28B(1).

13.4.2   Second, a responsible body will act unlawfully if it fails to take such steps as it is reasonable for it to have to take to ensure that:

(a) in relation to the arrangements it makes for determining the admission of pupils to the school, disabled persons are not placed at a substantial disadvantage in comparison with persons who are not disabled[1]; and
(b) in relation to education and associated services provided for, or offered to, pupils at a school by it, disabled pupils are not placed at a substantial disadvantage in comparison with pupils who are not disabled[2].

This second type of discrimination, otherwise known as a 'failure to make reasonable adjustments'[3] or, perhaps more correctly, a 'failure to take reasonable steps' (discussed at 13.6), applies to admissions and education and associated services but not to exclusion.

1 DDA 1995, s 28C(1)(a).
2 DDA 1995, s 28C(1)(b).
3 See Code of Practice (Schools), Chap 4.

These two types of discrimination will be considered in more detail below[1]. **13.4.3**

1 See 13.5 and 13.6.

Discrimination through less favourable treatment   13.5

Although all discrimination is, in effect, less favourable treatment, the DDA   **13.5.1**
1995 differentiates between discrimination which involves treating a person less favourably than a person who is not disabled ('discrimination through less favourable treatment')[1] and failing to take reasonable steps to ensure that a disabled person is not placed at a substantial disadvantage in comparison with persons who are not disabled[2]. This section will deal with the first category.

1 DDA 1995, s 28B.
2 DDA 1995, s 28C.

A responsible body will discriminate against a disabled person if: **13.5.2**

(a) for a reason which relates to his disability, it treats him less favourably than it treats or would treat others to whom that reason does not or would not apply; and
(b) it cannot show that the treatment in question is justified[1].

1 DDA 1995, s 28B(1).

This type of discrimination will apply to the arrangements a responsible   **13.5.3**
body makes in respect of admission to a school, in the education or associated services provided for, or offered to, pupils at the responsible body's school or the exclusion of a pupil, whether permanently or temporarily[1].

1 DDA 1995, s 28A(1) to (3).

The 'lack of knowledge defence'

The taking of a particular step by a responsible body in relation to a person   **13.5.4**
does not amount to less favourable treatment if the responsible body shows that at the time in question it did not know, and could not reasonably have been expected to know, that the person was disabled[1]. This is known as 'the lack of knowledge defence'[2]. In the majority of cases, schools will be aware of a pupil's disability because of the arrangements made for children with special educational needs or else parents will normally be only too willing to provide the necessary information[3]. Responsible bodies will, nonetheless, need to be proactive in seeking out information, otherwise they may not be able to use the lack of knowledge defence[4]. Thus schools are recommended to ensure there is an atmosphere in which parents and pupils are happy to disclose information about their disability, ask parents when they visit about any disability their child may have and provide space on admission forms to ask about disability. The lack of knowledge defence is also unlikely to be

available if a member of staff at the school knows of the disability but has not passed that information on. In effect, the responsible body will be considered to have deemed knowledge of the disability[5].

1 DDA 1995, s 28B(4).
2 Code of Practice (Schools), para 5:2.
3 Code of Practice (Schools), para 5:7.
4 Code of Practice (Schools), para 5:8.
5 Code of Practice (Schools), para 5:10.

The three tests

13.5.5   As the Code of Practice (Schools) makes clear[1], this means that there are, in effect, three tests to be met before less favourable treatment amounts to unlawful disability discrimination:

(a) the less favourable treatment is for a reason that is related to the child's disability;
(b) it is less favourable treatment than someone gets if the reason does not apply to them; and
(c) it is less favourable treatment that cannot be justified.

1 Code of Practice (Schools), para 3:7.

The less favourable treatment is for a reason that is related to the child's disability

13.5.6   The first test means that there must be a direct link between the reason for the less favourable treatment and the disability[1]. For example[2], if a school refuses to take a child who has epilepsy unless he stops having fits, the reason for the refusal will be the child's fits which are an intrinsic part of his disability and so the reason will relate to his disability[3]. In contrast, if pupils have been causing a nuisance in local stores through rowdy and disruptive behaviour and the school takes disciplinary action, even if one of the pupils has a disability, the disciplinary action will not be for a reason related to the pupil's disability[4].

1 Code of Practice (Schools), para 3:9.
2 Code of Practice (Schools), para 3:9A.
3 See also Code of Practice (Schools), paras 3:9B and 3:9C.
4 Code of Practice (Schools), para 3:10A.

It is less favourable treatment than someone gets if the reason does not apply to him

13.5.7   The second test involves a comparison between the disabled child who is being treated allegedly less favourably for a reason related to his disability and another child to whom that reason does not apply[1]. To assist in understanding this concept, the Code of Practice (Schools) gives three examples[2]. In the case of the child with epilepsy[3], if he is treated differently than a child who does not have fits, there will be less favourable treatment than another child for a reason related to his disability.

1 Code of Practice (Schools), para 3:11.
2 Code of Practice (Schools), paras 3:12A to 3:12C.
3 Code of Practice (Schools), para 3:12A.

It is less favourable treatment that cannot be justified

When considering whether less favourable treatment is justified, in addition **13.5.8**
to whatever guidance appears in the Code of Practice (Schools)[1], the DDA
1995 sets out a number of principles which should be applied in determining whether less favourable treatment is justified[2].

1 See Code of Practice (Schools), Chap 3 'What is discrimination? Less favourable
   treatment', paras 3:14 to 3:30.
2 DDA 1995, s 28B(5).

Thus, less favourable treatment of a person can be justified if it is the result **13.5.9**
of a permitted form of selection[1]. A permitted form of selection means:

(a) if the school is a maintained school which is not designated as a gram-
    mar school[2], any form of selection by ability or aptitude which is per-
    mitted by the SSFA 1998[3];
(b) if the school is a maintained school which is designated as a grammar
    school, any of its selective admission arrangements;
(c) if the school is an independent school, any arrangements which make
    provision for any or all of its pupils to be selected by reference to a gen-
    eral or special ability or aptitude, with a view to admitting only pupils
    of high ability or aptitude[4].

1 DDA 1995, s 28B(6).
2 Under the powers given to the Secretary of State so to do by SSFA 1998, s 104.
3 Permitted forms of selection by ability are: (a) any selection by ability authorised by
   SSFA 1998, s 100 (pre-existing arrangements); (b) any selection by ability authorised
   by SSFA 1998, s 101 (pupil banding); and (c) any selection by ability conducted in
   connection with the admission of pupils to the school for secondary education suitable
   to the requirements of pupils who are over compulsory school age: SSFA 1998,
   s 99(2).
     No admission arrangements for a maintained school may make provision for selection
   by aptitude unless they make provision for a permitted form of selection: SSFA 1998,
   s 99(3). The permitted forms of selection by aptitude are: (a) any selection by aptitude
   authorised by SSFA 1998, s 100 (pre-existing arrangements); and (b) any selection by
   aptitude authorised by SSFA 1998, s 102 (aptitude for particular subjects): SSFA 1998,
   s 99(4).
4 DDA 1995, s 28Q(9); and see Code of Practice (Schools), paras 3:24 to 3:30.

An example of selective arrangements justifying less favourable treatment is **13.5.10**
given[1] as a child with learning difficulties who applies to attend a selective
school, but fails a non-verbal reasoning test which is used to select the
school's intake and is refused admission. The refusal is because she has failed
her test and that failure is related to her disability (assuming that these learning difficulties amount to a disability). Because she is not selected because of
her disability, but other children without her disability would have passed and
therefore been admitted, she is treated less favourably than others to whom
that reason does not apply. However, so long as the school has operated its
selective criteria objectively, the treatment is likely to be justified.

1 Code of Practice (Schools), para 3:29A.

If the justification is not based upon a permitted from of selection, less **13.5.11**
favourable treatment will be justified only if the reason for it is both material
to the circumstances of the particular case and substantial[1].

1 DDA 1995, s 28B(7).

13.5.12 If, in a case where it is alleged that the responsible body have treated a disabled person less favourably, the responsible body is also under a duty to ensure that the disabled pupil is not substantially disadvantaged[1], but it fails without justification to comply with that duty, the treatment of that person cannot be justified as being material in the circumstances and substantial, unless that treatment would have been justified even if the responsible body had complied with that duty[2].

1 See 13.6.
2 DDA 1995, s 28B(8).

13.5.13 For a reason to be material, there has to be a clear connection between the reason that the responsible body gives and the circumstances of the particular case. The reason also has to be more than trivial or minor to be substantial[1]. The justification must also relate to the individual child; a blanket policy cannot constitute a material and substantial reason as it will fail to take account of the individual circumstances of the treatment[2]. In the example referred to above, the treatment of the epileptic child is unlikely to be justified[3]. If, however, a child with Tourette's Syndrome was excluded from a school trip[4], it would be less favourable treatment, but it might be justified if it would make the maintenance of discipline impossible. A material consideration, however, would be the extent to which the behaviour could be managed and what reasonable adjustments could be made to policies and procedures.

1 Code of Practice (Schools), para 3:17.
2 Code of Practice (Schools), para 3:21.
3 Code of Practice (Schools), para 3:18A.
4 Code of Practice (Schools), para 3:18B. For an example of treatment of a child with muscle spasms, see para 3.18B.

13.5.14 As seen from the last example, the Code of Practice (Schools) refers to reasonable adjustments and suggests[1] that a consideration when deciding whether less favourable treatment is justified will be whether there may have been reasonable adjustments which the responsible body could have made[2] and whether or not they tried to make them or made them. The term 'reasonable adjustments' does not appear in the disability discrimination in education part of the DDA 1995 and is in fact taken from the parts of the DDA 1995 dealing with employment[3] and goods and services[4] and it should perhaps more correctly be described as a duty to take reasonable steps to accord with the wording in the Act. As it features in the Code of Practice (Schools), though, it will be something responsible bodies have to have regard to. The Code suggests[5] that information sharing is key to avoid less favourable treatment and to enable a responsible body to make reasonable adjustments in response.

1 Code of Practice (Schools), paras 3:19 to 3:23.
2 Code of Practice (Schools), para 3:19.
3 DDA 1995, Pt II.
4 DDA 1995, Pt III.
5 Code of Practice (Schools), para 3:20.

13.5.15 Three further examples are given in the Code of Practice (Schools)[1]. First[2], a child with Hirschprung's Disease and lack of bowel control is refused admission by a school until the child is toilet trained as the school's policy is that all children must be toilet trained. The application of this blanket policy is unlikely to amount to sufficient justification. Second, a school refuses to allow a pupil with learning difficulties to attend a play on the basis the school believes he would not understand it[3]. If the belief is based on the assumption he would not understand it, rather than a material reason, this action is unlikely to be justified. Third[4], a wheelchair-bound child with cerebral palsy is prevented from accompanying their class on a 12-mile hike, but only after the school has carried out a risk assessment. This is likely to be treatment which can be justified in light of health and safety risks. In the absence of such a risk assessment, though, it may be that a similar justification would not apply.

1 Code of Practice (Schools), paras 3:23A to 3:23C.
2 Code of Practice (Schools), para 3:23A.
3 Code of Practice (Schools), para 3:23B.
4 Code of Practice (Schools), para 3:23C.

Failure to take reasonable steps to ensure no substantial disadvantage

13.6

The second type of discrimination is a failure to take reasonable steps to ensure that a disabled person is not substantially disadvantaged[1]. In the Code of Practice (Schools) draft issued for consultation, this element is described as 'A failure to make reasonable adjustments'[2]. As mentioned above[3], this phrase does not appear in the disability discrimination in education part of the DDA 1995 and is a concept expressed in other parts dealing with employment and services. The title in the draft code is therefore inaccurate and should, more correctly, refer to a failure to take reasonable *steps* rather than adjustments. Nonetheless, although the words used may be incorrect, the advice in the Code of Practice will be just as relevant and valid.

13.6.1

1 DDA 1995, s 28C(1).
2 Code of Practice (Schools), Chap 4 'What is discrimination? A failure to make reasonable adjustments'.
3 See 13.4.2.

A responsible body will act unlawfully if it fails to take such steps as it is reasonable for it to have to take to ensure that:

13.6.2

(a) in relation to the arrangements it makes for determining the admission of pupils to the school, disabled persons are not placed at a substantial disadvantage in comparison with persons who are not disabled[1]; and

(b) in relation to education and associated services provided for, or offered to, pupils at a school by it, disabled pupils are not placed at a substantial disadvantage in comparison with pupils who are not disabled[2]

but, in relation to a failure to take a particular step, a responsible body does not discriminate if it can show that its failure to comply was justified[3].

1 DDA 1995, s 28C(1)(a).
2 DDA 1995, s 28C(1)(b).
3 DDA 1995, s 28B(2).

13.6.3   This duty does not, however, require the responsible body to (a) remove or alter a physical feature (for example, one arising from the design or construction of the school premises or the location of resources), or (b) provide auxiliary aids or services[1].

1 DDA 1995, s 28C(2).

13.6.4   Schools are therefore not required to make physical alterations to buildings[1]. The improvement of the physical environment to increase access should instead be addressed through accessibility strategies and plans[2].

1 This applies insofar as addressing disability discrimination in education; schools may, however, need to meet their duties under other parts of the DDA 1995: see, for example, DDA 1995, Pts II and III.
2 Code of Practice (Schools), para 4:14; and see 13.7.

13.6.5   Special educational provision should include any educational aids and services where these are necessary to meet the child's identified needs. The disability discrimination duties do not provide an additional route to secure access to auxiliary aids and services[1].

1 Code of Practice (Schools), para 4:12.

13.6.6   Regulations may make provision:

(a) as to the circumstances in which it is reasonable for a responsible body to have to take steps of a prescribed description;
(b) as to the steps which it is always reasonable for a responsible body to have to take;
(c) as to circumstances in which it is not reasonable for a responsible body to have to take steps of a prescribed description;
(d) as to steps which it is never reasonable for a responsible body to have to take[1].

1 DDA 1995, s 28C(3).

13.6.7   In relation to a failure to take a particular step, a responsible body does not discriminate against a disabled person if it shows (a) that, at the time in question, it did not know and could not reasonably have been expected to know, that he was disabled, and (b) that its failure to take the step was attributable to that lack of knowledge[1].

1 DDA 1995, s 28B(3).

13.6.8   In considering whether it is reasonable for it to have to take a particular step in order to comply with this duty, a responsible body must have regard to any relevant provisions of a Code of Practice[1] issued under the DDA 1995[2].

1 See the Code of Practice (Schools), discussed at 11.2ff.
2 DDA 1995, s 28C(4); and see DDA 1995, s 53A.

The tests

13.6.9   As with less favourable treatment, there are a number of elements or tests to establish in order to found a claim for this type of discriminatory conduct:

(a) the disabled person has been placed at a disadvantage;

(b) the disadvantage is substantial;

(c) in comparison with persons who are not disabled;

(d) the responsible body could have taken reasonable steps to ensure that the disabled person was not placed at such a substantial disadvantage;

(e) the responsible body failed to take such steps; and

(f) its failure could not be justified.

The disadvantage is substantial

'Substantial' has the same meaning throughout the DDA 1995 and the **13.6.10** Code of Practice (Schools) and therefore means something more than minor or trivial[1]. In considering what may be a substantial disadvantage, a responsible body should take account of a number of factors which may include: the time and effort that might need to be expended by a disabled pupil, the inconvenience, indignity or discomfort suffered and the loss of opportunity or diminished progress that may be made in comparison to non-disabled pupils[2].

1 Code of Practice (Schools), para 4:6.
2 Code of Practice (Schools), para 4:8.

In comparison with non-disabled persons

The comparison here is directly between disabled children and children **13.6.11** who are not disabled[1].

1 Code of Practice (Schools), para 4:7

Failure to take reasonable steps

The duty to take reasonable steps is anticipatory[1] and therefore it is no **13.6.12** excuse for a responsible body to say it was waiting for a child to arrive before it thought about what it should do. The duty is also owed to all disabled children, not just to individual children[2]. For example[3], a school should check to ensure a field study centre could take disabled pupils[4] or change its policy to ensure that staff could administer medicines to pupils[5]. In contrast, if a school adopted a policy that its staff should not administer medicines it is unlikely to have taken reasonable steps.

1 Code of Practice (Schools), paras 4:9, 4:17 and 4:18.
2 Code of Practice (Schools), para 4:17.
3 See also Code of Practice (Schools), paras 4:17B to 4:17D.
4 Code of Practice (Schools), para 4:17B.
5 Code of Practice (Schools), para 4:17E.

In order to take reasonable steps in respect of individual pupils, a responsi- **13.6.13** ble body will need to have good information about children who will be attending the school[1]. Discussions with parents, pupils and the LEA will therefore be reasonable steps to take before a pupils starts. Thus, a small rural primary school may have little experience of disabled pupils. If it is proposed that a disabled child should attend, if the headteacher consults the parents, local voluntary organisations and devises a reasonable training and information programme for staff, the school is likely to have taken reasonable steps[2]. The need for good information is, however, a continuing need[3] For example, if a child's condition worsens or as they move up the school their curriculum needs change, if a school has arrangements in place to keep these changes under review and to make appropriate adjustments, it will probably have taken reasonable steps[4].

1 Code of Practice (Schools), para 4:21.
2 Code of Practice (Schools), para 4:20A.
3 Code of Practice (Schools), para 4:21.
4 See Code of Practice (Schools), paras 4:21A to 4:21C.

13.6.14 What steps are 'reasonable' will of course have to be objectively determined in the light of the individual pupil's disability and the circumstances of the responsible body. Responsible bodies will need to consider what steps could be taken and in deciding whether what has been considered is reasonable, they must have regard to the relevant provisions of the Code of Practice (Schools)[1] The Code assumes the involvement of disabled pupils in every aspect of school life[2] and suggests a careful consideration of how that participation is best facilitated will help the responsible body to determine what a reasonable step might be. Relevant factors may include[3]:

- the need to maintain academic, musical, sporting and other standards;
- the financial resources available to the responsible body;
- the cost of taking a particular step;
- the extent to which it is practicable to take the step;
- the extent to which aids and services will be provided to disabled pupils as special educational provision;
- health and safety requirements; and
- the interests of other pupils and persons who may be admitted to the school as pupils (and, it is suggested, school staff).

1 DDA 1995, s 28C(4).
2 Code of Practice (Schools), para 4:23.
3 Code of Practice (Schools), para 4:24.

13.6.15 Examples of how the reasonable step duty might work are given in the Code of Practice (Schools)[1]. A typical example may be where a school admits physically disabled pupils and has been adapted to accommodate wheelchairs and other equipment[2]. The school considers that the pupils' standing frames may pose a health and safety risk to other pupils. The frames are placed out of the way and are not consequently used by the disabled pupils, which has an adverse effect on their disabilities. The school, however, then obtains a health and safety assessment of the risk and this suggests that there is no significant risk. The school should therefore make the standing frames available, otherwise it is likely to be acting unlawfully.

1 See Code of Practice (Schools), paras 4:26A to 4:26C.
2 Code of Practice (Schools), para 4:26B.

Failure to take reasonable steps cannot be justified

13.6.16 The principles of justification are the same as with less favourable treatment[1] The justification must be both material to the circumstances of the particular case, ie no blanket policy, and substantial[2] There must be a clear connection between the reason the school gives and the circumstances of the particular case[3].

1 See DDA 1995, s 28B(5) to (8); and see 13.5.8ff.
2 DDA 1995, s 28B(7); and Code of Practice (Schools), para 4:27.
3 Code of Practice (Schools), para 4:28.

Confidentiality requests

Under the DDA 1995, a request can be made which is known as a 'confi- **13.6.17**
dentiality request'[1]. This is a request which asks for the nature, or for the
existence, of a disabled person's disability to be treated as confidential. The
request must be made either by a disabled person's parent or by the disabled
person himself where the responsible body reasonably believes that he has
sufficient understanding of the nature of the request and its effect[2]. Where
a confidentiality request has been made and the responsible body are aware
of the request[3], in determining whether it is reasonable for a responsible
body to have to take a particular step in relation to that person, regard shall
be had to the extent to which taking the step in question is consistent with
compliance with that request[4].

1 DDA 1995, s 28C(7).
2 DDA 1995, s 28C(7); and see also Code of Practice (Schools), paras 5:12 to 5:16.
3 DDA 1995, s 28C(5).
4 DDA 1995, s 28C(6).

Non-actionability

Section 28C of the DDA 1995 is stated, however, only to impose duties for the **13.6.18**
purpose of determining whether a responsible body has discriminated against
a disabled person and a breach of any such duty is not actionable as such[1].

1 DDA 1995, s 28C(8).

If, in case where it is alleged that the responsible body have treated a dis- **13.6.19**
abled person less favourably, the responsible body is also under a duty to
ensure that the disabled pupil is not substantially disadvantaged, but it fails
without justification to comply with that duty, the treatment of that person
cannot be justified as being material in the circumstances and substantial,
unless that treatment would have been justified even if the responsible body
had complied with that duty[1].

1 DDA 1995, s 28B(8).

Responsibility to prepare accessibility strategies and plans **13.7**

Every LEA must prepare, in relation to schools for which it is the responsi- **13.7.1**
ble body[1] (a) an accessibility strategy, and (b) further such strategies at
such times as may be prescribed[2].

1 Ie maintained schools, pupil referral units and maintained nursery schools.
2 DDA 1995, s 28D(1).

Accessibility strategies

An 'accessibility strategy' is a written[1] strategy for, over a prescribed period: **13.7.2**

(a) increasing the extent to which disabled pupils[2] can participate in the
     schools' curriculums;
(b) improving the physical environment of the schools for the purpose of
     increasing the extent to which disabled pupils are able to take advan-
     tage of education and associated services[3] provided or offered by the
     schools; and

(c) improving the delivery to disabled pupils (i) within a reasonable time and, (ii) in ways which are determined after taking account of their disabilities and any preferences expressed by them or their parents, of information which is provided in writing for pupils who are not disabled[4].

1 DDA 1995, s 28D(3).
2 'Disabled pupils' includes a disabled person who may be admitted to a school as a pupil: DDA 1995, s 28D(18).
3 Provision is made in the DDA 1995 for the Secretary of State to issue regulations which may prescribe services which are, or services which are not, to be regarded for the purposes of accessibility strategies and accessibility plans as being education or associated services: DDA 1995, s 28D(15).
4 DDA 1995, s 28D(2).

13.7.3   In preparing its accessibility strategy, an LEA must have regard to:

(a) the need to allocate adequate resources for implementing the strategy; and
(b) any guidance issued as to:
　(i)   the content of an accessibility strategy;
　(ii) the form in which it is to be produced; and
　(iii) the persons to be consulted in its preparation[1].

1 DDA 1995, s 28E(1). Guidance on accessibility strategies is not contained in the Code of Practice (Schools) but will be found in separate guidance issued by the Secretary of State.

13.7.4   Every LEA must also have regard to any guidance issued by the Secretary of State[1] with respect to the review and, if necessary, revision of its accessibility strategy[2].

1 DDA 1995, s 28E(3).
2 DDA 1995, s 28E(2).

13.7.5   Every LEA must keep its accessibility strategy under review during the period to which it relates and, if necessary, revise it[1]. Once an LEA has produced an accessibility strategy, it is the duty of the LEA to implement it[2]. Inspections of LEAs by OFSTED[3] may extend to the performance by an LEA of its functions in relation to the preparation,[4] review, revision and implementation of its accessibility strategy[5].

1 DDA 1995, s 28D(4).
2 DDA 1995, s 28D(5).
3 Office for Standards in Education; under EA 1997, s 38.
4 But not publication, in contrast to schools: see 13.7.12.
5 DDA 1995, s 28D(6).

13.7.6   If the Secretary of State, or, in Wales, the National Assembly, asks for a copy of the accessibility strategy, a copy must be provided[1]. If asked to do so, an LEA must also make a copy of its accessibility strategy available for inspection at such reasonable times as it may determine[2].

1 DDA 1995, s 28E(5) and (6).
2 DDA 1995, s 28E(7).

13.7.7   The Secretary of State retains certain reserve powers to ensure that LEAs have complied with their duties to produce, review and revise accessibility strategies. If the Secretary of State[1] is satisfied (whether on a complaint or otherwise) that a responsible body:

(a) has acted, or is proposing to act, unreasonably in the discharge of a
  duty in respect of an accessibility strategy; or
(b) has failed to discharge a duty imposed in respect of such a strategy,

the Secretary of State may give that responsible body such directions as to
the discharge of the duty as appear to it to be expedient[2]. These directions
may be given even if the performance of the duty is contingent upon the
opinion of the responsible body[3]. Such directions may be varied or revoked
by the Secretary of State (or, in Wales, the National Assembly) and may be
enforced, on the application of the directing authority, by a mandatory
order obtained in accordance with s 31 of the Supreme Court Act 1981[4].

1 In Wales, the National Assembly: DDA 1995, s 28M(8).
2 DDA 1995, s 28M(1).
3 DDA 1995, s 28M(4).
4 DDA 1995, s 28M(7).

Accessibility plans

Whilst accessibility strategies relate to all schools for which an LEA is   **13.7.8**
responsible, accessibility plans relate to individual schools both within the
maintained and also within the independent and non-maintained sectors[1].

1 DDA 1995, s 28D(7).

The responsible body for a school[1] must prepare (a) an accessibility plan,   **13.7.9**
and (b) further such plans at such times as may be prescribed[2].

1 Which in this context will be governing bodies in respect of maintained schools, the LEA
  in respect of pupil referral units and maintained nursery schools and the proprietor in
  respect of other schools.
2 DDA 1995, s 28D(8).

An 'accessibility plan' is a written[1] plan for, over a prescribed period: **13.7.10**

(a) increasing the extent to which disabled pupils can participate in the
  school's curriculum;
(b) improving the physical environment of the school for the purpose of
  increasing the extent to which disabled pupils are able to take advantage of education and associated services[2] provided or offered by the
  school; and
(c) improving the delivery to disabled pupils (i) within a reasonable time,
  and (ii) in ways which are determined after taking account of their disabilities and any preferences expressed by them or their parents, of
  information which is provided in writing for pupils who are not disabled[3].

1 DDA 1995, s 28D(10).
2 Provision is made in the DDA 1995 for the Secretary of State to issue regulations which
  may prescribe services which are, or services which are not, to be regarded for the
  purposes of accessibility strategies and accessibility plans as being education or associated
  services: DDA 1995, s 28D(15).
3 DDA 1995, s 28D(9).

When preparing its accessibility plan, the responsible body must have regard   **13.7.11**
to the need to allocate adequate resources for implementing the plan[1].

1 DDA 1995, s 28E(4).

13.7.12   Once produced, it is the duty of the responsible body[1] to implement the school's accessibility plan[2]. During the period to which the accessibility plan relates, the responsible body must keep it under review and, if necessary, revise it[3]. When a school or pupil referral unit or maintained nursery school is inspected by OFSTED[4], that inspection may extend to the performance by the responsible body of its functions in relation to the preparation, publication, review, revision and implementation of its accessibility plan[5].

1 Ie governing bodies in respect of maintained schools (see also DDA 1995, s 28D(14)), the LEA in respect of pupil referral units and maintained nursery schools and the proprietor in respect of other schools.
2 DDA 1995, s 28D(12).
3 DDA 1995, s 28D(11).
4 Under the School Inspections Act 1996.
5 DDA 1995, s 28D(13).

13.7.13   In the governing body's annual report[1], information as to the following must be included:

(a) the arrangements for the admission of disabled persons as pupils at the school;
(b) the steps taken to prevent disabled pupils from being treated less favourably than other pupils;
(c) the facilities provided to assist access to the school by disabled pupils; and
(d) the accessibility plan prepared by the governing body[2].

1 Ie the report prepared each year by a governing body under SSFA 1998, s 42(1).
2 EA 1996, s 317(6).

13.7.14   The Secretary of State or, in Wales, the National Assembly, may ask for a copy of the accessibility plan prepared by the proprietor of an independent school (other than a city academy) and, if they do, the accessibility plan must be supplied[1]. If asked to do so, the proprietor of an independent school which is not a city academy must make a copy of his accessibility plan available for inspection at such reasonable times as he may determine[2].

1 DDA 1995, s 28E(5) and (6).
2 DDA 1995, s 28E(8).

13.7.15   The Secretary of State retains certain reserve powers to ensure that responsible bodies have complied with their duties to produce, review and revise accessibility plans. If the Secretary of State[1] is satisfied (whether on a complaint or otherwise) that a responsible body:

(a) has acted, or is proposing to act, unreasonably in the discharge of a duty in respect of accessibility plans; or
(b) has failed to discharge a duty imposed in respect of such a plan,

the Secretary of State may give that responsible body such directions as to the discharge of the duty as appear to it to be expedient[2].

1 In Wales, the National Assembly: DDA 1995, s 28M(8).
2 DDA 1995, s 28M(1).

The Secretary of State, or, in Wales, the National Assembly, may also issue   **13.7.16**
directions to non-maintained special schools and city academies[1] relating to
the discharge of their duties with respect to accessibility plans. Such directions may be given if the Secretary of State or National Assembly is satisfied
(whether on a complaint or otherwise) that the responsible body for a non-
maintained special school or a city academy:

(a) has acted, or is proposing to act, unreasonably in the discharge of a duty
     which that body has in relation to (i) the provision to the Secretary of
     State or National Assembly, as appropriate, of copies of that body's
     accessibility plan, or (ii) the inspection of that plan; or
(b) has failed to discharge that duty.

The Secretary of State or National Assembly may give such directions as to
the discharge of the duty as appear to him to be expedient[2]. These directions
may be given even if the performance of the duty is contingent upon the
opinion of the responsible body[3]. Such directions may be varied or revoked
by the Secretary of State or the National Assembly and may be enforced, on
the application of the directing authority by a mandatory order obtained in
accordance with s 31 of the Supreme Court Act 1981[4].

1 DDA 1995, s 28M(2) and (3).
2 DDA 1995, s 28M(3).
3 DDA 1995, s 28M(4).
4 DDA 1995, s 28M(7).

Residual duties of LEAs   **13.8**

The SENDA 2001 recognises that LEAs are responsible for a wide range of   **13.8.1**
functions[1] which may affect disabled persons and consequently, rather than
addressing each and every function, the DDA 1995 will, from September
2002, require LEAs to exercise all their functions, except those expressly
excluded, in a way which does not discriminate against disabled pupils or
disabled persons who may be admitted to a school as a pupil[2].

1 'Functions' are defined as including the LEA's powers and duties: EA 1996, s 579(1); or
   'all the duties and powers . . . : the sum total of the activities Parliament has entrusted to
   it': per Lord Templeman in *Hazell v Hammersmith and Fulham London Borough Council*
   [1992] 2 AC 1, [1991] 1 All ER 545.
2 DDA 1995, ss 28F and 28G.

It is difficult, if not impossible, to provide a comprehensive list of such   **13.8.2**
functions, but these will include:

* the provision of school transport[1];
* the provision of milk, meals and other refreshment[2];
* the provision of certain clothing to certain pupils[3];
* the provision of education for children of compulsory school age who,
  by reason of illness, exclusion from school or otherwise may not receive
  suitable education unless arrangements for the provision of such education are made[4];
* the exercise of the LEA's functions with respect to children with special educational needs[5];
* behaviour support[6];

- education welfare, school attendance orders and non-attendance issues[7];
- early years development and childcare[8]; and
- the general responsibilities with respect to admissions[9].

1 EA 1996, s 509.
2 EA 1996, s 512.
3 EA 1996, s 510.
4 EA 1996, s 19.
5 EA 1996, Pt IV.
6 EA 1996, s 527A.
7 EA 1996, ss 437 to 444.
8 SSFA 1998, ss 117 to 124.
9 SSFA 1998, ss 84 to 109.

13.8.3 Consequently, in discharging a function (except for those prescribed functions to which the duty does not apply[1] or the functions to which other parts of the DDA 1995 do apply) it is unlawful for an LEA to discriminate against (a) a disabled pupil, or (b) a disabled person who may be admitted to a school as a pupil[2]. However, an act done in the discharge of such a function is unlawful only if no other provision makes that act unlawful[3]. This stresses the residual nature of this provision; if an act is specifically made unlawful and covered by another provision of the DDA 1995, this residual or fall back duty cannot apply.

1 DDA 1995, s 28F(2).
2 DDA 1995, s 28F(3).
3 DDA 1995, s 28F(4).

13.8.4 For the purposes of this residual duty not to discriminate, the same meaning of 'discrimination' applies[1] with slight differences. The changes are that this residual duty applies only to LEAs; it does not apply to governing bodies or proprietors of schools and so the responsible body for this purpose can only be an LEA[2].

1 See DDA 1995, ss 28B and 28C; and see 13.6 and 13.7.
2 DDA 1995, s 28G(1)(a).

13.8.5 Thus, an LEA will discriminate against a disabled person if, in exercising its 'residual' functions:

(a) for a reason which relates to the person's disability, it treats him less favourably than it treats or would treat others to whom that reason does not or would not apply; and
(b) it cannot show that the treatment in question is justified[1].

1 As per DDA 1995, ss 28B(1) and 28G(1).

13.8.6 In addition, each LEA must take such steps as it is reasonable for it to have to take to ensure that, in discharging any of its 'residual' functions:

(a) disabled persons who may be admitted to a school as pupils are not placed at a substantial disadvantage in comparison with persons who are not disabled; and
(b) disabled pupils are not placed at a substantial disadvantage in comparison with pupils who are not disabled[1].

This duty does not, however, require an LEA to (a) remove or alter a physical feature, or (b) provide auxiliary aids or services[2].

1 DDA 1995, s 28G(2).
2 DDA 1995, s 28G(3).

As with the duty not to discriminate placed on responsible bodies, the residual duty imposes duties only for the purpose of determining whether an LEA has discriminated against a disabled person and thus a breach of such a duty is not actionable as a breach of statutory duty as such[1].

13.8.7

1 DDA 1995, s 28G(4).

Victimisation

13.9

Under the general provisions of the DDA 1995, protection is given to disabled persons who may be subject to victimisation because they may have brought a claim alleging disability discrimination or have given evidence in such a claim[1].

13.9.1

1 DDA 1995, s 55; and see 11.5.

These provisions are considered in detail in 11.5, and will apply to all types of disability discrimination in education[1]. For the avoidance of doubt however, both in relation to the duty not to discriminate against disabled pupils and prospective pupils[2] and the residual duty imposed on LEAs[3], in the case of an act which constitutes discrimination by virtue of the provisions protecting an individual from victimisation, those duties are stated to apply to discrimination against persons who are not disabled as well as those who are[4].

13.9.2

1 DDA 1995, s 55(1).
2 DDA 1995, ss 28A, 28B and 28C.
3 DDA 1995, s 28F.
4 DDA 1995, ss 28A(6) and 28G(5).

ENFORCEMENT

Bringing claims against responsible bodies in respect of residual duties

13.10

The general question of enforcement and the appropriate forum for bringing a claim has been considered in 11.9. This section will therefore deal with the specific points of bringing claims against responsible bodies or LEAs in respect of residual duties.

13.10.1

A claim that a responsible body:

13.10.2

(a) has discriminated against a person (A) in a way which is made unlawful by the DDA 1995; or
(b) is, because the responsible body is the employer of a person whose acts committed in the course of his employment are to be treated as also done by his employer[1], to be treated as having discriminated against a person (A) in such a way,

may be made to the Special Educational Needs and Disability Tribunal[2] by that person's (A's) parents[3].

1 By virtue of DDA 1995, s 58.
2 Which will be renamed the Special Educational Needs and Disability Tribunal from 1 September 2002.
3 DDA 1995, s 28I(1).

13.10.3 The jurisdiction of the Tribunal covers discrimination by all responsible bodies with the exception[1] of claims relating to admissions[2] or permanent exclusions[3], which are dealt with by independent appeal panels. The procedure for bringing a claim before the Tribunal has been considered in 11.9.

1 DDA 1995, s 28I(2).
2 See DDA 1995, s 28K.
3 See DDA 1995, s 28L.

13.10.4 In respect of claims for which it has jurisdiction, if the Tribunal considers that a claim made to it is well-founded:

(a) it may declare that the person (A) has been unlawfully discriminated against; and
(b) if it does so, it may make such order as it considers reasonable in all the circumstances of the case[1].

The power to make such orders may be exercised, in particular, with a view to obviating or reducing the adverse effect on the person concerned (A) of any matter to which the claim relates, but does not include the power to order the payment of any sum by way of compensation[2].

1 DDA 1995, s 28I(3).
2 DDA 1995, s 28I(4).

13.10.5 Provision is made to ensure that a responsible body complies with an order of the Tribunal. Where the Tribunal makes an order, if the Secretary of State is satisfied (whether on a complaint or otherwise) that the responsible body concerned:

(a) has acted, or is proposing to act, unreasonably in complying with the order; or
(b) has failed to comply with the order,

the Secretary of State may give the responsible body such directions as to compliance with the order as appear to him to be expedient[1]. Such directions may be varied or revoked by the Secretary of State (or, in Wales, the National Assembly) and may be enforced, on the application of the directing authority by a mandatory order obtained in accordance with s 31 of the Supreme Court Act 1981[2].

1 DDA 1995, s 28M(5) and (6).
2 DDA 1995, s 28M(7).

Admissions

13.10.6 In the maintained sector, every LEA has the duty to put in place arrangements to enable parents to express a preference for the maintained school they wish their children to attend[1]. The LEA will be the admissions authority for community and voluntary controlled schools (unless it has delegated the function to such schools) and each governing body will be the admissions authority in respect of every foundation and voluntary aided school. The admissions authority must make arrangements to enable parents whose preferences have not been met to appeal against the admission authority's decision to an independent appeal panel[2]. The constitution and procedure of independent admission appeals is set out in Schedule 24 to the SSFA 1998. In the case of city academies, the admission arrangements and appeal process will be set out in an agreement entered into by the academy and the Secretary of State[3]. In the independent and non-maintained sector, each school will determine its own admission arrangements and the process for making an appeal (if any) against a decision to refuse admission.

1 SSFA 1998, s 86.
2 SSFA 1998, s 94.
3 EA 1996, s 482.

If arrangements have been made enabling an appeal to be made against a **13.10.7** decision of an admissions authority or city academy under the statutory or agreed appeal arrangements,[1], a claim for disability discrimination or victimisation in relation to an admissions decision[2] must be made under the appeal arrangements[3].

1 DDA 1995, s 28K.
2 'Admissions decision' means a decision refusing to accept an expressed preference under SSFA 1998, s 94(1) or (2) or a decision taken as to the admission of a person to a city academy taken by the responsible body or on its behalf: DDA 1995, s 28K(5).
3 DDA 1995, s 28K(1) and (3).

Claims which may be considered as part of the appeal arrangements (and **13.10.8** they must be made under the appeal arrangements, not in separate appeals[1]) are that in relation to an admission decision, a responsible body:

(a) has discriminated against a person (A) in way which is made unlawful by the disability discrimination in education provisions of the DDA 1995; or
(b) is, by virtue of the provisions relating to the victimisation of complainants (ie by virtue of DDA 1995, s 58[2]), to be treated as having discriminated against a person (A) in such a way[3].

1 DDA 1995, s 28K(3).
2 See 11.5.
3 DDA 1995, s 28K(1).

This exception to the rule that claims should be made to the Tribunal will **13.10.9** therefore only apply to *admissions decisions* in respect of which an appeal is available to an independent appeal panel. It will not therefore apply to all aspects of the admissions process in the maintained sector. Thus a claim that there has been disability discrimination in an admissions authority's arrangements, including its policy or criteria for admission, rather than in respect of an individual decision to refuse admission, will have to be made to the Tribunal. And, of course, as the admission arrangements in independent or non-maintained schools do not fall within the statutory regime for admissions, any claim that their admission arrangements discriminate on the grounds of disability, whether generally or in respect of a refusal to admit a specific child, will have to be made to the Tribunal.

13.10.10   The body hearing the claim has the same powers which it has in relation to an appeal under the appeal arrangements[1].

1   DDA 1995, s 28K(4).

Exclusions

13.10.11   In the maintained sector, responsibility for the behaviour and disciplining of pupils in schools is placed on each school's governing body (in respect of policy) and headteacher (in respect of taking measures to promote good behaviour and deal with disciplinary problems)[1]. The headteacher has the ultimate sanction to exclude a pupil on disciplinary grounds from the school either for a fixed term period, not exceeding 45 school days in any one school year, or permanently[2]. In the case of permanent exclusions, once a governing body's pupil discipline committee has upheld the headteacher's decision, an LEA is under an obligation to make arrangements to enable a parent (or the pupil themselves if they are over 16) to appeal against the decision that they should not be reinstated into the school[3].

Appeals are made to independent appeal panels established by the LEA[4], whether the child has been excluded from a community, voluntary controlled, voluntary aided or foundation school. In the case of city academies, the appeal arrangements will be determined by the agreement entered into between the responsible body of the academy and the Secretary of State[5].

This statutory regime does not apply to independent or non-maintained schools and so the process by which a pupil can be excluded and the rights of appeal against such a decision (if any) will be a matter for the school, which will usually be incorporated into the contract between the school and the parents.

1   SSFA 1998, s 61.
2   SSFA 1998, s 64.
3   SSFA 1998, s 67.
4   See SSFA 1998, Sch 18 for their constitution and rules of procedure.
5   EA 1996, s 482.

13.10.12   Where the statutory arrangements, or, in the case of city academies, the agreed arrangements, are in place to enable a parent or the pupil to appeal against an exclusion decision[1], the parent or the pupil may raise a claim in relation to the exclusion decision that there has been unlawful disability discrimination or victimisation as part of that appeal[2]. Indeed, if the parent or pupil wishes to make such a claim they must make it through the appeal arrangements[3].

1   'Exclusion decision' means a decision of a governing body not to reinstate a pupil excluded by the headteacher or a decision not to reinstate a pupil who has been permanently excluded from a city academy by its headteacher, taken by the responsible body or on its behalf: DDA 1995, s 28L(5).
2   DDA 1995, s 28L(1).
3   DDA 1995, s 28L(3).

13.10.13   Thus a parent may claim that a responsible body[1]:

(a)   has discriminated against a person (A) in way which is made unlawful by the provisions relating to disability discrimination in education; or

(b) is, by virtue of DDA 1995, s 58 (ie the provisions protecting individuals from victimisation) to be treated as having discriminated against a person (A) in such a way[2].

1 In this context 'responsible body', in relation to a maintained school, includes the discipline committee of the governing body required to be established by Regulations made under SSFA 1998, Sch 11, para 4 to hear representations in respect of exclusions: DDA 1995, s 28L(6).
2 DDA 1995, s 28L(1).

The body hearing the appeal has the same powers which it has in relation to an appeal under the appeal arrangements[1].   **13.10.14**

1 DDA 1995, s 28L(4).

As with admissions, the jurisdiction of independent appeal panels applies only to 'exclusion decisions' in respect of individual pupils and, by the nature of that jurisdiction, in respect only of permanent exclusions. Claims that a school's discipline policy may infringe the DDA 1995 will therefore have to be brought in the Tribunal. Similarly, it will be for the Tribunal to determine claims, for example, that a headteacher discriminated against a pupil in imposing disciplinary sanctions less than exclusion, such as detention, or in excluding a pupil for a fixed term. With the latter, there is an apparent absurdity within the legislation that if a child is permanently excluded and raises a claim of discrimination, the appeal must be made within 15 school days to the independent appeal panel, but if the child is excluded for, say, one day and makes a similar claim, the time limit for appealing to the Tribunal will be six months, or eight months if conciliation is attempted.   **13.10.15**

With independent and non-maintained schools, all claims relating to decisions to exclude or expel a pupil will have to be made to the Tribunal.   **13.10.16**

Agreements relating to enforcement   **13.11**

Any term in a contract or other agreement made by or on behalf of a responsible body is void so far as it purports to: **13.11.1**

(a) require a person to do anything which would contravene any provision relating to disability discrimination in education;
(b) exclude or limit the operation of any provision relating to disability discrimination in education;
(c) prevent any person from making a claim for such discrimination[1].

1 DDA 1995, s 28P(1).

In effect, schools, and this will probably most usually apply to independent and non-maintained schools, will be prohibited from requiring parents to exclude any right to bring a claim under the DDA 1995 in their contracts. It would also prevent maintained schools from including any such term in a home-school agreement[1] albeit that such agreements do not create any legal obligation in contract or tort[2].   **13.11.2**

1 EA 1996, s 110.
2 EA 1996, s 111(6).

13.11.3 If, however, an agreement is entered into seeking to settle a claim to the Tribunal or to an independent appeal panel in respect of an admission or exclusion decision, (b) and (c) above do not apply to such an agreement[1]. Any person interested in such an agreement can apply to the county court, which can make such order as it thinks just for modifying the agreement to take account of the effect of the above provisions, ie to bring the agreement in line with these provisions[2]. An order made in these circumstances can be retrospective[3]. Such an order cannot, however, be made unless all persons affected have been given (save where the rules of court permit notice to be dispensed with[4]) notice of the application and afforded an opportunity to make representations to the court[5].

1 DDA 1995, s 28P(2).
2 DDA 1995, s 28P(3).
3 DDA 1995, s 28P(1).
4 DDA 1995, s 28P(5).
5 DDA 1995, s 28P(4).

Chapter 14

Disability discrimination in further and higher education

Introduction   14.1

To a certain extent, the provisions of the Disability Discrimination Act   **14.1.1**
(DDA) 1995 had been applied to further and higher education to a greater
degree than in schools. Nonetheless, the DDA 1995 still exempted further
education and higher education institutions from obligations under the Act,
insofar as the provision of education was concerned.

The one concession in the DDA 1995 towards disabled students was that it   **14.1.2**
amended the Further and Higher Education Act (FHEA) 1992. Under the
FHEA 1992, the then Further Education Funding Councils (FEFCs) were
required to act in a strategic manner to secure sufficient and adequate provision of further education. They would do this by placing conditions upon
the financial support the FEFC could give to educational establishments[1].
The most important and specific was the requirement placed on governing
bodies of further education colleges to publish annual disability statements
containing information about the provision of facilities for education made by
the institution in respect of 'disabled persons'[2]. The content of the disability
statement is prescribed by regulations[3]. The annual disability statement
therefore has to contain (and will continue to do so) the following items[4]:

(a) policies of the institution relating to the provision of facilities for education;
(b) names of the member or members of staff with special responsibility
    for disabled persons;
(c) admission arrangements;
(d) educational facilities and support including academic and curriculum
    support, relevant staff expertise and technology and equipment avail-
    able;
(e) additional support or special arrangements during examinations and
    assessments;
(f) facilities and support associated with educational facilities and support
    including counselling and welfare arrangements; and
(g) physical access to educational and other facilities.

Reference to complaints handling and appeals, where appropriate, should
also be included within the statement.

---

1 Further and Higher Education Act (FHEA) 1992, s 5.

2 FHEA 1992, s 5(7A).
3 See FHEA 1992, s 5(7A) and (7B) and the Education (Disability Statements for Further Education Institutions) Regulations 1996, SI 1996/1664.
4 Education (Disability Statements for Further Education Institutions) Regulations 1996, SI 1996/1664, reg 2.

14.1.3   FEFCs themselves were required each year to provide a written report to the Secretary of State on the provision of further education for disabled students in their area during the previous year. In particular, these reports had to refer to progress they had made and their plans for future provision of further education for disabled students[1].

1 FHEA 1992, s 8(6).

14.1.4   So far as LEAs carried out further education functions, the DDA 1995 placed LEAs under a duty to publish disability statements, containing information on the provision of facilities for the further education made by the LEA in respect of disabled persons[1].

1 Education Act (EA) 1996, s 528.

14.1.5   The provisions in respect of LEAs continue to remain in force. As far as the FEFC is concerned, in view of its abolition under the Learning and Skills Act 2000, the duty is now transferred to the local Learning and Skills Councils[1].

1 See Learning and Skills Act 2000, s 82.

14.1.6   In higher education, Higher Education Funding Councils (HEFCs) have been required to have regard to the requirements of disabled persons when exercising their statutory functions[1]. Loans can be made as well as grants or other payments by HEFCs to the governing bodies of universities or higher education institutes on condition that the governing body of those institutes should publish disability statements[2]. As in the further education sector, a 'disability statement' is a statement containing information about the provision of facilities for education and research made by the university or institution in respect of disabled persons[3]. Guidance on the production of disability statements and the detail they should contain has been published by the Higher Education Funding Council for England[4] and by the Higher Education Funding Council for Wales[5]. A disability statement should therefore contain[6] information on the policies and procedures adopted by universities and higher education institutes relating to disabled students in respect of the following:

(a) equal opportunities;
(b) access and admissions;
(c) examinations and assessment;
(d) quality assessment and monitoring and evaluation of support services;
(e) staff development and training programmes;
(f) provision of financial assistance to disabled students; and
(g) charging students for certain facilities.

The disability statement should also describe the nature and range of the current provision provided at the university or institution for disabled students, including:

(a) examples of the type of information, advice, services, materials and support provided;

(b) support and provision relating to academic services including for example special arrangements for examinations;

(c) information technology provision;

(d) the physical environment; and

(e) details of the members of staff responsible for assisting and supporting disabled students.

1 FHEA 1992, s 62(7A).
2 FHEA 1992, s 65(4A).
3 FHEA 1992, s 65(4B).
4 See HEFCE Circular 8/96.
5 See HEFCW Circular W96/43HE.
6 HEFCE Circular 8/96, paras 12 to 13.

Scope of the chapter

This chapter will consider the new obligations imposed on further and higher education institutions by the amendments made to the DDA 1995 by the Special Educational Needs and Disability Act (SENDA) 2001. Many of the principles are the same as for disability discrimination in primary and secondary education considered in Chapter 13, and cross-reference will therefore be made to those sections where appropriate. A separate Code of Practice – the Code of Practice (Post 16): New duties (from 2002) in the provision of post-16 education and related services for disabled persons and students (referred to here as 'the Code of Practice (Post 16)')[1] – will be produced by the Commission which, as we will see, although dealing with similar principles to disability discrimination in schools, contains slightly different guidance. **14.1.7**

1 As to which, see 11.2ff.

Although this chapter and the Code of Practice (Post 16) deal with post-16 education, please note that this only relates to the provision of education in further education and higher education institutes. Discrimination against disabled pupils who are educated post-16 in school sixth forms is considered to fall within the school based provisions of the DDA 1995, and therefore the appropriate guidance is contained in the Code of Practice (Schools), the effect of which has been considered in Chapter 13. **14.1.8**

DEFINITIONS, RULES AND RESPONSIBILITIES

Unlawful discrimination **14.2**

The above, then, are the provisions in force prior to the commencement of the SENDA 2001. The SENDA 2001 itself will, with effect from 1 September 2002 in the majority of cases, impose further and far more specific duties on responsible bodies within the further education and higher education sector. Unlike the school provisions of the SENDA 2001, it is intended that not all the post-16 provisions will come into force on the same date, in order to allow time for responsible bodies to comply with the relevant provisions. Hence, whilst the duties not to discriminate against disabled students will come into force from September 2002, it is intended that **14.2.1** the duties on responsible bodies to make adjustments that involve the provision of auxiliary aids and services will take effect from 1 September 2003, and those relating to making adjustments to physical features of premises, from 1 September 2005[1].

1   See Code of Practice (Post 16), Foreword.

14.2.2   The Commission is given the power to prepare and issue Codes of Practice, giving practical guidance on how to avoid discrimination[1]. The Commission will therefore be issuing a code of practice in respect of post-16 education in the same way as it will issue a code of practice in respect of pre-16 education[2]. In accordance with the general principles[3], all bodies and persons exercising responsibilities in the further education and higher education sector will have to have regard to the Code of Practice when carrying out their functions.

1   DDA 1995, s 53A(1).
2   A draft Code of Practice – Draft Code of Practice (Post 16): New duties (from 2002) in the provision of post-16 education and related services for disabled persons and students – was issued by the Commission for consultation in July 2001; references in this chapter to the 'Code of Practice' are therefore references to this draft, which was the only document available at the time of writing.
3   See DDA 1995, s 53.

14.2.3   From 1 September 2002, it will therefore be unlawful for the body responsible[1] for an educational institution to discriminate against a disabled person:

(a)   in the arrangements it makes for determining admissions to the institution;
(b)   in the terms on which it offers to admit into the institution;
(c)   by refusing or deliberately omitting to accept an application for admission to an institution[2].

1   See 14.3.
2   DDA 1995, s 28R(1).

14.2.4   In addition, it is unlawful for the body responsible for an educational institution to discriminate against a disabled student in the student services it provides or offers to provide[1] and it is unlawful for the body responsible for an educational institution to discriminate against a disabled student by excluding him from the institution whether permanently or temporarily[2].

1   DDA 1995, s 28R(2).
2   DDA 1995, s 28R(3).

14.2.5   'Student services' means services of any description which are provided wholly or mainly for students[1] and regulations may make provision as to services which are or are not to be regarded as student services[2]. Draft regulations[3] were issued for consultation in autumn 2001, but the author is not aware of these having been confirmed at the time of writing.

1   DDA 1995, s 28R(11).
2   DDA 1995, s 28R(12).
3   The draft Disability Discrimination (Student Services) Regulations 2001.

Responsible bodies **14.3**

An 'educational institution', which is subject to the provisions of the DDA **14.3.1**
1995, is an institution[1]:

(a) within the higher education sector;
(b) within the further education sector; or
(c) designated in an order made by the Secretary of State.

1 DDA 1995, s 28R(6).

For each educational institution there will be a body responsible for its con- **14.3.2**
duct[1]. The body responsible, known as the 'responsible body'[2], will be the
governing body of an institution within the further education sector, a university, or an institution other than a university within the higher education
sector or, in the case of an institution designated by the Secretary of State,
the body specified in the order[3].

1 DDA 1995, s 28R(5).
2 DDA 1995, s 28R(5).
3 DDA 1995, Sch 4B, para 1.

Unlawful discrimination against disabled students or **14.4**
prospective students

A responsible body will discriminate against a disabled person if: **14.4.1**

(a) for a reason which relates to his disability it treats him less favourably
than it treats or would treat others to whom that reason does not or
would not apply; and
(b) it cannot show that the treatment in question is justified[1].

1 DDA 1995, s 28S(1).

A responsible body will also discriminate against a disabled person if: **14.4.2**

(a) it fails, to the person's detriment, to take such steps as it is reasonable
for it to take to ensure that, in relation to the arrangements it makes for
determining admissions to the institution or in relation to student services provided for, or offered to, students by it, disabled students are not
placed at a substantial disadvantage in comparison with students who
are not disabled[1]; and
(b) it cannot show that its failure to comply is justified[2].

1 DDA 1995, ss 28S(2) and 28T(1).
2 DDA 1995, s 28S(2).

As with pre-16 education, therefore, the DDA 1995 creates two intercon- **14.4.3**
nected types of discrimination: (a) less favourable treatment, and (b) a
failure to take reasonable steps to ensure a disabled student is not placed at
a substantial disadvantage. These two types of discrimination will be considered in turn.

14.5 Less favourable treatment

14.5.1 As indicated above, a responsible body will discriminate against a disabled person if:

(a) for a reason which relates to his disability, it treats him less favourably than it treats or would treat others to whom that reason does not or would not apply; and

(b) it cannot show that the treatment in question is justified[1].

1 DDA 1995, s 28S(1).

14.5.2 This type of discrimination will apply to the arrangements a responsible body makes in respect of admission to an institution, in the student services provided for, or offered to, students or the exclusion of a student, whether permanently or temporarily[1].

1 DDA 1995, s 28R(1) to (3).

Tests

14.5.3 Although the Code of Practice (Post 16)[1], does not repeat the view in the Code of Practice (Schools)[2] that there are, in effect, three tests to be met before less favourable treatment amounts to unlawful disability, the reality is that the following will apply to determine whether this type of discrimination is present:

(a) the less favourable treatment is for a reason that is related to the student's disability;

(b) it is less favourable treatment than someone gets if the reason does not apply to them; and

(c) it is less favourable treatment that cannot be justified.

1 Code of Practice (Post 16), Chap 4.
2 Code of Practice (Schools), para 3:7.

14.5.4 The taking of a particular step by a responsible body in relation to a person does not amount to less favourable treatment if the responsible body shows that at the time in question it did not know, and could not reasonably have been expected to know, that the person was disabled[1]. Responsible bodies will, nonetheless, need to be proactive in seeking out information for if they have failed to take reasonable steps to find out about a person's disability, the defence will not be available[2]. Thus, responsible bodies are encouraged to ensure there is an atmosphere in which people are happy to disclose information about their disability. This may mean asking applicants on courses to disclose their disabilities on application and enrolment forms; publicising the provision made for disabled people; providing opportunities for students to talk to staff in confidence; allowing students to provide information on their disability when applying for examinations etc[3]. The 'lack of knowledge defence' is also unlikely to be available if a member of staff at the institution knows of the disability but has not passed that information on. In effect, the responsible body will be considered to have deemed knowledge of the disability[4].

1 DDA 1995, s 28S(3).
2 Code of Practice (Post 16), para 4:17.
3 Code of Practice (Post 16), para 4:19.
4 Code of Practice (Post 16), para 4:18.

The Code of Practice (Post 16) deals with elements of less favourable treat-   **14.5.5**
ment in a slightly different way to the Code of Practice (Schools). It thus
examines the nature of the correct comparison[1], considers less favourable
treatment in respect of admissions[2], exclusions[3] and services[4] and then provides guidance on what may amount to justification[5].

1 Code of Practice (Post 16), para 4:4 to 4:10.
2 Code of Practice (Post 16), paras 4:11 to 4:13.
3 Code of Practice (Post 16), para 4:14.
4 Code of Practice (Post 16), para 4:15.
5 Code of Practice (Post 16), paras 4:22 to 4:32.

Comparison with treatment of others

The Code of Practice (Post 16) stresses that for a disabled person to be   **14.5.6**
treated less favourably, the responsible body must have treated him less
favourably in comparison with how other people are treated or would be
treated and the reason for the less favourable treatment must relate to the
disabled person's disability[1]. A basic example[2] is if a university says it refuses
to take dyslexic students on English degrees[3]. If however, a hearing impaired
student is turned down for a dentistry course because she does not have the
necessary qualifications, the rejection is not connected to the disability and
so there is no less favourable treatment[4].

1 Code of Practice (Post 16), para 4:4.
2 Other examples specifically with reference to admissions, exclusions and student services
   can be found in Code of Practice (Post 16), paras 4:11 to 4:14.
3 Code of Practice (Post 16), para 4:4A.
4 Code of Practice (Post 16), para 4:4.B.

If the treatment is caused by the fact that the person is disabled, then the   **14.5.7**
treatment relates to the disability. This is the case even if other people are
also treated unfavourably for a broadly similar reason[1]. For example, a
Tourette's Syndrome student is excluded because he has been verbally abu-
sive to staff. The college's regulations ban such conduct. However, the
swearing is directly linked to the student's disability and therefore in this
case the appropriate comparison should be made with a student who does
not swear at staff. The exclusion is probably therefore due to his disability
and unlawful[2]. This does not mean, however, that disabled students may
have a general excuse for misbehaviour[3].

1 Code of Practice (Post 16), para 4:5.
2 Code of Practice (Post 16), para 4:5B.
3 Code of Practice (Post 16), para 4:6 and see para 4:6A.

Bad treatment of a disabled person is also not necessarily less favourable   **14.5.8**
treatment. If a member of staff is rude to all students, including disabled
students, the disabled student is not being treated less favourably than non-
disabled students[1].

1 Code of Practice (Post 16), paras 4:7 and 4:7A.

A disabled student does not have to prove that others *were* treated more   **14.5.9**
favourably, only that others *would* have been treated better[1].

1 Code of Practice (Post 16), para 4:9.

Justification

14.5.10   If a student establishes that there has been less favourable treatment, it may be justified if it is necessary in order to maintain[1]:

(a) academic standards; or
(b) standards of any other prescribed kind.

Less favourable treatment would also be justified if it is of a prescribed kind, it occurs in prescribed circumstances or it is of a prescribed kind and it occurs in prescribed circumstances[2]. In all other circumstances, however, less favourable treatment or a failure to comply with the duty not to substantially disadvantage disabled students will be justified only if the reason for it is both material to the circumstances of a particular case and substantial[3].

1 DDA 1995, s 28S(6).
2 DDA 1995, s 28S(7).
3 DDA 1995, s 28S(8).

14.5.11   The onus to prove justification will be on the responsible body[1]. The reason for the treatment must be both material to the circumstances of the particular case and substantial ie not minor or trivial. To be material the reasons must relate to the individual circumstances[2] and therefore a blanket policy will not normally suffice.

1 And see Code of Practice (Post 16), para 4:24.
2 Code of Practice (Post 16), para 4:31; and see also paras 4:31A, 4:32 and 4:32A.

14.5.12   Academic standards may provide a reason for less favourable treatment. The DDA 1995 does not require a responsible body to do anything that would undermine the academic standards of a particular course or other prescribed standards[1]. For example, a person with learning difficulties applies to do a biology course, but does not meet the entry requirements. If no steps can be taken to eliminate any disadvantage, refusing him entry is likely to be justified on the grounds of maintaining the academic standards of the course[2]. But academic standards cannot be a blanket excuse to bar particular groups[3]. Thus, it is likely to be unlawful for a college to bar dyslexic students from journalism courses[4].

1 Draft regulations specifying prescribed standards and the institutions to which they relate were issued for consultation in autumn 2001– see the draft Disability Discrimination (Justification) Regulations.
2 Code of Practice (Post 16), para 4:26A.
3 Code of Practice (Post 16), para 4:27.
4 Code of Practice (Post 16), para 4:27B.

14.5.13   If, in a case where it is alleged that the responsible body has treated a disabled person less favourably, the responsible body is also under a duty to ensure that the disabled pupil is not substantially disadvantaged[1], but it fails without justification to comply with that duty, the treatment of that person cannot be justified as being material in the circumstances and substantial, unless that treatment would have been justified even if the responsible body had complied with that duty[2].

1 See 14.6.
2 DDA 1995, s 28S(9).

Failure to take reasonable steps to prevent substantial disadvantage **14.6**

The second type of discrimination is a failure to take reasonable steps to **14.6.1**
ensure that a disabled person is not substantially disadvantaged[1]. In the
Code of Practice (Post 16) draft issued for consultation, this element is
described as 'A duty to make reasonable adjustments'[2]. This phrase does not
appear in the disability discrimination in education part of the DDA 1995
and is a concept expressed in other parts dealing with employment and
services. The title in the draft code is therefore inaccurate and should, more
correctly, refer to a duty to take reasonable *steps* rather than adjustments.
Nonetheless, although the words used may be incorrect, the advice in the
Code of Practice will be just as relevant and valid.

1 DDA 1995, s 28T(1).
2 Code of Practice (Post 16), Chap 5.

A responsible body will act unlawfully if it fails to take such steps as it is rea- **14.6.2**
sonable for it to have to take to ensure that:

(a) in relation to the arrangements it makes for determining admissions to
     the institution, disabled persons are not placed at a substantial dis-
     advantage in comparison with persons who are not disabled[1]; and
(b) in relation to student services provided for, or offered to, students by
     it, disabled students are not placed at a substantial disadvantage in
     comparison with students who are not disabled[2],

but, in relation to a failure to take a particular step, a responsible body does
not discriminate if it can show that its failure to comply was justified[3].

1 DDA 1995, s 28T(1)(a).
2 DDA 1995, s 28T(1)(b).
3 DDA 1995, s 28S(2).

As in the case of less favourable treatment, a 'lack of knowledge defence' **14.6.3**
may be available if the responsible body was not aware of the student's disability[1]. In relation to a failure to take a particular step, a responsible body
does not discriminate against a disabled persons if it shows (a) that, at the
time in question, it did not know and could not reasonably have been
expected to know, that he was disabled, and (b) that its failure to take the
step was attributable to that lack of knowledge[2].

1 DDA 1995, s 28S(3) and (4); and see 14.5.4.
2 DDA 1995, s 28S(3).

In contrast to discrimination in schools, the obligation is not limited by the **14.6.4**
DDA 1995 stating that the duty does not require the responsible body to
remove or alter a physical feature or provide auxiliary aids or services[1].

1 See in contrast DDA 1995, s 28C(2).

In considering whether it is reasonable for a responsible body to have to take **14.6.5**
a particular step in order to comply with its duty, a responsible body must
have regard to any relevant provisions of the Code of Practice (Post 16)[1].
Detailed guidance on this particular duty can be found in Chapters 5 and 6
of the Code of Practice (Post 16).

1 DDA 1995, s 28T(2).

Tests

14.6.6 As with less favourable treatment, there are a number of elements or tests to establish in order to found a claim for this type of discriminatory conduct. Although these are not explicitly set out in the Code of Practice (Post 16), the following are involved:

(a) the disabled person has been placed at a disadvantage;
(b) the disadvantage is substantial;
(c) in comparison with persons who are not disabled;
(d) the responsible body could have taken reasonable steps to ensure that the disabled person was not placed at such a substantial disadvantage;
(e) the responsible body failed to take such steps; and
(f) its failure could not be justified.

14.6.7 Most reasonable steps or adjustments need to be made from 1 September 2002, but reasonable adjustments relating to auxiliary aids and services must be implemented by 1 September 2003 and reasonable adjustments to physical features from 1 September 2005[1].

1 Code of Practice (Post 16), para 5:3.

14.6.8 'Substantial disadvantage' has the same meaning throughout the DDA 1995 and the Code of Practice (Post 16), and therefore means something more than minor or trivial[1]. In considering what may be a substantial disadvantage, a responsible body should take account of the time, inconvenience, effort or discomfort entailed in comparison with other students[2].

1 Code of Practice (Post 16), para 5:2.
2 Code of Practice (Post 16), para 5:2 and see examples at paras 5:2A to 5:2E.

14.6.9 The duty to take reasonable steps is anticipatory[1] and therefore it is no excuse for a responsible body to say it was waiting for a student to arrive before it thought about what it should do. The issue of anticipatory reasonable adjustments is especially relevant in respect of buildings[2] so, for example, if a university keeps its building works department briefed on all aspects of physical access and every time work is undertaken an assessment is made so that visual or acoustic issues are addressed, the responsible body will be anticipating reasonable adjustments that might need to be made[3]. The duty is a continuing one[4] and so a responsible body should keep the steps it may need to take constantly under review.

1 Code of Practice (Post 16), paras 5:5 and 5:6, and see examples at paras 5:6A to 5:6D.
2 Code of Practice (Post 16), para 5:7.
3 Code of Practice (Post 16), para 5:7A, see also paras 5:7B and 5:7C.
4 Code of Practice (Post 16), para 5:9.

14.6.10 In deciding what steps are 'reasonable', a responsible body will have to take into account all the circumstances of the case. Responsible bodies will need to consider what steps could be taken and in deciding whether what has been considered is reasonable, they must have regard to the relevant provision of the Code of Practice (Post 16)[1]. The Code explains that the steps will vary according to[2]:

(a) the type of services being provided;

(b) the nature of the institution or service and its size and resources;
(c) the effect of the disability on the individual disabled person or student.

1   DDA 1995, s 28T(2).
2   Code of Practice (Post 16), para 6:1.

Relevant factors for the responsible body to consider may include[1]:   **14.6.11**

* the need to maintain academic and other prescribed standards[2];
* the financial resources available to the responsible body[3];
* grants or loans likely to be available to disabled students (and only disabled students) for the purpose of enabling them to receive student services, such as Disabled Students' Allowances[4];
* the cost of taking a particular step[5];
* the extent to which it is practicable to take the step[6];
* the extent to which aids and services will otherwise be provided to disabled pupils as special educational provision[7];
* health and safety requirements[8]; and
* the interests of other people including other students[9].

1   Code of Practice (Post 16), para 6:2.
2   And see Code of Practice (Post 16), paras 6:3 to 6:6.
3   And see Code of Practice (Post 16), para 6:7.
4   And see Code of Practice (Post 16), paras 6:8 to 6:9.
5   See Code of Practice (Post 16), para 6:10.
6   And see Code of Practice (Post 16), para 6:11.
7   And see Code of Practice (Post 16), para 6:12.
8   And see Code of Practice (Post 16), paras 6:13 to 6:15.
9   And see Code of Practice (Post 16), paras 6:16 and 6:17.

Confidentiality requests

Under the DDA 1995, a request can be made which is known as a 'confi-   **14.6.12**
dentiality request'[1]. This is a request made by a disabled person which asks
for the nature, or for the existence, of his disability to be treated as confidential. Where a confidentiality request has been made and the responsible
body are aware of the request[2], in determining whether it is reasonable for
a responsible body to have to take a particular step in relation to that person,
regard shall be had to the extent to which taking the step in question is consistent with compliance with that request[3].

1   DDA 1995, s 28T(5).
2   DDA 1995, s 28T(3); and see Code of Practice (Post 16), paras 6:18 to 6:20.
3   DDA 1995, s 28T(4).

Non-actionability

Section 28T of the DDA 1995 is stated, however, only to impose duties for   **14.6.13**
the purpose of determining whether a responsible body has discriminated
against a disabled person and a breach of any such duty is not actionable as
such[1].

1   DDA 1995, s 28T(6).

If, in a case where it is alleged that the responsible body has treated a dis-   **14.6.14**
abled person less favourably, if the responsible body is also under a duty to
ensure that the disabled student is not substantially disadvantaged, but it
fails without justification to comply with that duty, the treatment of that

person cannot be justified as being material in the circumstances and substantial, unless that treatment would have been justified even if the responsible body had complied with that duty[1].

1 DDA 1995, s 28S(9).

14.7 Occupation of premises by educational institutions

14.7.1 In order to enable responsible bodies to take reasonable steps or make reasonable adjustments in respect of premises which they do not own, specific provision is made in the DDA 1995[1].

1 DDA 1995, s 28W.

14.7.2 If premises are occupied by an educational institution under a lease[1] and the responsible body would not normally be entitled to make a particular alteration to the premises and the alteration is one which the responsible body proposes to make in order to comply with its duty to take reasonable steps to ensure that a disabled person does not suffer substantial disadvantage[2], the lease is modified by the DDA 1995. Thus, except to the extent which it expressly so provides, the lease is deemed to have effect as if it provided[3]:

(a) for the responsible body to be entitled to make the alteration with the written consent of the lessor;
(b) for the responsible body to have to make a written application to the lessor for consent if it wishes to make the alteration;
(c) if such application is made, for the lessor not to withhold his consent unreasonably; and
(d) for the lessor to be entitled to make his consent subject to reasonable conditions.

1 'Lease' includes a tenancy, sub-lease or sub-tenancy and an agreement for a lease, tenancy, sub-lease or sub-tenancy; and 'sub-lease' and 'sub-tenancy' shall have such meaning as may be prescribed: DDA 1995, s 28W(3).
2 DDA 1995, s 28W(1).
3 DDA 1995, s 28W(2).

14.7.3 If the terms and conditions of a lease:

(a) impose conditions which are to apply if the responsible body alters the premises; or
(b) entitle the lessor to impose conditions when consenting to the responsible body's altering the premises,

the responsible body is to be treated for these purposes as not being entitled to make the alteration[1] and so the specific powers of modification to the lease will apply.

1 DDA 1995, s 28W(4).

14.7.4 If any question or dispute occurs in which it is suggested that a responsible body has been in breach of its duty to take reasonable steps to ensure disabled persons are not substantially disadvantaged by failing to make a particular alteration to premises, any constraint attributable to the fact that the premises are occupied by the educational institution under a lease is to be ignored, unless the responsible body has applied to the lessor in writing for consent to the making of the alteration[1].

1 DDA 1995, Sch 6, para 10.

If a responsible body has applied in writing to the lessor for consent to the **14.7.5** alteration and that consent has been refused or the lessor has made his consent subject to one or more conditions, that responsible body or a disabled person who has an interest in the proposed alteration may refer the matter to the county court[1]. The court must determine whether the lessor's refusal was unreasonable or whether the condition(s) is or are unreasonable[2].

If the court determines that the refusal was unreasonable or that the condition is or conditions are unreasonable, it may make such a declaration as it considers appropriate or an order authorising the responsible body to make the alteration specified in the order[3]. A responsible body may be required to comply with conditions specified in the court's order[4]. If a claim is brought against a responsible body in the county court alleging unlawful discrimination, the claimant or the responsible body may ask the court to direct that the lessor be joined as a party to the proceedings[5] and, as part of those proceedings, the court may examine whether a refusal of consent, or condition(s) imposed, by the lessor were unreasonable[6]. The court may also order the lessor instead of the responsible body to pay compensation[7].

1 DDA 1995, Sch 6, para 11(1)
2 DDA 1995, Sch 6, para 11(2).
3 DDA 1995, Sch 6, para 11(3).
4 DDA 1995, Sch 6, para 11(4).
5 DDA 1995, Sch 6, para 12(1).
6 DDA 1995, Sch 6, para 12(5).
7 DDA 1995, Sch 6, para 12(6)(c) and (8).

Regulations may be made by the Secretary of State as to the circumstances **14.7.6** in which lessors will be taken to have withheld their consent, withheld their consent unreasonably or reasonably and which conditions may be reasonable or unreasonable[1]. Similarly, Regulations may be made to deal with the situation where an institution occupies premises under a sub-lease or sub-tenancy[2].

1 DDA 1995, Sch 6, para 13; and see the draft Disability Discrimination (Educational Institutions) (Alteration of Leasehold Premises) Regulations 2001, issued for consultation in 2001.
2 DDA 1995, Sch 6, para 14.

Further education provided by LEAs and schools   14.8

Where[1]:   **14.8.1**

(a) a course of higher education has been secured by a Local Education Authority (LEA) under s 120 of the Education Reform Act 1988; or
(b) a course[2] of further education has been secured by an LEA or provided by the governing body of a maintained school under s 80 of the School Standard and Frameworks Act 1998; or
(c) recreational or training facilities[3] have been secured by an LEA,

it is unlawful for the LEA or governing body to discriminate against a disabled person[4]:

(a) in the arrangements it makes for determining who should be enrolled[5] on the course;

(b) in the terms on which it offers to enrol him on the course; or

(c) by refusing or deliberately omitting to accept an application for his enrolment on the course.

1 DDA 1995, s 28U.

2 'Course' includes each of the component parts of a course of further education if, in relation to the course, there is no requirement imposed on persons registered for any component part of the course to register for any other component part of that course: DDA 1995, s 28R(8) as modified by DDA 1995, Sch 4C, para 1 as inserted by SENDA 2001, Sch 5.

3 'Recreational or training facilities' means any facilities secured by an LEA under EA 1996, s 508(1) or provided by it under EA 1996, s 508(1A): DDA 1995, s 28R as modified by DDA 1995, Sch 4C, para 1 as inserted by SENDA 2001, Sch 5.

4 DDA 1995, s 28R(2) as modified by DDA 1995, Sch 4C, para 1 as inserted by SENDA 2001, Sch 5.

5 'Enrolment' in relation to a course of further education secured by an LEA, includes registration for any one of the component parts if, in relation to the course, there is no requirement imposed on persons registered for any component part of the course to register for any other component part of that course: DDA 1995, s 28R(8) as modified by DDA 1995, Sch 4C, para 1 as inserted by SENDA 2001, Sch 5.

14.8.2 It is similarly unlawful for the LEA or governing body to discriminate against a disabled person who has enrolled on the course in the services which it provides or offers to provide[1]. 'Services' means services of any description which are provided wholly or mainly for persons enrolled on the course[2]. It is also unlawful for an LEA to discriminate against a disabled person in the terms on which it will provide, or offer to provide, recreational or training facilities[3].

1 DDA 1995, s 28R(3) as modified by DDA 1995, Sch 4C, para 1 as inserted by SENDA 2001, Sch 5.

2 DDA 1995, s 28R(4) as modified by DDA 1995, Sch 4C, para 1 as inserted by SENDA 2001, Sch 5.

3 DDA 1995, s 28R(5) as modified by DDA 1995, Sch 4C, para 1 as inserted by SENDA 2001, Sch 5.

14.8.3 The LEA or governing body must also take such steps as it is reasonable for it to have to take to ensure that:

(a) in relation to its arrangements for enrolling persons on a course of further or higher education provided by it; and

(b) in relation to services provided, or offered, by it,

disabled persons are not placed at a substantial disadvantage in comparison with persons who are not disabled[1]. For a detailed consideration of this duty see 14.6.

1 DDA 1995, s 28RT(1) as substituted by SENDA 2001, Sch 5, para 2.

14.9 Victimisation

14.9.1 Under the general provisions of the DDA 1995, protection is given to disabled persons who may be subject to victimisation because they may have brought a claim alleging disability discrimination or have given evidence in such a claim[1].

1 DDA 1995, s 55; and see 11.5.

These provisions are considered in detail in 11.5, and will apply to all types of disability discrimination in education[1]. For the avoidance of doubt, however, in relation to the duty not to discriminate against disabled students[2] in the case of an act which constitutes discrimination by virtue of the provisions protecting an individual from victimisation, those duties are stated to apply to discrimination against persons who are not disabled as well as those who are[3].   **14.9.2**

1 DDA 1995, s 55(1).
2 DDA 1995, ss 28R, 28S and 28T.
3 DDA 1995, s 28R(4).

ENFORCEMENT

Rules for making claims   **14.10**

The provisions dealing with enforcement are somewhat more straightforward in the case of post-16 education than pre-16. All claims of discrimination in further and higher education (including further education provide by LEAs and schools) should be brought in the county court[1] by way of civil proceedings. Claims should be instituted within six months of the act complained of, unless the dispute is referred to conciliation, in which case the period for making a claim will be extended by two months[2].   **14.10.1**

For further details on the procedure for making a claim, see 11.9.

1 DDA 1995, s 28V(3).
2 DDA 1995, Sch 3, para 13(1) and (2).

Chapter 15

The Disability Rights Commission

The Disability Discrimination Act (DDA) 1995 originally introduced a **15.1.1**
National Disability Council, a modified and limited version of the Equal
Opportunities Commission (EOC) and the Commission for Racial Equality
(CRE), to advise the Secretary of State on certain disability issues. These
included:

(a) matters relevant to the elimination of discrimination against disabled
    persons;
(b) measures to reduce or eliminate such discrimination; and
(c) matters relating to the operation of the DDA 1995[1].

1 DDA 1995, s 50(2).

Unlike the two Commissions, however, the National Disability Council **15.1.2**
(NDC) had no power to investigate complaints and/or to take action on
behalf of disabled persons. It also had no power, again in contrast to the
EOC and CRE, to monitor particular aspects of the impact of the DDA
1995 or to carry out investigations into the operation of the Act in individual organisations or industries.

In response to these concerns, the newly-elected Labour government in **15.1.3**
1997 asked the Disability Rights Task Force to examine the role of the
National Disability Council and produce proposals for a body more in line
with the EOC and CRE. Consequently, the Disability Rights Task Force
recommended the creation of a Disability Rights Commission (DRC) with
certain functions[1], which led to the Disability Rights Commission Act
(DRCA) 1999.

1 Disability Rights Task Force, *Recommendations to Government on the Proposed Role and
   Functions of a Disability Rights Commission* (March 1998).

DUTIES AND COMPOSITION OF THE COMMISSION

15.2   Duties

15.2.1   The Disability Rights Commission Act 1999 established the DRC ('the Commission'), a body corporate[1] with statutory functions, including the following duties[2]:

(a) to work towards the elimination of discrimination[3] against disabled persons;
(b) to promote the equalisation of opportunities for disabled persons;
(c) to take such steps as it considers appropriate with a view to encouraging good practice in the treatment of disabled persons; and
(d) to keep under review the working of the DDA 1995 and the DRCA 1999.

1   DRCA 1999, Sch 1, para 1.
2   DRCA 1999, s 2(1).
3   Which includes disability discrimination in education: see DRCA 1999, s 2(5) (as amended by Special Educational Needs and Disability Act (SENDA) 2001, Sch 7, para 2).

15.2.2   The Commission may, for any purpose connected with the performance of its functions[1]:

(a) make proposals or give other advice to any Minister of the Crown as to any aspect of the law or a proposed change to the law;
(b) make proposals or give other advice to any government agency or other public authority as to the practical application of any law;
(c) undertake, or arrange for or support (whether financially or otherwise), the carrying out of research or the provision of advice or information.

1   DRCA 1999, s 2(2).

15.2.3   The Commission shall also make proposals or give other advice on any matter specified in a request from a Minister of the Crown[1] and may charge for facilities or services made available by it[2].

1   DRCA 1999, s 2(3).
2   DRCA 1999, s 2(4).

Composition

15.2.4   The Commission comprises[1] at least ten, and not more than 15, Commissioners appointed by the Secretary of State. The Secretary of State may only appoint a Commissioner who is not disabled if satisfied that after the appointment more than half of the Commissioners will be disabled persons or persons who have had a disability[2]. The conditions of appointment, terms of office, disqualification and removal of Commissioners are governed by Schedule 1 of the DRCA 1999[3].

1   DRCA 1999, Sch 1, para 2(1).
2   DRCA 1999, Sch 1, para 2(2).
3   See DRCA 1999, Sch 1, paras 3 to 5.

One Commissioner is appointed as chairman of the Commission by the Secretary of State[1] and there is provision for one or two of the other Commissioners to be appointed as deputy chairmen, one of whom should be a disabled person or a person who has had a disability[2].

1 DRCA 1999, Sch 1, para 6(1).
2 DRCA 1999, Sch 1, para 6(2).

15.2.5

The Commission is required to employ a Chief Executive, whose appointment is subject to approval by the Secretary of State[1] and may employ such other staff as it may appoint, subject to the numbers and terms and conditions of service being approved by the Secretary of State[2].

1 DRCA 1999, Sch 1, para 10(2).
2 DRCA 1999, Sch 1, para 10(1)(b).

15.2.6

POWERS OF THE COMMISSION

Formal investigations

15.3

One of the most significant features of the DRCA 1999, which ensured that the Commission had greater power than its predecessor, was the granting of power for the Commission to undertake formal investigations. The Commission may therefore decide[1] to conduct a formal investigation for any purpose connected with the performance of its duties[2]. It must also conduct a formal investigation if directed to do so by the Secretary of State for any such purpose[3]. The Commission may at any time stop or suspend the conduct of a formal investigation, but if that investigation was directed by the Secretary of State, his approval must be obtained[4].

1 DRCA 1999, s 3(1).
2 For a list of the Commission's duties, see 15.2.1.
3 DRCA 1999, s 3(2).
4 DRCA 1999, s 3(3).

15.3.1

The Commission may nominate one or more Commissioners to conduct the investigation[1] (and may appoint additional Commissioners for the purpose of that investigation[2]). The Commission shall authorise the appointed Commissioners and additional Commissioners to exercise such of the Commission's functions (which may include drawing up or revising terms of reference) in relation to the investigation as the Commission may determine[3].

1 DRCA 1999, s 3(4)(a).
2 DRCA 1999, s 3(5) and Sch 2.
3 DRCA 1999, s 3(4)(b).

15.3.2

Before taking steps to conduct a formal investigation, the Commission must ensure that terms of reference for the investigation have been drawn up and notice of the holding of the formal investigation and the terms of reference have been served or published[1]. The terms of reference shall be drawn up by the Commission, except where the formal investigation is held at the direction of the Secretary of State, in which case the terms of reference should be drawn up by the Secretary of State after consulting the Commission[2]. Where the terms of reference confine the formal investigation to the activities of one or more named persons, notice of the formal investigation and the terms of

15.3.3

reference should be served on each of those persons[3]. If the formal investigation is not confined to named persons, notice of the formal investigation and the terms of reference should be published in such manner as appears to the Commission to be appropriate to bring it to the attention of persons likely to be affected by it[4]. If the terms of reference are revised, a similar process of notice or publication has to be followed[5].

1 DRCA 1999, Sch 3, para 2(1).
2 DRCA 1999, Sch 3, para 2(2).
3 DRCA 1999, Sch 3, para 2(3).
4 DRCA 1999, Sch 3, para 2(4).
5 DRCA 1999, Sch 3, para 2(5).

15.3.4   As part of a formal investigation, the Commission may propose to investigate whether:

(a) a person has committed or is committing an unlawful act;
(b) any requirement imposed by a non-discrimination notice[1] served on a person (including a requirement to take action specified in an action plan) has been or is being complied with;
(c) any undertaking given by a person in an agreement made with the Commission[2] is being or has been complied with[3].

If it does propose one or more of these actions, the Commission may not investigate unless the terms of reference of the formal investigation confine it to the activities of one or more named persons (and the person concerned is one of those persons)[4].

1 See 15.4.
2 See 15.5.
3 DRCA 1999, Sch 3, para 3(1).
4 DRCA 1999, Sch 3, para 3(2).

15.3.5   Further, the Commission may not investigate whether a person has committed or is committing any unlawful act (which includes an act which amounts to unlawful disability discrimination in education[1]) unless (a) it has reason to believe that the person concerned may have committed or may be committing the act in question, or (b) that matter is to be investigated in the course of a formal investigation into his compliance with any requirement in a non-discrimination notice or undertaking given in an agreement with the Commission[2]. The Commission must serve a notice on the person concerned offering him the opportunity to make written and oral representations about the matters being investigated[3]. If the formal investigation concerns whether or not the person has committed or is committing an unlawful act (otherwise than in breach of a requirement of a non-discrimination notice or an undertaking), the Commission must include in the notice a statement informing the person that the Commission has reason to believe that he may have committed or may be committing an unlawful act[4]. The Commission may, however, refuse to receive oral representations made on behalf of the person under investigation by a person, not being a solicitor or counsel, to whom the Commission reasonably objects as being unsuitable[5], but must give written reasons for its objection[6].

1 DRCA 1999, Sch 3, para 3(1).
2 DRCA 1999, Sch 3, para 3(3).
3 DRCA 1999, Sch 3, para 3(4).

4 DRCA 1999, Sch 3, para 3(5).
5 DRCA 1999, Sch 3, para 3(7).
6 DRCA 1999, Sch 3, para 3(8).

The Commission cannot make any findings in relation to a matter whether: **15.3.6**

(a) a person has committed or is committing an unlawful act;
(b) any requirement imposed by a non-discrimination notice[1] (including a requirement to take action specified in an action plan) has been or is being complied with;
(c) any undertaking given by a person in an agreement made with the Commission is being or has been complied with[2],

without giving the person concerned or his representative a reasonable opportunity to make written and oral representations[3].

1 See 15.4.
2 See DRCA 1999, Sch 3, para 3(1); and see 15.5.
3 DRCA 1999, Sch 3, para 3(6).

For the purposes of a formal investigation, the Commission may serve a **15.3.7**
notice on any person requiring him to (a) give such written information as may be described in the notice, or (b) attend and give oral information about any matter specified in the notice and to produce all documents in his possession or control relating to any such matter[1]. Such a notice, though, may only be served on the written authority of the Secretary of State unless the terms of reference confine the investigation to the activities of one or more named persons and the person being served is one of those persons[2].

A person cannot, however, be required to (a) give information or produce a document which he could not be compelled to give in evidence, or produce, in civil proceedings before the High Court, or (b) attend at any place unless the necessary expenses of his journey are paid or tendered to him[3]. Where a person has been served with a notice, the Commission may apply to a county court for an order requiring the person to comply with the notice or with directions contained in the notice if that person has failed to comply with the notice or the Commission has reasonable cause to believe that he intends not to comply with it[4].

1 DRCA 1999, Sch 3, para 4(1).
2 DRCA 1999, Sch 3, para 4(2).
3 DRCA 1999, Sch 3, para 4(3).
4 DRCA 1999, Sch 3, para 5.

In light of the findings the Commission may make during, or as a result of, **15.3.8**
a formal investigation, it may make recommendations[1]. Such recommendations may be made both before and after the conclusion of a formal investigation[2]. The recommendations may be[3]:

(a) recommendations to any person for changes in his policies or procedures, or as to any other matter, with a view to promoting the equalisation of opportunities for disabled persons or persons who have had a disability; or
(b) recommendations to the Secretary of State for changes in the law or otherwise.

1 DRCA 1999, Sch 3, para 6(1).

2 DRCA 1999, Sch 3, para 6(3).
3 DRCA 1999, Sch 3, para 6(2).

15.3.9 At the end of every formal investigation, the Commission must prepare a report of its findings[1]. The Commission must exclude from its report, however, any matter which relates to an individual's private affairs or any person's business interests if (a) publication of that matter might, in the Commission's opinion, prejudicially affect that individual or person, and (b) its exclusion is consistent with the Commission's duties and the object of the report[2]. The report of a formal investigation carried out at the direction of the Secretary of State shall be published by the Secretary of State, or, but only if the Secretary of State directs, by the Commission[3]. The reports of all other formal investigations shall be published by the Commission[4].

1 DRCA 1999, Sch 3, para 7(1).
2 DRCA 1999, Sch 3, para 7(2).
3 DRCA 1999, Sch 3, para 7(3).
4 DRCA 1999, Sch 3, para 7(4).

15.4 Non-discrimination notices

15.4.1 If, in the course of a formal investigation, the Commission is satisfied that a person has committed or is committing an unlawful act[1], it may serve on him a notice (a 'non-discrimination notice') which:

(a) gives details of the unlawful act which the Commission has found that he has committed or is committing; and

(b) requires him not to commit any further unlawful acts of the same kind and, if the finding is that he is committing an unlawful act, to cease doing so[2].

1 Which includes any act of disability discrimination in education.
2 DRCA 1999, s 4(1).

15.4.2 The Commission, before issuing a non-discrimination notice, must first serve on the person concerned a notice informing him that the Commission is considering issuing a non-discrimination notice and of the grounds for so doing and offering him the opportunity to make written and oral representations[1] within a period specified in the notice of not less than 28 days[2]. The Commission may, however, refuse to receive oral representations made on behalf of the person concerned by a person, not being a solicitor or counsel, to whom the Commission reasonably objects as being unsuitable[3], but must give written reasons for its objection[4]. On issuing a non-discrimination notice, the Commission must serve a copy on the person to whom it is addressed[5].

1 DRCA 1999, Sch 3, para 8(2).
2 DRCA 1999, Sch 3, para 8(3).
3 DRCA 1999, Sch 3, para 8(4).
4 DRCA 1999, Sch 3, para 8(5).
5 DRCA 1999, Sch 3, para 9.

Appeal against a non-discrimination notice

15.4.3 A person on whom a non-discrimination notice is served may, within the period of six weeks beginning on the day after the day on which the notice is served on him, appeal against any requirement imposed by the non-discrimination notice[1]. Such an appeal is brought in the employment tribunal or the county court, in respect of requirements relating to acts outside the employment tribunal's jurisdiction[2].

The court or tribunal may quash any requirement against which the appeal is brought if (a) it considers the requirement to be unreasonable, or (b) in the case of a requirement that the person cease an unlawful act, if it considers that the Commission's finding that the person had committed or is committing the unlawful act in question was based on an incorrect finding of fact[3]. On quashing a requirement, the court or tribunal may direct that the non-discrimination notice shall have effect with such modification as it considers appropriate[4], which may include the substitution of a requirement in different terms and, in the case of a requirement not to do an unlawful act or to cease committing an unlawful act, modifications to the details given describing the unlawful act[5]. The person cannot, however, appeal again against a non-discrimination notice modified by the court or tribunal[6].

If the court or tribunal allows an appeal but does not quash the entire non-discrimination notice, the Commission may by notice to the person concerned, vary the non-discrimination notice (a) by revoking or altering any recommendation, or (b) by making new recommendations in pursuance of the Commission's powers to make recommendations as to the steps a person could reasonably be expected to take to comply with a requirement not to commit further unlawful acts or to cease committing such acts[7].

1 DRCA 1999, Sch 3, para 10(1).
2 DRCA 1999, Sch 3, para 10(2).
3 DRCA 1999, Sch 3, para 10(3).
4 DRCA 1999, Sch 3, para 10(4).
5 DRCA 1999, Sch 3, para 10(5).
6 DRCA 1999, Sch 3, para 10(6).
7 DRCA 1999, Sch 3, para 10(7).

When notices become final

15.4.4 A non-discrimination notice becomes final when (a) an appeal brought against it has been dismissed, withdrawn or abandoned, or (b) the time for appealing expires without an appeal having been brought or an appeal is allowed without the whole non-discrimination notice being quashed[1].

The Commission is required to maintain a register of non-discrimination notices which have become final[2]. Where the non-discrimination notice imposes a requirement to propose an action plan, the Commission shall note on the register the date on which the action plan has become final[3]. The register shall be available for inspection at all reasonable times and the Commission shall arrange for certified copies of any entry to be provided if required by any person[4].

1 DRCA 1999, Sch 3, para 11.
2 DRCA 1999, Sch 3, para 13(1).
3 DRCA 1999, Sch 3, para 13(2).
4 DRCA 1999, Sch 3, para 13(3).

15.4.5   Once a non-discrimination notice has become final, during the period of five years from that date the Commission may apply to a county court for an order, if:

(a) it appears to the Commission that the person concerned has failed to comply with any requirement imposed by the notice not to commit any further unlawful acts or to cease committing such acts; or
(b) the Commission has reasonable cause to believe that he intends not to comply with any such requirement[1].

The county court may make an order requiring the person concerned to comply with the requirement or with such directions for the same purpose as are contained in the court order[2].

1   DRCA 1999, Sch 3, paras 12(1) and (2).
2   DRCA 1999, Sch 3, para 12(3).

Action plans

15.4.6   The non-discrimination notice may include recommendations as to the action which the Commission considers the person could reasonably be expected to take with a view to complying with any requirement not to commit any further unlawful acts or to cease committing such acts[1]. The non-discrimination notice may also require the person concerned:

(a) to propose an adequate action plan with a view to securing compliance with such a requirement; and
(b) once an action plan proposed by him has become final, to take any action which is specified in the plan and he has not already taken at the time or times specified in the action plan[2].

1   DRCA 1999, s 4(2).
2   DRCA 1999, s 4(3).

15.4.7   An 'action plan' for these purposes is a document drawn up by the person concerned (not the Commission) specifying action (including action he has already taken) intended to change anything in his practices, procedures or other arrangements which caused or contributed to the commission of the unlawful act or is liable to cause or contribute to a failure to comply with a requirement not to commit any further unlawful act or to cease committing an unlawful act. An action plan is adequate if the action specified in it would be sufficient to ensure, within a reasonable time, that the person is not prevented from complying with that requirement by anything in his practices, policies, procedures or other arrangements[1]. The action specified may include ceasing an activity or taking continuing action over a period[2].

1   DRCA 1999, s 4(4).
2   DRCA 1999, s 4(4).

15.4.8   Where a non-discrimination notice has become final and includes a requirement for a person to propose an action plan, Part III of Schedule 3 to the DRCA 1999 lays down the necessary action which that person must take[1]. The person must serve his proposed action plan on the Commission within such period as may be specified in the non-discrimination notice[2]. If the person fails to do so, the Commission may apply to the county court for an order directing him to serve his proposed action plan within such period as the order specifies[3]. If, however, the person complies and serves a proposed action plan, the action plan becomes final at the end of the prescribed period unless the Commission gives notice that it is not adequate[4].

1 DRCA 1999, Sch 3, para 14(1).
2 DRCA 1999, Sch 3, para 15(1).
3 DRCA 1999, Sch 3, para 15(2).
4 DRCA 1999, Sch 3, para 15(3).

If the Commission considers that the proposed action plan is inadequate, it **15.4.9** may give notice to the person (a) stating its view that the plan is not adequate, and (b) inviting the person to serve on the Commission a revised action plan which is adequate within such period as may be specified in the notice[1]. The notice may also include the Commission's recommendations on what might be included to make the action plan adequate[2]. If the person serves a revised action plan within the specified time, it will supersede the original and become final at the end of the specified period unless the Commission apply to the court for an order that it is inadequate[3]. If the person fails to serve a revised action plan, the original action plan becomes final at the end of the specified period, unless, as will be likely, the Commission apply to the county court for an order that that action plan is inadequate[4].

1 DRCA 1999, Sch 3, para 16(1).
2 DRCA 1999, Sch 3, para 16(2).
3 DRCA 1999, Sch 3, para 16(3).
4 DRCA 1999, Sch 3, para 16(4).

If the Commission considers that a proposed action plan is not adequate, it **15.4.10** may apply to the county court for an order[1]:

(a) declaring that the proposed action plan in question is not an adequate action plan;
(b) requiring the person to revise his proposal and serve on the Commission an adequate action plan within such period as the order may specify; and
(c) containing such directions (if any) as the court considers appropriate as to the action which should be specified in the adequate action plan required by the order[2].

1 DRCA 1999, Sch 3, para 17(1).
2 DRCA 1999, Sch 3, para 17(3).

The Commission cannot, however apply for such an order unless: **15.4.11**

(a) a notice requiring the person to revise the proposed action plan has been served; and
(b) the person has not served a revised action plan on the Commission in response to the notice within the specified period[1].

If the court declines to make an order, the proposed action plan becomes final at the end of the prescribed period[2]. If, however, the court orders the person to serve an adequate action plan on the Commission, if he serves such a plan, it shall become final at the end of the prescribed period unless the Commission applies again to the court on the basis that it considers it to be inadequate[3].

1 DRCA 1999, Sch 3, para 17(2).

2 DRCA 1999, Sch 3, para 17(4).
3 DRCA 1999, Sch 3, para 18(2).

15.4.12 An action plan may be varied by agreement in writing between the Commission and the person[1].

1 DRCA 1999, Sch 3, para 19.

15.4.13 If, during the period of five years after the action plan has become final, the Commission considers that the person has failed to comply with the requirement to carry out any action specified in the action plan, it may apply to the county court for an order requiring the person to comply with that requirement or with such directions for the same purpose as are contained in the order[1].

1 DRCA 1999, Sch 3, para 20.

15.4.14 To enable it to determine whether an action plan is adequate or the person is complying with the requirement to take the specified action, the Commission may serve notice on any person requiring him to give such information in writing, or copies of documents in his possession or control, relating to those matters as may be described in the notice[1]. A person may not be required to give information or produce a document which he could not be compelled to give in evidence or produce in civil proceedings before the High Court[2]. If a person fails to comply with a notice, the Commission may apply to the county court for an order requiring the person to comply with it or with such directions for the same purpose as may be contained in the order[3].

1 DRCA 1999, Sch 3, para 21(1).
2 DRCA 1999, Sch 3, para 21(2).
3 DRCA 1999, Sch 3, para 21(3) and (4).

15.5 Agreements in lieu of enforcement action

15.5.1 If the Commission has reason to believe that a person has committed or is committing an unlawful act, it may enter into an agreement in writing with that person on the assumption that that belief is well founded (whether or not the person admits to the unlawfulness)[1]. An agreement for these purposes is one by which:

(a) the Commission undertakes not to take any relevant enforcement action[2] in relation to the unlawful act in question; and
(b) the person concerned undertakes (i) not to commit any further unlawful acts of the same kind (and, where appropriate, to cease committing the unlawful act in question), and (ii) to take such action (which may include ceasing any activity or taking continuing action over any period) as may be specified in the agreement[3].

1 DRCA 1999, s 5(1).
2 'Relevant enforcement action' means: (a) beginning a formal investigation into the commission by the person of the unlawful act in question; (b) if a formal investigation has begun, taking any further steps in the investigation of that matter; and (c) taking any steps, or further steps, with a view to the issue of a non-discrimination notice based on the commission of the unlawful act in question: DRCA 1999, s 5(4).
3 DRCA 1999, s 5(2).

The undertakings are binding on the parties[1] and the action specified in an   **15.5.2**
undertaking given by the person must be action intended to change anything
in the practices, policies, procedures or other arrangements of the person
concerned which (a) caused or contributed to the commission of the unlawful act, or (b) is liable to cause or contribute to a failure to comply with his
undertaking[2]. An agreement may include terms providing for such incidental or supplementary matters (including the termination of the agreement or
the right of either party to terminate it in certain circumstances) and may be
varied or revoked by agreement between the Commission and the person[3].
Terms other then those specified above may not be included unless authorised by regulations issued by the Secretary of State[4].

1 DRCA 1999, s 5(3).
2 DRCA 1999, s 5(5).
3 DRCA 1999, s 5(6).
4 DRCA 1999, s 5(7).

If the person who has entered into an agreement fails to comply with any   **15.5.3**
undertaking which he has given or the Commission has reasonable cause to
believe that he intends not to comply with any such undertaking, the
Commission may apply to the county court for an order requiring that
person to comply with the undertaking or with such directions for the same
purpose as are contained in the order[1].

1 DRCA 1999, s 5(8) and (9).

Persistent discrimination   **15.6**

Where: **15.6.1**

(a) a non-discrimination notice has become final; or
(b) there has been a finding[1] in proceedings before a court, tribunal or
     adjudicating body[2] that a person has committed an act which is unlaw-
     ful discrimination (including unlawful disability discrimination in edu-
     cation); or
(c) there has been a finding[3] by a court or tribunal in other proceedings
     that a person has committed an act prescribed by the Secretary of
     State,

if, during the period of five years beginning on that date, it appears to the
Commission that unless restrained the person concerned is likely to do one
or more unlawful acts, the Commission may apply to the county court for an
injunction restraining him from doing so[4]. If satisfied that the application is
well-founded, the county court may grant the injunction in the terms
applied for or in more limited terms[5].

1 A finding becomes final when an appeal against it is dismissed, withdrawn or abandoned
   or when the time for appealing expires without an appeal having been brought.
2 Including independent appeal panels.
3 See note 1 above.
4 DRCA 1999, s 6(1) and (2).
5 DRCA 1999, s 6(3).

15.7 Assistance in relation to proceedings

15.7.1 Perhaps the most important power of the Commission, in the context of disability discrimination in education, is the Commission's ability to provide assistance in relation to certain proceedings. This power is available[1] in proceedings which an individual has brought or proposes to bring in respect of claims for disability discrimination, but also and most importantly for these purposes, to complaints and claims for disability discrimination to the Special Educational Needs and Disability Tribunal[2], in admission appeals to independent admission appeal panels[3], in exclusion appeals to independent exclusion appeal panels[4] and civil proceedings[5]. Other proceedings in which the Commission may give assistance may be prescribed by the Secretary of State[6].

1 DRCA 1999, s 7(1)(a).
2 Under DDA 1995, s 28I.
3 Under DDA 1995, s 28K.
4 Under DDA 1995, s 28L.
5 Under DDA 1995, s 28V.
6 DRCA 1999, s 7(1)(b).

15.7.2 Where an individual applies to the Commission for assistance, it may grant the application on any of the following grounds:

(a) that the case raises a question of principle;
(b) that it is unreasonable to expect the applicant to deal with the case unaided (because of its complexity, the applicant's position in relation to another party or for some other reason);
(c) that there is some other special consideration which makes it appropriate for the Commission to provide assistance[1].

1 DRCA 1999, s 7(2).

15.7.3 If the Commission grants an application it may:

(a) provide or arrange for the provision of legal advice;
(b) arrange for legal or other representation (which may include any assistance usually given by a solicitor or counsel);
(c) seek to procure the settlement of any dispute;
(d) provide or arrange for the provision of any other assistance which it thinks appropriate[1].

1 DRCA 1999, s 7(3).

15.7.4 Where the Commission has given an individual assistance and any costs or expenses have become payable to him (however arising) by another person in respect of the matter in which assistance was sought, a sum equal to any expenses incurred by the Commission in providing the assistance shall be a first charge for the benefit of the Commission on the costs and expenses recovered[1]. This charge is subject to any charge under the Legal Aid Act 1988 and any provision under that Act for payment of any sum to the Legal Aid Board[2].

1 DRCA 1999, s 8(1) and (2).
2 DRCA 1999, s 8(4)(a).

Codes of Practice and conciliation of disputes   **15.8**

The role of the Commission in respect of the preparation and issuing of **15.8.1**
Codes of Practice giving practical guidance[1] and in making arrangements for
the provision of conciliation services[2] has been considered in Chapter 11.

1   DDA 1995, s 53A.
2   DDA 1995, s 28.

Offences   **15.9**

To enable the Commission to carry out its functions properly and effectively, **15.9.1**
the DRCA 1999 creates two offences to deal with persons who may attempt
to frustrate its work.

A person who deliberately alters, suppresses, conceals or destroys a docu- **15.9.2**
ment required to be produced as part of a formal investigation[1] or in
pursuance of the Commission's power to seek information[2] is guilty of an
offence and is liable on summary conviction to a fine not exceeding level 5
on the standard scale[3].

1   Under DRCA 1999, Sch 3, para 4.
2   Under DRCA 1999, Sch 3, para 21.
3   DRCA 1999, Sch 3, para 24.

A person who makes any statement which that person knows to be false or **15.9.3**
misleading in a material particular or recklessly makes such a statement
when complying with:

(a)   a notice served by the Commission in respect of a formal investigation
     or in pursuance of its powers to seek information,
(b)   a non-discrimination notice;
(c)   an agreement in lieu of enforcement; or
(d)   a court order,

is guilty of an offence and is liable on summary conviction to a fine not
exceeding level 5 on the standard scale[1].

1   DRCA 1999, Sch 3, para 24.

Disclosure of information   **15.10**

No information given to the Commission by any person in connection with **15.10.1**
a formal investigation or the exercise of any of the Commission's functions
with respect to non-discrimination notices shall be disclosed by the
Commission or by any person who is or has been a Commissioner, an additional Commissioner or an employee of the Commission[1].

1   DRCA 1999, Sch 3, para 22(1).

A person who discloses information in breach of this prohibition is guilty of **15.10.2**
an offence and is liable on summary conviction to a fine not exceeding level
5 on the standard scale[1].

1   DRCA 1999, Sch 3, para 22(3).

15.10.3 The exceptions to this prohibition are where disclosure is made[1]:

(a) on the order of the court;

(b) with the consent of the person who gave the information to the Commission;

(c) in the form of a summary or other general statement published by the Commission which does not identify that person or any other person to which the information relates;

(d) in a report of the formal investigation published by the Commission;

(e) to a Commissioner, an additional Commissioner or an employee of the Commission, or, so far as is necessary for the proper performance of the Commission's functions, to other persons; or

(f) for the purpose of any civil proceedings to which the Commission is a party, or of any criminal proceedings.

1 DRCA 1999, Sch 3, para 22(2).

Appendices

Appendix 1

Extracts from the Education Act 1996 (c 56), as amended by the Special Educational Needs and Disability Act 2001 (c 10)

Education Act 1996

*****

PART IV
SPECIAL EDUCATIONAL NEEDS

CHAPTER I
CHILDREN WITH SPECIAL EDUCATIONAL NEEDS

Introductory

312 Meaning of 'special educational needs' and 'special educational provision' etc

(1) A child has 'special educational needs' for the purposes of this Act if he has a learning difficulty which calls for special educational provision to be made for him.

(2) Subject to subsection (3) (and except for the purposes of section 15A or 15B a child has a 'learning difficulty' for the purposes of this Act if—

(a) he has a significantly greater difficulty in learning than the majority of children of his age,

(b) he has a disability which either prevents or hinders him from making use of educational facilities of a kind generally provided for children of his age in schools within the area of the local education authority, or

(c) he is under compulsory school age and is, or would be if special educational provision were not made for him, likely to fall within paragraph (a) or (b) when of . . . that age.

(3) A child is not to be taken as having a learning difficulty solely because the language (or form of the language) in which he is, or will be, taught is different from a language (or form of a language) which has at any time been spoken in his home.

(4) In this Act 'special educational provision' means—

(a) in relation to a child who has attained the age of two, educational provision which is additional to, or otherwise different from, the educational provision made generally for children of his age in schools maintained by the local education authority (other than special schools) . . ., and

(b)   in relation to a child under that age, educational provision of any kind.

(5)   In this Part—

'child' includes any person who has not attained the age of 19 and is a registered pupil at a school;

'maintained school' means any community, foundation or voluntary school or any community or foundation special school not established in a hospital.

Code of Practice

313 Code of Practice

(1)   The Secretary of State shall issue, and may from time to time revise, a code of practice giving practical guidance in respect of the discharge by local education authorities and the governing bodies of maintained schools, of their functions under this Part.

(2)   It shall be the duty of—

(a)   local education authorities, and such governing bodies, exercising functions under this Part and

(b)   any other person exercising any function for the purpose of the discharge by local education authorities, and such governing bodies, of functions under this Part,

to have regard to the provisions of the code.

(3)   On any appeal under this Part to the Tribunal, the Tribunal shall have regard to any provision of the code which appears to the Tribunal to be relevant to any question arising on the appeal.

(4)   The Secretary of State shall publish the code as for the time being in force.

(5)   In this Part 'the Tribunal' means the Special Educational Needs and Disability Tribunal.

314 Making and approval of code

(1)   Where the Secretary of State proposes to issue or revise a code of practice, he shall prepare a draft of the code (or revised code).

(2)   The Secretary of State shall consult such persons about the draft as he thinks fit and shall consider any representations made by them.

(3)   If he determines to proceed with the draft (either in its original form or with such modifications as he thinks fit) he shall lay it before both Houses of Parliament.

(4)   If the draft is approved by resolution of each House, the Secretary of State shall issue the code in the form of the draft, and the code shall come into effect on such day as the Secretary of State may by order appoint.

Special educational provision: general

315 Review of arrangements

(1)   A local education authority shall keep under review the arrangements made by them for special educational provision.

(2) In doing so the authority shall, to the extent that it appears necessary or desirable for the purpose of co-ordinating provision for children with special educational needs, consult the governing bodies of community, foundation and voluntary and community and foundation special schools in their area.

316 Duty to educate children with special educational needs in mainstream schools
(1) This section applies to a child with special educational needs who should be educated in a school.

(2) If no statement is maintained under section 324 for the child, he must be educated in a mainstream school.

(3) If a statement is maintained under section 324 for the child, he must be educated in a mainstream school unless that is incompatible with-

(a) the wishes of his parent, or
(b) the provision of efficient education for other children.

(4) In this section and section 316A 'mainstream school' means any school other than—

(a) a special school, or
(b) an independent school which is not—
    (i)   a city technology college,
    (ii)   a city college for the technology of the arts, or
    (iii) a city academy.

316A Education otherwise than in mainstream schools
(1) Section 316 does not prevent a child from being educated in—

(a) an independent school which is not a mainstream school, or
(b) a school approved under section 342,

if the cost is met otherwise than by a local education authority.

(2) Section 316(2) does not require a child to be educated in a mainstream school during any period in which—

(a) he is admitted to a special school for the purposes of an assessment under section 323 of his educational needs and his admission to that school is with the agreement of—
    (i)   the local education authority,
    (ii)   the head teacher of the school or, if the school is in Wales, its governing body,
    (iii) his parent, and
    (iv)   any person whose advice is to be sought in accordance with regulations made under paragraph 2 of Schedule 26;
(b) he remains admitted to a special school, in prescribed circumstances, following an assessment under section 323 at that school;
(c) he is admitted to a special school, following a change in his circumstances, with the agreement of—
    (i)   the local education authority,
    (ii)   the head teacher of the school or, if the school is in Wales, its governing body, and
    (iii) his parent;
(d) he is admitted to a community or foundation special school which is established in a hospital.

(3) Section 316 does not affect the operation of—

    (a)   section 348, or
    (b)   paragraph 3 of Schedule 27.

(4) If a local education authority decide—

    (a)   to make a statement for a child under section 324, but
    (b)   not to name in the statement the school for which a parent has expressed a preference under paragraph 3 of Schedule 27,

they shall, in making the statement, comply with section 316(3).

(5) A local education authority may, in relation to their mainstream schools taken as a whole, rely on the exception in section 316(3)(b) only if they show that there are no reasonable steps that they could take to prevent the incompatibility.

(6) An authority in relation to a particular mainstream school may rely on the exception in section 316(3)(b) only if it shows that there are no reasonable steps that it or another authority in relation to the school could take to prevent the incompatibility.

(7) The exception in section 316(3)(b) does not permit a governing body to fail to comply with the duty imposed by section 324(5)(b).

(8) An authority must have regard to guidance about section 316 and this section issued—

    (a)   for England, by the Secretary of State,
    (b)   for Wales, by the National Assembly for Wales.

(9) That guidance shall, in particular, relate to steps which may, or may not, be regarded as reasonable for the purposes of subsections (5) and (6).

(10) 'Prescribed', in relation to Wales, means prescribed in regulations made by the National Assembly for Wales.

(11) 'Authority'—

    (a)   in relation to a maintained school, means each of the following—
        (i)   the local education authority,
        (ii) the school's governing body, and
    (b)   in relation to a maintained nursery school or a pupil referral unit, means the local education authority.

317 Duties of governing body or LEA in relation to pupils with special educational needs

(1) The governing body, in the case of a community, foundation or voluntary school and the local education authority, in the case of a maintained nursery school, shall—

    (a)   use their best endeavours, in exercising their functions in relation to the school, to secure that, if any registered pupil has special educational needs, the special educational provision which his learning difficulty calls for is made,
    (b)   secure that, where the responsible person has been informed by the local education authority that a registered pupil has special educational needs, those needs are made known to all who are likely to each him, and
    (c)   secure that the teachers in the school are aware of the importance of identifying, and providing for, those registered pupils who have special educational needs.

(2) In subsection (1)(b) 'the responsible person' means—

(a)   in the case of a community, foundation or voluntary school the head teacher or the appropriate governor (that is, the chairman of the governing body or, where the governing body have designated another governor for the purposes of this paragraph, that other governor), and

(b)   in the case of a nursery school, the head teacher.

(3) To the extent that it appears necessary or desirable for the purpose of co-ordinating provision for children with special educational needs—

(a)   the governing bodies of community, foundation and voluntary schools shall, in exercising functions relating to the provision for such children, consult the local education authority . . . and the governing bodies of other such schools, and

(b)   in relation to maintained nursery schools, the local education authority shall, in exercising those functions, consult the governing bodies of community, foundation and voluntary schools.

(4) Where a child who has special educational needs is being educated in a community, foundation or voluntary school or a maintained nursery school, those concerned with making special educational provision for the child shall secure, so far as is reasonably practicable and is compatible with—

(a)   the child receiving the special educational provision which his learning difficulty calls for,

(b)   the provision of efficient education for the children with whom he will be educated, and

(c)   the efficient use of resources,

that the child engages in the activities of the school together with children who do not have special educational needs.

(5) Each governors' report shall include a report containing such information as may be prescribed about the implementation of the governing body's policy for pupils with special educational needs.

(6) The annual report for each community, foundation or voluntary school shall also include a report containing information as to—

(a)   the arrangements for the admission of disabled pupils;

(b)   the steps taken to prevent disabled pupils from being treated less favourably than other pupils; and

(c)   the facilities provided to assist access to the school by disabled pupils;

and for this purpose 'disabled pupils' means pupils who are disabled persons for the purposes of the Disability Discrimination Act 1995.

(7) In this section 'annual report' means the report prepared under section 42 of the School Standards and Framework Act 1998.

317A Duty to inform parent where special educational provision made
(1) This section applies if—

(a)   a child for whom no statement is maintained under section 324 is a registered pupil at—

(i)   a community, foundation or voluntary school, or

(ii)   a pupil referral unit,

(b)   special educational provision is made for him at the school because it is considered that he has special educational needs, and

    (c)   his parent has not previously been informed under this section of special educational provision made for him at the school.

(2) If the school is a pupil referral unit, the local education authority must secure that the headteacher informs the child's parent that special educational provision is being made for him at the school because it is considered that he has special educational needs.

(3) In any other case, the governing body must inform the child's parent that special educational provision is being made for him there because it is considered that he has special educational needs.

318 Provision of goods and services in connection with special educational needs

(1) A local education authority may, for the purpose only of assisting—

    (a)   the governing bodies of community, foundation or voluntary schools (in their or any other area) in the performance of the governing bodies' duties under section 317(1)(a), or

    (b)   the governing bodies of community or foundation special schools (in their or any other area) in the performance of the governing bodies' duties,

supply goods or services to those bodies.

(2) The terms on which goods or services are supplied by local education authorities under this section to the governing bodies of community, foundation or voluntary schools or community or foundation special schools in any other area may, in such circumstances as may be prescribed, include such terms as to payment as may be prescribed.

(3) A local education authority may supply goods and services to any authority or other person (other than a governing body within subsection (1)) for the purpose only of assisting them in making for any child to whom subsection (3A) applies any special educational provision which any learning difficulty of the child calls for.

(3A) This subsection applies to any child—

    (a)   who is receiving relevant nursery education within the meaning of section 123 of the School Standards and Framework Act 1998, or

    (b)   in respect of whose education grants are (or are to be) made under section 1 of the Nursery Education and Grant-Maintained Schools Act 1996.

(4) This section is without prejudice to the generality of any other power of local education authorities to supply goods or services.

319 Special educational provision otherwise than in schools

(1) Where a local education authority are satisfied that it would be inappropriate for—

    (a)   the special educational provision which a learning difficulty of a child in their area calls for, or

    (b)   any part of any such provision,

to be made in a school, they may arrange for the provision (or, as the case may be, for that part of it) to be made otherwise than in a school.

(2) Before making an arrangement under this section, a local education authority shall consult the child's parent.

320 Provision outside England and Wales for certain children

(1) A local education authority may make such arrangements as they think fit to enable a child for whom they maintain a statement under section 324 to attend an institution outside England and Wales which specialises in providing for children with special needs.

(2) In subsection (1) 'children with special needs' means children who have particular needs which would be special educational needs if those children were in England and Wales.

(3) Where a local education authority make arrangements under this section in respect of a child, those arrangements may in particular include contributing to or paying—

(a)   fees charged by the institution,
(b)   expenses reasonably incurred in maintaining him while he is at the institution or travelling to or from it,
(c)   his travelling expenses, and
(d)   expenses reasonably incurred by any person accompanying him while he is travelling or staying at the institution.

(4) This section is without prejudice to any other powers of a local education authority.

Identification and assessment of children with special educational needs

321 General duty of local education authority towards children for whom they are responsible

(1) A local education authority shall exercise their powers with a view to securing that, of the children for whom they are responsible, they identify those to whom subsection (2) below applies.

(2) This subsection applies to a child if—

(a)   he has special educational needs, and
(b)   it is necessary for the authority to determine the special educational provision which any learning difficulty he may have calls for.

(3) For the purposes of this Part a local education authority are responsible for a child if he is in their area and—

(a)   he is a registered pupil at a maintained school,
(b)   education is provided for him at a school which is not a maintained school but is so provided at the expense of the authority,
(c)   he does not come within paragraph (a) or (b) above but is a registered pupil at a school and has been brought to the authority's attention as having (or probably having) special educational needs, or
(d)   he is not a registered pupil at a school but is not under the age of two or over compulsory school age and has been brought to their attention as having (or probably having) special educational needs.

322 Duty of Health Authority, Primary Care Trust or local authority to help local education authority

(1) Where it appears to a local education authority that any Health Authority, Primary Care Trust or local authority could, by taking any specified action, help in the exercise of any of their functions under this Part, they may request the help of the authority or trust, specifying the action in question.

(2) An authority or a trust whose help is so requested shall comply with the request unless—

    (a)   they consider that the help requested is not necessary for the purpose of the exercise by the local education authority of those functions, or

    (b)   subsection (3) applies.

(3) This subsection applies—

    (a)   in the case of a Health Authority or Primary Care Trust, if that authority or trust consider that, having regard to the resources available to them for the purpose of the exercise of their functions under the National Health Service Act 1977, it is not reasonable for them to comply with the request, or

    (b)   in the case of a local authority, if that authority consider that the request is not compatible with their own statutory or other duties and obligations or unduly prejudices the discharge of any of their functions.

(4) Regulations may provide that, where an authority or a trust are under a duty by virtue of subsection (2) to comply with a request to help a local education authority in the making of an assessment under section 323 or a statement under section 324 of this Act, they must, subject to prescribed exceptions, comply with the request within the prescribed period.

(5) In this section 'local authority' means a county council, a county borough council, a district council (other than one for an area for which there is a county council), a London borough council or the Common Council of the City of London.

323 Assessment of educational needs

(1) Where a local education authority are of the opinion that a child for whom they are responsible falls, or probably falls, within subsection (2), they shall serve a notice on the child's parent informing him—

    (a)   that they are considering whether to make an assessment of the child's educational needs,

    (b)   of the procedure to be followed in making the assessment,

    (c)   of the name of the officer of the authority from whom further information may be obtained, and

    (d)   of the parent's right to make representations, and submit written evidence, to the authority within such period (which must not be less than 29 days beginning with the date on which the notice is served) as may be specified in the notice.

(2) A child falls within this subsection if—

    (a)   he has special educational needs, and

    (b)   it is necessary for the authority to determine the special educational provision which any learning difficulty he may have calls for.

(3) Where—

    (a)   a local education authority have served a notice under subsection (1) and the period specified in the notice in accordance with subsection (1)(d) has expired, and

    (b)   the authority remain of the opinion, after taking into account any representations made and any evidence submitted to them in response to the notice, that the child falls, or probably falls, within subsection (2),

they shall make an assessment of his educational needs.

(4) Where a local education authority decide to make an assessment under this

section, they shall give notice in writing to the child's parent of that decision and of their reasons for making it.

(5) Schedule 26 has effect in relation to the making of assessments under this section.

(6) Where, at any time after serving a notice under subsection (1), a local education authority decide not to assess the educational needs of the child concerned they shall give notice in writing to the child's parent of their decision.

324 Statement of special educational needs

(1) If, in the light of an assessment under section 323 of any child's educational needs and of any representations made by the child's parent in pursuance of Schedule 27, it is necessary for the local education authority to determine the special educational provision which any learning difficulty he may have calls for, the authority shall make and maintain a statement of his special educational needs.

(2) The statement shall be in such form and contain such information as may be prescribed.

(3) In particular, the statement shall—

(a) give details of the authority's assessment of the child's special educational needs, and
(b) specify the special educational provision to be made for the purpose of meeting those needs, including the particulars required by subsection (4).

(4) The statement shall—

(a) specify the type of school or other institution which the local education authority consider would be appropriate for the child,
(b) if they are not required under Schedule 27 to specify the name of any school in the statement, specify the name of any school or institution (whether in the United Kingdom or elsewhere) which they consider would be appropriate for the child and should be specified in the statement, and
(c) specify any provision for the child for which they make arrangements under section 319 and which they consider should be specified in the statement.

(4A) Subsection (4)(b) does not require the name of a school or institution to be specified if the child's parent has made suitable arrangements for the special educational provision specified in the statement to be made for the child

(5) Where a local education authority maintain a statement under this section, then—

(a) unless the child's parent has made suitable arrangements, the authority—
(i) shall arrange that the special educational provision specified in the statement is made for the child, and
(ii) may arrange that any non-educational provision specified in the statement is made for him in such manner as they consider appropriate, and
(b) if the name of a maintained school is specified in the statement, the governing body of the school shall admit the child to the school.

(5A) Subsection (5)(b) has effect regardless of any duty imposed on the governing body of a school by section 1(6) of the School Standards and Framework Act 1998.

(6) Subsection (5)(b) does not affect any power to exclude from a school a pupil who is already a registered pupil there.

(7)   Schedule 27 has effect in relation to the making and maintenance of statements under this section.

325 Appeal against decision not to make statement

(1)   If, after making an assessment under section 323 of the educational needs of any child for whom no statement is maintained under section 324, the local education authority do not propose to make such a statement, they shall give notice in writing of their decision to the child's parent.

(2)   In such a case, the child's parent may appeal to the Tribunal against the decision.

(2A)· A notice under subsection (1) must inform the parent of the right of appeal under subsection (2) and contain such other information as may be prescribed.

(2B)   Regulations may provide that where a local education authority are under a duty under this section to serve any notice, the duty must be performed within the prescribed period.

(3)   On an appeal under this section, the Tribunal may—

    (a)   dismiss the appeal,
    (b)   order the local education authority to make and maintain such a statement, or
    (c)   remit the case to the authority for them to reconsider whether, having regard to any observations made by the Tribunal, it is necessary for the authority to determine the special educational provision which any learning difficulty the child may have calls for.

326 Appeal against contents of statement

(1)   The parent of a child for whom a local education authority maintain a statement under section 324 may appeal to the Tribunal—

    (a)   when the statement is first made,
    (b)   if an amendment is made to the statement, or
    (c)   if, after conducting an assessment under section 323, the local education authority determine not to amend the statement.

(1A)   An appeal under this section may be against any of the following—

    (a)   the description in the statement of the local education authority's assessment of the child's special educational needs,
    (b)   the special educational provision specified in the statement (including the name of a school so specified),
    (c)   if no school is specified in the statement, that fact.

(2)   Subsection (1)(b) does not apply where the amendment is made in pursuance of—

    (a)   paragraph 8 (change of named school) or 11(3)(b)(amendment ordered by Tribunal) of Schedule 27, or
    (b)   directions under section 442 (revocation of school attendance order);

and subsection (1)(c) does not apply to a determination made following the service of notice under paragraph 2A (amendment by LEA) of Schedule 27 of a proposal to amend the statement.

(3)   On an appeal under this section, the Tribunal may—

    (a)   dismiss the appeal,
    (b)   order the authority to amend the statement, so far as it describes the author-ity's assessment of the child's special educational needs or specifies the

special educational provision and make such other consequential amendments to the statement as the Tribunal think fit, or

(c)   order the authority to cease to maintain the statement.

(4)   On an appeal under this section the Tribunal shall not order the local education
authority to specify the name of any school in the statement (either in substitution for
an existing name or in a case where no school is named) unless—

(a)   the parent has expressed a preference for the school in pursuance of arrangements under paragraph 3 (choice of school) of Schedule 27, or

(b)   in the proceedings the parent, the local education authority, or both have
proposed the school.

(5)   Before determining any appeal under this section the Tribunal may, with the
agreement of the parties, correct any deficiency in the statement.

326A Unopposed appeals

(1)   This section applies if—

(a)   the parent of a child has appealed to the Tribunal under section 325, 328,
329 or 329A or paragraph 8(3) of Schedule 27 against a decision of a local
education authority, and

(b)   the authority notifies the Tribunal that they have determined that they will
no, or will no longer, oppose the appeal.

(2)   The appeal is to be treated as having been determined in favour of the appellant.

(3)   If an appeal is treated as determined in favour of the appellant as a result of subsection (2), the Tribunal is not required to make any order.

(4)   Before the end of the prescribed period, the authority must—

(a)   in the case of an appeal under section 325, make a statement under section
324 of the child's educational needs,

(b)   in the case of an appeal under section 328, 329 or 329A, make an assessment
of the child's educational needs,

(c)   in the case of an appeal under paragraph 8(3) of Schedule 27 against a
determination of the authority not to comply with the parent's request,
comply with the request.

(5)   An authority required by subsection (4)(a) to make a statement under section
324 must maintain the statement under that section.

(6)   Regulations under this section, so far as they relate to Wales, require the agreement of the National Assembly for Wales

327 Access for local education authority to certain schools

(1)   This section applies where—

(a)   a local education authority maintain a statement for a child under section
324, and

(b)   in pursuance of the statement education is provided for the child at a school
maintained by another local education authority.

(2)   Any person authorised by the local education authority shall be entitled to have
access at any reasonable time to the premises of any such school for the purpose of
monitoring the special educational provision made in pursuance of the statement for
the child at the school.

328 Reviews of educational needs

(1) Regulations may prescribe the frequency with which assessments under section 323 are to be repeated in respect of children for whom statements are maintained under section 324.

(2) Where—

- (a) the parent of a child for whom a statement is maintained under section 324 asks the local education authority to arrange for an assessment to be made in respect of the child under section 323,
- (b) no such assessment has been made within the period of six months ending with the date on which the request is made, and
- (c) it is necessary for the authority to make a further assessment under section 323,

the authority shall comply with the request.

(3) If in any case where subsection (2)(a) and (b) applies the authority determine not to comply with the request—

- (a) they shall give notice in writing of that fact to the child's parent, and
- (b) the parent may appeal to the Tribunal against the determination.

(3A) A notice under subsection (3)(a) must inform the parent of the right of appeal under subsection (3)(b) and contain such information as may be prescribed.

(3B) Regulations may provide that where a local education authority are under a duty under this section to serve any notice, the duty must be performed within the prescribed period.

(4) On an appeal under subsection (3) the Tribunal may—

- (a) dismiss the appeal, or
- (b) order the authority to arrange for an assessment to be made in respect of the child under section 323.

(5) A statement under section 324 shall be reviewed by the local education authority—

- (a) on the making of an assessment in respect of the child concerned under section 323, and
- (b) in any event, within the period of 12 months beginning with the making of the statement or, as the case may be, with the previous review.

(6) Regulations may make provision—

- (a) as to the manner in which reviews of such statements are to be conducted,
- (b) as to the participation in such reviews of such persons as may be prescribed, and
- (c) in connection with such other matters relating to such reviews as the Secretary of State considers appropriate.

329 Assessment of educational needs at request of child's parent

(1) Where—

- (a) the parent of a child for whom a local education authority are responsible but for whom no statement is maintained under section 324 asks the authority to arrange for an assessment to be made in respect of the child under section 323,
- (b) no such assessment has been made within the period of six months ending with the date on which the request is made, and
- (c) it is necessary for the authority to make an assessment under that section,

the authority shall comply with the request.

(2) If in any case where subsection (1)(a) and (b) applies the authority determine not to comply with the request—

(a)   they shall give notice in writing of that fact to the child's parent, and

(b)   the parent may appeal to the Tribunal against the determination.

(2A) A notice under subsection (2)(a) must inform the parent of the right of appeal under subsection (2)(b) and contain such other information as may be prescribed.

(3) On an appeal under subsection (2) the Tribunal may—

(a)   dismiss the appeal, or

(b)   order the authority to arrange for an assessment to be made in respect of the child under section 323.

329A Review or assessment of educational needs at request of responsible body

(1) This section applies if—

(a)   a child is a registered pupil at a relevant school (whether or not he is a child in respect of whom a statement is maintained under section 324),

(b)   the responsible body asks the local education authority to arrange for an assessment to be made in respect of him under section 323, and

(c)   no such assessment has been made within the period of six months ending with the date on which the request is made.

(2) If it is necessary for the authority to make an assessment or further assessment under section 323, they must comply with the request.

(3) Before deciding whether to comply with the request, the authority must serve on the child's parent a notice informing him—

(a)   that they are considering whether to make an assessment of the child's educational needs,

(b)   of the procedure to be followed in making the assessment,

(c)   of the name of their officer from whom further information may be obtained, and

(d)   of the parent's right to make representations, and submit written evidence, to them before the end of the period specified in the notice ('the specified period').

(4) The specified period must not be less than 29 days beginning with the date on which the notice is served.

(5) The authority may not decide whether to comply with the request until the specified period has expired.

(6) The authority must take into account any representations made, and any evidence submitted, to them in response to the notice.

(7) If, as a result of this section, a local education authority decide to make an assessment under section 323, they must give written notice to the child's parent and to the responsible body which made the request, of the decision and of their reasons for making it.

(8) If, after serving a notice under subsection (3), the authority decide not to assess the educational needs of the child—

(a)   they must give written notice of the decision and of their reasons for making it to his parent and to the responsible body which made the request, and

(b)   the parent may appeal to the Tribunal against the decision.

(9) A notice given under subsection (8)(a) to the child's parent must—

(a)   inform the parent of his right to appeal, and
(b)   contain such other information (if any) as may be prescribed.

(10)   On an appeal under subsection (8) the Tribunal may—

(a)   dismiss it, or
(b)   order the authority to arrange for an assessment to be made in respect of the child under section 323.

(11)   This section applies to a child for whom relevant nursery education is provided as it applies to a child who is a registered pupil at a relevant school.

(12)   'Relevant school' means—

(a)   a maintained school,
(b)   a maintained nursery school,
(c)   a pupil referral unit,
(d)   an independent school,
(e)   a school approved under section 342.

(13)   'The responsible body' means—

(a)   in relation to a maintained nursery school or a pupil referral unit, the head teacher,
(b)   in relation to any other relevant school, the proprietor or head teacher, and
(c)   in relation to a provider of relevant nursery education, the person or body of persons responsible for the management of the provision of that nursery education.

(14)   'Relevant nursery education' has the same meaning as in section 123 of the School Standards and Framework Act 1998, except that it does not include nursery education provided by a local education authority at a maintained nursery school.

(15)   'Prescribed', in relation to Wales, means prescribed in regulations made by the National Assembly for Wales.

330 Assessment of educational needs at request of governing body of grant-maintained school
[*Repealed by the School Standards and Framework Act 1998.*]

331 Assessment of educational needs of children under two
(1) Where a local education authority are of the opinion that a child in their area who is under the age of two falls, or probably falls, within subsection (2)—

(a)   they may, with the consent of his parent, make an assessment of the child's educational needs, and
(b)   they shall make such an assessment if requested to do so by his parent.

(2) A child falls within this subsection if—

(a)   he has special educational needs, and
(b)   it is necessary for the authority to determine the special educational provision which any learning difficulty he may have calls for.

(3) An assessment under this section shall be made in such manner as the authority consider appropriate.

(4) After making an assessment under this section, the authority—

    (a)   may make a statement of the child's special educational needs, and
    (b)   may maintain that statement,

in such manner as they consider appropriate.

332 Duty of Health Authority, Primary Care Trust or National Health Service trust to notify parent etc

(1) This section applies where a Health Authority, a Primary Care Trust or a National Health Service trust, in the course of exercising any of their functions in relation to a child who is under compulsory school age, form the opinion that he has (or probably has) special educational needs.

(2) The Authority or trust—

    (a)   shall inform the child's parent of their opinion and of their duty under paragraph (b), and
    (b)   after giving the parent an opportunity to discuss that opinion with an officer of the Authority or trust, shall bring it to the attention of the appropriate local education authority.

(3) If the Authority or trust are of the opinion that a particular voluntary organisation is likely to be able to give the parent advice or assistance in connection with any special educational needs that the child may have, they shall inform the parent accordingly.

332A Advice and information for parents

(1) A local education authority must arrange for the parent of any child in their area with special educational needs to be provided with advice and information about matters relating to those needs.

(2) In making the arrangements, the authority must have regard to any guidance given—

    (a)   for England, by the Secretary of State,
    (b)   for Wales, by the National Assembly for Wales.

(3) The authority must take such steps as they consider appropriate for making the services provided under subsection (1) known to—

    (a)   the parents of children in their area,
    (b)   the head teachers and proprietors of schools in their area, and
    (c)   such other persons as they consider appropriate.

332B Resolution of disputes

(1) A local education authority must make arrangements with a view to avoiding or resolving disagreements between authorities (on the one hand) and parents of children in their area (on the other) about the exercise by authorities of functions under this Part.

(2) A local education authority must also make arrangements with a view to avoiding or resolving, in each relevant school, disagreements between the parents of a relevant child and the proprietor of the school about the special educational provision made for that child.

(3) The arrangements must provide for the appointment of independent persons with the function of facilitating the avoidance or resolution of such disagreements.

(4) In making the arrangements, the authority must have regard to any guidance given—

(a)   for England, by the Secretary of State,
(b)   for Wales, by the National Assembly for Wales.

(5)   The authority must take such steps as they consider appropriate for making the arrangements made under subsections (1) and (2) known to—

(a)   the parents of children in their area,
(b)   the head teachers and proprietors of schools in their area, and
(c)   such other persons as they consider appropriate.

(6)   The arrangements cannot affect the entitlement of a parent to appeal to the Tribunal.

(7)   In this section—

'authorities' means the governing bodies of maintained schools and the local education authority,

'relevant child' means a child who has special educational needs and is a registered pupil at a relevant school.

(8)   For the purposes of this section a school is a relevant school in relation to a child if it is—

(a)   a maintained school or a maintained nursery school,
(b)   a pupil referral unit,
(c)   a city technology college, a city college for the technology of the arts or a city academy,
(d)   an independent school named in the statement maintained for the child under section 324, or
(e)   a school approved under section 342

Special Educational Needs Tribunal

333 Constitution of Tribunal
(1)   The Tribunal shall exercise the jurisdiction conferred on it by this Part.

(2)   There shall be appointed—

(a)   a President of the Tribunal (referred to in this Part as 'the President'),
(b)   a panel of persons (referred to in this Part as 'the chairmen's panel') who may serve as chairman of the Tribunal, and
(c)   a panel of persons (referred to in this Part as 'the lay panel') who may serve as the other two members of the Tribunal apart from the chairman.

(3)   The President and the members of the chairmen's panel shall each be appointed by the Lord Chancellor.

(4)   The members of the lay panel shall each be appointed by the Secretary of State.

(5)   Regulations may—

(a)   provide for the jurisdiction of the Tribunal to be exercised by such number of tribunals as may be determined from time to time by the President, and
(b)   make such other provision in connection with the establishment and continuation of the Tribunal as the Secretary of State considers necessary or desirable.

(6)   The Secretary of State may, with the consent of the Treasury, provide such staff and accommodation as the Tribunal may require.

334 The President and members of the panels

(1) No person may be appointed President or member of the chairmen's panel unless he has a seven year general qualification (within the meaning of section 71 of the Courts and Legal Services Act 1990).

(2) No person may be appointed member of the lay panel unless he satisfies such requirements as may be prescribed.

(3) If, in the opinion of the Lord Chancellor, the President is unfit to continue in office or is incapable of performing his duties, the Lord Chancellor may revoke his appointment.

(4) Each member of the chairmen's panel or lay panel shall hold and vacate office under the terms of the instrument under which he is appointed.

(5) The President or a member of the chairmen's panel or lay panel—

  (a)   may resign office by notice in writing to the Lord Chancellor or (as the case may be) the Secretary of State, and
  (b)   is eligible for re-appointment if he ceases to hold office.

335 Remuneration and expenses

(1) The Secretary of State may pay to the President, and to any other person in respect of his service as a member of the Tribunal, such remuneration and allowances as the Secretary of State may, with the consent of the Treasury, determine.

(2) The Secretary of State may defray the expenses of the Tribunal to such amount as he may, with the consent of the Treasury, determine.

336 Tribunal procedure

(1) Regulations may make provision about the proceedings of the Tribunal on an appeal under this Part and the initiation of such an appeal.

(2) The regulations may, in particular, include provision—

  (a)   as to the period within which, and the manner in which, appeals are to be instituted,
  (b)   where the jurisdiction of the Tribunal is being exercised by more than one tribunal—
     (i)   for determining by which tribunal any appeal is to be heard, and
     (ii)   for the transfer of proceedings from one tribunal to another,
  (c)   for enabling any functions which relate to matters preliminary or incidental to an appeal to be performed by the President, or by the chairman,
  (d)   . . .
  (e)   for hearings to be conducted in the absence of any member other than the chairman,
  (f)   as to the persons who may appear on behalf of the parties,
  (g)   for granting any person such disclosure or inspection of documents or right to further particulars as might be granted by a county court,
  (h)   requiring persons to attend to give evidence and produce documents,
  (i)   for authorising the administration of oaths to witnesses,
  (j)   for the determination of appeals without a hearing in prescribed circumstances,
  (k)   as to the withdrawal of appeals,
  (l)   for the award of costs or expenses,
  (m)   for taxing or otherwise settling any such costs or expenses (and, in particular, for enabling such costs to be taxed in the county court),

    (n) for the registration and proof of decisions and orders, and
    (o) for enabling the Tribunal to review its decisions, or revoke or vary its orders, in such circumstances as may be determined in accordance with the regulations.

(2A) Proceedings before the Tribunal shall be held in private, except in prescribed circumstances.

(3) The Secretary of State may pay such allowances for the purpose of or in connection with the attendance of persons at the Tribunal as he may, with the consent of the Treasury, determine.

(4) Part I of the Arbitration Act 1996 shall not apply to any proceedings before the Tribunal but regulations may make provision corresponding to any provision of that Part.

(4A) The regulations may make provision for an appeal under this Part to be heard, in prescribed circumstances, with a claim under Chapter 1 of Part IV of the Disability Discrimination Act 1995.

(5) Any person who without reasonable excuse fails to comply with—

    (a) any requirement in respect of the discovery or inspection of documents imposed by the regulations by virtue of subsection (2)(g), or
    (b) any requirement imposed by the regulations by virtue of subsection (2)(h),

is guilty of an offence.

(6) A person guilty of an offence under subsection (5) is liable on summary conviction to a fine not exceeding level 3 on the standard scale.

336A Compliance with orders
(1) If the Tribunal makes an order, the local education authority concerned must comply with the order before the end of the prescribed period beginning with the date on which it is made.

(2) Regulations under this section, so far as they relate to Wales, require the agreement of the National Assembly for Wales.

CHAPTER II

SCHOOLS PROVIDING FOR SPECIAL EDUCATIONAL NEEDS

Special schools

337 Special schools
(1) A school is a special school if it is specially organised to make special educational provision for pupils with special educational needs.

(2) There are the following categories of special school—

    (a) special schools maintained by local education authorities, comprising—
        (i)   community special schools, and
        (ii) foundation special schools; and
    (b) special schools which are not so maintained but are for the time being approved by the Secretary of State under section 342.

Establishment etc of special schools

338 Power of funding authority to establish grant-maintained special school
[*Repealed by the School Standards and Framework Act 1998.*]

339 Establishment, etc of maintained or grant-maintained special schools
[*Repealed by the School Standards and Framework Act 1998.*]

340 Procedure for dealing with proposals
[*Repealed by the School Standards and Framework Act 1998.*]

341 Approval of premises of maintained or grant-maintained special schools
[*Repealed by the School Standards and Framework Act 1998.*]

Approval of non-maintained special schools

342 Approval of non-maintained special schools
(1) The Secretary of State may approve under this section any school which—

  (a) is specially organised to make special educational provision for pupils with special educational needs, and

  (b) is not a community or foundation special school,

and may give his approval before or after the school is established.

(2) Regulations may make provision as to the requirements which are to be complied with as a condition of approval under subsection (1) above.

(3) Any school which was a special school immediately before 1st April 1994 shall be treated, subject to subsection (4) below, as approved under this section.

(4) Regulations may make provision as to—

  (a) the requirements which are to be complied with by a school while approved under this section, and

  (b) the withdrawal of approval from a school (including approval treated as given under subsection (3)) at the request of the proprietor or on the ground that there has been a failure to comply with any prescribed requirement.

(5) Without prejudice to the generality of subsections (2) and (4), the requirements which may be imposed by the regulations include requirements—

  (a) which call for arrangements to be approved by the Secretary of State, or

  (b) as to the organisation of any special school as a primary school or as a secondary school.

(6) Regulations shall make provision for securing that, so far as practicable, every pupil attending a special school approved under this section—

  (a) receives religious education and attends religious worship, or

  (b) is withdrawn from receiving such education or from attendance at such worship in accordance with the wishes of his parent.

343 Nursery education in grant-maintained special schools
[*Repealed by the School Standards and Framework Act 1998.*]

344 Government etc of special schools
[*Repealed by the School Standards and Framework Act 1998.*]

Maintained special school becoming grant-maintained

345 Maintained special school becoming grant-maintained special school
[*Repealed by the School Standards and Framework Act 1998.*]

Grouping of grant-maintained special schools

346 Groups including grant-maintained special schools
[*Repealed by the School Standards and Framework Act 1998.*]

Independent schools providing special education

347 Approval of independent schools
(1) The Secretary of State may approve an independent school as suitable for the admission of children for whom statements are maintained under section 324.

(2) Regulations may make provision as to—

  (a) the requirements which are to be complied with by a school as a condition of its approval under this section,
  (b) the requirements which are to be complied with by a school while an approval under this section is in force in respect of it, and
  (c) the withdrawal of approval from a school at the request of the proprietor or on the ground that there has been a failure to comply with any prescribed requirement.

(3) An approval under this section may be given subject to such conditions (in addition to those prescribed) as the Secretary of State sees fit to impose.

(4) In any case where there is a failure to comply with such a condition imposed under subsection (3), the Secretary of State may withdraw his approval.

(5) No person shall so exercise his functions under this Part that a child with special educational needs is educated in an independent school unless—

  (a) the school is for the time being approved by the Secretary of State as suitable for the admission of children for whom statements are maintained under section 324, or
  (b) the Secretary of State consents to the child being educated there.

(5A) But that does not apply to a local education authority deciding, for the purposes of section 324(5), whether a parent has made suitable arrangements.

348 Provision of special education at non-maintained schools
(1) This section applies where—

  (a) special educational provision in respect of a child with special educational needs is made at a school which is not a maintained school, and
  (b) either the name of the school is specified in a statement in respect of the child under section 324 or the local education authority are satisfied—

(i)   that his interests require the necessary special educational provision to be made for him at a school which is not a maintained school, and

(ii)   that it is appropriate for the child to be provided with education at the particular school.

(2)   Where this section applies, the local education authority shall pay the whole of the fees payable in respect of the education provided for the child at the school, and if—

(a)   board and lodging are provided for him at the school, and

(b)   the authority are satisfied that the necessary special educational provision cannot be provided for him at the school unless the board and lodging are also provided,

the authority shall pay the whole of the fees payable in respect of the board and lodging.

(3)   In this section 'maintained school' means a school maintained by a local education authority.

Variation of deeds

349 Variation of trust deeds etc by order
(1)   The Secretary of State may by order make such modifications of any trust deed or other instrument relating to a school as, after consultation with the governing body or other proprietor of the school, appear to him to be necessary to enable the governing body or proprietor to meet any requirement imposed by regulations under section 342 or 347.

(2)   Any modification made by an order under this section may be made to have permanent effect or to have effect for such period as may be specified in the order.

. . .

SCHEDULE 26
MAKING OF ASSESSMENTS UNDER SECTION 323

Section 323

Introductory

1   In this Schedule 'assessment' means an assessment of a child's educational needs under section 323.

Medical and other advice

2   (1) Regulations shall make provision as to the advice which a local education authority are to seek in making assessments.

(2)   Without prejudice to the generality of sub-paragraph (1), the regulations shall require the authority, except in such circumstances as may be prescribed, to seek medical, psychological and educational advice and such other advice as may be prescribed.

Manner, and timing, of assessments, etc

3   (1) Regulations may make provision—

(a)   as to the manner in which assessments are to be conducted,

(b)   requiring the local education authority, where, after conducting an assessment under section 323 of the educational needs of a child for whom a
statement is maintained under section 324, they determine not to amend the
statement, to serve on the parent of the child a notice giving the prescribed
information, and

(c)   in connection with such other matters relating to the making of assessments
as the Secretary of State considers appropriate.

(2) Sub-paragraph (1)(b) does not apply to a determination made following the
service of notice under paragraph 2A of Schedule 27 (amendment of statement by
LEA) of a proposal to amend the statement.

(3) Regulations may provide—

(a)   that where a local education authority are under a duty under section 323,
329, or 329A to serve any notice, the duty must be performed within the prescribed period,

(b)   that where a local education authority have served a notice under section 323(1)
or 329A(3) on a child's parent, they must decide within the prescribed period
whether or not to make an assessment of the child's educational needs,

(c)   that where a request has been made to a local education authority under section 329(1), they must decide within the prescribed period whether or not to
comply with the request, and

(d)   that where a local education authority are under a duty to make an assessment, the duty must be performed within the prescribed period.

(4) Provision made under sub-paragraph (3)—

(a)   may be subject to prescribed exceptions, and

(b)   does not relieve the authority of the duty to serve a notice, or assessment,
which has not been served or made within the prescribed period.

Attendance at examinations

4   (1) Where a local education authority are considering whether to make an assessment, they may serve a notice on the parent of the child concerned requiring the child's
attendance for examination in accordance with the provisions of the notice.

(2) The parent of a child examined under this paragraph may be present at the
examination if he so desires.

(3) A notice under this paragraph shall—

(a)   state the purpose of the examination,

(b)   state the time and place at which the examination will be held,

(c)   name an officer of the authority from whom further information may be
obtained,

(d)   inform the parent that he may submit such information to the authority as he
may wish, and

(e)   inform the parent of his right to be present at the examination.

Offence

5 (1) Any parent who fails without reasonable excuse to comply with any requirements of a notice served on him under paragraph 4 commits an offence if the notice

relates to a child who is not over compulsory school age at the time stated in it as the time for holding the examination.

(2) A person guilty of an offence under this paragraph is liable on summary conviction to a fine not exceeding level 2 on the standard scale.

SCHEDULE 27
MAKING AND MAINTENANCE OF STATEMENTS UNDER SECTION 324

Introductory

1   In this Schedule—

'amendment notice' has the meaning given in paragraph 2A,

'statement' means a statement under section 324,

'periodic review' means a review conducted in accordance with section 328(5)(b), and

're-assessment review' means a review conducted in accordance with section 328(5)(a).

Copies of a proposed statement

2   (1) Before making a statement, a local education authority shall serve on the parent of the child concerned a copy of the proposed statement.

(2) But that is subject to sub-paragraphs (3) and (4).

(3) The copy of the proposed statement shall not specify any prescribed matter.

(4) The copy of the proposed statement shall not specify any matter in pursuance of section 324(4).

Amendments to a statement

2A   (1) A local education authority shall not amend a statement except—

(a)   in compliance with an order of the Tribunal,
(b)   as directed by the Secretary of State under section 442(4), or
(c)   in accordance with the procedure laid down in this Schedule.

(2) If, following a re-assessment review, a local education authority propose to amend a statement, they shall serve on the parent of the child concerned a copy of the proposed amended statement.

(3) Sub-paragraphs (3) and (4) of paragraph 2 apply to a copy of a proposed amended statement served under sub-paragraph (2) as they apply to a copy of a proposed statement served under paragraph 2(1).

(4) If, following a periodic review, a local education authority propose to amend a statement, they shall serve on the parent of the child concerned—

(a)   a copy of the existing statement, and
(b)   an amendment notice.

(5) If, at any other time, a local education authority propose to amend a statement, they shall proceed as if the proposed amendment were an amendment proposed after a periodic review.

(6) An amendment notice is a notice in writing giving details of the amendments to the statement proposed by the authority.

Provision of additional information

2B   (1) Sub-paragraph (2) applies when a local education authority serve on a parent—

- (a)   a copy of a proposed statement under paragraph 2,
- (b)   a copy of a proposed amended statement under paragraph 2A, or
- (c)   an amendment notice under paragraph 2A.

(2) The local education authority shall also serve on the parent a written notice explaining (to the extent that they are applicable)—

- (a)   the arrangements under paragraph 3,
- (b)   the effect of paragraph 4, and
- (c)   the right to appeal under section 326.

(3) A notice under sub-paragraph (2) must contain such other information as may be prescribed.

Choice of school

3   (1) Every local education authority shall make arrangements for enabling a parent—

- (a)   on whom a copy of a proposed statement has been served under paragraph 2,
- (b)   on whom a copy of a proposed amended statement has been served under paragraph 2A, or
- (c)   on whom an amendment notice has been served under paragraph 2A which contains a proposed amendment about—
  - (i)   the type or name of a school or institution, or
  - (ii)   the provision made for the child concerned under arrangements made under section 319,
  to be specified in the statement,

to express a preference as to the maintained school at which he wishes education to be provided for his child and to give reasons for his preference.

(2) Any such preference must be expressed or made within the period of 15 days beginning—

- (a)   with the date on which the written notice mentioned in paragraph 2B was served on the parent, or
- (b)   if a meeting has (or meetings have) been arranged under paragraph 4(1)(b) or (2), with the date fixed for that meeting (or the last of those meetings).

(3) Where a local education authority make a statement in a case where the parent of the child concerned has expressed a preference in pursuance of such arrangements as to the school at which he wishes education to be provided for his child, they shall specify the name of that school in the statement unless—

- (a)   the school is unsuitable to the child's age, ability or aptitude or to his special educational needs, or

(b)   the attendance of the child at the school would be incompatible with the provision of efficient education for the children with whom he would be educated or the efficient use of resources.

(4) [*Deleted by Special Educational Needs and Disability Act 2001, Sch 1, para 6.*]

Consultation on specifying name of school in statement

3A   (1) Sub-paragraph (2) applies if a local education authority are considering—

(a)   specifying the name of a maintained school in a statement, or
(b)   amending a statement—
    (i)   if no school was specified in the statement before the amendment, so that a maintained school will be specified in it,
    (ii) if a school was specified in the statement before the amendment, so that a different school, which is a maintained school, will be specified in it.

(2) The local education authority shall—

(a)   serve a copy of the proposed statement or amended statement, or of the existing statement and of the amendment notice, on each affected body, and
(b)   consult each affected body.

(3) 'Affected body' means—

(a)   the governing body of any school which the local education authority are considering specifying; and
(b)   if a school which the local education authority are considering specifying is maintained by another local education authority, that authority

Representations

4   (1) A parent on whom a copy of a proposed statement has been served under paragraph 2, or on whom a proposed amended statement or an amendment notice has been served under paragraph 2A may—

(a)   make representations (or further representations) to the local education authority about the content of the proposed statement or the statement as it will have effect if amended in the way proposed by the authority, and
(b)   require the authority to arrange a meeting between him and an officer of the authority at which the proposed statement or the statement as it will have effect if amended in the way proposed by the authority can be discussed.

(2) Where a parent, having attended a meeting arranged by a local education authority under sub-paragraph (1)(b) in relation to (a) a proposed statement, or (b) an amendment proposed following a reassessment review, disagrees with any part of the assessment in question, he may require the authority to arrange such meeting or meetings as they consider will enable him to discuss the relevant advice with the appropriate person or persons.

(3) In this paragraph—

'relevant advice' means such of the advice given to the authority in connection with the assessment as they consider to be relevant to that part of the assessment with which the parent disagrees, and

'appropriate person' means the person who gave the relevant advice or any other person who, in the opinion of the authority, is the appropriate person to discuss it with the parent.

(4) Any representations under sub-paragraph (1)(a) must be made within the period of 15 days beginning—

   (a) with the date on which the written notice mentioned in paragraph 2B was served on the parent, or
   (b) if a meeting has (or meetings have) been arranged under sub-paragraph (1)(b) or (2), with the date fixed for that meeting (or the last of those meetings).

(5) A requirement under sub-paragraph (1)(b) must be made within the period of 15 days beginning with the date on which the written notice mentioned in paragraph 2B was served on the parent.

(6) A requirement under sub-paragraph (2) must be made within the period of 15 days beginning with the date fixed for the meeting arranging under sub-paragraph (1)(b).

Making the statement

5   (1) Where representations are made to a local education authority under paragraph 4(1)(a), the authority shall not make or amend the statement until they have considered the representations and the period or the last of the periods allowed by paragraph 4 for making requirements or further representations has expired.

(2) If a local education authority make a statement, it may be in the form originally proposed (except as to the matters required to be excluded from the copy of the proposed statement) or in a form modified in the light of the representations.

(2A) If a local education authority amend a statement following service of a proposed amended statement under paragraph 2A, the amended statement made may be in the form proposed or in a form modified in light of the representations.

(2B) If a local education authority amend a statement following service of an amendment notice, the amendments may be those proposed in the notice or amendments modified in the light of the representations.

(3) Regulations may provide that, where a local education authority are under a duty (subject to compliance with the preceding requirements of this Schedule) to make a statement, the duty, or any step required to be taken for performance of the duty, must, subject to prescribed exceptions, be performed within the prescribed period.

(4) Such provision shall not relieve the authority of the duty to make a statement, or take any step, which has not been performed or taken within that period.

Service of statement

6   (1) Where a local education authority make or amend a statement they shall serve a copy of the statement, or the amended statement, on the parent of the child concerned.

(2) They shall, at the same time, give the parent written notice of his right to appeal under section 326(1) against

   (a) the description in the statement of the authority's assessment of the child's special educational needs,
   (b) the special educational provision specified in the statement (including the name of a school specified in the statement), or
   (c) if no school is named in the statement, that fact.

(3) A notice under sub-paragraph (2) must contain such other information as may be prescribed.

Keeping, disclosure and transfer of statements

7   (1) Regulations may make provision as to the keeping and disclosure of statements.

(2) Regulations may make provision, where a local education authority become responsible for a child for whom a statement is maintained by another authority, for the transfer of the statement to them and for Part IV to have effect as if the duty to maintain the transferred statement were their duty.

Change of named school

8   (1) Sub-paragraph (2) applies where—

(a)   the parent of a child for whom a statement is maintained which specifies the name of a school or institution asks the local education authority to substitute for that name the name of a maintained school specified by the parent, and

(b)   the request is not made less than 12 months after—
   (i)   an earlier request under this paragraph,
   (ii)   the service of a copy of the statement or amended statement under paragraph 6,
   (iii) . . .
   (iv)   if the parent has appealed to the Tribunal under section 326 or this paragraph, the date when the appeal is concluded,

whichever is the later.

(2) The local education authority shall comply with the request unless—

(a)   the school is unsuitable to the child's age, ability or aptitude or to his special educational needs, or

(b)   the attendance of the child at the school would be incompatible with the provision of efficient education for the children with whom he would be educated or the efficient use of resources.

(3) Where the local education authority determine not to comply with the request—

(a)   they shall give notice in writing of that fact to the parent of the child, and

(b)   the parent of the child may appeal to the Tribunal against the determination.

(3A) A notice under sub-paragraph (3)(a) must inform the parent of the right of appeal under sub-paragraph (3)(b) and contain such other information as may be prescribed.

(4) On the appeal the Tribunal may—

(a)   dismiss the appeal, or

(b)   order the local education authority to substitute for the name of the school or other institution specified in the statement the name of the school specified by the parent.

(5) Regulations may provide that, where a local education authority are under a duty to comply with a request under this paragraph, the duty must, subject to prescribed exceptions, be performed within the prescribed period.

(6) Such provision shall not relieve the authority of the duty to comply with such a request which has not been complied with within that period.

Appendix 1   Extracts from the Education Act 1996

Procedure for amending or ceasing to maintain a statement

9   (1) A local education authority may not . . . cease to maintain, a statement except in accordance with paragraph . . . 11.

(2) Sub-paragraph (1) does not apply where the local education authority—

(a)   cease to maintain a statement for a child who has ceased to be a child for whom they are responsible, or

(b)   . . .

(c)   are ordered to cease to maintain a statement under section 326(3)(c), . . .

(d)   . . .

10   [*Deleted by paragraph 17 Schedule 1 Special Educational Needs and Disability Act 2001.*]

11   (1) A local education authority may cease to maintain a statement only if it is no longer necessary to maintain it.

(2) Where the local education authority determine to cease to maintain a statement—

(a)   they shall give notice in writing of that fact to the parent of the child, and

(b)   the parent of the child may appeal to the Tribunal against the determination.

(2A) A notice under sub-paragraph (2)(a) must inform the parent of the right of appeal under sub-paragraph (2)(b) and contain such other information as may be prescibed.

(3) On an appeal under this paragraph the Tribunal may—

(a)   dismiss the appeal, or

(b)   order the local education authority to continue to maintain the statement in its existing form or with such amendments of—

(i)   the description in the statement of the authority's assessment of the child's special educational needs, or

(ii)   the special educational provision specified in the statement,

and such other consequential amendments, as the Tribunal may determine.

(4) Except where the parent of the child appeals to the Tribunal under this paragraph, a local education authority may only cease to maintain a statement under this paragraph within the prescribed period beginning with the service of the notice under sub-paragraph (2).

(5) A local education authority may not, under this paragraph, cease to maintain a statement if—

(a)   the parent of the child has appealed under this paragraph against the authority's determination to cease to maintain the statement, and

(b)   the appeal has not been determined by the Tribunal or withdrawn.

Appendix 2

Extracts from the Disability Discrimination Act 1995 (c 50), as amended by the Special Educational Needs and Disability Act 2001 (c 10)

Disability Discrimination Act 1995

An Act to make it unlawful to discriminate against disabled persons in connection with employment, the provision of goods, facilities and services or the disposal or management of premises; to make provision about the employment of disabled persons; and to establish a National Disability Council.

[20th November 1995]

PART I

DISABILITY

1 Meaning of 'disability' and 'disabled person'

(1) Subject to the provisions of Schedule 1, a person has a disability for the purposes of this Act if he has a physical or mental impairment which has a substantial and long-term adverse effect on his ability to carry out normal day-to-day activities.

(2) In this Act 'disabled person' means a person who has a disability.

2 Past disabilities

(1) The provisions of this Part and Parts II to 4 apply in relation to a person who has had a disability as they apply in relation to a person who has that disability.

(2) Those provisions are subject to the modifications made by Schedule 2.

(3) Any regulations or order made under this Act may include provision with respect to persons who have had a disability.

(4) In any proceedings under Part II, 3 or 4 of this Act, the question whether a person had a disability at a particular time ('the relevant time') shall be determined, for the purposes of this section, as if the provisions of, or made under, this Act in force when the act complained of was done had been in force at the relevant time.

(5) The relevant time may be a time before the passing of this Act.

3 Guidance

(1) The Secretary of State may issue guidance about the matters to be taken into account in determining—

   (a)   whether an impairment has a substantial adverse effect on a person's ability to carry out normal day-to-day activities; or
   (b)   whether such an impairment has a long-term effect.

(2) The guidance may, amongst other things, give examples of—

   (a)   effects which it would be reasonable, in relation to particular activities, to regard for purposes of this Act as substantial adverse effects;
   (b)   effects which it would not be reasonable, in relation to particular activities, to regard for such purposes as substantial adverse effects;
   (c)   substantial adverse effects which it would be reasonable to regard, for such purposes, as long-term;
   (d)   substantial adverse effects which it would not be reasonable to regard, for such purposes, as long-term.

(3) An adjudicating body determining, for any purpose of this Act, whether an impairment has a substantial and long-term adverse effect on a person's ability to carry out normal day-to-day activities, shall take into account any guidance which appears to it to be relevant.

(3A) 'Adjudicating body' means—

   (a)   a court;
   (b)   a tribunal; and
   (c)   any other person who, or body which, may decide a claim under Part 4

[*3(4) to (12) set out the process by which the Secretary of State produces guidance.*]

PART II

EMPLOYMENT

★ ★ ★ ★ ★

PART III

DISCRIMINATION IN OTHER AREAS

19 Discrimination in relation to goods, facilities and services
(1) It is unlawful for a provider of services to discriminate against a disabled person—

   (a)   in refusing to provide, or deliberately not providing, to the disabled person any service which he provides, or is prepared to provide, to members of the public;
   (b)   in failing to comply with any duty imposed on him by section 21 in circum-stances in which the effect of that failure is to make it impossible or unreasonably difficult for the disabled person to make use of any such service;
   (c)   in the standard of service which he provides to the disabled person or the manner in which he provides it to him; or
   (d)   in the terms on which he provides a service to the disabled person.

(2) For the purposes of this section and sections 20 and 21—

   (a)   the provision of services includes the provision of any goods or facilities;

(b)   a person is 'a provider of services' if he is concerned with the provision, in the United Kingdom, of services to the public or to a section of the public; and

(c)   it is irrelevant whether a service is provided on payment or without payment.

(3)   The following are examples of services to which this section and sections 20 and 21 apply—

(a)   access to and use of any place which members of the public are permitted to enter;

(b)   access to and use of means of communication;

(c)   access to and use of information services;

(d)   accommodation in a hotel, boarding house or other similar establishment;

(e)   facilities by way of banking or insurance or for grants, loans, credit or finance;

(f)   facilities for entertainment, recreation or refreshment;

(g)   facilities provided by employment agencies or under section 2 of the Employment and Training Act 1973;

(h)   the services of any profession or trade, or any local or other public authority.

(4)   In the case of an act which constitutes discrimination by virtue of section 55, this section also applies to discrimination against a person who is not disabled.

(5)   Except in such circumstances as may be prescribed, this section and sections 20 and 21 do not apply to—

(a)   . . .

(b)   any service so far as it consists of the use of any means of transport; or

(c)   such other services as may be prescribed.

(5A)   Nothing in this Part applies to the provision of a service in relation to which discrimination is made unlawful by section 28A, 28F or 28R.

(6)   . . .

[*Ss 20 to 28 omitted.*]

PART IV
DISABILITY DISCRIMINATION IN EDUCATION

CHAPTER 1
SCHOOLS

Duties of responsible bodies

28A Discrimination against disabled pupils and prospective pupils

(1)   It is unlawful for the body responsible for a school to discriminate against a disabled person—

(a)   in the arrangements it makes for determining admission to the school as a pupil:

(b)   in the terms on which it offers to admit him to the school as a pupil; or

(c)   by refusing or deliberately omitting to accept an application for his admission to the school as a pupil.

(2)   It is unlawful for the body responsible for a school to discriminate against a disabled pupil in the education or associated services provided for, or offered to, pupils at the school by that body.

(3) The Secretary of State may by regulations prescribe services which are, or services which are not, to be regarded for the purposes of subsection (2) as being—

(a)   education; or
(b)   an associated service.

(4) It is unlawful for the body responsible for a school to discriminate against a disabled pupil by excluding him from the school, whether permanently or temporarily.

(5) The body responsible for a school is to be determined in accordance with Schedule 4A, and in the remaining provisions of this Chapter is referred to as the 'responsible body'.

(6) In the case of an act which constitutes discrimination by virtue of section 55, this section also applies to discrimination against a person who is not disabled.

28B Meaning of 'discrimination'
(1) For the purposes of section 28A, a responsible body discriminates against a disabled person if—

(a)   for a reason which relates to his disability, it treats him less favourably than it treats or would treat others to whom that reason does not or would not apply; and
(b)   it cannot show that the treatment in question is justified.

(2) For the purposes of section 28A, a responsible body also discriminates against a disabled person if—

(a)   it fails, to his detriment, to comply with section 28C; and
(b)   it cannot show that its failure to comply is justified.

(3) In relation to a failure to take a particular step, a responsible body does not discriminate against a person if it shows—

(a)   that, at the time in question, it did not know and could not reasonably have been expected to know, that he was disabled; and
(b)   that its failure to take the step was attributable to that lack of knowledge.

(4) The taking of a particular step by a responsible body in relation to a person does not amount to less favourable treatment if it shows that at the time in question it did not know, and could not reasonably have been expected to know, that he was disabled.

(5) Subsections (6) to (8) apply in determining whether, for the purposes of this section

(a)   less favourable treatment of a person, or
(b)   failure to comply with section 28C,

is justified.

(6) Less favourable treatment of a person is justified if it is the result of a permitted form of selection.

(7) Otherwise, less favourable treatment, or a failure to comply with section 28C, is justified only if the reason for it is both material to the circumstances of the particular case and substantial.

(8) If, in a case falling within subsection (1)—

(a)   the responsible body is under a duty imposed by section 28C in relation to the disabled person, but

(b)   it fails without justification to comply with that duty,

its treatment of that person cannot be justified under subsection (7) unless that treatment would have been justified even if it had complied with that duty.

28C Disabled pupils not to be substantially disadvantaged

(1)   The responsible body for a school must take such steps as it is reasonable for it to have to take to ensure that—

(a)   in relation to the arrangements it makes for determining the admission of pupils to the school, disabled persons are not placed at a substantial disadvantage in comparison with persons who are not disabled; and

(b)   in relation to education and associated services provided for, or offered to, pupils at the school by it, disabled pupils are not placed at a substantial disadvantage in comparison with pupils who are not disabled.

(2)   That does not require the responsible body to—

(a)   remove or alter a physical feature (for example, one arising from the design or construction of the school premises or the location of resources); or

(b)   provide auxiliary aids or services.

(3)   Regulations may make provision, for the purposes of this section—

(a)   as to circumstances in which it is reasonable for a responsible body to have to take steps of a prescribed description;

(b)   as to steps which it is always reasonable for a responsible body to have to take;

(c)   as to circumstances in which it is not reasonable for a responsible body to have to take steps of a prescribed description:

(d)   as to steps which it is never reasonable for a responsible body to have to take.

(4)   In considering whether it is reasonable for it to have to take a particular step in order to comply with its duty under subsection (1), a responsible body must have regard to any relevant provisions of a code of practice issued under section 53A.

(5)   Subsection (6) applies if, in relation to a person, a confidentiality request has been made of which a responsible body is aware.

(6)   In determining whether it is reasonable for the responsible body to have to take a particular step in relation to that person in order to comply with its duty under subsection (1), regard shall be had to the extent to which taking the step in question is consistent with compliance with that request.

(7)   'Confidentiality request' means a request which asks for the nature, or asks for the existence, of a disabled person's disability to be treated as confidential and which satisfies either of the following conditions—

(a)   it is made by that person's parent; or

(b)   it is made by that person himself and the responsible body reasonably believes that he has sufficient understanding of the nature of the request and of its effect.

(8)   This section imposes duties only for the purpose of determining whether a responsible body has discriminated against a disabled person; and accordingly a breach of any such duty is not actionable as such.

28D   Accessibility strategies and plans

(1)   Each local education authority must prepare, in relation to schools for which they are the responsible body—

(a)   an accessibility strategy;
(b)   further such strategies at such times as may be prescribed.

(2)   An accessibility strategy is a strategy for, over a prescribed period—

(a)   increasing the extent to which disabled pupils can participate in the schools' curriculums;
(b)   improving the physical environment of the schools for the purpose of increasing the extent to which disabled pupils are able to take advantage of education and associated services provided or offered by the schools; and
(c)   improving the delivery to disabled pupils—
   (i)   within a reasonable time, and
   (ii)   in ways which are determined after taking account of their disabilities and any preferences expressed by them or their parents,

of information which is provided in writing for pupils who are not disabled.

(3)   An accessibility strategy must be in writing.

(4)   Each local education authority must keep their accessibility strategy under review during the period to which it relates and, if necessary, revise it.

(5)   It is the duty of each local education authority to implement their accessibility strategy.

(6)   An inspection under section 38 of the Education Act 1997 (inspections of local education authorities) may extend to the performance by a local education authority of their functions in relation to the preparation, review, revision and implementation of their accessibility strategy.

(7)   Subsections (8) to (13) apply to—

(a)   maintained schools;
(b)   independent schools: and
(c)   special schools which are not maintained special schools but which are approved by the Secretary of State, or by the National Assembly, under section 342 of the Education Act 1996.

(8)   The responsible body must prepare—

(a)   an accessibility plan;
(b)   further such plans at such times as may be prescribed.

(9)   An accessibility plan is a plan for, over a prescribed period—

(a)   increasing the extent to which disabled pupils can participate in the school's curriculum;
(b)   improving the physical environment of the school for the purpose of increasing the extent to which disabled pupils are able to take advantage of education and associated services provided or offered by the school; and
(c)   improving the delivery to disabled pupils—
   (i)   within a reasonable time, and
   (ii)   in ways which are determined after taking account of their disabilities and any preferences expressed by them or their parents,

of information which is provided in writing for pupils who are not disabled.

(10)   An accessibility plan must be in writing.

(11)   During the period to which the plan relates, the responsible body must keep its accessibility plan under review and, if necessary, revise it.

(12)   It is the duty of the responsible body to implement its accessibility plan.

(13)   An inspection under the School Inspections Act 1996 may extend to the performance by the responsible body of its functions in relation to the preparation, publication, review, revision and implementation of its accessibility plan.

(14)   For a maintained school, the duties imposed by subsections (8) to (12) are duties of the governing body.

(15)   Regulations may prescribe services which are, or services which are not, to be regarded for the purposes of this section as being—

(a)   education; or
(b)   an associated service.

(16)   In this section and in section 28E, 'local education authority' has the meaning given in section 12 of the Education Act 1996.

(17)   In relation to Wales—

'prescribed' means prescribed in regulations; and

'regulations' means regulations made by the National Assembly.

(18)   'Disabled pupil' includes a disabled person who may be admitted to the school as a pupil.

(19)   'Maintained school' and 'independent school' have the meaning given in section 28Q(5)

28E   Accessibility strategies and plans: procedure
(1)   In preparing their accessibility strategy, a local education authority must have regard to—

(a)   the need to allocate adequate resources for implementing the strategy; and
(b)   any guidance issued as to—
      (i)   the content of an accessibility strategy;
      (ii)   the form in which it is to be produced; and
      (iii)   the persons to be consulted in its preparation.

(2)   A local educational authority must have regard to any guidance issued as to compliance with the requirements of section 28D(4).

(3)   Guidance under subsection (1)(b) or (2) may be issued—

(a)   for England, by the Secretary of State; and
(b)   for Wales, by the National Assembly.

(4) In preparing an accessibility plan, the responsible body must have regard to the need to allocate adequate resources for implementing the plan.

(5)   If the Secretary of State asks for a copy of—

(a)   the accessibility strategy prepared by a local education authority in England, or

(b)   the accessibility plan prepared by the proprietor of an independent school (other than a city academy) in England,

the strategy or plan must be given to him.

(6) If the National Assembly asks for a copy of—

(a)   the accessibility strategy prepared by a local education authority in Wales, or
(b)   the accessibility plan prepared by the proprietor of an independent school in Wales,

the strategy or plan must be given to it.

(7) If asked to do so, a local education authority must make a copy of their accessibility strategy available for inspection at such reasonable times as they may determine.

(8) If asked to do so, the proprietor of an independent school which is not a city academy must make a copy of his accessibility plan available for inspection at such reasonable times as he may determine.

Residual duty of education authorities

28F Duty of education authorities not to discriminate
(1) This section applies to—

(a)   the functions of a local education authority under the Education Acts; and
(b)   [*Scotland*]

(2) But it does not apply to any prescribed function.

(3) In discharging a function to which this section applies, it is unlawful for the authority to discriminate against—

(a)   a disabled pupil; or
(b)   a disabled person who may be admitted to a school as a pupil.

(4) But an act done in the discharge of a function to which this section applies is unlawful as a result of subsection (3) only if no other provision of this Chapter makes this act unlawful.

(5) In the case of an act which constitutes discrimination by virtue of section 55, this section also applies to discrimination against a person who is not disabled.

(6) In this section and section 28G, 'local education authority' has the meaning given in section 12 of the Education Act 1996.

(7) 'The Education Acts' has the meaning given in section 578 of the Education Act 1996.

(8) [*Scotland*]

28G Residual duty: supplementary provisions
(1) Section 28B applies for the purposes of section 28F as it applies for the purposes of section 28A with the following modifications—

(a)   references to a responsible body are to be read as references to an authority; and
(b)   references to section 28C are to be read as references to subsections (2) to (4).

(2) Each authority must take such steps as it is reasonable for it to have to take to ensure that, in discharging any function to which section 28F applies—

   (a) disabled persons who may be admitted to a school as pupils are not placed at a substantial disadvantage in comparison with persons who are not disabled; and

   (b) disabled pupils are not placed at a substantial disadvantage in comparison with pupils who are not disabled.

(3) That does not require the authority to—

   (a) remove or alter a physical feature; or
   (b) provide auxiliary aids or services.

(4) This section imposes duties only for the purpose of determining whether an authority has discriminated against a disabled person; and accordingly a breach of any such duty is not actionable as such.

(5) A reference in sections 28I, 28K(1), 28M(6) and 28P to a responsible body is to be read as including a reference to a local education authority in relation to a function to which section 28F applies.

(6) A reference in section 28N and 28P to a responsible body is to be read as including a reference to an education authority in relation to a function to which section 28F applies.

(7) 'Authority' means—

   (a) in relation to England and Wales, a local education authority; and
   (b) [*Scotland*]

Enforcement: England and Wales

28H Special Educational Needs and Disability Tribunal
(1) The Special Educational Needs Tribunal—

   (a) is to continue to exist; but
   (b) after the commencement date is to be shown as the Special Educational Needs and Disability Tribunal.

(2) It is referred to in this Chapter as 'the Tribunal'.

(3) In addition to its jurisdiction under Part 4 of the Education Act 1996, the Tribunal is to exercise the jurisdiction conferred on it by this Chapter.

(4) 'Commencement date' means the day on which section 17 of the Special Educational Needs and Disability Act 2001 comes into force.

28I Jurisdiction and powers of the Tribunal
(1) A claim that a responsible body—

   (a) has discriminated against a person ('A') in a way which is made unlawful under this Chapter, or
   (b) is by virtue of section 58 to be treated as having discriminated against a person ('A') in such a way,

may be made to the Tribunal by A's parent.

(2) But this section does not apply to a claim to which section 28K or 28L applies.

(3) If the Tribunal considers that a claim under subsection (1) is well founded—

(a)   it may declare that A has been unlawfully discriminated against; and
(b)   if it does so, it may make such an order as it considers reasonable in all the circumstances of the case.

(4) The power conferred by subsection (3)(b)—

(a)   may, in particular, be exercised with a view to obviating or reducing the adverse effect on the person concerned of any matter to which the claim relates; but
(b)   does not include power to order the payment of any sum by way of compensation.

28J Procedure

(1) Regulations may make provision about—

(a)   the proceedings of the Tribunal on a claim of unlawful discrimination under this Chapter; and
(b)   the making of a claim.

(2) The regulations may, in particular, include provision—

(a)   as to the manner in which a claim must be made;
(b)   if the jurisdiction of the Tribunal is being exercised by more than one tribunal—
   (i)   for determining by which tribunal any claim is to be heard, and
   (ii)   for the transfer of proceedings from one tribunal to another;
(c)   for enabling functions which relate to matters preliminary or incidental to a claim (including, in particular, decisions under paragraph 10(3) of Schedule 3) to be performed by the President or by the chairman;
(d)   enabling hearings to be conducted in the absence of any member other than the chairman;
(e)   as to the persons who may appear on behalf of the parties;
(f)   for granting any person such disclosure or inspection of documents or right to further particulars as might be granted by a county court;
(g)   requiring persons to attend to give evidence and produce documents;
(h)   for authorising the administration of oaths to witnesses;
(i)   for the determination of claims without a hearing in prescribed circumstances;
(j)   as to the withdrawal of claims;
(k)   for enabling the Tribunal to stay proceedings on a claim;
(l)   for the award of costs or expenses;
(m) for taxing or otherwise settling costs or expenses (and, in particular, for enabling costs to be taxed in the county court)
(n)   for the registration and proof of decisions and orders; and
(o)   for enabling prescribed decisions to be reviewed, or prescribed orders to be varied or revoked, in such circumstances as may be determined in accordance with the regulations.

(3) Proceedings before the Tribunal are to be held in private, except in prescribed circumstances.

(4) Unless made with the agreement of the National Assembly, regulations made under this section do not apply to Wales.

(5) The Secretary of State may pay such allowances for the purposes of or in connection with the attendance of persons at the Tribunal as he may, with the consent of the Treasury, determine.

(6) In relation to Wales, the power conferred by subsection (5) may be exercised only with the agreement of the National Assembly.

(7) Part 1 of the Arbitration Act 1996 does not apply to proceedings before the Tribunal but regulations may make provision, in relation to such proceedings, corresponding to any provision of that Part.

(8) The regulations may make provision for a claim under this Chapter to be heard, in prescribed circumstances, with an appeal under Part 4 of the Education Act 1996.

(9) A person who without reasonable excuse fails to comply with—

(a) a requirement in respect of the disclosure or inspection of documents imposed by the regulations by virtue of subsection (2)(f), or
(b) a requirement imposed by the regulations by virtue of subsection (2)(g),

is guilty of an offence.

(10) A person guilty of an offence under subsection (9) is liable on summary conviction to a fine not exceeding level 3 on the standard scale.

(11) Part 3 of Schedule 3 makes further provision about enforcement of this Chapter and about procedure.

28K Admissions
(1) If the condition mentioned in subsection (2) is satisfied, this section applies to a claim in relation to an admissions decision that a responsible body—

(a) has discriminated against a person ('A') in a way which is made unlawful under this Chapter; or
(b) is by virtue of section 58 to be treated as having discriminated against a person ('A') in such a way.

(2) The condition is that arrangements ('appeal arrangements') have been made—

(a) under section 94 of the School Standards and Framework Act 1998 or
(b) under an agreement entered into between the responsible body for a city academy and the Secretary of State under section 482 of the Education Act 1996,

enabling an appeal to be made against the decision by A's parent.

(3) The claim must be made under the appeal arrangements.

(4) The body hearing the claim has the powers which it has in relation to an appeal under the appeal arrangements.

(5) 'Admissions decision' means—

(a) a decision of a kind mentioned in section 94(1) or (2) of the School Standards and Framework Act 1998;
(b) a decision as to the admission of a person to a city academy taken by the responsible body or on its behalf.

28L Exclusions
(1) If the condition mentioned in subsection (2) is satisfied, this section applies to a claim in relation to an exclusion decision that a responsible body—

(a) has discriminated against a person ('A') in a way which is made unlawful under this Chapter; or

(b)   is by virtue of section 58 to be treated as having discriminated against a person ('A') in such a way.

(2)   The condition is that arrangements ('appeal arrangements') have been made—

(a)   under section 67(1) of the School Standards and Framework Act 1998, or
(b)   under an agreement entered into between the responsible body for a city academy and the Secretary of State under section 482 of the Education Act 1996,

enabling an appeal to be made against the decision by A or by his parent.

(3)   The claim must be made under the appeal arrangements.

(4)   The body hearing the claim has the powers which it has in relation to an appeal under the appeal arrangements.

(5)   'Exclusion decision' means—

(a)   a decision of a kind mentioned in section 67(1) of the School Standards and Framework Act 1998;
(b)   a decision not to reinstate a pupil who has been permanently excluded from a city academy by its headteacher, taken by the responsible body or on its behalf.

(6)   'Responsible body', in relation to a maintained school, includes the discipline committee of the governing body if that committee is required to be established as a result of regulations made under paragraph 4 of Schedule 11 to the School Standards and Framework Act 1998

(7)   'Maintained school' has the meaning given in section 28Q(5).

28M   Roles of Secretary of State and the National Assembly
(1)   If the appropriate authority is satisfied (whether on a complaint or otherwise) that a responsible body—

(a)   has acted, or is proposing to act, unreasonably in the discharge of a duty imposed by or under section 28D or 28E, or
(b)   has failed to discharge a duty imposed by or under either of those sections,

it may give that body such directions as to the discharge of the duty as appear to it to be expedient.

(2)   Subsection (3) applies in relation to—

(a)   special schools which are not maintained special schools but which are approved by the Secretary of State, or by the National Assembly, under section 342 of the Education Act 1996; and
(b)   city academies.

(3)   If the appropriate authority is satisfied (whether on a complaint or otherwise) that a responsible body—

(a)   has acted, or is proposing to act, unreasonably in the discharge of a duty which that body has in relation to—
     (i)   the provision to the appropriate authority of copies of that body's accessibility plan, or
     (ii)   the inspection of that plan, or
(b)   has failed to discharge that duty,

it may give that body such directions as to the discharge of the duty as appear to it to be expedient.

(4) Directions may be given under subsection (1) or (3) even if the performance of the duty is contingent upon the opinion of the responsible body.

(5) Subsection (6) applies if the Tribunal has made an order under section 28I(3)

(6) If the Secretary of State is satisfied (whether on a complaint or otherwise) that the responsible body concerned—

(a) has acted, or is proposing to act, unreasonably in complying with the order, or
(b) has failed to comply with the order,

he may give that body such directions as to compliance with the order as appear to him to be expedient.

(7) Directions given under subsection (1), (3) or (6)—

(a) may be varied or revoked by the directing authority; and
(b) may be enforced, on the application of the directing authority, by a manda-tory order obtained in accordance with section 31 of the Supreme Court Act 1981.

(8) 'Appropriate Authority' means—

(a) in relation to England, the Secretary of State; and
(b) in relation to Wales, the National Assembly.

(9) 'Directing Authority' means—

(a) the Secretary of State in relation to a direction given by him; and
(b) the National Assembly in relation to a direction given by it.

Enforcement: Scotland

28N [*Scotland*]

Agreements relating to enforcement

28P Validity and revision of agreements of responsible bodies
(1) Any term in a contract or other agreement made by or on behalf of a responsi-ble body is void so far as it purports to—

(a) require a person to do anything which would contravene any provision of, or made under, this Chapter;
(b) exclude or limit the operation of any provision of, or made under, this Chapter; or
(c) prevent any person from making a claim under this Chapter.

(2) Paragraphs (b) and (c) of subsection (1) do not apply to an agreement settling a claim—

(a) under section 28I or 28N; or
(b) to which section 28K or 28L applies.

(3) On the application of any person interested in an agreement to which subsection (1) applies, a county court . . . may make such order as it thinks just for modifying the agreement to take account of the effect of subsection (1).

(4) No such order may be made unless all persons affected have been—

- (a)   given notice of the application; and
- (b)   afforded an opportunity to make representations to the court.

(5) Subsection (4) applies subject to any rules of court providing for notice to be dispensed with.

(6) An order under subsection (3) may include provision as respects any period before the making of the order.

Interpretation of Chapter 1

28Q Interpretation

(1) This section applies for the purpose of interpreting this Chapter.

(2) 'Disabled pupil' means a pupil who is a disabled person.

(3) 'Pupil'—

- (a)   in relation to England and Wales, has the meaning given in section 3(1) of the Education Act 1996; and
- (b)   [*Scotland*].

(4) Except in relation to Scotland . . . 'school' means—

- (a)   a maintained school;
- (b)   a maintained nursery school
- (c)   an independent school;
- (d)   a special school which is not a maintained school but which is approved by the Secretary of State, or by the National Assembly, under section 342 of the Education Act 1996;
- (e)   a pupil referral unit.

(5) In subsection (4)—

'maintained school' has the meaning given in section 20(7) of the Schools Standards and Framework Act 1998;

'maintained nursery school' has the meaning given in section 22(9) of the School Standards and Framework Act 1998;

'independent school' has the meaning given in section 463 of the Education Act 1996; and

'pupil referral unit' has the meaning given in section 19(2) of the Education Act 1996.

(6) 'Responsible body' has the meaning given in section 28A(5).

(7) 'Governing body', in relation to a maintained school, means the body corporate (constituted in accordance with Schedule 9 to the School Standards and Framework Act 1998) which the school has as a result of section 36 of that Act.

(8) 'Parent'—

- (a)   in relation to England and Wales, has the meaning given in section 576 of the Education Act 1996; and
- (b)   [*Scotland*].

(9) In relation to England and Wales 'permitted form of selection' means—

(a) if the school is a maintained school which is not designated as a grammar school under section 104 of the School Standards and Framework Act 1998, any form of selection mentioned in section 99(2) or (4) of that Act;

(b) if the school is a maintained school which is so designated, any of its selective admission arrangements;

(c) if the school is an independent school, any arrangements which make provision for any or all of its pupils to be selected by reference or special ability or aptitude, with a view to admitting only pupils of high ability or aptitude.

(10) [*Scotland*]

(11) [*Scotland*]

(12) 'City academy' means a school which is known as a city academy as a result of subsection (3) or (3A) of section 482 of the Education Act 1996.

(13) 'Accessibility strategy' and 'accessibility plan' have the meaning given in section 28D.

(14) 'The National Assembly' means the National Assembly for Wales.

CHAPTER 2
FURTHER AND HIGHER EDUCATION
Duties of responsible bodies

28R Discrimination against disabled students and prospective students
(1) It is unlawful for the body responsible for an educational institution to discriminate against a disabled person—

(a) in the arrangements it makes for determining admissions to the institution;
(b) in the terms on which it offers to admit him to the institution; or
(c) by refusing or deliberately omitting to accept an application for his admission to the institution.

(2) It is unlawful for the body responsible for an educational institution to discriminate against a disabled student in the student services it provides, or offers to provide.

(3) It is unlawful for the body responsible for an educational institution to discriminate against a disabled student by excluding him from the institution, whether permanently or temporarily.

(4) In the case of an act which constitutes discrimination by virtue of section 55, this section also applies to discrimination against a person who is not disabled.

(5) The body responsible for an educational institution is to be determined in accordance with Schedule 4B, and in the remaining provisions of this Chapter is referred to as the 'responsible body'.

(6) 'Educational institution', in relation to England and Wales, means an institution—

(a) within the higher education sector;
(b) within the further education sector; or
(c) designated in an order made by the Secretary of State.

(7) [*Scotland*]

(8) Subsection (6) is to be read with section 91 of the Further and Higher Education Act 1992.

(9) The Secretary of State may not make an order under subsection (6)(c) or (7)(e) unless he is satisfied that the institution concerned is wholly or partly funded from public funds.

(10) [*Scotland*]

(11) 'Student services' means services of any description which are provided wholly or mainly for students.

(12) Regulations may make provision as to services which are, or are not, to be regarded for the purposes of subsection (2) as student services.

28S Meaning of 'discrimination'
(1) For the purposes of section 28R, a responsible body discriminates against a disabled person if—

- (a) for a reason which relates to his disability, it treats him less favourably than it treats or would treat others to whom that reason does not or would not apply; and
- (b) it cannot show that the treatment in question is justified.

(2) For the purposes of section 28R, a responsible body also discriminates against a disabled person if—

- (a) it fails, to his detriment, to comply with section 28T; and
- (b) it cannot show that its failure to comply is justified.

(3) In relation to a failure to take a particular step, a responsible body does not discriminate against a person if it shows—

- (a) that, at the time in question, it did not know and could not reasonably have been expected to know, that he was disabled; and
- (b) that its failure to take the step was attributable to that lack of knowledge.

(4) The taking of a particular step by a responsible body in relation to a person does not amount to less favourable treatment if it shows that at the time in question it did not know, and could not reasonably have been expected to know, that he was disabled.

(5) Subsections (6) to (9) apply in determining whether, for the purposes of this section—

- (a) less favourable treatment of a person, or
- (b) failure to comply with section 28T,

is justified.

(6) Less favourable treatment of a person is justified if it is necessary in order to maintain—

- (a) academic standards; or
- (b) standards of any other prescribed kind.

(7) Less favourable treatment is also justified if—
- (a) it is of a prescribed kind;
- (b) it occurs in prescribed circumstances; or
- (c) it is of a prescribed kind and it occurs in prescribed circumstances.

(8)   Otherwise less favourable treatment, or a failure to comply with section 28T, is justified only if the reason for it is both material to the circumstances of the particular case and substantial.

(9)   If, in a case falling within subsection (1)—

    (a)   the responsible body is under a duty imposed by section 28T in relation to the disabled person, but

    (b)   fails without justification to comply with that duty,

its treatment of that person cannot be justified under subsection (8) unless that treatment would have been justified even if it had complied with that duty.'

28T Disabled students not to be substantially disadvantaged
(1)   The responsible body for an educational institution must take such steps as it is reasonable for it to have to take to ensure that—

    (a)   in relation to the arrangements it makes for determining admissions to the institution, disabled persons are not placed at a substantial disadvantage in comparison with persons who are not disabled; and

    (b)   in relation to student services provided for, or offered to, students by it, disabled students are not placed at a substantial disadvantage in comparison with students who are not disabled.

(2)   In considering whether it is reasonable for it to have to take a particular step in order to comply with its duty under subsection (1), a responsible body must have regard to any relevant provisions of a code of practice issued under section 53A.

(3)   Subsection (4) applies if a person has made a confidentiality request of which a responsible body is aware.

(4)   In determining whether it is reasonable for the responsible body to have to take a particular step in relation to that person in order to comply with its duty under subsection (1), regard shall be had to the extent to which taking the step in question is consistent with compliance with that request.

(5)   'Confidentiality request' means a request made by a disabled person, which asks for the nature, or asks for the existence, of his disability to be treated as confidential.

(6)   This section imposes duties only for the purpose of determining whether a responsible body has discriminated against a disabled person; and accordingly a breach of any such duty is not actionable as such.

Other providers of further education or training facilities

28U Further education etc provided by local education authorities and schools
(1)   Part 1 of Schedule 4C modifies this Chapter for the purpose of its application in relation to—

    (a)   higher education secured by a local education authority;

    (b)   further education—

        (i)   secured by a local education authority; or

        (ii)   provided by the governing body of a maintained school;

    (c)   recreational or training facilities secured by a local education authority.

(2)   [*Scotland*]

Enforcement, etc

28V Enforcement, remedies and procedure

(1) A claim by a person—

- (a) that a responsible body has discriminated against him in a way which is unlawful under this Chapter,
- (b) that a responsible body is by virtue of section 57 or 58 to be treated as having discriminated against him in such a way, or
- (c) that a person is by virtue of section 57 to be treated as having discriminated against him in such a way,

may be made the subject of civil proceedings in the same way as any other claim in tort or (in Scotland) in reparation for breach of statutory duty.

(2) For the avoidance of doubt it is hereby declared that damages in respect of discrimination in a way which is unlawful under this Chapter may include compensation for injury to feelings whether or not they include compensation under any other head.

(3) Proceedings in England and Wales may be brought only in a county court.

(4) [*Scotland*]

(5) The remedies available in such proceedings are those which are available in the High Court . . .

(6) The fact that a person who brings proceedings under this Part against a responsible body may also be entitled to bring proceedings against that body under Part 2 is not to affect the proceedings under this Part.

(7) Part 4 of Schedule 3 makes further provision about the enforcement of this Part and about procedure.

28W Occupation of premises by educational institutions

(1) This section applies if—

- (a) premises are occupied by an educational institution under a lease;
- (b) but for this section, the responsible body would not be entitled to make a particular alteration to the premises; and
- (c) the alteration is one which the responsible body proposes to make in order to comply with section 28T.

(2) Except to the extent to which it expressly so provides, the lease has effect, as a result of this subsection, as if it provided—

- (a) for the responsible body to be entitled to make the alteration with the written consent of the lessor;
- (b) for the responsible body to have to make a written application to the lessor for consent if it wishes to make the alteration;
- (c) if such an application is made, for the lessor not to withhold his consent unreasonably; and
- (d) for the lessor to be entitled to make his consent subject to reasonable conditions.

(3) In this section—

'lease' includes a tenancy, sub-lease or sub-tenancy and an agreement for a lease, tenancy, sub-lease or sub-tenancy; and 'sub-lease' and 'sub-tenancy' have such meaning as may be prescribed.

(4) If the terms and conditions of a lease—

(a) impose conditions which are to apply if the responsible body alters the premises, or

(b) entitle the lessor to impose conditions when consenting to the responsible body's altering the premises,

the responsible body is to be treated for the purposes of subsection (1) as not being entitled to make the alteration.

(5) Part 3 of Schedule 4 supplements the provisions of this section.

28X Validity and revision of agreements
Section 28P applies for the purposes of this Chapter as it applies for the purposes of Chapter 1, but with the substitution, for paragraphs (a) and (b) of subsection (2), of 'under section 28V'.

29 Education of disabled persons
[*Omitted—see Special Educational Needs and Disability Act 2001, s 40(1).*]

30 Further and higher education of disabled persons
(1) The Further and Higher Education Act 1992 is amended as set out in subsections (2) to (6).

(2) In section 5 (administration of funds by further education funding councils), in subsection (6)(b), after 'may' insert ', subject to subsection (7A) below,'

(3) After section 5(7) insert—

'(7A) Without prejudice to the power to impose conditions given by subsection (6)(b) above, the conditions subject to which a council gives financial support under this section to the governing body of an institution within the further education sector—

(a) shall require the governing body to publish disability statements at such intervals as may be prescribed; and

(b) may include conditions relating to the provision made, or to be made,

by the institution with respect to disabled persons.

(7B) For the purposes of subsection (7A) above—

"disability statement" means a statement containing information of a prescribed description about the provision of facilities for education made by the institution in respect of disabled persons;

"disabled persons" means persons who are disabled persons for the purposes of the Disability Discrimination Act 1995; and

"prescribed" means prescribed by regulations.'

(4) In section 8 (supplementary functions) add, at the end—

'(6) As soon as is reasonably practicable after the end of its financial year, each council shall make a written report to the Secretary of State on—

(a) the progress made during the year to which the report relates in the provision of further education for disabled students in their area; and

(b) their plans for the future provision of further education for disabled students in their area.

(7) In subsection (6) above—

"disabled students" means students who are disabled persons for the purposes of the Disability Discrimination Act 1995; and

"financial year" means the period of twelve months ending with 31st March 1997 and each successive period of twelve months.'

(5) In section 62 (establishment of higher education funding councils), after sub-section (7) insert—

'(7A) In exercising their functions, each council shall have regard to the requirements of disabled persons.

(7B) In subsection (7A) "disabled persons" means persons who are disabled persons for the purposes of the Disability Discrimination Act 1995.'

(6) . . .

(7) The Education Act 1944 is amended as set out in subsections (8) and (9).

(8) In section 41 (functions of local education authorities in respect of further edu-cation), after subsection (2) insert—

'(2A) It shall be the duty of every local education authority to publish disability state-ments at such intervals as may be prescribed.

(2B) For the purposes of subsection (2A) above—

"disability statement" means a statement containing information of a Prescribed description about the provision of facilities for further education made by the local education authority in respect of persons who are disabled persons for the purposes of the Disability Discrimination Act 1995; and

"prescribed" means prescribed by regulations made by the Secretary of State.'

(9) In section 41(7), (8) and (11), for 'this section' substitute 'subsections (1) and (6) above'.

31 Further and higher education of disabled persons: Scotland
[*Scotland*]

Interpretation of Chapter 2

31A Interpretation
(1) Subsections (2) to (4) apply for the purpose of interpreting this Chapter.

(2) 'Disabled student' means a student who is a disabled person.

(3) 'Student' means a person who is attending, or undertaking a course of study at, an educational institution.

(4) 'Educational institution', 'responsible body' and 'student services' have the meaning given in section 28R.

CHAPTER 3
SUPPLEMENTARY

31B Conciliation for disputes

(1) The Disability Rights Commission may make arrangements with any other person for the provision of conciliation services by, or by persons appointed by, that person in connection with disputes.

(2) In deciding what arrangements (if any) to make, the Commission must have regard to the desirability of securing, so far as reasonably practicable, that conciliation services are available for all disputes which the parties may wish to refer to conciliation.

(3) No member or employee of the Commission may provide conciliation services in connection with disputes.

(4) The Commission must ensure that arrangements under this section include appropriate safeguards to prevent the disclosure to members or employees of the Commission of information obtained by any person in connection with the provision of conciliation services in accordance with the arrangements.

(5) Subsection (4) does not apply to information which is disclosed with the consent of the parties to the dispute to which it relates.

(6) Subsection (4) does not apply to information which—

    (a)   does not identify a particular dispute or a particular person; and
    (b)   is reasonably required by the Commission for the purpose of monitoring the operation of the arrangements concerned.

(7) Anything communicated to a person providing conciliation services in accordance with arrangements under this section is not admissible in evidence in any proceedings except with the consent of the person who communicated it.

(8) 'Conciliation services' means advice and assistance provided to the parties to a dispute, by a conciliator, with a view to promoting its settlement otherwise than through a court, tribunal or other body.

(9) 'Dispute' means a dispute arising under Chapter 1 or 2 concerning an allegation of discrimination.

(10) 'Discrimination' means anything which is made unlawful discrimination by a provision of Chapter 1 or 2.

31C Application to Isles of Scilly

This Part applies to the Isles of Scilly—

    (a)   as if the Isles were a separate non-metropolitan county (and the Council of the Isles of Scilly were a county council), and
    (b)   with such other modifications as may be specified in an order made by the Secretary of State.

PART V
PUBLIC TRANSPORT

★ ★ ★ ★ ★

PART VI
THE NATIONAL DISABILITY COUNCIL

★ ★ ★ ★ ★

PART VII
SUPPLEMENTAL

53 Codes of practice prepared by the Secretary of State

[*Repealed by the Disability Rights Commission Act 1999, with effect from 25/4/00 by virtue of the Disability Rights Commission Act 1999 (Commencement) No 2 and Transitional Provision) Order 2000, SI 2000/880.*]

53A Codes of practice

(1) The Disability Rights Commission may prepare and issue codes of practice giving practical guidance on how to avoid discrimination, or on any other matter relating to the operation of any provision of Part 2, 3 or 4, to—

  (a)   employers;
  (b)   service providers;
  (c)   bodies which are responsible bodies for the purposes of Chapter 1 or 2 of Part 4; or
  (d)   other persons to whom the provisions of Parts 2 or 3 or Chapter 2 of Part 4 apply.

(1A) The Commission may also prepare and issue codes of practice giving practical guidance to any persons on any other matter with a view to—

  (a)   promoting the equalisation of opportunities for disabled persons and persons who have had a disability; or
  (b)   encouraging good practice in the way such persons are treated,

in any field of activity regulated by any provision of Part 2, 3 or 4.

(1B) Neither subsection (1) nor (1A) applies in relation to any duty imposed by or under sections 28D or 28E.

(2) The Commission shall, when requested to do so by the Secretary of State, prepare a code of practice dealing with the matters specified in the request.

(3) In preparing a code of practice the Commission shall carry out such consultations as it considers appropriate (which shall include the publication for public consultation of proposals relating to the code).

(4) The Commission may not issue a code of practice unless—

  (a)   a draft of it has been submitted to and approved by the Secretary of State and laid by him before both Houses of Parliament; and
  (b)   the 40 day period has elapsed without either House resolving not to approve the draft.

(5) If the Secretary of State does not approve a draft code of practice submitted to him he shall give the Commission a written statement of his reasons.

(6) A code of practice issued by the Commission—

   (a)   shall come into effect on such day as the Secretary of State may by order appoint;

   (b)   may be revised in whole or part, and re-issued, by the Commission; and

   (c)   may be revoked by an order made by the Secretary of State at the request of the Commission.

(7) Where the Commission proposes to revise a code of practice—

   (a)   it shall comply with subsection (3) in relation to the revisions; and

   (b)   the other provisions of this section apply to the revised code of practice as they apply to a new code of practice.

(8) Failure to observe any provision of a code of practice does not of itself make a person liable to any proceedings.

(8A) But if a provision of a code of practice appears to a court, tribunal or other body hearing any proceedings under Part 2, 3 or 4 to be relevant, it must take that provision into account.

(9) In this section—

'code of practice' means a code of practice under this section;

'discrimination' means anything which is unlawful discrimination for the purposes of any provision of Part II, 3 or 4; and

'40 day period' has the same meaning in relation to a draft code of practice as it has in section 3 in relation to draft guidance.

54 Further provision about codes issued under section 53

(1) In preparing a draft of any code under section 53, the Secretary of State shall consult such organisations representing the interests of employers or of disabled persons in, or seeking, employment as he considers appropriate.

(2) Where the Secretary of State proposes to issue a code, he shall publish a draft of it, consider any representations that are made to him about the draft and, if he thinks it appropriate, modify his proposals in the light of any of those representations.

(3) If the Secretary of State decides to proceed with a proposed code, he shall lay a draft of it before each House of Parliament.

(4) If, within the 40-day period, either House resolves not to approve the draft, the Secretary of State shall take no further steps in relation to the proposed code.

(5) If no such resolution is made within the 40-day period, the Secretary of State shall issue the code in the form of his draft.

(6) The code shall come into force on such date as the Secretary of State may appoint by order.

(7) Subsection (4) does not prevent a new draft of the proposed code from being laid before Parliament.

(8) The Secretary of State may by order revoke a code.

(9) In this section '40-day period', in relation to the draft of a proposed code, means—

(a) if the draft is laid before one House on a day later than the day on which it is laid before the other House, the period of 40 days beginning with the later of the two days, and

(b) in any other case, the period of 40 days beginning with the day on which the draft is laid before each House, no account being taken of any period during which Parliament is dissolved or prorogued or during which both Houses are adjourned for more than four days.

[*Section 53 repealed except for subsection (a) from 25/4/00 – see note to section 53.*]

55 Victimisation

(1) For the purposes of Part II, Part 3 or 4, a person ('A') discriminates against another person ('B') if—

(a) he treats B less favourably than he treats or would treat other persons whose circumstances are the same as B's; and

(b) he does so for a reason mentioned in subsection (2).

(2) The reasons are that—

(a) B has—
   (i) brought proceedings against A or any other person under this Act; or
   (ii) given evidence or information in connection with such proceedings brought by any person; or
   (iii) otherwise done anything under this Act in relation to A or any other person; or
   (iv) alleged that A or any other person has (whether or not the allegation so states) contravened this Act; or
(b) A believes or suspects that B has done or intends to do any of those things.

(3) Where B is a disabled person, or a person who has had a disability, the disability in question shall be disregarded in comparing his circumstances with those of any other person for the purposes of subsection (1)(a).

(3A) For the purposes of Chapter 1 of Part 4—

(a) references in subsection (2) to B include references to—
   (i) a person who is, for the purposes of that Chapter, B's parent; and
   (ii) a sibling of B; and
(b) references in that subsection to this Act are, as respects a person mentioned in sub-paragraph (i) or (ii) of paragraph (a), restricted to that Chapter.

(4) Subsection (1) does not apply to treatment of a person because of an allegation made by him if the allegation was false and not made in good faith.

56 Help for persons suffering discrimination

(1) For the purposes of this section—

(a) a person who considers that he may have been discriminated against, in contravention of any provision of Part II, is referred to as 'the complainant'; and

(b) a person against whom the complainant may decide to make, or has made, a complaint under Part II is referred to as 'the respondent'.

(2) The Secretary of State shall, with a view to helping the complainant to decide whether to make a complaint against the respondent and, if he does so, to formulate and present his case in the most effective manner, by order prescribe—

(a) forms by which the complainant may question the respondent on his reasons for doing any relevant act, or on any other matter which is or may be relevant; and

(b)   forms by which the respondent may if he so wishes reply to any questions.

(3)   Where the complainant questions the respondent in accordance with forms prescribed by an order under subsection (2)—

(a)   the question, and any reply by the respondent (whether in accordance with such an order or not), shall be admissible as evidence in any proceedings under Part II;

(b)   if it appears to the tribunal in any such proceedings—
   (i)   that the respondent deliberately, and without reasonable excuse, omitted to reply within a reasonable period, or
   (ii)   that the respondent's reply is evasive or equivocal, it may draw any inference which it considers it just and equitable to draw, including an inference that the respondent has contravened a provision of Part II.

(4)   The Secretary of State may by order prescribe—

(a)   the period within which questions must be duly served in order to be admissible under subsection (3)(a); and

(b)   the manner in which a question, and any reply by the respondent, may be duly served.

(5)   This section is without prejudice to any other enactment or rule of law regulating interlocutory and preliminary matters in proceedings before an industrial tribunal, and has effect subject to any enactment or rule of law regulating the admissibility of evidence in such proceedings

57 Aiding unlawful acts

(1)   A person who knowingly aids another person to do an unlawful act is to be treated for the purposes of this Act as himself doing the same kind of unlawful act.

(2)   For the purposes of subsection (1), an employee or agent for whose act the employer or principal is liable under section 58 (or would be so liable but for section 58(5)) shall be taken to have aided the employer or principal to do the act.

(3)   For the purposes of this section, a person does not knowingly aid another to do an unlawful act if—

(a)   he acts in reliance on a statement made to him by that other person that, because of any provision of this Act, the act would not be unlawful; and

(b)   it is reasonable for him to rely on the statement.

(4)   A person who knowingly or recklessly makes such a statement which is false or misleading in a material respect is guilty of an offence.

(5)   Any person guilty of an offence under subsection (4) shall be liable on summary conviction to a fine not exceeding level 5 on the standard scale.

(6)   'Unlawful act' means an act made unlawful by any provision of this Act other than a provision contained in Chapter 1 of Part 4.

58 Liability of employers and principals

(1)   Anything done by a person in the course of his employment shall be treated for the purposes of this Act as also done by his employer, whether or not it was done with the employer's knowledge or approval.

(2) Anything done by a person as agent for another person with the authority of that other person shall be treated for the purposes of this Act as also done by that other person.

(3) Subsection (2) applies whether the authority was—

  (a)   express or implied; or
  (b)   given before or after the act in question was done.

(4) Subsections (1) and (2) do not apply in relation to an offence under section 57(4).

(5) In proceedings under this Act against any person in respect of an act alleged to have been done by an employee of his, it shall be a defence for that person to prove that he took such steps as were reasonably practicable to prevent the employee from—

  (a)   doing that act; or
  (b)   doing, in the course of his employment, acts of that description.

59 Statutory authority and national security etc
(1) Nothing in this Act makes unlawful any act done—

  (a)   in pursuance of any enactment; or
  (b)   in pursuance of any instrument made by a Minister of the Crown under any enactment; or
  (c)   to comply with any condition or requirement imposed by a Minister of the Crown (whether before or after the passing of this Act) by virtue of any enactment.

(2) In subsection (1) 'enactment' includes one passed or made after the date on which this Act is passed and 'instrument' includes one made after that date.

(3) Nothing in this Act makes unlawful any act done for the purpose of safeguarding national security.

PART VIII
MISCELLANEOUS

60 Appointment by Secretary of State of advisers

. . .

61 Amendment of Disabled Persons (Employment) Act 1944

. . .

64 Application to Crown etc
(1) This Act applies—

  (a)   to an act done by or for purposes of a Minister of the Crown or government department, or
  (b)   to an act done on behalf of the Crown by a statutory body, or a person holding a statutory office, as it applies to an act done by a private person.

(2) . . .

(3) The provisions of Parts II to IV of the 1947 Act apply to proceedings against the Crown under this Act as they apply to Crown proceedings in England and Wales; but

section 20 of that Act (removal of proceedings from county court to High Court) does not apply.

(4) [*Scotland*]

. . .

(8) In this section—

'the 1947 Act' means the Crown Proceedings Act 1947;

. . .

'Crown proceedings' means proceedings which, by virtue of section 23 of the 1947 Act, are treated for the purposes of Part II of that Act as civil proceedings by or against the Crown;

. . .

'statutory body' means a body set up by or under an enactment;

'statutory office' means an office so set up; and

. . .

65 Application to Parliament
(1) This Act applies to an act done by or for purposes of the House of Lords or the House of Commons as it applies to an act done by a private person.

. . .

67 Regulations and orders

(1) Any power under this Act to make regulations or orders shall be exercisable by statutory instrument.

(2) Any such power may be exercised to make different provision for different cases, including different provision for different areas or localities.

(3) Any such power includes power—

  (a) to make such incidental, supplemental, consequential or transitional provision as appears to the Secretary of State to be expedient; and
  (b) to provide for a person to exercise a discretion in dealing with any matter.

(4) No order shall be made under section 50(3) unless a draft of the statutory instrument containing the order has been laid before Parliament and approved by a resolution of each House.

(5) Any other statutory instrument made under this Act, other than one made under section 3(9), 52(8), 54(6) or 70(3), shall be subject to annulment in pursuance of a resolution of either House of Parliament.

(6) Subsection (1) does not require an order under section 43 which applies only to a specified vehicle, or to vehicles of a specified person, to be made by statutory instrument but such an order shall be as capable of being amended or revoked as an order which is made by statutory instrument.

(7) Nothing in section 34(4), 40(6) or 46(5) affects the powers conferred by subsections (2) and (3).

68 Interpretation

(1) In this Act—

'act' includes a deliberate omission;

'benefits', in Part II, has the meaning given in section 4(4);

'conciliation officer' means a person designated under section 211 of the Trade Union and Labour Relations (Consolidation) Act 1992;

'employment' means, subject to any prescribed provision, employment under a contract of service or of apprenticeship or a contract personally to do any work, and related expressions are to be construed accordingly;

'enactment' includes subordinate legislation and any Order in Council;

'mental impairment' does not have the same meaning as in the Mental Health Act 1983 or [*Scotland*] but the fact that an impairment would be a mental impairment for the purposes of either of those Acts does not prevent it from being a mental impairment for the purposes of this Act;

'Minister of the Crown' includes the Treasury;

'occupational pension scheme' has the same meaning as in the Pension Schemes Act 1993;

'premises' includes land of any description;

'prescribed' means prescribed by regulations;

'profession' includes any vocation or occupation;

'provider of services' has the meaning given in section 19(2)(b);

'regulations' means regulations made by the Secretary of State;

'section 6 duty' means any duty imposed by or under section 6;

'section 15 duty' means any duty imposed by or under section 15;

'section 21 duty' means any duty imposed by or under section 21;

'trade' includes any business;

'trade organisation' has the meaning given in section 13.

69 Financial provisions

. . .

SCHEDULES

SCHEDULE 1
PROVISIONS SUPPLEMENTING SECTION 1

Section 1(1)

Impairment

1   (1) 'Mental impairment' includes an impairment resulting from or consisting of a mental illness only if the illness is a clinically well-recognised illness.

(2) Regulations may make provision, for the purposes of this Act—

(a)   for conditions of a prescribed description to be treated as amounting to impairments;

(b)   for conditions of a prescribed description to be treated as not amounting to impairments.

(3) Regulations made under sub-paragraph (2) may make provision as to the meaning of 'condition' for the purposes of those regulations.

Long-term effects

2   (1) The effect of an impairment is a long-term effect if—

(a)   it has lasted at least 12 months;
(b)   the period for which it lasts is likely to be at least 12 months; or
(c)   it is likely to last for the rest of the life of the person affected.

(2) Where an impairment ceases to have a substantial adverse effect on a person's ability to carry out normal day-to-day activities, it is to be treated as continuing to have that effect if that effect is likely to recur.

(3) For the purposes of sub-paragraph (2), the likelihood of an effect recurring shall be disregarded in prescribed circumstances.

(4) Regulations may prescribe circumstances in which, for the purposes of this Act—

(a)   an effect which would not otherwise be a long-term effect is to be treated as such an effect; or
(b)   an effect which would otherwise be a long-term effect is to be treated as not being such an effect.

Severe disfigurement

3   (1) An impairment which consists of a severe disfigurement is to be treated as having a substantial adverse effect on the ability of the person concerned to carry out normal day-to-day activities.

(2) Regulations may provide that in prescribed circumstances a severe disfigurement is not to be treated as having that effect.

(3) Regulations under sub-paragraph (2) may, in particular, make provision with respect to deliberately acquired disfigurements.

Normal day-to-day activities

4   (1) An impairment is to be taken to affect the ability of the person concerned to carry out normal day-to-day activities only if it affects one of the following—

(a)   mobility;
(b)   manual dexterity;
(c)   physical co-ordination;
(d)   continence;
(e)   ability to lift, carry or otherwise move everyday objects;
(f)   speech, hearing or eyesight;
(g)   memory or ability to concentrate, learn or understand; or
(h)   perception of the risk of physical danger.

(2) Regulations may prescribe—

   (a)   circumstances in which an impairment which does not have an effect falling within sub-paragraph (1) is to be taken to affect the ability of the person concerned to carry out normal day-to-day activities;

   (b)   circumstances in which an impairment which has an effect falling within sub-paragraph (1) is to be taken not to affect the ability of the person concerned to carry out normal day-to-day activities.

Substantial adverse effects

5   Regulations may make provision for the purposes of this Act—

   (a)   for an effect of a prescribed kind on the ability of a person to carry out normal day-to-day activities to be treated as a substantial adverse effect;

   (b)   for an effect of a prescribed kind on the ability of a person to carry out normal day-to-day activities to be treated as not being a substantial adverse effect.

Effect of medical treatment

6   (1) An impairment which would be likely to have a substantial adverse effect on the ability of the person concerned to carry out normal day-to-day activities, but for the fact that measures are being taken to treat or correct it, is to be treated as having that effect.

(2) In sub-paragraph (1) 'measures' includes, in particular, medical treatment and the use of a prosthesis or other aid.

(3) Sub-paragraph (1) does not apply—

   (a)   in relation to the impairment of a person's sight, to the extent that the impairment is, in his case, correctable by spectacles or contact lenses or in such other ways as may be prescribed; or

   (b)   in relation to such other impairments as may be prescribed, in such circumstances as may be prescribed.

Persons deemed to be disabled

7   (1) Sub-paragraph (2) applies to any person whose name is, both on 12th January 1995 and on the date when this paragraph comes into force, in the register of disabled persons maintained under section 6 of the Disabled Persons (Employment) Act 1944.

(2) That person is to be deemed—

   (a)   during the initial period, to have a disability, and hence to be a disabled person; and

   (b)   afterwards, to have had a disability and hence to have been a disabled person during that period.

(3) A certificate of registration shall be conclusive evidence, in relation to the person with respect to whom it was issued, of the matters certified.

(4) Unless the contrary is shown, any document purporting to be a certificate of registration shall be taken to be such a certificate and to have been validly issued.

(5)   Regulations may provide for prescribed descriptions of person to be deemed to have disabilities, and hence to be disabled persons, for the purposes of this Act.

(6)   Regulations may prescribe circumstances in which a person who has been deemed to be a disabled person by the provisions of sub-paragraph (1) or regulations made under sub-paragraph (5) is to be treated as no longer being deemed to be such a person.

(7)   In this paragraph—

'certificate of registration' means a certificate issued under regulations made under section 6 of the Act of 1944; and

'initial period' means the period of three years beginning with the date on which this paragraph comes into force.

Progressive conditions

8 (1) Where—

  (a) a person has a progressive condition (such as cancer, multiple sclerosis or muscular dystrophy or infection by the human immunodeficiency virus),

  (b) as a result of that condition, he has an impairment which has (or had) an effect on his ability to carry out normal day-to-day activities, but

  (c) that effect is not (or was not) a substantial adverse effect, he shall be taken to have an impairment which has such a substantial adverse effect if the condition is likely to result in his having such an impairment.

(2)   Regulations may make provision, for the purposes of this paragraph—

  (a) for conditions of a prescribed description to be treated as being progressive;

  (b) for conditions of a prescribed description to be treated as not being progressive.

SCHEDULE 2
PAST DISABILITIES

Section 2(2)

1   The modifications referred to in section 2 are as follows.

2   References in Parts II to 4 to a disabled person are to be read as references to a person who has had a disability.

2A References in Chapter 1 of Part 4 to a disabled pupil are to be read as references to a pupil who has had a disability.

2B References in Chapter 2 of Part 4 to a disabled student are to be read as references to a student who has had a disability.

3   In section 6(1), after 'not disabled' insert 'and who have not had a disability'.

4   In section 6(6), for 'has' substitute 'has had'.

4A In section 28B(3)(a) and (4), after 'disabled' insert 'or that he had had a disability'.

4B   In section 28C(1), in paragraphs (a) and (b), after 'not disabled' insert 'and who have not had a disability'.

4C   In section 28S(3)(a) and (4), after 'disabled' insert 'or that he had had a disability'.

4D   In subsection (1) of section 28T, after 'not disabled' insert 'and who have not had a disability'.

4E   In that subsection as substituted by paragraphs 2 and 6 of Schedule 4C, after 'not disabled' insert 'and who have not had a disability'.

5   For paragraph 2(1) to (3) of Schedule 1, substitute—

'(1) The effect of an impairment is a long-term effect if it has lasted for at least 12 months.

(2) Where an impairment ceases to have a substantial adverse effect on a person's ability to carry out normal day-to-day activities, it is to be treated as continuing to have that effect if that effect recurs.

(3) For the purposes of sub-paragraph (2), the recurrence of an effect shall be disregarded in prescribed circumstances.'

SCHEDULE 3
ENFORCEMENT AND PROCEDURE

Sections 8(8) and 26(6)

PART I
EMPLOYMENT

* * * * *

PART II
DISCRIMINATION IN OTHER AREAS

Restriction on proceedings for breach of Part III

5   (1) Except as provided by section 25 no civil or criminal proceedings may be brought against any person in respect of an act merely because the act is unlawful under Part III.

(2) Sub-paragraph (1) does not prevent the making of an application for judicial review.

Period within which proceedings must be brought

6   (1) A county court or a sheriff court shall not consider a claim under section 25 unless proceedings in respect of the claim are instituted before the end of the period of six months beginning when the act complained of was done.

(2) Where, in relation to proceedings or prospective proceedings under section 25,

the dispute concerned is referred for conciliation in pursuance of arrangements under section 28 before the end of the period of six months mentioned in sub-paragraph (1), the period allowed by that sub-paragraph shall be extended by two months.

(3) A court may consider any claim under section 25 which is out of time if, in all the circumstances of the case, it considers that it is just and equitable to do so.

(4) For the purposes of sub-paragraph (1)

(a) where an unlawful act of discrimination is attributable to a term in a contract, that act is to be treated as extending throughout the duration of the contract;

(b) any act extending over a period shall be treated as done at the end of that period; and

(c) a deliberate omission shall be treated as done when the person in question decided upon it.

(5) In the absence of evidence establishing the contrary, a person shall be taken for the purposes of this paragraph to decide upon an omission—

(a) when he does an act inconsistent with doing the omitted act; or

(b) if he has done no such inconsistent act, when the period expires within which he might reasonably have been expected to do the omitted act if it was to be done.

Compensation for injury to feelings

7 In any proceedings under section 25, the amount of any damages awarded as compensation for injury to feelings shall not exceed the prescribed amount.

Evidence

8 (1) In any proceedings under section 25, a certificate signed by or on behalf of a Minister of the Crown and certifying—

(a) that any conditions or requirements specified in the certificate were imposed by a Minister of the Crown and were in operation at a time or throughout a time so specified, or

(b) that an act specified in the certificate was done for the purpose of safeguarding national security, shall be conclusive evidence of the matters certified.

(2) A document purporting to be such a certificate shall be received in evidence and, unless the contrary is proved, be deemed to be such a certificate.

PART 3
DISCRIMINATION IN SCHOOLS

Restriction on proceedings for breach of Part 4, Chapter 1

9 (1) Except as provided by sections 28I, 28K and 28L, no civil or criminal proceedings may be brought against any person in respect of an act merely because the act is unlawful under Chapter 1 of Part 4.

(2) Sub-paragraph (1) does not prevent the making of an application for judicial review.

Period within which proceedings must be brought

10   (1) The Tribunal shall not consider a claim under section 28I unless proceedings in respect of the claim are instituted before the end of the period of six months beginning when the act complained of was done.

(2) If, in relation to proceedings or prospective proceedings under section 28I, the dispute concerned is referred for conciliation in pursuance of arrangements under section 31B before the end of the period of six months mentioned in sub-paragraph (1), the period allowed by that sub-paragraph shall be extended by two months.

(3) The Tribunal may consider any claim under section 28I which is out of time if, in all the circumstances of the case, it considers that it is just and equitable to do so.

(4) But sub-paragraph (3) does not permit the Tribunal to decide to consider a claim if a decision not to consider that claim has previously been taken under that sub-paragraph.

(5) For the purposes of sub-paragraph (1)—

   (a)   if an unlawful act of discrimination is attributable to a term in a contract, that act is to be treated as extending throughout the duration of the contract;
   (b)   any act extending over a period shall be treated as done at the end of that period; and
   (c)   a deliberate omission shall be treated as done when the person in question decided upon it.

(6) In the absence of evidence establishing the contrary, a person shall be taken for the purposes of this paragraph to decide upon an omission—

   (a)   when he does an act inconsistent with doing the omitted act; or
   (b)   if he has done no such inconsistent act, when the period expires within which he might reasonably have been expected to do the omitted act if it was to be done.

Evidence

11   (1) In any proceedings under section 28I, 28K or 28L, a certificate signed by or on behalf of a Minister of the Crown and certifying that any conditions or requirements specified in the certificate—

   (a)   were imposed by a Minister of the Crown, and
   (b)   were in operation at a time or throughout a time so specified,

shall be conclusive evidence of the matters certified.

(2) A document purporting to be such a certificate shall be received in evidence and, unless the contrary is proved, be deemed to be such a certificate.

PART 4
DISCRIMINATION IN FURTHER AND HIGHER EDUCATION INSTITUTIONS

Restriction on proceedings for breach of Part 4, Chapter 2

12   (1) Except as provided by section 28V, no civil or criminal proceedings may be brought against any person in respect of an act merely because the act is unlawful under Chapter 2 of Part 4.

(2) Sub-paragraph (1) does not prevent the making of an application for judicial review.

Period within which proceedings must be brought

13   (1) A county court or [*Scotland*] shall not consider a claim under section 28V unless proceedings in respect of the claim are instituted before the end of the period of six months beginning when the act complained of was done.

(2) If, in relation to proceedings or prospective proceedings under section 28V, the dispute concerned is referred for conciliation in pursuance of arrangements under section 31B before the end of the period of six months mentioned in sub-paragraph (1), the period allowed by that sub-paragraph shall be extended by two months.

(3) A court may consider any claim under section 28V which is out of time if, in all the circumstances of the case, it considers that it is just and equitable to do so.

(4) For the purposes of sub-paragraph (1)—

   (a)   if an unlawful act of discrimination is attributable to a term in a contract, that act is to be treated as extending throughout the duration of the contract;
   (b)   any act extending over a period shall be treated as done at the end of that period; and
   (c)   a deliberate omission shall be treated as done when the person in question decided upon it.

(5) In the absence of evidence establishing the contrary, a person shall be taken for the purposes of this paragraph to decide upon an omission—

   (a)   when he does an act inconsistent with doing the omitted act; or
   (b)   if he has done no such inconsistent act, when the period expires within which he might reasonably have been expected to do the omitted act if it was to be done.

Compensation for injury to feelings

14   In any proceedings under section 28V, the amount of any damages awarded as compensation for injury to feelings shall not exceed the prescribed amount.

Evidence

15   (1) In any proceedings under section 28V, a certificate signed by or on behalf of a Minister of the Crown and certifying that any conditions or requirements specified in the certificate—

(a)   were imposed by a Minister of the Crown, and

(b) were in operation at a time or throughout a time so specified,

is conclusive evidence of the matters certified.

(2) A document purporting to be such a certificate is to be—

(a)   received in evidence; and

(b)   deemed to be such a certificate unless the contrary is proved.

SCHEDULE 4
PREMISES OCCUPIED UNDER LEASES

PART 1
OCCUPATION BY EMPLOYER OR TRADE ORGANISATION

★ ★ ★ ★ ★

PART 2
OCCUPATION BY PROVIDER OF SERVICES

★ ★ ★ ★ ★

PART 3
OCCUPATION BY EDUCATIONAL INSTITUTIONS

Failure to obtain consent

10   If any question arises as to whether a responsible body has failed to comply with the duty imposed by section 28T, by failing to make a particular alteration to premises, any constraint attributable to the fact that the premises are occupied by the educational institution under a lease is to be ignored unless the responsible body has applied to the lessor in writing for consent to the making of the alteration.

Reference to court

11   (1) If the responsible body has applied in writing to the lessor for consent to the alteration and—

(a)   that consent has been refused, or

(b)   the lessor has made his consent subject to one or more conditions,

that body or a disabled person who has an interest in the proposed alteration to the premises being made, may refer the matter to a county court . . .

(2)   On such a reference the court must determine whether the lessor's refusal was unreasonable or (as the case may be) whether the condition is, or any of the conditions are, unreasonable.

(3)   If the court determines—

(a)   that the lessor's refusal was unreasonable, or

(b)   that the condition is, or any of the conditions are, unreasonable, it may make such declaration as it considers appropriate or an order authorising the responsible body to make the alteration specified in the order.

(4) An order under sub-paragraph (3) may require the responsible body to comply with conditions specified in the order.

Joining lessors in proceedings under section 28V

12   (1) In proceedings on a claim under section 28V, in a case to which this Part of this Schedule applies, the claimant, . . . or the responsible body concerned may ask the court to direct that the lessor be joined . . . as a party to the proceedings.

(2) The request must be granted if it is made before the hearing of the claim begins.

(3) The court may refuse the request if it is made after the hearing of the claim begins.

(4) The request may not be granted if it is made after the court has determined the claim.

(5) If a lessor has been so joined . . . as a party to the proceedings, the court may determine—

   (a)   whether the lessor has—
      (i)   refused consent to the alteration, or
      (ii) consented subject to one or more conditions, and
   (b)   if so, whether the refusal or any of the conditions was unreasonable.

(6) If, under sub-paragraph (5), the court determines that the refusal or any of the conditions was unreasonable it may take one or more of the following steps—

   (a)   make such a declaration as it considers appropriate;
   (b)   make an order authorising the responsible body to make the alteration specified in the order;
   (c)   order the lessor to pay compensation to the complainant.

(7) An order under sub-paragraph (6)(b) may require the responsible body to comply with conditions specified in the order.

(8) If the court orders the lessor to pay compensation it may not order the responsible body to do so.

Regulations

13   Regulations may make provision as to circumstances in which—

   (a)   a lessor is to be taken, for the purposes of section 28W and this Part of this Schedule to have—
      (i)   withheld his consent;
      (ii) withheld his consent unreasonably;
      (iii) acted reasonably in withholding his consent;
   (b)   a condition subject to which a lessor has given his consent is to be taken to be reasonable;
   (c)   a condition subject to which a lessor has given his consent is to be taken to be unreasonable.

Sub-leases etc

14   Regulations may make provision supplementing, or modifying, section 28W or any provision made by or under this Part of this Schedule in relation to cases where the premises of the educational institution are occupied under a sub-lease or sub-tenancy.

SCHEDULE 4A
RESPONSIBLE BODIES FOR SCHOOLS

Section 28A

1   (1)   The bodies responsible for schools in England and Wales are set out in the following table.

(2)   In that Table—

'the local education authority' has the meaning given by section 22(8) of the School Standards and Framework Act 1998; and

'proprietor' has the meaning given by section 579 of the Education Act 1996.

Table

Type of school	Responsible body
1 Maintained school.	The local education authority or governing body, according to which has the function in question.
2 Pupil referral unit.	The local education authority.
3 Maintained nursery school.	The local education authority.
4 Independent school.	The proprietor.
5 Special school not maintained by a local education authority.	The proprietor.

2   [*Scotland*]

SCHEDULE 4B
RESPONSIBLE BODIES FOR EDUCATIONAL INSTITUTIONS

Section 28R

1   (1)   The bodies responsible for educational institutions in England and Wales are set out in the following table.

(2)   In that Table 'governing body' has the meaning given by section 90 of the Further and Higher Education Act 1992.

Table

Type of institution	Responsible body
1 Institution within the further education sector.	The governing body.
2 University.	The governing body.
3 Institution, other than a university, within the higher education sector.	The governing body.
4 Institution designated under section 28R(6)(c).	The body specified in the order as the responsible body.

2   [*Scotland*]

SCHEDULE 4C
MODIFICATIONS OF CHAPTER 2 OF PART 4

Section 28U

PART 1
MODIFICATIONS FOR ENGLAND AND WALES

1   For section 28R, substitute—

'28R Further education etc provided by local education authorities and schools

(1) Subsections (2) and (3) apply in relation to—

   (a)   any course of higher education secured by a local education authority under section 120 of the Education Reform Act 1988;

   (b)   any course of further education—

       (i)   secured by a local education authority; or

       (ii)   provided by the governing body of a maintained school under section 80 of the School Standards and Framework Act 1998.

(2) It is unlawful for the local education authority or the governing body to discriminate against a disabled person—

   (a)   in the arrangements they make for determining who should be enrolled on the course;

   (b)   in the terms on which they offer to enrol him on the course; or

   (c)   by refusing or deliberately omitting to accept an application for his enrolment on the course.

(3) It is unlawful for the local education authority or the governing body to discriminate against a disabled person who has enrolled on the course in the services which they provide, or offer to provide.

(4) "Services", in relation to a course, means services of any description which are provided wholly or mainly for persons enrolled on the course.

(5) It is unlawful for a local education authority to discriminate against a disabled person in the terms on which they provide, or offer to provide, recreational or training facilities.

(6) In this Chapter "responsible body" means—

   (a) a local education authority, in relation to—
     (i)   a course of further or higher education secured by them;
     (ii) recreational or training facilities; and
   (b) the governing body of a maintained school, in relation to a course of further education provided under section 80 of the School Standards and Framework Act 1998.

(7) "Further education"—

   (a) in relation to a course secured by a local education authority, has the meaning given in section 2(3) of the Education Act 1996; and
   (b) in relation to a course provided under section 80 of the School Standards and Framework Act 1998 means education of a kind mentioned in subsection (1) of that section.

(8) In relation to further education secured by a local education authority—

"course" includes each of the component parts of a course of further education if, in relation to the course, there is no requirement imposed on persons registered for any component part of the course to register for any other component part of that course; and

"enrolment", in relation to such a course, includes registration for any one of those parts.

(9) "Higher education" has the meaning given in section 579(1) of the Education Act 1996.

(10) "Local education authority" has the meaning given in section 12 of the Education Act 1996.

(11) "Governing body" and "maintained school" have the same meaning as in Chapter 1.

(12) "Recreational or training facilities" means any facilities secured by a local education authority under subsection (1), or provided by it under subsection (1A), of section 508 of the Education Act 1996 (recreation and social and physical training).'

2 For subsection (1) of section 28T, substitute—

'(1) Each responsible body must take such steps as it is reasonable for it to have to take to ensure that—

   (a) in relation to its arrangements for enrolling persons on a course of further or higher education provided by it, and
   (b) in relation to services provided, or offered by it,

disabled persons are not placed at a substantial disadvantage in comparison with persons who are not disabled.'

3   In section 28W(1)(a) for 'by an educational institution' substitute 'by a responsible body wholly or partly for the purpose of its functions'.

4   Omit section 31A.

PART 2

MODIFICATIONS FOR SCOTLAND

[*Scotland*]

Index

References are to paragraph numbers. References in *italics* refer to page numbers of the appendices.